CALLING PHILOSOPHERS NAMES

CALLING PHILOSOPHERS NAMES

On the Origin of a Discipline

CHRISTOPHER MOORE

PRINCETON UNIVERSITY PRESS

Princeton and Oxford

Published by Princeton University Press
41 William Street, Princeton, New Jersey 08540
6 Oxford Street, Woodstock, Oxfordshire OX20 1TR

press.princeton.edu

LCCN 2019935934
ISBN 9780691195056
ISBN (e-book) 9780691197425

British Library Cataloging-in-Publication Data is available

Editorial: Rob Tempio and Matt Rohal
Production Editorial: Natalie Baan
Text and Jacket Design: Pamela Schnitter
Production: Merli Guerra and Brigid Ackerman
Publicity: Alyssa Sanford and Julia Hall
Copyeditor: David Robertson

Jacket art: Anne Wilson, *Bump* (still from *Errant Behaviors*), 2004.
Video and sound installation. Composer: Shawn Decker; Animator: Cat Solen;
Post-production Animator and Mastering: Daniel Torrente. Copyright 2004
Anne Wilson. Courtesy of the artist and Rhona Hoffman Gallery.

This book has been composed in Times New Roman and Adobe Garamond

Printed on acid-free paper. ∞

Printed in the United States of America

10 9 8 7 6 5 4 3 2 1

For Sandra Peterson

παρέχω ἐμαυτὸν ἐρωτᾶν, καὶ ἐάν τις βούληται ἀποκρινόμενος ἀκούειν ὧν ἂν λέγω.

Surely this was a touch of fine philosophy; though no doubt he had never heard there was such a thing as that. But, perhaps, to be true philosophers, we mortals should not be conscious of so living or so striving. So soon as I hear that such or such a man gives himself out for a philosopher, I conclude that, like the dyspeptic old woman, he must have "broken his digester."

—MELVILLE, MOBY-DICK

Why do I wish to call our present activity philosophy, when we also call Plato's activity philosophy? Perhaps because of a certain analogy between them, or perhaps because of the continuous development of the subject. Or the new activity may take the place of the old because it removes mental discomforts the old was supposed to.

—WITTGENSTEIN

CONTENTS

ACKNOWLEDGMENTS

This book concerns the origins of the term "philosopher," not of my becoming a professional one, but my having written it depends on my employment, and the love of wisdom, or its direction and refinement, that occasioned it and for both I have many debts here to acknowledge.

In college, Nancy Crumbine and Roy Sorensen modeled two ways to think philosophically. Amplifying their salutary effects were Jim Moor, Amy Allen (see below), Sam Levey, Christie Thomas, and Bernie Gert. Bill Scott taught me Greek.

In graduate school, Sandra Peterson gave me a direction for a sort of ancient philosophy I could emulate, then respond to, and draw inspiration from. Her writings on the origins of the term "philosophy" have motivated the whole of my own work, especially when our views have differed. My classmate Josh Kortbein brought me into the richest conversations about philosophy, its aspirations, and its disciplinary norms.

This project began when I taught at Skidmore and received early encouragement at a research presentation from the late classicist and college president David Porter. Elizabeth Belfiore provided early advice on the resulting paper, as she did so often, and a certain anonymous referee, in rejecting that paper, observed that I had a project much larger than an article in my hands. I presented studies for this monograph at Penn State, Bryn Mawr, the Center for Hellenic Studies, Duquesne, Vassar, Penn State–Altoona, and at the annual conferences of CAMWS, SAGP, and NPSA, and two meetings of the West Coast Plato Workshop.

I wrote much of the book at Harvard's Center for Hellenic Studies in Washington, DC. I cannot imagine a more commodious, welcome, beautiful, and bibliographically well-outfitted place to live and work. Gregory Nagy and Lanah Koelle served exemplarily as hosts. I had critical conversations about Pindar with Sven Schipporeit and about Alcmaeon with Stavros Kouloumentas. Some of the book's leading arguments and narrative elements took shape in the crucible of questioning by Paul Kosmin, who also provided a model of scholarly presentation. I thank Radcliffe Edmonds for additional support. The Dean of the College of the Liberal Arts at Penn State, Susan Welch, made my semester in Washington possible, and supported me in other fundamental ways. I revised the book with research leave funded by the Penn

State Center for Humanities and Information, for which I thank its director, Eric Hayot.

I had valuable early email exchanges on relevant topics with Robin Boyes and Del Reed. My student Brendan Bernicker read the first three chapters with assiduity. Amy Allen, now my department head at Penn State, arranged and funded a seminar for my manuscript; thus my colleagues Vincent Colapietro, Eduardo Mendieta, Mark Munn, and Mark Sentesy read the whole thing, giving me many useful suggestions and much encouragement. The three outside readers—Andrew Ford, Doug Hutchinson, and Chris Raymond—discussed the project with me at heroic lengths during the seminar and for months following; their interest and commitment has meant the most to my continued understanding of the nature and value of the project. Benjamin Randolph and Joshua Billings read and commented on the penultimate draft, with canny advice for improving its rhetorical shape. Kate Baldanza helped me sharpen up the introduction. Kris Klotz proofread the book, and Blythe Woolston prepared the index.

Rob Tempio at Princeton University Press identified this book project as one worth taking on; his commitment to intellectual history and to philosophy in its ancient cultural context made him the ideal editor. His four readers for the manuscript each helped, in his or her own way, to make the work rather less disappointing than it otherwise would have been. I am thankful to the rest of the Princeton University Press staff involved in this complicated project, especially Natalie Baan.

To be sure, despite my deep appreciation for all named above, none is to be taken to agree with all or any particular claims I make in what follows. Then again, that might be a necessary condition of our sharing in the disciplinary life of *philosophia*.

During copyediting, my daughter was born, whose name, Lydia, as luck would have it, has particular aptness for this book. She is already a conversationalist after her fashion, and I eagerly await our learning together how to obey the Delphic *"Philosophos ginou!"*

SELECTED ABBREVIATIONS
AND EDITIONS

Aesch.	Aeschylus. Page, D., ed. *Aeschyli Septem Quae Supersunt Tragoedias*. Oxford: Oxford University Press, 1972.
fr.	fragment (in *TrGF*)
Sept.	*Seven against Thebes*
Supp.	*Suppliant Maidens*
Alcm.	Alcman (in **PMG**)
Ambrose	Migne, J. P., ed. *Sancti Ambrosii Mediolanensis Episcopi Opera Omnia*. Patrologia Latina 14–17, Paris: Migne, 1845.
Ammonius	Busse, A., ed. *Ammonius in Porphyrii Isagogen sive Quinque Voces*. Commentaria in Aristotelem Graeca 4.3. Berlin: Reimer, 1891.
Anac.	Anacreon (in **P**)
Anon. Iambl.	Anonymus Iamblichi (in **LM**)
Apul.	Apuleius. Jones, C. P., ed. *Apuleius. Apologia, Florida, De Deo Socratis*. Loeb Classical Library. Cambridge, MA: Harvard University Press, 2017.
Apol.	*Apologia*
Flor.	*Florida*
Ar.	Aristophanes. Wilson, N. G., ed. *Aristophanis Fabulae*. 2 vols. Oxford: Oxford University Press, 2007.
Ach.	*Acharnians*
Av.	*Birds*
Eccl.	*Ecclesiazusae (Assemblywomen)*
Eq.	*Knights*
Nub.	*Clouds*
Ran.	*Frogs*
Thesm.	*Women at the Thesmophoria*
Vesp.	*Wasps*
Arist.	Aristotle
An. post.	*Posterior Analytics*
Ath. Pol.	*Constitution of the Athenians*
Cael.	*De Caelo (On the Heavens)*

De an.	*De Anima (On the Soul)*
Eth. Nic.	*Nicomachean Ethics.* Bywater, I, ed. *Aristotelis Ethica Nicomachea.* Oxford: Oxford University Press, 1894.
Gen. corr.	*On Generation and Corruption*
M. A	*Metaphysics.* Primavesi, O., ed. "Aristotle, *Metaphysics* A: A New Critical Edition with Introduction." In *Aristotle's "Metaphysics" Alpha: Symposium Aristotelicum*, edited by C. Steel, 385–516. Oxford: Oxford University Press, 2012.
M. B–N	*Metaphysics.* Jaeger, W., ed. *Aristotelis Metaphysica.* Oxford: Oxford University Press, 1957.
[MXG]	*On Melissus, Xenophanes, and Gorgias*
Part. an.	*Parts of Animals*
Phys.	*Physics*
Poet.	*Poetics*
Pol.	*Politics*
Rh.	*Rhetoric.* Ross, W. D., ed. *Aristotelis Ars Rhetorica.* Oxford: Oxford University Press, 1959.
Soph. el.	*Sophistical Refutations*
Top.	*Topics*
Bacchyl.	Bacchylides. Snell, B. and H. Maehler, eds. *Bacchylides. Carmina cum fragmentis.* 10th ed. Leipzig, Teubner, 1970.
BNJ	Worthington, I., ed. *Brill's New Jacoby.* 2nd ed. Leiden: Brill, 2018–.
BNP	Schneider, H., M. Landfester, and H. Cancik, eds. *Brill's New Pauly.* Leiden: Brill, 1996–.
Cic.	Cicero
Tusc.	*Tusculan Disputations.* Fohlen, G., ed. *Cicéron: Tusculanes.* 2 vols. Paris: Les Belles Lettres, 1930–31.
Clem.	Clement of Alexandria
Strom.	*Stromata (Miscellanies).* Stählin, O., ed. *Clemens Alexandrinus: Stromata.* Leipzig: J. C. Henrichs, 1906.
DK	Diels, H. and W. Kranz, eds. *Die Fragmente der Vorsokratiker.* 6th ed. Berlin: Weidmann, 1951.
DL	Diogenes Laertius. Dorandi, T., ed. *Diogenes Laertius: Lives of Eminent Philosophers.* Cambridge: Cambridge University Press, 2013.
DS	Diodorus Siculus. *Diodore de Sicile: Bibliothèque Historique.* Paris: Les Belles Lettres, 1972–.

Diss. Log.	*Dissoi Logoi* (in **LM**)
EGF	Davies, M., ed. *Epicorum Graecorum Fragmenta.* Göttingen: Vandenhoeck and Ruprecht, 1988.
EGM	Fowler, R. L., ed. *Early Greek Mythography.* 2 vols. Oxford: Oxford University Press, 2001 and 2013.
Eur.	Euripides. Diggle, J, ed. *Euripides Fabulae.* 3 vols. Oxford: Oxford University Press, 1981–94.
Andr.	*Andromache*
El.	*Electra*
Hec.	*Hecuba*
Hel.	*Helen*
Heracl.	*Children of Heracles*
Hipp.	*Hippolytus*
IA	*Iphigenia at Aulis*
IT	*Iphigenia among the Taurians*
Phoen.	*Phoenician Women*
[Rhes.]	*[Rhesus]*
fr.	fragment (in *TrGF*)
Euseb.	Eusebius
Chron.	Helm, R., ed. *Eusebius Werke: Die Chronik des Hieronymus.* Bd. 7. Berlin: Akademie-Verlag, 1913–26.
Praep. evang.	Mras, K., ed. *Eusebius Werke: Die Praeparatio evangelica.* Bd. 8. Berlin: Akademie-Verlag, 1954–56.
Flor. Monac.	Munich Florilegium
Gnom. Vat.	Vatican Gnomologium
Gorg.	Gorgias of Leontini (in **LM**)
Hdt.	Herodotus. Wilson, N. G., ed. *Herodoti Historiae.* 2 vols. Oxford: Oxford University Press, 2015.
Hermias	Lucarini, C. M. and C. Moreschini, eds. *Hermias Alexandrinus: In Platonis Phaedrum Commentarii.* Berlin: De Gruyter, 2008.
Hes.	Hesiod. Most, G. W., ed. *Hesiod.* Rev. ed. 2 vols. Loeb Classical Library. Cambridge, MA: Harvard University Press, 2018.
Op.	*Works and Days*
[Sc.]	*Shield of Heracles*
Theog.	*Theogony*
HJ	Hutchinson, D. S. and M. R. Johnson, eds. *Aristotle: Protrepticus.* Cambridge: Cambridge University Press, forthcoming.

Homer	Monro, D. R. and T. W. Allen, eds. *Homeri Opera*. 2nd ed. 4 vols. Oxford: Oxford University Press, 1922.
Il.	*Iliad*
Od.	*Odyssey*
Iambl.	Iamblichus of Chalcis
DCMS	*On General Mathematical Science*. Festa, N., ed. *Iamblichi De communi mathematica scientia*. Leipzig: Teubner, 1891.
Pro.	*Protrepticus (Exhortation to Philosophy)*. Pistelli, E. ed. *Iamblichi Protrepticus*. Stuttgart: Teubner, 1967.
VP	*On the Pythagorean Way of Life*. Nauck, A. ed. *Iamblichi De vita Pythagorica*. St. Petersburg: Eggers, 1884.
Ibyc.	Ibycus (in ***PMG***)
IG	Kirchhoff, A. and U. von Wilamowitz Moellendorff, eds. *Inscriptiones Graecae*. 62 fasc. Berlin: Walter de Gruyter, 1873–.
Isid.	Isidore of Seville. Lindsay, W. M., ed. *Isidori Hispalensis Episcopi Etymologiarum sive Originum Libri XX*. Oxford: Clarendon Press, 1911.
Isoc.	Isocrates. Mandilaras, B. G., ed. *Isocrates: Opera Omnia*. 3 vols. Munich and Leipzig: Teubner/Saur, 2003.
LM	Laks, A. and G. Most. *Early Greek Philosophy*. 9 vols. Loeb Classical Library. Cambridge MA: Harvard University Press, 2017.
LSJ	Liddell, H. G., R. Scott, and H. S. Jones. *A Greek-English Lexicon*. 9th ed. Oxford: Clarendon Press, 1925–40.
Lys.	Lysias. Carey, C., ed. *Lysiae Orationes cum Fragmentis*. Oxford: Oxford University Press, 2007.
Nicom.	Nicomachus of Gerasa. Hoche, R., ed. *Nicomachi Geraseni Pythagorei Introductionis Arithmeticae Libri II*. Leipzig: Teubner, 1866.
Ench.	*Manual of Harmonics*
Isag. Arithm.	*Introduction to Arithemetic*
OCD	Hornblower, S., A. Spawforth, and E. Eidinow. *Oxford Classical Dictionary*. 4th ed. Oxford: Oxford University Press, 2012.
OED	Simpson, J. A. and E.S.C. Weiner. *Oxford English Dictionary*. 2nd ed. 20 vols. Oxford: Clarendon Press, 1989.

P	Page, D. L., ed. *Poetae Melici Graeci*. Oxford: Oxford University Press, 1962.
PCG	Kassel, R. and C. Austin, eds. *Poetai Comici Graeci*. 8 vols. Berlin: De Gruyter, 1983–95.
Pind.	Pindar. Race, W. H., ed. *Pindar*. Rev. ed. 2 vols. Loeb Classical Library. Cambridge, MA: Harvard University Press, 2012.
Isthm.	*Isthmian Odes*
Nem.	*Nemean Odes*
Ol.	*Olympian Odes*
Pae.	*Paeans*
Pyth.	*Pythian Odes*
Pl.	Plato. Burnet, J. ed. *Platonis Opera*. Oxford: Oxford University Press, 1900–7.
Alc.	*Alcibiades*
Alc. II	*Alcibiades II*
Ap.	*Apology of Socrates*
Chrm.	*Charmides*
Cra.	*Cratylus*
Criti.	*Critias*
Epin.	*Epinomis*
Euthyd.	*Euthydemus*
Grg.	*Gorgias*
Hp. mai.	*Hippias Major*
Hp. mi.	*Hippias Minor*
Leg.	*Laws*
Menex.	*Menexenus*
Phd.	*Phaedo*
Phdr.	*Phaedrus*
Phlb.	*Philebus*
Prm.	*Parmenides*
Prt.	*Protagoras*
R.	*Republic*. S. R. Slings, ed. *Platonis Rempublicam*. Oxford: Oxford University Press, 2003.
RL	(*Rival*) *Lovers* (*Erastai* or *Anterastai*)
Symp.	*Symposium*
Soph.	*Sophist*
Tht.	*Theaetetus*
Tim.	*Timaeus*

PLF	Lobel, E. and D. Page, eds. *Poetarum Lesbiorum Fragmenta.* Oxford: Clarendon Press, 1968.
Plut.	Plutarch. Nachstädt, W., W. Sieveking, and J.B. Titchener, eds. *Plutarchi Moralia.* 7 vols. Leipzig: Teubner, 1966–71.
PMG	Davies, M. and D. L. Page, eds. *Poetarum Melicorum Graecorum Fragmenta.* Vol. 1. Oxford: Clarendon Press. 1991.
Porph.	Porphyry
VP	*Life of Pythagoras.* des Places, Édouard, ed. *Porphyre: Vie de Pythagore, Lettre à Marcella.* Paris: Les Belles Lettres, 1982.
Quint.	Quintilian
Inst.	*Institutes of Oratory.* Winterbottom, M., ed. *M. Fabi Quintiliani Institutionis Oratoriae Libri Duodecim.* 2 vols. Oxford: Oxford University Press, 1970.
Ross	Ross, W. D., ed. *Aristotelis Fragmenta Selecta.* Oxford: Oxford University Press 1955.
Σ	Scholiast
Simon.	Simonides (in **P**)
Sol.	Solon (in **W**)
Soph.	Sophocles. Lloyd-Jones, H. and N. G. Wilson, eds. *Sophoclis Fablulae.* Oxford: Oxford University Press, 1990.
Ant.	*Antigone*
El.	*Electra*
OC	*Oedipus at Colonus*
fr.	fragment (in ***TrGF***)
SSR	Giannantoni, G., ed. *Socratis et Socraticorum Reliquiae.* Napoli: Bibliopolis, 1991.
Stob.	Stobaeus. Wachsmuth, C. and O. Hense, eds. *Joannis Stobaei Anthologium.* 5 vols. Berlin: Weidmann, 1884–1912.
TCT	Grafton, A., G. Most, and S. Settis. *The Classical Tradition.* Cambridge, MA: Harvard University Press, 2010.
Thgn.	Theognis (in **W**)
Thuc.	Thucydides. Jones, H. S. and J. E. Powell, eds. *Thucydidis Historiae.* 2 vols. Oxford: Oxford University Press, 1942.

TrGF	Snell, B., R. Kannicht, and S. Radt, eds. *Tragicorum Graecorum Fragmenta.* 6 vols. Göttingen: Vandenhoeck and Ruprecht, 1971–2004.
Val. Max.	Valerius Maximus. Shackleton Bailey, D. R., ed. *Valerius Maximus: Memorable Doings and Sayings.* 2 vols. Loeb Classical Library. Cambridge, MA: Harvard University Press, 2000.
VM	*De Vetere Medicina.* Schiefsky, M. J., ed. *Hippocrates: On Ancient Medicine.* Leiden: Brill, 2005
W	West, M. L., ed. *Iambi et Elegi Graeci.* 2 vols. Oxford, Oxford University Press, 1989–92.
Xen.	Xenophon. Marchant, E. C., ed. *Xenophontis Opera Omnia.* 2nd ed. 5 vols. Oxford: Clarendon Press, 1921.
An.	*Anabasis*
Cyn.	*Cynegeticus (On Hunting with Dogs)*
Cyr.	*Cyropedia*
Hell.	*Hellenika (History of Greece)*
Mem.	*Memorabilia (Memoirs of Socrates)*
Oec.	*Oeconomicus (On Estate Management)*
Symp.	*Symposium (Banquet)*
YC	Yuen-Collingridge, Rachel. "Historical Lexicography and the Origins of Philosophy: Herodotus' Use of φιλοσοφέειν, σοφιστής and Cognates." PhD diss., Macquarie University, 2012.

Note on Reference to "Presocratic" Fragments

The text of ancient writings by and about the early Greek writers eventually called "philosophers" comes from LM, unless noted, and is cited by both DK and LM number, if available. In DK, "A" precedes testimonia, "B" precedes fragments. In LM, "P" precedes information about the philosopher, "D" precedes fragments or doctrinal statements, and "R" precedes later reception of the philosopher's thought.

Other abbreviations are generally from *OCD*. Translations are my own unless otherwise credited.

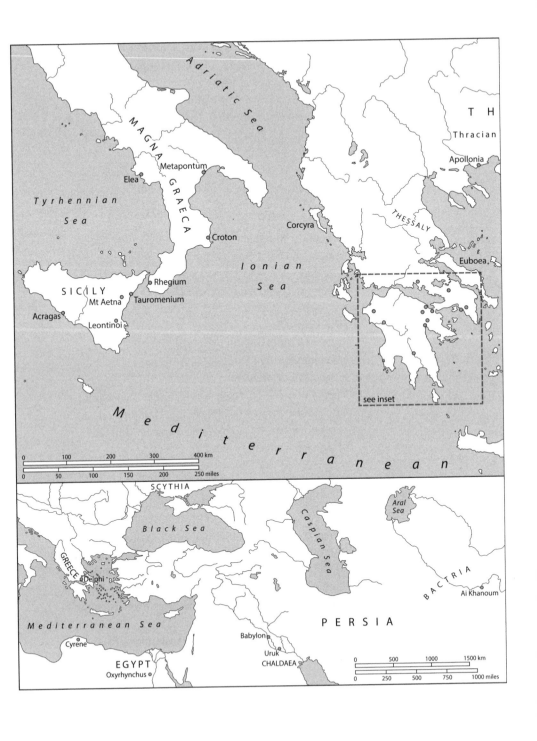

Adriatic Sea

MAGNA GRAECA

Metapontum
Elea

Tyrhennian
Sea

Corcyra

Croton

Ionian
Sea

Rhegium

SICILY

Mt Aetna

Tauromenium

Acragas

Leontinoi

T H
Thracian

Apollonia

THESSALY

Euboea

see inset

M e d i t e r r a n e a n

| 0 | 100 | 200 | 300 | 400 km |

| 0 | 50 | 100 | 150 | 200 | 250 miles |

SCYTHIA

Black Sea

Caspian Sea

Aral
Sea

BACTRIA

GREECE

Delphi

Ai Khanoum

Mediterranean Sea

PERSIA

Cyrene

Babylon

Uruk

EGYPT

CHALDAEA

Oxyrhynchus

| 0 | 500 | 1000 | 1500 km |

| 0 | 250 | 500 | 750 | 1000 miles |

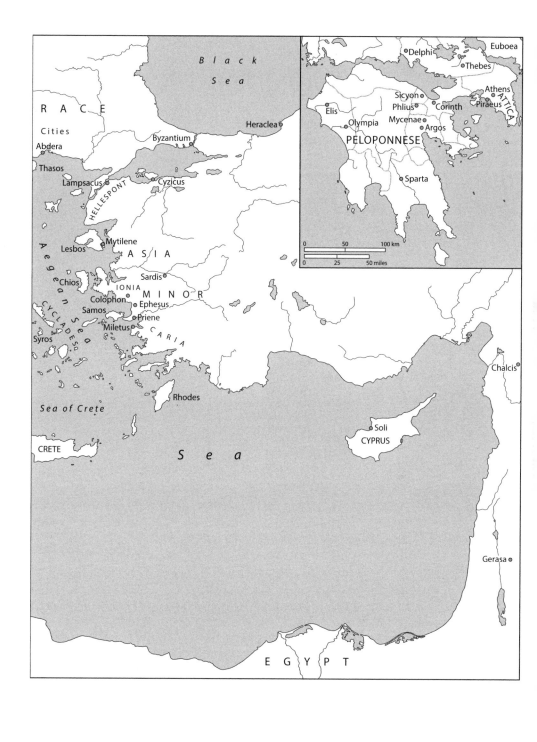

Black
Sea

THRACE

Cities

Abdera

Thasos

Byzantium

Heraclea

Lampsacus

Cyzicus

HELLESPONT

Aegean Sea

Mytilene

Lesbos

ASIA

CYCLADES

Chios

Sardis

IONIA

MINOR

Colophon

Ephesus

Samos

Priene

Syros

Miletus

CARIA

Sea of Crete

Rhodes

CRETE

Sea

Soli

CYPRUS

Chalcis

Gerasa

EGYPT

Delphi

Euboea

Thebes

Athens

Sicyon

ATTICA

Elis

Phlius

Corinth

Piraeus

Olympia

Mycenae

Argos

PELOPONNESE

Sparta

0   50   100 km

0   25   50 miles

CALLING
PHILOSOPHERS
NAMES

1

Introduction: The Origins of *Philosophia*

A History of *Philosophia*, Not of Philosophy

This book tells a new story of the origin of *philosophia*—the Greek name, and the discipline that it came to name. It begins around 500 BCE, with the coinage not of a self-lauding "love of wisdom" but with a wry verbal slight, and concludes a century and a half later, in the maturity of an institution that is continuous with today's departments of philosophy. This phenomenon—accommodating a name-calling name and consolidating a structured group around it—recurs through history, as the cases of the Quakers, Shakers, Freaks, and queer activists illustrate.[1] A norm-policing name, at first distasteful, gets appropriated, facilitates a new and ennobling self-understanding, and then governs a productive and tight-knit social enterprise. I argue that such is the origin of *philosophia*.

The name *philosophos* seems to have begun as "sage-wannabe," a bemused label for a person's repetitive and presumed excessive efforts to join the category of *sophoi*, the political advice-giving sages of the Greek world. The label stuck. Eventually, a fashion for etymological invention glossed *philosophos* as "lover of wisdom." The gloss caught on, but not because it had recovered a historical truth; rather, it sounded good, and provided a happy construction on what those called it were feeling. In this way, every philosophy instructor's class-opening exhortation to philosophy anachronizes, retrojecting fourth-century BCE linguistic play onto the term's coinage many generations earlier. Relatedly, most historians of ancient philosophy, guilty not of anachronism but of partiality to the fourth century, ignore the word's early years, treating it as an unremarkable term meaning "cultivator of one's intellect," a word that on

---

[1] For the Shakers, see Evans 1859, ch. 1, ¶26 (with ¶¶15–22): "Sometimes, after sitting awhile in silent meditation, they were seized with a mighty trembling, under which they would often express the indignation of God against all sin. At other times, they were exercised with singing, shouting, and leaping for joy, at the near prospect of salvation. They were often exercised with great agitation of body and limbs, shaking, running, and walking the floor, with a variety of other operations and signs, swiftly passing and repassing each other, like clouds agitated with a mighty wind. These exercises, so strange in the eyes of the beholders, brought upon them the appellation of Shakers, which has been their most common name of distinction ever since."

their reading happened to catch Plato's fancy, who then singlehandedly made it a technical term and a distinctive life-defining goal. Neither view—"lover of wisdom" or "intellectual cultivator"—squares with the evidence from the first century of the expression's use, and neither attends to the way reflection on the expression contributed to the very thing to which the fraught term applied. Just as a sand grain irritates the oyster into making a pearl, a once-irritating word, PHILOSOPHOS, helped bring about the discipline of *philosophia* among the pearls of fourth-century BCE Athens.

In its focus on the origin of *philosophia*, this book differs from studies that seek the origin of philosophy, whether in Greece or elsewhere. Such studies must start by deciding what counts for us moderns as philosophy, then figure out what kind of ancient evidence would justify our finding philosophy in some early practice, and finally gather whatever evidence is available and explain how this evidence could identify the origin of such practices.[2] These studies have cogent goals, to be sure, tracing back our distinctive reason-giving enterprise, studying the conditions under which it arose, and reconstructing the dialectical process by which familiar concepts, distinctions, and problems became salient. Their work is genuinely philosophical, because recognizing reasons *as* reasons means acknowledging and evaluating the normative force of various claims. But they confront serious methodological challenges when they encounter the equivocal evidence on which the issue of origins must rely. The basis on which we are to ascertain the existence of some "philosophy" way back when seems undecideable. After all, what counts as philosophy *now* is hardly obvious, given the complexity of our practices, not to mention the diversity and disagreements within the field. What counts as ancient evidence for (our idea of) philosophy is no easier to decide. Some might look for explicit dialectical engagement, others for explicit argumentative inference, and yet others for non-theistic explanation. Adding to the difficulty, our evidence for the earliest candidate philosophers comes to us pre-interpreted by later philosophers, such as Aristotle, who might perhaps have to take responsibility for *making* them philosophical in our sense. To be sure, the best such studies confront these methodological challenges explicitly and provide deep insight into the nature of philosophy, whatever it may be, in the ancient world. Yet none avoids a fealty to present-day ideas. Perhaps a rational demonstration is a rational demonstration, in 500 BCE as much as now. But was any particular case of rational demonstration philosophy? Was anything nondemonstrative or

---

[2] Sassi 2018 provides one of the clearest recent examples of this approach (see p. 277n50 below for her application of this method to Thales). Frede 2000 and Palmer 2009 contain subtle reflections on the historiography of the development of ancient philosophy. See also Lloyd 1970, "Preface" and 1–15; Collins 2000, 82–92.

nonrational philosophy? How many people had to share in this demonstrative practice for "philosophy" to become recognizable or count as a practice, institution, and discipline? These are intractable questions, and there is no ready criterion to which one might appeal.

Fortunately, there is a criterion for *something*, when we shift approaches. Rather than struggle to apply our own complicated concepts to a complicated past, we might study the concepts that our forebears used. This is the contextualist or historicizing approach. Unable to decide on the first "philosophers," we can still decide on the first "*philosophoi.*" Whereas for historians of philosophy, the earliest known philosophers may have been Thales and Anaximander, for historians of *philosophia*, the earliest known *philosophoi* were those called *philosophoi* in the earliest attestations of the term: as it seems to turn out, people associated with Pythagoras or early fifth-century BCE Ionians. The history of *philosophia* eventually includes Thales and Anaximander, but only once early Academic (fourth century BCE) authors strove to identify and baptize precursors. The evidence we have allows us to see the development of a cultural phenomenon that the Greeks could themselves see, reflect on, react to, and consciously or unconsciously modify, one that may have begun in Magna Graeca rather than Asia Minor.[3] The Greeks certainly talked about *philosophia*; why they did so, and what effect on *philosophia* came about as a result, is the concern of this book.

A new approach to the origins of the discipline is encouraged not just by the desire to track ancient rather than modern concepts, to discuss social rather than purely rational phenomena. It is also encouraged by a puzzling feature of ancient histories of philosophy. Over more than a millennium of accounts, and with provocative regularity, ancient authors advert to the origin of the very word *philosophos*. No other discipline pauses with such care to reflect on the introduction of its name—not astronomy, not poetics, not mathematics. Not only that, but from at least the fourth century BCE, these historians, otherwise impresarios of disagreement, partisans of some school, or skeptics about all factions, took a single and unwavering view of that origin; we know of no rejections, suspicions, or alternative accounts.[4] The story they told of that lexical origin, the analysis of which provides a narrative thread for my book, took varied forms, and differences among them are important; but the striking consensus about the core claim is even more important. We find the account in Aristotle, and in his once-famous colleague Heraclides Ponticus; in a rig-

[3] Ionia may have had the conditions for coinage of the term (see Emlyn-Jones 1980, 97–111, 164–77), but we lack any evidence for the coinage of the term there.
[4] We do of course know of differing accounts of the *development* of the discipline; see, for example, Laks 2018.

orous second-century BCE historian of philosophers, Sosicrates of Rhodes; in the (conjectured) first-century CE encyclopedist of philosophy Aëtius; in the Roman philosopher-rhetorician Cicero and rhetorician-philosopher Quintilian; in the omnivorous historians Valerius Maximus and Diodorus Siculus; in the Platonist intellectuals Apuleius and Maximus; in the neo-Platonist scholars Iamblichus and Hermias; in the Christian-philosophical apologists Augustine and Clement; in the Church Fathers Ambrose and Isidore; and in two biographers of Greek philosophers who may have read more sources than anyone else, Diogenes Laertius and Eusebius.[5]

The version attributed to Sosicrates (fl. < 145 BCE) provides a conveniently compressed starting place.[6] We find it in Diogenes Laertius's *Life of Pythagoras*, one of the late chapters of his *Lives of Eminent Philosophers* (ca. third century CE), a sequence of biographies of earlier Greek thinkers and the essential extant source for ancient philosophy anecdotes. In his work, Sosicrates sets out the history of philosophical teacher-student relationships, and Diogenes generally relies on him for his rigorous historical skepticism.[7] Here he quotes or paraphrases Sosicrates's work on academic lineages, called *Successions*:

[Pythagoras], being asked by Leon tyrant of Phlius what he was (τίς εἴη), said [he was] a *philosophos* (φιλόσοφον).[8] And he likened life to a festival, since some come to it to compete, some for business, some, indeed the best, as spectators; thus in life some are slavish, he said, born (φύονται)[9] as hunters after reputation and excess, but *philosophoi* [are hunters] after truth (ἀληθείας).[10] (DL 8.8)

[5] Aët. 1.3.7; Cic. *Tusc.* 5.3.8–9; Quint. *Inst.* 12.1.19; Val. Max. 8.7 ext. 2; DS 10 fr. 24; Apul. *Apol.* 4.7; *Flor.* 15.22; Max. Tyr. 1.2a; Iambl. *VP* 12 with *Pro.* 9; Hermias *In Phdr.* 278a; August. *De civ. D.* 8.2; *De trin.* 14.1.2; Clem. *Strom.* 1.61.4; Ambrose *De Abr.* 2.7.37; Isid. 8.6, 14.6; DL 1.12, 8.8; Euseb. *Praep. evang.* 10.14.3; *Chron.* 14.2–4 Helm. See the Appendix for all texts.

[6] For the date, see Strabo 10.4.3, with discussion in Giannattasio Andria 1989 and *BNJ* 461.

[7] Contrarian views on life-dates: 1.38 (Thales), 1.49 and 1.62 (Solon), 1.68 (Chilon), 1.95 (Periander), 1.101 (Anacharsis); contrarian views on literary authenticity: 2.84 (Aristippus), 6.80 (Diogenes), 7.163 (Ariston of Chion); precise anecdotes: 1.75 (Pittacus), 1.106–7 (Myson's father), 6.82 (Monimus, a student of Diogenes), 6.13 (first cloak-doubler). See also Ath. 4.163f (a Pythagorean's fashion innovations), 10.422c (Crates, cf. DL 6.90). This Sosicrates may have written a famously rigorous *History of Crete* (DS 5.80; Ath. 6.263f; Σ Eur. *Hipp.* 47; Σ Ar. *Av.* 521).

[8] One version of this text (Φ, the Vatican excerpt) prints φιλόσοφος as direct speech; this presents Pythagoras as having actually used the term, and might present this brief account as abstracting from a longer dramatic version.

[9] Marcovich 1999 conjectures φαίνονται ("appear") for φύονται, against all manuscripts. The verb one chooses determines the degree of Pythagorean doctrine of soul-transmigration found in this passage, and may affect one's view of its sources.

[10] For the Greek of this passage, see Appendix, p. 321.

On the surface, this two-sentence tale is simple; but it also has important implications. Pythagoras calls himself a *philosophos*; uses an analogy to describe *philosophoi* and to differentiate them from other kinds of people; and says that *philosophoi* strive after an elusive truth. That Leon, from a city neighboring Corinth between the Peloponnese and Attica, has to ask what Pythagoras takes himself to be suggests that Pythagoras acts or speaks in an unfamiliar way. That the story takes place during Pythagoras's life, around the end of the sixth century or early in the fifth century BCE, and that Leon does not know the word *philosophos*, or at least not when applied to oneself, implies the word's coinage in that period. That Pythagoras has to provide an elaborate analogy to explain the term tells us that the meaning of *philosophos* is not transparent or apparent from its putative parts even to elite Greek speakers. That Pythagoras does not find it appropriate to define the word *philosophos* in terms either of love or of wisdom, but only in the rhyming terms of observation (*theatai*) and hunting (*thêratai*),[11] implies that he did not coin the term himself: were the implausibility of describing oneself with a private neologism not enough, he would need to explain why he created and used the word *philosophos* in particular. That *philosophoi* are compared as a group to Olympic athletes and traveling salespeople suggests that they could be recognized as a type.[12] Finally, that Pythagoras is the protagonist of this story means that Pythagoras was viewed as an archetypal *philosophos*.

Already we see reasons against accepting the standard accounts of "philosopher" as meaning (etymologically) "lover of wisdom" or (initially) "intellectual cultivator"; other versions of the Pythagoras story provide similar reasons. If the former meaning were obvious, Pythagoras would not have needed to explain who *philosophoi* are; at most he might have discussed the way his actions or speeches reveal his love of wisdom. If the latter were valid, again he would not have needed to explain who *philosophoi* are; Leon would have to be obtuse not to appreciate the basic idea of cultivating one's intellect. Nothing said here precludes people from *later* saying that *philosophos* means "lover of wisdom" or using it to mean "intellectual cultivator." In fact, we find both in the fourth century BCE, as early as the work of Plato and Alcidamas, and then more prominently in Aristotle. But calling *philosophoi* "lovers of wisdom" is

---

[11] One might wonder, given Sosicrates's late date, whether this metaphor relies on Plato's "hunting for what's real" (τὴν τοῦ ὄντος θήραν, *Phd.* 66c2; cf. Iambl. *Pro.* 13.64,2 and 20.99,15), but since the metaphorical use of hunting for a quasi-abstract object exists from the fifth century BCE, this cannot be determined. Other important fourth-century BCE hunting references are at Xen. *Cyn.* 12–13; Pl. *Soph.* 218d–223b.

[12] It may be worth noting that Pythagoras's adopted hometown, Croton, enjoyed amazing success at athletic festivals (Dunbabin 1948, 369–70), and that Pythagoras's contemporary Xenophanes also vaunted his intellectual *sophia* over athletic glory (B2/D61).

a conscious achievement; of course, using the term to mean "intellectual cultivator" in a broad and undifferentiated sense is another achievement, though this one is perhaps less deliberate.[13]

This book's argument has two parts. The first concerns the coinage of the word *philosophos*. *Phil*- prefixed terms in the sixth and early fifth centuries BCE, at the time *philosophos* was coined, tend to be name-calling names. They tend to call out those so named for excessive activity related to a social practice referred to synecdochally by the word's second element; there is no evidence that the *phil*- prefix indicated the affection of "love." For example, *philaitios*, with the second element *aitia*, "cause," or in its social context, "legal motion," means excessive activity in lawsuits, or "litigious." This word has pejorative rather than laudatory valence, and it does not impute an *affection* for causes or legal motions.[14] The second element in *philosophos* is *soph*-, the root of *sophos*, which, as I argue later, referred at the end of the sixth century BCE particularly to "sages," culturally prominent, socially elite, intellectually wide-ranging civic and domestic advisers typified though not exhausted by the "Seven *Sophoi*" of the early sixth century BCE. So calling someone *philosophos* would seem to impute an excessive tendency to act like sages or to seek after the status of sages (broadly construed), presumably through advice-giving and study, where this practice or aspiration would seem dubious, problematic, or even ridiculous. Word invention would satisfy the impulse to label certain people who act in ways that are not adequately described by any other label. The political, intellectual, and religious circle of Pythagoreans in late sixth-century and early fifth-century BCE Magna Graeca provides the most plausible agent for occasioning this linguistic creation and subsequent diffusion (whatever the nature of that group's constitution).

The second part of my argument concerns the trajectory of the term *philosophos*. Through the fifth century BCE it was applied to people acting like those Pythagoreans: giving sage advice about ethical and existential

---

[13] The earliest extant Greek use known to me of *philein sophian*, "loving wisdom," is in the Septuagint *Prov.* 29.3 (second century–first century BCE); the earliest use of *philian sophias*, "love of wisdom," in Nicomachus's *Introduction to Arithmetic* 1.1.1.2 (60–120 CE—John Philoponus attributes to Nicomachus this definition of philosophy [*In Nic. Isag. Arithm.* 1.8; cf. 1.52, 15.2, 21.20]); and the earliest use of *philos sophias*, "lover of wisdom," in Euseb. *Vit. Const.* 4.2.8 (fourth century CE). Pl. *Lys.* 212d8 (. . . ἂν μὴ ἡ σοφία αὐτοὺς ἀντιφιλῇ) admittedly gets close.

[14] Aesch. fr. 326a.14 (attributed to the poet's voice); *Supp.* 485; there is a maxim, Μὴ φιλαίτιος ἴσθι ("Don't be litigious"), found in an addendum to the (fourth-century BCE) list attributed to Sosiades (Stob. 3.1.173, in the Brussels codex).

issues, making arguments that are grounded in hypotheses about the nature of the *kosmos*, and talking with erudition and precision about political matters of no immediate relevance. In time, the word could sometimes shake off the pejorative sense, becoming a sort of neutral label, for example for the self-constituting group of people who practiced formal debate about important matters for the sake of the debate, as an exercise of dialectical skill, rather than for political or forensic purposes, as an expression of Sage wisdom. As a neutral label, it could be self-applied, as increasingly it was around the turn of that century—but not universally so, since its original negativity had not yet been, and may never have been, entirely eradicated. Those being called *philosophoi* or calling themselves *philosophoi* sought to vindicate the appellation, and did so in various ways. Some gave new explanations for the very actions that led to the scornful name; some invented alternative etymologies of the term *philosophos*; and some looked backward and assembled a noble lineage of great thinkers, with whom they could carry on current debates, calling them the first and paradigmatic *philosophoi*. It is worth noting that a story of similar structure could perhaps be told about the *sophistai*, another group of people whose name is formed from the *soph-* root, perhaps around the same time and in parallel, though probably without significant interchange with the *philosophoi* until the end of the fifth century BCE.[15]

In brief, past scholarship has treated the word *philosophos* as definable by a phrase. I think we should treat it as defined rather more by application— "those people are akin to those we call *philosophoi*"—and the choice of word a result of name-calling name conventions. Treated this way, *philosophos* is defined, at the start, as in a family resemblance with the Pythagoreans, and the specific word *philosophos* serves to denote this family resemblance because the Pythagoreans were, in effect, *sophos*-wannabes. Only later could processes of abstraction liberate the term *philosophos* from its archetype.

Though this account of the origin of *philosophia* differs from an account of the origin of philosophy, it complements rather than replaces it. The name is reactive, not motivating. What got philosophy going may indeed have been wonder, or the leisured pursuit of scientific understanding, or the appreciation

[15] The word *sophistês* first appears in Pind. *Isthm.* 5.28 (after 480 BCE), and must have been in circulation before that. The *-istês* ending denotes a professional status, referring initially to clever advice-giving and musical instruction. There develops a canonical set of practitioners certainly by the early fourth century BCE (cf. Pl. *Prt.* 316c5–317c2), though probably by the late fifth century BCE, and gains a technical meaning by the time of Aristotle's works. Much more ought to be said, but space does not allow it here. See Edmunds 2006; Billings and Moore forthcoming, "Introduction."

of and confidence in large-scale claims defended by reasons.[16] Perhaps it was the moral seriousness that drove Socrates to avoid wrongdoing by learning what he could learn. Perhaps it was the fear of death and the Empedoclean quest for self-purification and psychic health. Perhaps nautical astronomy, or agricultural meteorology, or genealogical grandstanding played a role; perhaps it was influence from Egypt or Babylon or Chaldaea.[17] Scholarship on ancient philosophy has learned much from pursuing these hypotheses. But none alone explains why people got called *philosophoi*, and none explains the development of an enduring discipline—a mutually self-aware group of coordinated practitioners with a historical consciousness of their forerunners—named precisely *philosophia*. What they do aim to explain is why people like the Pythagoreans did what they did, what they did, and why and how others after the Pythagoreans did what they did. An account of the origins of philosophy takes an internal perspective, asking why, for example, Thales put water at the center of a unified cosmic account, whereas an account of the origins of *philosophia*, which I attempt to provide in this book, takes an external perspective, asking why someone would ever call Thales *philosophos*.

Internal and external accounts of origins both rely on thinner evidentiary bases than we would hope for. We no more have independent statements of Pythagoras's self-descriptions than we do of the reasoning that brought him to theorize the soul, life, or the *kosmos*. Our interpretation of the patterns of *phil-* prefixed names depends on infrequent uses at somewhat indeterminate moments after their coinage. My primary theses, which are my best explanations for the broad range of evidence that is mustered here, must still count ultimately as open to doubt and revision. In light of this weak evidentiary tissue, the story I tell may be judged a merely likely story. Even if so, it should appear likelier than the alternatives. My methodology is to study the meaning of a compound name by reconstructing the morphosemantic limitations and the historical occasions for its coinage; track the changes to its meaning with an eye to patterns of diffusion; and treat its ascendency to discipline-name on a parallel with other reappropriated names. At the book's conclusion, I reflect on the relevance of this study to our understanding of philosophy today. What I think seemed most incredible to contemporary observers of Pythagoreans or their look-alikes was their commitment to the precise discussion of (seemingly) background issues—issues that amount neither to urgent decisions nor to salacious social gossip—as instrumental for, even constitutive of, the good life.

---

[16] For the latter, see, e.g., Barnes 1982, 3–12; Osborne 2004, 133–35.

[17] For an ancient perspective on the non-Greek origins of or influences on *philosophia*, see, e.g., DL 1.1–11; for a more recent perspective, see West 1971.

The same incredulity, I believe, characterizes present-day popular attitudes toward philosophy.

Heraclides Ponticus's History of *Philosophia*

Sosicrates's version of the story about Pythagoras's self-appellation as *philosophos* provides key evidence about the origins of *philosophia*, with respect to both the word and the origin of the discipline it eventually came to name. To the extent that something about the story is true or plausible, we learn something important and distinctive about the earliest uses of the term *philosophos*. To the extent that people told the story—as we will see, by the fourth century BCE, just when we also see the formation of a recognizable discipline—we learn something important and distinctive about the uses of the term *philosophos* at the time that the discipline eventually came to be. Thus, this book addresses three questions about the story. What about it is historically reliable? Why would the term *philosophos* still be worth discussing in the fourth century BCE? And how did this story come to be told in this form?

The earliest name associated with the authorship of the Pythagoras story is Heraclides Ponticus, a member of Plato's Academy. Born around 390 BCE, Heraclides grew up in Heraclea, a town on the Pontus, the Black Sea. Now a city named Karadeniz Ereğli and Turkey's leading steel town, classical Heraclea forged intellectuals, including the mythographer Herodorus and his Socratic-aligned son Bryson.[18] Like many others, Heraclides moved to Athens in his youth, and rose to prominence; his school of choice was the Academy, by then a decade old.[19] Early school histories tell us that he served as acting director during one of Plato's sojourns to Sicily, and at Plato's death he was deemed a candidate for the permanent post.[20] The esteem may speak to his administrative skill or social graces, but it probably also reflects the breadth of his interests and his literary flair, insofar as he wrote philosophical dialogues and treatises with a Platonic vigor.[21] Dozens in number, they ranged from argumentative engagements with Heraclitus and Democritus to literary criticism of Homer, Hesiod, Euripides, and Sophocles, and from histories of invention

---

[18] On Heraclea's intellectual scene, see Burstein 1976, 5, 39–66; Desideri 1991, esp. 8–11, 14–15. Famous names include the Academic Chion, the Pythagorean Zopyrus, the Peripatetic Chamaeleon, and the Stoic Heracleotes.

[19] DL 3.46, 5.86; see Gottschalk 1980, 2–6; Mejer 2009.

[20] Acting director: *Suda* η 461, though doubt is expressed by Guthrie 1978, 483, and the claim is denied by Voss 1896, 11–13. Candidate for post: *PHerc.* 1021 col. vi.41–vii.10.

[21] Vigor: DL 5.89.

and discovery to political, legal, and ethical studies.[22] Cicero treated the dialogues in particular as vital models of the genre,[23] and others expressed their
appreciation as well.[24]

Heraclides gave special attention to the history of Pythagoreanism. Diogenes Laertius attributes to him works of historical research (ἱστορικά), one
of which is called *On the Pythagoreans*, and says that he studied with Pythagoreans.[25] In Porphyry's study of vegetarianism, Heraclides provides his earliest source for the gustatory and sacrificial practices of Pythagoras and the
Pythagoreans, their most promiment and telling idiosyncrasies.[26] Clement of
Alexandria cites Heraclides for Pythagoras's core ethical beliefs.[27] And the fact
that several doxographers of philosophy cite Heraclides's remarkable cosmological view that each star is its own *kosmos* as a view of the Pythagoreans
suggests that Heraclides himself cited the sharing and did so with approval.[28]

A version of the story of Pythagoras's self-naming elsewhere attributed to
Sosicrates appears in Heraclides's work called variously *On Diseases*, *Causes
of Diseases*, or, from a famous episode, *On the Woman Not Breathing*.[29] The
work is lost, but Diogenes Laertius quotes or paraphrases parts of it throughout his *Life of Empedocles*; we also have secondhand citations in Galen, Pliny,
and Origen.[30] None gives a plot summary, and none gives the context for the
Pythagoras-as-*philosophos* episode. Nevertheless, these fragments hint at
a work concerned with Empedocles and Pythagoras, and so (presumably)
Pythagoras as an essential predecessor of Empedocles. This context provides clues to the provenance or plausibility of the Pythagoras story, and thus
about the origin of the term *philosophia*. We begin with the material about
Empedocles.

---

[22] List of works: DL 5.86–88.

[23] Cic. *Att.* 13.19.4, 15.4.3, 15.13.3, 15.27.2, 16.2.6, 16.11.3, 16.12; *QFr.* 3.5.1.

[24] E.g., Gell. *NA* 8 fr. xv; the extent of the reception of his work through antiquity is powerful evidence.

[25] DL 5.88, 5.86 (διήκουσε). *Suda* ε 1007 probably suggests that Heraclides wrote about
Pythagoras himself.

[26] Porph. *Abst.* 1.26.2–4.

[27] Clem. *Strom.* 2.21.130.3 (~ Theodoret *Graec. aff. cur.* 11.8), namely, "knowledge of the
perfection of the numbers of the soul is happiness" (or ". . . of the numbers is happiness of the
soul").

[28] Aët. 2.13; Euseb. *Praep. evang.* 15.30.8; ps-Gal. *Hist. phil.* 52; Theodoret *Graec. aff. cur.*
4.20.

[29] Source: Cic. *Tusc.* 5.3.9 with DL 1.12. Names: Αἰτίαι περὶ νόσων: DL 5.87; Περὶ νόσων:
DL 8.51, 8.60; Περὶ τῆς ἄπνου: DL 1.12; Ἄπνους: Gal. *De loc. aff.* 6.5, *De diff. R.* 1.8. None are
sure to go back to Heraclides.

[30] Fragments collected in Schütrumpf 2008, frr. 82–95 (A–D); Wehrli 1969, frr. 76–89; Voss
1896, frr. 67–78.

Diogenes treats *On Diseases* as historically authoritative about Empedocles's life.[31] As for its details of Empedocles's pyroclastic death in Mt. Aetna, he treats it as a plausible contender. In the dialogue, he says, Heraclides narrates what happened after Empedocles cured an intractable patient (the "woman not breathing"). Empedocles held a sacrifice and feast on the land of Peisianax, the patient's father. The attendees then left for the night's sleep, leaving Empedocles by himself. When they returned in the morning, nobody could find him. A servant reported having heard, in the middle of the night, an exceedingly loud sound calling to Empedocles, and then saw a heavenly light and the illumination of torches. Pausanias, a special friend of Empedocles's, started to tell people to resume their search, but then reversed himself, telling them rather to pray and to sacrifice to Empedocles "as to one having become a god" (καθαπερεὶ γεγονότι θεῷ, DL 8.67–68). In this way, Heraclides describes the origins of Empedocles's apotheosis and cult following. The fact that Timaeus of Tauromenium, a fourth-century BCE historian, is said to have taken issue with aspects of the story shows the extent to which contemporaries and successors took Heraclides's detailed account as a basically valid position in biographical debate. It also shows the centrality of Empedocles's death in understanding the sort of person—and thus perhaps what sort of philosopher—he really was.

As *On Disease*'s colloquial title, *On the Woman Not Breathing*, implies, a therapeutic marvel captured the attention of an audience—and, structurally, it led directly to Empedocles's disputed apotheosis. Heraclides says that Empedocles explained to Pausanias what was going on with the unbreathing woman (τὴν ἄπνουν), presumably at the feast celebrating his success in saving her (DL 8.60). He had preserved the body of this woman, Pantheia of Acragas, for thirty days despite a lack of breath or pulse (8.61). Other doctors had failed to understand the case.[32] It is on these grounds (ὅθεν), Diogenes says, that Heraclides calls Empedocles both a doctor and a seer, but also from the following lines (λαμβάνων ἅμα καὶ ἀπὸ τούτων τῶν στίχων, 8.61), which are ten of the first twelve lines of Empedocles's poem (or one of them):

Friends, you who dwell in the great city beside the yellow Acragas   1
On the lofty citadel and who care for good deeds

---

[31] DL 8.51. In the following paragraph (8.52), Diogenes may attribute to Heraclides Empedocles's death at 60 (the manuscripts print "Heraclitus," but F. W. Sturz conjectured "Heraclides" in 1805, and Dorandi 2013 thinks this may be right). That Diogenes actually first attributes the view to Aristotle, "and also" (ἔτι τε) to Heraclides, suggests that Aristotle may have cited Heraclides for the information.

[32] Gal. *De loc. aff.* 6 (they were greatly puzzled); DL 8.69 (citing Hermippus: the other doctors had given up hope).

. . .

I greet you! I, who for you am an immortal god, no longer mortal
I go among you, honored, as I am seen,   5
Crowned with ribbons and with blooming garlands.
Whenever I arrive with these in the flourishing cities,
I am venerated by men and by women; they follow me,
Thousands of them, asking where is the road to benefit:
Some of them desire prophecy, others ask to hear,   10
For illnesses of all kinds, a healing utterance,
. . . [33]   (Empedocles B112/D4, trans. Laks and Most)

Empedocles says that people ask him to heal and predict the future (10–11). Diogenes seems to say that Heraclides includes these lines in his work—how else could he know that Heraclides relied on them?—but whether put in Empedocles's or another character's mouth, or presented by the narrator (Heraclides?) himself, we do not know. In any event, Diogenes treats the Pantheia episode as clinching the claim that Empedocles rather than other doctors knew both how to bring the woman back alive and how to foresee that she would return to the living. Diogenes does not, however, indicate why Heraclides wanted to show Empedocles's superiority, which he may well have taken to be factual.[34] We must turn to the two extant Pythagoras passages for information.

In his *Life of Pythagoras*, Diogenes says that Heraclides presented Pythagoras telling the following detailed story about himself.[35] He had been born a

---

[33] DL 8.62. See DS 13.83.1 for line 3: "Respectful harbors for strangers, inexperienced in wickedness," and Clem. *Strom.* 6.30.1 for line 12: "Pierced for a long time by terrible \<pains\>."

[34] As Origen (*C. Cels.* 2.15.40) observes, Plato's Myth of Er presents a similar situation; more convincingly, Aristotle speaks of suspended animation in his lost *Eudemus, or On the Soul* (frr. 9 and 11 Ross), and the phenomenon is not unknown in the contemporary world. In 2014, a Polish woman was declared dead, as having no pulse or breath, and left in a body bag for eleven hours (http://www.bbc.com/news/world-europe-30048087). Heraclides may have been inspired by Democritus's work, which was eventually called Περὶ τῶν ἐν Ἅιδου (DL 9.46; *Suda* τ 1019; Procl. *In R.* 2.113.6–9; a work by the same name is attributed to Protagoras at DL 9.55, and Socrates in Pl. *Ap.* 29b4–5 says that he does not know sufficiently "about those [things] in Hades" [περὶ τῶν ἐν Ἅιδου], apparently a topic appropriate for *sophoi* to know), a collection of reports about seemingly dead people who came back to life. The symptomatology had recurrent interest (Tert. *De anim.* 43; Aët. 5.25.3 [Leucippus], 4.4.7 [Democritus]), and assertions of death remained challenging (Celsus *Med.* 2.6). For details see Leszl 2006.

[35] DL 8.4–5. Though Diogenes does not cite the work, all editors attribute this story to *On Diseases* (even if with reservations; Gottschalk 1980, 14, does not use it in his reconstruction of the dialogue) rather than to the book the title of which alone we know, *On the Things* [or: *Those*] *in Hades*; though Pythagoras is *said* to have narrated about Hades, this quotation or paraphrase includes no such narration itself, and this passage points to a work concerned with Pythagoras's retained memory and metempsychosis rather than with the events in Hades themselves.

man named Aethalides and was believed to be a son of Hermes. When Hermes came to him to grant him any wish he desired except for immortality, he chose to retain all his memories through both life and death. So when, having died, he ended up reincarnated as, or, literally, "came into" (εἰς . . . ἐλθεῖν) Euphorbus—the Trojan hero eventually struck by Menelaus—he reported his earlier experiences as human, as flora, and as fauna, both on Earth and in Hades. When he died as Euphorbus he went into (μεταβῆναι . . . εἰς) Hermotimus, who wished to make the curious history of his soul credible, and did so by identifying a relic from his run-in with Menelaus. Then he became a Delian fisherman and finally Pythagoras, who remembered everything. This story serves to prove Pythagoras's theory of metempsychosis, for Pythagoras's divine memory allows him to remember the transfers of his soul.

One passage definitively known from *On Diseases* tells of Pythagoras's self-application of the name *philosophos*. We have seen what looks like a loose abridgment in Sosicrates; also, we know a closer version with an explicit attribution, translated into Latin, from Cicero.[36] It comes in the final quarter of the preamble to Book 5 of his *Tusculan Disputations*. Cicero is explaining that philosophy does not get the credit it deserves because its benefits predate its naming. Cultural benefactors were once called "wise men" rather than philosophers, he says; only with Pythagoras did this change.

> This name [sc. *sapientes*] for them [sc. the descendants of the wise men] spread all the way to the time of Pythagoras. People say that he went to Phlius, as Heraclides Ponticus writes, the pupil of Plato and a man foremost in learning (*quem, ut scribit auditor Platonis Ponticus Heraclides, uir doctus in primis, Phliuntem ferunt uenisse*), and discussed certain issues learnedly and at length with Leon, the ruler of the Phliusians. When Leon marveled at his talent and eloquence, he asked him to which profession (*arte*) he most dedicated himself. He in turn said that it was not a profession that he knew, but that he was a "philosopher." Leon, astonished at the novelty of the term, asked what kind of people philosophers were and what the difference was between them and the rest of mankind. Pythagoras answered that he thought human life was similar to the kind of festival which is held with a magnificent display of games in a gathering from the whole of Greece. For there some people seek the glory and distinction of a crown by training their bodies, and others are drawn by the profit and gain in buying or selling, but there is a certain class of people, and this quite the most free, who look for neither applause nor gain, but come for the sake of seeing and look

---

[36] On differences between Cicero's and Sosicrates's versions that are irrelevant to the present argument, see YC 1.320n10.

thoroughly with great attention at what is being done and how. In the same way, he said, we have arrived into this life from another life and nature (*ex alia uita et natura*), as if from some city into some crowd at a festival, and some devote themselves to glory and others to money, but there are certain rare people who count all matters for nothing and eagerly contemplate the nature of things (*rerum naturam studiose intuerentur*). These people call themselves students of wisdom (*sapientiae studiosos*)—that is, philosophers (*philosophos*)—and just as there it was most fitting for a free character to watch while seeking nothing for oneself, so in life the contemplation and understanding of things (*studiis contemplationem rerum*) far surpasses all other pursuits.[37] (*Tusc.* 5.3.8–9, trans. Schütrumpf 2008, modified)

So, Heraclides (in *On Diseases*; see below) has Pythagoras travel to Phlius, display to Leon his intellectual wares, attribute his acumen to his being a *philosophos*, differentiate *philosophoi* from profit- and honor-seekers with an "Olympic games" analogy, and say that *philosophoi* "have come into this life from another life and nature" to study the nature of things. Because this closing language reflects the "coming into" language found in the metempsychosis passage (reflected in Sosicrates's φύονται; see p. 4 above), the passages fit well together. Perhaps for Heraclides it is Pythagoras's telling his life story to Leon that incites Leon's astonishment, and since that story does not advance Cicero's account, Cicero glosses it as a "learned" discussion of "certain issues." Alternatively, Pythagoras's story of his soul's adventure might follow the description of *philosophoi* in the conversation with Leon, perhaps as a personal justification; in this case, the learned and lengthy conversation might have been about the soul more generally.[38] The apparent unity of the Empedocles story (cure, explanation, and apotheosis) suggests unity here as well.

In *On Diseases*, Pythagoras explains what *philosophoi* do: they understand the world as befits free people, which includes recognizing the immortality and peregrinations of the soul. Empedocles, elsewhere assumed to belong in the Pythagorean tradition (see chapter 5, pp. 140–42), understands the relation between immortal soul and mortal body from a medical and prognostic perspective. Empedocles surely is himself being treated as a *philosophos*. What

---

[37] For the Latin of this passage, see Appendix, pp. 321–22.

[38] The Academic Dicaearchus reports that the three best known Pythagorean doctrines (the rest being mysterious) were soul-immortality and transformation of living things, a universal life cycle, and kinship of all living things (Porph. *VP* 19); these were publicly known around the time of Pythagoras's life (Xenophanes B7/D64; Hdt. 4.95) (see chapter 4). If the conversation occurred at an athletic event, maybe Pythagoras's dietetics are at issue (see Guthrie 1962, 187–95, for references). Or might he be giving leadership advice (cf. Hdt. 1.30–32)?

we have in Heraclides's work, then, is a celebration of *philosophia*. This celebration asserts the following: *philosophia* befits noble people, seeks knowledge
on its broadest construal, gives insight into the nature of death and the soul,
cures otherwise hopeless patients, and contributes in a fashion to one's own
immortality—as a recognition of it, or the purification that is a prerequisite
to it. Given the vibrant prose formulation, the fascination of the episodes, and
their historical relevance, this work appears to be a wholehearted exhortation
to *philosophia*, an early instance of the *protreptikos logos* genre.

Admittedly, not all readers of the fragmentary *On Diseases* have judged it
to be an exhortation to philosophy. Its most recent commentator, Philip van
der Eijk, follows an interpretative tradition that puts it in the history of medicine.[39] He allows that it is an unusual medical text, one mixed with the lives
and sayings of famous healers, and spiced by stories of the miraculous, but
one that still asserts an intriguing physiological view. Galen treated the section
on the unbreathing woman seriously as an analysis of seizures. Yet van der
Eijk's view, like those of his predecessors, takes almost no account of the Pythagoras story.[40] Nor does his view show how many lines of the dialogue those
who later cited it actually knew. I suspect that they had only brief excerpts
or paraphrases, the latter suggested by their disagreement over basic facts.[41]
The putatively medical sections of philosophical works were sometimes excerpted by later authors; if one should rely on the ancient citations of Plato's
Charmides, for example, that dialogue would appear basically medical, even
though it is in fact a protreptic to Socratic philosophizing.[42] A further point is

[39] Van der Eijk 2009, 239–40, 244–48; earlier, Lonie 1965, 133–43; Mayhew 2010, 460–61.

[40] Van der Eijk gives it only about a page, 243–44; neither Lonie 1965, Guthrie 1978, 483–90,
nor Mayhew 2010 mention the *philosophos* story at all; and it plays no real role in Dillon 2003,
204–15. Seeing no clear relevance to the overall dialogue, though admitting that Pythagoras
and Empedocles had medical interests, citing Celsus's *On Medicine* (proem 7–9), van der Eijk
wonders whether the *philosophos* passage even comes from a different work, e.g., *On the Pythagoreans* or *On Those in Hades*.

[41] There is no evidence that sources other than Diogenes Laertius actually read the work
(and he himself may not have). Origen (*C. Cels.* 2.16) cites Heraclides's story, along with Plato's
myth of Er, about those who spend twelve days in Hades, as an example of resurrection that
non-Christians believe, and Pliny (*HN* 7.52.175) cites Heraclides's "celebrated book" about the
woman who revived after not breathing for seven days as an example of the curability of the
feminine disease of "a turning of the womb." Galen cites Heraclides or his work (τὸ βιβλίον
ἄπνους) three times: at *De trem.* 6 as a familiar reference point about shivering; at *De diff. R.*
1.8 for the unbreathing woman representing the condition, as opposed to fever, where breathing
(and by parallel the pulse) slows so much as to make the person look dead; and at *De loc. aff.* 6
for one kind of hysteria, in which Heraclides's woman experiences the most puzzling kind of
condition, having effectively no breath or pulse, only some core warmth. All these accounts
could come from very short excerpts or paraphrases.

[42] The densest set of ancient references to the *Charmides* are to the "Thracian doctors of
Zalmoxis" section (156d3–157b1), which we know was excerpted (at least in Stob. 4.37.23, under

that the excerpts suggest authorship for a lay audience rather than for technical practitioners.

The more plausible view, that *On Diseases* is a protreptic to philosophy, is found in H. B. Gottschalk's 1980 book, *Heraclides of Pontus*. He argues persuasively that Heraclides sought "to make propaganda for the contemplative life by drawing an idealized portrait of one of its greatest exponents [sc. Empedocles], who was shown on the last day of his life on earth which was also the day of his ultimate triumph."[43] He sees Heraclides's dialogue as combining the banquet format of Plato's *Symposium* with the death and exaltation format of the *Phaedo*: people talk about Empedocles's resurrection of the unbreathing woman at a festal celebration, and then Pausanias or others talk about Empedocles's disappearance at its conclusion. Both parts of the dialogue reflect on the nature of soul, as immortal and independent from the body, and present philosophy as the right way to understand it. The Pythagoras scene in particular "contains a statement of the ideals underlying Empedocles's way of life": the superiority of *philosophia*, as a reflection on the nature of things, over the mere medical skill of non-philosophical doctors.

What matters here is that Pythagoras's self-appellation fits a historical narrative about philosophy's power, and the story is read by Cicero and Diogenes Laertius as historically reliable about the sorts of things Pythagoras said as well as about the last days of Empedocles. The consequence is that the Pythagoras self-appellation story appears to be part of an ennobling account of the history of philosophy that, whatever poetic license Heraclides must have taken for *his* account to become read over the ensuing centuries, seemed basically true.

From Sosicrates's précis of this story, we have inferred a late sixth- or early fifth-century BCE coinage date for the term *philosophos*, the term's opacity, and Pythagoras's archetypal role in the image of the *philosophos*. Cicero's Heraclidean version confirms and expands these inferences. The word *philosophos* entered the vernacular around the time, and even the place, of Pythagoras; the word is new to Leon, but Heraclides appears not to say that Pythagoras invented it. Pythagoras's surprising self-labeling is occasioned by, and apparently explains, his talented and eloquent discussion of questions of interest to a political leader like Leon. Pythagoras does link the word *philosophos* to something

---

the chapter heading "On Health and Considering One's Survival," immediately following a citation from Hippocrates): Apul. *Apol.* 26.4; Clem. *Strom.* 1.15.58.3; Jul. *Or.* 8.244a; *Caesars* 309c; Max. Tyr. 28.4; Hermias *In Phdr.* 274c, Maximus Planudes *Compendia e Platonis dialogis* 143. On the dialogue, see Moore and Raymond 2019.

[43] Gottschalk 1980, 32 (this quotation), 13–22 (structure of dialogue), 23–33 (Pythagoras passage).

like its roots, which may be expressed in Latin as *sapientiae studiosus*. And this apparently plausible story was told in the middle of the fourth century BCE, when Heraclides wrote *On Diseases*. Thus we have a reasonable account of a founding moment in the history of *philosophia*.

A Related Account of Pythagoras's Self-Appellation

A surprising fact about Diogenes Laertius's inclusion, in Book 8 of his *Lives of the Eminent Philosophers*, of the story about Pythagoras's self-naming that he takes from Sosicrates, is that he had already included a different version of the story in Book 1.[44] More remarkable again is that the Book 1 version, found in the treatise's Preface, mentions Heraclides's story—which Sosicrates's must ultimately have relied on—but then rejects it in favor of another source of information. The functions of the two versions of the story differ, to be sure: in the Book 8 *Life of Pythagoras*, Diogenes gathers anecdotes about Pythagoras, whereas in the Book 1 Preface he argues that *philosophia* began in Greece, on the grounds that *philosophia* is a Greek word. This is his evidence:

> Pythagoras first called *philosophia* by its name and himself *philosophos*, in Sicyon when talking to Leon tyrant of the Sicyonians, or of Phliusians as Heraclides Ponticus in the *Woman Not Breathing* says; for nobody is wise (σοφόν) but god. Previously (θᾶττον δέ),[45] people spoke of *sophia*, and a *sophos*

---

[44] The magnitude of the *Lives*, and the importance of the present story in two distinct contexts, perhaps excuses Diogenes here; the basic historical compatibility of the two stories (identified below) perhaps does too. Nevertheless, it seems clear that he is drawing from distinct archives at these two points, and he may not have completed an overall consistency-ensuring revision of his treatise; see Most 2018.

[45] There has been confusion about θᾶττον δέ. Hicks 1925 translates: "All too quickly the study was called wisdom and its professor a sage, to denote his attainment of mental perfection; while the student who took it up was a philosopher or lover of wisdom"—but it would be absurd to write that as soon as Pythagoras started calling *sophia* "*philosophia*," it started being called *sophia* again. Similarly Caponigri 1969, 5; YC 1.1, 1.318 ("rapidly"); Mensch 2018, 8 ("before very long"). Reale 2005, 17: "too readily [*troppo facilmente*] was the name 'wisdom' given," but this would need to be better relativized to the time of Pythagoras's self-naming. Reich 1967 argues for "all too quickly [*allzu schnell*]," which he then glosses "all too hastily [*allzu voreilig*]," in explicit contrast to "formerly [*ehedem*]," on the grounds that, from Pythagoras's perspective, people spoke of wisdom too hastily, without thinking enough about what they are doing; but this is overly nuanced and without evidence. Nor can θᾶττον δέ here mean "often," since it would not make sense of the linguistic advance marked by Pythagoras's self-appellation. θᾶττον [δέ] means "earlier, sooner, before," at DL 2.39, 2.120, 2.139, 5.39, 6.56 (Mericus Causobonus translating as *antea*, according to Dorandi 2013 ad loc., who refers to 1.12), and LSJ s.v. ταχύς C.i.2. The adverb is correctly translated by Anonymous 1758; Zevort 1847; and Yonge 1901.

as the promulgator (ἐπαγγελλόμενος) of it—he who has a perfected soul in the highest degree—but [now in Pythagoras's time] the one eagerly welcoming (ἀσπαζόμενος) *sophia* is [called] a *philosophos*.[46] (DL 1.12)

The similarities with Heraclides's version are apparent. Pythagoras calls himself *philosophos* but does not invent the term, he does so famously in a conversation with Leon, he has to explain his use of the term, and the meaning of the term is basically the same: being receptive of truth and wisdom (though Sosicrates's telling provides a more active emphasis). The key difference with Heraclides's version is also clear. Aside from the geographical dispute, to which we will return, Pythagoras gives a different explanation for calling himself *philosophos*, using no festival analogy or reference to athletes, merchants, and spectators. Leon might have expected him to call himself *sophos*, presumably because people in the past treated those who spoke from and lived with *sophia*—as Pythagoras appeared to do—as *sophoi*.[47] But Pythagoras has come to find the name inappropriate, as befitting only a god. The name *philosophos* works better; it means "eagerly welcoming" or "following" *sophia*, which makes no epistemically hazardous claims about the possession of wisdom.[48] Heraclides's version emphasizes the *philosophos*'s differential objects of pursuit—truth rather than glory and profit—whereas this version emphasizes differential orientations toward one object—invitation rather than embodiment.

This story is obviously not the Heraclidean one we know from Cicero and Sosicrates. Nor should we assume it is from an otherwise unquoted section of *On Diseases*. Tiziano Dorandi's recent edition of Diogenes's *Lives*, adopted by the editors of the Loeb Classical Library's *Early Greek Philosophy*, rightly punctuates the passage such that Heraclides is cited only for the alternative citizenry over whom Leon might be tyrant, the "Phliusians."[49] Many earlier editors did not include a comma after "Sicyons," however, which leaves Heraclides saying, absurdly, that Leon was tyrant "over the Sicyonians or Phliu-

---

[46] For the Greek of this passage, see Appendix, p. 324. Indicating the importance ascribed to this passage, *Suda* σ 806 replicates this passage verbatim from καὶ σοφός ("and a *sophos* . . .").

[47] By the fifth century BCE, the verb ἐπαγγέλλω, which here in the middle I translate "promulgate," can mean "offer willingly" (LSJ s.v. A.4); only in the fourth century BCE can it also mean "profess" or "make a profession of," especially in description of Sophists (A.5). The story does not clarify which connotation is meant—the latter implies presentation of oneself as lecturer or even as professional, whereas the former does not—though perhaps Pythagoras himself could only have used the earlier connotation.

[48] Before the fifth century BCE, ἀσπάζομαι means "greet, welcome" (LSJ s.v. A.1); only in the late fifth and early fourth century BCE can the term mean "eagerly follow, cling to" (A.3); again, the story does not clarify which connotation is meant, and again perhaps Pythagoras himself could only have used the earlier connotation.

[49] See Dorandi 2013 ad loc. and LM 4.374.

sians." Yet Heraclides does not in fact say this according to Sosicrates or Cicero, and such ambivalence would quite gainsay the vibrancy and determinate detail of Heraclides's famous story.[50] Diogenes often cites authorities only for divergent details, even when there are major narrative differences between his sources (typified by his uses of Sosicrates, cited in note 3 above).

The existence of this non-Heraclidean version of the Pythagoras story has a fundamental consequence. There must be a core story shared by both versions, in which Pythagoras calls himself *philosophos* to Leon and has to explain its use. We see that for some reason Diogenes prefers the non-Heraclidean version, the one that includes the "not-*sophos*" explanation, since he quotes or paraphrases it and not Heraclides's in his Preface, even though both would support his claim about the Greek origin of *philosophia*. (As we will see in chapter 3, other fourth-century BCE authors follow the non-Heraclidean version rather than that of Heraclides.) There is no reason to believe that the non-Heraclidean version—whose author I will call the "Sicyon author" (i.e., "Sicyon-version author")—derives from Heraclides. There might even be reason to believe that Heraclides took a credible pre-existing story and adapted Pythagoras's reasons to suit his protreptic goals.[51] The Sicyon author's version emphasizes continuity with *sophoi*; as we will see in later chapters, the ambition to assemble lineages of *sophoi* dates back to the mid-fifth century BCE, and so we would expect some attempts to fit Pythagoras, Pythagoreans, and similar *philosophoi* into such "*sophos* lineages," as we might call them.[52] The disagreement about Leon's place of tyranny is not surprising: Phlius and Sicyon share borders near Corinth; political upheaval struck Sicyon during the relevant period, perhaps making the determination of rulership confusing; associates of Aristotle and Heraclides engaged in new research into Sicyon in the fourth century BCE; and Phlius played an important role in early Pythagoreanism.[53] The overwhelming sense is that Heraclides's version of the

[50] For the debate, see, e.g., Joly 1956, 21–28; Malingrey 1961, 30–31; Guthrie 1962, 164–45. Editors who attribute the disjunction to Heraclides rather than Diogenes include Cobet 1878a; Long 1964; Marcovich 1999; Schütrumpf 2008 ad fr. 84. Anonymous 1833 puts commas on either side of ἢ Φλιασίων, with unclear meaning. Genaille 1965 hides behind modern citation conventions, translating ". . . Leon, tyran des Sicyoniens, *appelés parfois* Phliasiens (*cf.* Héraclide du Pont, livre sur l'*Apnon*)" (my italics).

[51] Riedweg 2004 and 2005, 94–96, describes the sufficient fifth-century BCE materials available to such a historian; see note 67 below for fuller assessment.

[52] This is not especially controversial; see the opening paragraph of *OCD* s.v. "philosophy, history of."

[53] Leon is not otherwise known. The controversy over Phlius and Sicyon has much to do with Pythagorean history (similar controversies: Euseb. *Praep. evang.* 10.3.4.5–9), but in no simple way. The cities were neighbors on the Corinthian Gulf (Xen. *Hell.* 7.2.20; Skalet 1928, 26–27; Lolos 2011, 22), whence settlers to Croton departed (Dunbabin 1948, 250, 269). Phlius

Pythagoras story is neither the only nor the first, even as his account is the longest, is the most detailed, and is distinguished as the only one attributed to an author. Because of the conflation in latter-day scholarship of all versions of the Pythagoras story to his account, the historical reality of any version— and thus any evidence about the origins of the discipline we might infer from one—tends to stand on the plausibility of Heraclides's exposition.[54]

Burkert against Heraclides: An Academic Fiction?

From the fourth century BCE to the sixth century CE, Heraclides's story was taken as fact. Now, however, it has little currency, and thus plays almost no role in attempts to understand the origins of *philosophia*. This is not altogether

---

had also sent settlers to Pythagoras's home island of Samos, among whom were Hippasus, a purported great-grandfather of Pythagoras (Paus. 2.13.2; DL 8.1; cf. Delatte 1922, 148; Burnet 1930, 87n5; Minar 1942); Porphyry also cites early views that Phlius was Pythagoras's hometown (*VP* 5). Phlius was the home place of at least four fifth-century BCE Pythagoreans, including Echecrates (Iambl. *VP* 35.251, 267; DL 8.46; *BNP* s.v. "Leon [2]"; Zhmud 2013, 148; this does not require, as Riedweg 2004 asserts, that any Pythagoras story must postdate their establishment there). Sicyon was Greece's oldest city (Euseb. *Chron.* 62), and in the early sixth century BCE it hosted the "best of the Greeks," in the form of the suitors of Agariste, daughter of its tyrant Cleisthenes, leading Greek of his generation, and mother of Athens's democratizer Cleisthenes (Hdt. 6.126–30; see Hammond 1956, 46; Griffin 1982, 52–56, 97; Parker 1994, 423–24). In the following decades, the city supported Greece's most consequential musical innovators (Skalet 1928, 178–80; Griffin 1982, 57, 158–62), a lineage of which appeared in Heraclides's history of music (Barker 2014, 50). Despite the cultural knowledge we have of these cities, we know nothing of their political histories at the time of Pythagoras, and thus cannot resolve the controversy. Sicyon might have had a tyrant after Cleisthenes's death around 569 BCE and before its last tyrant, Aischines, had the latter, in fact, been deposed by the Spartans at the end of the sixth century BCE; our source, *Rylands Papyrus* 18 (see BNJ 105 ad F1), is unclear. This possibility has its supporters (e.g., Cavaignac 1919; White 1958; Parker 1992; BNP s.v. "Sicyon"; Leahy 1968, 4n12, includes older bibliography), though others support an earlier date for the last tyrant, which would make a Pythagorean meeting with one impossible (e.g., Hammond 1956; Leahy 1968; OCD s.v. "Sicyon"). *BNJ* 105 ad F2 takes Aristotle to assert in the *Politics* that Cleisthenes was Sicyon's last tyrant (*Pol.* 1316a30–31), but this passage marks instead only a regime change between Myron and Cleisthenes. For general histories of the pertinent ("Orthagorid") period, see Skalet 1928, 52–62; Andrewes 1956, 54–61; Griffin 1982, 37–61; Lolos 2011, 61–65. Should Sicyon have had a tyrant during the maturity of Pythagoras, this fact would presumably have been recorded in Aristotle's lost *Constitution of the Sicyonians* (Poll. *Onom.* 9.77; cf. Arist. *Pol.* 1315b10–21), though there were other likely sources for Sicyon's political history by the later fourth century (*POxy.* 1365, containing a work possibly by Ephorus of Cyme [ca. 400–330 BCE]). Should Sicyon not have had a tyrant during that time—if Aischines had been deposed in the mid-sixth century BCE, as some interpretations prefer—it still must have had rulers anyway, and they might still have been called "tyrants." If they were not, then Leon must have been tyrant not of Sicyon but of Phlius.

[54] Such conflation is found in, e.g., Burkert 1960 and Riedweg 2004; contrast Gottschalk 1980, 23–36.

surprising. The loss of almost all Heraclides's works except some fantastical excerpts establishes him as an impresario of myth.[55] His Pythagorean partisanship hardly helps, given the disfavor into which the man from Samos, demoted to cult leader, at best a symbol of mystical magniloquence and ostentatious erudition, has fallen, especially for philosophers proud of their discipline's modest rigor.[56] The decisive moment in the rejection of Heraclides's account of Pythagoras came in 1960. Walter Burkert (1931–2015) was at that time writing the century's most important book on Pythagoras, published as *Weisheit und Wissenschaft: Studien zu Pythagoras, Philolaos und Platon* in 1962, and in a revised translation as *Lore and Science in Ancient Pythagoreanism* in 1972. Burkert took as his task the reassessment of all ancient testimony for Pythagoras's philosophical acumen, attitudes, and endeavors—especially his purported mathematical, cosmological, and psychological discoveries—from the classical and Hellenistic periods through the Neopythagoreanism of Nicomachus of Gerasa (ca. 60–120 CE) and Iamblichus of Chalcis (ca. 245–325 CE). Burkert debunked practically all of it as mere retrojecting and idealizing fictions by later Pythagoreans. Among the lore he sought to reassess was Heraclides's Pythagoras story. Was it true, he asked, or pure hagiographical invention?

As a kind of advanced guard for his book, Burkert published, in 1960, an article titled "Platon oder Pythagoras? Zum Ursprung des Wortes 'Philosophie,'" arguing unqualifiedly for invention.[57] In this masterpiece of breadth, concision, and acuity, Burkert vindicates suspicions about the story that had occupied philosophers and philologists since Eduard Zeller's monumental *Philosophy of the Greeks in Its Historical Development* (1844–52), and had come to a head in Werner Jaeger's *Aristotle: Fundamentals of the History of his Development*.[58] Having assumed that the version discussed above, found in Diogenes Laertius's Preface (DL 1.12), also comes from Heraclides but in a part of his work not quoted in Sosicrates or Cicero, Burkert makes two interlocking claims: we have a strong reason against believing that Pythagoras could or would ever have defined *philosophos* as either "one spec-

---

[55] Ancient negative evaluations are found in the hypercritical Timaeus, who accuses Heraclides of "always being such a paradoxologist" (DL 8.72), though Polybius states that Timaeus was overly critical (Polyb. 12.4a6, 12.14, 25c2); in Plutarch (*Cam.* 22.2–4); and in Cicero (*Nat. D.* 1.13.34), though not in his own voice: in the voice, rather, of an Epicurean given to reviling Academics. Guthrie 1978, 484, redeems Heraclides's supposed "weakness for fantasy and superstition" by noting that Plato, too, tells far-fetched tales though always in appropriate contexts.

[56] Burnyeat 2007 captures the present-day tone.

[57] "Plato or Pythagoras: On the Origin of the Word 'Philosophy'": this contribution was never translated into English nor included in the book, though Burkert cites its results at 5n11, 8, 65, 74, 77, and 106 (in the 1972 edition).

[58] Jaeger 1923, 2nd ed. 1948; Engl. in 1934, 2nd ed. 1962; see esp. 1962, 97–98, 432.

tating the universe" (from the Cicero version) or "one lacking but striving for *sophia*" (from the DL 1.12 version); and yet, by contrast, we have a strong reason in favor of believing that Heraclides could or would have concocted his story on inspiration from Plato's *Phaedrus* (for example), which in effect includes both definitions (at *Phdr.* 278d and 249b5–d3). I will address these claims in turn.

According to Burkert, a range of reasons tell against Pythagoras's defining the *philosophos* in either way. First, the biographical reasons. Pythagoras, full of self-conceit, would never have called attention to an abyss between himself and *sophia* or divinity—after all, as his successor Empedocles did, he vaunted his own immortality—and yet this is what the "not-*sophos*" definition would require.[59] Nor would it have been relevant for him to treat himself as a lover of observation or hunter after truth, for this would explain only his calling himself *theôrêtikos* or *philotheamôn*, not *philosophos*. Second, the evidentiary reasons. There is no independent evidence that Pythagoras invented the word *philosophos*, even if classical authors suggest that Pythagoreans used the term. And what evidence may exist for the fifth-century BCE use of *philosophos*, for example by Zeno and Heraclitus, has its own problems of authenticity and proves neither gloss on *philosophos* (as striving for an as-yet-unpossessed *sophia* or spectating the universe). Third, the linguistic reasons. A survey of the earliest *phil-* prefixed terms shows that *phil-* never meant "lacking and desiring *x*," but rather its (almost) exact opposite, "close acquaintance and familiarity, or habitual dealings, with *x*."[60]

In favor of a fourth-century BCE confabulation of Heraclides's Pythagoras story, Burkert has another set of assertions. Every version of the Pythagoras story goes back to Heraclides, he claims; Aristotle cannot be a source. The Academy and Lyceum actively debated Pythagoras's commitment to the practical or contemplative life, both as a historical/theoretical matter and in the context of broader ethical/metaphysical debates, familiar to all readers, from Plato's *Gorgias* and Aristotle's *Nicomachean Ethics*. Heraclides's story looks suspiciously like a tendentious contribution to that discussion. Indeed, Burkert conjectures the coinage of the term *philosophos*, or at least its dissemination and popularization, in the (late) fifth century BCE, at a time when *phil-* prefixed terms (as illustrated by Aristophanes's *Wasps*, of 422 BCE, and Plato's *Lysis*, of the early fourth century BCE, discussed below, in chapters 3 and 8) proliferated to capture favorite pastimes, hobbies, and even

---

[59] Others are doubtful that Pythagoras would ever have said that he lacked wisdom: Morrison 1956, 136–38; Chroust 1964a, 427n17, 432–33; Kahn 2001, 2, 5–6; Riedweg 2005.

[60] Burkert 1960, 176–77, 161 (biographical reasons); 169–71 (evidentiary reasons); 172–73 (linguistic reasons).

life-determining passions. An expanding democratic middle class sought the former trappings of the elites and formulated *sophia* for itself—hence the idea of the *philosophoi* as amateur seekers of wisdom. Plato sharpened the idea of this "striving while lacking" to contrast the *philosophoi* with conceited "Sophists" and to describe Socrates's incessant questioning as phenomenologically akin to love.[61]

Burkert rejected Heraclides's account decisively,[62] and appeared to have put to rest a deep puzzle—what sense to make of an instance of philosophy's discussing its own essence at its very foundation—that engaged not only Zeller and Jaeger but also many other prominent scholars of philosophy's founding, including Erwin Rohde, Ulrich von Wilamowitz-Moellendorf, Isidore Lévy, Robert Joly, Augusto Rostagni, Fritz Wehrli, John Burnet, and J. S. Morrison. To a large extent his argument has been accepted, most notably in two of Andrea Nightingale's books, *Genres in Dialogue* (1995) and *Spectacles of Truth* (2004), which have been cited more times than any other work that addresses the early history of the word *philosophos*.[63] In her 1995 book, for example, Nightingale argues that "Plato appropriated the term 'philosophy' for a new and specialized discipline," which before him "did not have a technical sense that indicated a specific group of thinkers practicing a distinct discipline or profession," but instead "was used to designate 'intellectual cultivation' in a broad and unspecified sense." Nightingale allows that, even were Heraclides's "rather dubious claim" about Pythagoras true, it would not show that Pythagoras used the term in a "technical" way. Nor, looking at the other fifth-century BCE uses of *philosophos* and cognates, does Nightingale see any instance of a "special subgroup of intellectuals that had appropriated the title of '*philosophoi*'" or a "specific group of professional thinkers."[64] I qualify Nightingale's claim about Plato in chapter 8 and her claims about fifth-century BCE uses in chapter 5. What is particularly relevant here is her reaction to Heraclides's story, as assessed by Burkert: she takes it to be useless for understanding the early history of *philosophia*, and treats pre-fourth century BCE usage as having neither complexity, traceable origin, nor semantic diffusion. Burkert's claim that Heraclides's history of *philosophia* is a fourth-century BCE fantasy

---

[61] Burkert 1960, 166n1 (Heraclides as sole source); 166–69 (Aristotle not a source); 159–60 with Burkert 1972, 106–9 (Heraclides's tendentious contribution); 174–76 (Plato sharpened the sense).

[62] Burkert 1960, 175.

[63] See Burkert 1960 for older references and Riedweg 2004, 148nn6–8, for more recent ones. Notable doubters include Havelock 1963, 306n8; Chroust 1964a, 427–28; Kahn 2001, 68; Hadot 2002, 14n1. Guthrie 1962, 164–66, 204–5, not having seen Burkert's article, takes a mixed attitude; Lloyd 2009, 9n1, remains agnostic.

[64] Nightingale 1995, 14–15.

has had the effect of inaugurating the history of *philosophia* in the fourth century BCE.

Before evaluating this claim, we must determine precisely what Burkert has demonstrated. He says that Pythagoras would not have exposited *philosophos* as the one "striving after wisdom," whereas Heraclides, by contrast, could or even would have. True enough. But we also have reason to doubt that Heraclides himself attributed the "not-*sophos*" definition to Pythagoras. It looks rather as if Heraclides tells a version of a pre-existing story. Even if we grant Burkert's conflation of the two stories, contrary to evidence, we can see that Burkert's bolder move is to reject the whole of Heraclides's Pythagoras story because he can reject a part, the speech Pythagoras gives in response to Leon's question. Yet we can reject the part without rejecting the whole. The speech, indeed, has the least cause for acceptance: speeches are notoriously difficult to preserve or remember, and might provide the best occasion for invention, as Thucydides famously implies (Thuc. 1.22).

Even with the rejection of Pythagoras's speech of explanation, however, much remains untouched from Heraclides's account. I will mention three items. First, the dramatic context: a meeting between Pythagoras and Leon the tyrant. Burkert never doubts the plausibility of such an interaction; and while the tale may loosely fit the generic structure of the "sage advisor of tyrants" trope, it is no less likely for that.[65] Second, the historical claim: Pythagoras was the first to call himself *philosophos*. Burkert never doubts the possibility of the self-application, though he does think that Pythagoras is being said to "invent" the word and that he does so by explaining what it means. But the story need not imply invention of the adjective/noun, only its self-application (and, in some versions, invention of the abstract noun); the historical implication could be that the term was already used for other people, and that Pythagoras innovated with his self-application. Nothing holds him to applying it to himself to "mean" either of the things Burkert believes Heraclides put into his mouth. What remains after abandoning Pythagoras's speech, third, is a more general historical implication: fifth-century BCE Pythagoreans had good reason to allow themselves to be called *philosophoi*. They could, with truth or fiction, retroject this appellation onto their only slightly earlier representative, Pythagoras.[66] In sum, then, much of Heraclides's story of Pythagorean (redemptive) self-ascription might still be taken seriously.

---

[65] On the story's structure and on the wise advisor trope, see Hdt. 1.30, with Bischoff 1932; Lattimore 1939; Joly 1956; Gottschalk 1980, 23–27; Martin 1993; Sharp 2004; Riedweg 2005, 94; YC 1.113–18. Nevertheless, our fragments do not indicate that Pythagoras *advises* Leon.

[66] On such retrojection, see Burkert 1972, 91. I assume nothing in particular about the delineation of "Pythagorean," following the caution of Zhmud 2013.

The Structure of This Book

Why did Heraclides propound the Pythagoras story in particular, and why did so many ancient historians of philosophy find him believable? My answer is that the general historical implications that accompany the story may well be true. I thus break with Burkert and the past sixty-some years of scholarship on the origins of *philosophia*.[67] The two main implications of my answer are the following:

1. The word *philosophos* existed early in the Pythagorean movement;
2. That the Pythagoreans had reason to call themselves *philosophoi* and presented an explanation of their doing so suggests they were already being called it and that the name was neither obvious in meaning nor laudatory in application.

There are, then, secondary implications that one might expect. If these are sound, they would support the main implications.

3. The earliest non-Pythagorean uses of *philosophos* would develop from this original Pythagorean-derived meaning;
4. The uses of *philosophos* would show negative valence in the earliest cases, and then instances of neutral and redemptive valence later;
5. Plato's works themselves can be treated as instances of saving the appearances and redeeming the practices theretofore called *philosophia*.

These fifth- and early fourth-century BCE phenomena provide a context for the mid-fourth century BCE trends:

6. Heraclides's story contributes to ongoing protreptic efforts to redeem *philosophoi* by explaining their positive value, and does so, in part, in a way familiar from Aristotle, by displaying a historical disciplinary consciousness.

---

[67] The most thorough response to Burkert heretofore is, as I mentioned above, Riedweg 2004, an article that argues persuasively for the fifth-century BCE existence of all of Heraclides's story elements (meaning that the story *could* predate Heraclides's version), but who does not treat closely of the etymology, coinage, or fifth-century BCE uses of *philosoph-* words, etc. Mallan 2005 also argues for the Pythagorean heritage of the ideas found in Heraclides's version. I note that Aristophanes, by 423/17 BCE, could speak of "desiring wisdom" (ὦ τῆς μεγάλης ἐπιθυμήσας ἄνθρωπε, *Nub.* 412).

By this book's end, my hope is that the reader may see what allowed Heraclides to write the Pythagoras story in a way that convinced his readers. The result will be a clearer understanding of the origin of the word *philosophos* (and *philosophia*) and of the discipline called *philosophia*. The structure of the narrative falls into three parts.

Part One: Origins

The first part of the book, chapters 2–4, focuses on the origins of the term *philosophos*. In chapter 2, I argue for what we might call the "lexical precondition" for Heraclides's story: the existence of the word *philosophos* at the time of Pythagoras or at least in the period of the early Pythagorean generations. The evidence is a fragment from Heraclitus, quoted by Clement: "philosophical men really quite ought to be researchers into much" (B35/D40). Burkert accepted the familiar and casual skepticism about Heraclitus's authorship of this—after all, it predates the next earliest attestation of the word by at least several decades, and seems in conflict with Heraclitean fragments that decry polymathy (e.g., B40/D20, B129/D26)—and claimed that, even were it authentic, it would not support either definition of *philosophia* found in the Pythagoras stories.[68] I argue, first, that we have no reason to doubt Clement's accuracy of quotation for either source-critical or epistemological reasons. I show, second, that while Heraclitus's use does not support the "explanations" of *philosophos* found in the Pythagoras stories, it in fact supports the view that I have said the stories imply: that the term was applied, and perhaps with pejorative implication, to the Pythagoreans. Both positions have had their proponents in earlier scholarship, but with a full defense of those positions we can better see their centrality not just for Heraclitean epistemology but for the history of *philosophia*.

In chapter 3, I show what the term *philosophos* could have meant at the time for which it is attested, and thus what meaning Pythagoras or his followers would have sought to spin in accepting the term for themselves, had they done so. Burkert rejected the analysis of *phil-* prefixed terms as "striving for *x* which one lacks," suggesting instead "familiar with *x*."[69] For his purposes, that analysis sufficed, but it does not suffice for us. He did not pay close enough attention to the peculiar archaic use of *phil-* prefixed names, their normative valence, their application, or the contribution of their second element to the overall meaning. Nor did he pay close enough attention to the meaning of that

---

[68] Burkert 1960, 171; Burkert 1972, 131, 209–10.

[69] Burkert 1960, 172–74; confirming his negative argument, see Landfester 1966 and Cipriano 1991.

particular second element, *soph-*, at the end of the sixth century BCE. This chapter begins by turning again to Cicero's version of the Pythagoras story, and in more detail to a non-Heraclidean but probably still fourth-century BCE version, found in Diodorus Siculus, which in effect dramatizes the thesis of this book: that the word *philosophos* was formed in reference to *sophoi* considered as "sages." Important support for this ancient perspective comes from Aristotle's analysis, written in Heraclides's prime, of *phil-* prefixed names as usually having a negative valence; from the *phil-* prefixed names that surely predate the coinage of the term *philosophos*; from the precursors of those names in *Pi-ro-* prefixed Mycenaean (Linear B) names; and from, quite importantly, the sense of the term *sophos* in sixth-century BCE Greek.

In chapter 4, I pick up a claim made in the previous chapter, that a term like *philosophos* would have been coined in response to certain sorts of unusual activity. I accumulate the earliest evidence that the Pythagoreans would have been excellent targets of this term. This is because their public face was politically notorious and influential, with their cohesion and even efficacy seeming to depend on their pedagogical and research exercises. I thereby develop Burkert's acknowledgment of the organized political side of their existence.[70] Additional evidence comes from what looks to be Aristotle's support of Heraclides's account, if we can reconstruct Iamblichus's late citations of Aristotle correctly. Burkert asserts that Pythagoras was not really a philosopher; what concerns me is only the beliefs that observers had about him and the names that they had reason to call him—since, for his contemporaries, *philosophos* hardly meant what academic philosophers now mean by "philosopher."

Part Two: Development

The next part of the book, chapters 5–7, focuses on the development of uses of the word *philosophos* before and outside of Plato's Academy. In chapter 5, I draw on the fifth-century BCE uses of *philosophos* and cognates for two purposes: as corroboration for the coinage meaning set out in chapter 3 and the connection to Pythagoreans set out in chapter 4, and as description of the drift in meaning the term underwent across several generations of use. I focus on six authors, each of whom use the term once: Herodotus, Thucydides, the Hippocratic author of *On Ancient Medicine*, Gorgias, Aristophanes, and Lysias. (An appendix to the chapter assesses some less reliable but still possible evidence for early usage.) Burkert already referred to these authors in his observation that *philosophos* did not first mean "lacking

---

[70] Burkert 1972, 113–19, 132.

wisdom" or "spectating the universe."[71] Treated, however, in their respective literary and rhetorical contexts, they provide significant information about the fifth-century BCE career of the idea of being *philosophos*. It appears that at the end of that century, we see the term sometimes losing its wry implication and naming a quite specific mode of dialectic exchange about matters of abstract or broad significance.

In chapter 6, I turn to a fifth-century BCE figure as yet unmentioned, but whose importance to the later understanding of *philosophia* cannot be underestimated: Socrates. Many scholars, including Burkert and Nightingale, believe that Socrates's students inaugurated new thinking about *philosophia*; presumably Socrates's life, or at least his death, galvanized them to do so. This would be a central ingredient in the recipe for the redemptive story told by Heraclides, a grand-student of Socrates's. In fact, at least Xenophon and Plato, for whom we have the most evidence, never or only rarely call Socrates *philosophos*, even if we now think that, for both, Socrates modeled the philosophical life. This chapter makes this observation in part by focusing on both authors' attitude toward Socrates's connection to Anaxagoras, considered by later historicans to be the first to philosophize in Athens, and by focusing on Xenophon's hesitation to use the word *philosophos* with respect to Socrates. This suggests again that the term *philosophos* had a negative valence during Socrates's life and even, in some quarters, after his death. Plato and other Socratics do use the term *philosophia* positively, even putting it in Socrates's mouth. Their doing so in the fourth century BCE tracks the neutralizing trend we saw in chapter 5; it may also, however, reflect conscientious efforts to redeem a term that had been applied to Socrates. Socrates's discussion circles, which is what Plato most recurrently calls *philosophia*, were probably formalized in the "schools" of the so-called Minor Socratics and as the Academy, where Heraclides matured in his understanding of *philosophia*.

In chapter 7, I address non-Academic uses of *philosophia* in the fourth century BCE, which provides the background against which we can understand Heraclides's use of the term. We can see how *philosophia* became a discipline in the Academy only by understanding how the term *philosophia* was being used elsewhere. The key context comes from the educators Alcidamas, Isocrates, and the author of the *Dissoi Logoi*. I show that we have less reason to say that these educators competed over "ownership" of the term *philosophos* (even

---

[71] Burkert 1960, 173. Nightingale 1995, 14–15, treats the uses only as evidence that the authors did not know of *philosophia* as a professional discipline.

if at times they may have) or its true and universal meaning than that they gave varying retrospective reconstructions of the term's usage, differing, for example, in the relative emphases they give to practical teaching over the defensibility of research outcomes. To the extent that the Academic view of *philosophia* "won," this is not because that view was truer or more convincing, but because the Academy instigated a continued *discipline* that called itself *philosophia* more than Alcidamas or Isocrates did, neither of whom appear to have had success or interest in developing the sort of well-populated discipline crucial for maintaining a name.

Part Three: Academy

The final part of the book, chapters 8–10, focuses on the disciplinary development of the word *philosophos* in Plato's Academy. In chapter 8, I confront the use of *philosophia* by Heraclides's teacher, Plato. Burkert—and many others—views Plato's appropriation of *philosophia* as part of his effort to contrast Socrates's and his own practice with that of Sophists, rhetoricians, and other claimants to wisdom; he describes the etymological play, defining *philosophia* as "love of wisdom," as Plato's attempt to fit Socrates's interrogative approach. This may be so. Nightingale and, for example, John Cooper argue in particular that Plato creates a technical and professional formulation of *philosophoi* and *philosophia*, as though *ex nihilo*. This is less certain. I show that across his dialogues, Plato treats *philosophia* as a term in common parlance, and thus that he is, in effect, saving the appearances (of Thucydides and Gorgias, among others) when he presents it as conversations that conduce to virtue and flourishing. The dialogues dramatize or narrate just those conversations. Plato's reconstruction of past usages differs from Isocrates's, for example, in emphasizing the conversationality and the tendency to self-consciousness of its logic and argumentative rigor; but this is not expressly new—it is just a plausible interpretation of the past. Plato does provide something new, but it is not a new "meaning" of *philosophia*. It is, rather, a new explanation for the possibility that *philosophia*-style conversations could actually conduce to their end, human happiness. The epistemological and metaphysical considerations mooted in the dialogues concerning knowledge and universals do not determine what *philosophia* is (namely, conversations) but how *philosophia* could actually work (namely, by getting clearer about what is really true). Given how unappealing *philosophia* has been made out to be, a proponent needs to vindicate this apparently lazy pursuit. The Academy, an institution devoted to this pursuit, needed a defense. Yet, in most of Plato's dialogues—from the *Charmides* to

Protagoras, Phaedrus to *Republic, Lysis* to *Symposium*, and even from the *Parmenides* to the *Philebus*—*philosophia* still refers to person-to-person interactions, not to anything beyond those conversations; *philosophia* is not yet a discipline, a historically extended, increasingly distributed, and impersonal, concerted enterprise.

In chapter 9, proceeding from the belief that Heraclides's Pythagoras story implies a historical account of the development of the discipline of *philosophia*, I describe the rise of this historiography of philosophy, one that materializes only in the Academy. Aristotle's writings provide the clearest evidence. When in the intellectual-historical mode, Aristotle circumscribes *philosophia* as an engagement with the ideas of others, living or dead, whom one takes also to be or have been engaged in *philosophia*. This includes Thales's views, for example, since Aristotle can reconstruct them as addressing certain questions and open to critique by successors, including himself in particular, but not those of Hesiod, Orpheus, or other admittedly wise authors, who are not as amenable to this kind of virtual conversation. Aristotle does not explain his departure from Plato's interpersonal picture of *philosophia* to a disciplinary one, but the density of conversations, memories, texts, and positions found in the Academy probably prompted his new view. Since progress in philosophy matters, and is possible, one should bring to bear everything of relevance to any possible question, not just the ideas of one's immediate interlocutors.

In chapter 10, I focus on a set of fourth-century BCE cultural attitudes about *philosophia* different and on average later than those on which chapter 7 focused, a set that serves expressly as context and occasion for the versions of the protreptic story about Pythagoras told by Heraclides and by other fourth-century BCE writers. Positive and negative perceptions of *philosophia* coexisted. The positive feelings are most strikingly manifest in the Dephic maxim *philosophos ginou* ("be philosophical"), the existence for which comes from a 1966 discovery in Afghanistan. The negative feelings are best appreciated from fragments of the comic dramatist Alexis, from an anti-philosophical "apotreptic" found in a recently published Oxyrhynchus papyrus, and from apotreptics found in familiar philosophical texts. What becomes clear is that two ideas about *philosophia* operate simultaneously, one quasi- or fully disciplinary, the other mundanely ethical. Equivocation between these two ideas is prominent in certain parts of Aristotle's *Protrepticus* and in the Platonic *Rival Lovers*.

In an epilogue, this book concludes with a brief discussion of the relevance of this study to the way we might now think about *philosophia* and the history of philosophy in contemporary discussions of philosophy.

Conclusion: Three Observations about This Study

A feature of scholarship of ancient philosophy is its unremitting interrogation of the same old texts. What might seem boring or witless to outsiders in fact gives scholars both a deep and vivid sensitivity born of disciplinary familiarity and a confidence that they are laboring rightly, given that so many wise forebears have already tested the life lived reconstructing, analyzing, and evaluating these texts. There is also the competitive zest in seeking something as yet overlooked by past generations, and the pride of minute discovery, a feeling of distinction in a crowded field of greatness. Such desires and sentiments have driven the writing of this book, as it returns to canonical texts in Greek intellectual history: Heraclitus's fragments, Herodotus's and Thucydides's histories, the oeuvres of Plato, Xenophon, and Aristotle, and the great biographical efforts of Diogenes Laertius and Iamblichus of Chalcis, to name a few. I have drawn, even if inadequately, silently, and often unknowingly, from the accumulated centuries of study of these texts. But a real pleasure in writing this book about ancient beginnings has been the use of materials that are neither old nor well known. Some even postdate Walter Burkert's 1960 article. Of course, scholarship itself over the past six decades has often been groundbreaking, and I cite, if selectively, most often from it. But new archaeological finds and papyrological discoveries—primary rather than secondary sources—have come into play. Michael Ventris decoded Linear B in 1952, with gradual translations of Cretan tablets coming only in the ensuing decades, which have allowed me to write the section on Mycenaean onomastics. The Egyptian Exploration Fund published a satire on *philosophoi*, probably from the fourth century BCE, from an Oxyrhynchus (Egyptian) papyrus, in 1984. An ostracon also found in Oxyrhynchus, concerning Antisthenes's attitude toward *philosophia*, was first published in 1966 and 1967. The Derveni papyrus, which does not mention *philosophoi* but reveals a sympathy between theological and physical modes of philosophy in the fifth century BCE, came to light in Macedonia in 1962 and received its full official publication only in 2006. I hardly need mention the Strasbourg papyrus, published in 1999, allowing new joins of Empedocles's poem. A papyrus about Sicyon, from the Rylands collection, although published in 1911, did not get read properly until Mary White's reexamination in 1958; similarly, a papyrus in Erlangen, first published in 1942, may have gotten its correct attribution to Antisthenes only in 2014. Perhaps most remarkably, while not a papyrological discovery, Aristotle's *Protrepticus* (late 350s BCE) has been the subject of a major ongoing reconstruction by Doug Hutchinson and Monte Johnson; the editors have recovered both matters of form and of content from previously unsuspected direct quotations from Iamblichus; key parts of my work depend on their efforts.

As this sample of relevant new sources shows, a requirement for studying the origin of a word and a discipline is interdisciplinary methods. Thus, studying the origin of *philosophia*, and by extension philosophy, involves rather more than *philosophein*, and by extension, philosophizing. It takes philology: the full range of techniques appropriate for interpreting ancient texts with the goal of understanding the cultural formations that influenced them and that they influenced. This does not mean, however, that the book does not address philosophers or that it does not contribute to philosophy. It does so in at least four ways. It allows clearer formulations of an abiding question, "What is philosophy?," provides some historicized answers, and suggests avenues for answering the question at later periods. It allows better analysis of philosophical arguments that include the *philosophos*-word group in a premise or conclusion. It allows richer context for interpreting the methods and goals of classical-era philosophers, including Heraclitus, Socrates, Plato, and Aristotle. And it allows for philosophical practitioners' improved self-understanding, through improved appreciation of their discipline's earliest norms, ideals, and compromises, however much those delimiting features of the discipline have changed through the millennia.

As should by now be clear, this book has as its goal neither an ahistorical definition nor a universal praise of philosophy. It seeks instead its disciplinary origin. The Greeks loved studying such origins, apotheosizing or heroizing the inventors of the arts and sciences. We love it, too. Sometimes our love is defensive, underlining the nobility of science, the value of literature, or the urgency of scholarship, teaching, and theory. But sometimes our love has more than instrumental value, by contributing to self-understanding—about the norms to which we commit ourselves as members of a discipline, whether that discussion be medicine or social theory or ethics. Disciplinary origins, like political constitutions, project powerful limits or ideals onto our present-day practice, even if the means and extent of this projection occasion intra- and extra-disciplinary debate and disagreement. Philosophy provides a special case for the histories of disciplines. Its spokespeople may rightly claim that it birthed or sloughed off many of those disciplines themselves, such as psychology and physics. To be sure, it was no ur-discipline; it arose in a milieu spawning a range of disciplines, including linguistics, poetics, political science, and historiography, with the boundaries clear only in time. But unlike other disciplines, which at least seem to have relatively stable and uncontroversial objects of study—stars and orbits in astronomy, points and lines in geometry, melodies and instruments in music—the objects of philosophy have never been secure or subject to enduring consensus; and the twenty-first century promises no resolution. A discipline called philosophy nevertheless came to be, and, in time, quite self-consciously so.

ORIGINS

Heraclitus against the *Philosophoi*

The Earliest Attestation of the Word *Philosophos*: Heraclitus B35

According to Clement of Alexandria (ca. 150–215 CE), a Christian apologist and our most copious source for Heraclitean fragments,[1] Heraclitus gave a condition for being "philosophical men" (*Strom.* 5.140.6):

> B35/D40: For philosophical men really quite ought to be researchers into much, according to Heraclitus (χρὴ γὰρ εὖ μάλα πολλῶν ἵστορας φιλοσόφους ἄνδρας εἶναι καθ᾽ Ἡράκλειτον).[2]

Generally thought to have lived about 535–475 BCE, Heraclitus would have written this by the early fifth century BCE,[3] contemporaneous with Pythagoras's life or just after his death, which most historians place around 480 BCE.[4] The authenticity of this fragment would prove the existence of the word *philosophos* during Pythagoras's life. It would thus provide the lexical precondition for the truth of Heraclides's story, either in its literal version, taking Pythagoras to have actually used the word *philosophos*, or in a figurative sense, taking early Pythagoreans to have actually used the word *philosophos*. It would also help to date the coinage of the term, important for inferring its possible original meaning, on the basis of late sixth-century BCE use of the *phil-* prefix and the *soph-* second element.

Yet many scholars doubt the authenticity of the fragment, or believe that Clement paraphrased most of it, including the part with the word *philosophos*, which could not then be traced to Heraclitus's stylus. The first goal of this

---

[1] DK provide Clement as the source for 24 fragments; only Hippolytus comes close, with 18.

[2] Against LM, which prints ἵστορας, with a smooth breathing, I follow DK's rough breathing; nothing rests on it.

[3] DL 9.1 and *Suda* η 472 set his floruit at 503–500 BCE, the latter synchronizing his life with the reign of Darius, 521–487 BCE; Kahn 1979, 303n2, suggests Heraclitus wrote ca. 505–490 BCE.

[4] For Pythagoras's death at 480 BCE, see *BNP* s.v.; *TCT* s.v. gives 475 BCE; Guthrie 1962, 174, gives 495–90 BCE. Earlier authors claimed he died in 505 BCE, counting forward 75 years from 580 BCE.

chapter is to dispute this and defend Heraclitus's authorship of the entire fragment. The second goal is to suggest possible senses and referents of the phrase *philosophoi andres* at the beginning of the fifth century BCE, in the Greek that Heraclitus uses. Most who deny Heraclitean authorship of the word *philosophos* in B35 do so because they believe that it recommends a kind of polymathy that Heraclitus elsewhere rejects; they explain the word's existence in the fragment as Clement's paraphrastic contribution by pointing to the frequency with which Clement uses the word *philosophos* and even the phrase *philosophos anêr* in his writings. Yet B35 recommends polymathy only if it recommends being *philosophos*, and nothing supports this assumption. Heraclitus avows a normative relation between two kinds of people, not between his readers and the predicate. Indeed, the weight of evidence suggests that Heraclitus discourages being *philosophos*. This reading would allow consistency between B35 and other Heraclitean fragments.[5] Since neither textual nor source-critical difficulties impugn the fragment, we would have no reason to doubt its authenticity. Further, acceptance of authenticity would suggest that, at Heraclitus's time, *philosophos* lacked, or could lack, a positive connotation; it would not be a state worthy of universal emulation. Finally, since Heraclitus repeatedly impugns Pythagoras for his devious polymathy, B35 may refer specifically to Pythagoreans. Something like this idea—that here Heraclitus is reporting a popular view of philosophers, or speaks ironically, or refers to Pythagoras— has already been suggested by Francis Cornford, Walther Kranz, William Guthrie, and Gregory Kirk. This chapter puts these oft-forgotten suggestions by eminent scholars of early Greek philosophy on a stronger footing.

A Challenge to Interpreting the Fragment: Ambivalence about Polymathy

The main difficulty with B35 is that it appears to represent a laudatory attitude toward extensive inquiry that stands in tension with the Heraclitean statements that charge other thinkers with too much inquiry.

> B40/D20: Polymathy does not teach intelligence (πολυμαθίη νόον οὐ διδάσκει): for it would have taught it to Hesiod and Pythagoras, and again to Xenophanes and Hecataeus.

---

[5] Admittedly, we know very little about the structure or purpose of Heraclitus's writing, and thus about the relationship, if any, between fragments (see Granger 2004); but we probably can expect consistency.

B57/D25a: Teacher of most is Hesiod: they know him to know most (ἐπίστανται πλεῖστα εἰδέναι), he who did not recognize (ἐγίνωσκεν) day and night: for they are one.

B129/D26: Pythagoras of Mnesarchus practiced *historia* most of all men and, selecting out these writings, made his own wisdom, polymathy, fraudulence (ἱστορίην ἤσκησεν ἀνθρώπων μάλιστα πάντων, καὶ ἐκλεξάμενος ταύτας τὰς συγγραφὰς ἐποιήσατο ἑαυτοῦ σοφίην, πολυμαθίην, κακοτεχνίην).

B81/D27: [Pythagoras] leader of imposters (κοπίδων ἐστὶν ἀρχη||[γός]).

We need to get clear about the target of Heraclitus's criticism. B40 states categorically that *polumathia* does not teach *nous* ("intelligence," "insight"), which the structure of the statement suggests is more valuable. Because it had to be at least *prima facie* plausible that it *did* teach *nous*, *polumathia* cannot simply mean the bare accumulation of facts or data, which people might find impressive and useful but not a source of special mental competence. *Polumathia* must instead mean extensive learning, study, and the consequent integration or deployment of that experience to make one seem an authority. The lexical evidence, meager as it is, supports this.[6] So, too, does the biography of the four men Heraclitus derides in B40.[7] Among other taxonomic projects, the seventh-century poet Hesiod wove diverse threads of Panhellenic mythology into a consistent narrative in *Theogony*, and in *Works and Days* he assembled sage wisdom, calendarized auspicious days, explicated the laws of justice, and taught the myriad techniques of farming. From the earliest reception, he acquired an impressive authority on account of his far-reaching knowledge.[8] This is reflected in B57, which says that people believe, with great certitude, that Hesiod knows many things (πλεῖστα)—

---

[6] In Aristophanes's *Wasps* (422 BCE), it is "learned (πολυμαθῶν) and clever (δεξιῶν) men present" (Ar. *Vesp.* 1175) who will provide the audience for a defiantly unlearned father; that they expect "impressive" (σεμνούς, 1174; μεγαλοπρεπεῖς, 1187) and non-mythological (1179) stories implies their high level of worldliness and culture. In Plato's *Laws*, *polumatheis* are those who memorize wide swathes of poetry and gain much experience intending to become *sophos* (Pl. *Leg.* 810e6–811a5), but with "bad training" (κακῆς ἀγωγῆς) are at risk of becoming quite bad (ζημία) (819a1–6). Anaxarchus (mid- to late fourth century BCE) recognizes the equivocal value of polymathy (πολυμάθειαν κάρτα μὲν ὠφελεῖν, κάρτα δὲ βλάπτειν, Stob. 2.31.116). Stobaeus seems to attribute two instances of the *polumath-* word-group to Democritus: "many polymaths do not have intelligence" (πολλοὶ πολυμαθέες νοῦν οὐκ ἔχουσιν, B64/[27]D307) and "one ought to practice thoughtfulness, not polymathy" (πολυνοῦην, οὐ πολυμαθίην ἀσκέειν χρή, B65/[9]R104); but these seem mostly to recapitulate Heraclitus.

[7] Much scholarship reflects on the ordering of these names but none suggests its making a difference here. Some quotations of this fragment exclude the names (Ath. 13.610b; Clem. *Strom.* 1.93.1; Procl. *In Tim.* 102,22 Diehl; Stob. 2.31.116), but DL 9.1 includes all four, and Σ Pl. *Tht.* 179e includes Hesiod and Pythagoras.

[8] See Koning 2010 for evidence.

this vague object is related to πολλῶν from B35—but that this knowledge has so little point that he fails to "recognize" (ἐγίνωσκεν) a fundamental, familiar, and indeed omnipresent truth.[9] Hecataeus of Miletus (ca. 560–480 BCE) was considered the first substantial prose author, writing a systematic and rationalizing history of legendary personages, called either *Histories* or *Genealogies*, and a complete geographical and ethnographic account called *Around the World*. Like Hesiod before him, he collated and rationalized huge quantities of myth, natural history, and anthropology. This achievement could have contributed to his authority as political advisor to the Ionians concerning the Persian danger.[10] Hecataeus's contemporary Xenophanes of Colophon (ca. 570–470) wrote poetry similarly influenced by Milesian naturalizing, addressing the foundations of the cities of Elea and Colophon, proposing new views of cosmology and meteorology, and taking on the entire enterprise of Greek polytheism.[11] This vast learning could have contributed to his fame and success as a traveling poet. As we will see in chapter 3, Pythagoras won a remarkable public estimation from whatever investigative or analytic projects he engaged in, and we have no evidence that he was a mere accumulator of facts or figures. As we see from B129, his *historia* eventuates in *polumathia*, which amounts to his own idiosyncratic (and merely apparent) *sophia*, pointless in itself (cf. Heraclitus's B2/D2, B89/R56, B108/D43), and presumably the grounds for his devious and fictious self-presentation (κακοτεχνίη, B129; cf. κοπίδων ἀρχη‖[γός], B81).[12]

Heraclitus thus appears to treat *polumathia* as the collation and reinterpretation of extensive research and learning, specifically what would generate social, cultural, or political authority, albeit of the misplaced sort. That being a *pollôn histôr* basically means being *polumathês* is clear from B57, where polymathic Hesiod is believed to know the most things (πλεῖστα εἰδέναι) and B129, where polymathic Pythagoras has practiced the most *historia*—and, of course, from the fifth- and fourth-century BCE lexical evidence. Thus the paradox: whereas in B129, etc., Heraclitus abjures *polumathia*, in B35 he says that *philosophoi* must basically be *polumatheis*. On the assumption that Hera-

[9] Cf. Lesher 2016.

[10] Writings: *Suda* ε 738 with *BNJ* 1 ad T2; travel to Egypt and presenting lineage sixteen generations back: Hdt. 2.143 with Kosmin 2018, 1; advice to Aristagoras: Hdt. 5.36, 5.125–126; pace West 1991. See generally *EGM* 2.658–69, 677–80; on the connection between literacy, editorial collation, and historiography in Hecataeus and his contemporaries, see Thomas 1989, 155–95; Hawes 2014, 6–17.

[11] For the conflict between Heraclitus and Xenophanes, see Lesher 1994, 20–23. Xenophanes's city-founding poetry constituted 2000 lines (DL 9.20; see *BNJ* 450). Colophon had a complicated and legendary past; see *BNJ* 448. Elea, founded by settlers from Ionian Phocis around 540 BCE, was the hometown of Parmenides and Zeno.

[12] Sider and Obbink 2013 studies parallels between Pythagoras and Heraclitus without, however, attending to the latter's response to the former.

clitus thinks his readers should be *philosophoi*, resolution of the paradox requires either that we reject one or more of the fragments, or that we understand
the relevant fragments anew. Most interpreters have taken the first route, and
finding the evidence for Heraclitus's distaste of *polumathia* stronger than the
evidence against it, they reject the authenticity of B35 either in full or in part.
Of course, the assumption that Heraclitus enjoins us to be *philosophoi* may
well be dubious—in which case the apparent contradiction has no bite.

Suspicions of Clementine Meddling

The most recent instance of doubt about the authenticity of B35 comes in a
momentous publication: André Laks and Glenn Most's nine-volume collection of the early Greek philosophical fragments for the Loeb Classical Library
(2016)—a collection already supplanting Diels and Kranz's *Die Fragmente der
Vorsokratiker* for many readers. Their doubt appears to depend on two specific instances of misplaced skepticism about Clement's reliability, both of
which we can resolve.

In their collection of Heraclitean fragments, Laks and Most include twenty-
three quotations from Clement, regarding twenty-two of which they express
no substantive doubt.[13] For B35/D40, however, they print the following, putting in bold font all that they think comes reliably from the source text:

> B35/D40 Clement of Alexandria, *Stromata*
> For according to Heraclitus, men who love wisdom must be **investigators**
> into very many things.[1]
>
> [1] It is uncertain whether the whole sentence is to be attributed to Heraclitus or only
> some parts of it, and whether in particular the term *philosophoi* ("men who love wisdom")
> belongs to him and what exactly it means here.

Thus they accept only one word, "investigators" (ἵστορας), as reliable; despite
the equanimity of the footnote, they side with skepticism, by contrast to their
approach elsewhere. They cite no reasons, textual or source-critical, for their
uncertainty, nor any scholarship demonstrating the unique unreliability of this
Clementine quotation. A reader may get the impression, from this authoritative source, that everyone knows that we cannot base arguments on this fragment; and indeed, with attestations of *philosophos* from only 430 BCE or later,
that one would be hard-pressed to defend the present history of *philosophia*.

---

[13] They query the μᾶλλον δὲ ἀναπαύεσθαι in B20/D118, the ἀποθανών in B26/D71, and the
φυλάσσει in B28/D19; except perhaps the last, none count as significant exclusions.

Laks and Most's potentially decisive view has its precedents, even if readers of their text are not in the position to discern them. The editors do not cite
Heraclitus scholarship here, but throughout the nine volumes of the Loeb collection, they acknowledge six works on Heraclitus: Hermann Diels's 1901 edition of Heraclitus; Walther Kranz's 1951 revision of Diels's *Die Fragmente
der Vorsokratiker*; Miroslav Marcovich's 1967 critical edition of Heraclitus;
Charles Kahn's 1979 translation and commentary, the best known full-scale
analysis of Heraclitus's work in English; Thomas Robinson's 1987 convenient
translation and commentary for the University of Toronto Press; and Serge
Mouraviev's 1999 twenty-volume study of the reception of Heraclitus. Four
of these six texts actually accept the entirety of the fragment. Only Marcovich and Robinson do not; and since Robinson depends on Marcovich, only
Marcovich matters.

In fact, Marcovich accepts more of Clement's quotation-paraphrase than
Laks and Most did: "Men (?) must be acquainted with many things (πολλῶν
ἴστορας χρὴ [? ἀνθρώπους] εἶναι)."[14] Yet the upshot remains the same: he athe-
tizes the intensifiers and the accusative subject of the assertion, *philosophous
andras*. He cuts *philosophos* not because it would commit Heraclitus to a contradiction in promoting broad research, since even the overhauled version
promotes research. It is rather because of "Clement's predilection for [*philosophos*] used as adjective" and his use of the phrase "tribe of philosophical men"
(γένη φιλοσόφων ἀνδρῶν); the latter two words are the ones that we find in
the Heraclitus quotation, earlier in the *Stromata* (1.68.4).[15] These, however,
are specious reasons.[16]

Clement uses the term *philosophos* 133 times in his extant work. Hardly
anything follows from this, since those appear in four works, largely about
philosophy, comprising nearly 248,000 words; by comparison, Eusebius of
Caesarea (ca. 260–340 CE) uses the term 208 times in his *Praeparatio Evan-
gelica*, which is 12,000 words shorter. Nor have scholars suspected Clement
of inserting his favorite words into his other quotations from Heraclitus. Nor

---

[14] Marcovich 1967, 25–29. See below, pp. 46–47, for Reinhardt's severer reduction.

[15] Marcovich admits that several facts tell in favor, if not strongly enough, of the Heraclitean
provenance of *philosophos*: Herodotus's use of the verb in his *Histories* (discussed in chapter 5);
Heraclides's story itself (discussed in chapter 1); and Heraclitus's affinity for compound words,
including κακοτεχνίη (B129), πολυμαθίη (B40), and ἀγχιβασίη (B122/D61) (Finkelberg 2017,
88n16, adds ἀρηϊφάτους (B24/D122a), ἀείζωον (B30/D85), and παλίντροπος (B51/D49)).

[16] For Clement's working method related to this fragment, see Wiese 1963, 255–61; Dinan
2005, 54–57; Osborn 2005, 16–18, 144–46, 184–86.

does Marcovich explain why Clement would paraphrase whatever Heraclitus originally had—"men"?—with the much more limiting "philosophical men."[17]

It is true that Clement uses "philosophical men" on another instance (1.68.3), which proves the accessibility to him of that formulation—and thus for many nineteenth- and twentieth-century scholars, the smoking gun against Clement's reliability. Yet Clement's having used that locution only once suggests that he has no predilection for that formulation. In fact, in this other instance, he hardly does so from his own creative impulse or linguistic habit: he is essentially quoting from Plato's *Phaedo*.[18] That Clement's one (non-Heraclitean) use of *philosophos anêr* comes in discussing a text with a peculiar density of that formulation means that we cannot on that basis assume that he would attribute it to other authors.[19] One might even suppose that the fact that an early fourth-century BCE author, Plato, uses the formulation *philosophos anêr* eight times speaks in favor of its use by a predecessor only a hundred years earlier.[20] Even stronger evidence is the frequency with which sixth- and fifth-century BCE authors use the parallel formulation, *anêr sophos*,[21] which locution Heraclitus might have in mind, and other *x anêr* formulations for intellectuals, including *periphradês anêr* (Soph. *Ant.* 347, <441 BCE: a very thoughtful man)[22] and *anêr meteôrophanax* (Ar. *Nub.* 333, 423/17 BCE: a

---

[17] One may find similarly inadequate reflection on the word/phrase being paraphrased in Schuster 1872, 63–64; Robinson 1987, 104.

[18] Clement has just quoted *Phd.* 78a3–4, where Socrates says: "Greece is large, where there are, I'd suppose, good men (ἀγαθοὶ ἄνδρες), and the races of foreigners are many, too (πολλὰ δὲ καὶ τὰ τῶν βαρβάρων γένη)." Clement explains: "By the 'races of foreigners' (διὰ τοῦτο καὶ γένη βαρβάρων), [Plato] means 'the races of foreign philosophical men' (γένη φιλοσόφων ἀνδρῶν βαρβάρων), recognizing, in the *Phaedrus*, [Theuth, etc.], and in the *Charmides*, [Zalmoxis, etc.]." Marcovich is suspicious of this *philosophôn andrôn* as a Clementine invention." But in the first place, Plato writes *philosophos anêr* on three occasions in the *Phaedo* (64d2, 84a2–3, 95c1), the very dialogue that Clement has in front of him, and so he probably has that language in mind from that source (it also shows up at *Phdr.* 248d2–3, which dialogue he has just cited, and in four other Platonic dialogues: *Soph.* 216a4; *RL* 135e1, 136b10; *Euthyd.* 305c7; *Tim.* 19e5). In the second place, the construction of Socrates's sentence at *Phd.* 78a suggests that "men" (ἀνδρῶν) is the assumed noun in the second clause, carrying over from the first; Socrates can be heard to say πολλα . . . τὰ τῶν [ἀνδρῶν] βαρβάρων γένη (the formulation βαρβάρων ἀνδρῶν or ἀνδρῶν βαρβάρων is found at Pl. *Criti.* 113a2, and also Ar. *Ach.* 168; *Vesp.* 439; Hdt. 1.214.3, 6.106, 8.87; Eur. *Hel.* 1604). The collocation of *genos* and *philosophos* appears in Plato at *R.* 501e3, 581c4.

[19] YC 1.345 believes that Clement shows himself capable of introducing the term where it does not belong; but Clement does not present himself here as quoting, only explaining, and thus he cannot be charged with misquoting.

[20] In the fourth century BCE, it also shows up in Aeschin. 1.141.7, 3.257.6.

[21] Thgn. 120; Pind. *Ol.* 11.10; *Isthm.* 1.45; *Nem.* 8.41; *Pae.* 13 fr. 52s.3; Bacchyl. 13.164; Hdt. 2.49, 3.25, 3.85, 5.23, 7.130; and, e.g., Critias[?] "Sisyphus" 43F19.12 *TrGF* (= B25/[43]T63); Eur. *Autolycus* fr. 282.23.

[22] Eust. 135.25 reads ἀριφραδὴς ἀνήρ, "a clear-minded man," which makes the same point.

man with "high-flown pretension," in Henderson's translation). So, we have evidence that Heraclitus could use *philosophos anêr*, and no evidence that Clement would independently.

Though Marcovich does not mention it, one might wonder about the accuracy of Clement's adjacent quotations, to Empedocles (from a generation after Heraclitus) and Phocylides (a contemporaneous Milesian poet); Clement cites this triad in support of the view that one must wade through much Greek philosophy to come upon anything valuable. But nothing tells against their basic accuracy.[23] We therefore have no reason to believe that Clement is unreliable in this paragraph. Combined with the view that Clement introduces no important inaccuracies into his other Heraclitus quotations, and in particular that no recent editor has doubted the authenticity of the four other *kath' Herakleiton* ("according to Heraclitus") constructions, of which this is the fifth, I see no reason to doubt the existence of *philosophos* in Heraclitus's fragment B35.[24] The same goes for denying the Heraclitean provenance of the intensifying εὖ μάλα ("really quite").[25]

I have spent this time on Marcovich's skepticism because it remains authoritative for many readers, including Laks and Most, and because it consolidates a century of skepticism.[26] Of course, other careful readers of Heraclitus have accepted the whole fragment. I have already cited four, and there are many

---

[23] Laks and Most accept the accuracy of the Empedocles quotation: ὄλβιος, ὃς θείων πραπίδων ἐκτήσατο πλοῦτον, | δειλὸς δ' ᾧ σκοτόεσσα θεῶν πέρι δόξα μέμηλεν ("Happy, he who possesses the wealth of divine organs of thought; | Wretched, he who cares for an obscure doctrine about the gods") (B132/D8). Though Clement's formulation of Phocylides differs from the two other extant (and late) versions, his agrees with them in subject clause, and so apparently gets it right; this tells in favor of his quotation of *philosophous andras*, the subject clause of B35. Clement writes: "and it is truly necessary to have wandered much for the one seeking to be excellent" (καὶ τῷ ὄντι ἀνάγκη πολλὰ πλανηθῆναι διζήμενον ἔμμεναι ἐσθλόν). Plutarch has "much deceived (πόλλ᾽ ἀπατηθῆναι) is the one seeking to be excellent" (*De auditu* 47e); an anonymous manuscript has "suffering much that is unintended (παθεῖν, πόλλ᾽ ἀέκοντα) is the one seeking to be excellent" (Anon. An. Par. 1.166.18 Cramer).

[24] Other καθ' Ἡράκλειτον constructions: B40/D20 (though Clement abbreviates), B17/D3, B25/D122b, B86/D38.

[25] It may be important to the fragment's tone (as ironical, sarcastic, etc.). εὖ μάλα is available to Heraclitus (see Hom. *Il.* 23.761; *Od.* 4.96, 24.123; *Hymn. Hom. Ap.* 171; Hes. [*Sc.*] 355), and appears more than twenty times in Plato; and Clement's argumentative goals do not require that he introduce an intensifier into a fragment that did not have one. A more interesting question concerns what it intensifies, either the χρή or the πολλῶν (or, with Pradeau 2002, 272, a little implausibly, the ἵστορας); maybe it intensifies both.

[26] Those skeptical that Heraclitus used the term *philosophous* include Wilamowitz-Moellendorf 1880, 124–25; Gigon 1935, 140; Deichgräber 1935, 110n4; Wiese 1963, 260n3, 318; Dumont 1988, 780; Hadot 2002, 285n2; Pradeau 2002, 272–73; YC 1.328–48 (with refs.); Fronterotta 2013; Hülsz Piccone 2013, 281–82; and Hülsz Piccone 2014.

more.[27] From my perspective, the case for B35 goes beyond a preponderance of the evidence; I see nothing to provoke a reasonable doubt.

Recent Scholarship's Two-Step Model of Heraclitean Epistemology

If we want to accept the fragment as reported, we must resolve the obvious tension between it and Heraclitus's anti-polymathy fragments. My ultimate resolution involves rejecting the assumption that Heraclitus recommends being an "investigator into much" and seeing him as simply describing the necessary conditions for being such a person. A rejection of that assumption is equivalent to finding that, for readers of Heraclitus's Greek of the sixth and fifth centuries BCE, *philosophos* is not a term of aspiration, acclaim, or self-identification. In chapter 3, I will argue that we have good reason to believe that it was not a term of this sort, and thus that we have reason to accept the historical conditions for Heraclides's Pythagoras story. In this chapter I reject the assumption that in B35 Heraclitus is recommending polymathy, and I do this by pointing to four pieces of evidence. First, by speaking of *histores pollôn*, Heraclitus says that philosophical men ought to be polymathic. Second, Heraclitus directly rejects polymathy as his ideal. Third, in other fragments, Heraclitus advances a contrary ideal: undergoing a qualitative rather than a quantitative shift in insight, a shift that he treats in analogy to waking up, recognizing how things really are, and appreciating that *to sophon* ("what's wise," "wisdom") is "one" and distinct from all else. Fourth, Heraclitus says nothing to suggest that this qualitative shift is acquired through polymathy; in particular, Heraclitus's appreciation of sense perception does not entail advocacy of extensive empirical learning. I have already shown the first two parts of the argument, in the analysis of *polumathia* and of fragments such as B40 and B129. What I develop here is the third and fourth elements, arguing against the common view that Heraclitus can recommend *polumathia* in B35 by treating it as the first step in a two-step process of acquiring wisdom.

The view of a two-step process is found most clearly in the work of Marcovich, to whom we will return, and in Patricia Curd, in a sophisticated account

---

[27] E.g., Lassalle 1858; Bywater 1877; Diels 1901, 10; Walzer 1939, 74–75; Chroust 1947, 22, 25–26; Joly 1956, 30–31; Ramnoux 1959, 122; Malingrey 1961, 38; Bollack and Wismann 1972; Conche 1987; Sweet 1995; Mouraviev 1999, III.3.B/iii, 44–45; Pradeau 2002; Finkelberg 2017, 200n39.

from 1991, but also in some other scholars.[28] An impulse toward such a view is found in some interpretations that identify Heraclitus as an empiricist. In 1942, Karl Reinhardt, quite like Laks and Most, suspected that Clement paraphrases everything except ἵστορας; he thinks the original statement must have encouraged the reader to be a *histôr*. He infers this from one of Heraclitus's remarks that apparently deals with perception:

B101a/D32: For eyes are more precise witnesses (μάρτυρες) than ears.

Reinhardt takes *histores* to be those who seek direct experience of the world, eyes to be windows onto that direct experience, and ears to be mere entry points for secondhand testimony. B35 thus says that the wise must investigate with their own eyes. Reinhardt reasons that this is not simply because false tales are told, but that even when true tales are told, they are not believed (as Heraclitus claims in B1, discussed below). Only direct experience vindicates paradoxical reports, reports that would otherwise be dismissed. This skeptical Pyrrhonism is an interesting view, to be sure.[29] It is not clear, however, that Heraclitus excludes the possibility that some appearances, whether visual or otherwise, might be imprecise or deceptive. Nor is it clear how this

---

[28] E.g., von Fritz 1945, 230–36; Wheelwright 1959, 19, 23–24, 26–27; Lallot 1971; Bollack and Wismann 1973, 134; Cook 1975, 433–35; Hussey 1982, 37; Havelock 1983, 56–57; Finkelberg 2017, 200n40, 206, 219.

[29] W. J. Verdenius (1947, 280–84), a few years later, takes a similar route (as do Barnes 1982, 116, and Sweet 1995, 64: "The wise person is not one who has learned many different things (fr. 40), but rather one who has inquired into many things (frs. 35, 55) and has come to know the order which is common to all of them (frs. 2, 30)"). Verdenius says that ἱστορεῖν means "inquiring independently," in contrast to μανθάνειν, which means "borrowing other people's wisdom," the verb implied in πολυμαθίη (B40, B129). Thus Heraclitus praises self-reliant search, "persuad[ing] oneself by objective argument," and elsewhere denigrates "rely[ing] on personal authority." Verdenius acknowledges that in B129 Heraclitus says that Pythagoras engages in ἱστορίη, but he assumes that in saying this, Heraclitus is simply parroting the common but mistaken praise of Pythagoras as "inquirer"—a praise the Pythagoreans maintained—and then denouncing that praise. (For the claim that the Pythagoreans said their master practiced ἱστορίη Verdenius cites Burnet (1930, 97n1), who in turn cites Iambl. *DCMS* 25.78,5 (probably paraphrasing Aristotle's *Protrepticus*): ἐκαλεῖτο δὴ ἡ γεωμετρία πρὸς Πυθαγόρου ἱστορία ["geometry was called by Pythagoras '*historia*'"]; yet this is not compelling evidence for an "ironic" interpretation of "inquirer.") But, as we will see below, there is no evidence from archaic or classical Greece that *historia* or being *histôr* involves objective argument or independent inquiry. Nor is there evidence for or coherence in the presumed contrast between independent inquiry and reliance on others' wisdom; a person may inquire on his own among many people and take up their ideas (cf. Curd 1991, 544n2). Even if Heraclitus does denounce Pythagoras, B129 does not imply that Pythagoras's followers wrongly ascribed to him the practice of *historia*; it only suggests that his *historia* went to a bad end.

strict empiricism fits with the more generous empiricism in the following fragment:

B55/D31: Whatever sight, hearing, learning are of (ὅσων ὄψις ἀκοὴ μάθησις), that I prefer.

Thus while Heraclitus may esteem a sort of self-reliance or active self-application to problems, the nature of the reliable input remains uncertain.[30] This may be moot, anyway, to the extent we cannot justify Reinhardt's severe treatment of the Heraclitean fragment and his assumption that Clement would rely on Heraclitus's praise of *historia* by rewording nearly the entirety of Heraclitus's sentence.

As we saw above, Marcovich attributes four words to Heraclitus: χρὴ . . . πολλῶν ἵστορας . . . εἶναι. He interprets this skeletal fragment against the background of B101a and B55. Sense perception and experience, the two modes of inquiry that B55 appears to recommend, are essential for knowing the *logos*, the universal and unified object of knowledge. But B40, B57, and B129 show that these modes of inquiry alone get you only to the stage of polymathy, which is epistemically inadequate. So to polymathy one must add intelligence or interpretative ability.[31] B35 (on *philosophoi andres*), Marcovich concludes, "stress[es] the need of gathering many sense data as the first condition for the recognition of the Logos." The weaknesses of this view are readily apparent. B35 makes no reference to sense data, or to being only the first stage in anything, or to recognizing the *logos*.[32]

Thomas Robinson tries to broaden the evidence base for Marcovich's claims.[33] "Of course," Robinson says, wisdom is not achieved "from a mere mindless accumulation of facts." But in support of the view that Heraclitus believes accumulation to be important nevertheless, Robinson cites the following three fragments:

---

[30] The syntax and meaning of *mathêsis* is disputed; I follow Marcovich 1967, 21. Barnes 1982, 115, translating instead "The things we learn of by sight and hearing . . ." (similarly LM 3.155), takes the fragment as evidence for Heraclitus's empiricism and sensationalism: "knowledge must be built on . . . sense-experience." This is consistent with an anti-polymathism.

[31] The former Marcovich defines negatively with language from B107/D33: having [οὐ] βάρβαρος ψυχή, "a [non-] barbaric soul." (Pressure on this interpretation comes from Nussbaum 1972, 9–13; Wilcox 1991; Robb 1991.) The latter he defines as the skill inferred from B93/D41, whatever one deploys to understand Delphic oracles.

[32] For a persuasive view about Heraclitean *logos*, see Johnstone 2014 against West 1971, 115–16, 124–29; see also Hoffman 2006, 1–18; Hülsz Piccone 2013, 283–96.

[33] Robinson 1987, 104.

B18/D37: If he does not expect the unexpected he will not find it out (ἐξευρήσει), it being unsearchable (ἀνεξερεύνητον) and impassable.

B22/D39: Those seeking out (διζήμενοι) gold dig up much (πολλήν) earth and find little.

B123/D35: Nature tends to conceal itself.

These three fragments, Robinson says, "suggest the difficulties involved in exploring the real, which reveals its secrets (B123) only to the persevering (B22) and open-minded (B18) enquirer." Robinson assumes that only a sufficient quantity of inquiry unlocks the world's mysteries.[34] This does seem to be something like Clement's view; the genuine love of wisdom demands, and indeed cannot avoid, much trial and error.[35] Yet B22 appears to dissuade one from digging around too much rather than to encourage it.[36] And neither

---

[34] Cf. Kahn 1979, 105: "Even if the *logos* is common to all, so that the structure of reality is 'given' in everyday experience, recognition comes hard. It requires the right kind of openness on the part of the percipient . . . [a]nd it requires inquiry and reflection—digging up a lot of earth and judging it with discretion. The 'gnosis' which Heraclitus has in mind is rational *knowledge*, and it has to be gained by hard work; it is not the miraculous revelation of a moment of grace."

[35] Clement takes the claim that philosophical men "ought" (χρή) to be "researchers into much" to mean mean that one can hardly avoid the dead-ends and vain wandering on the way to wisdom. Yet the modal claim, on this reading, is ambiguous. It may mean that it is *inevitable* that seekers, presumably of wisdom, will have many false starts, follow mistaken clues, or otherwise abide lots of confusion, ignorance, and reversal. They "ought to" confront these challenges; if they do not, they are doing something wrong. The "much" that one ends up researching is not instrumentally or constitutively valuable to attaining wisdom; it is merely an incidental though unavoidable byproduct of the path to the attainment of wisdom. The matter of epistemic value is not the vain wandering, or even something learned *because of* the vain wandering; the vain wandering simply slows down the acquisition of the object(s) of epistemic value. Cognizance of the vain wandering at best allows one to brace oneself for the long and often disappointing slog; or, to put a positive spin on it, it reaffirms that one might be going in the right direction ("you ought to pass eight traffic lights before seeing my street"). The other possible interpretation of the χρή is that the seemingly vain wandering is valuable in itself, instrumentally or constitutively. Heraclitus might be saying that one has to do a lot of research, to be sure, but the research *itself* brings one to wisdom. The research bridges rather than blocks. This may feel like vain wandering and as instrumentally or constitutively useless; yet it is exactly the naïve dismissal of investigative work on the basis of feelings of toil that Heraclitus warns his reader against. The discrimination necessary for knowledge may require lots of experience. We can even specify three ways in which extensive experience could be necessary: as the connoisseur's accumulated experience of distinctions and quality, as the experimental or empirical scientist's systematic experience of variety and norms, or as the Socratic inquirer's introspective experience of repeated failure and *aporia* (where wisdom just is the true appreciation of one's ignorance, etc.).

[36] Finding even a little gold would require, on one reading, the unfortunate digging of much dirt besides. On another reading, the experience with geology or mineralogy acquired through much digging would be necessary even to recognize gold as gold rather than, say, iron pyrite. The second possibility might seem less likely. Recognition of gold (in contrast with less shiny and popular minerals) may not seem, to Heraclitus's mind, to require the accumulation of knowledge

of the other fragments encourage polymathy. B18 seems to advise a certain mental state during exploration; B123 seems to speak to the manner of the world's intelligibility.

The most promising argument for Heraclitus's exhorting his readers to do something in addition to knowledge-accumulation comes from Patricia Curd (1991). She attributes to Heraclitus the belief that one should start with a "collection of material" or an "accumulation of true beliefs," and then "link them together into a network in which the beliefs are mutually supporting and explanatory." Knowledge, Curd says, is "the comprehension of the system as a whole." On this reading, in his advocacy of knowing the *logos*, Heraclitus means knowing the deep relations among all the things there are. Heraclitus intervenes in pre-Socratic philosophy by moving away from the early Greek "naïve metaphysics," whereby we know discrete and unconnected things, and by moving toward a search "for justification . . . seeing that and how [each] single belief is part of a system that is a unified whole."[37] In support of her view, Curd references B17, B35, B40, B41, B54, B107, B108, B112, and B114. We have already looked at B35 (on *philosophoi andres*) and B40 (on the failure of polymathy to teach intelligence). These are the other relevant fragments:

B17/D3: For most people do not understand such things as they encounter, nor having learned do they recognize, but they seem to themselves [to have done so].

B41/D44: The wise is one: to know a judgment that steers all through all.

B54/D50: Unapparent harmony is better than apparent.

B107/D33: Eyes and ears are bad witnesses for men, should they have barbarian souls.

---

of what is not gold. This is in large part because whereas Heraclitus surely thinks that people do not readily recognize wisdom, he would likely think that people do immediately recognize gold. Thus B22 does not support the view that wisdom requires polymathy only accidentally or non-constitutively. Indeed, in some sense, B22 seems ultimately not to be about the requirements for finding gold (contra Burnet 1930, 132, who paraphrases: "If men cared to dig for the gold they might find it"). Heraclitus seems to be saying instead that "those who seek silly things [e.g., gold] hardly even find them; and they put an awful lot of effort into it." To this extent the case of gold does not provide an analogy to that of wisdom (with Fränkel 1938, 322, citing B9/D79 ["Asses would choose sweepings rather than gold," ὄνους σύρματ᾽ ἂν ἑλέσθαι μᾶλλον ἢ χρυσόν, trans. LM 3.177], and contra Mourelatos 1965, 352). The story would be different, to be sure, if Heraclitus meant by "gold" anything objectively valuable and thus wrote B22 to claim that even eking out a little something valuable takes much effort and dealing with much that is not objectively valuable; but we do not have evidence that "gold" does mean that for Heraclitus (see B9), or that he believes that it takes effort—rather than, say, a change in perspective—to get at what is objectively valuable. (Marcovich 1967, 38, strikes me as naïve here.)

[37] Curd 1991, 531, 535–36.

B108/D43: Of those whose *logoi* I have heard not one arrives at recognizing what wisdom is, separated from all.

B112/D114a + b: To exercise discipline is greatest virtue and wisdom, to speak and act truly, perceiving in accordance with nature.

B114/D105: For, those speaking with intelligence must rely on the common among all, just as a city on its law and even more reliably: for all human laws are nourished by the one divine law: for it is as strong as it is willing to be and is sufficient for all and exceeds all.

These fragments support the view that Heraclitus thinks that wisdom is a unity or a concord (B41, B54, perhaps B108), that wisdom and understanding should be our goal (B108, B112, B114), and that this wisdom is not mere familiarity with the surface of things (B17, B54, B107). Yet of all these fragments, *only* B35 could plausibly be taken to support Curd's contention that polymathy is necessary for wisdom. For, without that fragment, nothing Heraclitus says in B40 or the seven fragments above suggests any value in accumulating information, multiple true beliefs about the world, or familiarity with diverse phenomena that may later be susceptible to systematization. In fact, then, for Curd, B35, which she understands as recommending diverse inquiry, provides the *sole* grounds for her view that Heraclitus accepts Milesian or Pythagorean research when accompanied by systematization and the appreciation of the stable *logos*. Given the vehemence with which Heraclitus seems to dismiss the methodology of the polymaths and the fact that his fragments arguably do not themselves show the results of any "diverse inquiry" of his own, we should check the interpretation of B35 rather than reinterpret many other fragments.[38]

This review of the important recent scholarship on B35 reveals a tendency to suppose that Heraclitus advocates the *historia* and even *polumathia* associated with Pythagoras, Hesiod, Xenophanes, and Hecataeus, but qualifies his advocacy by treating *historia* and *polumathia* as starting points rather than as goals. This tendency places Heraclitus squarely in the shared Ionian-Italic research tradition.[39] Heraclitus would thus contribute to this tradition an appreciation for an underlying unity, or harmony, or explanatory schema, in addition to a reliance on direct verification and experience of challenging material. As we have seen, however, this popular view depends exclusively on B35. This is a problematic dependence, both because it is just one fragment

[38] Indeed, debates about the superiority of having a single big idea over having many little ideas ("the hedgehog and the fox") were contemporaneous with Heraclitus: see Węcowski 2004; Stokes 1971, 86–89, argues for Heraclitus's firm preference for the one big idea.

[39] On the hazards of doing so, see Graham 1997.

against a range of apparently contradictory fragments and because it is a fragment characterized by the pragmatic ambiguity of not explicitly recommending to its readers that they become *histores pollôn*, besides the fact that the concept of *polumathia* probably already includes some degree of synthesis of that which has been learned. In fact, Heraclitus probably favors an alternative view, and this can be shown by reconstructing his epistemology.

A Reconstruction of Heraclitus's Epistemology

In our attempt to understand B35, we can hypothesize a contrasting pair of reconstructions for Heraclitus's epistemological thought. We have just seen the two-stage model. The necessary first stage is research into much; by contrast, the necessary second stage is somehow adding to, abstracting from, or linking together the results of the first stage, with the goal of attaining unified understanding. The reason for the first stage, and the operations to be done in the second stage, may be accounted for in various ways; all fall into the category of "research." An alternative reconstruction of Heraclitus's epistemology is a one-stage model, in which it is unnecessary and may even be useless to research or inquire into much.

Heraclitus treats as the primary desideratum of thought the comprehension of the "*logos*," the unifying structure of the world at all levels of analysis. Such comprehension constitutes wisdom. The nature of this *logos* seems related to the harmony of opposites and the continuity of change.[40] The question of Heraclitean epistemology concerns the way one comes to know the *logos*. We have already seen the absence of compelling evidence for the view that one must journey far, do a lot of research, or undergo manifold trials and tribulations. It seems rather that one must recognize what is really in front of oneself—and this requires a change in oneself. After all, Heraclitus's fragments regularly provide mundane examples: rivers, the sun, roads, beverages, games, bows, lyres, combs.[41] Their wide range has pedagogical but not epistemic purpose. Any single one would suffice for his argument about the nature of the *logos*; the multiplicity of instances helps the reader catch that argument. It would appear that Heraclitus wants to show that our naïve notion of things need not therefore be the correct notion of them. In this respect, Heraclitus's epistemology shares something with Parmenides's, the premises of whose "Way of Truth" tell against research (even if his "Way of Opinion" does not), or Zeno's, whose paradoxes hardly require diverse inquiry to generate or explain them.

[40] Guthrie 1962, 415–54, remains an eloquent argument for and exposition of this basic view.
[41] River: B12/D65a, B49a/R9, A6/D65; sun: B3/D89b; road: B60/D51; beverage: B125/D59; game: B52/D76; bow and lyre: B48/D53 and B51/D49; carding-comb: B59/D52.

Heraclitus's dismissal of inferential or systematized knowledge does not thereby make his epistemology easy to understand. If the prized epistemic state—comprehension, understanding, knowledge—does not depend on the systematic integration of diverse beliefs and perceptions, it must come from somewhere else.[42] One might wonder whether it comes from a special feature of knowable objects themselves.[43] Yet Heraclitus lacks the stark distinction, familiar from Plato's dialogues, between unchanging knowables and changing believables. If the criterion of knowledge comes not (primarily) from the objects of belief or the relation between the beliefs, what remains is the subject of the beliefs, the person and her mind. This seems in fact Heraclitus's choice. He exhorts his readers to wake up and have a kind of self-knowledge they do not yet have. A sequence of fragments treats human ignorance as the effect not of inadequate research or wrong focus, but of living as though one were asleep. Seeing how they do so will help us, ultimately, to understand Heraclitus's vision and critique of "philosophical men."

> B1/D1: The *logos* being always men are not understanding, both before hearing and having heard it already: for all things coming to be in accordance with this logos, they are like the inexperienced when they have experienced words and deeds of the sort I go through distinguishing each by its nature and saying how they are; and men take no notice of what they do when awake just as those asleep do not take cognizance.[44]

In the opening statement of his work,[45] Heraclitus presents the human ignorance of the *logos* in three ways, three avenues through which to make sense of his epistemology and thus his attitude toward *pollôn histores*.

People do not understand (ἀξύνετοι) despite having heard (ἀκούσαντες), as though they were deaf, distracted, or spoke only a foreign language.[46] The *logos*

---

[42] Drozdek 2011, 102, claims that *noos*, what we need for wisdom, is not "reasoning" but instead "intuition, insight, seeing the essence of things"; unfortunately, it is quite unclear what these amount to.

[43] On the view that knowledge comes about with respect to its proper objects, see Gerson 2009, which however does not address Heraclitus's epistemology.

[44] τοῦ δὲ λόγου τοῦδ᾽ ἐόντος ἀεὶ ἀξύνετοι γίνονται ἄνθρωποι, καὶ πρόσθεν ἢ ἀκοῦσαι, καὶ ἀκούσαντες τὸ πρῶτον· γινομένων γὰρ πάντων κατὰ τὸν λόγον τόνδε ἀπείροισιν ἐοίκασι, πειρώμενοι καὶ ἐπέων καὶ ἔργων τοιούτων, ὁκοίων ἐγὼ διηγεῦμαι κατὰ φύσιν διαιρέων ἕκαστον καὶ φράζων ὅκως ἔχει. τοὺς δὲ ἄλλους ἀνθρώπους λανθάνει ὁκόσα ἐγερθέντες ποιοῦσιν ὅκωσπερ ὁκόσα εὕδοντες ἐπιλανθάνονται.

[45] Arist. *Rh.* 1407b16–17 and Sext. Emp. *Math.* 7.132 confirm its initial position in his book or collection.

[46] Hussey 1982, 37, hints at the importance of knowing the right language: "the step from the obvious to the latent truth is like the translation of utterances in a language which is foreign

is being presented to them directly, without any requirement that they travel, gather up information, assemble fragments, or run the gauntlet of puzzlement. The problem is internal to the potential knowers. Either they lack some basic capacity for understanding, or ignore what they should not, or despite paying attention fail to deal correctly with the object of their attention. The first possibility is unlikely. Heraclitus's pessimism bottoms out at epistemic disappointment, not fatalism; he thinks people can understand the *logos*, but can do so only if they follow his critical lead. The second possibility fits his texts better. Distractions abound—tradition, convention, authority, private imagination, wish-fulfillment—and they obscure what must be appreciated in particular. Coming to know might require not the acquisition of more facts, but exactly the reverse, the purging or cabining of everything else. We ought to have fewer assumptions, not more.[47] This brings with it another epistemological task, determining the nature of that post-purge remainder. We can barter that task for another with the third possibility, which fits the texts just as well. It is wrong to deem people distracted; rather, they simply fail to interpret or recognize correctly. What they hear or see or otherwise experience lacks sense or relevance or clarity. Only having acquired the skills of or commitment to interpretation or recognition does the noise of the *logos* become a voice. The extra task now is determining the nature of that interpretative or recognitional capacity and what gets interpreted or recognized. Even without taking up this task now, we can see that it does not obviously require copious research.

In the next part of B1, Heraclitus says that people are like the inexperienced (ἀπείροισιν) even when they experience (πειρώμενοι). This presents, on the practical dimension, the problem that the first part of the fragment presents on the linguistic or auditory dimension. Presented with the relevant material, the inexperienced do not know what to do with it. Novices lack the right habits, or judgments of salience, or sense of form.

In the last part of B1, Heraclitus says that the failure to take notice when awake parallels a similar failure when asleep. Sleepers dream, and in those dreams they feel awake and aware and active. Yet that feeling misleads them; they do not really take cognizance. Heraclitus's fragment does not specify the object of that cognizance. One might provide: of their dream world, on its own terms. They may have at best a superficial appreciation of it, overlooking its inconsistencies, lapses, and implausibilities. They fail to integrate or

---

to most men"; "To reach the truth from the appearances, it is necessary to interpret, to guess the riddle, or divine the meaning of the oracle." See also Clements 2014, in the section "Senses as 'Bad Witnesses.'"

[47] This view is argued persuasively by Dilcher 2013, and diverges from, e.g., West 1971, 114–17.

systematize all their true dream beliefs. We have no reason to think that Heraclitus valorizes integrated or systematic beliefs by identifying such beliefs with knowledge. Nor would Heraclitus find it bad that dreamers overlook their dreamworld's erratic rendering. More probably, he notes that dreamers fail to realize that their world *is* a dreamworld, that it is *illusory*. The problem is that one's dreamworld, populated by the appearance of objects from the real world, looks quite like the real world, and one's orientation in it, structured by one's own personality, feels like one's real orientation. "Looking like" and "feeling like" do not, however, entail "actually being like"; asleep, we forget or do not take cognizance of this. Yet remembering and recognizing our sleeping does not require extensive research or system-building. It simply takes waking up.[48] Barring that, it takes peeling one's consciousness away from the dreamworld and realizing that "it is only a dream" and fighting the temptation to rejoin that sleep-bamboozled perspective. In either case, being awake is enough, either to see the world or to know that the world you thought you saw was not the world. You need go no further than acknowledging or refraining from acknowledging what you see. The analogy, then, is that people awake fail to acknowledge what they ought in the way that asleep they fail to acknowledge what they ought. (Marcel Proust, in *Le Temps Retrouvé*, says that recognizing the utter subjectivity of our dreamworld helps us see the pervasive subjectivity of our waking life and perhaps adjust for it.)[49] Heraclitus speaks of this elsewhere in terms of private rather than public understanding. Our idiosyncratic obsessions must have that quilted, cogent aspect of a dream, reasonable to the person passively undergoing its narrative thrust and variety. Relieving ourselves of that muffled phenomenology does not involve picking at the logical failures or deficiencies alone but an utter change in consciousness. What this change in consciousness amounts to, I can only guess. It might have something to do with answering a riddle, which requires seeking similarities where otherwise there seem to be only differences, a simultaneous abstraction and attention to concrete detail; or it might require a second-order perspective on one's own representations, accommodating the subjectivity of our perspective by juxtaposing it with an ideal of objectivity; who knows. But that Heraclitus has something in mind here seems plain.

What we see in B1 is that Heraclitus convicts people of failing to use their linguistic competence, practical abilities, and consciousness. These are three versions of the same failure. In each case, what is important is already present: the words in some language, the objects of some discipline, and the surround-

---

[48] On the challenges in distinguishing sleeping and waking, see Pl. *Tht.* 157e2–58d6. For alternative views of Heraclitus's remarks on sleep, see West 1971, 147–49; Dilcher 1995, 18–19.

[49] Proust 1927, 2.63.

ings in which one sleeps. Understanding the *logos* and so coming to wisdom is a matter of something clicking into place, a shift. Perhaps that shift is mostly passive; usually we just wake up, or finally realize what language the speaker is speaking, or recognize the tools in front of us. But perhaps we might adopt an active stance toward this. As long as it does not require research, however, the nature of the procedure does not matter.

Heraclitus returns to these three dimensions of critique in other fragments:

> B34/D4: Not understanding though having heard, they resemble the deaf: the saying testifies to them: being present they are absent.

> B19/D5: Knowing how neither to listen nor to speak.

> B56/D22: Men are deceived in the recognition of what is obvious.

> B17/D3: Most people do not understand such things as they encounter, nor having learned do they recognize, but they seem to themselves [to do so].

> B2/D2: The *logos* being common the many live as though having private reason.

> B89/R56: The awake have a common *kosmos* but each of the sleeping turns to his own.

B34 begins as B1 did, with the observation that hearing need not bring understanding. The fragment goes on to identify the problem. It is not that people research too little. What they need to know may be right before them, in their immediate presence, and yet they do not acknowledge it for what it is. They may as well have already left, or have never arrived in the first place, so little do they respond to what is given to them. B19 clarifies that whatever human characteristic "deafness" stands in for, we are not to take it as a congenital defect of the auditory function. Heraclitus says that it is not that people *cannot* hear, but that they do not know how to listen. They lack some competence to deal with what is present. Their ignorance about speaking is presumably an immediate correlate; just as they do not hear the intelligible articulation of the *logos*, they cannot reproduce that intelligible articulation as a response. On this line of interpretation, B56 says that what would seem totally apparent, "what is obvious" (τῶν φανερῶν), is still misunderstood. Again, people fail to deal with what is right in front of them. B17 says the same thing at greater length: people may take in aspects of the world without understanding, recognizing, or knowing. Finally, B2 and B89 present people as overly interior or subjective, caught up in their own imagination, thoughts, or dreams, and therefore blinded to the reality about them.[50]

---

[50] Cf. B71–75/D54–55, all of which are recorded in M. Aur. *Med.* 4.46 and 4.42.

Heraclitus repeatedly claims that the world is available for us if only we were to acknowledge it. Our understanding of it is not automatic; we must first push beyond whatever quotidian modes of perception and reflection we dwell in. But understanding is not impossible; Heraclitus does not express the epistemic qualifications that Xenophanes does. His attitude seems to be summarized in the following fragment:

> B93/D41: The lord whose shrine is in Delphi neither tells nor conceals but indicates.

The world does not speak our humdrum language; but neither does it obscure its message entirely.

For all this, Heraclitus does not say what would bring us to this heightened consciousness, this language of the *logos*. Probably it involves recognizing the formal structure or necessary nature of the *kosmos*, the conflict-in-unity adumbrated—in whatever form—in his most famous fragments. What this recognition requires or amounts to, or how it comes about, he does not really say. But his everyday examples, of roads and tops and drinks, suggest that recognition requires only a fresh vision of our world, a vision cleansed both of theoretical bias and of personal inclination or habit.[51]

A variant of looking right in front of ourselves is looking "within" ourselves—"I searched out (ἐδιζησάμην) myself" (B101/D36)—though with vigilance against taking the sense of interiority too seriously.[52] It is a variant, and not something completely different, because while self-knowledge may take a certain skill of attention or interpretation, it does not seem to take lots of introspection. W.K.C. Guthrie and Charles Kahn think that for Heraclitus, the inside recapitulates the outside, since both partake of the *logos*, and they infer from this premise that knowing oneself just is knowing everything else—*hen kai pan*.[53] Perhaps so, but the more plausible significance of this fragment is that understanding oneself has no less value than understanding the world, and that neither proves a shortcut to the other. Another fragment concerning self-knowledge, "it belongs to all people to know themselves and exercise discipline" (B116/D30), may present a self-constitutional view of self-knowledge.

---

[51] Other scholars have advanced "understanding" or relatedly non-research views, e.g., Fränkel 1938, 313–27; Kirk 1961, 108–10; Lesher 1983 (grasping connections, paying attention) and 1994, 3–5, 8–10, 12–23 (deep and puzzle-induced reflection); Pritzl 1985 (relating the stability of a name to the unfolding of an activity); Mackenzie 1988 (meditation on paradoxes); Schofield 1991, 18–19, 33 (redescribing what is present to all); Hölscher 1993, 233 (grasping through intuition).

[52] Cf. Moore 2015b, 16–17; Moore 2018a.

[53] Guthrie 1962, 416–19; Kahn 1979, 105.

We come to know ourselves *as* epistemic agents, which means acknowledging for the first time our epistemic responsibility (and thus epistemic hazards, that is, the possibility that we have false beliefs). We presumably become "awake" or "experienced" or "fluent" toward the world and the *logos* through the development of our self-knowledge—not through the piecemeal acquisition of knowledge wrought from an expanded inquiry into nature.

The Non-Exhortative Reading of B35

I have just argued that Heraclitus does not recommend *polumathia*. That means he cannot be recommending being *philosophos*.[54] Walther Kranz thought that Heraclitus might have coined the term, and in the fragment represents the opinion of the "many."[55] A good sentiment, but the idea in this form is hardly promising: we have no evidence for other Heraclitean neologisms, and no reason to think the "many" would have a view about a group labeled with a neologism. Wilhelm Nestle expressed a related sentiment through a one-letter emendation: he changed the εὖ to οὐ, such that we have "men who are philosophers must *not* be inquirers into many things indeed."[56] Philosophical men have apparently been trying to inquire into much, wasting their time or deluding themselves. But εὖ μάλα is only a little less common in the sixth and fifth centuries BCE than οὐ μάλα,[57] and the mistake would be inexcusable

---

[54] Thus the translation of Barnes 1982, 147, cannot be borne out: "We must be knowers of very many things" (he adds: "it only remains to transmute that mass of dross into the gold of knowledge"). The fact that there is a χρή does not matter, despite the claim of Verdenius 1947, 280–84, that Heraclitus always uses χρή with "admonitory force," that is, to direct a command to his readers. None of the four fragments Verdenius cites in support match B35's syntactic structure (χρή + emphatic + predicate noun + subject noun + copula). All are infinitive + χρή without emphasis: B43/D112 (ὕβριν χρὴ σβεννύναι), B44/D106 (μάχεσθαι χρὴ τὸν δῆμον ὑπὲρ τοῦ νόμου), B80/D63 (εἰδέναι χρὴ τὸν πόλεμον ἐόντα ξυνόν), and B114/D105 (ξὺν νόῳ λέγοντας ἰσχυρίζεσθαι χρὴ τῷ ξυνῷ πάντων). B44 specifies the *dēmos* as subject to the relevant norms. Further, χρή is the word in Clement's quotation most open to doubt (see YC 1.340–41), and thus the one that can bear the least interpretative weight. It is worth noting that the precise meaning of χρή (moral, social, subjective, or cosmic) does not determine its pragmatic force; the question here is the audience for the articulation of that force and the way they are supposed to understand it. For debate on the force, see Goodell 1914, 93, 97 ("the whole field of *must, ought, should, is necessary, it behoves, is fitting, is the divine will,*" in contrast to "there is a lack, a need"); Redard 1953, 47–56 (used for gnomic phrases and norms of conduct, especially those ordained by god); Benardete 1965 (subjective, where morality is objective); Wiltshire 2007, 10–11; Mourelatos 2008, 277–78.

[55] DK ad loc.

[56] Nestle 1942, 16 and 249n3.

[57] See n. 25 above for evidence.

and implausible for Clement or his sources; no other Heraclitean fragment has been thought to be lacking a negative particle.[58] Francis Cornford, long before Kranz and Nestle, and, after them, William Guthrie and Gregory Kirk among others, interpret B35, in its Clementine form, as consistent with the rest of Heraclitus, by understanding it as directed negatively at Pythagoras or Pythagorean types.[59] Cornford gives the fullest formulation:

> I understand . . . "Lovers of Wisdom must know a great many things indeed," as an ironical sneer at 'polymaths,' perhaps especially directed at Pythagoras, whose humility led him to call himself not "wise," but a "lover of wisdom." To Heracleitus, convinced that "wisdom is one," and that he possessed it, such humility seemed mawkish and hypocritical. πολλῶν ἵστορες in his language is a term of contempt.

Cornford must implicitly assume that this claim is ironical or sarcastic, set off by the εὖ μάλα, rather than simply an analytic or descriptive claim; Pythagoras would be known to Heraclitus's readers as "philosophical"; Pythagoras would be known to Heraclitus's readers as polymathic, that is, as a *pollôn histôr*; Heraclitus would not have also called himself "philosophical" or assumed his readers would call themselves "philosophical"; and Heraclitus would think that calling Pythagoras polymathic would take him down a notch. As I have argued in this chapter, every one of Cornford's implicit assumptions is borne out. In brief, Heraclitus would be saying what so-called *philosophoi andres*, exemplified in the Pythagoreans, are committed to.[60]

Who the *Pollôn Histores* Might Be

Heraclitus has described philosophical men as *pollôn histores*. Though I have been translating *histôr* as "researcher," the sense might be broader than that;

---

[58] The closest possibility of such error is found in B29/D13, where Clement provides in one place a disanalogy (οὐχ ὥσπερ, *Strom.* 4.50.2) which elsewhere he presents as an analogy (ὅπως, *Strom.* 5.59.5); Bernays has conjectured ὅκωσπερ, which is accepted by DK and LM. The central claim of that fragment is supported either way.

[59] Cornford 1912, 186n3; Guthrie 1962, 204, 417; Kirk 1962, 395 with 238; similarly, Delatte 1922, 166; Lallot 1971; Gottschalk 1980, 30; Lloyd 2002, 41; Riedweg 2004, 179–82, and 2005, 96–97; Lloyd 2009, 9; Peterson 2011, 202n7; Smith 2016, 21–22, Finkelberg 2017, 34n66 (but seemingly rejecting this reading later in his book).

[60] The view that Heraclitus focuses on the Pythagoreans would be corroborated were the intuitions presented in Marcovich 1967, 73, 76–77, 80, that B28a/D19, B28b/D28, and B81 allude to Pythagoras, also borne out.

and insofar as it is the first characterization of *philosophoi* men in Greek literature, we would like to know what it means. Its meaning turns out to be rather
ambiguous; in the end, that very ambiguity may serve Heraclitus's purposes.

The standard Greek-English lexicon (LSJ) claims that the *histôr* is "one who
knows law and right" or "judge." "Judge" does suit Agamemnon's role as *histôr*
in the funeral games at *Iliad* 23.486, though at *Iliad* 18.511, the *histôr* depicted
on Achilles's shield seems rather to be a third party officiating a dispute, with
the council of elders given the real decision-making power. On average, as it
were, these two uses describe a sort of neutral magistrate providing the deliberative structure for decision-making; whether he appoints himself to make
that final decision seems optional. On this construal of the noun, the *pollôn
histôr* would be a person who must find a structure to deal continually with a
range of contentions and contradictions.

Yet the language of the *Iliad* predates Heraclitus by more than a century,
and we see in all other uses, even those probably contemporary with the *Iliad*,
something less obviously a "judge." For example, at *Odyssey* 21.26, Heracles
is called "*epi-histôr* (ἐπιίστορα) of great deeds" just before being said to slay
Iphitus. With the prefix, *histôr* becomes connected to competent or bold action; what that action "rests on" (*epi-*) would seem not to be judgment but skill
or knowledge or insight; after all, Heracles is not said to exercise careful judgment in doing great deeds, but to be able to do them. The genitive object of *epi-
histôr* is the deeds themselves. Perhaps similarly, at *Works and Days* 792–93,
Hesiod speaks of the birth of an *histôr* man, whose "mind (νόον) is really quite
sound (πεπυκασμένος)." This looks like a synonym for the *sôphrôn* ("disciplined") person unaffected by extraneous or heedless desires or accidents. No
object is specified.

In both the *Homeric Hymn to Selene* 2 and Bacchylides 9.44, *histores* are
skillful women, the first "of song (ᾠδῆς)," and thus able to sing of the moon,
the second "in spear-work (κοῦραι)." The genitive of the first identifies their
particular competence or excellence; the second uses a dative. But in the later
fifth century BCE, the term seems to mean simply "knowledgeable about" or
"aware of."[61] By the beginning of the fifth century BCE, then, being *histôr*
means being good at some ability, and later in the century, it means being aware

---

[61] Having just moaned "I know, I know" (οἶδ᾽ οἶδ᾽, Soph. *El.* 846), acknowledging the un-
happy fate confronting her time and again, Sophocles's Electra thinks she has learned of her
brother's death and thus of her irredeemable position, and reiterates: "I am *istôr, huper-istôr*"
(ἴστωρ, ὑπερίστωρ, *El.* 850). This seems to be: "I recognize [it], I more than recognize [it]!" The
same meaning is found in Euripides's *Iphigenia among the Taurians*, when Thoas says that the
women were "*histores* about the plots (βουλευμάτων)" (*IT* 1431), that is, secretly in the know.
The genitive in these two examples identifies the content of that knowledge or awareness.

of something significant. On these definitions, Heraclitus's *pollôn histôr* would either have lots of skills or lots of awareness.

In the centuries on either side of Heraclitus, the meanings of *histôr* range from judge or mediator, to having the mental grounds for action and an imperturbable mind, to having skills and factual awareness. With the genitive object *pollôn*, we have "judge of much," "mediator of much," "capable of much," "impervious to much," "skilled in much," and "aware of much." Scholarship on this confusing range of meanings has generally subordinated the Heraclitean problem to a Herodotean problem,[62] but some have taken the archaic uses seriously.[63] The most promising recent effort has been by Carl Huffman, who offers a two-part definition of *histôr*: an "arbitrator" and a "person having knowledge or skill."[64] He does not speculate on the relationship between these two parts; we might guess that the skillfulness of the arbitrator came to stand in for skillfulness in general, since, as we will see in chapter 3, the term *sophos* undergoes such a despecialization. But his key insight comes from discussing Heraclitus's critique of Pythagoras's *historia* in B129. He argues that it refers to his compiling, digesting, surveying, and borrowing of other literature—in short, his use of "hearsay evidence."[65] If the meaning of *historia* redounds to that of *histôr*, being an *histôr* amounts to extensive surveying and potentially unprincipled sorting through gathered information. The stories of Pythagoras's wide-ranging education, travel, and advice-giving (surveyed in chapter 4) fit Heraclitus's charge. This would mean that the *pollôn histôr* would do a lot of assembling, collating, organizing, and presenting of material. This is, after a fashion, the work of a researcher or inquirer into much. Granted, we have no extant use of *histôr* that confirms this usage, one that is considerably more cognitively and practically complex than coordinating a

---

[62] See, e.g., Sigurdarson 2003, 20–24 (recognizing two uses of the term) and 25–27 (recognizing the ambiguity for Heraclitus); Schepens 2007, 40–43 (emphasizing the judicial sense, with Herodotus as an innovator); Darbo-Peschanski 2007a, 29–35.

[63] Floyd 1990 judges ἵστωρ to share a root with ἵζειν ("to seat"), not ἰδεῖν ("seeing," most recently Watkins 2000 s.v. "weid-" II.6: "*histôr*: wise, learned, learned man"), and to refer to someone who relies on others' views and therefore convenes and sits the real judges down; he explains away the post-Homeric meanings connected to witnessing or knowledge as dependent on retrojective folk-etymology from ἰδεῖν. The abstract ἱστορίη, referring to the historian's or ethnographer's activity, involves the judge-like task of "rigorous questioning" and "adjudicat[ing] among conflicting versions and differing assessments of blame"; this view he shares with Connor 1993; Pradeau 2002, 272–73. Granger 2004, 238 (cf. Conche 1987, 99), thinks ἵστωρ can refer also to first-hand observation, and properly names the activities of Heraclitus's systematizing and rationalizing contemporaries (on which practices see Moore 2013b and 2014b), but seems not to provide evidence for this. See, generally, Darbo-Peschanski 2007b.

[64] Huffman 2008, 32n32.

[65] Also on B129 see Mansfeld 1989 and Zhmud 2017's corrective to Huffman's claims.

meeting for an important decision, being skilled at singing or spear-throwing, recognizing one's fate, or knowing a secret plan. But as a development or derivative of these, it sounds plausible, and it certainly does have corroboration in *historia*.

Some questions remain. What is Heraclitus doing using a term that, for us at least, seems quite ambiguous between the contentless but form-rich (and publicly recognized) ability characteristic of the resolution expert and the formless but content-rich (and publicly recognized) ability of the expert in song or spear? What is he doing using an empty plural object when we never see such an object as an argument in the other instances of *histôr*? Whatever *histôr* means, Heraclitus is linking being *philosophos* with dealing somehow with plurality or diversity in a way that has a knowing appearance, yet nowhere else does Heraclitus praise a connection to plurality or diversity, and he always expresses skepticism about appearances of knowledge. This would suggest that, whatever he means, he expresses doubt about the promise of being *philosophos*. There is even a chance that his contemporaries experienced much of the uncertainty about the meaning of *histôr* that we do, such that they were supposed to conclude that *whatever* the cognitive or practical effort to the "much stuff" the *philosophos* must apply, it cannot be good; in this way, the vagueness or indeterminacy provides a more strongly derisive claim. And even if the term *histôr* did not baffle early fifth-century BCE readers, they may have bounced between an increasingly ambiguous emphasis on either the contentlessness or the formlessness of its skill of judgment and acknowledgment—that is, on the *histôr*'s admitted lack of any real field of wisdom except a competence at judging the wisdom of others, or on the *histôr*'s presumed competence in some branch of wisdom. This would, with surprising neatness, track the two connotations of being *philosophos* that the Pythagoras stories seen in chapter 1 attribute to Pythagoras, the self-conscious lack of wisdom with concomitant pursuit of wisdom, and the self-conscious orientation toward wisdom in contrast to the banausic orientation toward money or honor.

Conclusion: The Unbearable Lightness of Being *Philosophos*

Heraclitus castigates Pythagoras at least three times in his extant fragments for his conniving imposture, a stance that is dependent on apparently broad research. He does not otherwise praise the accumulation of diverse ideas, opinions, and pieces of knowledge. In B35, Heraclitus observes that, whatever might seem definitive of being *philosophos*—for example, political power or cultural esteem—it is really defined by apparent expansive research. I say "apparent" because the term I have translated as "researcher," *histôr*, is a person seen by the public to be an inquirer, judge, or expert. So Heraclitus here says that the real way to be *philosophos* is to investigate much. We also know, however, that Heraclitus does not recommend investigating much, and indeed attributes such extensive investigation (with a negative inflection) to Pythagoras. Thus Heraclitus means in this fragment that his readers should *not* aim to be philosophical men. For if they did, they would get their sought-after insight, power, and esteem only with (ostentatious) research; and yet such research would not confer to them the insight (*nous*) or wisdom (*to sophon*) that they ought really to seek.

This chapter has argued for the authenticity of this fragment. Further, its best interpretation confirms a Pythagorean-era origin of the word *philosophos*, and its early denotation and connotation as applied wryly to those groups of people who strove to become (seen as) *sophoi* by means of study. (Charles Kahn even saw that *philosophoi andres* could be read as "men who want to become sages.")[66] Heraclitus's fragment does not expressly say that Pythagoras was called a *philosophos*. But in the context of Heraclitus's oeuvre, it would seem to imply that Pythagoras was one. Even if it did not, it presents a view and evaluation of the term *philosophos* consistent with the basic account suggested in the previous chapter and defended in the next. That account argues that the word *philosophos* did not begin with the meaning "intellectual cultivator" or "lover of wisdom." Neither meaning is plausibly glossed as "researcher into much," since intellectual cultivation seems not to require "research," and love of wisdom seems not to require "much" or "many" as its object(s).

This claim does not represent the standard view. Most commentators have simply doubted that Clement correctly quotes Heraclitus here. Many suspect that nearly every word in the fragment is paraphrase or retrojection. Even those who have found a residue of Heraclitean language excise the term *philosophos*. Their doubt has arisen from two distinct sources. First, some commentators have noted that after this supposed use in Heraclitus, *philosophos*-group words show up again only in the last decades of the fifth century BCE. This half-century gap weakens the credibility of the earlier instance. Of course this reasoning is itself only weakly credible. We might suppose that the word simply had little value to or metrical compatibility in tragic or epinician verse, and

---

[66] Kahn 1979, 105. But he continues in what I believe to be a mistaken way: "It would be in character for him to introduce the theme of wisdom in the compound form *philo-sophos*, as the object of ardent desire." Heraclitus uses only the verb (*philein*), not the adjective or noun *philos/ philia*, and when he does, it only ever governs infinitive verbs, meaning "tends to" (B87/D8, B123/D35). For Heraclitus, the *phil-* prefix or root might not mean "ardent desire."

no argumentative purpose in the longest extant pieces of intellectual verse between Heraclitus and Herodotus, namely, the fragments of Parmenides's poem on Being. (Prose works during the period are entirely lost.) The second source of doubt is more interesting and is not so readily dismissed. On a traditional or unexamined construal, B35 appears to conflict with the fragments denouncing Pythagorean research (*historia*, B129), expressing skepticism about pre-Socratic breadth of learning (*polumathia*, B40), and adumbrating Heraclitus's vision of wisdom's unity (B41). That apparent conflict arises because, on this traditional construal, this fragment *approves* of broad research. Since Heraclitus more frequently *scorns* broad research, however, something has to go. What goes is the fragment supporting the (apparently) minority view.

Yet some commentators have given Clement the benefit of the doubt, and have suspected not his correctness but the popular interpretation of Heraclitus's thinking about wisdom. They have argued that the apparent incompatibility between B35 and B40, B41, and B129 is merely apparent. A coherent epistemology, as they propose it, accepts that diverse research is *insufficient* for understanding and wisdom; but while insufficient it remains *necessary*. On this proposal, the men whom Heraclitus scorns stopped short in their quest for knowledge or wisdom, namely, at the mere accumulation of information. These men should have proceeded on to reflection and unification.

The doubters and the accepters of Clement's text, despite their differences in methodology and the boldness of their epistemological theorizing, share a core and determinative assumption. They believe the same thing about Heraclitus's use of the word *philosophos*. They think that Heraclitus uses it as a term of praise or self-identification. Taken as positively inflected, this fragment tells us what we readers, as aspiring or actual philosophers, should do. Heraclitus is saying: be *pollôn histores*, "researchers into much!" It is this assumption about the meaning and use of the term *philosophos* that makes the passage seem on the one hand not Heraclitus's, thereby requiring that we modify or reject an otherwise important fragment, or on the other an advocate of a specific two-step method of inquiry, thereby requiring that we hypothesize an unsupported epistemology. But none of these commentators has defended his or her assumption that Heraclitus must be using the word *philosophos* as a term of praise or self-identification, and that he thereby exhorts his readers to be *pollôn histores*.

This chapter has shown that we should not assume that Heraclitus urges his readers to become *philosophoi andres*. We should thus withhold the inference that he exhorts his readers to be *pollôn histores*, researchers or inquirers into much. This argument will receive corroboration later in the book. We will see in chapter 3 the philological claim that *philosophos* need not originally have been a term of praise or self-identification. Thus Heraclitus need not be taken as saying that *sophia*, which is eminently desirable in Heraclitus's eyes, comes through being a *philosophos*, and thus through being a researcher into much. Further, this chapter adds the epistemological argument that it is simply implausible to ascribe to Heraclitus a view that *to sophon* ("wisdom") comes through the systematization of broad and diverse pieces of information. The extant fragments do not support the claim that he advocates a two-step model for the acquisition of wisdom, where expansive perceptual discovery precedes or underwrites some second-order treatment of those discoveries. In the background is a hermeneutic assumption that, in any event, a simplistic reading of this passage does not fit with the polyvalent, ambiguous, and riddling nature of the other fragments of Heraclitus, as the past decades of scholarship have acknowledged.[67] It is irresponsible to reduce the words of B35 to the straightforward exhortation *be researchers into much*, without at least showing it to be the only possible reading.

I have taken B35 to identify the costs of being a (Pythagorean) philosophical man. You have your work cut out for you. You have to take up the yoke of extensive research, inquiry, expert arbitration, or whatever it is that the Pythagoreans (and *histores*) do. This burden may be necessary for becoming *philosophos*. But it is not for that reason necessary for becoming *sophos*. The irony, as Heraclitus might see it, is that those people whose name seemingly encodes the very commitment to being *sophos* are committed to it in the wrong way. This is not to say that Heraclitus uses the term *philosophos* ironically or sarcastically. To say so would be to take *philosophos* as having a positive surface meaning, and we have no reason to believe it does. It is rather to say that an apparently neutral definition has at the same time implications that *philosophoi* are doing the wrong thing, or that despite the second element, *-sophoi*, the *philosophoi* remain far from being *sophoi*. Whether these *philosophoi* need to learn a lot because that is what wisdom requires or because that is what their (Pythagorean-sourced) norms require—or even because that is what their self-delusion requires!—is the real question for Heraclitus's reader.[68]

Scholars have been right to see B35 as a lynchpin for their interpretations of Heraclitean epistemology. But they have been wrong to present Heraclitus as thinking that *philosophoi*, in being "investigators into much," are on track to becoming *sophoi*. The *philosophoi* are going the wrong way. What exactly constitutes a reversal of course remains an open question. This chapter has suggested some directions an answer might take. It has also shown the impor-

---

[67] E.g., Kahn 1979; Mackenzie 1988; Most 1999, 357–59.
[68] Cf. Lesher 1994, 19n38.

tance a history of the term *philosophos* has in the histories of philosophy and of epistemology.

In many aspects of his thought, Heraclitus had few immediate followers. Among them we might include Socrates and Plato. As we will see in later chapters, both hear their compatriots' use of *philosophos* with a connotation of "researcher into much," and both dislike that connotation. The Socrates-inflected disagreement is with research as such, in light of our ignorance about matters much closer at hand. The Plato-inflected disagreement (if such a distinction lends any conceptual clarity) is with the curiosity about multitude, in light of the epistemic priority of unity or unification. Thus a Heraclitean reactivity to the term *philosophos* recurs a century later. That is not to say that they acquired that reactivity from their reading of Heraclitus or his followers, but that Heraclitus had already flagged some perennial concerns.

3

What *Philosophos* Could Have Meant: A Lexical Account

A New Route to an Etymology

The term *philosophos* entered early into the Ancient Greek practice of coining *phil-* prefixed names, among the first several dozen of an eventual nine hundred. This chapter seeks to understand its original sense by reconstructing the original sense of contemporaneous *phil-* prefixed names. This requires an inquiry both into coinage patterns and into the term's second element, *soph-*, at the time of coinage, which the Heraclitean evidence discussed in chapter 2 puts at about 500 BCE. The two parts of this chapter describe the two parts of the word.

Philosophy teachers often proclaim, on the first day of the semester, that *philosophos* means "lover of wisdom," glossing this as "one lacking-but-striving-for-wisdom." Walter Burkert argued for the implausibility of the gloss (as we saw in chapter 1); the earliest *phil-* prefixed names admit no such lack, actually implying the opposite: the regular presence of the second element's referent. True enough, but not the whole story—Burkert's crucial discovery provides only the foundation for our closer scrutiny of early *phil-* prefixed names.

In the previous chapter, I argued that Heraclitus used the term *philosophos* as something of a wry name, not as a one-word description for those who love wisdom or seek mental culture. Yet the label had to come from somewhere, and its incorporation of the root *soph-* gives us direction. It suggests that we look for the ways the *soph-* root was used in that era that parallel the way other second-element roots were used in *phil-* prefixed names of that era. It turns out that second-element roots in *phil-* prefixed names were used synecdochally to refer to some social practice. As cattle ranchers speak of "heads" of beef while caring mainly for the "sides," the second element need refer only to a salient (as easily countable) but not critical item. The *soph-* in *philosophos* seems to refer to *sophoi*, sage advisors, with the relevant social practice probably being something like "acting or preparing to act as a *sophos*."

This chapter begins with a look at the way some ancient authors understood the origins of the term *philosophos*, with reference to two versions of the Pythagoras story. First is Cicero's context for Heraclides's account. Second is Diodorus Siculus's account, one relatively unstudied in scholarship about the origins of *philosophia*, but perhaps of all versions the most plausible. The core of the chapter then vindicates Diodorus's version, arguing first for the sixth-century BCE patterns of formation of *phil-* prefixed terms, and second for the use of the *soph-* element at that time.

From *Sophoi* to *Philosophoi* in Cicero and Diodorus Siculus

We saw in chapter 1 Cicero's reproduction of Heraclides's Pythagoras story of self-naming *philosophoi* (Lat. *sapientiae studiosos*), which continues the story he has told about the *sophoi* (Lat. *sapientes*): "this name for them spread all the way to the time of Pythagoras" (*Tusc.* 5.3.8). Earlier in the preamble to Book 5 of the *Tusculan Disputations*, Cicero has been praising the value of philosophy: it has brought about personal, social, and civic security (5.1.1–2.6). But he also recognizes that its illustrious history has been obscured by the relative novelty of the name: not all its successes have redounded to "philosophy" so called. People used to speak only of "wise men" (*sapientes*) and their "wisdom" (*sapientia*), which amounts to "the knowledge of the origin and causes of all things divine and human" and "the contemplation of nature." Among those deemed "wise" he includes historical, legendary, and mythical examplars: the "Seven *Sophoi*"; Lycurgus, Odysseus, and Nestor; and Atlas, Prometheus, and Cepheus, whose mythic apotheoses as constellations testify to their more-than-human knowledge of the heavenly bodies (5.3.7–8). The name *sapientes* was used down to the time of Pythagoras, at which point *philosophos* became the relevant name, applying to Anaxagoras, Archelaus, Socrates, and Plato (5.4.10).[1]

---

[1] This preface is rather jumbled (cf. Nutting 1909, 233–34; Dougan and Henry 1934, 201; Douglas 1990, 144): philosophy, while still called wisdom, brought about the origins of cities, but Socrates brings "philosophy," once called philosophy, into the cities. The earliest philosophers, while still called wise men, sought the best life and to make themselves virtuous, but Atlas, Prometheus, and Cepheus represent a wisdom concerned instead with the contemplation of nature, as astronomy. This confounded chronology tells against assuming Cicero has a single source. HJ suggest that sections 5–6 may rely on Posidonius (whose work is epitomized in, and known from, Sen. *Ep.* 90.5–25), and that Heraclides provides, in addition to 8–9, also 7, on the legendary and historical *sophoi*, and 10, including the passage on Socrates. This latter view is difficult to accept, given Cicero's citation of Heraclides in the midst only of an anecdote rather than a historical lineage, the difficulty of imagining *On Diseases* claiming that *Socrates* made philosophy relevant to human life (rather than Pythagoras or Empedocles!), and Cicero's similar claim about Socrates's innovation at *Brut.* 8.30–31 but with a different account (Socrates refuted

For Cicero and his Greek sources, *sophos* gave way to *philosophos*. This implies some essential connection between the words. What the connection is, however, Cicero does not explain: he does not say why the term *sophos* went out of fashion or was not used by Pythagoras. Some readers of Cicero conjecture that, at the point in the (lost) Greek source of Cicero's text when Leon asks Pythagoras, in Cicero's translation, what *ars* he professes, he asks what *sophia* he professes.[2] Pythagoras's answer would be, in effect, that he practices no specific *sophia*, but rather something that transcends all *sophiai* ("technical expertises"), perhaps something architectonic, a master knowledge; the implication is that *philosophia* replaces *sophia* as the best intellectual practice.[3] This conjecture is hardly assured.[4] Cicero has already been translating *sophia* as *sapientia*, not as *ars*. As we will see below, by the end of the sixth century BCE, and certainly in the fourth century BCE, trades or skills were not generally referred to as various *sophiai*. Most detrimentally to the conjecture, the *sophoi*, especially the "Seven *Sophoi*," who had "wisdom," are treated as having the *same* transcendent breadth as that of Pythagoras. Indeed, Cicero's discussion rather obscures what novelty the term *philosophos* brings to a language that already includes the term *sophos*.

The connection between *sophoi* and *philosophoi* is drawn more clearly in an author contemporaneous with Cicero, who likely draws from some fourth-century BCE source contemporaneous with Heraclides. This is Diodorus of Sicily, whose forty-volume *Library of History* (60–30 BCE), an account of the world from mythological to Roman times, draws on a range of fourth-century BCE Greek writers; perhaps, in the present case, he draws from Aristoxenus the Peripatetic.[5] We will recognize the general form from the version of the Pythagoras story presented in Diogenes Laertius's preamble (chapter 1):

the views of Gorgias, Thrasymachus, Protagoras, Prodicus, Hippias, and other unnamed men, thereby giving rise to ethical discussion and his popularity). On the prefaces in *Tusculan Disputations* in general, see Douglas 1995, esp. 203; Gildenhard 2007, esp. 203–6.

[2] E.g., Gottschalk 1980, 23n30, 26–27; Riedweg 2005, 92.

[3] Riedweg 2005, 97, thus suggests that the *phil-* prefix denotes "an intensification."

[4] YC 1.320 suggests τέχνη. Note that in Sosicrates, Leon simply asks "what he [Pythagoras] is" (τίς εἴη, DL 8.8), allowing that no play on words is an essential part of the story.

[5] Long treated as unreliable, recent scholarship has shown the accuracy of Diodorus (Sacks 1990; Rubincam 1998; Sulimani 2011, 1–162). For whatever reason, this passage is almost never dealt with in histories of *philosophia* or analyses of the Pythagoras stories; those who do mention it simply assimilate it to DL 1.12 (Burkert 1960, 161n5; Malingrey 1961, 29n1; Chroust 1964a, 427n17; Gottschalk 1980, 31–32; YC 1.323n29, 1.325n42). Among Diodorus's evident early sources are Hecataeus of Abdera, Ephorus, Theopompus, and Timaeus of Tauromenium. Attribution of Diodorus's Pythagoras story to Aristoxenus comes from Lévy 1926, 87, followed by Thesleff 1961, 109; for Aristoxenus's methods, see, recently, Stavru 2018. Alternatively, Gottschalk 1980, 32n63, follows Corssen 1912, 35, in suggesting attribution to an earlier fourth-century BCE text, Andron's *Tripod*.

Pythagoras called (ἐκάλει) his particular choice of life (αἵρεσιν) *philosophia* but not *sophia*. For, finding fault with the ones before him, the so-called Seven *Sophoi*, he said that though no human is *sophos*—usually, natural weaknesses leave one without the strength to succeed in everything (πάντα κατορθοῦν)—the one emulating (ζηλῶν) the character and life of the *sophos* may suitably be called *philosophos*.[6] (DS 10 fr. 24)

According to Diodorus, Pythagoras explains the name *philosophos* by reference to and contrast with the name and description *sophos*. As in Cicero's version, there were *sophoi* and then with Pythagoras there were *philosophoi*. In this version, Pythagoras claims that the name *sophos*, the designation for the Seven Sages, does not in fact suit humans, but since the people to whom the name refers provide suitable models for living, the name he accepts for himself is built from the name *sophos*.

This story assumes that the legendary Seven *Sophoi* ("Seven Sages") were popularly thought to have a more-than-human success in everything (πάντα κατορθοῦν).[7] Diodorus's pages immediately before these ones show that they were. Solon caused the decadent Athenians to simplify and become virtuous, and to revolt against the tyrannical Peisistratids. Pittacus, a wonderfully wise and a great legislator, freed his land from tyranny, strife, and war. Bias, an excellent speaker, used his gifts to help the wronged.[8]

To explain the shift from *sophos* to *philosophos*, Diodorus says that Pythagoras found fault (καταμεμφόμενος) with his predecessors the *sophoi*, although their name denotes a status beyond what is accessible to humans. A strange though not unique charge, Pythagoras apparently means to criticize the fact that *sophoi* are being called *sophos*, not the men themselves.[9] After all, Pythagoras mentions nothing they have done, and does not say that

---

[6] For the Greek of this passage, see Appendix, p. 321.

[7] It is uncertain whether this means "straighten out, fix" (Eur. *Hipp.* 1445; *Andr.* 1080; Hippoc. *Fract.* 16 [of bones]), used literally or figuratively for something bent or broken, or "accomplish successfully" (Eur. *Hel.* 1067; *Hipp.* 680; Hdt. 1.120; Lys. 18.13; Pl. *Meno* 99c9; *Tht.* 203b9; Xen. *Mem.* 3.1.3; Isoc. 7.11; D. 2.20, 21.106, 24.7), or something in between (Soph. *El.* 416; *OC* 1487). Parallels from Aristotle (*Eth. Nic.* 1106b28–31: one can fail in many ways, but succeed [κατορθοῦν] only in one) and Demosthenes (*Or.* 18.289–90, citing a poem that says only gods can succeed at all) suggest the non-reparative version.

[8] Solon: DS 9 frr. 1–5, 31–32; Pittacus: 9 frr. 16–20; Bias: 9 frr. 21–23. Tell 2015 describes the Sages' legendary dispute-resolution.

[9] Damon of Cyrene, a Platonist of the second century BCE, similarly "chastises" (ἐγκαλεῖ) all the *Sophoi*, especially the Seven (DL 1.40). Ammonius, who wrote at the end of the fifth century CE, evidently following Nicomachus of Gerasa's (60–120 CE) *Introduction to Arithmetic* 1.1, said that Pythagoras "was the first to assail the error found among the ancients," who called just any random expert *sophos* (*In Isag.* proem 9.7).

they erroneously or pridefully called themselves *sophos*. In fact, according to Diodorus, they do quite the opposite. Diodorus has just worked through the stories, which we know to go back to the fifth century BCE, that the Seven *Sophoi* disavowed the description *sophos*, repeatedly and famously, and that, indeed, they claimed that only god, Apollo, deserves the title.[10] Pythagoras thus *continues* a Sage tradition in criticizing the name and in querying its appropriateness for mere mortals. The existence of that critical tradition and efforts to slough off a name suggests that people *were* called and considered *sophoi* or *sophos*; we will see the evidence for this below. Perhaps some even accepted the name, or were thought to accept it; but this critical tradition also hints that the truly *sophos*, the true *sophoi*, acknowledge the inaccessibility of *sophia*. Socrates was apparently not the first to discover epistemic modesty or the moral power that such modesty confers. Pythagoras joins the *sophoi* in vindicating the intimations of one's mental excellence by rejecting them.

Pythagoras disparages public claims to the attainment of the ideal of wisdom, but not the ideal itself. Modesty is not epistemic skepticism or pessimism. As a *philosophos*, Pythagoras wishes to avoid the charges of hubris he would deserve should he own to a more-than-human state, a quasi-divine superiority over his neighbors. But as a *philosophos*, he also wishes to orient his life toward being *sophos*, since that provides the right pattern to which to fit himself. Pythagoras wants to have it both ways: to reveal his knowingness about human limitations, and to push against those human limitations. The *sophoi* set political things aright: they advised the most headstrong of kings, understood the fragility of human life, and found civic benefit in thoughtfulness and virtue rather than in athletic prowess. They crystallized a life of experience and reflection in lapidary precepts, expressed in a riddling or riddlingly blunt way that has bite against the naïve, the self-deluding, and the simply mistaken people in the world.[11] The *sophoi*'s powers therefore are pragmatic, advisory, and analytic; they set institutions, individuals, and conceptions aright. It is this ideal theory-praxis combination at which Pythagoras takes aim.

On Diodorus's account, then, Pythagoras took up the name *philosophos* insofar as it meant a choice of life (αἵρεσιν) to emulate (ζηλῶν) the *sophos*.[12] Diodorus's account implies that this conscious choosing and emulating is a

---

[10] DS 9 frr. 6–7; cf. DL 1.27–33. For the pre-Academic *sophoi* stories from Miletus, Priene, and Athens that assume that only god is *sophos,* see Wiersma 1933.

[11] DS 9 frr 7, 9–15, 24–25, 31–32, 38–39, and fragments cited earlier.

[12] The noun αἵρεσις, "choice," could even refer to a "group" or "intentional community," since that is what, non-metaphorically, would have been chosen. "Emulation" can imply "being a disciple," as in Plut. *Them.* 2.4, in which Themistocles is the disciple (ζηλωτής) of Mnesiphilus, who chose a life (αἵρεσις) concerned with *sophia* in a pedagogical lineage coming down (ἐκ διαδοχῆς) from Solon.

surprising thing to do. His earlier chapters show why. For almost none of the *sophoi*—Anacharsis, Myson, Periander, Chilon, or Bias—does Diodorus describe or even mention a route to achieving status as *sophos*; Solon is the exception that proves the rule.[13] Other authors similarly have nothing to say about any education, study, tutelage, or concentrated effort that the *sophoi* may have taken on themselves to attain their status. This silence suggests that the ascension to *sophos* status comes simply through hard and long experience, or perhaps by a special dispensation, or that, in a sense, the route does not matter. The reflective intention to achieve that status through disciplined means, focusing on the route, would therefore be remarkable. This seeking of a previously unsought status would deserve a special name. This special name, *philosophos* here, could be accepted by Pythagoras in explaining himself to others.

As Diodorus tells it, Pythagoras would be the sort to call by a special name. In adjacent paragraphs he writes that Pythagoras studied with Pherecydes and learned geometry from the Egyptians. With his students he exercised memory and self-control; they aimed to increase their knowledge and capacity for judgment. This work had a visible result. Pythagoras spoke with such charm and effectiveness that everyone wanted to listen. He presented in himself a highly appealing mode of life, disciplined and devoid of the decadence that charismatic people risk falling into, and he argued for this mode of life as well. His society and its views drew considerable attention. Its members manifested inexplicably powerful bonds of friendship and loyalty, and they had unusual views about the soul, expressed in terms of metempsychosis, the recollection of past lives, vegetarianism, and other theories of diet and health. Their influence grew so great as to advance Greece and to earn them disastrous envy. So the Pythagoreans appear to have tried to become like *sophoi*, and the direction of their self-education, and the success they attained through that self-education, supports that appearance.[14]

Indeed, we find what Diodorus writes in Book 10 of the *Library* in compact form in Valerius Maximus's version of the story, in his *Memorable Deeds and Sayings* (ca. 14–37 CE), one that appears to rely on a source shared at some remove by Diodorus but not by Cicero:[15]

---

[13] Solon is presented as a late addition to the ranks of the *sophoi*. Diodorus says that Solon was by nature excellent, but that he also applied himself to all learning, and got the best teachers, and (anachronistically) spent time with the men greatest "in philosophy" (ἐπὶ φιλοσοφίᾳ) (DS 9 fr. 1). See also Hdt. 1.30 (discussed in chapter 5, pp. 128–31).

[14] DS 10 frr. 4 (Pherecydes), 11 (geometry), 7–8 (memory and self-control), 3.2, 23 (appealing mode of life), 4–6, 14–15 (friendship), 9–13 (views of soul), 24.2, 25 (envy).

[15] Bloomer 1992, 62–64, 78–108, discusses the difficulties in identifying Valerius's sources, and concludes that Valerius evidently never relied on Diodorus, which he obviously does not here.

To pass to a more ancient performance of diligence: Pythagoras, who from his youth embarked upon the work of most perfect wisdom (*sapientiae*) with the desire of acquiring knowledge and all that is good (for everything destined to arrive at its ultimate goal also begins early and rapidly), repaired to Egypt. There familiarizing himself with the writings of that people and scrutinizing the memoranda left by priests of ages gone by, he learned the observations of countless cycles. From Egypt he went to Persia and gave himself over to the finished wisdom of the magi for them to mold. His docile mind absorbed what they ungrudgingly displayed to him: the motions of the stars, the courses of the planets, the force, individuality, and effect of each one. Then he sailed to Crete and Lacedaemon, and after inspecting their laws and manners came to the Olympic competition. There he displayed a specimen of his multifarious knowledge amid the enthusiastic admiration of all Greece. Asked under what title he was registered (*cognomine censeretur*), he professed himself (*edidit*), not a wise man (*sapientem*)—for that had been preempted (*occupaverant*) by the surpassing Seven—but a lover of wisdom (*amatorem sapientiae*), that is, in Greek, a *philosophos*. He also proceeded to that part of Italy which was then called Greater Greece, in which he commended the results of his studies to many flourishing cities.[16] (8.7 ext. 2, trans. Shackleton Bailey)

The key difference from Diodorus's version is clear: rather than criticizing the Seven *Sophoi* for their name, Pythagoras simply allows that the name already belongs to them.[17] But the story's moral remains the same: the name *philosophos* must be understood in relation to that of the *Sophoi*. And one detail remains the same: Pythagoras, so often called an inventor of words and practices, is not said to have invented the word *philosophos*, only to have called himself it.[18]

Should Pythagoras have been called *philosophos*, it need not have been any great compliment. The naming could have been a wry observation that he strove ludicrously for a status for which people normally do not strive. It could have expressed a bemused qualification: "Who knows whether he *counts* as a *sophos*, but he sure *wants* to be a *sophos*!" It might have registered his thirst for limitless self-improvement and influence, a harmless if nevertheless nakedly egoistic ambition, what the Greeks might call *philautia* ("egoism"; see below) crossed with *philotimia* ("ambition"; again, see

---

[16] For the Latin of this passage, see the Appendix, p. 322.

[17] Valerius's version also emphasizes that Pythagoras studied concertedly with teachers, in Egypt and Persia, and studied political institutions, in Crete and Sparta, and then displayed this novel knowledge; the number of stages suggests exercise and association.

[18] De Vogel 1966, 218–20, identifies more than a dozen inventions attributed to Pythagoras.

below). Yet while the name *philosophos* need not have had a laudatory tone, it could easily have later been spun to have a positive or at least conciliatory sound, and our passages from Diodorus and Valerius appear to record that spinning.

Pythagoras as spin doctor has left its trace in the care Diodorus and Valerius take with the etymological situation. They do not claim that Pythagoras coined either *philosophos* or *philosophia*. They present him as simply having used those terms in self-reference. If there is an implied dramatic situation, in which someone asks what kind of person he is, Pythagoras is havingto explain the self-application. This would imply either that the self-application of *philosophos* is counterintuitive or that the term is unfamiliar to his audience. In the first case, it would be because the name is hardly self-recommending. In the second, the meaning of the term would not shine through transparently, as it would if it actually and obviously meant "lover of wisdom" or "acknowledger of the impossibility of *sophia* and yet the goodness of striving for it nevertheless." In either case, the term *philosophos* would not sound like something a person would self-interestedly apply to himself.

The First Element, *Phil-*: Aristotle's Theory

Diodorus's story prompts us to think of the *phil-* prefix as an instrument for coining names that would only awkwardly be applied to oneself. Aristotle provides the earliest sustained analysis of *phil-* prefixed names and vindicates this view, even if earlier authors (e.g., Hesiod, Aristophanes, Plato) had acknowledged the peculiarity of these names. Aristotle's view—not heretofore studied by scholars—is that such names generally have or start with a negative connotation. As a native Greek speaker with a high-grade sensitivity to morally inflected language, his insight is worth taking very seriously. It provides the earliest theoretical evidence in support of this book's negative thesis, that the term *philosophos* probably did not begin as one of praise of the sort that is expressed in phrases like "lover of wisdom" or "intellectual cultivator."

Aristotle apparently coins the term *philotoioutoi*, "*phil*-whatevers," and uses this metalinguistic term in the *Nicomachean Ethics* (Books 1, 2, and 4) to discuss the use of various (first-order) *phil-* prefixed names.[19] Aristotle treats

---

[19] For analysis of ethical issues in these passages, see Lefebvre 2011. Aristotle's neologism finds uptake only in late antique and medieval commentaries on these very passages. It is always associated with a form of *legetai*, "being called" or "being said to be" (implied: *phil-* something); it does not mean "amateurs" or "aficionados."

phil- prefixed names as names, as one-word adjectival or nominal appella-tions. He recognizes that people start out using them to label others by treating one feature as representative or indexical for their whole public persona. He never decomposes a *phil-* prefixed name into a noun-object phrase ([*toioutou*] *philos*) as though it were a description.[20] Doing so would wrongly presume that the combination of two morphological elements into a single word has no effect on the ultimate meaning of that word. He assumes that all *phil-* prefixed terms work in about the same way.

Aristotle introduces the term *philotoioutoi* in *Nicomachean Ethics*, Book 1. He has just observed—in a modified version of the "three lives at a festival" comparison—that at the Olympic games the wreath goes not to the most at-tractive or strongest in the stadium but to the one who competes (1099a3–5). His point is about activity; he goes on to assert that the life of excellent activ-ity is universally pleasant.[21] There are, by contrast, the sorts of objects that please only idiosyncratically:

> to each person that item is pleasurable in respect to which he is called (ἡδὺ πρὸς ὃ λέγεται) a *philotoioutos*, for instance a horse (ἵππος) to the *philippos*, sights (θέαμα) to the *philotheoros*;[22] and in the same way, justice (τὰ δίκαια) to the *philodikaios* and, generally, things in accordance with virtue (τὰ κατ' ἀρετήν) to the *philaretos*.[23] Now the pleasures with respect to most people conflict, since such things are not pleasurable by nature, but with respect to the *philokaloi*,[24] pleasures are pleasurable by nature. (*Eth. Nic.* 1099a7–13)

[20] This fact is often hidden in translation, as, e.g., in Broadie and Rowe 2002.

[21] For further context, see Gauthier and Jolif 1959, 2.1.67–68.

[22] Aristotle's word for the *phil-*sights or -spectacles person differs from Plato's, *philotheamôn* (see chapter 8, pp. 251–55), which contains the root noun, *theama*, cited by Aristotle here. The difference is between a *phil-* name built from an action, *theorein*, and from the object of that action. There are no extant comparisons of the two forms of this word, and both are extremely rare in the classical period. The arbitrary creation of the name shows that the object need not be expressly stated by the *phil-* name; this finding will be consistent with what we show below.

[23] *Philaretos* is found only once in classical Greek; perhaps its rarity suggests a coinage as "scrupulous," "sedulous."

[24] Before Aristotle, *philokalos* emphasized a concern for appearances (into which "nobility" readily fits); even for him, the peacock is *philokalos* (*Hist. an.* 488b24), dubiously so: linked here with *phthoneros*, the Revised Oxford Translation renders the pair "jealous and self-conceited." Gorgias's Funeral Oration refers to the "*philokalos* peace" (B6/D28; cf. Thuc. 2.40.1 and chap-ters 5, p. 133, and 8, pp. 234–36, below), presumably the lovely pleasant time outside of war. In Xenophon, being *philokalos* involves being concerned with one's physical appearance (*Cyr.* 1.3.3, 2.1.22), one's social appearance (*Symp.* 4.15.5), the appearances of events one arranges (*Cyr.* 8.3.5), and the looks of women (*Mem.* 3.11.9). In Isocrates, *philokaloi* have the right con-cern for dress, being elegant (μεγαλοπρεπές) rather than excessive (περίεργος) in the fashion of the dandy (καλλωπιστής) (Isoc. 1.27; cf. 1.10); those who are *philokaloi* and *philoponoi* are "subservient (λατρεύοντας) to beauty" (10.57). I suspect this term was coined snidely, pointing

Aristotle schematizes: people who are called a particular *philotoioutos* find their particular *toioutos* pleasurable. He does not say whether the compound name encodes the goodness, normality, or intensity of the pleasure taken in the object indicated by the word's second element. While some of the exemplary objects of pleasure (justice, virtue) seem to us evidently good, Aristotle does not say whether the *phil-* prefixed names encode a laudatory attitude, either in the fourth century BCE or at the time of coinage. Nor does Aristotle say what relation the subject has to that pleasing object, whether it be possession, lack, availability to reflection, or something else. Nor does he even suggest that the *philotoioutos* experiences love or friendship (*philein, philia, philos*). The *phil-* prefixed word points only to a simple psychological state, a life-organizing pleasure that is oriented toward the thing named by the word associated with the second element. Of course, Aristotle realizes that this is not just any pleasure whatsoever, but rather a pleasure distinct and notable enough to be worth naming. But he does not specify the criteria of distinctiveness or notability; he addresses the pleasure in no way other than as a *pleasurable* state.[25]

Aristotle returns once to this austere analysis of the *philotoioutos*, in a somewhat richer but less textually certain parallel account found in the *Rhetoric*. There, Aristotle says that when people desire something (ὧν ἐπιθυμοῦντες τυγχάνουσιν) that befits the sort of people they are (πρὸς ἃ τοιοῦτοι or φιλοτοιοῦτοι),[26] not only does that thing please them, but it also appears good (οὐ . . . μόνον ἡδὺ ἀλλὰ καὶ βέλτιον φαίνεται).[27] Such it is with "victory in the case of *philonikoi*, honor in the case of *philotimoi*, money in the case of *philochrêmatoi*, and the others likewise" (*Rh.* 1363a37–b3). The key point is that the appearance-as-good does not mean that onlookers judge the desire as good.

out a zeal for aesthetic self-presentation, and like *philotimos* (discussed below) only later and sometimes taking on broader, more neutral, and even positive inflections.

[25] As recent translations go, the rendering by Crisp 2014, 14, "each person finds pleasure in that of which he is said to be fond," while it decomposes the term, at least maintains the non-obtrusive psychological language; Broadie and Rowe 2002, 104, by contrast, writing "in relation to which he is called 'lover of' that sort of thing," import the concept of "love," which is indefensible unless we accept a strong version of the single quotation marks, where by "lover of" we mean not someone who loves something but the first half of a compound name in which "lover" does not really mean "one who loves."

[26] The manuscripts print πρὸς ἃ τοιοῦτοι. An anonymous commentary on the *Rhetoric* (Rabe 1896, 27) seems to have read or inferred φιλοτοιοῦτοι. Both Ross 1959 and Kassel 1976 follow Vahlen 1903 in emending the text.

[27] Cipriano 1990, 42, claims that Aristotle distinguishes between being inclined toward something, loving something, and feeling pleasure in the attainment of that toward which one is inclined; she also notes that Aristotle's attention to these experiences has dialectical and not purely linguistic motivation. I leave aside whether such differentiation is possible; for the sake of the argument here we can call all of them descriptive psychological states.

Two books later in the *Nicomachean Ethics* Aristotle gives a new analysis, this time with normative judgments. He has just been discussing a deficiency in discipline (σωφροσύνη), exemplifying it with the so-called belly-crazy (γαστρίμαργοι), who eat too much. He generalizes:

> Regarding idiosyncratic (ἰδίας) pleasures many people make errors in many ways. For as the *philotoioutoi* are so-called (λεγομένων) for enjoying (τῷ χαίρειν) what they ought not, or more than the many do, or not as they ought, the intemperate for their part go too far (δ᾽ οἱ ἀκόλαστοι ὑπερβάλλουσιν) in all these respects. For they enjoy some things that they ought not—given that those things are hateful—and if they ought to enjoy some of them, they enjoy them rather more than they ought or than most people do. (*Eth. Nic.* 1118b21–27)

Aristotle now asserts that the label denotes the breaking of a norm. It not only identifies an intentional psychological state, "enjoying"; it also censures the person to whom the name has been applied. It conveys to the listener of the speech containing the *phil-* prefixed term a negative judgment as well as a claim about the ground of that judgment. Since calling someone *akolastos* ("intemperate," "undisciplined") obviously imputes blame and charges him with a wholesale excess in his tastes, calling someone a *phil-* prefixed name also imputes blame, but somewhat less, charging him with tastes that are excessive in at least certain respects. Someone might very much enjoy gambling on horses, and indeed get so much enjoyment from doing so as to forget about life's other pleasures and obligations; his character is not altogether damned, as the *akolastos*'s character might be, but still he is a little, so to say, *philippos*. A qualified deprecation remains something of a deprecation. And Aristotle says that the name is used *for* (τῷ) excessive or incorrect attitudes. The label is in itself always pejorative, not merely a neutral name to be used with an excoriating speaker's intention.[28] In the *Eudemian Ethics* Aristotle gives the concrete example of Philoxenus, whom he censures for being a gourmand (ὀψοφάγος, 1231a5–17), a term that, according to Athenaeus, he elsewhere glosses with a *phil-* prefixed name, dinner-lover (φιλόδειπνος), and that others gloss as fish-lover (φίλιχθυς).[29] Thus *philodeipnos* and *philichthus* fit Aristotle's analysis, in that they are words simultaneously referring to a pleasure and

---

[28] For discussion of other aspects of this passage, see Steward 1892, 314–15; Gauthier and Jolif 1959, 2.1.245; Taylor 2006, 200. Aspasius *In Eth. Nic.* 91,10 seems to have a corrupt text of Aristotle, leading him to read Aristotle as distinguishing two kinds of pleasures: those toward bad objects, and those toward appropriate objects and felt with greater poignancy than the majority does (see Konstan 2006, 93, with 195nn187–88).

[29] Ath. 1.6d; see Davidson 1997, ch. 1, for fish mania.

denoting something inappropriate. Similarly, in the *Rhetoric*, Aristotle diagnoses youthful immaturity as excessively and problematically *philophiloi* and *philetairoi*, "friend/companion crazy" (1389a35–b2).[30]

Aristotle's third remark about the *philotoioutos* goes beyond the simple "pleasure" analysis of Book 1 and the simple "excessive pleasure" analysis of Book 3. It comes in Aristotle's account of the nameless virtue concerned with honor (τιμή). According to Aristotle, three kinds of people have a drive (ὄρεξις) toward honor: those with a drive greater than one ought to have; those with a drive less than one ought to have; and those with a drive for honor that comes from an appropriate source, in an appropriate way, and to an appropriate degree. The first two, manifesting the extremes of those drives, get labeled. We censure as ambitious (φιλότιμον ψέγομεν) those who pursue (ἐφιέμενον) honor to an inappropriately great extent, or from an inappropriate source.[31] We censure as unambitious (ἀφιλότιμον) those who avoid honor even for admirable things. But the case of *philotimia* is more complicated than that, because sometimes we praise (ὅτε . . . ἐπαινοῦμεν) an ambitious person as being manly and noble (φιλόκαλον), and sometimes we praise the unambitious person as being measured and disciplined (σώφρων). Aristotle generalizes:

> Clearly, deploying the [terms] *philotoioutos* in multiple ways (πλεοναχῶς τοῦ φιλοτοιούτου λεγομένου), we do not use the [term] *philotimos* for the same thing every time (οὐκ ἐπὶ τὸ αὐτὸ φέρομεν ἀεὶ τὸ φιλότιμον), but, when praising, for pursuing honor more than most people, and when censuring, for pursuing honor more than one ought. The moderate position being nameless, apparently the extremes competed for the unclaimed borderland. (*Eth. Nic.* 1125b14–18)

Aristotle goes on to reiterate that a praiseworthy moderate position does exist, but because it lacks its own name, it borrows the name of one of the extremes, which deceives people into thinking that there are only two exhaustive categories, ambition and unambition (*Eth. Nic.* 1125b18–25; cf. 1108b29–1109a5).

---

[30] *Philetairos* seems to mean something like "loyal," "driven by peer esteem," maybe "hungry for social acknowledgment" (Thuc. 3.82.4; Xen. *Cyr.* 8.3.49), though later, positively, "companionable" (Theophr. *Char.* 29.4). *Philophilos* is also "loyal" and "concerned for friends" (Arist. *Rh.* 1381b27; *Eth. Nic.* 1155a29, 1159a34).

[31] Greek literature supports Aristotle's point about the badness of *philotimia*: Hdt. 3.54.4; Eur. *Phoen.* 531–6; *IA* 337–42, 527; Thuc. 3.82.8 (paired with *pleonexia*); Ar. *Thesm.* 383–84; *Ran.* 280–82, 678–79. Some cases are ambiguous: Thuc. 2.65.7 and 8.89.3 say that acting on "private (ἴδιος) *philotimia*" seems obviously bad, but context does not clarify whether *idios* modifies or emphasizes; similarly Pind. fr. 210, which speaks of evident pain in "excessive (ἄγαν) *philotimia*."

This analysis finds normative variety—ambivalence—where the earlier analyses did not.[32] The ambivalence could take two forms. It could be that every *phil-* prefixed term can be used in multiple ways, or that some *phil-*prefixed terms can be used in one way, some in another, and some in multiple ways.[33] In the first (strong) case, you can never tell, just by looking at it, whether a particular *phil-* prefixed term counts as censure or praise or neither. In the second (weak) case, you can never tell by knowing that a word has a *phil-* prefix whether it counts as censure or praise or neither. The warning has a remediating effect on those who assume they know what words mean by looking at their parts and ignoring the kind of word in which they find those parts.

Related to that ambiguity, there is further difficulty concerning what we might call Aristotle's speech act theory. In the Book 3 analysis, Aristotle claims that *phil-* prefixed words are intrinsically evaluative; describing somebody as *phil-* such-and-such carries one's disapprobation. It is their application and not the manner of their use that registers the judgment. In Book 4, Aristotle seems to maintain this view. You can call someone *philotimos*, and simply by doing so you censure him. It is like a slur, expressively rather than neutrally descriptive. But we soon run into a problem: Aristotle says that the word *philotimos* can be used both for praise and for blame. This Janus-faced usage seems to displace any evaluation from the word itself to its use.

Another alternative is the one Aristotle argues for in the case of *philotimos*. The term was first coined to indicate an excess. Something untoward had to be noted, and this compound adjective did the job. A mild adjective, to be sure. But the mere fact that a name came to be created shows that something other than mere observation or description—"Oh, he cares about honor!"—motivates the name-calling. A sentence or a phrase suffices for description. At some point, a class of distinctly problematic people were identified, those who so lacked ambition as to warrant grave concern. They came to be called

---

[32] Dover 1974 gives a similar analysis of *philotimos*, which while in a positive light is reputation bought at a cost to oneself, patriotism rather than shameful living, through its competitive realization it may shade into "aggression, pride, and boastfulness" (230–34, 236); *philonikia*, which while sometimes thought a virtue early in the fourth century BCE, was also a derogatory name for being "quarrelsome, factious, contentious" (233–34); *philanthrôpia*, which though happily linked with compassion is, at least in Demosthenes, seen as servile (201–2); *philodikos*, *philoloidoros*, and *philopragmôn*, all of which may be used as terms of reproach for being litigious and quarrelsome (187–89). See also Whitehead 1983, 56–62 (who provides copious evidence for the negative use of *philotimos* early on, in contradiction to his unsupported claim [56] that the term "began as an uncomplicatedly favorable one, lacking any suggestion that τιμή was not a proper object of 'love' "), and Christ 1998.

[33] Aspasius *In Nic. Eth.* 116,27–117,18, and Steward 1892, 348–49, suppose the latter.

aphilotimos. The alpha-privative feature of this word proves its posteriority to *philotimos*; its morphosemantic parallel proves its censoriousness.[34]

The binary form of the names suggests that they exhaust the possibilities, but they do not. They may point to a single norm that may be disobeyed in two opposite ways and obeyed in one. Obedience is the measured, decorous, and well-aimed pursuit of honor. While this intermediate kind of pursuit can readily be described, it has no specially tailored name. Presumably there was little reason to draw attention to this standard way of being, and certainly not with a flashy word. Thus the ethical state of affairs is this: three ways to be (excessive, deficient, and on point) and two names for them. Eventually, the middle position did need a name. It took its name from the position of excess, presumably because the middle position, in most contexts, means pursuing honor quite often, rather than a mere lack of an excessive commitment to honor. Now *philotimos* referred both to the excess and to the mean; for the one, it served as censure, and for the other, as praise. (*Philokalos* would have been a good candidate for the mean state; see note 24 above.)

This turn of events could mean one of two things. One might suppose the excoriative content of *philotimos* was wholly blanched out, such that moral outrage or appreciation would have to be colored in on subsequent uses. But this blanching is implausible, since Aristotle thought that *philotimos* retained the power of censure. So it must mean instead that there are two names, which are spelled the same but with different meanings: *philotimos*$_{\text{excess}}$ and *philotimos*$_{\text{mean}}$. When the first is addressed at someone, it censures. When the second is addressed to someone, it praises.

So Aristotle thinks that the *phil-* prefix creates names for labeling norm-breaking behavior. Often this is the only thing to label. Following the norm may then go nameless. When it needs a name, it may take it from one of the extremes. This development makes the word equivocal. The result of this Book 4 analysis means that the Book 3 analysis is basically true: *phil-* prefixed terms censure or start as censures. But it also means that the Book 1 analysis is sometimes safer: because *phil-* prefixed terms, as we now use them, sometimes do not censure, what is common to both the censorious and the encouraging terms is that they denote some distinctive (and posited) desire. So the three analyses develop dialectically.

Several results follow from Aristotle's series of analyses. *Phil-* prefixed terms are used first for other people. The *phil-* prefix does not itself create a word

---

[34] The English word "ambition" has undergone a related change; see the *OED* s.v. 1: "The ardent (*in early usage, inordinate*) desire to rish to high position, or to attain rank, influence, distinction or other preferment" (my italics).

with laudatory sense. Indeed, we may suspect that such words generally begin with a censuring tone, even if they later acquire an approbative one.[35] Thus, too, *philosophos*: applied to others and (plausibly) not positive at coinage.[36] Corroboration comes from a parallel analysis found in *Nicomachean Ethics*, to which we will now turn.[37]

While treating of friendship, Aristotle comes to meditate on what is usually translated the "self-lover," but could be construed as the "egoist": the *philautos* (*Eth. Nic.* 9.8). Aristotle notes that there is a puzzle whether one should love (φιλεῖν) oneself the most. On the one hand, many people think that like goes best with like, and nobody is more like you than you yourself. On the other hand, those who care (ἀγαπῶσι) most of all for themselves, or at any rate more than they do for other people, are criticized (ἐπιτιμῶσι), being denounced (ἀποκαλοῦσι) as so-called *philautoi*. This name, Aristotle reiterates, is used in reproach (ὡς ἐν αἰσχρῷ).[38] It is an other-applied, pejorative label for selfish people.

[35] See already Dover 1974, 10–11.

[36] In fact, Aristotle may provide an *ex post facto* etymology of *philosophos* in his *Protrepticus* (as reconstructed by HJ), one that mirrors those found in Plato's works and studied in chapter 8 (pp. 242–56). In a sinuous sentence, we read: "The *philosophos* seems—as with the other desires (ὀρέξεις) proper [to their bearer] that are named after their affection (φιλοστοργίᾳ) for one kind of object—if one ought fasten to him as well the proper name due to the passion (πάθους)—to have a drive (ἔφεσιν) for a certain knowledge honored for itself, and not for anything separate resulting from it" (Iambl. *DCMS* 23.70,26–71,4). In Aristotle's words, the name of a kind of person comes from the name of that kind of person's distinctive desire, and this desire *specifies* its particular object, and in the case of the *philosophos* the object is wisdom (*sophia*). This does not confirm the view that *phil-* prefixed terms tend to start negatively. But it also does not overturn that view. In the first place, Aristotle sets this etymology not in a scientific lecture but the persuasive setting of a dramatized exhortation to *philosophia*. In the same dialogue, he gives a series of starkly different definitions of *philosophia* (e.g., precise discussions of truth: Iambl. *DCMS* 26.83,7; possession and use of *sophia*: Iambl. *Pro.* 6.40,2–3; knowledge deployed with correct judgment, use of reason, and contemplation of the whole of the good: Iambl. *Pro.* 6.37,3–22). Second, treating *sophia* as an object of knowledge that people considered intrinsically valuable as early as the sixth century BCE tends toward anachronism, as we will see below. Third, and crucially, Aristotle's analysis here undermines itself. *Philostorgia*, the term Aristotle uses to describe the character trait of desiring one kind of object named by *phil-* prefixed terms, is precisely a *phil-* prefixed term that fails this analysis. After all, *philostorgia* does not mean a desire, passion, or affection *for* love or affection (στοργή), but a continual having of affection, that is, being characterized by or inclined to love or affection. (The term *philostorgia* may have itself been the subject of Sophistic interest; Antiphon of Rhamnous (fr. 73 Blass) is said to have deployed the terms *astorgia, philostorgia,* and *storgê* in his "rhetorical handbooks." For a history of the word's use see Roskam 2011, 178–81.) If Aristotle had taken *philostorgia* as his model, then *philosophia* would have to have meant a continual *having* of wisdom; this may not be inconsistent with a drive toward or an appetite for wisdom, but it is a misleading way of presenting it.

[37] Yet another parallel would be found in the analysis of φίλερις ("captious person") at Arist. *Soph. el.* 171b26.

[38] These passages: *Eth. Nic.* 1168a28–30. The chapter goes through 1169b2.

Philautos is a label in part because it is not merely a combination of the words for "self" and "lover," as the standard English translation suggests. We can see this for both parts of the compound. First, Aristotle says that the attitude the self-lover has toward himself is *agapê*, not *philia*.[39] Aristotle describes this person's character with words other than the ones that appear to form the two elements of the compound. When Plato, perhaps in the same period of time, has occasion to talk about someone who loves himself, he does not use the name, and thus the reproach; reproach is not appropriate to his context.[40] Second, the *philautos* does not especially love the self (*autos*). In Aristotle's first explanation, the *philautos* fails to act in accordance with what is excellent, presumably preferring pleasure or ease or his current whim (1168a33). In his second explanation of this reproach (ὄνειδος), Aristotle says the *philautos* assigns to himself the most goods, honors, and bodily pleasures (1168b15–18). If names were transparent, *philautos* would be much less meaningful and useful than *philochrêmatos*, *philotimos*, or *philêdonês*.

So how could this name have come to be? We want to pick on people for their failures in communal activities—in particular their shortcomings in distributive justice—but we wish to avoid crassness. *Autos* does not alone pick out or stand for anything bad, and thus being notably related to it is not bad as such. But it would be meaningless to say that for someone their "self is dear" (if people even think of themselves *as* selves, which is questionable), since this is the case for everyone, trivially. To justify the name-calling, the name must be understood to involve a second element (*autos*) that actually stands in for the distribution of goods, and the compound must be understood to pick out an improper distribution of goods. *Phil-* does not literally mean "mania for" or "excessive desire for." It is attached to nouns to create censorious names.[41] Two parallels are the names *philozôos* (with the second element "life") and

---

[39] That Aristotle elsewhere uses *philein* means only that the verbs of affection are interchangeable; it does not change the fact that *philautos* does not entirely mean *philôn heauton*.

[40] When Plato is describing the phenomenon of preference for oneself over others, he uses a descriptive phrase (ὃ λέγουσιν ὡς φίλος αὐτῷ, *Leg.* 731e1; τὴν σφόδρα ἑαυτοῦ φιλίαν, *Leg.* 731e4), not this name. Since the *Laws* would not have been written much earlier than the *Ethics*, since Aristotle does not speak of the name as an in-vogue slang, and since Plato does use many *phil-* prefixed names, I think Plato would have used it if it were anything other than a nickname.

[41] After Aristotle and before Philo, there are at most two extant uses of *philautos* (Timaeus of Tauromenium in DL 8.66, if Diogenes is quoting rather than paraphrasing; Phld. *On Anger* in *PHerc.* 182, fr. 17, col. 28.33), and none of *philautia*. Perhaps it came to sound too strident or colloquial (as with "selfish" or "egomaniacal"). It does suggest that *phil-* prefixed names are not transparent; for obviously egoism has always been a perennial issue, especially in the context of *eudaimonia*, and were *philautos* transparent, it would be an eminently suitable name for it, and we would expect to see it more often.

philopsuchos ("soul").[42] On the conventional translation they both mean "life-loving"; but since most people love life itself (e.g., *Eth. Nic.* 1169b27–1170b4), "life" stands in for protection of one's own in battles, and the *phil-* prefix creates a name-calling name, and so the compounds mean "coward."

Interestingly, Aristotle goes on to redeem the term *philautos* heard in an artificially transparent way, saying that it is, in some respects, admirable to love oneself. Of course this redemption of the name for Aristotle's philosophical purposes does not by itself change the public connotations of the word.[43] We see something very similar in the contemporaneous dialogue *Hipparchus*, possibly by Plato or his Academic students. There Socrates and his interlocutor analyze *philokerdês* ("profit"). The "profiteer" is obviously a bad name, and Socrates innovates when he argues that it means "lover of the good."[44]

For all the significance and credibility of Aristotle's hypotheses about *phil-*prefixed names, however, they remain incomplete. Aristotle makes two related but unquestioned assumptions that limit his insight into the phenomenon of *phil-* prefixed names. Both assumptions follow his psychological reading of these terms. The psychological reading has two parts: the "attitudinal" condition, where a *philotoioutos* is so named for desiring, getting pleasure, or otherwise having some positive feeling toward something; and the "object" condition, where a *philotoioutos* is so named for that positive feeling about the apparent referent of the second element of a *phil-* prefixed name. For example, the attitudinal condition for naming someone *philotimos* is that that person has some positive feeling toward something. The object condition is that that positive feeling is toward honor. So the fact that a *phil-* prefixed term is used brings with it the (often negative) evaluation discussed above; the *first* element brings the psychological state; and the *second* element brings the intentional object of the state. As it turns out, neither condition looks promising in light of

---

[42] *Philozôos* as coward(ly): Eur. fr. 816.6; Plato Com. 19 *PCG*; Arist. *Rh.* 1389b32; *philopsuchos* as coward(ly): Eur. *Phoen.* 597; *Hec.* 348; Anon. Iambl. 4.2. The fact that *philozôos* can also mean "fond of animals" (Xen. *Mem.* 1.4.7) supports the theory of coinage described below.

[43] Elsewhere Aristotle uses the term negatively: *Rh.* 1389b35 (among the elderly's many bad qualities is their being *philautoi*, linked to their being *philozôoi* ("cowardly") and embracing *mikropsuchia* ("small-heartedness"), living for the useful, rather than *kalon*, more than they ought); *Pol.* 1263b2 ("*to philauton* is rightly blamed; this is not 'loving oneself' (τὸ φιλεῖν ἑαυτόν) but 'loving more than one ought' (τὸ μᾶλλον ἢ δεῖ φιλεῖν), as in *to philochrêmaton*, for everyone at least loves (φιλοῦσί), so to speak, each of these things"; *Mag. mor.* 1212a28–33 (the *philautos* does everything for his own advantage; the *phaulos* [bad person] is *philautos*; the opposite personage is the *philagathos* [b19]). At *Rh.* 1371b20–21, Aristotle instances a weak rehabilitation (or neutralization) of the term: everyone is more or less *philautos*, in that all get pleasure from what is their own—their words, works, honor, or children.

[44] Cf. Moore 2015b, 239–44. In favor of Platonic authorship: Calogero 1938; Friedländer 1964, 108–16.

further evidence about Greek *phil-* prefixed terms. To that we now turn, focusing on the earliest known *phil-* prefixed terms.

Testing Aristotle's Theory on Pre-Classical Greek *Phil-* Prefixed Names

Greek has upwards of 900 *phil-* prefixed names.[45] By the period of Aristophanes, many *phil-* prefixed names could be heard as though they were built from a verbal first element, *philein*, and an objective second element, the accusative argument of the verb. The verb *philein* would, by that time, be understood attitudinally as "to desire," "to like," or "to love." But what late fifth- or early fourth-century BCE speakers could hear in a term need not be what seventh- or sixth-century BCE speakers heard. It has long been appreciated by scholars that in Greek *phil-* prefixed names up through the middle of the fifth century BCE, the *phil-* first element would not yet have been understood verbally. It would have been understood instead as a *bahuvrihi* compound meaning "to whom *x* is *philon* ('dear' or 'one's own')."[46] In that pre-classical period, *philon* would not have the attitudinal inflection of enduring desire that it later acquired. It meant, depending on grammatical role and context, dear, united, friend, shared, convenient, trustworthy, benign, welcome, particular, relevant, or inherent.[47] This is the realization Burkert had in his 1960 paper.[48] Modern scholarship has sought the date by which the first element came to sound different, and why.[49] But parties to this investigation agree that the shift begins only after Pythagoras and Heraclitus, and finishes later; so the coinage of *philosophos* predated the shift to the classical paradigm.

We will test Aristotle's hypothesis by looking at *phil-* prefixed terms attested by the beginning of the fifth century BCE. This means nine in Homer, a half-dozen in sixth-century BCE poetry, and some from Pindar.[50] That they lack an explicit attitudinal component (the "desire for") has been observed in previous scholarship. It has not been appreciated, however, that we cannot take the second element transparently, as though it simply stood in for the similarly

---

[45] Landfester 1966, 108; LSJ s.vv. φιλάβουλος–φιλωρείτας.

[46] Cipriano 1990, 43, 97–100; Meissner 2006, 168–70; Tribulato 2015, 168, 334–35.

[47] Landfester 1966, 95–107; Hooker 1987; Cipriano 1990, 14–24; Intrieri 2013, 213–25.

[48] Burkert 1960, 172–73; see chapter 1, p. 22.

[49] Especially Osthoff 1878, 145–60; Landfester 1966; Cipriano 1990, 25–38, 97–110.

[50] Cunliffe 1963, 408–9; Cipriano 1990, 48–55.

spelled noun.[51] Indeed, the second element points rather obliquely at what the name is about. Nor has it been appreciated that most of these names are originally or generally other-applied epithets, not self-descriptions.[52] Finally, and most importantly, it has not been appreciated that many of these names are not used in congratulation or approval; many include a bemused, skeptical, or even censorious judgment. Thus in the following analysis, I will discuss the presence of these four features: (i) the lack of explicit attitudinal component; (ii) the lack of concern for an object transparently referred to by the cognate noun of the second element; (iii) the status as an epithet, adjective, or name applied to other people; and (iv) a built-in evaluation of the person or state tagged with the word.

I turn first to Homer. Parentheses surround the English translation of the noun related to the word's second element.

Φιλήρετμος ("oar"). Homer used this epithet, which may look to us like "oar-loving," for the Phaeacians and the Taphians. The Phaeacians had wonderful seafaring skills, as their other epithets, "famed for ships" (ναυσικλυτός), "with long oars" (δολιχήρετμος), and "convoying safely" (πομπός ἀπήμων) confirm.[53] The Taphians were pirates (ληϊστῆρες) who raided and traded in metals and slaves.[54] Both would be seen as repeatedly rowing, although the Taphians surely would row with a frequency that would make the coastal peoples comfortable. The adjective, even in non-formulaic contexts, cannot seriously be taken to impute to these groups a feeling of pleasure, enjoyment, or desire for oars, or indeed any attitude at all toward the oars. Oars are mere instruments for traveling by ship—an important instrument, to be sure, as the point at which a human interacts, often with great toil, with a rowed vessel. The sense of the name must be something like "using oars an awful lot," "engaging in the hard task of rowing more than one would think reasonable." "Oar" stands in for a social practice, naval rowing, and the name signifies a way of life that accommodates that normally unpleasant or incidental institution. *Philêretmos* may even have something bemused about it, as coming first

---

[51] While Cipriano 1990, 107, notes in passing that the different semantic connotations the second member can assume does determine the possible meanings of the compound, it does not play an important part in the analysis, despite the fact that in her book she is ultimately comparing *philologos* to *logophilos* (cf. 8).

[52] This fact is made little of by Cipriano 1990, 97, even when she notes that *phil-* compounds tend to be stereotypical epithets, poetic descriptions of abstract entities, and adjectives applicable to large sets of individuals.

[53] φιλήρετμος: *Od.* 5.386, 8.96, 8.386, 8.535, 11.349, 13.36; excellence in seafaring: e.g., 7.34–36; their other epithets: 8.191, 8.369, 8.566, 13.166, 13.174; useful discussion: Louden 2011, 2.649–51.

[54] Epithet: *Od.* 1.181, 1.419; piracy: 15.427, 16.426.

from the mouth of a landlubber; it is hard to imagine why a Phaeacian would deem himself *philêretmos*, or to whom he would express himself in this way. Maybe the term was coined by some overland transportation guild, smirking at the Phaeacians's reliance on the irregular seas. Or it was first used for Taphian-like pirates, bemusedly marking their avarice by highlighting how much harder they pull at the oars than at their own work.

Φιλομμειδής ("smiling"). This epithet applies almost exclusively to Aphrodite, the goddess of sexual love, and only in early epic.[55] It never picks out a psychological state.[56] Nor does it suggest that Aphrodite has any attitude toward smiles as such. It refers instead to the performance of seduction she personifies, with its characteristically coy smiling.[57] Akin to a great many epithets applied to her that mean "scheming" (ποικιλόφρων, δολοφρονέουσα, δολιόφρων, δόλιος, δολομήδες, δολόπλοκος), though in possible contrast to a pair connected to crowns (φιλοστεφάνος, εὐστέφανος), this one appears to have a notably negative inflection in meaning as "deceptive" or "untrustworthy."[58]

Hesiod pretends to hear this epithet as φιλο(μ)μηδέα, where the second element comes from μήδεα ("genitals," though also "ploys"); this would account for the rest of his line, ὅτι μηδέων ἐξεφαάνθη ("because she came forth from genitals," *Theog.* 200). This would imply not "lover of genitals" but "characterized in an important way with reference to the genitals"—and perhaps with the double entendre on Aphrodite's relevance for sexuality. (Even were the second element μῆδος, it would probably actually be the homonym "mind.") Hesiod's etymological play suggests that Greeks recognized at an early date the nontransparency of *phil-* prefixed terms, and thus that their meaning is not to be found solely in a naïve decomposition of the compound.

Φιλοψευδής ("lies"). Zeus is called this a single time in the Homeric poems, where he faces accusations of misrepresenting his allegiances (*Il.* 12.164). But

---

[55] *Il.* 3.424, 4.10, 5.375, 14.211, 20.40; *Od.* 8.362; *Hom. Hymn Aphr.* 5, 49, 56, 65, 155; Hes. *Theog.* 200, 990; Hes. fr. 247.1; *Cypr.* 5.1 *EGF.* It is once used for Glauconome, an otherwise unknown Nereid (Hes. *Theog.* 256; cf. Apollod. *Bibl.* 1.2.7).

[56] Boedeker 1974, 20–36, contra Beekes 2010, s.v. φίλος, who defines *philommeidês* as "with a friendly smile."

[57] Faulkner 2008, 92.

[58] Jackson 2010, 157: It is used "most often when Aphrodite is being shamed or subordinated on account of her association with sexuality"; "Zeus, by belittling Aphrodite and encouraging Athena, seeks to replace Aphrodite's model of excessively intimate interaction with Athena's more appropriate model of friendship" (161). Cf. Boedeker 1974, 35; Friedrich 1982, 105; Bouchard 2015. Φιλοστεφάνος (*Hom. Hymn Dem.* 102) is obviously not a matter of "loving crowns" per se; Boedeker 1974, 21, thinks that this word is originally a formulaic invention to deal with a metrical puzzle, drawing from φιλομμειδής and εὐστέφανος, not part of the overall epithet system, which would explain its oddly positive nature. Might it have originally meant "hungry for victory," "vainglorious," or "vain"? *Eustephanos*: *Od.* 8.267. The others are cited at Bouchard 2015, 13.

he is not accused of enjoying such representations or of preferring lies in some general way.[59] The charge is that Zeus is characteristically deceptive about his intentions. Thus "lies" themselves are not even at issue, but rather a very specific thing about which one might not speak truly. Aristotle clarifies Homer's usage when he later uses the word to refer to people who are not sincere about their capacities, who either boast about or underrepresent them (*Eth. Eud.* 1234a3). Thus the word is not used for those who get pleasure from lying, or even for those who simply lie often.

Φιλοκέρτομος ("jeering"). In the *Odyssey*, Ctessipus, son of Polytherses, is characterized by jeering and disrespectful behaviors associated with jeering (22.287). Odysseus gives no reason to believe that Ctessipus *enjoys* jeering. We learn too little about Ctessipus himself to know whether he actually jeers frequently. We know only that this is a negative other-applied name.

Φιλοπτόλεμος ("war"). Various peoples are said to be warlike: the Myrmidons, Trojans, Greeks, and Leleges.[60] Whether they like or desire war is not at issue, nor even "war" as such. These groups are distinguished by irascibility or a proclivity to fighting, and perhaps do not make the normal efforts to ensure peace. None of Homer's characters applies this term to himself. It is used as an epithet here; later literature makes clear its negative connotation.

Φιλοκτέανος ("possession"). The Atrides are said to be "most covetous" (*Il.* 1.122). While they may indeed enjoy their possessions more than most do, presumably the point is neither to identify their enjoyment nor their possessions as such, but (outside Homer's formulaic use) to censure a grasping spirit, especially of money or land, but really of whatever can be competed for or sought out.

Φιλόξενος ("stranger"). People referred to as "hospitable" may enjoy the company of or the hosting of strangers or foreigners.[61] This adjective does not determine whether *philoxenoi* enjoy the company of strangers *qua* foreigners (as do "host families" for high school students from abroad), or are fastidious about meeting the obligations of *xenia*, or are simply broadly accommodating. It is probably safest to assume something like the second, that it has to do with good participation in *xenia*, rather than some attitude toward *xenoi* per se.

Φιλοπαίγμων ("play"). In the first extant usage of this word, a dance tune is called "sportive."[62] Presumably it is used metaphorically, on the model of

---

[59] Earlier in the *Iliad* Zeus was said not to help liars (οὐ γὰρ ἐπὶ ψευδέσσι πατὴρ Ζεὺς ἔσσετ᾽ ἀρωγός, *Il.* 4.235).

[60] Myrmidons: *Il.* 16.65, 23.129; Trojans: 16.90, 16.835, 17.194; Greeks: 17.224, 19.269, 20.351; Leleges: 21.86.

[61] *Od.* 6.121, 8.576, 9.176, 13.202.

[62] *Od.* 23.134.

people enjoying play. Humans who are *philopaigmones* could enjoy play and childishness, but they might not.[63]

I will now cite a few non-Homeric *phil-* prefixed terms that are used as mainly negative epithets that refer neither to a desire nor to the literal object of some desire. **Φιλαίματος** ("blood") describes Ares and Fear.[64] These divinities surely do not enjoy blood itself; rather, they are distinguished by their connection to war, violence, and destruction. This epithet seems negatively inflected in meaning. **Φιλοδέσποτος** ("master") modifies δῆμος ("people") in its first extant use.[65] Here it is clearly pejorative; it is as though the only way to describe the "subservience" of some people is to imagine them, absurdly, as partial to their master. But the subservient person doubtfully loves his master; he simply accommodates the wishes of some authority. The man who is **φιλοκερδής** ("profit") is similarly not to be applauded.[66] One would not want to be called **φιλόμωμος** ("blame"). In Simonides's poem we find a disavowal of the name: "I am not censorious."[67] Thus this is a negative other-applied name, used defensively here. And once again, there is little sense that the censorious person *likes* or *desires* to blame; the point is rather that he is characterized by behavior that can be interpreted as blaming.

Finally, a few more poetic uses that (i) lack an attitudinal component, (ii) lack a literal object, and (iii) are other-applied epithets: **φιλάγλαος** ("splendor"), meaning "resplendent"/"vain," said of Agrigento (Pind. *Pyth.* 12.1); **φιλόμαχος** ("battle"), meaning "pugnacious," said of the race of Perses (Pind. fr. 164); and **φιλόνεικος** ("victory"), meaning "contentious," denied by a speaker (Pind. *Ol.* 6.19).

The preceding analysis shows that the *phil-* prefix generates fairly opaque names. These names caricature some distinctive personal quality. Walter Burkert glossed the *phil-* prefix as "close acquaintance and familiarity with." We see that this is much too concrete, narrow, and selective.[68] A truer formula-

[63] Φιλοφροσύνη (*Il.* 1.256) appears not to be a *phil-* prefixed term (which would explain the difficulty faced by Cipriano 1990, 43n21); it seems to mean something like "disposed to treating others as *philos*."

[64] Anac. fr. 100D.3; Aesch. *Sept.* 45; cf. Eur. *Phoen.* 174; [*Rhes.*] 932.

[65] Thgn. 849.

[66] Thgn. 199; cf. Pind. *Isthm.* 2.6.

[67] Simon. fr. 4.22.

[68] Cf. Chroust 1964a, 427n16 and 432n28. Hadot 2002, 16, is too narrow in saying that the prefix "designate[s] the disposition of a person who found his interest, pleasure, or *raison de vivre* in devoting himself to a given activity," and gives only the examples of *philoposia* (not extant from before Xenophon's *Memorabilia* [1.2.22] and Plato's *Phaedo* [87e10], where it has distinctly negative connotation) and *philotimia* (which LSJ s.v. says is "frequently in bad sense in early writers," as we have already seen).

tion, were a unified formulation required, would be "marked somehow by a counter-normative relation to, perhaps especially one of repetition." The above analysis also shows that the second element usually stands in for something less concrete or natural than if it were the cognate independent word. Many of these names come from legal contexts; to the above we can add **φιλαίτιος** ("cause") = "litigious"[69] and **φιλόψογος** ("censure") = "censorious."[70] Also, from the field of economic relations: **φιλάργυρος** ("silver") and **φιλόπλουτος** ("wealth") = "avaricious."[71] Others come from norms of warfare, servitude, and competition. We can infer that the second element—often a concrete object (oar, smile, silver, soul)—stands for some conventional practice or system (navy, seduction, monetary accumulation, protecting external values). In every conventional practice, a participant must modulate his participation. He must be involved to some degree: defending his property, seeking romantic partners, or promoting the welfare of his hometown. That involvement is, in an important respect, set by the common good it facilitates. Be involved too much, however, and the directing good can come to seem to be merely one's own private good. One explains a person's overwhelming helpfulness by diagnosing the self-directed benefit; the public good is being sacrificed for the private good. Criticism is difficult because participation in the conventional practice is nonetheless important. But criticism is also necessary because such participation must be corrected. The name-calling allowed by *phil-* prefix names allows sensitive policing of these conventional practices. A name-caller can seem simply to draw attention to a person's participation in a neutral activity: for example, "that guy is always filing legal motions; he's a real motions-filer" (φιλαίτιος). Since legal motions themselves are appropriate for many situations, the name-caller is not criticizing harshly, in the way that using an obscene name is. But since one's relation to legal motions usually is not a matter for discussion, calling attention to it by creating a name for it implies that the relation is not merely notable; it is worrisome. An important aim of making a name for someone is to regulate behavior; and most regulation-worthy behavior is problematic behavior.

A Legacy of Mycenaean Onomastics

Phil- prefixed names begin as other-applied terms. Personal names are also, in a sense, other-applied terms—by parents of their children. Already in Homer

---

[69] Aesch. *Supp.* 803.
[70] Eur. *El.* 904, cf. *Phoen.* 198.
[71] Soph. *Ant.* 1055; fr. 528; Eur. *IT* 411.

there are five: the famous Philoctêtês; Philoitios, Odysseus's faithful herdsman; the father and son Philêtor and Philêtoridês; and Philomêleidês, king of Lesbos. Such *phil-* prefixed personal names are multiplied to the hundreds in the classical and Hellenistic periods; even in Rome we know of thirty-three such names.[72] This formula predates Homer, too; in the Mycenaean period, there are more than two dozen names that start with *pi-ro-* (𐀠 𐀫; Greek *phil-*); at least seventeen of them have second elements, not simply dependent suffixes.[73] These personal names—which have been known only since the 1950s—do not, however, simply add to the supply of *phil-* prefixed names suitable for our analysis. They may seem to be counterexamples to the Aristotelian position that *phil-* prefixed names serve to point out some problematic disposition. It would be surprising (though not impossible) for a parent to give a child a name that refers to some dubious trait.

In fact these names may provide positive evidence for the theory outlined here. Of the 2000 known Mycenaean personal names, wholly thirty percent are compounds.[74] Many of these names must have been coined in an appellative environment that provided a range of apparent patterns on which to build. Building on apparent patterns allows for mutations in morphosemantic understanding, which thus opens up new possibilities. It is hard to know exactly the early meaning of the *pi-ro-* first element, but let us suppose it was something like belongingness, dearness, or love.[75] Imagine then (though without real evidence) that a name like *Pi-ro-pa-ta-ra* > Φιλοπάτρα ("ancestor") was coined to mean "[has a] loving ancestor."[76] But then imagine it came later to be understood as "cares for her ancestor." This new analysis, applied to

[72] Pape and Benseler 1911, 2.1616–32; Solin 2003, 1.161–73. Among names attested by the sixth century BCE are Φιλόδημος ("the people"), Φιλόκωμος ("merry-making"), Φιλόλαος ("the people"), Φιλόμβροτος ("mankind"), Φιλόμηλος ("herd"), Φιλόξενος ("host/guest"). See Tribulato 2015, 421–22.

[73] *Pi-ro* (Φίλων), *Pi-ro-i-ta* (Φιλοίτας), *Pi-ro-ka-te* (Φιλογάθης or Φιλοκαρτής?), *Pi-ro-na* (Φιλώνα?), *Pi-ro-ne-ta* (Φιλονέστας, Φιλονείτας ["save, rescue"] or Φιλωνήτας ["price paid"]), *Pi-ro-pa-ta-ra* (Φιλοπάτρα ["ancestor"]), *Pi-ro-pe-se-wa*, *Pi-ro-qa-wo*, *[.]pi-ro-qe-mo*, *Pi-ro-qo-[*, *Pi-ro-ta-wo*, *Pi-ro-te-ko-to*, *Pi-ro-we-ko* (Φιλοῦργος ["work"]), *Pi-ra-jo* (Φιλαῖος), *Pi-ra-ka-ra* (Φιλάγρα), *Pi-ra-ka-wo* (Φιλάχαιϝος), *Pi-ra-ki*, *Pi-ra-ki-jo* (Φιλάρχιος?), *Pi-ra-me-no* (Φιλαμενός?), *Pi-ra-qo*, *Pi-re-ta*, *Pi-ri-no* (Φιλῖνος), *Pi-ri-sa-ta* (Φιλίστης), *Pi-ri-ta* (Φιλίστα), *Pi-ri-ta-wo*, *Pi-ri-to-jo* (Φίλιστος). For the conjectured Greek translations, see Aura Jorro 1993, 2.121–29, as well as Landau 1958, 165; Bartonek 1999, 123, 128.

[74] See Ilievski 1983 for discussion.

[75] On the Proto-Indo-European root, see Buck 1949, 1110; Watkins 2000, 60 s.v. *prî*; Rendich 2010, 188 s.v. *phi-*. Boisacq 1938, 1027, s.v. φίλος surveys earlier scholarship and declares the origins to be obscure.

[76] For this transformation and more on compound personal names, see Meissner and Tribulato 2002, 311, and generally Morpurgo Davies 2000.

Pi-ro-we-ko > Φιλοῦργος ("work"), makes "hardworker" possible. The range of names is limited only by the combinations that could sound auspicious.

Mycenaean has no examples of *pi-ro-* (*phil-*) words that are not proper names. The limits of our documentary evidence and the fact that much of our lexicon comes from bureaucratic lists and other materials may explain this exclusion. But I conjecture that the negatively inflected adjectives, and indeed the *phil-* prefixed adjectives in general, are derivative of the personal names. *Phil-* prefixing, let us say, first served as a proper name creator. These names were transparent to their coiners and perhaps to some parents when choosing a name. After that, they became identifiers, not descriptions. This would make *phil-* prefixing now appropriate for name-calling labels. It would have the advantage of *sounding* positive (because people call their children similar names) while potentially *meaning* quite the opposite (because the instance of name-calling is not one of christening but of norm policing). In other words, to make a wry or bemused name that lacks the harshness of an insult, a person could borrow the name-creating technique of *phil-* prefixing. The name's creation for someone who already has a proper name tips the hearers off to its special (bemused or censorious) meaning. Because it was coined in order to make such a negatively inflected name, we do not have to posit an original "descriptive" or "neutral" or "positive" meaning. This theory would rescue Aristotle's view. It would also allow some *phil-* prefixed terms always to have had positive evaluations as adjectivizations of actual proper names (on the model of Philopatra, and maybe Philoxenus).[77]

Classical Reflection on *Phil-* Prefixed Names: A Corroboration

Aristophanes's play of 422 BCE, the *Wasps*, opens with a comic set piece about the formation of *phil-* prefixed name-calling names; it provides further corroboration for the present argument. The play dramatizes the obsession of its *phil-* prefixed protagonist, Philocleon, with exercising the power that jury duty affords. Philocleon cannot get enough of jury duty; the action of the play involves his non-*phil-* prefixed son Bdelycleon's attempts to curb his mania. The

---

[77] An added consideration: extant Greek includes two *philêso-* prefixed words, both *hapax* forms found in Pindar: φιλησίμολπος (*Ol.* 14.14), glossed at line 16 with another epithet of the Graces, ἐρασίμολπος (also a *hapax*; the terms here are defined by a scholiast as φίλη τῶν μολπῶν and τῶν μολπῶν ἐρῶσα); and φιλησιστέφανος (*Pae.* 1 fr. 52a.8), modifying a celebratory feast. Both words exist in versions without -*ês*-, suggesting this short-lived (?) compositional form derives from the more compact form, perhaps trying to avoid the negative overtone. For reflections on this form, see Bréal 1897, 181–82; Gildersleeve 1885, xli–xlii.

household's slaves ask the audience to guess what trait they should ascribe to the father.

> XANTHIAS: . . . [Philocleon] is ill from a bizarre illness
> that nobody will recognize or diagnose;
> they'll have to learn what it is from us. So: start guessing!
> —Amynias here, son of Pronapses, claims the man
> is a *philokubos* ("dice").
> SOSIAS: He's talking nonsense, by Zeus,
> judging the illness by his own symptoms!
> XANTHIAS: True enough, though *"philo-" is* the start of the evil.
> Here next is Sôsias' claiming to Derclyus that
> the man is a *philopotês* ("drinking").
> SOSIAS: Not at all; since
> that illness is an affliction of gentlemen.
> XANTHIAS: And now Nicostratus of Scambonidae claims
> the man to be a *philothutês* ("sacrifice") or a *philoxenos* ("hosting").
> SOSIAS: By the dog, O Nicostratus, not a *philoxenos*; since Philoxenus is a bugger.
> XANTHIAS: You're all just driveling; you're not going to find it;
> if you're really eager to know it, quiet down and listen:
> I'll tell you now what's plaguing the master.
> A *philêliastês* ("Eliaia") is what he is, like none other,
> passionate (*eraô*) for this—judging—and he groans
> unless he sits in the front row. (Ar. *Vesp.* 71–90)

Aristophanes seems to have coined the word *philêliastês*, combining the naming element *phil-* and the name of the body of 6000 citizens from which individual juries would be empanelled, the *Eliaia*.[78] The word is an opaque label: the slaves have to gloss it with a description, "passionate for judging." It is also evaluative, describing a bad state to be in (see "plaguing," "groans"). It mimics the other *phil-* terms treated in the lines above as the names of diseases (76, 80, 87).[79] All are bemused slanders.

Taken compositionally, each of the *phil-* terms could seem simply to imply that the second element somehow characterizes the subject of the term. Indeed, if *phil-* meant "love of," and the second element were taken as it were directly or literally, the names could seem to mean the following: "lover of dice [a game]," "lover of drinking [a way of staying hydrated]," "lover

---

[78] On the Eliaia, see MacDowell 1986, 30.
[79] Cf. Cipriano 1990, 39; Thorburn 2005.

of sacrifice [a way to propitiate the gods]," "lover of hosting [a part of hospitality]," and "lover of the jury [a venue of democratic practice]." But this is not quite right. *Philokubos* means profligate gambling.[80] *Philopotês* means wallowing in alcoholic excess.[81] *Philothutês* means, at least here, acting piously for the sake of eating the meat produced in the sacrifice; elsewhere it might mean "acting superstitiously."[82] We have already seen *philoxenos* used without moral indignation in Homer; here the use suggests that the term could apply to those who throw decadent parties, but also, jokingly and more pungently, to those who purchase foreign male prostitutes in Athens.[83] Each is, at least, a way of calling a person out for his excessive engagement with a common social institution: gambling, drinking, feasting, and partying. These names are humorous because the positive-sounding second element refers only indirectly to the characteristic that the comedian is lambasting.

The word invented by Aristophanes here follows this pattern. The jury is a preexisting social institution, to which a person's orientation must be rightly modulated. The name *philêliastês* is funny because while its naïvely literal reading—"somehow repeatedly concerned with the jury"—would be anodyne and possibly trivially patriotic or democratic, its actual use, in name-calling, expresses a counter-normative involvement with something that this social institution implies.[84] It is not that Philocleon likes the jury pool, or likes it a lot, or likes it in the wrong way. Philocleon's attitude toward the jury pool itself is not really at issue. The slaves point out that he likes to wield arbitrary coercive power over others. He has access to this power when he is empanelled on a jury. It is funnier and more poignant, however, to say that he is *philêliastês* than that he enjoys abusing his civic power: *phil-* names point to some social

[80] Aristotle uses the term, for which the Revised Oxford Translation provides "addicted to gaming" (*Phgn.* 808a31), in a parallel with *philoloidoros* ("abusive," 808a32), *philogunaios* ("fond of women," 808a36), and *philupnos* ("somnolent," 808b6). The Alcidamean *Odysseus* 27 presents the "great badness" of dice: it harms the losers, ridicules the winners, and the proceeds are almost always spent straightaway.

[81] Hdt. 2.174.1 expresses his low esteem of the Egyptian Amasis: "a *philopotês* and a real jester (φιλοσκώμμων) and never a get-down-to-business kind of guy"). Hippoc. *Aer.* 1 contrasts the ones who are "*philopotai* and eat multiple big meals and are indulgent" with those who exercise and labor and refrain from drinking. Antiphon the Sophist is cited to have said "nor to be called *philopotês*, seeming to neglect your business, having been drowned in wine" (μήτε φιλοπότην κληθῆναι καὶ δοκεῖν τὰ πράγματα καταμελεῖν ὑπὸ οἴνου ἡσσώμενου), B76/D72. Pendrick 2002, 422–23, is misleading when he says that Aristophanes, at least here, treats the term "as a virtue," but see his note on ancient accusations of *philopotia*.

[82] Starkie 1897 ad 82.

[83] Cf. Gilula 1983, contra MacDowell 1971 ad 84.

[84] Cf. Konstan 1985, 27–28, 31–33: humor comes about only if an otherwise salutary desire "is represented as a pure obsession, detached, in the final analysis, from the acknowledged public value of its goal."

institution in which one can choose (wrongly) how involved one might be. The playful slaves can more safely evaluate their master negatively by building a name on a "positive" institution and letting name-calling patterns induce the listener to understand their negative judgment.

The Second Element, *Soph-*: A Focus on *Sophoi* ("Sages")

I have so far argued that the term present in the second element of a *phil-* pre-fixed name refers synecdochally to a social practice in which the person so named has excessively or at least markedly involved himself. But we need to identify the term before we can seek out the relevant social practice and excessive involvement. This may be easy for "oars" or "coy smiles," but is not for the root *soph-*, whose related terms, *sophos* and *sophia*, underwent radical changes from their earliest attestation in epic to their period of greatest philosophical familiarity, the Athenian fourth century BCE. Even if Plato and Aristotle did not themselves innovate when they treated *sophia* as a comprehensive wisdom concerning the nature of the world, more than a century had passed since the likely coinage of *philosophos*; and given the term *sophos*'s profound changes in meaning from 600 to 500 BCE, we can allow a change of similar magnitude during the subsequent century, one marked by ever-increasing consciousness of intellectual practice and status. Thus we cannot retroject the picture of *sophia* we see in their works; we need instead to historicize and study the words at the relevant time.

At the end of the sixth century BCE, the term *sophos* refers especially to the insight appropriate to giving advice for living, especially at the political level, though also at the social, domestic, and personal levels. By that period, *sophoi* had as archetypes the *Sophoi*, "Sages," of two generations earlier, intellectually and verbally prestigious consultants to cities and their denizens. The second element of the term *philosophos* points to some social practice for which *sophoi* play a key role, and to which *philosophoi* could be judged excessively or at least markedly and repeatedly involved. This surely includes giving guidance about living well, with the presumption of epistemic authority, with something like the goal of achieving the elite social status of the Sages.

We must begin with the Archaic background, where *sophos* means excellent at a specific skill, and then Theognis, where it broadens to mean excellent at living and advising. In Simonides and Pindar we get clear evidence for the term *sophos* as the valorization for those giving grave advice, typically with existential, social, or political moment, and not just in technical categories.

Epigraphical use shows conservativism, but it too eventually recapitulates the shift from specific skills to a general condition of excellence in living. We can rely little on the evidence from Heraclitus, who as we saw in the last chapter counts rather as a radical epistemologist than as a passive recorder of language, but the use of *sophos* in his fragments corroborates the shift in meaning we will have already seen. I close this section by hypothesizing the origins of *Sophoi* legends, which we can place in the century or more before Plato's *Protagoras*, which provides the first extant reference to the "Seven Sages," and thus to the period of probable coinage of the term *philosophos*—I look to the *polis* system, Persian incursion, and Babylonian precursors. Before turning to the lexical evidence, however, we will study a few late classical discussions of early uses of the term *sophos*.

Diodorus's story about Pythagoras presented *philosophoi* as emulators of a certain kind of person. This story assumes that the *soph-* second element does not refer simply to *sophia* conceived as "wisdom," a superlative degree of intelligent competence in living, but to membership in an elite social class with archetypal *Sophoi*, "Sages." The historical-linguistic question is whether by the time of the coinage of *philosophos*, in the late sixth or early fifth century BCE, the adjective/noun *sophos* or the abstract noun *sophia* could and commonly did refer to such a class. It is well known that by the fourth century BCE, Greeks saw in their sixth-century BCE past a cultural category of *Sophos*, "Sage," most recognizable in the stories of the Seven *Sophoi*.[85] But the Seven *Sophoi* are attested for the first time only in Plato's *Protagoras* (343a1–b3), written in the early fourth century BCE. This has led some people to believe that he invented the category.[86] This view is not utterly implausible, given that, as we will see, the term *sophos* appears to have meant "technically skilled" early in its career.[87]

Yet there are historiographical reasons for accepting the basic reality of Diodorus's story. In the first-generation Peripatetic Demetrius of Phalerum's chronological *List of Archons*, which is concerned to synchronize important Greek events, he says that Thales was the first to be called (a) *sophos*, dating this naming to the archonship of Damasias in 582 BCE, and that it is from that

[85] Recently, Martin 1993; Sharp 2004; Nightingale 2007, 173–78; Tell 2011, 15–17; Kurke 2011.

[86] Fehling 1985, critiqued by, among others, Martin 1993, 112–13; Bollansée 1998a and 1999; Leão 2010b, esp. 413–14; Engels 2010, 9–40; YC 1.267–71.

[87] The etymology of *sophos* is famously confounded; Boisacq 1938, 888 (with bibliography showing slight consensus around "seeing clearly"); Buck 1949, 1213–14; Frisk 1954, 4.754; Chantraine 1968 s.v.; Beekes 2010, s.v.; Rendich 2010, 268–69 ("good illumination"); Floyd 2012 ("sharp," "wedge"); Vernhes 2014a and 2014b; Sauge 2014, n10 (related to τεύχω, τυγχάνω).

date that the others of the Seven *Sophoi* came to be so called.[88] If this story is true—and all or most of the Seven *Sophoi* did live in the early sixth century BCE[89]—then the concept *sophos*, as a laudable status to be granted or recognized, would have existed from the time of the Sages themselves. Thus the idea would predate the coinage of *philosophos*, and allow the formation of a recognized status for which I argue. Unfortunately, the story does not say who certified Thales as *sophos*, or for what, even if we suspect that it was for winning a verbal competition at a Panhellenic festival.[90] Given Demetrius's calendrical preoccupations, he may simply have meant that Thales came to Panhellenic prominence, for example for predicting an eclipse, around 582 BCE. Yet we need not doubt Demetrius's story altogether. Demetrius collected and published "Sayings of the Seven *Sophoi*," revealing his explicit interest in the *sophoi* as *Sophoi* (Stob. 3.1.172). Earlier writers anticipated his account of Thales and his colleagues. In Plato's *Protagoras*, Socrates, speaking of Thales and others, says that the "so-called Seven . . . came together and dedicated the first fruits of their *sophia* to Apollo at his temple in Delphi."[91] This might imply that the Oracle claimed Thales to be *sophos* or *sophôtatos*, as it claimed of Socrates in the fifth century BCE (and that Chaerephon's idea to ask about Socrates came from such stories circulating in the fifth century BCE), or that at the Pythian games, founded at that period, Thales won an award or competition in something related to being (what was then considered) *sophos*. Andron of Ephesus, a contemporary of Plato, agreed that "those also denoted *Sophoi* were contemporaneous with Thales."[92] Andron is responsible for one of the famous "competition of the *Sophoi*" stories circulating in Greece: "the Argives gave a tripod as an award for virtue to the *sophôtatos* of the Greeks; Aristodemus of Sparta

---

[88] DL 1.22: πρῶτος σοφὸς ὠνομάσθη . . . καθ' ὃν καὶ οἱ ἑπτὰ σοφοὶ ἐκλήθησαν. For discussion of this story, see Mosshammer 1976; Leão 2010a, 28–31; Rossetti 2015a, 214–21; and on Peripatetic research into the Seven *Sophoi*, see Fortenbaugh 2014, 115–19. Compare the story found at Hdt. 2.160.

[89] Hellenistic chronographers dated the apogee of the Seven to 585, at the midpoint of Alyattes's reign, when Thales supposedly predicted the eclipse.

[90] DL 1.29–30 attributes to the Academic Eudoxus of Cnius and to a certain Eunathus of Miletus the claim that a friend of Croesus is the one who honored Thales as wisest of the Greeks.

[91] Pl. *Prt.* 343a5–b2 (for discussion see Leão 2010b). Pind. fr. 209 may provide evidence for a provenance of this story from at least the early fifth century BCE: τοὺς φυσιολογοῦντας ἔφη Πίνδαρος· ἀτελῆ σοφίας καρπὸν δρέπ(ειν) ("the physiologists, says Pindar, 'pick wisdom's unripe fruit'"). If only the second half is Pindaric, we wonder to whom Pindar originally referred; but he seems to have in mind people related to but worse than those who pick *sophia* when ripe, presumably the *sophoi* themselves.

[92] Clem. *Strom.* 1.129.4: συνεχρόνισαν δὲ οἱ συγκαταλεγέντες σοφοὶ τῷ Θαλεῖ. Andron's dates: Bollansée 1998b.

won, but he gave it to Chilon" (DL 1.30–31). Other tellers claim that a golden tripod drinking-cup was found and given to a *Sophos* for his reputed wisdom, but then passed along to other *Sophoi* out of modesty, and eventually dedicated to Apollo in Delphi. Yet another version, apparently partway between Andron's and these, posits a single person awarding the prize to the wisest of the Greeks, the ownership transferred from one to another, and then dedicated to Apollo or, on Apollo's request, left with the final recipient. Though we know these folktales only from the early fourth century BCE, their variety points to a long and early provenance for the concept of *sophos* and an archetypal class of *Sophoi*.[93] Whether the concept goes all the way back to 582 BCE, as a literal reading of Demetrius requires, remains uncertain. We must instead assess the meaning of *sophos* across its earliest uses, to see when it could designate the kind of widely prized practical competence represented by the (Seven) *Sophoi*. We will find that it in fact does designate this by Pythagoras's era, the end of the sixth century BCE, and thus becomes available to be built into a *phil*-prefixed name that means what Diodorus's presumably fourth-century BCE source took it to mean.

Evolving Pre-Classical Uses of *Sophos*

In the earliest extant uses of *sophos*, the term refers to laudable competence in a to-be-specified practice. Archilochus, in the seventh century, speaks of a "good fisherman(?) and *sophos* pilot."[94] Homer speaks of a *sophos* builder (τέκτων) and of a builder who knows all (pertinent) *sophiai*.[95] Hesiod uses the related verb in reference to skill at seafaring.[96] The Homeric *Margites*, written by the time of Archilochus' adulthood, has a man who is neither digger nor plowman, "nor indeed *sophos* in any other way, falling short in all *technai*"

---

[93] Hes. *Op.* 657 testifies to the awarding of tripods to poets; see Bollansée 1998a; Kurke 2011, 110–11; Verhasselt forthcoming, §3. Hdt. 8.124.1–2 says that after the victory at Salamis, Themistocles was "reputed wisest" (ἐδοξώθη . . . σοφώτατος) and received a wreath from the Spartans for his wisdom (σοφίης). Isoc. *Antid.* 313 says that Solon was the first Athenian to receive the name "sophist" (λαβόντα τὴν ἐπωνυμίαν ταύτην [sc. σοφιστής]); since Isocrates refers to the Seven *Sophoi* as the Seven *Sophistai* (*Antid.* 235), he too implies an early tradition of deeming people exemplarily *sophos*.

[94] Fr. 211 W: τρίαιναν ἐσθλὸς καὶ κεβερνήτης σοφός. The *sophos*-pilot trope arises again at Aesch. *Supp.* 770. The meaning of τρίαιναν is unclear; cf. LSJ s.v. A ("three-pronged fish-spear," "the badge of Poseidon") against Edmonds 1931 ad loc. ("steersman").

[95] Hom. *Il.* 23.712 (σοφὸς ἤραρε τέκτων, a variant reading found in Philoponus and referred to in Eustathius's comments on *Iliad* 15.412 [instead of κλυτὸς]; see "Homerus" F2 *EGF*); *Il.* 15.411–12 (πάσης | εὖ εἰδῇ σοφίης). On Homeric *tektôn* see YC 1.46–50.

[96] Hes. *Op.* 649 (οὔτε τι ναυτιλίης σεσοφισμένος οὔτε τι νηῶν); see YC 1.162–69.

(fr. 2 W).[97] *Sophiai*—or more properly, ways of being *sophos*—are differentiated in the way *technai* are.[98] There is no being *sophos* simpliciter. Assume, contrafactually, that there is a state of *sophos toioutôi*, "*sophos* in whatever." This would make *sophoi* or *sophoi andres* mean something like "professionals." We could imagine a class of professionals—especially when doing macroeconomics or social theory—but not of the Seven Professionals. So it does not yet mean anything like "Sage."

By the sixth century BCE the use of *sophos* changes drastically. Theognis (fl. 544 BCE) writes that the *sophos* man can spot counterfeit gold and silver.[99] He speaks not of an expert or professional in metallurgy but of the person who, with a worldly sensibility, sees through deceit and confusion. Elsewhere Theognis uses *sophos* and *sophia* to refer to this worldliness and a competence with respect to human nature, opposites of a credulous naïveté or social ignorance. Theognis does not conceptualize or typify *sophoi* as Sages. But he does use the term *sophos* to refer collectively to qualities that the Greeks came to apply to the Sages: keen judgment about others, the wherewithal to persuade them, and a self-knowledge that amounts to turning that social sensitivity on oneself.[100] *Sophos* takes this most general form in the "Ages of Man" poem by Theognis's contemporary, Solon: according to the poem, a sixty-year-old

---

[97] Arist. *Eth. Nic.* 1141a15 + Clem. *Strom.* 1.25.1: τὸν δ᾽ οὔτ᾽ ἂρ σκαπτῆρα θεοὶ θέσαν οὔτ᾽ ἀροτῆρα | οὔτ᾽ ἄλλως τι σοφόν· πάσης δ᾽ ἡμάρτανε τέχνης. See Gostoli 2007, 11 and 75, for dating and analysis of *sophos* as "expertise."

[98] *Sophos* again modifies *tektôn* in (Pindar's?) description of Alcman, reconstructed as τέκτον(-) πα]ρθενίων σοφῶν, "carpenter of skillfully-produced maiden songs" (Alcm. fr. 13(a), first published in 1957). Alcm. fr. 2(i).1 and Anac. fr. 72.2 (μ᾽ οὐδὲν εἰδέναι σοφόν) have *sophos* in terms of horsemanship (the latter metaphorically for the skill of sexual conquest). Bacchyl. 10.37–45 says that different men take different paths, specializing in different "fields of knowledge" (*epistêmai*), such that one man is *sophos* by sharing the honor of the Graces; one by having knowledge of prophecy; one by aiming an artful bow at boys; and one in animal husbandry, presumably including horsemanship.

[99] Thgn. 120: καὶ ἐξευρεῖν ῥάδιον ἀνδρὶ σοφῷ; cf. LSJ s.v. σοφός A.2, "worldly-wise."

[100] Thgn. 876: "the one having a measured wisdom" (μέτρον ἔχων σοφίης) knows that wine deserves both praise and blame; this involves an appreciation of variable effects on people. 1074: the *sophia* that involves turning a versatile *êthos* toward one's various friends is better than "great virtue" (and contrasted with inflexibility at 218). 563–65: one ought to learn from a good man who knows all *sophiai* sitting next to you whenever he says something *sophos*; apparently this means tips on how to live, not lessons in particular technical skills. 790: the narrator would substitute nothing for his "excellence in/and *sophia*" (ἀρετῆς σοφίης), the cultivation of his mind among good people (μετὰ τῶν ἀγαθῶν ἐσθλὸν ἔχοιμι νόον, 792), which must again refer to social competence. 502: drunkenness puts to shame the person previously *sophos*, which means either that it undoes one's careful comportment or that it shows that that comportment and self-control do not go deep; see Ford 2002, 40–41, for context.

lacks the power of speech and *sophia* for great acts of excellence that he once had.[101]

In two poets who came of age (and thus linguistic maturity) in the late sixth century BCE we see irrefutably the rise of the relevant concept of *sophos* as Sage. Pindar (b. 518 BCE) has a delightfully paradoxical verse: "even about the saying *mêden agan* ['nothing in excess'] the *sophoi* spoke excessively!"[102] In a victory ode from around 470 BCE, Pindar cites another maxim, "money, money is the man"; joking that only those in great distress think this is true, he dismisses such talk by acknowledging that his listener is *sophos*.[103] Being *sophos* thus means being familiar with universalizing maxims and their human contexts of application.[104] Alcaeus had already attributed this maxim to Aristodemus of Sparta, a man later to be considered one of the Seven Sages.[105] In 462 BCE, Pindar presents a speech by Jason that begins with gnomic insight about the minds of mortals, the priority of justice over deceit, the importance of self-control, and the responsibility one must take for one's eventual success, and calls this a speech of "*sophos* words."[106]

One reference, in Pindar's Seventh *Olympian*, deserves close scrutiny because it provides, if ambiguously, the closest we might find to an origin of the idea of the Seven Sages, the group mentioned in Diodorus's Pythagoras story. As part of the epinician's celebration of the Rhodian tyrant Diagoras, Pindar narrates the island's founding myth: Helius fathered with Rhodos the sons who were the "seven wisest in thought of that earlier generation of men" (ἑπτὰ σοφώτατα νοήματ' ἐπὶ προτέρων ἀνδρῶν παραδεξαμένους | παῖδας, *Ol.* 7.72–73). This provocative collocation of "seven," "wisest," and "earlier generation" correlates with the background conditions appropriate to the rise of a concept of Seven *Sophoi*.[107] Earlier in the poem Pindar twice mentioned

[101] Sol. fr. 27.16. See Noussia-Fantuzzi 2010, 369–90, esp. 387–88.

[102] Pind. *Hymn* 1 fr. 35b: σοφοὶ δὲ καὶ τὸ μηδὲν ἄγαν ἔπος αἴνησαν περισσῶς.

[103] Pind. *Isthm.* 2.10–12: "χρήματα χρήματ' ἀνήρ" | ὃς φᾶ κτεάνων θ' ἅμα λειφθεὶς καὶ φίλων. | ἐσσὶ γὰρ ὢν σοφός.

[104] Pind. *Pyth.* 3.80–84 also treats of the depth of insight needed for understanding gnomic insight, with four epistemic terms (though none are *sophos*-group terms): "Hieron, if you know correctly how to comprehend the epitome(?) of sayings (εἰ δὲ λόγων συνέμεν κορυφάν, Ἱέρων, ὀρθὰν ἐπίστᾳ), then having learned (μανθάνων) the ancient ones (προτέρων), you understand (οἶσθα): [a gnomic statement found in Hom. *Il.* 24.527–530]"; on κορυφάν as either "sum total," "sense," or "height of," see LSJ s.v. II.1–2 with Ford 2002, 79 (who translates "a choice part").

[105] Alcaeus fr. 360 *PLF*: χρήματ' ἄνηρ, πένιχρος δ' οὐδεὶς πέλετ' ἔσλος (though with spelling of οὐδεὶς at DL 1.31).

[106] Pind. *Pyth.* 4.138–41: σοφῶν ἐπέων... ἐντὶ μὲν θνατῶν φρένες ὠκύτεραι | κέρδος αἰνῆσαι πρὸ δίκας δόλιον τραχεῖαν ἑρπόντων πρὸς ἐπιβδαν ὅμως· | ἀλλ' ἐμὲ χρὴ καὶ σὲ θεμισσαμένους ὀργὰς ὑφαίνειν λοιπὸν ὄλβον; cf. *Dithyramb* 2 fr. 70b.24.

[107] On groups of seven in Greek mythology, see Roscher 1904, 4–53 (20–21 on Helius) and Gernet and Boulanger 1970, 82. Bresson 1979, 32–33, 41, 121, and Verdenius 1972, 23, 27, deny

sophos-group terms, both times in reference to a generalized human excellence.[108] All the while, Pindar uses the poem to retail a two-tier provision of the goods of civilization: first Athena's *technai*, especially in pottery and culture, and then Helius's *sophôtatoi*, implicated in Rhodian political success, in particular in the founding of three polities.[109] Zeno of Rhodes (mid-second century BCE) clarifies that this myth treats Rhodes as the cradle of *all* civilization—including the techniques of learning, astrology, navigation, and time-keeping—even of Egypt, which served merely as high ground for their discoveries when they were flooded out.[110] This story is in turn quite like the account the Hellenistic Babylonian historian Berossus, which involves flood-prediction, burial of writings, and a sail to safety,[111] and another Babylonian account of Seven Babylonian sages mentioned below. Thus, since we know of no Rhodian mythology of Seven *Sophoi* (or *Sophôtatoi*) before Pindar, and Zeno of Rhodes's account seems to be in some way an elaboration of Pindar's, it is possible that Pindar himself came up with this formulation, influenced (if indirectly) by Babylonian ideas. The efficacy of Pindar's mythmaking is well-known.[112] The fact that *Olympian* 7 was famous for being inscribed in gold

---

a reference here to the Seven *Sophoi* on the—to my mind, weak—grounds that whereas Sages have moral wisdom, Helius's sons have technical ability (Farnell 1932, 55, believes that when Pindar, in line 53, refers to *sophia* he means the artist's skill, but does not coordinate this with line 72), whereas Hirzel (cited in Martin 1993, 127n45) entertains the idea. For disagreements about the meaning of the line itself, including the source and relative superiority of the sons' wisdom, see Paley 1868, 36n2; Seymour 1889, 116; Fennell 1893, 81; Wilamowitz-Moellendorff 1922, 366–68; Fernandez-Galiano 1956, 228; and Gentili 2013, 495. For the founding myth of Rhodes, see *EGM* 2.591–93. We know about Helius's seven sons only from this poem and DS 5.57.1, where their excellence in "astrology" and thus in navigation and meteorology is noted (οἱ δ᾿ Ἡλιάδαι διάφοροι γενηθέντες τῶν ἄλλων ἐν παιδείᾳ διήνεγκαν καὶ μάλιστ᾿ ἐν ἀστρολογίᾳ. εἰσηγήσαντο δὲ καὶ περὶ τῆς ναυτιλίας πολλὰ καὶ τὰ περὶ τὰς ὥρας διέταξαν).

[108] First, Pindar says that even someone *sophos* can lose his mind (αἱ δὲ φρενῶν ταραχαί | παρέπλαγξαν καὶ σοφόν) but then still go to the Oracle (*Ol.* 7.30–31); Pindar is thinking of the self-controlled person who, while imperfect and sub-divine, recognizes where authority and prudence lie. Second, Pindar defends the excellence of *sophia*—here associated though not identified with craftsmanship—as free of the deception or inauthenticity such apparent skill might be thought to involve (δαέντι δὲ καὶ σοφίᾳ μείζων ἄδολος τελέθει, 53).

[109] Pind. *Ol.* 7.74–76: ἀπάτερθε δ᾿ ἔχον | διὰ γαῖαν τρίχα δασσάμενοι πατρωίαν, | ἀστέων μοῖραν, κέκληνται δέ σφιν ἕδραι. This account appears to presage Protagoras's "Great Speech" about Prometheus and Epimetheus in Plato's *Protagoras* (320c8–323d2), in its reference to προμαθέος αἰδώς (*Ol.* 7.44; see Moore 2015a, 408–15), its two-tier promulgation of technical and then political capabilities, and the parallel between Epimetheus's failure to distribute competencies to humans and the gods' failure to distribute land to Helius (58), which is solved by cunning and foresight (61–70). It is notable that the *Protagoras* is also the dialogue in which the Seven Sages are first discussed in extant literature.

[110] DS 5.55–57.

[111] *BNJ* 680 F4b.

[112] See Morgan 2015 for Pindar's political efficacy.

letters on the Temple of Athena Lindia makes this poem uniquely situated to contribute to the idea of the Seven *Sophoi*.[113]

Aside from these speculations about the Seven in *Olympian* 7, the passage shows that, for Pindar, *sophia* refers to more than poetic skill, even if it also means this in Pindar.[114] Indeed, the poetic *sophos* might just be a special case or instantiation of a generally good and insightful counselor.[115] Even when *sophos* does refer specifically to poetic skill, Pindar's poetic skill has a deep and systemic function as political advice-giving.[116] His greatest poems are written to activate and manage the norms accepted by the leading great and mighties of early fifth-century BCE Greece. This advisory competence is thought of as distinct from mechanical abilities or facts and theories learned by rote, and thus it is considered as potentially universally available. Pindar says that the *sophoi* have their knowledge by nature, in contrast to those who merely learn, who are boisterous and chattering.[117] This is consistent with later doxographers, who, like Diodorus, almost never mention the education of the Sages.[118] The wise, Pindar says, are deemed

---

[113] Gorgon of Rhodes in Σ Pind. *Ol.* 7.

[114] For *sophos* as referring to the poet's skill in Pindar, see the references in Slater 1969, s.v. b, and discussion of pre-474 usages in YC 2.16–41. Earlier: Hes. fr. 256 (παντοίης σοφίης δεδαηκότα, referring to the citharist Linus); Sol. fr. 13.52 (ἱμερτῆς σοφίης μέτρον ἐπιστάμενος, referring to that provided by the Olympian muses; see Ford 2002, 18; Noussia-Fantuzzi 2010, 184–85); Ibyc. S151.23 (καὶ τὰ μὲ[ν ἂν] Μοῖσαι σεσοφι[σ]μέναι | εὖ Ἑλικωνίδ[ες] ἐμβαίεν †λόγω[ι; see Murray 1981, 90n21; Verdenius 1983, 42n132; Woodbury 1985, 200); Stesichorus S89.7–8 *PMG* (δαεὶς ... μέτ[ρα] τε καὶ σοφίαν του[; see Lehnus 1972). Alcm. 16.2–3 (context: those who would judge Alcman's skill; but παρὰ σοφοῖσιν is marked uncertain); *Hom. Hymn Herm.* 483, 511. See generally Noussia-Fantuzzi 2010, 359–61. Sappho 56.2 *PLF*, in which Sappho says that she does not expect another maiden to surpass her addressee (or herself?) in *sophia*, has uncertain meaning.

[115] Pindar thanks his divinely supported "wise mind" for his success in praising Hagesidamus (ἐκ θεοῦ δ᾽ ἀνὴρ σοφαῖς ἀνθεῖ πραπίδεσσιν ὁμοίως, *Ol.* 11.10–11). Cf. *Nem.* 8.40–41: αὔξεται δ᾽ ἀρετά ... <ἐν> σοφοῖς ἀνδρῶν. On a more banal level, later in *Ol.* 11, Pindar praises the Locrians in southern Italy for being welcoming, experienced in excellent things (καλῶν), martially accomplished, and "most wise" (ἀκρόσοφόν, 16–19).

[116] Thus the vaunting by Xenophanes B2/D61 of the civic value of his own (poetic, reformative, intellectual) *sophia* over the physical prowess of athletes (lines 11–14); see Ford 2002, 49–52.

[117] Pind. *Ol.* 2.87–88: σοφὸς ὁ πολλ᾽ εἰδὼς φυᾷ· μαθόντες δὲ λάβροι | παγγλωσσίᾳ; cf. *Pyth.* 1.42, where the wise are born that way (σοφοὶ ... ἔφυν). In *Ol.* 9.28–29, the wise become so in accordance with the divine (ἀγαθοὶ δὲ καὶ σοφοὶ κατὰ δαίμον᾽ ἄνδρες | ἐγένοντ᾽); cf. *Pyth.* 5.12–13, 8.74–76.

[118] In Diogenes Laertius, this means Solon, Chilon, Pittacus, Bias, Cleobulus, Periander, Anacharsis, and Epimenides. Thales is said to have had no teacher (οὐδεὶς δὲ αὐτοῦ καθηγήσατο, 1.27), except that he once spent time with (συνδείτριψεν) some priests in Egypt. Pherecydes, only sometimes taken to be a *Sophos*, learned from (διακήκοεν) Pittacus. As we saw earlier in this chapter, Diodorus Siculus provides educational anecdotes only for Solon. In some cases, *Sophoi* are said to have travelled (Szegedy-Maszak 1978; Montiglio 2000, 88–89; Ker 2000; Nightingale 2004; Kurke 2011, 112–15), but travel differs from study, lessons, or mentorship.

so by their fellow citizens when they have triumphed over difficulties; they may have wisdom about the gods and justice unavailable to other mortals; and they recognize the unpredictability of the future, the dangers of self-interest, and the prudence of restraint.[119] Putting this evidence together, we see that Pindar has a sense of the *sophoi* as notable persons, including poet advisors, characterized by the use of maxims and gnomic statements, where their having *sophia* means living a successful way of life—one that does not come explicitly through striving—and an understanding of fundamental aspects of human life and practices.

In case any question remains that Pindar could have a notion of the *sophoi* who use maxims and compete for position in a cultural-intellectual hierarchy, we need only look to his older contemporary Simonides (ca. 556–468 BCE). In his *Ode to Scopas*, which is analyzed in Plato's *Protagoras*, Simonides calls Pittacus *sophos* for having expressed the maxim "hard it is to be good (χαλεπὸν ἐσθλὸν ἔμμεναι)."[120] Pittacus came to be one of the legendary Seven, and here Simonides seeks to dislodge him from his status as advice-giver to the Greeks. Elsewhere Simonides challenges Cleobulus, another of the eventual Seven, on the question of fame.[121] What we see in Pindar and Simonides we see, simultaneously, in (mostly Attic) epigraphical evidence. In the later sixth century BCE, *sophia* and *sophos* refer to excellence in specific skills.[122] But by the first decades of the fifth century BCE, on the Athenian Acropolis, we can read:

[ἐσθλὸν] τοῖσι σοφοῖσι σο[φ]ίζεσθ[αι κ]ατ[ὰ τέχνων]
[hὸς γὰρ] *héχει τέχνεν λοῖ[ο]ν· héχει β[ίοτον]* (*IG* I³ 766)

admirable it is for sophoi to exercise themselves in their skill—
for he who has a skill leads a better life

While this does not refer to a College of *Sophoi*, it points to the increasing genericization and collectivization of *sophoi*, the abstraction of their competence to goodness, and the boon to overall livelihood (*bioton*).

---

[119] Pind. *Ol.* 5.16; *Pae.* 6 fr. 52f.50–53; *Nem.* 7.17–18, 5.18.

[120] Simon. fr. 542, Pl. *Prt.* 343b7; cf. Moore 2016.

[121] Simon. fr. 581; see Ford 2002, 105–9. Simonides may have had competitive success; Pl. *R.* 335e9–10 includes him with Bias and Pittacus among the illustrious *Sophoi*, and he spent time with *turannoi*; cf. Slings 2000, 62–63; Wallace 2015, 6–8, 14–15.

[122] *Sophia*: medicine (*IG* I³ 1393; cf. Wickkiser 2008, 18–19), pottery (*IG* I² 522), unknown (*IG* I³ 949), poetry (*IG* I³ 833 bis; 480–70 BCE); *sophos*: sculpture (*IG* I³ 1265), horsemanship and hospitality (*IG* VII 3501; Boeotia).

Pindar and Simonides have a contemporary in Heraclitus. In four fragments he substantivizes the adjective *sophos*, referring to *to sophon*. This could refer to the *content* of *sophia*, were *sophia* an intentional state, like knowledge; it could also refer to the state of being *sophos*. In these four fragments he speaks of *to sophon* as "one" and distinct, separate, presumably, from the range of pieces of knowledge a person might otherwise have.[123] The abstract noun *sophia* apparently objectifies this state of being *sophos*. Heraclitus speaks of the *sophôtatos* person as like an ape relative to god in terms of *sophiai*; exercising discipline is the greatest virtue and *sophia*; and, as we saw in chapter 2, Pythagoras is said to have devised a personal and highly dubious *sophia*.[124] Heraclitus does not speak explicitly of *sophoi* as Sages. But he speaks of being *sophos* as a unified state, in contrast to the earlier "professional of *x*" state; he talks about gnomic maxims and their understanding as characteristic of the *sophoi*; he refers to the political relevance of *sophia*; and he praises Bias— eventually thought of as the leading *Sophos*—as better than all other men. Thus even Heraclitus seems to have an (implicit or abstract) idea of the Sages.

Thus we have sufficient reason to posit an idea of *sophoi* as sages by the late sixth century BCE. It matters little that this fails to get us all the way back to Thales himself, as Demetrius supposed. Indeed, we might suppose that the idea could only have succeeded the lives of its archetypes. Here I conjecture a dynamic of formation, though it would take another book to substantiate it. The Greek *polis*-system that arose in the late seventh and early sixth centuries BCE underwent remarkable strain in the late sixth century, with Ionia experiencing increasing threat from the Persians, colonial enterprises feeling mixed allegiances, and cities dividing along class and Medizing lines. Citizens looked to models that promised civic amelioration. Adopting the skepticism of mythical paradigms found in Xenophanes and Hecataeus, they restricted their horizon to historical time and thus waxed nostalgic for their grandparents' generation.[125] There they found a series of successful political advisors, some

---

[123] Heraclitus B32/D45: ἓν τὸ σοφόν, μοῦνον λέγεσθαι οὐκ ἐθέλει καὶ ἐθέλει Ζηνὸς ὄνομα; B41/D44: ἓν τὸ σοφόν, ἐπίστασθαι γνώμην, ὅτέη ἐκυβέρνησε πάντα διὰ πάντων; B50/D46: οὐκ ἐμοῦ ἀλλὰ τοῦ λόγου ἀκούσαντες ὁμολογεῖν σοφόν ἐστιν ἓν πάντα εἶναι; B108/D43: ὁκόσων λόγους ἤκουσα, οὐδεὶς ἀφικνεῖται ἐς τοῦτο ὥστε γινώσκειν ὅτι σοφόν ἐστι πάντων κεχωρισμένον.

[124] Heraclitus B83/D77: ἀνθρώπων ὁ σοφώτατος πρὸς θεὸν πίθηκος φανεῖται καὶ σοφίη καὶ κάλλει καὶ τοῖς ἄλλοις πᾶσιν; B112/D114a+b: σωφρονεῖν ἀρετὴ μεγίστη καὶ σοφίη ἀληθέα λέγειν καὶ ποιεῖν κατὰ φύσιν ἐπαίοντας (cf. B118/D103: αὐὴ ψυχή, σοφωτάτη καὶ ἀρίστη); B129/D26.

[125] A similar dynamic is apparent from, e.g., Aristophanes's *Frogs* where the city's salvation seems to be in replicating its best citizens from two generations earlier, 490–80 BCE. Compare this "nostalgic" view with Wallace 2015, 13: "During the seminal decades 600–580, in response to the corruption of tyrants and the ineffectiveness of laws, a new type of political figure, the

never *tyrannoi* themselves, others—Solon, Pittacus, and Periander—having
had constitutional roles.[126] Bias, for example, was persuasive in legal contexts,
advised the Ionians to flee to Sardinia to escape the Persians, tried to broker
a deal between Samos and Priene, and deceived Alyattes into abandoning his
siege of Priene; he may also have written a two-thousand-line poem about a
path to Ionian prosperity.[127] Chilon was the first ephor of Sparta, strengthen-
ing that position's role against the kings' position, and opposing tyrannies
in Greece.[128] Dicaearchus later remembered these sagely *sophoi* as "shrewd
legislators."[129] These same eminent forebears were vaguely remembered for
having shared their grandparentish wisdom, expressed in easy-to-recall gnomic maxims. With this political and linguistic skill we might include, as derivatives or adjuncts, religious knowledge and poetic skill, but without any
specific competence in mind.[130]

    This formation of the legends of various *sophoi*, initially in their respec-
tive cities, could develop, with itinerant poets and traders, into a generalized
category.[131] Their hebdomality would have postdated this incremental accumulation. One possibility is that the pattern "Group of Seven" found in
Greek mythology set its mark on this category. But groups of nine and three
also proliferated, and the Sages are not mythological. A better possibility presents itself from evidence from Babylon, as I mentioned above. In 1960,

---

sophos or *sophistês*, offered wise counsel, mediation in civil strife, and political leadership to
many Greek communities."

[126] On Solon as politician see Noussia-Fantuzzi 2010, 19–44. Pittacus was a legal expert and
creator of laws (νόμων δημιουργός, Arist. *Pol.* 1274b18; νομοθέτης τε γὰρ ἀγαθός, DS 9 fr. 16;
νόμους δὲ ἔθηκε, DL 1.76), a "chosen tyrant" (αἰσυμνήτας, Arist. *Pol.* 1285a30); and removed
tyranny, civil strife, inequality, and war; see generally Bowra 1961, 136; Gagarin 1986, 59.
Periander planned a track across the Isthmus (DL 1.99) and arbitrated Athens's dispute with
Mytilene over Sigeon (Hdt. 5.95.2), all the while maintaining connections with Arcardia, Delphi, Olympia, Miletus, Lydia, and Egypt.

[127] Persuasive: Hipponax fr. 123 W; Demodocus fr. 6 W; Heraclitus B39/D11; diplomacy:
Hdt. 1.170; Plut. *Quaest. graec.* 20 295e; poem: DL 1.85 (see Martin 1993, 118; *BNP* s.v. "Bias
[2]"; *BNJ* 439). He received special honors after his death (DL 1.85, 1.88). See also Konstantakos
2005. The claim by Ford 2002, 78, that he was a "tyrant-sage," probably fits Pittacus better (see
Arist. *Pol.* 1285a35–39; DL 1.74–76, 79).

[128] DL 1.68; *BNJ* 105 F1; cf. DL 1.73, Paus. 3.16.4, *BNP* s.v. "Chilon [1]."

[129] DL 1.40: συνετοὺς δέ τινας καὶ νομοθετικούς; *sunetoi* means understanding in practical affairs, per Arist. *Eth. Nic.* 1142b34–43a18. Cf. Plut. *Them.* 2.4 on Themistocles's teacher
Mnesophilus, whose *sophia*, sourced in Solon, concerns "political cleverness and practical understanding" (δεινότητα πολιτικὴν καὶ δραστήριον σύνεσιν); on this passage, see Kerferd 1950,
9; Kurke 2011, 173; Tell 2015, 10–11.

[130] Lattimore 1939; Chroust 1947, 20–22; Kerferd 1950, 8–9; Kerferd 1976, 26–28; Kerferd
1981, 24; Vernant 1982 [= Vernant 1962], 69–81; Munn 2000, 16; Hadot 2002, 18–21. For a collection of sources see Snell 1943.

[131] Tell 2007, 266–72, speculates that *sophoi* did in fact associate as an "international elite."

German archaeologists unearthed a tablet from Anu's Bīt Rēš temple, where Gilgamesh ruled nearly five millennia ago.[132] That tablet, the "Uruk List of Kings and Sages," which is from 165 BCE but is copied from an earlier version, lists the seven "sages" (*apkallu*) of antediluvian Mesopotamia, each yoked to the king he advises. After the flood, there are no further groups of seven, only a single sage and eight scholars who again advise their respective rulers (*unmânu*).[133] Though the Babylonians listed their sages serially, not in parallel, the Greeks could have adopted the "Seven *Sophoi*" from them and distributed them geographically rather than temporally, as befits Greece's decentralized political organization.[134]

The point relevant to the coinage of *philosophos* is that in the late 500s BCE, *sophos* labeled less an exceptional intelligence or prudence than a kind of person who could give exceptional practical advice to political figures as well as timeless advice to fellow citizens in the generations to come.[135] This usage may have evolved from the earlier "excellent sailor" usage: as Socrates points out in Plato's *Apology* (22e1), those who are masters of their craft often gain a reputation as masters of much more. This extension can have firm grounding: a good sailor may need good captaining skills as well, which include insight into matters of justice and thoughtfulness; anyway, as the moral virtues seem unified in some respects, so too might the skills.[136] By and large, excepting the uses found in Heraclitus, which prove the rule in their self-conscious innovation, being *sophos* is a term for social engagement and problem-solving in a way that is publicly determined and applauded. This suggests that, when -*êretmos* is attached as second element to *phil*-, the term *philêretmos* points to being a hardy sailor; -*meidês* makes a term pointing to a practice of coy lovers, -*sophos* to a practice of exceptional civic advisors. So, just as "lover of oars" does not rightly gloss the meaning of *phileretmos*, "lover of wisdom" misrepresents the meaning of *philosophos*. The word does not just clinch the phrase; it coins a new one.

---

[132] Panel W 20030,7, published by van Dijk 1962 and reproduced in van Dijk and Mayer 1980, vol. 2, no. 89.

[133] See Reiner 1961 for another Akkadian text, LKA 76 rev., that speaks of "seven *apkallu*," with an argument (now perhaps otiose) that sages differ from their paired rulers. For the relation between sages and scribes, see Lambert 1957, 1, 9; Lambert 1962, 74. For discussion of the Uruk List of Kings and Sages, see Lenzi 2008.

[134] Cf. Burkert 1992, 106–14; Martin 1993, 121–23 (adding Vedic Sanskrit tradition and his own hypothesis).

[135] For an evolution of *sophia* that does not focus on the rise of the status of *sophoi*, see Ford 1993, 34–35; Kurke 2011, 95–102; Wolfsdorf forthcoming b.

[136] Compare the philosophical navigator of the Platonic "ship of state" (*R.* 488d5–489d1).

Conclusion: Occasioning the Composition of a *Phil-* Prefixed Name-Calling Name

The pattern familiar from the history of *phil-* prefixed names is that they lack an attitudinal component; lack a literally-referred-to object; are other-applied; are often bemused or derisive; and have the second element, typically on the surface a neutral or good thing, that stands in for some conventional social practice or system.

The following is what I take to be a plausible coinage-situation for *philosophos*. Suppose there were certain young men earnestly engaged in study and conversation. Such study would not appear to onlookers to be connected to any of the usual sort of learned trades. Perhaps these men act like students or apprentices. But students of what discipline, apprentices to what experts? It looks like they want to know about the *kosmos*, about the gods, about justice, about life and death. Expertise in such abstract and general topics is the province of the *sophoi* considered as wise advisors ("sages"). Thus it seems that one could explain these people only by saying they want to become *sophoi*. But in the traditional patterns one does not train to become a *sophos*; at some mature age, one simply has become deserving of the name *sophos*. A young man studying to become *sophos* is an odd, even risible idea. It is not obvious that such study could be successful; it may even be hubristic. The *sophoi* of legend got that way through remarkable self-application in warfare, leadership, agriculture, writing, and travel. Such practical experience, even if accompanied by copious reflection and discussion, is what contributes to one's wisdom. Aspirants to *sophos*-status would, it would seem, be better off trying to live well than thinking about living well. That is the eudaimonistic paradox. All the same, here are some people who seem to be trying to shortcut the route to *sophos* status. These aspirants are a funny group, with a funny social longing. They are marked by their peculiar attitude to the convention called "being *sophos*." The *phil-* prefix denotes this markedness. *Philosophoi* would be coined to classify certain people as, at least on the surface, aiming to be deemed *sophoi*.

It is important to distinguish this from the psychological translation, "love of wisdom." To say that someone loves wisdom is to purport to make a factual claim about the objects of that person's interest. The person who loves wisdom is a person who cares about, aims toward, or desires a certain cognitive achievement, a kind of knowledge or intellectual competence or theoretical virtue. Contrast this with name-calling connected to social conventions. In name-calling situations, to say that someone traffics in being *sophos* is to say that it looks as though a person strives to gain a certain cultural status and authority, a status and authority that likely cannot be attained in the manner on display.

What students would these be? They would need to be numerous, publicly visible, and influential enough to be worthy of classification or castigation. They would also need to exist over a long enough period for the name to acquire durability. In the next chapter, I propose that they may be Pythagoreans.

Pythagoreans as *Philosophoi*

Pythagoreans in Croton

Chapter 1 showed that the Pythagoras story, one version of which depends on Heraclides, links the term *philosophos* to Pythagoras. Chapter 2 showed that Heraclitus speaks of *philosophoi andres* in ways that suggest a possible reference to Pythagoreans. Chapter 3 showed that the coinage of the term *philosophos* probably came from the impulse to name a group of people who acted abnormally with respect to sagehood. This chapter argues that the Pythagoreans—a politically-organizing, quasi-religious group in southern Italy, according to Walter Burkert (1972, 113–19, 132)—could be this group, and it supports a historical linkage between Pythagoreans and *philosophoi*. Admittedly, no pre-Academic text explicitly calls any Pythagorean a *philosophos*; we are working with circumstantial evidence. Yet Heraclides's claim that Pythagoras called himself *philosophos* proves completely plausible, as does the inference that he had already been called *philosophos* by others. And at least one instance of the social situation underwriting the coinage of the term *philosophos* appears to have existed. So we need not posit an obscurely occasioned late sixth-century BCE desire to have a word designating the "love of wisdom" or "intellectual cultivation," which would be implausible, especially in the face of other perfectly acceptable phrases meaning the same thing. The idiosyncratic shape that is cut by fifth-century BCE uses of *philosophos*-group words can be accounted for as downstream versions of a term defined ostensively by Pythagorean activity rather than as the result of random chance. Finally, we can solve a paradox in recent Pythagorean studies, one that is emphasized most directly by Burkert: the confusing fact that people call Pythagoras a *philosophos* despite his apparent lack of almost all the intellectual attainments generally attributed to philosophers. In effect, Pythagoras need not even have been considered a philosopher in order to be called a *philosophos*.

The first (or among the first) objects of name-calling as *philosophoi* seem to have been the participants in the Pythagorean movement in Magna Graeca that lasted for nearly three-quarters of a century.[1] Such people lived in commercially vibrant cities throughout Italy, many of which had large oligarchic or quasi-democratic governments that could be readily influenced by like-minded voting blocs, and traveled enough to be seen by many people, not all of whom would have understood or appreciated their studious activity. The name could easily have traveled far, given the likely quantity of gossip about political developments in Magna Graeca. The stories that tell of Pythagoras naming his "practice" *philosophia* suggest that he was being treated as accommodating an initially other-applied name and vindicating it. If Pythagoras never in fact called himself *philosophos*, presumably those in his near circle did, and they retrojected the idea for doing so onto their intellectual leader.[2] At some later point, during the era of the Socratics after their master's death, the name may have come to refer to a particular discipline separate from the Pythagorean lineage.

The most plausible details of Pythagoras's admittedly fantasial biography support these possibilities. According to the sources, he resided in Samos until age forty, emigrating once he judged his liberal existence impossible under the tyranny of Polycrates.[3] In that first half of his life he is said to have studied broadly and far afield, zealously pursuing foreign wisdom, and adopting ascetic and purificatory practices.[4] He may have initiated Samian community discussions and have taken associates into caves for deeper conversation.[5] A dubious story that he harbored Zalmoxis, to be recounted in chapter 5, at least implies movement in aristocratic society, business connections, and notoriety for his intellectual ingenuity.[6] He probably had similarly elite connections to ritual practice, as anecdotes linking him to Apollo and Delphi imply.[7] He is said to have arrived in Croton with charisma, rhetorical versatility, and innovative ideas for institution building; all of these qualities suggest that he had Samian experience exercising all three, especially reflection on political egalitarianism, local self-reliance, and personal self-

---

[1] On this period, see, among others, von Fritz 1940; Minar 1942; Dunbabin 1948, 360–62, 366–67; Morrison 1956; Morrison 1958, 202; Philip 1966, 25–26; Burkert 1972, 109–20; Kahn 2001, 6–9.

[2] Ebert 2001.

[3] Strabo 14.1.16.1; Apul. *Flor.* 15; DL 8.3; Porph. *VP* 9, 16.

[4] Porph. *VP* 1, 6–8, 17; DL 8.2–3; Strabo 14.1.16.2.

[5] Porph. *VP* 9 (though Rowett 2014, 112n4, expresses doubt).

[6] Two stories similar to Hdt. 4.95 are told at Porph. *VP* 14–15. Rossetti 2013 thinks Pythagoras published a book while in Samos, taking Heraclitus fr. 129 as evidence; this is rather uncertain (cf. DL 8.6).

[7] See DL 8.5, 8, 21, and 8.11, 13, with Kurke 2011, 108–11; Rowett 2014, 113–14; Huffman 2014, 288.

improvement.[8] Even if Polycrates' rule may once have supported a public life of cultural critique—as his patronage of Alcmaeon and Ibycus might suggest[9]—Pythagoras may eventually have found himself *too* public and *too* critical.

Life in non-tyrannical Croton may have given freer reign to Pythagoras's novel or outspoken way of life. Showing himself thoughtful, educated, well-traveled, and gifted, he is said to have persuaded the Council of Elders to organize age- and gender-graded groups, to which he then addressed himself.[10] While he appears to have inspired the young especially,[11] he influenced people broadly enough to be considered practically a lawmaker, an avatar of the nomothetic sages Charondas and Zaleucus;[12] this probably means that his emphasis on virtue, friendship, and the sharing of property caused notable changes in legislative and executive action as those young people grew up.[13] His political power would come, then, from an unusual direction: the intellectual or ideological *Bildung* of a broad class of soon-to-be leaders, perhaps constituting hundreds or thousands of acolytes, partisans, or allies.[14] His combination of learning, eloquence, fresh ideas, and an orientation to self-development would plausibly have been distinctive at such high political levels. For those outside his force field of persuasion and mental revolution, these aspirations would have deserved a name if anything deserves a name.

---

[8] DL 1.13 implies that he did some philosophizing before moving to Italy.

[9] Ibyc. fr. S151.47–48; Hdt. 3.121.1; Strabo 14.1.6.1; *PBerol.* 7927, 1.24–33.

[10] Porph. *VP* 18, attributed to Dicaearchus, discussion at Rowett 2014, 114–16, 119–20. Huffman 2014, 281–84, observes that the verb Dicaearchus uses to refer to Pythagoras's effect on the elders is ψυχαγωγέω, which means that he is portrayed "as employing illegitimate appeals to the emotions to 'beguile' and 'bewitch' his audience," and thus "as a charismatic charlatan." But his account of the verb does not look to the abstract noun, which in Plato's *Phaedrus* (half a century before the Peripatetic author) is not obviously dubious; see Moore 2014c.

[11] Isoc. *Bus.* 29; Iambl. *VP* 17.71, 18.88, 35.254; Just. *Epit.* 20.4.14; Minar 1942, 25, 104; Rowett 2014, 118.

[12] Lawmaker: DL 8.3; Charondas and Zaleucus: DS 12.20.1; Sen. *Ep.* 90; DL 8.16; Porph. *VP* 21; *Suda* ζ 12.

[13] Because we cannot determine the precise route by which coiners came up with the word *philosophos*, I mention here a possibility connected to Pythagorean alienation of private property. Perhaps his circle disdained being *philochrêmatos* (adjective first attested in Andoc. 4.32 and related verb in Antiphon B103) or *philokerdês* (first attested in Thgn. 199; Pind. *Isthm.* 2.6), and encouraged self-improvement over tyrannical *philotimia* (first attested in Pind. fr. 210)—thus perhaps they were called *philosophoi* in their pursuit not of money or power but the esteem owed to a good advisor.

[14] DL 8.3: about three hundred. Pythagoras judged the best education to be citizenship in a well-governed city (Aristoxenus in DL 8.16).

Pythagoras's Contemporaneous and Near-Contemporaneous Reputation

Our identifiable sources for Pythagoras's self-application of the term *philosophos* date no earlier than Heraclides's writings from after the 370s. But Heraclides probably relied on an internal tradition, from sources with social, sentimental, or intellectual connections to Pythagoras's circle; at least his writings on Pythagoreanism—and other early philosophers—suggest as much. Time and perhaps secrecy have obscured this internal tradition and its sources. Yet an early external tradition remains. This range of outsider observations about Pythagoras take various perspectives, from bemused distance to fulsome praise. Scholars of ancient Pythagoreanism have studied this evidence often. We will analyze it for something particular: Pythagoras's salient and popular features, which support the hypothesis that he was labeled a *philosophos*, in particular for his combination of intellectual and political influence, and his connections to the term *sophos* and to legendary *sophoi*.

The earliest reference to Pythagoras is from Xenophanes of Colophon, his contemporary and a traveling poet, epistemologist, and critic of religion.[15] Xenophanes tells a story that when Pythagoras heard a dog yelping in pain, he asked its master to stop beating him; the tone of its cry informed Pythagoras as to which friend it had reincarnated.[16] The story testifies to the notoriety of Pythagoras, the intellectual provocativeness of his theory of palingenesis during his own lifetime, the ridicule it earned, and, crucially, Xenophanes's aiming, as Heraclitus did, to compete with Pythagoras in the realm explicitly of *sophia*.[17]

We studied Heraclitus's attitude toward Pythagoras in chapter 2, but we should reprise its key testaments. The fragment espousing that attitude most directly is B129: "Pythagoras of Mnesarchus practiced research more than anybody else, and selecting from some writings, made his own *sophia*,

---

[15] Xenophanes B7/D64. Diogenes Laertius introduces his quotation of this story as supporting the view that Pythagoras had lived a number of lives (ἄλλοτε ἄλλον αὐτὸν γεγενῆσθαι, DL 8.36). Since the quotation itself begins with "And when" (καί ποτέ), Xenophanes may have told other such tales about Pythagoras (Burkert 1972, 121). Xenophanes, likely living mostly in Western Greece, may have lived a few decades longer than Pythagoras (Guthrie 1962, 157).

[16] Lesher 2001, 78–81, argues that Xenophanes directs his critique not against the theory but against Pythagoras's claim to superhuman perceptual sensitivity. The common view that Xenophanes was "manifestly bent on exposing Pythagoras and his teachings to ridicule" (Cameron 1938, 15) must be tempered by the fact that Xenophanes found it worthwhile to mention him and his teaching, and by the fact that, in this passage at least, he does not explicitly reduce the idea of reincarnation to absurdity.

[17] For Xenophanes's competition in *sophia*, see B2/D61.12–14.

polymathy, and mischievous doings (κακοτεχνίη)."[18] Heraclitus asserts that Pythagoras strove consciously for *sophia*, and did so through quasi-scholarly techniques of collection and collation. This is in contrast to attaining a universal *sophia* through less overtly scholarly ways, such as the hard experience of life, self-investigation, and concentration. In B40—"Polymathy does not teach insight, for then it would have taught it to Hesiod and Pythagoras, and again to Xenophanes and Hecataeus"—Heraclitus says that what ought to be *sophia* or *nous* is, in the unifying program of these early rationalizing and systematizing researchers, just a mass of opinions. Heraclitus judges this factitious wisdom not merely epistemically suspect but, in its use as clever oratory, as leading to bad public or moral consequences. This explains Heraclitus's calling Pythagoras "leader of the imposters."[19] Heraclitus elsewhere recognizes the degree to which people trust those who seem the most learned. These three fragments present Pythagoras as notoriously learned (in a way) and a marketer of himself *as* learned (in another way).[20] Heraclitus thus criticizes Pythagoras's self-presentation as a person with epistemic authority, and consequent intellectual, religious, and civic authority.[21]

What Heraclitus indicts Pythagoras for—accumulating passels of knowledge and turning them into charismatic speech—becomes, in Empedocles's eyes, cause for celebration. "And there was among them a man of surpassing knowledge, a supreme master of all kinds of wise (σοφῶν) deeds, who had acquired an immense treasury of understanding. For, whenever he extended all his understanding, he readily saw each of all the things that are, in ten and even twenty generations of men."[22] The unspecified "man" has generally been thought to be Pythagoras.[23] Unlike Heraclitus, Empedocles claims that Pythagoras's

---

[18] For further discussion, see, e.g., Cameron 1938, 23n11; Guthrie 1962, 157–58; Huffman 2008; Rossetti 2013.

[19] Heraclitus B81; see Baron 2013, 160–61.

[20] Cameron 1938, 23 (with 30), claims that in scorning Pythagoras's inquisitiveness Heraclitus refers "not [to] an other-worldly navel-contemplating wisdom, but [to] an active pursuit of wisdom through observation"; this claim seems without evidence.

[21] There is a tradition that Heraclitus "listened to . . . Hippasus" (*Suda* s.v. Ἡράκλειτος), an apostate Pythagorean (Iambl. *VP* 18.81), and could have learned from him. But Hippasus may simply have been likened to Heraclitus for treating fire rather than the Pythagoreans' number as the first principle (Arist. *M.* A 984a7; see also Cameron 1938, 24–26).

[22] Empedocles B129/D38 (= Porph. *VP* 30): ἦν δέ τις ἐν κείνοισιν ἀνὴρ περιώσια εἰδώς, | παντοίων τε μάλιστα σοφῶν <τ᾿> ἐπιήρανος ἔργων, | ὅς δὴ μήκιστον πραπίδων ἐκτήσατο πλοῦτον. | Ὁππότε γὰρ πάσησιν ὀρέξαιτο πραπίδεσσιν, | ῥεῖ᾿ ὅ γε τῶν ὄντων πάντων λεύσσεσκεν ἕκαστα, | καί τε δέκ᾿ ἀνθρώπων καί τ᾿ εἴκοσιν αἰώνεσσιν (precise text disputed). For debate about the meaning, especially of the final line, see Burkert 1972, 138; Inwood 2001, 63, 213; Kahn 2001, 12.

[23] DL 8.54 gives an abbreviated version of the poem; he cites Timaeus for the claim that Empedocles means Pythagoras, but admits that others believe he meant Parmenides. See Baron 2013, 164–68.

capacious knowledge is superlative, providing him with a wealth of understanding, generating effective action, and giving him insight into the nature of reality. That insight amounts to a historical sensibility conjoined with a capacity to forecast the future and a sensitivity to the human lot. Empedocles treats Pythagoras as practical in the way that the *Sophoi* are practical.

Ion of Chios, the fifth-century BCE tragedian and belletrist, speaks yet again to Pythagoras's polymathy and intellectual influence, taking a careful and perhaps ironic middle ground between Heraclitus and Empedocles. He claims that although Pherecydes of Syros is dead, his soul lives on happily, "if truly (εἴπερ . . . ἐτύμως) the *sophos* Pythagoras saw and learned the *gnômê* [thoughts?] of all men."[24] This poetic fragment attributes to Pythagoras a view of a personal soul's endurance after death, and treats it as provocative enough both to cite and to express reservations about its truth.[25] It links Pherecydes, sometimes counted among the Seven *Sophoi*, to Pythagoras treated as *sophos*.[26] It also suggests that Pythagoras accumulated extensive knowledge, either "about" the "thoughts" of all men or "from" all men, namely, all those from whom a person might learn.[27] In another fragment, Ion says that Pythagoras attributed to Orpheus some verses he himself wrote.[28] In doing so, Pythagoras placed himself in the midst of Greek religious culture, perhaps with the devious goal of leveraging for himself Orpheus's authoritativeness. Orpheus was sometimes considered the first *philosophos*, and definitely a legendary *sophos* person.[29]

[24] Ion B4: εἴπερ Πυθαγόρης ἐτύμως ὁ σοφὸς περὶ πάντων | ἀνθρώπων γνώμας εἶδε καὶ ἐξέμαθεν. The translation is fraught, especially the target of "truly" (ἐτύμως) and the referent of *gnômê*; on the latter, compare Cameron 1938, 22 ("destinies"); Edmonds 1931 ("marks," citing Thgn. 60); and Guthrie 1962, 158 ("minds"). Cf. Minar 1942, 124.

[25] On εἴπερ in Ion's Ionic as ironic or skeptical, see Dover 1986, 30.

[26] Pherecydes, deemed by some the first prose writer about nature and the gods (DL 1.116, citing Theopompus), was sometimes included among the Seven *Sophoi* (DL 1.13, 1.42, 1.122) or as relevantly contemporary with them (*Suda* φ 214). Ancient authors often thought Pherecydes taught Pythagoras: DS 10 fr. 4; DL 1.13, 8.2; Porph. *VP* 2; Iambl. *VP* 2.9; Tzetz. *Chil.* 11.74–75. Schibli 1990, 2 (with 11–13), argues that he was born around 585 BCE, making this possible; see also West 1971, 1–9, 213–18 for details. Granger 2007 gives an overall account.

[27] On the view that Ion claims that Pythagoras got his wisdom from all men, thus recapitulating Heraclitus's view, see Kranz 1934, 227; Huxley 1965, 40; Schibli 1990, 12. Dover 1986, 30, gives: "achieved knowledge and understanding *beyond* that of all men" (my emphasis); similarly, Kahn 2001, 11.

[28] DL 8.8 B2. For Ion's historiographical interests, see Huxley 1965, 37–40; West 1985, 74–76; Dover 1986, 32; *BNJ* 392; *EGM* 2.698–99. For his political interests, see Jacoby 1947.

[29] Orpheus as *philosophos*: DL 1.5. As *sophos*: see chapter 9, pp. 265–66.

Herodotus, in the final quarter of the fifth century BCE, refers explicitly to Pythagoras twice.[30] The first time is in his discussion of Egyptians, where he notes that certain Egyptian religious prohibitions agree with rites called Orphic and Bacchic, but that they are really Pythagorean (Hdt. 2.81).[31] This implies that Pythagorean spiritual practices had taken broad hold by Herodotus's time and had so established themselves that people forgot their provenance. It also implies, as Ion had implied, similarities between Orphic and Pythagorean practices, however those might be defined.[32] The second reference concerns Thrace and the Getae, a religious group that accepted Zalmoxis as god and believed in an immortal soul (Hdt. 4.93–5; cf. DL 8.2 and Pl. *Chrm.* 156d5–6), as Pherecydes and Pythagoras famously did. A rationalized version of this story circulating in the Pontus, where Herodotus picked it up, knew Zalmoxis as a manumitted slave of Pythagoras's from his time living in Samos.[33] Apparently Zalmoxis learned soul-immortality from Pythagoras. He may also have learned how to make money and move in aristocratic society. Herodotus observes, by a litotes, that Pythagoras was "not the weakest Greek sophist" (οὐ τῷ ἀσθενεστάτῳ σοφιστῇ),[34] casting him instead as the strongest. As we will see in chapter 5, Herodotus uses *sophistês* as his word for *Sophos* (of the Seven Sages variety), and it is putative *sophistai* who practice *philosophein* (1.30). Herodotus also observes that Pythagoras contributed to Zalmoxis's gaining insight into Ionian ways of life (δίαιτιάν τε Ἰάδα) and a deeper character (ἤθεα βαθύτερα).[35] All this suggests that while he was in Samos, Pythagoras had political, intellectual, and cultural traction, and shared it with Zalmoxis.

---

[30] Herodotus is often thought to allude to Pythagoras (and Empedocles) on a third occasion, at 2.123, when he says that some to-be-left-unnamed Greeks presented the Egyptian view of transmigration of souls as their own discovery; see, e.g., Burkert 1972, 126; Kahn 2001, 13.

[31] This may mean that Herodotus believes that Pythagoras's views come from Egypt, as Schorn 2014, 298–99 suggests.

[32] See Cameron 1938, 5–7, 15–16, 33n19; Guthrie 1952, 46–47, 216–21; Burkert 1972, 125–33; Livingstone 2001, 157–59; Kahn 2001, 19–22; Betegh 2014.

[33] See Cameron 1938, 12–15; Minar 1942, 4–6; YC 1.306–10, for complications raised by this passage. Herodotus's reference to Pontus is an interesting one: Heraclea on the Pontus had a strong intellectual tradition, and two of its citizens, Herodorus and Heraclides, had pronounced Pythagorean interests. Its relative proximity to Thrace may have given currency to Zalmoxian tales (which may have appealed primarily to the nobility: Schorn 2014, 301).

[34] Contrast the translation of LM 4.37: "one who was not at all the weakest, the sage Pythagoras." It is not clear whether Herodotus treats travel as a central characteristic of *sophistai*, though LM 1.29 might suggest he does.

[35] These remarks led Lévy 1926, 6, to say that Herodotus treats Pythagoras with respect, in contrast to Heraclitus's and Xenophanes's acrimony. If so, we may wonder what redeemed Pythagoras's reputation in the intervening half century. (Perhaps his students were no longer a political or cultural threat?) Schorn 2014, 300–2, exercises more caution, showing Herodotus's (deliberate?) obfuscation about his attitude toward Pythagoras.

Probably not long after Herodotus wrote his *History*, the first-generation Socratic Antisthenes of Athens declared that Pythagoras had a great reputation for making speeches, fitting manner to audience, and that this capacity revealed a great skill—"it is part of *sophia* to discover the form of *sophia* (τρόπον τῆς σοφίας) suitable to each person" (V A 187 *SSR*)—that again relates him to *sophia*.[36] "Pythagoreans" are mentioned at *Dissoi Logoi* 6.8 as *sophistai* and successful teachers of *sophia* and virtue (on the work's date, see chapter 7). Three other authors from the same period, Glaucus of Rhegium, Democritus, and Anaximander of Miletus, provide corroborating evidence.[37]

Isocrates writes about Pythagoras once, in the *Busiris* (ca. 370s BCE), explicitly connecting him to *philosophia* and relying, apparently, on earlier traditions. Discussing Egyptian piety, Isocrates describes "Egyptian *philosophia*" and the putative divisions of labor it involves. Egyptian priests introduced medicines for the body and *philosophia* for the soul, which had the power not just to form laws but also to investigate reality; since the elders kept civic order, and the young did astronomy and geometry, we might guess that Isocrates means that it is the latter who did *philosophia*.[38] Isocrates says that Pythagoras studied this Egyptian piety and thus brought "*philosophia* in general" (τὴν τ᾽ ἄλλην φιλοσοφίαν) to the Greeks.[39] He goes on to say that

[36] On this fragment see Horky 2013, 88–90; Prince 2014 ad loc. Another first-generation Socratic, Aeschines (if Plut. *De curios.* 2.516c relies on his work; see VI A 90 *SSR*), may have treated Socrates as curious about Pythagoras's exemplary skill of persuasion (Σωκράτης δὲ περιήει διαπορῶν τί Πυθαγόρας λέγων ἔπειθε).

[37] Glaucus says that his contemporary Democritus studied with Pythagoreans; Thrasyllus says that he wrote an admiring work on Pythagoras himself (DL 9.38), indicating the early importance of such studies. Anaximander, an allegorist from the same period, wrote an "exegesis of Pythagorean symbola" (*Suda* α 1987). Anaximander's perceived need for an exegesis of these sayings implies a long-standing impression that Pythagoras had something serious and nonobvious to say. Anaximander also interpreted Homer (Xen. *Symp.* 3.6) and wrote about first inventors (*BNJ* 9 F3), which may suggest that he perceived Pythagoras as a *sophos*-level personage. See generally Burkert 1972, 166.

[38] Isoc. *Bus.* 22–23. Isocrates does not mention here whether Egyptians believed in the immortality of the soul; at any rate, Guthrie 1962, 160, asserts that the Egyptians certainly did not recognize transmigration.

[39] Isoc. *Bus.* 28. Livingstone 2001, 157–59, argues that Isocrates followed Herodotus on this (cf. Kahn 2001, 6, 12–13). The phrase τὴν τ᾽ ἄλλην φιλοσοφίαν has confused translators: Norlin 1928 has "all philosophy"; Mirhady in Mirhady and Too 2000, 56, has "the rest of philosophy"; and Horky 2013, 90–95, has "the other philosophy," meaning other than Isocrates's philosophy, thus specifically the Egyptian study of mathematics as a study of nature (perhaps implying that Isocrates is the second inventor of philosophy?). But this noun-phrase is found in Philostr. *V A* 4.25: Menippus was erotically overcome, despite τὴν . . . ἄλλην φιλοσοφίαν ἔρρωτο, which appears to mean "being strong in philosophy generally/usually"; see Smyth 1920 §1276 for the construction ("usual, general"), citing Antiph. 3.b.1. This would suggest that Isocrates means "philosophy in general," as I have translated it (and recently, LM 4.25). Still, the matter is uncertain.

Pythagoras gave serious and conspicuous attention to sacrificial and purificatory matters, with the hope that it would bring him human if not also divine favor. He succeeded in this: "for by so much did he exceed others in reputation that all the young desired to be his students, and their elders preferred to see their children associating with him than doing their own work; and this account [Isocrates adds] cannot be disbelieved, since to this day those claiming to be (προσποιουμένους) his students are more impressive when silent than are people famed for their great eloquence."[40] Isocrates had already warned that those who present themselves as having greater wisdom (κατεσχημάτισαν . . . σοφίαν) or virtue than they really have do harm to those taken in by their pretensions.[41] He leaves open whether Pythagoras benefited from or benefited others by his Egypt-sourced philosophy. He emphasizes instead that, for Pythagoras, doing *philosophia* was a way to seem intellectually impressive, as befits a teacher, concerning the topic of highest value, namely divinity. It is doubtful that Isocrates invented this story's key elements, an Egyptian *philosophia* and a period of study by Pythagoras in Egypt. So Pythagoras must already have been linked to *philosophia*, and his *philosophia* to his public intellectual and pedagogical influence.[42]

Isocrates's contemporary Alcidamas, a rhetorician we will study in chapter 7, calls Pythagoras a *sophos*, parallel in his importance to Italy with people like Archilochus, Homer, Sappho, Chilon, and Anaxagoras to their respective cities of honor.[43] He may also say that just as Athenians benefited from Solon's laws, and Spartans from Lycurgus's, Thebes flourished "once the leaders came to be *philosophoi*."[44] These revitalizing leaders seem to be Epaminondas and Pelopidas, who liberated Thebes from Spartan hegemony in the early

---

[40] Isoc. *Bus.* 28–29.

[41] Isoc. *Bus.* 24. Livingstone 2001, 155–61, thinks that Isocrates insinuates that Pythagoras learned "not religious wisdom but religious charlatanism," an ability to impress humans but not gods, and that because Isocrates did not have to mention the "marginal, mysterious figure" Pythagoras, his doing so is a tip-off that the point of the *Busiris* is to draw out the parallels between the restrictive Egyptian state and Pythagorean society.

[42] Livingstone's view that the *Busiris* responds throughout the text to Plato's *Republic*, such that the view of Egypt here is the *Republic*'s city, and *philosophia* here is the *Republic*'s *philosophia*, suggests that he would not believe that Isocrates provides independent evidence for Pythagoras's philosophicality. Kahn 2001, 12, makes the safer point that Isocrates's remarks already indicate a proliferation of stories about Pythagoras.

[43] Arist. *Rh.* 1398b11–16.

[44] Arist. *Rh.* 1398b17–20. Ross 1959 punctuates the passage on the belief that both remarks are from Alcidamas; Freese 1926, by contrast, thinks that "something has fallen out" after the remarks about Anaxagoras and thus the Thebes remark may not be Alcidaman. Both Cameron 1938, 34, and Ebert 2001, 432, refer to this passage in support of the claim that Pythagoreans were called *philosophoi* from an early date. Pl. *Phd.* 61d6–7 with 64b4–6 support the view that Pythagoreans, including Philolaus, spent time in Thebes.

fourth century BCE. Epaminondas was an outstanding philosophical student of the Pythagorean Lysis.[45] If the Pythagoreans were specially called *philosophoi*, then Epaminondas would be called *philosophos* on account of his Pythagoreanism.

Isocrates's and Alcidamas's contemporary Plato mentions Pythagoras and the Pythagoreans only twice explicitly, both times in the *Republic*.[46] Socrates mentions the "Pythagoreans" for having treated music and astronomy as sister sciences (*R.* 7.530d6–9). Three books later, Socrates observes that in contrast to Homer, who won no acolytes, Pythagoras gained the affections of his followers to an unusual degree (διαφερόντως . . . ἠγαπήθη), teaching them a "way of life" (ὁδόν τινα; τρόπον . . . τοῦ βίου, *R.* 10.600a10–b3). Here Socrates reveals Pythagoras's social and intellectual legacy, mentioning two possibly coincident groups: people called (ἐπονομάζοντες) "Pythagoreans" and some devoted followers who adopted the way of life he taught or modeled. The first had views about mathematics, in particular that (the same) mathematical principles underlie both auditory and spatial relations, and these views can probably be traced, at least minimally, to Pythagoras.[47] The second group, the followers, came to live like one another but unlike others. This group was drawn together in its idiosyncrasy by Pythagoras's emphasis on the value of changing one's life and by his personal lovability. Whereas the "Pythagoreans" adopted a mode of reasoning shareable across disciplines, the followers adopted a mode of deciding what to do and how to be. These two groups shared a self-conscious reformation of their respective practices: scientific and investigative on the one hand, practical and existential on the other. It would seem therefore that Pythagoras, according to Plato's Socrates, stood for the deliberate effort to change for the better. The followers, in adopting a new mode of life, would make this effort quite public. Even the Pythagoreans would stick out in their pursuits of cross-disciplinary work, which, like contemporary interdisciplinary projects, cannot be readily explained by appeal to the usual goods of the individual disciplines, in this case playing and teaching music, or developing the skills for surveying, navigation, and astronomy.

Plato's talk of people related to Pythagoras reveals Pythagoras's distinctive and public approach to self-improvement, a scholarly, wholehearted, and

---

[45] Corn. Nep. *Ep.* 2; see also Cic. *De or.* 3.34; *Off.* 1.4; Paus. 9.14; Ael. *VH* 3.17; Iambl. *VP* 35.250.

[46] Kahn 2001, 13–14, affirms the tradition that Prometheus in Plato's *Philebus* (16c2d–7) stands for Pythagoras, and Palmer 2014 tracks Pythagorean influences through *Gorgias*, *Phaedo*, *Republic* (see also Rowett 2014, 115, 120), *Philebus*, and *Timaeus*. See especially Ebert 2001 for the *Phaedo* as evidence that Pythagoreans were distinctively called *philosophoi*.

[47] Cf. Guthrie 1962, 161–62; Kahn 2001, 13 (supposing Socrates refers to Archytas); Horky 2013, 98–99.

concerted effort. In preceding authors, Pythagoras is seen to seek copious knowledge, especially from others, and to project the results. Those early authors continually describe him with the language of *sophos, sophistês,* and *philosophia.* He has notable views of the soul; it is plausible that his psychological insight contributed to his attractiveness and to his success at getting people to change their lives. In general, then, the contemporary and near-contemporary attitudes toward Pythagoras are of just the sort we would expect for someone who has been called by a name, *philosophos,* that means wanting distinctively to become a scion of the Seven (or however many) *Sophoi,* an initiate in that legendary class of cultural elites.

Aristotle's *Protrepticus* as Evidence, via Iamblichus

Earlier in this book we have seen that others (probably all) in the fourth century BCE accepted that Pythagoras was called *philosophos,* at least by himself: Heraclides and the sources for Diodorus and Diogenes, but also Heraclides's predecessor or contemporary, the person I have called the Sicyon author. Obviously later authors shared that belief, notably Cicero, who had much greater access to classical materials than we do, and can hardly be cited for zealous credulity. The most interesting corroboration for reliability of the Pythagoras tale, however, comes from Aristotle, in work now known only through excerpts by Iamblichus of Chalcis. Aristotle, apparently in his own voice in his *Protrepticus,* seems to accept Heraclides's story, which places in Phlius a Pythagoras who has to explain the name *philosophos.* Aristotle's research into Pythagoreanism, which catalogued its legends and analyzed its philosophical tenets, and his research into the history of philosophy, were theretofore unparalleled. As a long-term member of the Academy, he would have heard nearly every story in circulation about early philosophical machinations. Whatever his reconstructive tendencies, Aristotle is classical Athens's most reliable source on philosophy. And he seems to accept Heraclides's account. This is a strong argument in favor of it, and thus the early connection between Pythagoras and the name *philosophos.*

In chapter 12 of his late third-century CE *Pythagorean Way of Life* [*VP*], Iamblichus presents a version of Pythagoras's festival explanation remarkably similar to the one that Cicero attributes to Heraclides. It differs in excising the dramatic context, Leon's talking with Pythagoras, and extending the explanation about the objects of philosophy's study, to include remarks about number, beauty, and priority. Each chapter in Iamblichus's work begins with a summary of his own devising. This chapter begins: "His discourse about *philosophia*: the fact that he was the first to call himself a *philosophos* and the reasons for that word." Iamblichus assembles his works from verbatim but unattributed excerpts interspersed with his own remarks, and, according to Doug Hutchinson and Monte Johnson, the most recent editors of this passage and related passages, his chapter summaries always pertain to the source from which he draws. This means that Iamblichus will quote in this chapter from the passage of some work in which Pythagoras explicitly discusses philosophy and in which his inauguration of the self-appellation is made explicit. Below is the bulk of the chapter; I emphasize the lines that most echo Cicero's lines:

> And it is said that Pythagoras was the first to call (προσαγορεῦσαι) himself a *philosophos*, not only initiating this new use of a word (καινοῦ μόνον ὀνόματος ὑπάρξας), but also usefully teaching beforehand its proper objects (πρᾶγμα οἰκεῖον προεκδιδάσκων).[48] **For he said that the entrance (πάροδον) of human beings into life is like a crowd meeting at festivals. For as there, while all sorts of humans gather, each arrives with its own business: one hurries to sell wares for the sake of money and gain; another comes to display bodily strength for the sake of reputation, and there is a third group—and this one is at least the most free—that assembles for the spectacle (θέας) of the place, the beautiful works of manufacture, and the excellent performances and speeches, the displays of which usually occur at festivals. So also in life all sorts of men martial themselves together (συναθροίζεσθαι)[49] in the same place for what they each take seriously: longing for money and luxury seize some; desire for governing and leadership, rivalrousness and a mania for reputation possess others. But the purest way of life for a human being is the one satisfied by (ἀποδεξάμενον) the observation of the most beautiful things (τὴν τῶν καλλίστων θεωρίαν), which one may also term (προσονομάζειν) "philosophical."** Beautiful, for a start, is the spectacle of the entire heaven and the stars revolving in it, if one observes (καθορῷη) their order; for, after all, it is this way by participation in the primary and intelligible. And the primary is the nature

---

[48] Against all manuscripts, which print προεκδιδάσκων ("teaching beforehand"), Cobet 1878b, 338, followed by Nauck 1884, reads προσεκδιδάσκων ("teach in addition"), on the grounds that Cic. *Tusc.* 5.4.10 writes that Pythagoras invented the name and later amplified the thing itself (*sed rerum etiam ipsarum amplificator fuit*). But, as I argue below, Iamblichus is surely not drawing on Cicero; and it is rather to be expected that Pythagoras would be doing first what he is later named for, not vice versa. In any event, προσεκδιδάσκων is a rare and late word, found elsewhere only in Them. *Or.* 32.358b and perhaps in Joseph. *AJ* 17.6.1 (scribes may have replaced it with the more familiar ancient word, according to Hudson 1720 ad loc.), which suggests that it would be Iamblichus's remark, not a quotation, that would be at issue.

[49] This is found in MS P; Deubner prints ἀθροίζεσθαι.

of numbers and ratios running through all things, according to which all these things are harmoniously arranged and suitably ordered. And wisdom (σοφία) is truly a knowledge concerned with first things, beautiful, divine, undefiled, and always the same and in the same state, by participation in which all other things may be called beautiful. And philosophy is zealous pursuit of such observation (ἡ ζήλωσις τῆς τοιαύτης θεωρίας). Beautiful also is this care bestowed on education which is directed to improvement of human beings.[50] (Iambl. *VP* 12 58–59)

The close similarity of Cicero's and Iamblichus's passages, despite minor differences, points to a shared source.[51] It does not seem that Iamblichus relies on Cicero himself, both because Iamblichus goes further and because the part in excess of the Ciceronian overlap seems not his own extension of Cicero's words—they are stylistically continuous with the preceding prose and necessary to the explanation found in the overlap. Iamblichus could well be relying directly on Heraclides's work, then, for the greater part of *VP* 12. This might involve his having *On Diseases* before him, or something else that excerpts or embeds a direct quotation.

Actually, we have reason to wonder whether Iamblichus may have read Heraclides through an intermediary. He wrote about the Pythagorean explanation at Phlius in the next volume of his multivolume *On Pythagoreanism*, called the *Protreptic to Philosophy*. Chapter 9 has this summary: "An approach to exhortation from the intention of nature, according to the reply Pythagoras gave to those in Phlius who found out from him who he was and for the sake of what he has been born, attending to which we reach the conclusion of the protreptic as a whole" (Iambl. *Pro.* 4,9–13).[52] As in the previous work, the chapter summary always refers to material found in Iamblichus's source text. This is important because Iamblichus neither mentions nor quotes anything concerning Phlius in the chapter itself. The closest we get is the following:

[50] For the Greek of this passage, see Appendix, pp. 325–26.

[51] Only Cicero explains that the festival is "a magnificent display of games in a gathering from the whole of Greece"; but, on the assumption that Iamblichus quotes from a fourth-century BCE author, we would not suspect his source to need to explain festivals—Sosicrates does not either. Similarly, only Cicero adds that winners at festivals earn crowns, another detail that is irrelevant for classical Greeks. Cicero condenses, relative to Iamblichus's account, the objects the spectators take in, to "what is being done and how." He also condenses, relatively speaking, when giving the gloss on the analogy, the pursuits of the non-philosophers, from six items divided among two groups to two items divided among two groups. He adds a Latin expansion of the Greek term *philosophos*. Finally, he concludes by emphasizing that insofar as the high worth of observation is underlined by its lack of acquisitiveness, philosophy surpasses all other pursuits.

[52] For the Greek of this and the next two passages, see Appendix, p. 325.

Being asked [sc. what we were generated by nature and the god in order to do],
Pythagoras said, "to study the heavens (τὸ θεάσασθαι . . . τὸν οὐρανόν)," and
he claimed he was a spectator of nature (θεωρὸν . . . τῆς φύσεως), and for this
sake had passed into (παρεληλυθέναι) his way of life. (Iambl. *Pro.* 9 51,6–8)

We recall the final line, about "passing into" a life, from the middle of Cicero's
passage and the beginning of *VP* 12. The quotation "to study the heavens,"
and the gloss "spectator of nature," appear to condense the sentences of *VP* 12
that immediately follow the Cicero overlap. The chapter summary implies that
in the source material Pythagoras is responding in Phlius to some questions.
So it appears that Iamblichus is citing from some highly compressed version
of Heraclides's story that preserves some of the dramatic context but saves
little of the direct speech. We do not here get any of the festival analogy. It
shows up only a page later, when the source text goes its own way:

For just as we travel abroad to Olympia for the sake of the spectacle (θέας) itself,
even if nothing more will come from it—for the observation (ἡ θεωρία) itself
surpasses much money—and as we attend (θεωροῦμεν) the Dionysia not to
get anything from the actors—indeed we rather pay for it—and as we would
choose many other spectacles over much money, so too the observation of the
whole [i.e., universe] ought to be honored over all that is judged to be useful.
For surely one must not travel with great seriousness for the sake of watching
(θεάσασθαι) people acting as women and slaves, or fighting and racing, and not
think that one must be a spectator of the nature of what exists, and the truth—
for free. (Iambl. *Pro.* 9 53,19–54,5)

This is a free-associating gloss on the Pythagoras story, and its reference to
the Dionysia puts it in the voice of a fifth- or fourth-century BCE Athenian.
The prose, with its parentheticals, multiple examples, and sinuous argument,
looks rather like Aristotle's. And indeed it is Aristotle's: scholars have long
understood that Iamblichus's *Protreptic* relies on two main sets of works: Plato's dialogues (readily identified, because we have all of them), and Aristotle's
Protrepticus of 353 BCE (not so readily identified, because it is lost). Doug
Hutchinson and Monte Johnson have recently clarified the way Iamblichus relies on Aristotle's work and have shown in particular that this chapter itself
comes from Aristotle.[53] So, to spell out the consequence, Aristotle has written in the *Protrepticus* about Pythagoras's responding to a question in Phlius
about his being a *philosophos*.

---

[53] Hutchinson and Johnson 2005. My reconstruction in these pages owes much to HJ.

This means that Heraclides and Aristotle, contemporaries in Plato's Academy from 367 BCE, both wrote about Pythagoras in Phlius. They could have done so independently, sharing some unknown source for the Phlius detail and the core of the festival idea, or one could have relied on the other. If Heraclides relied on Aristotle,[54] Heraclides might still get the credit for developing the explanation as he did; however, Cicero, an assiduous reader of Aristotle's *Protrepticus*,[55] credits Heraclides not only for that, but also for the location and dramatic details, which on this hypothesis he should (more justly) have credited to Aristotle. So, it is probable that, instead, Aristotle relied on Heraclides. This may mean that he summarized Heraclides's account, or, more likely given the evidence we have, referred at least to some dramatic details—Pythagoras, Phlius, a question—and then put the upshot of the festival explanation into his own words. Hutchinson and Johnson's recent reconstruction of Aristotle's *Protrepticus* complicates matters a bit, since they show it to be a dialogue that features—as they conjecture—both Heraclides and Aristotle as characters.[56] So it is not clear who would have presented either a full or simplified version of the Pythagoras story. I judge most probable that the character Aristotle acknowledges the Heraclidean provenance of a story which he goes on to adumbrate.

There is one more telling piece of Iamblichean evidence, this one not obviously ascribed to Aristotle: the eighth chapter of *On the Pythagorean Life*. It is the first in a sequence of four chapters (8–11) concerning Pythagoras's first trip to Croton. Iamblichus summarizes this one as "When and how he traveled to Croton, what he did on his first appearance, and what words he spoke to the youth." In the latter part of the chapter, Iamblichus says that Pythagoras encouraged the youth toward education (παιδεία), and gives some content. The language recalls the fourth-century BCE prose moralists. The chapter concludes:

> Education (ἀγωγαῖς) basically accounts for the differences between human beings and animals, between Greeks and barbarians, between the free and servants, and between *philosophoi* and any random person. In sum, there is so much superiority here that while those found running faster than others at Olympia were seven from one city, those superior in wisdom (σοφίᾳ) from the whole

---

[54] This is the view of Jaeger 1962, 98; see Burkert 1960, 166–69.

[55] Cicero modeled his (lost) *Hortensius* on Aristotle's *Protrepticus* (evidence in HJ); he even defended *philosophia* in that work by explaining its name, according to Boethius *De topicis differentiis* 1188a.

[56] See Hutchinson and Johnson 2018, 112–13 for the characters, and 127–36 (and *passim*) for the argument that the work is a dialogue.

inhabited world numbered seven. And in later times, in which he himself [sc. Pythagoras] lived, one man alone surpassed all others in *philosophia*. For he called himself by this name (τοῦτο τὸ ὄνομα), rather than "wise" (σοφοῦ).[57] (Iambl. *VP* 8 44,5–15)

Iamblichus seems to be claiming that education is so far from having a trivial effect as to be responsible for the qualitative difference in *sophia* between the Seven *Sophoi* and other putative *sophoi*, and even in *philosophia* between Pythagoras and other putative *philosophoi*. This fits well enough with the preceding discussion. But then Iamblichus gives an explanation for Pythagoras's referring to himself as extraordinary in *philosophia*, rather than as a *sophos*. Thus we meet again, in strange form, the not-*sophos* version of the Pythagoras story we have attributed to the Sicyon author and have seen again in Diodorus. This alternative account, which crowns chapters 8–11, probably does not come from Heraclides's *On Diseases*, which appears to have focused on Empedocles, and, as Gottschalk has argued, probably abjures this pessimistic view of wisdom's inaccessibility (Gottschalk 1980, 26–36).[58] And the final two sentences must be Iamblichus's own chapter wrap-up.[59] He is free associating to a non-Heraclidean linkage he has read elsewhere between the *philosophoi* and the *sophoi*. He stands in a long tradition of people viewing Pythagoras and the Pythagoreans specifically as *philosophoi*.

Conclusion: The Plausibility of Such Name Calling

A final piece of evidence comes again from Iamblichus. The following passage appears to come from some fourth-century BCE source.

And first, exhorting (προτρεψάμενος) in the most famous city Croton, he gained many aspirants (ζηλωτάς), so that it is said that he got six hundred people not only moved toward the philosophy that he shared with them, but also toward the so-called common life (τὸ λεγόμενον κοινοβίους), according to his command.

---

[57] For the Greek of this passage, see Appendix, p. 326.

[58] Reference to Olympic games is a common *topos*; see, e.g., Arist. *M.* α.2 994a22–23 (even as Jaeger secludes here); Iambl. *VP* 8.40.

[59] The chapter has already mentioned *philosophia* without providing any contrasts with *sophia*; the sentence is not worded quite right (for the sake of parallelism, the antecedent of τοῦτο τὸ ὄνομα, "this name," should be *philosophos*, not *philosophia*); there is actually no explanation for Pythagoras's preference for *philosophos/philosophia*; and as we have seen from *VP* 12, the meaning of *philosophia* is so important to Iamblichus's sources as to justify presenting the matter at length.

And these were the ones philosophizing (οἱ φιλοσοφοῦντες), but many others were listeners, whom they called (καλοῦσιν) *akousmatikoi*.[60] On one occasion, so they say, the first he held after arriving alone in Italy, the man got more than two thousand by his speeches. (Iambl. *VP* 6.29–30)

This passage, which attends to language peculiar to the Pythagorean circle, suggests that a certain group of Pythagoreans was called "the ones philosophiz- ing" in the same way another group was called "*akousmatikoi*." How early they were called this, we cannot say, but the author seems to imply an early date. (The lore concerning the silence of the Pythagorean acolytes may em- phasize the centrality of good conversation to that life: talk is cheap, yet the skills of worthwhile talk may take years of training to acquire.)

This chapter has aimed to show that the Pythagoreans would be plausible and even likely candidates to be called *philosophoi*, on the grounds that they were seen and spoken about as acting in a way that would give rise to the coin- age of the term *philosophos*. As chapter 3 had it, to be so called, someone would need to appear to be repeatedly and (thus) excessively concerned with a social institution denoted synecdochally by the second element *soph-*. The most likely such referent would be the deeming of people as culturally elite *sophoi*, in the context of political, social, and personal advice-giving. So, it looks like *philosophoi* would have been coined for people who appeared to be striving to be *sophoi*, in a way that was not altogether admirable. Targets of the coinage of *philosophoi* would thus have to be people who acted in ways that would at least appear to conduce to the special advice-giving competence of *sophoi*, did so with enough notoriety as to deserve a name and allow that name to outlive them, and were engaged in a pursuit that people judged either impractical, imprudent, or improper. The scarcity of historical records from the late sixth century BCE means that there may have been, unbeknownst to us, numerous such persons. We do know, however, of at least one such group, the Pythagoreans, who fit these three parameters. They did study, talk, and adopt ways of life that apparently constituted their attempts to live well; they came to prominence in Greece's largest commercial colonies; and their het- erodox views and ambitious politics earned them intellectual criticism and political violence. The evidence surveyed in this chapter has focused on the ways near-contemporary authors commented on the Pythagoreans' being thought to be (aspiring to be) *sophoi*, and their noteworthy avenues of per- sonal exercise meant to satisfy their ambition. This sort of evidence and this

---

[60] Deubner secludes from "it is said . . ." to ". . . *akousmatikoi*" and Nauck the first clause of that seclusion, against manuscripts.

sort of account might be considered a mere adjunct to histories of philosophy, since it is simply unclear whether Pythagoras or his nearest political associates "philosophized" in the way most contemporary readers would understand the term. But it is at the heart of the history of *philosophia*, if, for better or worse, it is their behaviors that occasioned the coinage of the term.

Whereas this chapter studied people for whom the *philosophos* word group might have been used, the next chapter studies people who actually used the *philosophos* word group. The way they do so tracks what we might expect, should those words have been formed in the way described so far in this book.

DEVELOPMENT

Fifth-Century *Philosophoi*

Diffusion and Dynamism after Pythagoras and Heraclitus

The term *philosophos* and its cognates show up hardly a half-dozen times in fifth- or very early fourth-century BCE Greek—that is, before Alcidamas, Isocrates, and the Socratics. Blame this largely on the devastation of the century's prose works. But even in surviving treatises, none uses instances of the word family more than once. The selectivity with which authors use them suggests strict limits on its application. Besides being an important consideration on its own—it speaks against *philosophos* meaning something as broadly relevant as "given to intellectual cultivation"—the constellation of several narrow uses allows us to infer an earlier and tighter range of meanings from which each diverged.[1]

This chapter focuses on six texts: Herodotus's Croesus-Solon exchange in his history of the Persian Wars, Pericles's Funeral Oration in Thucydides's history of the Peloponnesian War, the Hippocratic treatise *On Ancient Medicine*, Gorgias's playful encomium *Helen*, Aristophanes's comedy *Ecclesiazusae* (*Assemblywomen*), and one of Lysias's forensic speeches. Only the *Ecclesiazusae* has a firm date (392 BCE); the others have windows of possibility of several decades, from the early 430s till as late as 380 BCE. Thus a few may overlap with usages of *philosophos* cognates discussed in chapters 6 and 7. Most, however, surely come from the 430s, 420s, or 410s. (No substantial prose work predates Herodotus.)[2] These instances exhibit enough of both unity and variety to allow meaningful retrospective reconstruction of the earliest history of the term *philosophos*.

What we find from this survey is that being *philosophos* means doing what might position a sage to make definitive claims about the good life (Herodotus); discussing fundamental political and social issues before the decisions

[1] Divergence could vary according to the *philosoph-* parts of speech, but the paucity of evidence prevents tracking such fine-grained change or constancy, and what evidence there is from the fifth century BCE does not warn that such variance could be large.

[2] The closest competition is the so-called Old Oligarch's (difficult to date) *Constitution of the Athenians*.

which they underlie become urgent (Thucydides); doing medicine by reliance on hypotheses about the underlying principles of human nature and their cosmic analogues rather than on practical assessment of diet and environment (*On Ancient Medicine*); debating deep issues that are neither politically nor meteorologically exigent and probably turn on logical considerations (Gorgias); revolutionizing a city's constitutional arrangements rather than propounding incremental legislative or policy change (*Ecclesiazusae*); and seeking ways out of personal difficulties reflectively (Lysias). Taken as a whole, then, being *philosophos* means continuously investigating, usually in conversational exchange, the underlying and significant normative structures that constitute city- and life-guiding principles. This supports the linguistic hypothesis of chapter 3, that the term *philosophos* points to the idea of acting, repetitively, to become like political-advising and maxim-spouting *sophoi*. We also see diversity by the end of the fifth century BCE: the Hippocratic treatise shows a natural-scientific side to *philosophia*; Gorgias recognizes its formalized performance; and Lysias, probably the latest author, domesticates *philosophia* into self-directed, albeit exceptional, life planning. The behavior that prompted the coinage of *philosophos* may have already included these scientific, formalized, and self-directed elements, along with the more prominent political and existential elements, and only certain later users of the term emphasized them; alternatively, one or another element—my guess is the one found in Gorgias's formalized usage—shows actual innovation.

An appendix of three likely uses of *philosophos* or *philosophia* in the fifth century BCE, connected to Zeno, Simon, and Democritus, follows this chapter. They corroborate claims made here, but with such evidentiary challenges as to warrant only subsidiary consideration.

Herodotus's Solon and His Sage Wisdom (Hdt. 1.30)

Early in the first book of his *History* (ca. 425–15 BCE),[3] Herodotus puts a use of the verb *philosophein* (Hdt. 1.30) squarely in the context of sagely *sophoi* (whom he calls *sophistai*), which we would expect from the conjectured coinage situation.[4] Herodotus introduces the scene by describing the

---

[3] For the date of authorship, see Fornara 1971; Munn 2000, 43; and bibliography at YC 1.1n1.

[4] Cf. DL 1.12 and Aristid. *Or.* 3.677; see Ford 1993, 36–37, and *FGH* 1005 ad F7, for discussion. The practice continued to Aristotle, who called the Seven Sages both *sophistai* (*On Philosophy* fr. 5 Ross) and *sophoi* (fr. 8 Ross), and Isoc. *Antid.* 235, who says that Solon is called *sophistês* but that the word is now a dishonorable appellation. I suspect that, for Herodotus in the

imperial successes of the Lydians in the early sixth century BCE, the details of which provide the important "sage" context. In his final episode about King Alyattes's life, Herodotus observes that Periander of Corinth, considered by later authors as one of the Seven *Sophoi*, brought peace to Sardis and Miletus by intercepting a Delphic oracle.[5] Herodotus then describes the first actions of Alyattes's son, Croesus: the subjugation of the Greeks of Asia Minor and the plotting about the subjugation of the islands of its coast. At this point a certain sage—either Bias of Priene or Pittacus of Mytilene, Herodotus is not sure which—comes to Sardis and analyzes Croesus's and the islanders' respective expectations. Croesus is "exceedingly pleased with his reasoning and, thinking he had spoken appropriately," decides to sue for peace with the islanders.[6] He has other ways to expand his empire, and thus the wealth of Sardis still grows. At its height came "all the other Greek *sophistai* alive at the time, each for his own reason."[7] Herodotus must have in mind Periander, Bias, Pittacus, and their ilk. Since he later mentions Thales and Chilon in their capacity as political advisors,[8] and the Lydian Sandanis,[9] such men are probably included, too. Herodotus then says that even (καὶ δὴ καί) Solon of Athens

---

late fifth century BCE, the term *sophos* had become broader than it once was, and therefore less appropriate for a political advisor than the professional name *sophistês*.

[5] Hdt. 1.20–22. Periander was notoriously excluded from some lists of the Seven *Sophoi* because he was a tyrant (cf. Paus. 1.23.1; Stamatopoulou 2016). Hdt. 1.96–101 describes the pattern of devolution from *sophos* to intimidating tyrant in his account of Deiokes.

[6] Hdt. 1.27. About fifteen years later, Herodotus says, Bias tries to rescue the Ionians from their slavery to the Persians by advising, at a counsel of all Ionians, that they emigrate to Sardinia; he adds that, before the Ionian defeat, another core sage, Thales of Miletus, had recommended political unification of Ionia (Hdt. 1.170).

[7] Hdt. 1.29: οἵ τε ἄλλοι πάντες ἐκ τῆς Ἑλλάδος σοφισταί, οἳ τοῦτον τὸν χρόνον ἐτύγχανον ἐόντες, ὡς ἕκαστος αὐτῶν ἀπικνέοιτο. "For his own reason" seems the best way to express ὡς ἕκαστος, in light of the ensuing lines that take up Solon's reasons for coming, though Sage 1985, 12, has "As each one of these sages came, so came Solon." How and Wells 1912 suspect that some of them may have come because of the wealth, arguing that "sophists" are later associated with venery; but Herodotus does not have "sophists" of Protagoras's ilk in mind. There is also a question about the meaning of the ἄλλοι; I have taken it to mean "all the other *sophistai* (sc. the ones not yet mentioned in Book 1), but Sage 1985, 12, has "there came . . . many [visitors], among whom were all the Greek sages."

[8] Thales: Hdt. 1.170; Chilon, as ἀνήρ . . . σοφώτατος: Hdt. 7.235.2, with a Chilon of Lacedaemon who gives advice at 1.59.2 and a Chilon son of Demarmenos who does not (perhaps the sage's grandson, as Macan 1895 guesses) at 6.65.2.

[9] Herodotus says that Sandanis, already considered a *sophos*, became more famous for giving clever though unheeded advice to Croesus about the austerity of the Persians and the pointlessness of conquering them (Hdt. 1.71). Herodotus also mentions, on three occasions, the legendary prophet Melampus, a *sophos anêr*, whose prophetic followers he calls *sophistai,* and who brings Dionysian ritual from Egypt to Greece and, when asked to cure madness in women caused by Dionysus, ruthlessly extorts half a kingship: Hdt. 2.49, 7.221, 9.34.

came,[10] after visiting Amasis in Egypt.[11] Solon had recently made laws for the Athenians. So as not to have his laws repealed, which could happen only with his express approval, he went abroad for ten years. He claimed for his purpose "observation" (κατά θεωρίης πρόφασιν, Hdt. 1.29).[12] Herodotus believes that Solon in fact traveled for both reasons—constitutional stability and observation (theôria). Solon is received by Croesus in his palace, and after several days, Croesus arranges for him to see his treasury in its blessed greatness (μεγάλα τε καὶ ὄλβια). Having given Solon time to observe (θεησάμενον) and investigate or appraise (σκεψάμενον) all of it, Croesus makes a remark and asks a question:

> Athenian visitor, much word has arrived to us about you concerning both your wisdom (σοφίης) and your wandering (πλάνης), that, philosophizing (φιλοσοφέων), you have covered much of the earth for the sake of *theôria*. So the desire came to me to ask you whether you have by now seen the most blessed (ὀλβιώτατος) of all men.[13] (Hdt. 1.30.1)

Croesus expects and hopes that Solon will say that he has, and that it is Croesus himself. But Solon describes the more blessed lives of three other men (Hdt. 1.30.3–1.31). When Croesus asks whether he is being deliberately insulted, Solon lectures him about the tenuousness of human life, gives detailed calculations about the number of days in a human life, contrasts the ways a rich and

---

[10] The structure of this and Herodotus's previous paragraphs implies that he includes Solon among the *sophistai* (contra: Stein 1869; How and Wells 1912); see Powell 1938 s.v. σοφιστής; Sage 1985, 244; McNeal 1986, 119, citing Hdt. 1.1 (τῇ τε ἄλλῃ χώρῃ ἐσαπικνέεσθαι, καὶ δὴ καὶ ἐς Ἄργος); YC 1.395–400. Thus καὶ δὴ καί must mean "and even," where Solon either would not immediately have been expected or is to be focalized. Andrea Purvis's formulation, "Of particular note" (in Strassler 2007), gets the force right.

[11] Herodotus says that Solon adopted "an admirable law" from Amasis, that each person each year must declare his occupation—as a just and honest one—to his respective governor: Hdt. 2.177.2. (Herodotus's next and final mention of Solon is his trip to Cyprus and praise of its king as best of tyrants: 5.113.2.) Arist. *Ath. Pol.* 11 says only that Solon went to Egypt "for business (ἐμπορίαν) and for *theôria*."

[12] On *prophasis*, see Pearson 1952, esp. 209n18; on Solon's wandering, see Montiglio 2000, 88. Havelock 1963, 280–81, presents *theôria* and its object too vaguely with his gloss "desire to see the world."

[13] Ξεῖνε Ἀθηναῖε, παρ' ἡμέας γὰρ περὶ σέο λόγος ἀπῖκται πολλὸς καὶ σοφίης εἵνεκεν τῆς σῆς καὶ πλάνης, ὡς φιλοσοφέων γῆν πολλὴν θεωρίης εἵνεκεν ἐπελήλυθας· νῦν ὦν ἵμερος ἐπειρέσθαι μοι ἐπῆλθέ σε εἴ τινα ἤδη πάντων εἶδες ὀλβιώτατον. The MSS disagree about the clause following φιλοσοφέων, some replacing γῆν πολλὴν with τὴν πολλὴν, τὴν πόλιν, or τῆς πολλῆς, resulting in the following translations: for the sake of *theôria* you have "gone through much" or "come to the city." This provocative variation makes little difference for my argument. The most thorough analysis of the text is at YC 2.99–115.

a fortunate man can be happy, and observes the impossibility of perfection in any part of life (Hdt. 1.32).[14]

Croesus's use of *philosophein* gives an important insight into the early uses of the term.[15] Croesus says that Solon has a reputation for having *sophia*,[16] which implies that he takes him to be *sophos*—and thus also, I believe, a *sophos*.[17] Midway through his *Histories*, Herodotus describes the *sophos* Anacharsis of Scythia as "having done *theôria* over much of the earth" (γῆν πολλὴν θεωρήσας) and as "presenting his copious *sophia*" (ἀποδεξάμενος κατ᾽ αὐτὴν σοφίην πολλήν, Hdt. 4.76.2).[18] It is as a *sophos*, then, and one who has seen and judged many people and their appurtenances and situation, that Croesus queries Solon for his view about the most blessed of men.[19] The first clause's "wisdom . . . wandering" matches the second clause's "*theôria* . . . covered much land." The participle, *philosopheôn*, must therefore gloss and give a name to Solon's travel and concern for understanding the world that is, according to Croesus, characteristic of his efforts to be a *sophos*.[20] *Philosophein* seems to name the way of life that appears oriented toward becoming a *sophos*.

It is not trivial that Herodotus uses *philosophos*-group words only once. The word must have for him a special, charged, and narrowly tailored meaning, used not for just any intellectual cultivation (many instances of which

---

[14] The passage from Hdt. 1.29–32 has received much scholarly attention; see, e.g., Benardete 1969, 16–19; Redfield 1985, 102; Belloni 2000, 160–64; Nightingale 2004, 63–64; Sharp 2004, 90–93; Ker 2000, 312–13; Asheri, Lloyd, and Corcella 2007, 97–104; YC 1.400–6.

[15] YC, the most sustained inquiry into this passage, seems to assume that Herodotus provides the earliest extant use of the entire *philosophos* group and perhaps implies that Herodotus coined the term; obviously I disagree. Riedweg 2004, 167–68; Riedweg 2005, 96, recognizes that the "natural way" Herodotus uses the word shows that the word "had been in use for some time."

[16] Croesus is probably saying that news has arrived "concerning" (εἵνεκεν) his *sophia*, not that the news has come "because of" his *sophia*, though this is possible.

[17] Cf. Peterson 2011, 203. If Solon's advice represents Herodotus's worldview, as Shapiro 1996 argues, we do not need to reject the equation of Solon with *sophos* on the grounds that it would entail, absurdly, that Herodotus is also a *sophos*; *sophoi* just are *sophoi* if they influence other people's views for certain kinds of reasons (like those of Herodotus).

[18] At 4.42.1, Herodotus says that he is the only one known for wisdom (σοφίης πέρι) in the Pontus. Anacharsis is explicitly included among the Seven *Sophoi* at DL 1.41–42. See Redfield 1985 on the rich concept of touristic travel in Herodotus.

[19] The long cap on this story at Hdt. 1.86.3 follows the familiar model of *sophos* advice to leaders cited above; see generally Bischoff 1932 and Lattimore 1939.

[20] This is obscured in many translations: Nightingale 2004, 63–65, "how you have traveled much of the earth philosophizing and pursuing *theôria*," as though it were an independent activity; De Sélincourt 1954, "how widely you have travelled in the pursuit of knowledge," conflating participle and explanation for Solon's travel; Legrand 1932, "le gout du savoir et la curiosité"; Rawlinson 1862, "from love of knowledge and a wish to see the world"; and recently Purvis in Strassler 2007, "We hear you have wandered through much of the world in search for knowledge."

Herodotus references through the *Histories*).[21] What this tightly worked set
piece shows is that *philosophein* is, according to Herodotus's Croesus, the activity appropriate to those aiming to become members of that Panhellenic
cultural elite, equally known as *sophoi* or *sophistai*, where expansive travels
and spectatorship prepare a person to give profound judgment about the human
experience. It is a stereotyped practice connected with sagehood, and one that
provides people like Solon, a lawmaker, adequate cover. It is not a commonplace, broadly distributed activity; it is not obviously what Milesian researchers are doing when they investigate, systematize, and write; it is not obviously
deliberative or political; and it is practiced by a fluid but delineable group of
people.[22]

Thucydides's Pericles and Defense of Athenian *Philosophein* (Thuc. 2.40)

Thucydides's *History of the Peloponnesian War* also includes a single use of
a *philosophos*-group word, again the verb *philosophein*, this time specifically
connected to deliberation about politically relevant matters before they become urgent.[23] Midway through his Funeral Oration of 431 BCE, Pericles

[21] Why Herodotus has only Croesus apply it only to Solon is uncertain—perhaps it is Solon's
travel to Egypt and Sardis or his being Athenian, perhaps it is Solon's fame for gnomic poetry,
perhaps it is the mere fact that this is the only conversation with a *sophistês* that Herodotus records—but the connection must have struck Herodotus's contemporaries and later audiences as
particularly apt. Solon comes to seem a paradigmatic sort of (non-disciplinary) *philosophos*:
see, e.g., Pl. *Chrm.* 154e8–155a3 (implied); *RL* 133c3–4 (implied); Xen. *Symp.* 8.39; [Dem.]
Erot. 50.5 (ca. 350–30 BCE); Aeschin. *In Ctes.* 108, 257 (ca. 330 BCE); cf. *In Tim.* 41 (ca. 345 BCE);
DS 9 frr. 1.2, 4.2; Plut. *Solon* 3; Malalas 6.6.
[22] This argument is contra Chroust 1947, 22; Morrison 1958, 208; Hadot 2002, 16; Frede
2004, 23; Nightingale 2004, 63–65. While Herodotus himself may have a Milesian investigatory
sensibility, even if Solon serves in some way as his avatar (per Shapiro 1996), Solon need not
himself have that sensibility.
[23] The book may have been written as late as the mid-390s BCE; see Pouilloux and Salviat
1983, 391–403, and 1985; and Munn 2000, 5–6, 11–12, 305–6, 316–27, 433n57, 434n61, who argues
that Thucydides could have written only after the war, after Socrates's execution, and during the
reconstruction of democracy and empire. Others have thought that because the *History* breaks
off at 411, he must have died then; or because Paus. 1.23.9 states that he was murdered en route to
Athens, it was shortly after 404 that he stopped writing. In any event, the speech may faithfully
record Pericles's speech of 431: Thucydides seems to have taken close notes of speeches from
the beginning of the war (Thuc. 1.22); many people would have been at Pericles's speech and
so could have corroborated Thucydides's sketch; and if anyone were worth quoting verbatim, it
would be Pericles. See also Gomme 1945, 2.104, 2.126, 2.129–30, 2.136, who argues that some
passages would be appropriate as spoken in the 430s but not after 404. But nothing rides on the
matter except chronological bookkeeping.

defends the Athenians from slander. "We beautify with economy, and we *philosophein* without softness" (φιλοκαλοῦμέν τε γὰρ μετ᾽ εὐτελείας καὶ φιλοσοφοῦμεν ἄνευ μαλακίας, 2.40.1). Critics of Athenian hegemony, it appears, have slung these names at the Athenians; Pericles accepts the names but not the negative imputations. The charges and nature of Pericles's corrections are not exactly obvious, since Thucydides uses these verbs only once; "beautify" (φιλοκαλέω) makes its first appearance in Greek here (and only appearance in classical Greek), and "philosophize" (φιλοσοφέω) makes one of the first appearances in Greek here. Both terms and their qualifications, novelties presented with such witty compression, call for a gloss; we get it in the subsequent five sentences:

> Wealth we use rather for timely activity (ἔργου) than for boastful speech (λόγου); and someone's admitting to poverty is not shameful—what's more shameful is for him not to flee actively (ἔργῳ) from it. Some of us concern ourselves with both household and political matters; while others, though occupied by activity (ἔργα), lack nothing in their appreciation for political matters. We alone consider the man who lacks any part in these to be, not unmeddling (ἀπράγμονα), but useless, and it is we ourselves who either decide or at least make correct sense of affairs (ἤτοι κρίνομέν γε ἢ ἐνθυμούμεθα ὀρθῶς τὰ πράγματα), not considering it to be speeches (λόγους) that undermine activity (ἔργοις) but rather the failure to have already come to understand, through speech (λόγῳ), how to act (ἔργῳ) when one must. For we so excel others in both our boldness and especially our thinking through (ἐκλογίζεσθαι) whatever it is we pursue; in other men, confidence is really ignorance, and calculation (λογισμός) brings hesitation. The men rightly judged strongest in soul are those who know (γιγνώσκοντες) most clearly what is terrible and what is pleasurable and who, on account of this, do not turn away from risks. (Thuc. 2.40.1–3)

The unnamed critics accuse the Athenians of being all show and all talk; Pericles explains that, far from being enervating, Athenian *philokalein* and *philosophein* contribute to agency and power—indeed, the word *ergon* shows up five times in the first three sentences, *logon* three times. He makes quick work of *philokalein*, apparently interpreted as the conspicuous consumption associated with the mid-century building program that much of the Delian League tribute funded. Pericles justifies the expenses as capital improvements necessary (and no more than necessary—μετ᾽ εὐτελείας) to prepare the city, and presumably Hellas at large, for likely eventualities. What looks like self-indulgent ornamentation counts as prudent outfitting. Pericles then generalizes to say that the real problem is complacency about the financial situation in which one might find oneself; such complacency would show a failure to prepare oneself for "timely activity."

This explanation applies equally to *philosophein*, apparently interpreted as the dithering and delay associated with the capacious network of formal and informal mid-century democratic decision-making bodies. This is a criticism familiar from Plato's Callicles: *philosophein* has its charms for the youth, but in adults it makes one incapable of facing the hard facts of political life, that one must simply act (*Grg.* 484c–85e). *Philosophein* reflects "softness" (μαλακία), taking the easy route of non-self-assertion.[24] Many readers have supposed that Pericles means to defend Athenian "philosophizing" as intellectual cultivation or scientific pursuits among the elite.[25] But he is really saying that *philosophein* is the citizenry's talking through fundamental political issues— including the nature and value of the expedient, bad, and pleasurable—before the political exigencies whose response relies on them arise. By implicit definition, the talking called *philosophein* does not realize itself in explicit political decision-making; but that is not because it is incompetent to eventuate in action—it precedes any such call for action, and when the call comes, the Athenians will be better prepared, having more considerations already fully and clearly in view, than anybody else. According to Pericles, then, not only is *philosophein* useful as a collective activity rather than harmful to the city (conducive of *malakia*); it is the best preparation for a city's prosperity—each citizen like a *sophos*.[26]

---

[24] A morally charged term, *malakia* characterizes people unwilling to confront politically or militarily important hardships, toil, and danger (Hdt. 6.11; Thuc. 1.122.4, 2.61.4, 2.85.2, 5.7.2, 5.75.3; Lys. 10.11); in the fourth century BCE it is fit explicitly into moral theorizing (Xen. *Symp.* 8.8; Arist. *Eth. Nic.* 1150a31).

[25] E.g., Ford 1993, 40 ("genteel refinement"); Hadot 2002, 16 ("intellectual activity and the interest in science and culture which flourished in their city"); and Laks 2002, 30 ("being attracted by the fine arts and literature"). Rusten 1985 is only half-right when he says that "it is no longer necessary to dilute the force of φιλοσοφοῦμεν to 'general culture', since it need not apply equally to every Athenian," and not right in claiming that "on an individual level . . . φιλοκαλεῖν is virtually a synonym for φιλοσοφεῖν." Gadamer 1982, 141, is too speculative when he argues that *philosophein* "means 'interest in theoretical questions,' for 'beautiful' refers to the domain of that which surpasses the necessary and useful and is sought for its own sake just because it is pleasing." Gomme 1945, 119–21, who mostly discusses *philokalein*, does not take the discussion of political preparation to gloss the meaning of "philosophize," but instead as a parallel—"the comparison is with other Greeks, Boeotians, and Peloponnesians, who would think a love of learning to be as inconsistent with courage as political discussion with decisiveness of action"— but this seems a misreading of Thucydides's logic.

[26] Isocrates says nearly the same thing in the mid-300s BCE: Athenian excellence comes from philosophizing, which is the education that prepares people to give and understand speeches (Isoc. *Antid.* 250).

In the Athenian context of Pericles's late 430s BCE, or in the ensuing decades during which Thucydides wrote his history, *philosophein* names a specific mode of political conversation, one in which all can participate but not one that characterizes every sort of discussion or practice of mental development. The focus is not on *sophia* or an attitude toward *sophia*, but on the proclivity to prepare to give advice and make decisions necessary for a city's being run well. This usage shares much with that of Herodotus's Croesus, who takes *philosophein* to refer to the actions that allow Solon at a moment's notice to advise him, a political leader, on the excellence of his life and life choices. A minor difference is that with the term, Thucydides emphasizes the verbal tendencies of the Athenians, whereas Croesus does not emphasize verbal tendencies; but Herodotus may presage Thucydides's usage of *philosophein* after all, since his Solon responds to Croesus's question loquaciously, with a range of moralizing stories, mathematical calculations, and disquisitions on gods, men, and mortality. Both would be glossed better as "doing what might make one be treated as a Seven Sage style *sophos*" than as "loving *sophia*" or "working to improve one's mind." We will see something similarly political, conversational, and preparatory in Gorgias's and Aristophanes's work. But first we shall take a detour into the Hippocratic corpus, to a less political use of the term, to see another way that *philosophein* involves the study of deep background considerations on which practical decisions are to be made.

The Hippocratic Critique of Empedoclean *Philosophia*-Inclined Doctors (Hippoc. *VM* 20.1)

Sometime perhaps around 420 BCE, an unknown Hippocratic author draws an explicit connection between Empedocles's writings on nature and so-called *philosophia* (probably the earliest extant occurrence of the abstract noun).[27] He does so in this text, *On Ancient Medicine*, to vivify a contrast between his favored medical approach and the more abstract and cosmological approach of other doctors and *sophistai* ("teachers," "experts") that he says "tend toward philosophy" (τείνει . . . ὁ λόγος ἐς φιλοσοφίην). While the text is not about *philosophia* per se—it is about the technical success of medicine as has long been practiced, not just with the influx of new thinking—it provides excellent evidence for a meaning of *philosophia* that seems best explained by a Pythag-

[27] 420 BCE: Schiefsky 2006, 64, arguing with "some confidence"; Lloyd 2006, 366, doubts that such confidence is warranted. In further support of Schiefsky's view: the reference only to Empedocles and no other thinker, and the language of "above and below the earth" (see below, pp. 138–40). On the text, see YC 1.351–54, and more broadly 1.348–60.

orean provenance, and that shares, with the political usages seen in Herodotus and Thucydides, the emphasis on reasoning through the fundamentals in some department of life removed from the pressure that comes from the urgency to make a decision.

Chapter 20 of *On Ancient Medicine*, the section with most relevance to our account, begins with an intradisciplinary dispute.[28] The author states that some doctors and sophists (presumably teachers of or lecturers on medicine) claim that successful treatment requires having learned "what the human is" (ὅ τι ἐστὶν ἄνθρωπος) and having learned it before they actually have to effect a cure of a human—as we saw Thucydides's Pericles say that Athenians talk about matters before they actually have to confront a problem.[29] The content of this "what is *x*" question, and thus the way to answer it, depends on the questioners' view of the proper knowledge of nature. For these sophists and doctors, this knowledge is cosmogonic and compositional. They think they must know the origins and parts of the universe. Given that humans are part of nature, this cosmogonic and compositional knowledge includes knowing the origins and parts of humans. The Hippocratic author disagrees with this inference, that knowing the whole of nature will allow one to know humans in a way relevant to health. He does not spell out his critique, but he seems to find several problems with the "philosophical" approach. First, the scale of those investigations is wrong; second, the creation stories that provide philosophical interest focus on isolated moments of becoming rather than on the interactions between the things that have come to be, which cause sickness and health; and, third, having simplified the world to a mixture of basic stuffs—"hot, cold, dry, wet, or whatever else you want"—the complexity that is material to human well-being gets forgotten.[30] He proposes as the proper knowledge of nature not *philosophia*, but rather something interactional in a fine-grained way. The doctor must know "what the human being is in light of what one eats and drinks, and what it is in relation to other things one does (ἐπιτηδεύματα), and how each thing will affect another (ὅ τι ἀφ᾽ ἑκάστου ἑκάστῳ συμβήσεται)."[31] This relational, dynamic, and particularistic view of the nature of medical knowledge conceives of knowledge in a way radically different from the way the *philosophia*-tending opponents do. They look back in time and space, seek-

---

[28] See Dunn 2005, 60–63, for the insightful sophistic moves the author makes throughout the text.

[29] Hippoc. *VM* 20.1: δεῖ καταμαθεῖν τὸν μέλλοντα ("one must learn [now] what in the future . . ."); compare to Thuc. 2.40.2, quoted above.

[30] This list and number of elements and the dismissive "or whatever you want" (ἢ ἄλλο τι ὅ ἂν θέλωσιν) open the treatise, Hippoc. *VM* 1.1.3.

[31] Hippoc. *VM* 20.3. This passage is paraphrased for the case of "rhetoric" in Pl. *Phdr.* 271d1–7.

ing from where and what something—a human—came to be, and then diagnose illness by projecting something anomalous onto that development or attained state. Our author, by contrast, exhorts doctors to observe, in the present, how humans are modified by the most intimate aspects of their environment, what humans take into their bodies, and what they work on, and then to diagnose illness by identifying troublemaking environmental causes. For example: too much unmixed wine for anyone or too much cheese for certain people. This clinical work in the natural history of human flourishing and illness may take as long as the environment is wide; but at least the evidence is visible and concrete, not merely hypothetical.

It is in describing his opponents' medical epistemology that the Hippocratic author appeals to the *philosophia* typified by Empedocles and the likeminded. In "tending toward" (τείνει)[32] that *philosophia*, such medical practitioners write "about nature from its origin what the human being is and how it first came to be and from what it was compounded."[33] His critique of *philosophia* actually has two parts. As we saw in the previous paragraph, the core of the criticism comes from his preference for the interactional model: the cosmogonic model simply does not provide "any clear knowledge" and it lacks "precision."[34] We can now add the filigree to this criticism, which is his claim that *philosophia*-inflected writings (γέγραπται) by doctors and sophists belong in the realm less of medicine than of "writing" (τῇ γραφικῇ). Our author appears to say that the "philosophical" writings fail to get through to the realities they purport to describe; their excellence is found not in their fit with the world but in their internal compositional arrangement.[35] He is probably not charging medical *philosophia* with absolute irrelevance, as being a theory that informs no practice, since he makes only a comparative claim. But he does suggest that its priorities are expositional, like persuasive power and explanatory simplicity and breadth, rather than the technical goals of efficacy and applicability.

Thus the Hippocratic author associates *philosophia* with advocating a method of simple, universal, logically fundamental explanations for tough

[32] LM 6.319 translate this as "belongs to"; the difference concerns the degree of overlap between what practitioners of medicine and practitioners of *philosophia* do, but the present analysis does not turn on it.

[33] The syntax of the first part of this phrase, οἳ περὶ φύσιος γεγράφασιν ἐξ ἀρχῆς ὅ τι ἐστὶν ἄνθρωπος, obscures the logical relation between writing "what the human being is" and writing "about nature from its origin." The final verb, συνεπάγη, from πήγνυμι, appears to be Empedoclean (found in B15/D52, B56/147b, B86/D213, B107/D241); see Schiefsky 2006, 305–6, for discussion and further occurrences of the verb in fifth-century BCE physics.

[34] Concerns about "precision" have already arisen, in Hippoc. *VM* 9, 12.

[35] For the history of this sentence's interpretation, see Schiefsky 2006, 306–10.

issues. At the beginning of his treatise, he calls this "using one or two hypothetical causes." This method of hypothesis is inappropriate for medicine, which deals with the manifest body and its surroundings, for it is suited rather to speaking about hidden matters, where access is otherwise blocked (τὰ ἀφανέα τε καὶ ἀπορεόμενα).[36] This includes, "for example, the things in the sky and the things below the earth" (οἷον περὶ τῶν μετεώρων ἢ τῶν ὑπὸ γῆν).[37] While study of the things in the sky and below the earth is not a definition of *philosophia*—*philosophia* is not mentioned in these opening pages—it is taken as an appropriate or stereotypical or legible occasion for *philosophia*. Thus the meaning of the phrase should give us more information about *philosophia* than we get in chapter 20, and so we will discuss it in detail.

In the Sky and below the Earth

The things in the sky (τὰ μετεώρα) include both the celestial and atmospheric bodies. Their study involves describing their motions, their ingredients, and their origins. One's physics determines one's belief about the effect of their relative positions on the mundane world, either as predictive or as causal. But studying *ta meteôra* is not just studying the stars, their patterns, and their powers. It is studying everything beyond our planet; and if our planet is to be considered somehow akin to the things beyond it, then it is in effect studying everything whatsoever and, to some degree, studying everything at once. This is cosmology. Abstracted from particular bodies, it is geometry and mathematics. Abstracted further and given a methodological spin, it may even include analysis as such.[38]

This totalizing view of "the things in the sky" as "everything" might seem to leave "the things under the earth" with relatively little territory of their own. This could suggest that the polarity simply emphasizes the totality.[39] But it is not the only possible way. Evidence for its importance comes from the fact that the nearly contemporaneous play, Aristophanes's *Clouds*, turns a joke on the very subject: a character's ignorance of the original referent of "below the earth." Strepsiades sees some denizens of Socrates's school bent over like animals. He eventually learns that their anuses are looking toward the heav-

---

[36] That these issues were fodder for fifth-century BCE debate is clear from Alcmaeon B1/D4 (= DL 8.83) and Euripides *Oenomaus* fr. 574 (τεκμαιρόμεσθα τοῖς παροῦσι τἀφανῆ; cf. fr. 811).

[37] Hippoc. *VM* 1.3. The word order suggests that a better translation is "subterranean things."

[38] On *analusis* in ancient Greek philosophy, see Menn 2002. Thanks to M. M. McCabe for prompting this idea.

[39] And it may have mythic origin: Pindar's story of Polydeuces allows him to choose to spend half his existence "under the earth" (γαίας ὑπένερθεν), the other half in the golden homes "of the heaven" (οὐρανοῦ) (Pind. *Nem.* 10.87–88).

ens (ἐς τὸν οὐρανόν) because they themselves are learning to do astronomy (ἀστρονομεῖν διδάσκεται).[40] In the meanwhile, however, he is baffled by their heads. "Why ever are they looking toward the earth (ἐς τὴν γῆν βλέπουσιν)"? His guide replies: "They are seeking what is *beneath* the earth" (ζητοῦσιν . . . τὰ κατὰ γῆς). "So they're seeking out bulbs?"[41] If that's the case, they should not strain so hard, Strepsiades says; he can help them find some wonderful ones. But why, he asks, are those others *really* (σφόδρ᾽) bending down? He is answered, paradoxically: "they are diving below Tartarus" (ἐρεβοδιφῶσιν ὑπὸ τὸν Τάρταρον) (Ar. *Nub.* 187–94).[42] This set piece requires that by around 420 BCE the Athenians already knew the polar expression. It also requires that there be something counterintuitive about the idea of studying the things under the earth. What is under the earth is in principle beyond human experience and perception.

Yet the reference to "below Tartarus" suggests that those who have passed on may come to know its denizens in the land of Hades; investigating beneath the earth is reflecting on death, the afterlife, judgment, and the career of the soul. This is probably because the underground is associated with burial, with the origins of plants, with the depths of the sea, and with all that is hidden from the clear light of living day. But the below is also associated with other sorts of investigative concern. Mining may be an important one, which would concern geology as such, but also theories and experiments concerning the pieces of land that contain mineral-rich ore. This would also include the exploration and creation of caves. The temperature of underground water, and its relation to flooding, would be another. Empedocles explains hot springs by appeal to underground fires; Oenopides of Chios, Thrasyalkes of Thasos, and others explain the Nile's fluctuations by appeal to the inverse proportion of atmospheric and geological temperature.[43]

Thus, as informative about the nature of *philosophia*, study of "the things in the sky and below the earth" is overdetermined, a pattern to fit a broad range of investigations, but also a pursuit directed toward (or not away from) the eventually practical. Some of those investigations have instrumental value: navigation, crop planning, and other sorts of forecasting; mineral extraction, irrigation, and the interpretation or prediction of earthquakes and volcanoes.

[40] In Ar. *Av.* 689–91 (414 BCE), Aristophanes jokingly has Prodicus include, in his study of the things above (περὶ τῶν μετεώρων), the nature of birds.

[41] Βολβοί usually refers to bulbs of the *Muscari comosum*, a Greek delicacy now called the tassel grape hyacinth.

[42] Tartarus is the lowest part of Hades (Hes. *Theog.* 119, 721–810).

[43] Empedocles A68/D110; Oenopides B11; Thrasyalkes (A)1; Anaxagoras A91/D66; Diogenes of Apollonius A18/D25. Plausibly influenced by this line of reasoning is Pl. *Phd.* 111c4–e4. See further Schiefsky 2006, 136–39.

Some address human choice at a life-defining level, connected to piety, self-care, and our respective dooms. Yet others have their application to life formulated in a roundabout way: acquiring a general and cogent comprehension of the entire world such that human nature, and thus the nature of human disease, may eventually be inferred. We see no emphasis on *philosophia* as a pursuit done purely for the pleasure of contemplation or the satisfaction of wonder, or for the intrinsic value of knowledge. Of course, nothing excludes the possibility of such emphasis. Yet, crucially, the Hippocratic author nowhere supposes that applying *philosophia* to medicine is a category error. His charges are against the rounding errors that accumulate when one goes to a general statement of the world and then back to an individual situation in the world.

Empedocles of Acragas

Rather than defining *philosophia* as investigating what is "in the sky and below the earth," the Hippocratic defines it ostensively: it is what Empedocles and those like him do, when they study nature. The citation of the Sicilian Empedocles does more than exemplify the relevant practice; it provides the archetype for it. Doing *philosophia* is basically doing what Empedocles does. This suggests that the Hippocratic author mentions Empedocles for reasons beyond, as Mark Schiefsky has put it in his careful study of the text, his "keen interest in anthropogony and embryology" and his status as "the first thinker to develop a clear concept of elemental constituent."[44] *Philosophia* itself manifests interest in biological generation and in analytic perspicuity, and it can be said to do so because *philosophia* names what Empedocles does.

This opens a question: why was Empedocles said to practice *philosophia*? There must be a strong connection between those first called *philosophoi* and Empedocles. We find such connections in two places: in the public linkages made between him and Pythagoreanism and in his fame for a life that combines politics, oratory, and intellectual investigation as Pythagoras's did.

Diogenes Laertius claims that Empedocles succeeded Pythagoras as representative of the Pythagorean school.[45] Timaeus of Tauromenium, a fourth-century BCE Sicilian with access to Italian documents, says that Empedocles listened to (ἀκοῦσαι) Pythagoras, obviously with some intermediation.[46]

---

[44] Schiefsky 2006, 302–3.

[45] DL 8.50. Diogenes Laertius discusses Pythagoras at 8.1–50 and Empedocles at 8.51–77. Hippolytus says that Empedocles came after the Pythagoreans and shared with them an interest in *daimones* and reincarnation (Hippol. *Haer.* 1.3).

[46] DL 8.54. Timaeus is cited again at 8.71–72 for his critical attitude toward stories about Empedocles's death and surrounding myths; this adds to the credibility of his claim about discipleship. Neanthes of Cyzicus, a reliable fourth-century BCE historiographer, says that Em-

Alcidamas, a student of Gorgias, who is in turn said to have been Empedocles's student, gives a more precise account. Both Zeno and Empedocles studied with Parmenides; Zeno then went off on his own, and Empedocles studied further with Pythagoreans and Anaxagoras.[47] As we saw in chapter 1, Heraclides wrote an account of Pythagoras's self-appellation of the term *philosophos* in his *On Diseases*, which otherwise celebrated Empedocles.[48] Clearly, fourth-century BCE historians, rhetoricians, and philosophers took Empedocles for a Pythagorean, and indeed perhaps as the most important Pythagorean; their evidence would likely have come from the fifth century BCE, which is the period of the sources that the Hippocratic author of *On Ancient Medicine* would have known.

The connection between Empedocles and Pythagoras goes beyond the pedagogical and the doctrinal. Pythagoras earned his fame as a dazzling public speaker, for the deep and systemic political influence he wrought in the oligarchies of southern Italy, and thanks to his mythic figure as wonderworker; he also had close ties to Western Greek medical innovators. In this respect, Empedocles recapitulates the Pythagorean model for winning familiarity and admiration across the eastern Mediterranean. Aristotle calls Empedocles the discoverer of rhetoric.[49] Elsewhere he notes Empedocles's impressive diction and poetic facility, and his production of historical verses, tragic drama, and political speeches.[50] The Peripatetic Satyrus says that Empedocles was a "top orator" and the teacher of Gorgias, who is now even more famous in rhetoric.[51] His oratory probably had more than belletristic and technical relevance; he weighed heavily in Acragas's political and social life.[52] But Gorgias also

---

pedocles poeticized Pythagoreanism, and studied with a Pythagorean (DL 8.55). Also on the Pythagoras-Empedocles connection, see DL 8.56; Philostr. *V A* 1.1, 6.5; Ath. 14.620c–d; Plut. *Quaest. conv.* 728e; Hierocl. *In Carm. Aur.* 23.2; Porph. *Antr.* 8; Olymp. *In Grg.* 35.12; and Euseb. *Praep. evang.* 10.14.15.

[47] DL 8.55–6; see again chapter 9. Empedocles lived at the right time to have studied with Anaxagoras and to have read his writings (Arist. *M.* A 984a11–13; see O'Brien 1968, 94–96).

[48] DL 8.67; Gottschalk 1980, 15–22; see again chapter 10.

[49] Arist. *Sophist* fr. 1 Ross.

[50] Arist. *On Poets* fr. 1 Ross.

[51] Quint. *Inst.* 3.1.8, DL 8.58, *Suda* ε 1002. In Pl. *Meno* 76c, Socrates speaks in the "manner of Gorgias" by citing Empedocles. See Spatharas 2001, 11 with bibliography, for reservations about the connection.

[52] DL 8.63–73: Empedocles spoke in favor of political equality, championed the people against tyrannical and self-serving magistrates and Council, and dissuaded his fellow citizens from civil strife (cf. Horky 2016). Thanks to his wealth and consequent influence on political decision-makers, he helped dissolve a newly instituted "One Thousand," presumably the oligarchic governing body. He is said to have been offered the kingship; he declined this position, and all leadership roles, to preserve his life of simplicity (λιτότητα) and freedom (ἐλεύθερον), according to Xanthus of Lydia and to Aristotle (see Schepens and Theys 1998; Kingsley 1990). He was forthright in

testifies to his teacher's wizardry. Timaeus recounts Empedocles's anemological feats. Heraclides recalls his medical and prognostic miracles as well as the posthumous stories of his apotheosis. Empedocles himself claims—echoing Pythagoras's entrance to Croton—that as he entered cities, men and women in the thousands revere and follow him, plying him with commercial, prophetic, and medical questions.[53]

At the same time, the scope of Empedocles's intellectuality surpassed that of virtually anyone else. As the Hippocratic author implies, it went from nature as a whole, what we would call cosmogony and physics, to all subordinated processes, especially those that recapitulate the macro-scale processes: speciation, embryology, and physiology. From these patterns of generation and constitution, Empedocles would draw moral conclusions about justice, animal rights, and self-improvement.[54] Empedocles's naturalizing program was a total system of inquiry and solution. Just so, the charismatic Pythagoras drew particular attention to himself and his associates thanks to their expansive research interests coupled with involvement in political upheaval on the eastern and western edges of the Greek world. Pythagoras's public (even if secretive) and concerted efforts looked like he sought recognition as the progeny of the incisive, canny, useful, and politically consequential *sophoi* of two generations earlier. This combination of public brilliance and unusual zeal provided good grounds for the coinage of *philosophos*. The term could then be applied to those who seemed relevantly similar to this Pythagorean archetype. The geographical, pedagogical, and research continuity between Pythagoras and Empedocles would support calling the latter *philosophos*.

If Empedocles's particular interests were tightly associated with his fame, then they could come to infuse the term *philosophos* with new meaning. If those first called *philosophoi* were not so called for their cosmogonic or physical interests—and of course they may have been—then those interests would not, early on, be denoted by the term; but with Empedocles's domination of certain intellectual trends in the following generations, those interests would come to be denoted by the term.[55] This usage we could then see in our Hippocratic author's text. And that is *philosophia* as specifically the investigation of macro-scale structures for eventual practical application to human life.

---

his critique of luxury and the compromise between power and integrity, forcing him to go into exile, not to return.

[53] DL 8.59 (wizardry), 8.60 (feats), 8.61, 67–68 (miracles and apotheosis), 8.62 (followers).

[54] Arist. *Rh.* 1373b6–17, Cic. *R.* 3.11.19, Iambl. *VP* 24.108.

[55] Contrast this view with McKirahan 2010, 252, who speaks of Empedocles as a "philosopher" only in the respect that he "articulated a complex and novel theory of the *kosmos*."

Gorgias and Quick-Witted Debates (Gorg. *Hel.* 13)

By the fourth century BCE people recognized an influence of Empedocles on his fellow-Sicilian, Gorgias (ca. 485–380 BCE), or at least a recapitulation. Probably Empedocles's oratory constituted some of that influence. But probably it would not have been limited to the practical application of *topoi* and figures of speech. Plato treats Gorgias as accepting Empedocles's theory of effluences, a theory meant to explain perception and perceptual reality (Pl. *Meno* 76c). Gorgias wrote a work called *On Non-Being*, which appears to respond to Parmenidean arguments about what exists.[56] His speeches about Palamedes and Helen contributed to epistemology, the philosophy of language, and reflection on justice, personal identity, and moral responsibility.[57] Isocrates grouped him with the Western Greek thinkers Parmenides, Zeno, and Melissus; an anonymous fourth-century BCE author analyzed him with Xenophanes and Melissus.[58] As the arguments mooted by Socrates in Plato's *Phaedrus* purport to show, successful rhetoric requires a surprisingly broad range of preliminary studies, psychology not the least of them. Thus it might be Empedocles's entire "philosophical" enterprise that contributed to Gorgias's rhetorical excellence.[59]

This may provide important background for understanding Gorgias's single extant use of a *philosophos*-group word, in his *Helen*, probably from around the end of the fifth century BCE.[60] The encomium investigates involuntary action in the context of Helen's removal to Troy. Absolving Helen of responsibility in case she was talked into going, Gorgias argues that persuasive speech does not facilitate choice; it instead compels the audience to carry out the will of the speaker, just as physical force does. In §13, he gives

[56] Its seriousness as a work of metaphysics is debated: see, e.g., Dodds 1959, 7–8 (a joke); Guthrie 1971, 192–200 (reductio ad absurdum); Kerferd 1981, 93–100 (sincere); Wardy 1996, 6–24 (deliberately ambiguous); Consigny 2001 (sincere in its radical antifoundationalism); Mc-Comisky 2002 (consistent with other works); and Palmer 2009, 35–36 (its doxography of metaphysics influenced Aristotle).

[57] Vitali 1971; MacDowell 1982; Mazzara 1999; Constantinidou 2008.

[58] Isoc. *Hel.* 3; *Antid.* 268; ps-Arist. *MXG.*

[59] Do Gorgias's brilliant antitheses and phrasal balances prosodize the elemental composition of the *kosmos*?

[60] Gorgias B11/D24. Olympiodorus (*In Grg.* proem 9) claims that *On Non-Being* inaugurated his writing career, in the late 440s CE. Gorgias traveled to Athens in 427 BCE, perhaps for the first time though maybe not for the last time (Spatharas 2001, 12), and wowed the Athenians with novel speeches (DS 12.53; Thuc. 3.86; Pl. *Hp. mai.* 282b4–c1; Timaeus in Dion. Hal. *Lys.* 3), but we have no evidence that the *Helen* was this text. Some scholars (e.g., Constantinidou 2008) find intertextual play between Gorgias's *Helen* and Euripides's *Trojan Women* (415 BCE) and even his *Helen* (412 BCE), suggesting that Gorgias presented his work in this half-decade.

three examples. The speeches of *meteorologoi* replace belief with belief, destroying the first, building up the second, thereby making what is initially unbelievable and unclear (τὰ ἄπιστα καὶ ἄδηλα) appear the opposite, namely true and clear, "to the eyes of belief" (whatever that poeticism means).[61] In "the compulsory competitions using speeches"—presumably those in legislative and forensic settings—words please and persuade the audience, apparently irrespective of their truthfulness.[62] Finally, in contests of philosophical speeches (or, less likely, philosophers' speeches, φιλοσόφων λόγων ἀμίλλας), quickness of judgment (γνώμης τάχος) reveals the mutability of belief-based opinions.[63]

Apparently these exemplary cases of persuasive effect occur in competition. Gorgias must have chosen them because they reveal change(s) of mind over a brief period, and because the criterion of success in these competitions is conviction: the best competitors will best exemplify Gorgias's point. They probably do not require competition, as solo recitals or cooperative panels display. But contest may be their default or salient mode. *Meteorologoi* seek for their interpretation of signs—from environmental changes to the future in farming, health, or other practical endeavor—to prevail over the interpretations of others.[64] The "compulsory" speakers compete for the allegiance of their audience. We are surely to understand "philosophical speeches" on this

---

[61] τοὺς τῶν μετεωρολόγων λόγους, οἵτινες δόξαν ἀντὶ δόξης τὴν μὲν ἀφελόμενοι τὴν δ' ἐνεργασάμενοι τὰ ἄπιστα καὶ ἄδηλα φαίνεσθαι τοῖς τῆς δόξης ὄμμασιν ἐποίησαν. A contemporary instance, from Aristophanes: "This is the thinkery of wise souls (ψυχῶν σοφῶν). | There men live who, speaking about | the heavens (τὸν οὐρανὸν | λέγοντες), persuade us (ἀναπείθουσιν) that it is an oven | and that it is around us, and we are embers" (Ar. *Nub.* 94–97). See, further, Pl. *Phd.* 96b1, 97a8, for Socrates's remarks about being persuaded back and forth by the speeches of *phusiologia*.

[62] τοὺς ἀναγκαίους διὰ λόγων ἀγῶνας, ἐν οἷς εἷς λόγος πολὺν ὄχλον ἔτερψε καὶ ἔπεισε τέχνῃ γραφείς, οὐκ ἀληθείᾳ λεχθείς. For the meaning of "compulsory contests" see MacDowell 1982, 39–40, but also Wardy 1996, 163n35. The Aldine edition of 1513 proposes ἀγοραίους in the place of ἀγῶνας, coming to about the same meaning, as well as ἔτρεψε ("turned") in place of ἔτερψε ("pleased"), which is plausible. LM 8.179 translate the passage quoted above as "contentions that constrain by means of speeches," but this is opaque in the context.

[63] φιλοσόφων λόγων ἀμίλλας, ἐν αἷς δείκνυται καὶ γνώμης τάχος ὡς εὐμετάβολον ποιοῦν τὴν τῆς δόξης πίστιν.

[64] Hippoc. *Aer.* 2.14–26 (recognizing that some people ignore the relationship between health and *meteôrologia/astronomia*); Eur. fr. 913 (contrasting *meteôrologoi*, who use deceptions [ἀπάτας], make random guesses on the basis of what is unknown [ἀφανῶν], and have no solid judgment [οὐδὲν γνώμης μετέχουσα], with the pious); Pl. *Crat.* 396c2 (*meteôrologoi* say that "looking at things above" [ὁρῶσα τὰ ἄνω] purifies the mind), 401b7 and 404c2 (*meteôrologoi* as the first namers of the gods, who are also *adoleschai*); *Pol.* 299b7 (condemning those *meteôrologoi* who presume to speak better, by appealing to climate, about navigation and health than sailors and doctors); *Phdr.* 270a1 (all great skills require *adoleschia* and *meteôrologia* about nature).

model, as concerned primarily with making their case against the speeches of opponents. This is not a cynical view, reducing philosophy to sophistry or rhetoric; rather, it means that their structure comes from the burden to articulate and defend an argument, not simply to appreciate reality, orient oneself toward the truth, or love wisdom.

Despite the similarities, Gorgias distinguishes philosophical exchange from the two other competitive modes. By "necessary" debates, Gorgias seems to mean those demanded by a city's constitution: persuasion seeks decision and action in the audience, while pleasure helps to effect the advocate's will. Philosophical exchanges might count contrastingly as "unnecessary" insofar as they lack an urgent decision-making role, or a legal-coercive structure, or an outcome that depends wholly on the preference of an audience whose sole task is to express its preference. This could imply that philosophical speech is leisured and optional, an intramural recreation without grave consequences to the city (the usual source of "necessity"); or that it unfolds in a freewheeling, conversational, and loose way; or that it has only internal or participant-judged criteria of success. Yet these possibilities might also be qualified.[65] Not all discussions with decision-making relevance are urgent, held in the moments before action is required. They could be for the sake of preparation, or deep background, or strategy, or eliminating possibilities that would always be bad or inappropriate. Nor do all debates outside the political-formal structure of a courtroom or assembly hall lack strongly held and policed practical norms. The symposium, for example, observes more or less definite rules of turn-taking, topical relevance, and verbal register. Finally, the criterion of success may not come from outside observers but also need not be the free choice of the competing parties; relatively self-enforcing standards of consistency, pertinence, and progress might suffice. A moderated view, then, is that philosophical exchanges probably lack the urgency that would make them count as necessary, and thus lack the attendant formal structures meant to ensure a decision no matter what disagreement (and thus delay) exists. While this does not entail that philosophical exchanges follow the argument absolutely wherever it goes, they can surely follow it further than "necessary" exchanges can.

Gorgias also distinguishes philosophical exchange from meteorological talk. This might surprise us, given the linkage in *On Ancient Medicine* of *philosophia* with the study of *ta meteôra*. Evidently Gorgias uses the term differently, even if (which is unlikely) he excludes anatomy, cosmogony, and physics from *meteôrologia*, leaving those fields for *philosophia*. He does not specify how he

---

[65] Pl. *Tht.* 172c8–175b7 stylizes the distinction between necessary (legal) and leisured (philosophical) speeches.

uses the latter term, but we might find its meaning at the handoff between Empedocles's and Gorgias's preoccupations, at what we might call a philosophical rhetoric. This would include the analysis of language, knowledge, perception, and the norms of agency and social comity. Such topics deal with the imperceptible and obscure, attitudes toward which, like the origins of the universe, max out epistemically at the "belief-based opinions" so vulnerable to change by philosophical debate. When Gorgias presents "quickness of judgment" (γνώμης τάχος) as the exemplary feature of philosophical debate, he seems to have in mind arguments in which the interlocutors respond directly to each other's speeches, without prepared set pieces. Success in such debate might depend on diagnosing weaknesses in opponents' syllogisms rather than on the accumulation of facts. Skill in logical diagnosis involves acute attention to language, reasoning, and belief as such.

Gorgias's mention of philosophical speeches in his triad of examples points to the notoriety, though not necessarily the popularity, of such talk.[66] The term "philosophizing" surely does not refer to all conversations between intellectually curious men and women, or between those who prefer truth over falsity. In the same way, meteorological talk is narrower than any casual talk of the weather or the night sky, and compulsory talk is narrower than any talk about the city's future and a criminal's past. In the familiar cases, the narrowness is well defined. So too in philosophical speech.

For Gorgias, philosophical speeches are public competitive diagnoses of an opponent's views about the topics at the nexus of Empedocles's and Gorgias's interests, notably those that devolve from the nature of language, reasoning, and knowledge. There is a family resemblance with the behavior of those who appeared to strive for *sophos*-hood. The conversations among the earlier generation would have seemed abstract but concerned nonetheless with social and existential, and thus political, questions, with unexpected hypotheses about the soul, web of life, ratios, harmony, and intuition undergirding the apparently practical answers. Perhaps this form of activity attributed to sixth-century BCE *philosophoi* had, for all its indirectness, an evident civic bias. By the late fifth century BCE, however, things had changed. Social observers may have seen an occasional differentiation within this *sophos*-striving group of people who preferred talking about *ta meteôra* and people who preferred talking about *ta legomena* or *ta noêmata* ("the things talked about" or "the things thought about"); the latter group struck them as more like the earlier

---

[66] DL 9.52 claims that Protagoras initiated verbal contests (λόγων ἀγῶνας), gave *sophismata* to "disputants" (πραγματολογοῦσι), and brought about "eristic competitors" (ἐριστικῶν); but since he says nothing about the dating or the relationship to *philosophia* or to Gorgias, we can infer nothing of relevance.

generation than the meteorologists did. They may also have noticed that some participants in more properly meteorological conversations oriented themselves less to political influence than the others. So, while the name *philosophos* may have been applied throughout the fifth century BCE to those who seemed sufficiently similar to those first called *philosophoi*, what counted as "similar" changed, with certain features becoming more pertinent. Gorgias, follower of Empedocles, Sicilian and Aegean traveler, would have both a conservatizing notion linked to Empedocles and a contemporizing notion linked to recent intellectual trends.

Aristophanes and Constitutional Innovation (Ar. *Eccl.* 571)

The political side of *philosophia*, connected to discussing and thinking through civic structures, which we have already seen explicitly in Thucydides and Gorgias, shows up again in Aristophanes, in his sole extant use of a *philosophos*-group term. In *Ecclesiazusae* (392 BCE), Praxagora has just won control of Athens for the women of the city. She waits to explain the plan that will bring about the benefits such rule entails.[67] The chorus tells Praxagora to delay no longer:

> Now indeed you must rouse a concentrated mind (πυκνὴν φρένα) and a philosophic
> thought (φιλόσοφον . . . φροντίδ᾽) that knows how (ἐπισταμένην)
> to defend (ἀμύνειν) your fellows.
> For, an idea (ἐπίνοια) comes from your tongue
> for a shared good fortune, exalting the citizen populace
> with myriads of benefits of life. Now's the time to clarify (δηλοῦν) what can be done;
> our city needs some wise invention (σοφοῦ . . . ἐξευρήματος).
> So go through the whole of it,
> leaving only what has been done and what has already been said earlier.
> For they hate if they spectate old things repeatedly.
>
> But don't delay—you've got to nail down those thoughts (διανοίας)—
> since quickness (ταχύνειν) contributes most to the satisfaction of the spectators.
>   (Ar. *Eccl.* 571–80)

---

[67] Ar. *Eccl.* 212–38, 441–53, 492, 560–67.

Editors only slowly accepted *philosophon* as scanning correctly in the text.[68] The meaning has remained uncertain. Yet as with Thucydides's Pericles, the chorus takes considerable effort to gloss the adjective which, given its position in the statement, looks somewhat wry. Being philosophical involves giving a verbal defense (ἀμύνειν . . . γλώττης), and thus a piece of spoken advocacy. The advocacy is for something thought out (ἐπίνοια, διανοίας), and thus perhaps more expansive than the normal run of self-directed notions. It takes up topics of universal or fundamental importance: the common prosperity (κοινῇ . . . εὐτυχίαισιν), the civic realm (πολίτην δῆμον), and flourishing in its fullest description (μυρίαισιν ὠφελίαισι βίου). It involves clarification (δηλοῦν) about possibility (δύναται), is connected to wisdom (σοφοῦ), and can propose something heretofore unimagined (ἐξευρήματος, μισοῦσι . . . τὰ παλαιά). Finally, its characteristic speed is fast (οὐ μέλλειν, ταχύνειν).

Much of this description is immediately familiar from our earlier authors. For the Hippocratic author, philosophy tended to the abstract and novel. For Thucydides and Herodotus, it took up deep questions of civic success and personal flourishing. Gorgias spoke of verbal advocacy motored by mental speed. For Aristophanes, then, being philosophical must be engaging in the specific kind of discussion about unseen and underappreciated norms governing the successful civic life that we saw in all those earlier authors.[69] He also presents it as quasi-competitive, instrumentally and socially valuable, and potentially radical. The practitioner may contribute to political success in the way a *sophos* would. Aristophanes uses the term with no sense of cosmology (as in the Hippocratic author), or primarily of disputation (as in Gorgias), or primarily of existential judgment (as in Herodotus). He confines the application to political problem-solving.[70]

---

[68] Dindorf 1826, looking to Ar. *Eq.* 787, and Blaydes 1881 give φιλόδημον; Meineke 1860 concedes the manuscript reading but suggests φιλόκοινον as much better; von Velsen 1883, looking to Ar. *Nub.* 358, and trying to maintain the dactyl, proposes φιλόμουσον; Rogers 1906, 84, 208, deletes φρένα καὶ φιλόσοφον as "useless to the sense, and destructive to the metre, and have plainly crept into the text from some gloss on the words πυκνὴν φροντίδα." Bergk 1872, noting an Archilochean meter and citing Ar. *Vesp.* 1526, amended only slightly to φιλόσοφον τ'; for metrical analysis, see Ussher 1986 ad 571–80; Sommerstein 1998, 188 (citing earlier scholarship).

[69] Huber 1974, 109–10, observes a hint of the pejorative tone in this passage. Van Leeuwen 1905 ad 571 glosses the chorus to be requesting a clever plan worthy of a (school) philosopher; this might get the wryness but is probably anachronistic. Halliwell 1997a, 280, suggests an "allusion to the currents of intellectual speculation on which Aristophanes has drawn for Praxagora's communistic scheme." Heberlein 1980, 59–60, and Rothwell 1990, 87, note that all the language in this passage is appropriate for sophists.

[70] Historians of *philosophia* have often thought that the absence of the term *philosophos* from Aristophanes's *Clouds* (423 BCE, revised after 418) gives reason to think it absent from contemporary Athens. It does not: (i) It is absent from many of Plato's Socratic dialogues (see p. 190); (ii) metrically ˘ ˘ ˘ ×, it requires a resolution, found only rarely in Aristophanes (in

Lysias and Personal Problem-Solving (24.10)

The terms *philosophia* and *sophia* had always been foreign to forensic or rhetorical address, Isocrates argued in the 350s BCE (*Antid.* 270). Excluding his own work, the extant speeches from the Ten Attic Orators bear out his claim.[71] Lysias's authentic work, which spans from 404 through the first quarter of the fourth century BCE, includes only one use of *philosophein*; a half-century later we see three trivial uses of *philosophos* in Aeschines (389–14 BCE), similar uses of the verb in a pseudo-Demosthenic speech and a pseudo-Lysianic speech, and some post-Isocratean uses in the pseudo-Demosthenic epideixis, *Eroticus.* They all show that *philosophos*-group terms describe a quite peculiar sort of person, argument, and practice, such that orators have rare occasion to deploy them. Indeed, *philosophos* cannot refer to just any sort of aspirant to self-improvement, *philosophia* to just any sort of scheme of intellectual cultivation, or *philosophein* to just any sort of reasoned pursuit of knowledge.

Lysias wrote the speech "On the Refusal of a Pension to a Handicapped Person" at some point in the period 403–380 BCE.[72] In it he says: "I recognized, council, that everyone having some misfortune investigates (ζητεῖν) and philosophizes (φιλοσοφεῖν) how to carry on least painfully" (Lys. 24.10.4). In the next sentence he glosses his activity as "I discovered" (ἐξηῦρον, Lys. 24.10.7). Thus for Lysias philosophizing is akin to investigating, perhaps hypothesizing and reflecting on various paths out of a difficulty. It might imply the use of sequential, branching arguments; it surely does not imply the love of wisdom or general intellectual cultivation. Lysias's use therefore shares something of Thucydides's and Aristophanes's uses, though Lysias does not specify a political or civic context. And as with those potentially contemporaneous uses, Lysias does not treat philosophizing as laudatory, but as appropriate for getting oneself out of a bad situation.[73]

Clouds, see 512, 1161, 1169; see Dover 1968, 164, and 233–35; and (iii) the (sole) uses in Herodotus, Thucydides, and Gorgias suggest a political relevance to *philosophoi* that does not especially characterize Aristophanes's Socrates.

[71] Cf. Todd 2007, 575.

[72] Schuckburgh 1890, 325; Todd 2000, 252.

[73] This use of the verb *philosophein* shows up again in Isocrates's *Antidosis* (121) and with negative connotation twice later. The pseudo-Lysianic "On an Accusation of Defamation: against Members of a Club" has the speaker claim that his defamers direct opposing arguments at him simply to "philosophize" rather than to assert their honestly held position (8.11.4; Todd 2000, 88–89, and 2007, 541–52, argues for a post-300 BCE date). In philosophizing they speak tactically and with ulterior motives. Whether or not the speaker rightly diagnoses his defamers' argumentative motivations—it is itself a debating trick to ascribe "debater's arguments" to one's opponents—"philosophizing" means the tricky use of debating words. Similarly, in a speech

Conclusion: The Earliest History of *Philosophia*

This chapter has studied six of the earliest post-Heraclitus uses of *philosophos*-group words. Looking backwards from them, they provide evidence for the claim that the term *philosophoi* referred first to people who, because they were seen always to be concertedly discussing and studying fundamental social, psychological, and cosmological matters, were thought to be striving to be *Sophoi*, the political and life advisors famous from the early sixth century BCE. In none of these uses does the word *philosophoi* or its cognates obviously mean "intellectual cultivators" or "lovers of wisdom," even if those to whom the term is applied could on occasion be truly described in such ways. The focus tends to be on something more concrete: making judgments about the best life; deliberating about politically salient questions before action on their basis is necessary; reasoning from cosmic structure to medical application; competing about ethical or psychological or epistemological matters; reflecting profoundly on political constitutions; and, eventually, tracing out paths around complicated life obstacles.

These six uses outline the meanings of the term available by the early fourth century BCE, notably among the Socratics, Xenophon and Plato in particular, and the rhetoricians, principally Isocrates and Alcidamas. They make less surprising the variety of meanings we find there, including examining oneself and others, arguing about the nature of justice, redirecting one's desires, learning about civic affairs, and practicing political speech giving. Ultimately, they provide several spans for the bridge between *philosophos* as used by Pythagoreans and by Heraclides in his *On Diseases*. The term underwent change and fissure; by studying its scions, we can see both whence it came and whither it might go.

Appendix to Chapter 5: Three More Fifth-Century Uses

This appendix discusses possible uses of the *philosophos* family by Zeno of Elea, Simon the Shoemaker, and the people of Abdera.

---

attributed to Demosthenes, "philosophized" means "contrived" (*Or.* 48.49; Scafuro 2011, 336, argues for inauthenticity and date ca. 341/0). This use seems to descend from the external observers of Gorgias's "philosophical speeches," speech used as quick-turning debate.

1. Zeno of Elea's Controversial Book

A contemporary of Parmenides and his monistic fellow traveler, Zeno of Elea was a mature thinker by 449 BCE and died in 430 BCE. The only reference to the name of his writings comes in the tenth-century Byzantine encyclopedia called the *Suda*. It refers to one as *Against the Philosophoi* (Πρὸς τοὺς φιλοσόφους). If the *Suda* correctly attributes this work to Zeno, it would provide the second-earliest attestation to the term *philosophos*. This would be obvious, had Zeno written the title. Even if did not, which is more likely, the title would imply that he used the word *philosophoi* in his text, perhaps in a phrase like "I argue against the *philosophoi* thus:. . . ." or "The *philosophoi* say . . . but this is impossible, for. . . ." After all, he and Parmenides were already considered *philosophoi* shortly after their deaths;[74] a posthumous title could hardly call his target *"philosophoi"*—later editors would not want to imply that Zeno also argued against himself. He must have been arguing against those *he* called *philosophoi*. This is even to be expected, since he apparently directed his paradoxes against pluralists, either Pythagoreans in particular or whomever someone like Heraclitus could call "researchers into much." That he contended is clear from the title or contents that the *Suda* ascribes to another of his books, *Quarrels* (Ἔριδες). That he dealt explicitly with those in the Pythagorean or research vein is suggested by the book title *Interpretation of [the Ideas of] Empedocles* (Ἐξήγησις τῶν Ἐμπεδοκλέους).[75]

For all this, many scholars do not accept such a book by Zeno. Some might judge the *Suda* unreliable in general, but without impugning the specific claim, this skepticism would miss its mark. Many believe Zeno wrote only one book, based on the purported absence of any reference to multiple books of Zeno's in Plato's *Parmenides* (127c–28e).[76] Yet the dialogue takes place in 449 BCE, leaving two decades for further authorship; and even then, the conversation between Socrates and Zeno hardly restricts Zeno to having written a single book.[77] Furthermore, no later reference to Zeno's arguments about plural-

---

[74] By the time Plato wrote the *Parmenides*, he could have his characters explain their being "quite philosophical" (μάλα φιλόσοφοι) by saying that they want to hear what Zeno used to talk about (Pl. *Prm.* 126b8–9).

[75] The dispute about the number of Empedocles's poems, and the reasonable assumption that there was only one, as argued by Inwood 2001, 8–19, 78–79, means that the plural τῶν probably refers to ideas, doctrines, arguments, etc. Zeno's works: *Suda* ζ 77.

[76] E.g., Heidel 1940, 22; Burkert 1960, 170; Graham 2010, 245. LM 5.165 treat any evidence for multiple books as potentially implying "the existence of apocryphal writings."

[77] We hear of τῶν . . . γραμμάτων (Pl. *Prm.* 127c3, 127d3, 128c7 [omitted by Proclus, secluded in Burnet 1901]); οἱ λόγοι (127e9, Socrates referring to individual arguments; Procl. *In Prm.* 694.18 says there are forty); τὸ γράμμα (Pl. *Prm.* 128a3, 128b8, 128c3, 128d3, all spoken by Zeno); singular pronouns (128d7, 128e2). Burnet 1930, 311, thinks these pages in fact imply

ity, place, motion, and compositionality includes a book title; while this may
imply their source in a single text, one that defended Parmenides's monism
against those who tried to lambaste it, the fact that Zeno's popularity came from
his forty paradoxes does not tell against his having written other works.[78] The
eleventh-century CE Arabic scholar Al-Mubassir, in his *Life of Zeno of Elea*,
claims that Zeno wrote "a single book, about nature";[79] but this is no more
persuasive an account than the *Suda*'s account.[80] Furthermore, our titles
could refer to various sections or editions of a single text.

Even if we are to accept the *Suda*'s account, there remains a question
about the number of titles it attributes to Zeno; the existence of an *Against
the Philosophoi* requires there to be four. The modern critical edition of the
Suda, Ada Adler's 1928 Teubner text, however, attributes only three to him:
ἔγραψεν Ἔριδας, Ἐξήγησιν τῶν Ἐμπεδοκλέους, Πρὸς τοὺς φιλοσόφους περὶ
φύσεως: "he wrote *Quarrels, Interpretation of [the Ideas of] Empedocles,
Against the Philosophoi on Nature*." Adler puts no comma after φιλοσόφους,
yielding a single title, Πρὸς τοὺς φιλοσόφους περὶ φύσεως (*Against the Philosophoi on Nature*), rather than two, *Against the Philosophoi* and *On Nature*.
On her punctuation, if Zeno did not provide the titles, we would lose evidence
that Zeno himself spoke of *philosophoi*, since later scholars could have referred to Pythagoreans, Empedocles, or whomever else as "philosophers on
nature" specifically to exclude Zeno and Parmenides, who, in Aristotelian
terms, were *not* philosophers of nature: after all, nature involves change, and
they reject the possibility of change. Yet Adler's punctuation is implausible.[81]
Texts called Περὶ φύσεως (*On Nature*) are attributed to nearly all other early
Greek philosophers, and indeed to Zeno by Al-Mubassir, so we should expect
one for Zeno; we should expect a comma before it. Nor does extant Greek elsewhere record the locution οἱ φιλόσοφοι περὶ φύσεως, so we should reject it
as a title.[82]

---

multiple books; he says that "Plato makes Zeno say the work by which he is best known . . . ,"
citing 128d6. To my eyes, however, that passage includes no such qualification.

[78] See Pl. *Prm.* 128d1 for Zeno's defense of Parmenides, and Lee 1936, 6–8, for the post-
Platonic philosophical understanding of Zeno's writings.

[79] Rosenthal 1937; Untersteiner 1963, 16–24.

[80] DL 1.16 does not include Zeno among those who have written a single book.

[81] The editors of Zeno A2/R35 punctuate such as to attribute four texts.

[82] To formulate the idea of "*philosophoi* on nature" properly, one should follow Arist. *Part. an.*
640a5, where περὶ φύσεως is governed by a verb that is in turn governed by a subject, *philosophoi*.
Strabo 16.2.24.3 might seem to provide a relevantly parallel construction—[the Sidonians are also]
φιλόσοφοι περί τε ἀστρονομίαν καὶ ἀριθμητικήν—but this means something like "*cultivate* the
practices of astronomy and arithmetic"; φύσις is not a practice to cultivate. Gal. *De plac. Hipp. et
Plat.* 9.6.54.5 might seem even closer—παρὰ δὲ τοῖς φιλοσόφοις περὶ τῶν τῆς ψυχῆς ἀρετῶν—but
Galen's propositional phrase seems to have an implied verb from the previous clause.

We thus have good reason to accept *Against the Philosophoi* as a title reflecting the words in something Zeno wrote, and can infer that *philosophoi* named Zeno's opponents, presumably combative intellectuals committed to making claims about plurality.

2. Simon the Shoemaker

Diogenes Laertius reports that Simon the Shoemaker, an Athenian craftsman at the time of Socrates whom he calls the first author of "Socratic dialogues," "made a sketch" of a Socratic conversation titled *On Philosophy* (Περὶ φιλοσοφίας). Whether Simon named it or not, the title implies a conversation about the term *philosophia* datable before 399 BCE. In fact we might date it even earlier, since Socrates became eminently quotable by the 420s BCE, as comedies by Cratinus, Eupolis, and Aristophanes witness, and an anecdote presents Simon as well-known to Pericles, who died in 429 BCE.[83] We can infer that the term or practice of *philosophia* was controversial or confusing or important enough to merit noteworthy discussion, as did, for example, on the topics of the teachability of virtue, the nature of beauty, and the art of conversation. This tells against dismissing Socrates-era *philosophia* as mere or unmarked intellectual cultivation; we do not see other sketches or dialogues from that time simply about *paideusis*, "learning" in general.

Even more than the evidence from Zeno, the value of this testimony has been doubted—indeed, I have never seen it adduced, even hypothetically, in accounts of the history of *philosophia*. The main problem is that we have no fragments from Simonic texts or other witnesses to them.[84] This alone might not trouble us, since many other fifth-century BCE authors met the same fate. More troubling, however, is the fact that Diogenes includes his Simon biography in a group of five other Socratics, although in the case of none of these Socratics do we have fragmentary evidence: Crito, Glaucon, Simmias, and Cebes.[85] The worry is that, even if Simon was a real person, and one with whom Socrates actually had conversations, and about whom other Socratics wrote, the texts listed in Diogenes were only fictitiously attributed to him, their topics imported from the interests of the Socrates character in fourth-century BCE authors.

---

[83] Plut. *Mor.* 776b implies that Socrates and Pericles met at Simon the Shoemaker's shop.

[84] Diogenes lists thirty-four dialogues that fit into a single volume. There are manuscript difficulties: Diogenes says he is listing thirty-three; three are presented in a second group (οἱ δέ); and the only dialogue-title without a *Peri*, τί τὸ καλόν, is listed twice. But the lists of works by known authors (e.g., Aristotle) face similar difficulties.

[85] DL 2.121–25.

Yet many scholars have expressed sympathy for Diogenes's attributions.[86] His notice of Simon as the first writer of Socratic dialogues distinguishes him from the other purported authors of Socratic literature.[87] The very rare term he uses, "sketch,"[88] fits what one might imagine early reports of Socratic conversation might look like: minutes of those exchanges useful to Simon for answering questions about the best new Socratic arguments. We know of a burgeoning and contemporaneous Athenian literature in anecdotes and recorded conversations, as, for example, those by Ion of Chios and Stesimbrotus of Thasos.[89] Socrates would plausibly talk to people in shoe shops.[90] Simon may well have been the owner of just such a shoe shop in the Athenian agora.[91] Other Socratics wrote about Simon.[92]

[86] Recently: Hock 1976, 41–43 (with bibliography); Sider 1980, 16; Brumbaugh 1991; Goulet 1997, 121–25 (attending to the evidence from Aristotle's commentators); Sellars 2001 [2003], 253–57; Cast 2008.

[87] DL 2.123: διελέχθη τοὺς λόγους τοὺς Σωκρατικούς. Diogenes acknowledges earlier authors of (non-Socratic) dialogues (DL 3.47–48), and grants Xenophon primacy in "having given to people" (εἰς ἀνθρώπους ἤγαγεν) his sketches of the things Socrates said (DL 2.48). He also retells an anecdote that Plato wrote *Lysis* while Socrates lived (DL 3.35); for the possibility that Socratic dialogues predated Socrates's death (a common assumption in the nineteenth century), see DL 2.60, 3.38; Sider 1980; Tomin 1997.

[88] The noun ὑποσημειώσεις is attested three times. Nicom. *Ench.* 1 *incip.*: "the handbook is a sort of sketch with which, by looking at the chapter headings, you may remember what is in the chapter contents, which are themselves much shorter than a proper treatment would provide for" (ἵνα ὑπὸ μίαν ἔχουσα αὐτὰ σύνοψιν ἐγχειριδίῳ τε ὡσανεὶ χρωμένη τῇ βραχείᾳ ταύτῃ ὑποσημειώσει ὑπομιμνήσκῃ ἐξ αὐτῆς τῶν ἐν ἑκάστῳ κεφαλαίῳ κατὰ πλάτος λεγεμένων τε καὶ διδασκομένων). In Iambl. *VP* 23.104,10–11, Pythagorean "dialogues and exchanges and memorabilia and sketches and treatises and publications" are said all to have used "symbols" and were difficult to interpret. DL 2.48 uses the verb ὑποσημειωσάμενος ("sketched") to describe Xenophon's Ἀπομνημονεύματα (*Memorabilia*) of Socrates.

[89] Dover 1986, 34–35, 37, speculates that Ion of Chios's Ἐπιδημίαι (428–422 BCE) recorded, from Ion's vantage, various conversations with interesting people, and may have made references to wise men, deserving "a place in the genealogy of the Socratic dialogues of Plato"; West 1985, 75, contains a similar view, likening Ion's work to Stesimbrotus's work *On Themistocles, and Thucydides, and Pericles* (so called at Ath. 13.589d).

[90] See Xen. *Mem.* 4.2.1 (discussion in Rossetti 2011). Stob. 4.32.21 relates a story about Crates's hearing a reading of Aristotle's *Protrepticus* in a shoemaker's shop. In Plato, Socrates speaks frequently about shoemaking: *Prt.* 319d; *Grg.* 447d, 491a; *Symp.* 221e; *R.* 333a, 397e, 443c; *Tht.* 146d.

[91] In the 1950s, archaeologists discovered, at the agora's edge, a shoemaker's shop with a ΣΙΜΟΝΟΣ scratched onto a potsherd: see Thompson 1960; Lang 1978, figures 12 and 13 and adjacent text.

[92] Phaedo of Elis wrote a *Simon* (DL 2.105; *Suda* φ 154), which Diogenes Laertius says is one of only two universally accepted dialogues by Phaedo. Synesius *Dio* 13.3 observes that even Simon the Shoemaker did not agree with everything Socrates said, which suggests a tradition of his general concurrence with Socrates; this tradition could come from Simon's narrative itself or, like the other evidence in Synesius's passage, from a dialogue, perhaps that of Phaedo. DL 2.105 mentions a *Skutikoi*, "Cobblers' Tales," which might be attributable to Aeschines: the MSS

So, as with Zeno of Elea, we have decent evidence for conversations by Socrates about *philosophia* as a charged and normatively relevant topic.

3. Democritus "Philosophia" of Abdera

The Roman author of *Varia Historia*, Aelian (ca. 175–235 CE CE), records that the citizens of Abdera, home also to Protagoras, named Democritus, born ca. 460 BCE, "*Philosophia*."[93] Should he have acquired this nickname before the end of his long life, this would be another early attestation to the word *philosophia*, its use in jokey names, and its relative novelty and sense that it counts as jargon. Democritus got called much by his compatriots, including "*Sophia*" and "Laughter" (*Gelasinos*); the Abderites told a story that when Hippocrates first met him he judged him crazy, but then came to admire him enormously.[94] All this suggests visible intellectual idiosyncrasy and a name to go with it; it cuts against the idea that *Philosophia* could mean something so general as "learning."

No decisive evidence puts the nickname in the fifth century BCE. But parallel nickname traditions allow it to be. The third-century BCE philosopher and satirist Timon of Phlius says that Anaxagoras "was called" *Nous*; Plutarch treats the name-calling as concurrent with Pericles.[95] The *Suda* says that Antiphon was called "Speech Chef" (Λογομάγειρος); both the encyclopedia article and Philostratus, the chronicler of early Sophists, say he was called Nestor. These nicknames could be contemporary, the latter especially, given that Plato's *Phaedrus* treats Nestor as a nickname for Gorgias as well, acknowledging, from early in the fourth century BCE, the possibility of contemporaneous fifth-century BCE nicknaming.[96] An Athenian founder of Thurii (444/3 BCE) named Dionysius gained the nickname *Chalkous* ("Bronze"), presumably near his lifetime, since later authors had to hypothesize its meaning.[97]

---

read *Skuthikoi*, "Scythians," but given *Suda* s.v., editors have often corrected it; see Goulet-Cazé 1997, 187–88.

[93] Ael. *VH* 4.20; the verb is ἐκάλουν.

[94] Ael. *VH* 4.20; Clem. *Strom.* 6.32.2.

[95] DL 2.6 (ἐπεκλήθη); Plut. *Per.* 4 (ὃν οἱ τότ᾿ ἄνθρωποι Νοῦν προσηγόρευον).

[96] Λογομάγειρος: *Suda* α 2744 (ἐκαλεῖτο); the term is *hapax*, and could well be a fifth-century BCE formulation on the model of λογοδαίδαλος (Pl. *Phdr.* 266e), λογογράφος (Thuc. 1.21), or λογοποιός (Hdt. 2.134). Nestor: *Suda* α 2745 (ἐκαλεῖτο) and Philostr. *V S* 1.15: "Having become most persuasive and having been called 'Nestor' for, when he spoke on anything, he would persuade. . . ." Nestor as Gorgias: Pl. *Phdr.* 261c. "Gorgias" and related terms themselves became nicknames: see Xen. *Symp.* 2.26; Philostr. *V S* 1.16.2; *Ep.* 73. Diogenes Laertius records many nicknames for fourth-century BCE or early third-century BCE philosophers: in Book 2 alone, at §63, 83 (and 86), 86 (and 100, 116), 109, 111–12, and 131. Linforth 1917 argues for οἱ ἀθανατίζοντοι as a nickname for Pythagoreans.

[97] Ath. 13.602c (ἐπικληθείς), 15.668e bis (καλούμενος, προσηγορεύθη).

Should contemporaneous nicknaming be a fifth-century BCE phenomenon, and should we find it odd to use "*philosophia*" as a distinguishing nickname once it grew into a common term (by the early or mid-fourth century BCE), we might hazard to include another entry into our catalogue of the earliest history of *philosophia*. Even if Abderites did not call Democritus "*Philosophia*" in the fifth century BCE, their nickname probably reflects a word used frequently by the author (as in Anaxagoras's case); so we might fairly assume that Democritus—who is not being called *Philosophos*—used the surprising word *philosophia* a lot. While not confirmed by his sparse fragmentary remains, it hardly seems improbable in view of the huge percentage of his work that has been lost.[98]

---

[98] I note a final (doubtful) fifth-century BCE use of *philosophos*. In his *On Poets*, Philodemus (first century BCE), writing about the connection between word sounds and pleasure, cites for evidence Antiphon, "one of the ancients—whether he believed himself to be *rhêtorikos* or *philosophos* (εἴτ᾽ οὖν ῥητορικὸς εἴτε καὶ φιλόσοφος ἠβούλετ᾽ εἶναι)" (Phld. *Poem.* [*PHerc.* 994] col. xxxviii.14–23). It is uncertain whether Philodemus has a fifth-century BCE Antiphon in mind, and even if he does, whether he has evidence for that Antiphon's having wondered whether he was *philosophos*, *ipsissima verba* (see Pendrick 2002, 243–44). Adding to the doubt is the fact that the earliest extant use of *rhêtorikos* appears not until Plato (in, e.g., the *Gorgias*—though, admittedly, treated as a word quite available to Gorgias during Socrates's life).

6

Socrates's Prosecution as *Philosophos*

Did Socrates Exemplify the *Philosophos*?

For intellectual historians since Aristotle, and thus since the time of Heraclides's Academy, Socrates has underwritten a crucial moment in the development of philosophy: either as a radical innovator, turning the discipline to ethics and human nature, or as a profound reformulator, advocating for the centrality of concepts, definition, and method in an ongoing practice.[1] But he represents a sea change not just for the thing, but also for the name. His death in 399 BCE coincides with the linguistic explosion of the term *philosophos* that is revealed by the earliest extant works of Alcidamas, Isocrates, Xenophon, Plato, and others. Indeed, some scholars attribute a new view of *philosophia* to the first-generation Socratics, and it is a fair hypothesis that Socrates had something to do with it. Plato, for instance, vaunts *philosophoi* and vaunts Socrates, featuring him as protagonist or impresario in all his dialogues except the *Laws*. One might think that his friends deemed Socrates the paradigmatic *philosophos*.[2]

Perhaps not, however: in our largest body of Socratic literature, Xenophon's memorabilia and Plato's dialogues, we either never or only rarely see Socrates call himself *philosophos* or get called it by his companions. This hardly seems an accident of usage, given the frequency with which both authors discuss or mention *philosophoi* and *philosophia*. The infrequency of such descriptions of Socrates would mystify, were *philosophos* to have meant "lover of wisdom" or "cultivator of one's intellect," since both authors treat Socrates as such a lover and cultivator without equal. But the original usage of *philosophos* and *philosophia* as described in chapters 2–5 should demystify this absence. The term presumably retained its wry, acerbic, or at least pointed quality, implying that its target acts akin to *sophoi* or seeks to be (judged to be) a sage. In Plato, Socrates stridently rejects the appellation *sophos anêr* ("wise man") and indeed the presumption or assumption that he is *sophos* about anything except his own lack of *sophia*.[3] In Xenophon, Socrates stridently rejects assimila-

---

[1] For these choices, see Laks 2018, 1–2.

[2] For Plato, see, e.g., Brown forthcoming.

[3] See Peterson 2011, 19–36.

tion to the distinctive caste of civically ambitious knowledge workers who pursue sterile, dubious, or even impious lines of argument. So, in their apologetic mission, Plato and Xenophon would hesitate to call Socrates a *sophos*-wannabe or to treat him as simply one in a club of book-studying aspirants to a wisdom-derived political success. Plato and Xenophon might have taken special care not to call Socrates *philosophos* if he had already been ensnared by the appellation; and much evidence allows that this might have been the case, principally the associations made between him and Anaxagoras.[4] So, what happens in the fifth century BCE does not wholly stay in the fifth century BCE, given the continued importance of Socrates to these fourth-century BCE writers. But the care taken toward Socrates does not prevent Plato, who has a different relation to Socrates than Xenophon does, from accepting the charge that Socrates philosophizes; he has, however, to explain the value latent in the idea, and eventually in the word itself. Details of Plato's redemptive project await chapter 8; in this chapter we will see the kernel of it, in the *Apology*.

Socrates was called *philosophos*. It is likely this name came, either directly or indirectly, from Anaxagoras's being so called, and thus from Anaxagoras we might learn the content of the imputation. So the first half of this chapter shows how Anaxagoras could be a vehicle for the travel of the term *philosophos* into the Athenian cultural scene and then in the application to Socrates. The second half treats of Xenophon's series of attempts to dissociate Socrates from or to qualify the imputation that he was a *philosophos*. At the chapter's end, I show the ways in which Plato's works mirror Xenophon's in this way. If these claims are borne out, the Anaxagoras–Socrates nexus stitches together the two parts of Heraclides's history of *philosophia*: the *content*, concerning Pythagoras and Empedocles, namely Presocratic philosophy; and the *form*, a dialogue reflecting on the discipline of its author, namely Academic philosophy.

Distancing Socrates from Anaxagoras

Demetrius of Phalerum, according to Diogenes Laertius, wrote that a twenty-year-old Anaxagoras "started to philosophize" (ἤρξατο δὲ φιλοσοφεῖν) in Athens at the time of the archon Callias (456 BCE).[5] That is, he was the first

---

[4] Riedweg 2004 tells a similar story for associating Socrates and Pythagoras, giving particular attention to Aristophanes's *Clouds*; the present story allows for Anaxagorean intermediation in that association.

[5] DL 2.7. Demetrius had other occasions to write about Anaxagoras and related topics: Anaxagoras's burying of his own children (Demetr. *On Old Age*, in DL 2.13, 9.20); his nearly

Athenian (according to later histories of the practice) said to philosophize (whatever they took that precisely to mean).[6] Chapter 3 presented a kind of corroborating evidence: Iamblichus quotes Aristotle's appeal to Pythagoras and Anaxagoras for views about philosophizing, presumably appealing to the first so-called philosopher and the first Athenian *philosophos*.[7] Demetrius seems also to say that great envy nearly brought great peril upon Anaxagoras. Post-Hellenistic authors record an accusation of impiety. Plutarch says that a fifth-century BCE Athenian seer named Diopeithes sought to criminalize the teaching of heaven-theory and the non-recognition of the gods; he specifically targeted Anaxagoras, and did so to implicate his friend Pericles; Pericles sent Anaxagoras away from Athens for his own safety (Plut. *Per.* 32). The reliability of Plutarch's account of this episode has come under considerable question,[8] yet utter skepticism about Plutarch's account

---

losing his life from the envy of others (*Apology of Socrates*, in DL 9.57); details about Democritus's absence from Athens (DL 9.37); the failures of Pericles (who was an associate of Anaxagoras) (Cic. *Off.* 2.17.60); and exact dates of Socrates's life (DL 2.44).

[6] I take ἤρξατο δὲ φιλοσοφεῖν as "started philosophizing," i.e., was the first to philosophize in Athens, with Curd 2007, 78, 131 (cf. Pl. *Cra.* 402b7), against the familiar Loeb translation "began to study philosophy at Athens" (Hicks 1925). The latter would imply that others in Athens taught Anaxagoras to philosophize; Diogenes cannot believe that, since he believes that Anaximenes of Miletus, who did not live in Athens, taught Anaxagoras (DL 2.6, cf. 9.57; the connection is perhaps unlikely; see Anaxim. A1, A2/D3, A3/P8, A7/D1). Further, Diogenes notes that Archelaus, from "Athens or Miletus, [was] student of Anaxagoras and teacher of Socrates. He was the first to bring natural philosophy from Ionia to Athens (οὗτος πρῶτος ἐκ τῆς Ἰωνίας τὴν φυσικὴν φιλοσοφίαν μετήγαγεν Ἀθήναζε)." Grammatically, the οὗτος refers to Archelaus; but Diogenes must have meant to refer to Anaxagoras. Diogenes's contemporary Clement of Alexandria writes that Anaximenes preceded "Anaxagoras [who] brought his pastime from Ionia to Athens (οὗτος μετήγαγεν ἀπὸ τῆς Ἰωνίας Ἀθήναζε τὴν διατριβήν)" (*Strom.* 1.63). A late summary of another source contemporary to Diogenes asserts that Anaxagoras left Miletus for Athens and inspired Archelaus, the first Athenian to become a philosopher (ps-Gal. *Hist. phil.* 3, following Aëtius).

[7] Iambl. *Pro.* 51,8–15.

[8] For doubt, given the lack of fifth-century BCE evidence, confusion in later centuries, and the suspicious similarity to Socrates's trial: Dover 1976; Filonik 2013, 26–36. Diogenes Laertius records four conflicting accounts (2.12–14). Sotion says: Cleon indicts Anaxagoras for the impious belief that the sun is a burning metal; Pericles's legal defense saves Anaxagoras at the cost of a heavy fine and exile. Hieronymus says: Pericles does little more than bring an illness-stricken Anaxagoras into court for pity to acquit his client. Satyrus says: Pericles's opponent Thucydides (not the historian) indicts Anaxagoras for both impiety and Persian sympathies; a jury sentences him to death. Hermippus says: while Anaxagoras awaits execution, Pericles proves to his audience's satisfaction that the good feelings they get from him depend on his tutelage from Anaxagoras, getting Anaxagoras released, but then a despondent Anaxagoras commits suicide anyway. Diodorus has it that people brought evidence of impiety against Anaxagoras the teacher of Pericles (DS 12.39); *Suda* α 1981 incoherently notes some legal trouble for Anaxagoras; see also Joseph. *Ap.* 2.265; Olymp. *In Mete.* 17.19.

seems misplaced.[9] Socrates's contemporaries presented wildly dissimilar accounts of *his* trial, but this does not undermine our belief in the trial's existence or basic purport.

Anaxagoras is said to have been the first philosophizer in Athens— that is, again, perhaps the first explicitly to be associated with the practice *philosophein*—and to have been exiled in connection with impiety and Pericles. There are also hints of a link to Socrates. Admittedly we have no evidence that Socrates ever met or spent time with Anaxagoras, despite the possibility.[10] But Theophrastus and later authors state that Socrates studied with Archelaus, who is best known as Anaxagoras's principal student.[11] Ion of Chios (490–21 BCE) specifies that a young Socrates traveled with Archelaus to Samos, the existence of which report suggests the contemporary public relevance of Socrates and his association with an Anaxagorean.[12] Similarly, Socrates seems acquainted with Damon, the notorious theorist of music, education, and politics in Pericles's and thus in Anaxagoras's orbit.[13] A thicker indirect connection is implied by Plato and Xenophon, both of whom defend Socrates against the impression that he was Anaxagoras's doppelgänger or follower. In what follows, I will show how those defenses describe that impression. Along the way we will see that the two defenses reveal surprising features of Anaxagoras's views, which most commentators have overlooked in their focus on his metaphysical and physical system.[14] These features help explain Anaxagoras's carrying the *philosophia* torch across the Aegean Sea.

[9] Curd 2007, 129, 136. For debate about the proliferation of stories about accused intellectuals, including Protagoras, Diagoras of Melos, and even Prodicus, see Dover 1976; L. O'Sullivan 2008; Filonik 2013.

[10] Curd 2007, 134–36. Anaxagoras's dates in Athens are a matter of contention; some believe he lived about 500 BCE to 428 BCE and came to Athens in 456 (Mansfeld 1979–80; Curd 2007, 131). *BNP* s.v. "Anaxagoras [2]" gives an arrival of 461. Some believe he came rather earlier to Athens, in 480, at the time of the Persian invasion, and accordingly have him leaving Athens by mid-century (O'Brien 1968; Woodbury 1981; Sider 2005; Graham 2006). Plato may have had literary reasons to avoid dramatizing a conversation between Socrates and Anaxagoras, even had they met. One dialogue of Socrates's youthful encounters with internationally known thinkers might suffice (the *Parmenides*); he does not give Socrates a dialogue with Archelaus, or Diogenes of Apollonia, or Diagoras, or any other naturalist alive in Athens; Anaxagoras may not have the corrective role of Parmenides and Zeno or the danger of sophistic teaching of Hippias, Gorgias, and Protagoras; and, as we will see, Plato appears to want to control the Socrates–Anaxagoras relationship.

[11] Theophrastus in Simpl. *In Phys.* 27,23; DL 2.16, 10.12; Sext. Emp. *Math.* 9.360. In general see Betegh 2016, 20–21; Betegh 2013 (for Aristophanes's attribution of Archelaus's views to the Socrates of the *Clouds*).

[12] DL 2.23; see Graham 2008. For Ion's dates, see Jennings and Katsaros 2007, 1–2, summarizing the literature.

[13] Pl. *Alc.* 118c; *R.* 3.400b–c, 4.424c; see Wallace 2015, 3–75.

[14] E.g., McKirahan 2010, 197: Anaxagoras "had a reputation for single-mindedly pursuing intellectual inquiry to the extent that . . . he had no concern with politics or worldly affairs."

In Plato's *Apology*, Meletus claims that Socrates believes in no gods. Socrates queries this: does he not agree with everyone in believing that the sun and the moon are gods? Meletus says no: Socrates, he asserts, claims the sun to be a stone, the moon to be earth. Socrates retorts that this is Anaxagoras's view, whose books are full of these statements. He adds that the Anaxagorean provenance of the claims is so well known that, were he to claim them for his own, even young people would ridicule him. Besides, Socrates concludes, this view of the sun and moon is really bizarre (οὕτως ἄτοπα ὄντα, Pl. *Ap*. 26c7–e2).[15] In the *Phaedo*, the dramatically later dialogue, Socrates clarifies his relation to Anaxagoras. He tells Cebes that when he was young he desired the *sophia* that people call research into nature (περὶ φύσεως ἱστορίαν). He used to investigate the causes of being and perishing, and appealed for explanatory resources to the four elements and various kinds of opposites. Socrates's particular interest concerned the causes of thought. Socrates wondered, for example, whether we think by means of blood, or by air, or by fire. Though he does not cite his sources, Socrates's hypotheses apparently come from Empedocles and those of his ilk, perhaps Diogenes of Apollonia and Heraclitus.[16] Socrates soon discovered the view that the brain explains cognitive activity, in particular the processes from perception to memory to opinion and stable knowledge. This encephalocentrism suggests the work of Alcmaeon (Pl. *Phd*. 96a6–b8). Socrates repeats that he finds this cognitive inquiry part of the same inquiry that studies "the heavens and earth" (96c1). Yet the "method" he followed to understand change and growth—and thus, presumably, all activity—led him into relentless paradoxes (96c1–97b7).

One day, however, he heard a man reading from a book he claimed to be Anaxagoras's, with the thesis that "mind is the organizer and cause of everything" (Pl. *Phd*. 97c1–2). This is exactly what Socrates wanted to hear. Yet if Anaxagoras accepted Socrates's assumption that mind organizes all for the best, Anaxagoras would have to go on to explain how all is organized for the best, including, for example, the shape of the earth and its position among the other bodies in the solar system (97c5–98b3).[17] So Socrates read Anaxagoras's books (τὰς βίβλους, 98b4) to learn the details.[18] Having investigated

[15] Burnet 1930, 193, observes that Socrates again calls Anaxagoras's views *atopa* in Pl. *Phd*. 98c2, and supposes it means "so strange, so singular," and thus memorable (not absurd?). Burnet also attributes to Anaxagoras belief in a flat world, to contemporary educated Athenians an outdated view.

[16] Socrates later describes the "vortex" (δίνη) and "kneading-trough" (κάρποδος) views of cosmology (Pl. *Phd*. 99b6–c1).

[17] On the significance of debates about the earth's shape, see Couprie 2011.

[18] For the plural, cf. Pl. *Ap*. 26e. Anaxagoras is thought to have written only one book, per DL 1.16; this may mean Socrates read multiple chapters or volumes.

them, Socrates felt himself sorely disappointed: Anaxagoras appealed to the usual sorts of causes for the order of things, such as air, ether, and water, seeming to give no thought to decisions about what is good (ἔδοξε βέλτιον, 98e2–3). Thus Socrates took a wholly different direction.

The explicit differentiation from Anaxagoras that we find in Plato we find again in Xenophon. When explaining Socrates's curricular ideas in *Memorabilia* Book 4, Xenophon describes Socrates's warnings against studying the "heavens" (τῶν οὐρανίων, Xen. *Mem.* 4.7.6),[19] with Anaxagoras as Socrates's sole case study. Socrates thinks that Anaxagoras held implausible views and sort of lost his mind (παρεφρόνησεν) thinking so highly of his explanation of divine celestial mechanisms. Xenophon then lends his own voice to a critique of Anaxagoras: it is paradoxical to hold that sun is fire or a fiery stone; cosmological discoveries exceed human grasp; and seeking them displeases the gods.[20] Xenophon had anticipated these charges in *Memorabilia* Book 1, when, explaining Socrates's innocence of the charges of impiety, he denies that Socrates jumped on the investigatory bandwagon. Unlike many others, he did not talk about "the nature of everything." Nor did he investigate the state of what the *sophistai* call the "*kosmos*," nor even by what laws each thing in "the heavens" comes about.[21] Xenophon commends Socrates's investigative reticence: human matters should not be neglected, and the reach of cosmic inquiry assures that neglect.[22]

Plato's and Xenophon's defenses of Socrates trace the shape of Anaxagoras's reputation. His fame appears to have ridden on the reduction of sun to stone and moon to dirt. Even Meletus, no *intellectuel engagé*, has heard the thesis, even if not as Anaxagoras's intellectual property. Xenophon has two formulations of it ready to hand. Its fame probably comes from its condescension to our two principal celestial bodies, and the realization that, because their hold on divinity was shaky to begin with, other presumed divinities may face similar demotion.[23] It also has a jingling polar quality—"the sun is fire, the moon is earth"—akin to the "things in the sky and below the earth" tag we

---

[19] On the Socratic curriculum according to Xenophon, see Moore 2018c.

[20] Xen. *Mem.* 4.7.7 and 4.7.6. Aristotle remonstrates Xenophon's position at *M.* A 982b29–983a11.

[21] Xen. *Mem.* 1.1.11: οὐδὲ γὰρ περὶ τῆς τῶν πάντων φύσεως, ᾗπερ τῶν ἄλλων οἱ πλεῖστοι διελέγετο σκοπῶν ὅπως ὁ καλούμενος ὑπὸ τῶν σοφιστῶν κόσμος ἔχει καὶ τίσιν ἀνάγκαις ἕκαστα γίγνεται τῶν οὐρανίων.

[22] Xen. *Mem.* 1.1.11.

[23] Burnet 1930, 191, claims that "it is essential to the argument that Helios and Selene were not regular objects of worship in the public religion of Athens," arguing that they were not yet identified with Apollo and Artemis; nevertheless, Athenians could "'think them to be gods,' since Helios was the great god of Rhodes, and Selene was worshipped at Elis and elsewhere."

studied in chapter 5; it could become shorthand for his purported atheism.[24] Interestingly, however, in the *Phaedo* Socrates never mentions it. Apparently the external and internal views of Anaxagoras come apart.

For Xenophon, Anaxagoras belongs to a category of people who concern themselves with the nature of everything, especially its organization (*kosmos*), processes, and origins. For Plato, Anaxagoras continues the naturalistic tradition but also distinguishes himself from it.[25] While Xenophon speaks of naturalism as concerned about "everything" (τῶν πάντων), he glosses this as a concern for the divine realm, the *kosmos*, the heavens: in short, astronomy or cosmology. Plato clarifies that within "everything" also goes biology, psychology, and the science of cognition. After all, in these debates Socrates explored questions about the physiological basis of thought. The current dialectic seemed to him inadequate. That is why he put his hopes in a theory that emphasizes "mind," Anaxagoras's unique contribution.

We might think that Socrates would look to Anaxagoras first for a theory of mind, moral psychology, or epistemology. Surprisingly, he instead says that he would begin with the shape and position of the earth, the movements of the heavenly bodies, and explanations for both. It is unclear whether Socrates is saying that Anaxagoras dealt only with macro-level topics or that he also dealt with micro-level topics.[26] I assume the latter, since Socrates does not say that Anaxagoras sidestepped the concerns of his predecessors, who did deal with mental phenomena.[27] Anaxagoras's elemental stuffs seem tailored to explain living organisms.[28] And, by speaking of "mind" as a basic constituent of the

[24] Harp. s.v. Ἀναξαγόρας presents only the claim about the sun and one other as Anaxagoras's relevant legacy; similarly, *Suda* α 1981, which adds biographical material. Earlier, Favorinus's *Miscellaneous Histories* (DL 9.35) presents Democritus's derision of the sun and moon doctrines as predating Anaxagoras. Plin. *NH* 2.149 links the sun thesis to the famous anecdote that Anaxagoras predicted a meteor fall, and so too, it seems, Plut. *Lys.* 12. Plut. *Nic.* 23 even suggests that Anaxagoras embargoed his views about the phases of the moon to avoid people's intolerance for his naturalistic ideas.

[25] So too Arist. *M.* A 984b15.

[26] Socrates's ensuing remarks leave these questions open. He likens Anaxagoras to *somebody* who explains (μοι ἔδοξεν ὁμοιότατον πεπονθέναι ὥσπερ ἂν εἴ τις λέγων ὅτι, Pl. *Phd.* 98c2–3) Socrates's presence in jail by appeal to the position of his muscles and bones rather than to the judgments by the Athenian jurors and by Socrates himself. He formulates in the optative an Anaxagorean explanation for talking, in terms of "sounds, air, and hearables" (98d6–e1). Neither indicates whether Socrates actually saw in Anaxagoras's work an explanation for human behavior, thought, or conversation.

[27] On Anaxagoras's possible interests in biology and medicine, see Jaeger 1947, 156–57; Vlastos 1950; Longrigg 1963, 158–67 (perhaps overly confident); Kucharski 1964; Müller 1965, 69–72, 126–37; Barnes 1982, 332. Advising caution, and arguing that our fragments that attribute such interests to Anaxagoras come through Aristotle and Theophrastus, is Schofield 1975.

[28] As the following fragments and testimonia suggest: B10/D21 (mentioning hair and flesh, in the context of reproduction; the larger context, apparently paraphrasing, includes hair, nails,

world distinct from other principles, Anaxagoras may have presented himself as at least attentive to consciousness, human purpose, the nature of the divine, and the normative.[29] In any event, Socrates judged Anaxagoras's explanations of the solar system to be somehow relevant to his human and political questions; he seems to have seen a powerful integration of cosmology and anthropology.

Both Xenophon and Plato discuss Anaxagoras specifically and at some length. For Xenophon, he is the only physicist mentioned in the whole of the *Memorabilia*. For Plato, he is the main physicist explicitly named in the *Apology* and the *Phaedo*. This suggests that Anaxagoras must have been the dominant thinker from whom one might distinguish Socrates, perhaps more even than Gorgias, Prodicus, or Protagoras.[30] This suggests that Socrates might have easily been confused with Anaxagoras and that both Xenophon and Plato worried about the muddling effects of such confusion. Socrates expressed interest in natural philosophy.[31] Even if he never contributed novel theses to natural philosophy, he certainly reflected on the nature of mind and human action; and it looks as though Anaxagoras did as well. Anaxagoras left Athens in fumes of suspicion. No mere head-in-the-clouds theorist, he must have been seen as a menace to society. His pernicious world theory challenged religious views, and he had the ear of leading politicians. We can hardly forget that Aristophanes had already attributed what seem to be Anaxagoras's doctrines to Socrates in the *Clouds*.[32]

Having shown the plausibility of a popular association between Anaxagoras and Socrates, and an effort to distinguish the latter from the former, I want now to suggest that Socrates came to be called *philosophos* for reasons connected to the appellation of *philosophos* in the case of Anaxagoras or the Anaxagoreans.

---

veins, arteries, muscles, bones); A41 (blood); A43/R15 (flesh, bone); A45 (genesis of "flesh bones veins muscles hair nails" from bread, and from water [for trees], "wood and bark and fruit"); A46/R14 (bone, flesh, marrow); and A52 (flesh, bone).

[29] See, for example, Drozdek 2005, 32–35; Drozdek 2011, 145–50. Yet Betegh 2016, 10, interpreting B4a/D12, believes that Anaxagoras has no account of agency or normative reasons, and thus about the origins of ethics, politics, and society.

[30] At the beginning of the Platonic *Rival Lovers* (132b9), the young men, who seem to Socrates to be talking about Anaxagoras or his ilk, are said by an uncultured onlooker to *philosophein*.

[31] Argued most forcefully in Taylor 1911.

[32] Ar. *Nub.* 225 (speculation about the sun [περιφρονῶ τὸν ἥλιον]; cf. DL 2.12), 227–30 (mixing mind with everything [κρεμάσας τὸ νόημα]), 372 (the whirl [Δῖνος]; cf. DL 2.12 [περιδινήσει]), and the ever-present atheism.

Distancing Socrates from *Philosophia*

Early in Plato's *Apology*, before addressing the present accusations, Socrates says that he will address his prosecutors' predecessors, the "old accusers." They supposedly said that "there is some Socrates, a wise man, a thinker about the things in the sky and investigator of everything below the earth, who makes the worse claim better" (ἔστι τις Σωκράτης σοφὸς ἀνήρ, τά τε μετέωρα φροντιστὴς καὶ τὰ ὑπὸ γῆς ἅπαντα ἀνεψητηκὼς καὶ τὸν ἥττω λόγον κρείττω ποιῶν, Pl. *Ap.* 18b8–10). These accusers classify him as a type of investigator. Socrates adds that such investigators are thought not to believe in gods (18c3–4). A short while later he repeats a modified version of the accusation, replacing "a wise man" with "doing injustice and meddling with things" (ἀδικεῖ καὶ περιεργάζεται, 19b5). He does not say whether wrongdoing and interference is a consequence of investigation and dialectical practice, but that seems implied; he appears to hear in the charge "wise man" (σοφὸς ἀνήρ) a pejorative gloss on the concrete accusations of investigation and dialectical practice, the negative evaluation of which he spells out as an imputation of wrongdoing and meddling. "Wise men," Socrates's rejection of the name suggests, give advice and expect it to be taken. Giving compelling advice counts as meddling; and if the advice is bad, or self-interested, or otherwise non-traditional, it counts as unjust as well.

Socrates denies the charge of being a "wise man," treating it as an imputation of injustice when used for him. He says the real "wise man" is Callias of Alopece, his neighbor and Athens's wealthiest man (and grandson of the Callias who was archon in 456 BCE).[33] Socrates does not impute injustice to Callias, saying only that Callias exceeds everyone else in his tuition payments to the most famous teachers: Gorgias, Prodicus, and Hippias. Should anyone count as wise and as desirous of being wise, accumulating and displaying wisdom, it is this Callias. Socrates lacks *sophia* in lacking knowledge about "the greatest matters" (*ta megista*), a divine knowledge that would presumably guide him in all action, even as he may possess *sophia* in recognizing that he lacks this knowledge.

Making sense of the attributions of *sophos* required that Socrates examine his fellow citizens. This lowered his already low approval ratings. At least it did among the adults he tested, those who thought themselves wise. The young, among them the children of the supposedly wise or their

---

[33] For Callias and the relationship to his grandfather, see Nails 2002, 68–74, 334, and below, pp. 182–87, 228–29.

children's friends, loved his examinations and his stock grew for them. But this caused him further trouble. The tenor of the accusations turned harsh. Now people say that Socrates is "a terrible person and corrupts the youth" (Pl. *Ap.* 23d2). Yet they can point to no specific teaching or action that would account for his wreaking terror or corruption. Presumably this is because Socrates has done no more than refuted them in conversation and inspired others to do so too. Wanting nevertheless to justify their aspersions, Socrates says that "they say the things ready at hand against all those who philosophize" (τὰ κατὰ πάντων τῶν φιλοσοφούντων πρόχειρα ταῦτα λέγουσιν); these include the catchphrases "*ta meteôra* and the things below the earth," "not believing in gods," and "making the worse claim better" (23d5–7). They are catchphrases: the first lacks a verb, leaving uncertain what unholy action those who philosophize are supposed to take toward the high and the low; the second fails the test of religious specificity; the third is notoriously mired in ambiguity.

Thus by 399 BCE, according to Plato, some people in Athens were said to "philosophize." Popular understanding of these people was weak, vague, and condemnatory. Philosophizers were at once defined and abused by their commitments to cosmology and tactical rhetoric, as well as to a resulting heterodox theology. These commitments were taken as corrosively influential on the children of the most highly reputed Athenian citizens—and thus on the upcoming leadership class. They were taken as politically poisonous. Of course, neither specific purposes and methods of the *philosophoi* as they saw them, nor their precise extent, registered much on the public mind. The Athenians had, as Plato's Socrates tells it, just those three points of reference, enough to draw a plane figure but too few for a solid body.

We have reason now to wonder whether this conception of *philosophoi* finds its archetype and realization in the person of Anaxagoras, with the causes of his exile, and with the associated thinkers, including Archelaus and the Periclean circle, who remained in Athens. Before answering this question, we should notice that as Plato does, Xenophon too presents Athenian ignorance about Socrates, ignorance about *philosophoi*, animosity toward both, and the resulting assimilation of Socrates to so-called *philosophoi*. Fuller discussion of Xenophon's attitude toward Socrates, *philosophia*, and the relation between Socrates and *philosophia* will come later in the chapter. Here I mention only one telling story. Xenophon recalls that, feeling insulted by Socrates, Critias retaliated: "He proscribed the teaching of the art of words, taking contumacious aim at him [Socrates] and, lacking any other way to take him down, attacked him with this disparagement commonly used by the masses against the *philosophoi* and slandering him before the masses" (*Mem.* 1.2.31). Thus

Xenophon too posits a group of people called *philosophoi* whom the masses disparage. Xenophon also presents the Athenians as uncertain about the number or identity of these *philosophoi* and thus about Socrates's position relative to them. Unlike Plato, at this point he limits their dubious trait to "teaching the art of words."

Linking Anaxagoras to *Philosophia*

The evidence from Xenophon, and even from Plato, might seem to require that we deny that the Athenian conception of the *philosophoi* originated around Anaxagoras. *Philosophia* is associated by Xenophon solely with teaching the art of words; he does not mention naturalist investigation or atheism. Similarly, Plato emphasizes "making the weaker claim stronger." The evidence reviewed above does not associate Anaxagoras with teaching the art of words. There might even seem to be opposed evidence. In Plato's *Hippias Major*, Socrates says that all or most of the *sophoi* down to Anaxagoras refrained from political activity (πολιτικῶν πράξεων, *Hp. mai.* 281c7). This claim is not decisive, however, since Socrates wants, tendentiously, to contrast Hippias, who does extensive ambassadorial work for Elis, with the *sophoi* into whose company he would like to include himself (281a3–c2).[34] Socrates does not deny that *sophoi* gave political advice and lessons, and bore considerable influence over civic affairs; he denies only that they held formal political office. Similarly opposed evidence might seem to come from Aristotle, who reports that people have said that Anaxagoras, as well as Thales and others, are *sophous* but not *phronimous* ("prudent"), given that they are ignorant about their advantage, and that while they know amazing, wondrous, difficult, and divine matters, they are useless, failing to seek (ζητοῦσιν) human goods (Arist. *Eth. Nic.* 1141b2–8).[35] This is again not decisive, since Aristotle simply articulates popular and latter-day opinion, in a way that heedlessly conflates men more than a century apart; he presents an idea of a type rather than reliable biographical information. It would be better to conclude that our sources report a tradition that prioritizes Anaxagoras's theoretical importance over whatever practical importance he may have had. Yet a combination of two pieces of evidence, from Thucydides and from Plato's *Phaedrus*, gives support for the ascription of *philosophia* to Anaxagoras (as "art of words," according to Xenophon).

---

[34] For more on Hippias, see chapter 9, pp. 262–67.

[35] Cf. DL 2.6–7 for a similar tradition—Anaxagoras's neglecting his household and homeland—that seems, actually, to show that people were inclined to consider Anaxagoras politically or managerially competent.

As we saw in chapter 5, in the Funeral Oration, Pericles acknowledges that Athenians "philosophize" (φιλοσοφοῦμεν), just as they "aspire to grandeur" (φιλοκαλοῦμεν), but the one without weakness, the other without prodigality. Pericles uses these words, otherwise absent from the *History* of Thucydides, only to qualify and then to gloss or redeem them. This suggests that Pericles is defending the Athenians—or himself, or those around him—against an accusation of detrimental "grandeur-aspiring" and "philosophizing." I have argued that Pericles re-explains the pejorative "philosophizing" to mean getting clear about the relevant background for making politically salient decisions in the face of emergencies. He continually emphasizes that, far from comprising sessions of aimless jabbering that yield only impractical abstractions, this kind of discussion, however eccentric or abstruse it may seem, prepares the citizenry to act well when it is called on to do so. This defense of Athenian "philosophizing" as a source of insightful civic courage implies that the word does connote lots of talking. For Pericles, specifically, it means persuasive talk. Throughout his speech Pericles lauds Athenian freedom of speech and embodies its strength in rhetorical ingenuity.

We can put this observation alongside the point in Plato's *Phaedrus*, where Socrates claims that Pericles studied with Anaxagoras.[36] He joins Anaxagoras's research interests to Pericles's political goals. Socrates starts by treating Pericles as a person who understands the nature of the art of rhetoric, and thus the content of the lessons for knowledgeable rhetoricians (Pl. *Phdr.* 269a6–c5). Indeed, he says, Pericles may be "the most perfect in rhetoric of anyone" (269e1–2). For evidence, Socrates points not to Pericles's oratorical or legislative and strategic successes but to his ongoing preparation and education. Each skill has its own content, but greatness in any skill requires "freewheeling" and "cosmological talk about nature (ἀδολεσχίας καὶ μετεωρολογίας φύσεως πέρι)" (270a1). Anaxagoras filled Pericles up with that cosmological talk and taught him the nature of mind[37] and its absence (φύσιν νοῦ τε καὶ ἀνοίας, 270a5).[38] From this Pericles drew what applies to the art of speech (ἐντεῦτεν

---

[36] Other fourth-century BCE evidence for Pericles's tutelage from Anaxagoras: Pl. *Alc.* 118c; *Ep.* 2.311a; Isoc. *Antid.* 235. Later evidence: Cic. *De or.* 3.138; DS 12.39; Plut. *Per.* 4.4–6.4, 16.5–7 (τῆς πολιτείας σύμβουλος, "counselor in government"); Olymp. *In Alc.* 136.1 (who says Pericles learned *philosophia* from Anaxagoras); see also Wallace 2015, 16–17. A political tenor to his relationship with Pericles probably explains Anaxagoras's eventual accession to (some formulations of) the Seven *Sophoi* (DL 1.42).

[37] Yunis 2011, 136, thinks the *Phaedrus* makes another allusion to Anaxagorean *nous*, since the dialogue's argument for immortality (Pl. *Phdr.* 245c5–246a2) shares structure and register with Anaxagoras B12/D27 (esp. lines 11–12), simply replacing *nous* with *psuchê*, a similar concept (cf. Curd 2011, §3.3, §5).

[38] The Greek word ἀνοίας is a crux; Burnet 1901 follows manuscript V and Aristides and prints διανοίας ("reason"); other manuscripts print ἐννοίας ("intention"). Yunis 2011 (with

εἵλκυσεν ἐπὶ τὴν τῶν λόγων τέχνην τὸ πρόσφορον αὐτῇ, 270a7). The relevance of cosmology to rhetoric Socrates describes through an analogy to medicine. In medicine, one sorts through a nature (διελέσθαι φύσιν, 270b4), namely of a body, to bring about health. So too in rhetoric, in which one sorts through the nature of a soul, to bring about beneficial belief and virtue. And just as in medicine, knowing the nature of the body takes knowing the nature of the whole, to understand the world's effect on it (as we see in *On Ancient Medicine*), so too knowing the nature of the soul takes knowing the nature of the whole, to understand the ways it is persuaded (270b4–71c4).[39]

Socrates's remarks suggest two constructions of Anaxagorean rhetorical pedagogy.[40] Anaxagoras may have taught Pericles about *ta meteôra* and *nous* and *anoia*. Together his curriculum comprises the world of nature and the world of human belief. The successful persuader knows everything natural and conventional. Anaxagoras might include the nature of the weather, engineering, navigation, and geology—all topics of great moment for political decision-making then as now—and of human intention, emotion, and necessity. Even instruction in meteorology would be useful for the prolific Peloponnesian War–era debates about mantic forecasting. Plutarch, for one, puts Anaxagoras's skills here. He writes that Anaxagoras vanquished superstition from Pericles's mind, especially about meteorological phenomena. Public speakers could have trouble convincing doom-and-gloomers. Plutarch also writes that when Pericles received a ram's head with a single horn, his friend Lampon interpreted it as a portent about the leadership of Athens, but Anaxagoras opened it up and gave a physical rather than political explanation for the ovine abnormality.[41] A tradition independent of Plutarch calls Anaxagoras a prognosticator, surely referring to his successful meteorological and climatological predictions.[42]

De Vries and Heindorf) accepts ἀνοίας and translates "lack of mind," which does not make sense to me. Ryan 2012 does not decide, but translates ἀνοίας as "what is not mind," wondering whether it is a pre-Socratic coinage, yet this is a strange interpretation and completely speculative. Verdenius 1955 takes a route similar to Ryan, glossing "that part of reality which does not consist of νοῦς." At Pl. *Hp. mai.* 283a6, Hippias deems Anaxagoras to "cogitate mindlessly" (ἀνόητα σοφίζεσθαι).

[39] Yunis 2011, 208, 212, suggests that Socrates's argument here may be deceptive, equivocating on the meaning of *phusis* across the inferential steps; this is very plausible (on which see Moore 2013a, 2014a, and 2014c), but irrelevant to this paper's claim about Anaxagoras.

[40] Cf. Gemin 2017. Contrast this charitable account with the deflationary one in Stadter 1991, 121–22, who argues that Pericles at most learned abstractions and other pomposities to sprinkle in his speeches. Yet Aristotle found Anaxagoras's writings "sober" compared to his predecessors (*M.* A 984b18), and Diogenes Laertius reports that Anaxagoras's book was "pleasantly and grandly written" (DL 2.6).

[41] Plut. *Per.* 4.4–6.3; cf. N. O'Sullivan 1995, 16–18.

[42] Philostr. *V A* 1.2.

Finally, and distinctively, Diogenes Laertius records a tradition whereby Anaxagoras dipped into Homeric interpretation and gnomic wisdom, and was helpful to Euripides (DL 2.10–11), which suggests incisive moral reflection.

Alternatively, Anaxagoras may have shown Pericles a method of inquiry freed of traditional strictures. Thus the importance of *adoleschia*—freewheeling conversation—and the study both of mind and its absence. Pericles may have learned or inferred that he ought not restrict himself to learning tropes, studying set texts, or absorbing policy briefings, the familiar content of the rhetorical art. He should think about his audiences in their cosmic situation. They are active and passive, physical and noetic, imperfect but improvable. Here Anaxagoras helps Pericles ascend the ranks of rhetoric not by telling him how the world works but by getting him to value *thinking about* how the world works.

Which mode of pedagogy we choose hardly matters. Xenophon's Athenians connect *philosophoi* with those whom they vaguely suspect of teaching the art of words. Plato's Athenians connect *philosophoi* with those who both investigate the world and make weaker arguments stronger. Plato's Socrates claims that Anaxagoras, who investigates the world, in a roundabout way also teaches the art of words. This suggests that Anaxagoras was called *philosophos* in the years before Socrates's death.

The Thucydidean passage now has additional relevance. Pericles is said to have been spokesman for Anaxagoras in his defense against a charge of impiety. Probably such a defense would have occurred in the early to mid-430s BCE, only a few years before the Funeral Oration. Indeed, some suppose that Anaxagoras was indicted as a proxy for Pericles, as Damon was, who might seem similarly scientific in his (musical) interests.[43] However that may be, had Anaxagoras and perhaps others in his and Pericles's circle been called *philosophoi*, we could explain Pericles's hearing of his neighbors or himself accused of "philosophizing." This would give Pericles a reason to defend them (or himself) from that imputation, by accepting and reframing the claim.

We might qualify the above argument by suggesting, as I did with Pythagoras and the Pythagoreans, that the term *philosophoi* may have applied initially, or as much, to so-called Anaxagoreans and others in his orbit rather than Anaxagoras himself. We know that they had serious cosmological interests. In Plato's *Cratylus*, Socrates has the Anaxagoreans explain moonlight.[44] Aristotle argues

---

[43] See Wallace 2015.

[44] Pl. *Cra.* 409b6. The reference to Anaxagoreans may suggest that Socrates takes this view to improve upon Anaxagoras's view, the novelty of which Socrates just claimed to undermine etymologically (409a7–b3). That he does not name the Anaxagoreans probably means both that they were not famous in their own right and that multiple people, each connected to Anaxagoras, held this view; see also Schofield 1980, 29.

at some length against the Anaxagoreans' view that the gallbladder causes acute disease, and identifies insight into the true nature of things as their overall orientation.[45] Others named as affiliates of Anaxagoras had literary interests, including Metrodorus of Lampsacus and potentially including the author of the Derveni papyrus.[46] According to Diogenes Laertius, Socrates's teacher Archelaus discussed ethics, law, justice, and goodness (DL 5.8). Some think the orator Polus of Acragas (best known from Plato's *Gorgias* and *Phaedrus*) was an Anaxagorean.[47] This ring of associates around Anaxagoras gives a larger target for the name *philosophos* to hit and to hold firm, to be picked up in the next round and hurled at the widening circle around him—now to include Socrates.

Xenophon's Non-Inclusion of Socrates among the *Philosophoi*

Xenophon provides good evidence that Socrates was included in this category of *philosophoi* but that this ascription was not universally laudatory. After all, Xenophon has no trouble presenting Socrates as a profound intellectual cultivator, someone who loves thinking, such that had the term *philosophos* been positive or even merely descriptive, we would expect Xenophon to use the word. Andrea Nightingale has already noticed that Xenophon does not call Socrates a "philosopher," in her *Genres of Dialogue*.[48] I expand on her observation, and take the opportunity to study Xenophon's conception of *philosophia*, which has not really been done;[49] doing it reveals a view of the career of the term *philosophos* consistent with our earlier studies. In not calling Socrates a *philosophos*, Xenophon seems to continue to hear the term as something other than a laudatory one and as referring to groups with which it would be better not to mix Socrates. I will start with four passages from the *Memorabilia*. In *Memorabilia* 4.2.24, *philosophein philosophia* ("philosophizing/practicing a philosophy") means following a program of political self-improvement through the accumulation and study of scholarship. In *Memorabilia* 1.2.19, those who philosophize crisply debate abstract views about the

---

[45] Arist. *Part. an.* 677a6–12; Iambl. *DCMS* 26.79,14 (= *Protrepticus* fr. 5 Ross). Aristotle cites Anaxagoreans in only these two places, which might suggest they have been eclipsed by the mid-fourth century BCE.

[46] On Anaxagorean allegoresis, see Morgan 2000, 98.

[47] See Pl. *Phdr.* 267b and *Grg.* 465d (τὸ τοῦ Ἀναξαγόρου ἂν πολὺ ἦν, ὦ φίλε Πῶλε—σὺ γὰρ τούτων ἔμπειρος) (discussion in Fowler 1997, 29; Cambiano 2012, 26). Aristotle in the *Metaphysics* quotes Polus on the nature of experience (*M.* A 981a3); cf. Pl. *Grg.* 448b5–7.

[48] Nightingale 1995, 16–17. See now Rossetti 2018, 288–92, and Peterson forthcoming for alternative views concerning Xenophon's use of *philosophia* group words.

[49] Moore 2018b contains a longer version of my discussion here.

nature of virtues (a use with parallels at *Anabasis* 2.2.12 and *Cyropaedia* 6.1.41). In *Memorabilia* 1.2.31, the clearest instance of *philosophos* as a term of abuse, *philosophoi* are understood to teach the art of words, which means, in effect, how to speak on fundamental political values. In *Memorabilia* 1.6.2–3, *philosophoi* are thought to charge tuition for instruction about the flourishing life. Then I turn to the *Symposium*, in which *philosophia* is instruction in speech about important topics (Xen. *Symp.* 1.5), and is preparation for legislation (8.39). Finally, in the *Oeconomicus* those who are "*philosophoi* men" proverbially enjoy learning things in the proper order. *Philosophia* is the explicit and concerted study of the topics appropriate for political success: justice and the other virtues, laws and government, and human well-being. In some contexts, people practice *philosophia* actually to attain these goods; in others, to talk about them; and in yet others, for spectacular display of such attainment. Thus *philosophia* has practical, theoretical, and rhetorical modes. As much as these modes differ in form, however, they share much in content. Xenophon emphasizes maturation toward civic success, not cosmological abstraction, meteorological speculation, diverse research and systemization, or delving deep into oneself. Thus Xenophon continues only one strand of the diffusion from a sixth-century BCE coinage of *philosophos*. He presents it from the outside, as a label for certain groups of people and their characteristic practices. What is important is that he does not see them as evidently laudatory or as a compliment to Socrates in including him among them, even as his idea of *philosophia* seems rather more Socratic than, say, Anaximandrian.

"Philosophizing a Philosophy": Efforts at a Political Education

Memorabilia 4.2 illustrates Socrates's teaching to those self-confident about their education and wisdom. An otherwise unknown Euthydemus has collected books from poets and wise people, and assumes that private possession or study of them suffices for political and rhetorical expertise. By asking a sequence of questions, Socrates undermines Euthydemus's assumption. He reminds Euthydemus that all the wisest politicians and experts had teachers, and shows him that to whatever use he has put his library, he remains ignorant about statesmanship's basic knowledge, what conforms with justice and what does not.[50] By undermining Euthydemus's confidence in his political preparations and competence, Socrates brings him to a salutary self-discovery:

[50] Xen. *Mem.* 4.2.1 (what is illustrated), 4.2.11 (collected books), 4.2.2–6, 12–19 (ignorance).

But by the gods, Socrates, [Euthydemus] says, I really thought I was philosophizing a philosophy (φιλοσοφεῖν φιλοσοφίαν), what I thought was the best way
for a man striving to be a gentleman to get an appropriate education; but now
what do you think of spiritless me, seeing that despite my earlier efforts I can't
even answer questions on the most obligatory topics, and have no other route to
improvement? (Xen. *Mem.* 4.2.23)

Euthydemus understands "philosophizing a philosophy" to be an effortful and
deliberately chosen intellectual route to improvement, where that improvement
would allow him to become a gentleman and thus also to answer questions
about the most important political topics.

For Euthydemus, the route to becoming a gentleman, the route he calls
"philosophizing a philosophy," has something to do with collecting books.[51]
Neither Socrates nor Euthydemus state what the latter has done or means to
do with those books. Consistent with Euthydemus's rejection of tutelage, he
probably has not acquired them to discuss them with others (cf. 1.6.14), but to
read alone, and, as he acquires ideas from them, to incorporate them as his
own ideas. Some books that he has read must be about justice; he admits that
he has reflected (κατανενόηκας) a lot on the relationship between justice and
goodness, and can explain (ἐξηγήσασθαι) what is and is not just. We might even
guess that Socrates uses, in his examination of Euthydemus's views about intentional injustice, the example of deliberate versus accidental misreading to
draw attention to Euthydemus's self-education through reading.[52]

Euthydemus couches his autodidactic sentiment in a comically earnest,
grammatically noteworthy construction. He uses a cognate accusative pleonasm, "philosophizing a philosophy" (equivalent to "practicing a philosophy"),
to intensify and draw attention to the action; this particular pleonasm is recorded only twice in Greek literature before the Christian period. Opening
his speech with this remark reveals the terms in which he thinks about his
practice of collecting books; it also expresses his surprise at the practice's
failure. He had conceived of his activity as *philosophein* and *philosophia*, very
much in these marked terms, and had intended to reap *philosophia*'s great
benefit, the development into a man of action, but nevertheless had failed to
reach his goal. We may be inclined to believe that his course of study had
been justified to him as *philosophia* and had promised wonderful results at
its completion, and here he is finding that "philosophizing a philosophy" can

---

[51] Xen. *Mem.* 4.2.1: γράμματα πολλὰ συνειλεγμένον; 4.2.8: ἔτι γε συνάγω, ἕως ἂν κτήσωμαι
ὡς ἂν δύνωμαι πλεῖστα; 4.2.9: κεκτημένους; 4.2.10: συλλέγεις.
[52] Xen. *Mem.* 4.2.12 (what Euthydemus thinks he can do), 4.2.20 (drawing attention to
self-education).

fail to produce those results. That "philosophizing a philosophy" has some
unity as a course of instruction and involves adopting a specific lifestyle—
such as collecting and reading books about justice and politics—is suggested
by a use of the same pleonasm a couple generations later. In Philemon's (ca.
363–262 BCE) play *Philosophoi*, somebody explains the odd traits of a main
character: "For he philosophizes a new philosophy; he teaches hunger and takes
students; one loaf, a fig for dessert, water for a drink."[53] The play appears to
treat "philosophizing a philosophy" as following a coherent and planned approach to self-improvement; the subject of the joke has developed a new approach, apparently based on *autarcheia* or desire-reduction. This dramatic
fragment includes no reference to philosophy's expected reliance on dialectical exchange, critical defense of one's reasoning, or mentorship. It suggests
instead a way of life that is unusual (teaching hunger!), seemingly indirect
(one fig!), but probably reasoned out (it's a three-course meal!). Euthydemus's
procedure is similarly unusual (Alcibiades, Critias, Pericles, and the other ambitious statesmen in the *Memorabilia* are not said to have read a lot of books),
indirect (management of a household, perfecting speeches, or fighting in war
would seem more direct routes), and yet reasoned out (the books are from the
authors purported to be wisest).

When Socrates replies to Euthydemus's consternation, he does not say that
Euthydemus was right to philosophize a philosophy and yet should from now
on philosophize a different and better philosophy. Nor does he say that Euthydemus thought he was philosophizing a philosophy but failed to, misled as
he was by mistaken authors. He goes on instead to encourage knowing himself, distinguishing good from bad things, and figuring out whom he means
to govern once he is a statesman.[54] These are presumably the most important
topics, those that a gentleman should know and about which he should be able
to answer questions. None of this Socrates calls "philosophy," neither here
nor anywhere else in Xenophon's Socratic works. (Euthydemus might on reflection come to think that Socratic conversation proves a better activity for
someone desiring the goal at which philosophizing a philosophy aims than the
activity he settled on.)

Since Xenophon does not present Socrates as speaking of his own or recommended actions as "philosophizing a philosophy," we might wonder why
Euthydemus does. Euthydemus overhears the brief conversations Socrates uses
specifically to draw him in;[55] but if Socrates uses the unusual phrase "phi-

---

[53] Fr. 88 *PCG*: Φιλοσοφίαν καινὴν γὰρ οὗτος φιλοσοφεῖ· | πεινῆν διδάσκει καὶ μαθητὰς
λαμβάνει. | εἷς ἄρτος, ὄψον ἰσχάς, ἐπιπιεῖν ὕδωρ.

[54] Xen. *Mem.* 4.2.24–30, 31–35, 36–39.

[55] Xen. *Mem.* 4.2.2–8.

losophize a philosophy" there, we would expect Xenophon to have had him use it elsewhere, and more importantly, we would expect Euthydemus, in the passage quoted above at 4.2.23, to say something like, "I thought I was—*as you put it*—'philosophizing a philosophy,'" and then to forego the gloss on that term, given that Socrates would obviously know exactly what it means. Euthydemus's motivation to collect and study books, and to call that activity "philosophizing a philosophy," must have come, therefore, from someone besides Socrates. Hippias, who becomes Socrates's interlocutor two chapters hence (4.4), advocates becoming *polumathês* for the sake of one's political education.[56] He or someone like him could have been one of the wise authors whose books Euthydemus had collected (σοφιστῶν, 4.2.1; τῶν σοφῶν ἀνδρῶν, 4.2.9). "Philosophizing (a philosophy)" thus would likely be a name, within a social circle of intellectual-political aspirants, for the studious preparation for a political career.[57]

Xenophon presents Socrates as helpful for people seeking a political career; indeed, the entire Book 4 of the *Memorabilia* shows a course of education apt for the political aspirant (even if it would benefit others as well). Yet *Memorabilia* 4.2 shows the Socratic education to comprise, at least in part, tough questions and indirect answers. Certainly it shows Socrates as more or other than simply a dispenser of sage bromides, etiological myth, allegorical thought experiments, and realist analyses of public institutions. These are the elements that we know to be in the writings of the fifth-century BCE writers called "wise men" or "sophists," including Hippias (cf. Xen. *Symp.* 1.5, 4.62), Protagoras (*Symp.* 1.5), and Prodicus (*Mem.* 2.1.21–34; *Symp.* 4.62). Those writings addressed problems of ethics, economy, and politics, and provided arguments or illustrations of views. From the uses of "philosophy" by Thucydides and Aristophanes (in chapter 5), it seems likely that sampling this written work could be called "philosophizing."

Socrates diagnoses the failures in Euthydemus's education. Euthydemus does not know himself (4.2.24–30); he seems persuaded by theological doubts (4.3.3–17); he does not understand justice (4.2.11–19), conceivably because Hippias, who could have been a favorite author of his, also does not understand justice (4.4.5–25);[58] he does not recognize the importance of *enkrateia* ("self-control") to the acquisition of pleasure (4.5.9); and he lacks precise understanding

---

[56] Cf. Pl. *Prt.* 318e1–319a2; *Hp. mai.* 281a1–283b4; *BNJ* 6. See further chapter 9, pp. 262–67.

[57] Cf. Dorion 2011, 83.

[58] I conjecture Hippias's influence on Euthydemus as an explanation for the odd incursion of an exchange between Socrates and Hippias into a sequence of four conversations between Socrates and Euthydemus.

of the moral concepts he so seeks to learn (4.6.2–12). These failures are not necessarily failures of *philosophia* itself. But they are failures that follow not studying with other people, in particular, not studying with Socrates. *Philosophia* must have had cultural capital with Euthydemus and those he admired. The high esteem given to *philosophia*, to the extent that it was a methodical study of the matters of highest import, is reasonable. But Xenophon shows that it is Socrates and conversation with him that is most useful, even essential; and he leads one to doubt whether *philosophia* as Euthydemus understands it gives an essential role to Socrates.

Xenophon's desire to laud Socrates rather than to link him to a novel pedagogical trend seems to explain Xenophon's insouciance about defining Socrates vis-à-vis *philosophia*. This could be parsed as Xenophon's lack of concern about *philosophia* and the jargon of the day. It could also be parsed as Socrates's concern to help Euthydemus in general rather than to correct his ideas about *philosophia*.

Self-Styled Philosophers

The first two chapters of the first book of the *Memorabilia* defend Socrates against the diverse charges historically levied against him. In chapter 2, Xenophon vindicates Socrates's association with Alcibiades and Critias. In section 19 of chapter 2, Xenophon responds to the claim that because that pair of men were bad at the end of their lives, Socrates must never have made them good in the first place:

> Now perhaps many of those claiming to philosophize (πολλοὶ τῶν φασκόντων φιλοσοφεῖν) might say that a just person never becomes unjust or a disciplined person hubristic or a person who has learned anything of which there is learning ignorant. But I do not acknowledge such things to be this way. (Xen. *Mem.* 1.2.19)

Xenophon epitomizes a common position among those who say of themselves that they "philosophize." Xenophon takes these claimants to *philosophia* to argue about justice, discipline, knowledge, and the permanence of virtue, and perhaps to form these arguments from abstract claims and deductions, for example, from the nature of opposites or from the relation of attributes to substances. Xenophon makes no charges against these topics or methods of argument. He even allows that other claimants to *philosophia* would, like himself, accept the impermanence of virtue. But Xenophon clearly distinguishes himself and Socrates from this group of "those who claim to philosophize." He does not speak of "*we* who claim to philosophize" or of "those who philosophize as opposed to those who have no grounds for their claims about virtue." There is a distinctive group of people who understand or present themselves as "philosophizing," and he is addressing something distinctive about them.

It is tempting to read Xenophon to be saying "those claiming (i.e., falsely) to philosophize," with the implication that he or Socrates might be among a different but related group, those who *truly* philosophize. But he seems really to be saying "those who pride themselves to philosophize," who actively consider themselves *philosophoi*.[59] Xenophon thus acknowledges the existence of a group of people who say of themselves that they philosophize. He does not say whether he thinks that they do so wrongly. As a consequence, he does not say whether he thinks that there are people who are actually *philosophoi* but do not claim, boast, or pretend to philosophize. But Xenophon seems not to think there are. He seems to think of philosophers as having an articulated, projected identity.

Twice in his non-Socratic writings Xenophon describes *philosophoi* as using abstract, deductive reasoning. I will mention one here (the other is at *Cyropaedia* 6.1.41). Early in the *Anabasis*, Xenophon's narrative of his mercenary campaign through present-day Turkey, an Athenian responds to Phalinus, who had encouraged the outnumbered Greeks to lay down their arms:

—Phalinus, now, as you see, there is nothing good (ἀγαθόν) for us except our arms and our virtue (ἀρετή). Having our arms we imagine that we could also use our virtue; but surrendering them, that we would be deprived of our bodies (τῶν σωμάτων). Do not imagine, then, that we will surrender to you our only goods: we will fight with them even over your goods.

—Hearing these things, Phalinus laughed and said, You seem a *philosophos* (φιλοσόφῳ . . . ἔοικας), young man, and you speak not without charm (λέγεις οὐκ ἀχάριστα); know, however, that you are foolish (ἀνόητος), if you imagine that your virtue would trump the power of the king. (Xen. *An.* 2.1.12–13)

A *philosophos* speaks of "goods" and "virtue," and draws connections between them and the "body," that is to say, being alive. Perhaps it is an additional point contributing to Phalinus's judgment of the Athenian's *philosophos*-like speech that he "speaks with charm"—with clarity, witty concision, and deductive reasoning, using an exhaustive disjunction. Phalinus also thinks that the Athenian is foolish. This need not mean that while the Athenian "seems" (ἔοικας)

---

[59] With Dorion 2003, 1.13; and Moore 2018b, against, e.g., Smith 1903, 22; Santoni 1989, 92n24.

a *philosophos*, he in fact is not because he is in fact foolish. The Athenian is obviously not a (characteristic) *philosophos*, given that he is in fact a soldier. Phalinus's point is only that his speech mimics that of *philosophoi*; and young men are prone to study with and thus mimic *philosophoi*. Since being like a *philosophos* is speaking in certain argumentatively precise ways and about the topics surrounding—at least in this case—fundamental questions of life, including virtue, death, and value, this must be what *philosophoi* do. This is more than intellectual cultivation, because it is the Athenian's specific way of talking that incites Phalinus's remark. It is not clear whether *philosophoi* are expected to have the right answers to these questions; but it might be assumed that they are not always eminently pragmatic.

A Disparagement Commonly Used against the Philosophers

Later in *Memorabilia* Book 1, Xenophon presents a case similar to that found in Plato's *Apology*, where Socrates says that people used the criticisms that were handy against philosophers (Pl. *Ap.* 23d2–6); he puts the claim in his own voice. He reports that Critias, the erstwhile associate of Socrates, avenged an insult from Socrates by using his legal powers as member of the Thirty against him. (Socrates insulted him by trying to discourage Euthydemus, the young man whom Xenophon discusses in Book 4, from associating with Critias: Xen. *Mem.* 1.2.29–30.) Xenophon explains:

> And in the laws he proscribed the teaching of the art of words (λόγων τέχνην μὴ διδάσκειν), taking contumacious aim at him [sc. Socrates] and, lacking any other way to bring him down, attacked him with this disparagement commonly (τὸ κοινῇ) used by the masses against the *philosophoi* and slandering him before the masses. But for myself, neither did I myself ever hear Socrates do this, nor was I aware of another claiming to have heard him do this. (Xen. *Mem.* 1.2.31)

We learn from this passage that by 404 BCE, the period of Critias's powers, there were so-called *philosophoi*. Presumably Xenophon does not say what people thought about *philosophoi* in general. He notes only that they were often disparaged (ἐπιτιμώμενον) and thus slandered (διαβάλλων) as teachers of the art of words. Apparently the masses despised this teaching and often (if not always) identified *philosophoi* as teachers of it.

Xenophon does not say that Socrates ought to be considered a *philosophos*. It is not even clear whether Critias judged Socrates a *philosophos*, as he understood the term. He seems to have been opportunistic instead, seeking out an accusation that would stick. He must have seen that the masses thought that

Socrates was a *philosophos*, and thus that the accusation was apt, or while not a *philosophos* himself, a teacher of the art of words, which was a role itself worthy of scorn.

In the following section, Socrates does not address the topic of *philosophia* head-on. Instead he interrogates the meaning of the obscure proscription.[60] The responses provide data on his interlocutors' vision of (at least a part of) *philosophia*. Socrates asks Critias (or Charicles, to whom he soon ends up talking) whether the edict prohibits correct or incorrect reasoning. Though Socrates may simply be trying to be provocative, he might rightly think that teachers of the art of words would teach people to use their words correctly. This is certainly what Xenophon thinks Socrates does in fact try to do (see *Mem.* 4.6); and he never calls the correct use of words *philosophia*. Charicles ignores Socrates's suggestion and says that the edict forbids Socrates only from having conversations with the youth. This hardly glosses the prohibition of teaching an art of words, since it would also prohibit talking with young merchants (which is not a form of teaching), and since many besides *philosophoi* have such conversations (which are not objectionable). Nevertheless, Charicles means to specify teaching by means of discussion (that is, by *philosophoi*) those who are still intellectually immature (οὔπω φρονίμοις), who may aspire to public and deliberative participation. He then makes his worries more explicit: it is the "asking of questions to which you know the answer" to which he objects, an obviously Socratic practice. But Socrates shows that this is still not objectionable as it stands. So Critias, taking a turn, reduces it to talking about "cobblers, builders, metal workers . . . cowherds," Socrates's familiar examples. Socrates loses patience with Critias's circumlocutions and tells him that what Critias wants to forbid is his talking (with the young) about that for which these are humdrum examples: justice, holiness, and similar topics, themselves presumably perfectly respectable topics. So Critias realizes, or admits, that what he really wants to forbid is Socrates's asking the youth the leading questions about ethical, political, and theological matters, matters they would need to think about before becoming public men.

"Teaching the art of words" may be euphemistic for this pedagogical activity that is supposedly typical of *philosophoi*. It might also be so general as to capture a broad range of activities—Anaxagoras's, Gorgias's, and Empedoclean doctors' activities. So general, it captures Socrates's activities too; neither he nor Xenophon would deny that he talks to ambitious youth about moral and political questions. Then why does Xenophon not admit that Socrates is fairly called a *philosophos* but not one worth vilifying? Xenophon presumably

[60] Xen. *Mem.* 1.2.34–37. Cf. Dorion 2003, 98–100.

believes that nothing good would come either from defending Socrates's status as *philosophos* or from showing that he distinguishes himself from the disparagement-worthy *philosophoi*. Doing either would associate Socrates on Xenophon's authority with an often disreputable crowd. It would also add an unnecessary term from which Socrates would have to be cautiously differentiated. Neither task would advance Xenophon's desire to demonstrate Socrates's exceptional life and goodness. The more important point is that, as we have already seen and will continue to see, for Xenophon *philosophos* is not a term of praise. It is a label of group membership, and not evidently a laudatory one.

Philosophers and Happiness

Whereas Critias treated *philosophoi* as teachers to outlaw Socrates's conversations, Antiphon treats *philosophoi* as teachers to deride Socrates's failure at teaching. Xenophon presents a set piece in which Antiphon aims to poach Socrates's associates. Antiphon addresses Socrates with the intention that their conversation be overheard by those around them. His gambit opens with two references to *philosophia*:

> Socrates, I thought that those philosophizing had to end up flourishing more (τοὺς φιλοσοφοῦντας εὐδαιμονεστέρους χρῆναι γίγνεσθαι). But you seem to me to have won the opposite from *philosophia*. [. . . After all, you are poor and do not charge tuition . . .] Now if just as the teachers of other practices show their students to be imitators of themselves, you too were to treat your associates in such a way, consider yourself to be a teacher of misery (κακοδαιμονίας). (Xen. *Mem.* 1.6.2–3)

Antiphon has a commercial view of *philosophia*.[61] He thinks that philosophizing amounts to teaching students and associates (cf. 1.6.12) and is thus a pedagogical profession (cf. Xen. *Poroi* 5.3). Antiphon also thinks that philosophizing, ideally practiced, makes one flourish. This view, that *philosophia* leads not merely to discoveries or mental diversion but actually to a more flourishing happy life, is familiar from Isocrates and Plato, as we will see. But Antiphon takes an instrumental approach to the connection between pedagogy and flourishing. He implies that philosophizing makes one flourish because

---

[61] Thus Smith 1903, 61, is misleading to gloss τοὺς φιλοσοφοῦντας as "lovers of knowledge" and to derive from Pl. *R.* 2.376b that this just means φιλομαθεῖς; Antiphon addresses Socrates not because Socrates loves wisdom or learning, but because although he has the trappings of a certain kind of teacher, he is not making any money from it. Santoni 1989, 321, has "engaged in a philosophy," which is better.

it brings tuition payments from one's students. Antiphon takes a fee from his students; they are glad to pay him because they believe that if they imitate him they will themselves mature into moneymaking and thus successful *philosophoi*.

Xenophon goes on to report a conversation in which Antiphon jokes that Socrates is just but not wise: because he charges no fees to those who spend time with him, his knowledge and wisdom must be empty; but at least he does not greedily mislead people about its value![62] The joke reveals three things about Antiphon's view of *philosophia*. First, *philosophia* involves spending time with people in knowledge-based discussion, in which wisdom counts for the most. Second, since these people might be willing to pay a fee, they are probably young people looking to improve their chances in the world. Third, though here Antiphon speaks explicitly of commercial justice, his joke would be really apt only if (certain) *philosophoi* aimed (or pretended to aim) for justice as well as for wisdom. Plato's *Republic* Book 2 and the Platonic *Clitophon* show that understanding justice had popular appeal, political relevance, and an intellectual imprimatur.[63] We might guess that Socrates exemplified this commitment to conversations about justice. All the same, Antiphon acts as though he appreciates Socrates's commitment to justice only as a fiduciary responsibility to potentially naïve or enthralled associates. He need not be dissembling or unusual in so acting. The contemporaneous discussions about justice we know about emphasized the external or instrumental benefits of being just; Antiphon perhaps believes that all *philosophoi*, given that they are paid teachers foremost, think about justice in a way that pays for them and would pay for their students, who after all need to justify paying their teachers. Thus Antiphon sees *philosophoi* as constituting a class of teachers on the basis of whose wisdom students will pay to learn about justice (potentially among other topics). This would be an unsurprising consequence, since the wise people that Euthydemus read (Xen. *Mem.* 4.2), the familiar topics of *philosophoi* (Xen. *Mem.* 1.2.16), and the content of Socrates's teaching when teaching the art of words (1.2.37) all include justice as the primary matter.

Again, Xenophon does not in his own words or through Socrates explicitly deny the implication that Socrates is a *philosophos*. But he does not explicitly accept or qualify the implication either. Instead Xenophon has Socrates explain what actually typifies him. In the midst of Socrates's discussion with Antiphon he gives a good example. Regarding the "treasures

---

[62] Xen. *Mem.* 1.6.11–12.
[63] Cf. Moore 2012.

of the wise men of old, which they left behind in the books they wrote, opening them up with my friends I [Socrates] go through them, and should we see anything good, we focus on it, and we consider it a great advantage should we become useful to one another" (Xen. *Mem.* 1.6.14). Xenophon says that from this practice he judges Socrates to be blessed (μακάριος) and prepared to lead his listeners to excellence (καλοκἀγαθία). We see the contrast with Euthydemus's practice discussed in *Memorabilia* 4.2. Looking at books is valuable only when exercising judgment in conversation about their best and useful elements, and applying one's discoveries to oneself and others. In the previous conversation with Antiphon, Socrates says that divinity comes through minimizing one's desires, which he practices (1.6.10). So Socrates reads carefully with friends, seeks the good, minimizes desire, and thinks about becoming more divine. For Xenophon, these traits are eminently useful.

In the *Memorabilia*, then, both Critias and Antiphon see Socrates as near enough to the group called *philosophoi* to charge him with the abuse thrown at *philosophoi* or to make fun of his failure to meet *philosophia*'s monetary ideals. In either case, the association of Socrates with this group of *philosophoi* makes sense. Socrates talks with others about the careful use of language and about justice and the other virtues. But Xenophon does not affirm the title of *philosophos* for Socrates. In the context of Socrates's encounter with Critias, Xenophon recognizes that much of the populace despises *philosophoi*. In Socrates's encounter with Antiphon, Xenophon knows that much of the populace, construing happiness in material terms, thinks *philosophoi* desire profit. Under neither perception does it help Socrates's case to associate him with *philosophoi*.

Callias the Philosophical Impresario

Xenophon's *Symposium* opens with Callias's planning to host a party for his beloved, a champion fighter named Autolycus. The three uses of *philosophos*-group words in the dialogue are directed toward Callias. This suggests that Xenophon deploys the words only to draw a portrait of Callias's reputation as an intellectual impresario.[64]

The dialogue's drama opens when Callias spots Socrates, Critobulus, Hermogenes, Antisthenes, and Charmides, and bids them come home with him. He exhorts them by telling Socrates that he and his friends' "purified souls"

---

[64] On Callias, Pl. *Ap.* 20c; *Tht.* 65a; *Alc.* 119a; Freeman 1938; Woldinga 1938, 20–23; Wolfsdorf 1998, 127–29; Bowen 1998, 13; Nails 2002, 68–74.

(ἐκκεκαθαρμένοις τὰς ψυχάς) would make his dinner brighter than military and political people would (Xen. *Symp.* 1.4). Socrates responds:

> You are always playing us for a joke and trivializing us, since you (σὺ μὲν) have given much money to Protagoras for wisdom (σοφίᾳ), and to Gorgias and Prodicus and to many others, but you regard us by contrast (ἡμᾶς δ') as being some sort of lay philosophers (αὐτουργούς τινας τῆς φιλοσοφίας). (Xen. *Symp.* 1.5)

Callias ignores the claims that he insults Socrates and his friends. He agrees with the middle claim, that he has paid much tuition to these sellers of wisdom. He says that until now he has hidden his ability to speak fluently and wisely (πολλὰ καὶ σοφὰ λέγειν), but that this party will allow him to show its attendees that he is worthy of much serious esteem (1.6).[65]

In this passage Socrates implies that Callias has an idea about the nature of *philosophia*. A practitioner of it has a purified soul and the capacity for wise speech. This is the only time Xenophon uses the verb for "to purify thoroughly" (ἐκκαθαίρω). In Plato or his imitators, "thorough purification" is connected three times to philosophy and once to politics, and means an expunging of any foreign matter or imperfection.[66] Presumably his Callias would think, even if implicitly, that practitioners of *philosophia* have undergone a purging, perhaps of confusion and of everyday concerns, through repeated and challenging effort.[67] This is not too esoteric an idea; it is what any refined practitioner does to attain his mastery. Callias's idea of the *philosophos* also includes oratorical excellence, an idea we have already connected to Euthydemus's and Critias's idea of the *philosophos*.

Socrates neither accepts nor rejects the imputation that he is a "lay" philosopher, the term "lay" usually being applied to a self-employed farmer, ben-

---

[65] On the importance of this passage, see Rettig 1879, 273; Woldinga 1938, 48–49; Gray 1992, 61.

[66] In the *Euthyphro* (3a1), Socrates says that Meletus wishes to "purify thoroughly" the city of corrupting influences; this leads him to prosecute even Socrates. In *Republic* Book 2 (2.361d5), Socrates calls Glaucon's hypothetical men, the just man stripped of all appearance of justice and the unjust man stripped of all appearance of injustice, "purified thoroughly," like statues, of all irregularities and foreign matter whatsoever. In *Republic* Book 6 (6.527d8), Socrates advocates for a long education in geometry and astronomy on the grounds that these studies purify the soul's organs and eliminate the blindness caused by everyday pursuits. In the dubious *Second Letter* (314a7), "Plato" tells Dionysius that his lessons are learned only through repeated hearings, "just as gold is purified thoroughly," the ore purged a little more with each pass.

[67] Woldinga 1938, 206–8, discusses other philosophical and mystical overtones.

efited by no assistants.[68] Socrates simply notes that Callias's claim that he and his friends are purified of soul, and are good dining companions, means that Callias takes them for incomplete—or, worse, ersatz—*philosophoi*. Neither Socrates nor Callias explicitly identifies the professional philosopher against whom Socrates stands in contrast. Nightingale thinks it is Callias, because he, like a professional farmer, employs others and is himself employed by nobody.[69] Socrates, too poor to contract out his philosophical labor, must do it all himself. This is a plausible view, and it is one that may track the Greek terms of contrast (μέν . . . δέ . . .). But contrary to the view of Nightingale, a professional philosopher could be the one with an expansive business, who works for others (for payment) and not just by himself; this would mean that Protagoras, Gorgias, and Prodicus, teachers of wisdom all, are the professional philosophers. Antiphon thought that philosophers worked for others. Others have thought that philosophers teach; and Callias seems rather to be a student.

We can leave aside the question concerning the professional philosopher, however, because the relevant point is that Socrates asserts that Callias sees him and his associates, including Critobulus, as lay but not full-blooded philosophers; and Callias does not disagree with this assertion. The joke is probably that Callias esteems only those to whom he is willing to pay cash rather than merely feed and entertain. The ensuing conversation vindicates Callias's assumption that Socrates and his friends have great facility in speaking cleverly. But Socrates remains distinct from Callias, Protagoras, and the others.

The word *philosophia* arises again when, in *Symposium* 4, Socrates returns to talk of Callias's studies. Explaining how Antisthenes acts as amatory intermediary, Socrates says to Antisthenes that he "intermediated with wise (σοφῷ) Prodicus, when you saw that [Callias] loved (ἐρῶντα) *philosophia* and the other one needed money" (Xen. *Symp.* 4.62). Antisthenes did the same with Hippias, from whom Callias learned mnemonic devices. We do not know whether Socrates considers Hippias a purveyor of *philosophia*

---

[68] See Xen. *Oec.* 5.4; *Cyr.* 7.5.67. Winans 1881, 48, gives an overly derisive translation, "'a sort of quacks,' 'independent dabblers,' '*amateurs*.'" Bartlett 1996, 134, translates "self-taught" (similarly Ollier 1961, 38, "autodidactes") but no other uses of the adjective support this view. Bowen 1998, 27, gives "do-it-yourself," rightly emphasizing the amateur aspect, but implying that Callias, who does not do it himself, is the real philosopher (cf. Watson 1857, 151, "workers for ourselves in the pursuit of wisdom"). See also Woldinga 1938, 213–15; Huß 1999, 86.

[69] Nightingale 1995, 16. Bartlett 1996, 134n7, classes Protagoras, Gorgias, and Prodicus as "Sophists or rhetoricians"; this implies that Callias, who is not self-taught, is the "philosopher." Higgins 1977, 15, also calls those three men Sophists, but Callias a "supporter" of them, and Socrates the "philosopher." Winans 1881, 48, judges Protagoras and the rest to be the philosophers.

as Callias understands it. Still, we know with certainty that Callias considers Prodicus a *philosophos*, that some *philosophoi* wish to work for money, and that the love of *philosophia* may lead one to study with a teacher of *philosophia*.[70]

The explicit idea of "philosophy" arises for a final time in the *Symposium* in the encomium to psychic love and self-improvement that Socrates addresses to Callias. Should he, Callias, wish to be a good partner to Autolycus,

> you should look into what kind of knowledge (ἐπιστάμενος) made Themistocles sufficient to free the Greeks, you should look into what Pericles could have known (εἰδώς) to be reputed the most powerful advisor among his people, you should observe how Solon, having philosophized (φιλοσοφήσας), could have established the most powerful laws in the city, and you should also seek out by what practices (ἀσκοῦντες) the Lacedaemonians are reputed to be the most powerful commanders. (Xen. *Symp.* 8.39)

Socrates puts four verbs in parallel: "having the knowledge to," "knowing how," "philosophizing," and "practicing." The first and second mean "an ability based in thought"; the fourth probably means something like the "purifying thoroughly" from *Symposium* 1.4 discussed above. The parallel construction implies that "philosophizing" also refers to a source of ability based in thought and its patient development. The reference to Solon's philosophizing recalls Herodotus's story about Croesus's meeting with Solon discussed in the previous chapter. Xenophon seems to be thinking of the account on which Herodotus drew, but he has modified it, putting the philosophizing ahead of lawmaking. This treats philosophizing as working up the political acuity or moral insight appropriate for effective laws.

Taking these three references to *philosophia* into account, we see that in the *Symposium* Xenophon treats *philosophia* as something Callias has a taste for and identifies some of the major intellectual players of the Socratic era as exemplars of *philosophia*. In Callias's view, at least as Socrates puts it, *philosophia* is the study of the skill highly valued in sympotic settings—public display of clever and novel speech, an ability prepared through much concerted effort. But Callias also accepts that it has a realization in legislation. Socrates supposes that Callias thinks of him, Socrates, as a sort of second-string or unaffiliated philosopher. Because we have little reason to believe that Callias has

---

[70] Bowen 1998, 63, obscures this in glossing Callias's love of *philosophia* as "passionate for learning." Huß 1999, 312–13, takes this use of "philosophy" to have an ironic coloring; this assumes the availability of a distinct non-ironic use.

an unusual view of *philosophia*, we may believe that his view is Xenophon's view. In other words, Xenophon may also think that *philosophia* is a rhetorical skill that has its realization in political action. Socrates is a marginal case of this sort of practitioner.

Socrates's Sole Self-Attribution as "Philosophos": As a Potential Cereals Grower

The word *philosophos* arises once in the *Oeconomicus*, when Ischomachus is teaching Socrates about agriculture. As Ischomachus offers to tell him more, Socrates compares his desires to those that a philosophical man would have:

> —So Socrates, [Ischomachus] said, from where do you wish (βούλει) we might begin reminding you about farming? For I know that I will say quite a lot that you already know about the necessities in farming.

> —Ischomachus, I said, it seems to me first pleasurable to learn (πρῶτον ἄν ἡδέως μανθάνειν)—for this is most of all [particular to] a philosophical man (φιλοσόφου γὰρ μάλιστά ἐστιν ἀνδρός)—how I might, should I wish to (βουλοίμην), get the most wheat and most barley from working the earth. (Xen. *Oec.* 16.9)

Socrates likens himself to a philosophical man but it is not clear why. The explanatory interjection could point either backwards or forwards, focusing on, as I see it, any of five points. (i) A focus on the order of instruction (πρῶτον . . . μανθάνειν). A philosophical man finds it pleasurable to learn things in a *specific order*, first things first, or at least to set things out in a specific order. It would be inefficient to go willy-nilly or in the wrong order. (ii) A focus on the "first." A philosophical man likes to learn the most fundamental matters first, in this case doing the most obvious thing farmers do, which is growing cereals. In either of these first two cases, the philosophical man would be the one who does not prefer to learn only whatever is easiest, lies most readily at hand, is most popular, or is most coolly sophisticated. (iii) A focus on "should I wish to." Socrates repeats Ischomachus's word "wish" (βούλομαι), now in the optative. A philosophical man gets pleasure from learning first how to do what he "might wish" to do. He learns in preparation, acquiring the knowledge on which likely future actions will have to be based.[71] This

---

[71] This is akin to what seems to be the view of Strauss 1970, 185, who gives three possible interpretations of the special characteristic of the philosopher in this passage, accepting only the third: the philosopher is the one who (i) wishes to *get* the richest harvest of crops, (ii) wishes

contrasts with learning only once necessity intervenes or bungling through something with no knowledge at all. The philosophical man recognizes that he is ignorant but also that he may later wish to act, so he learns what does not have immediate or self-evident importance. (iv) A focus on "pleasurable to learn." The philosophical man gets pleasure from learning. (v) A focus on "learn." The philosophical man is characteristically one who learns.[72]

While none of these five possibilities seems uniquely or even characteristically "philosophical," the third is compatible with the use of *philosophia* in *Memorabilia* 4.2. Euthydemus's philosophizing amounted to studying books for the sake of becoming an effective gentleman (which is what Socrates says he wants to know about in the *Oeconomicus*, e.g., 6.13–17, 11.5–6). Euthydemus did not admit to enjoying learning per se, but to learning what he would have to learn in order to succeed in the speeches and actions appropriate to political life. He seems to have understood the importance of a curriculum, even if he did not understand the prerequisites for it, such as knowing oneself first. The uses in *Memorabilia* Book 1, which have philosophers talking of justice and other virtue terms, might be compatible with any of the first three possibilities: learning what is fundamental, learning what needs to be talked about first (for example, before policy matters), or learning about topics that might arise in exigent circumstances. In the *Symposium*, Callias's love of *philosophia* means wanting to be able to talk cleverly and with apparent insight; and Solon's philosophizing means thinking incisively about law and public arrangements. Though neither is inconsistent with the fourth or fifth possibility, the enjoyment or characteristic practice of learning, neither is explained by it. Both are better approximated by the first three possibilities.

What "philosophical" means does not, of course, explain why Socrates makes this offhand remark. He is assuredly not just announcing, in the middle of another thought and sentence, that he is a *philosophos* man. He seems to be giving a defense of a somewhat peculiar kind of question, perhaps especially peculiar for the urban talker Socrates. "Philosophical men"

---

to *know how* to get the richest harvest of crops, or (iii) wishes to know *in case he should wish* to get the richest harvest of crops.

[72] Pomeroy 1994, 185, emphasizes the "desire to learn," translating "first I think I should like to learn (for it is very characteristic of a philosopher to *want to learn*)" (my italics); see also Nightingale 1995, 16n8, and Chantraine 1949, 95, who translates "cette curiosité est d'un vrai philosophe," and comments that philosophy amounts to searching for truth, and calls this a Socratic notion. Audring 1992, 99, by contrast, emphasizes the learning itself, "—den das Lernen steht einem Philosophen am meiste an—." Watson 1857, 129, leaves it indeterminate. Gabriel Danzig suggests to me that the philosophical man might be interested in making money, hence agriculture, given that Antiphon is interested in money.

pursue unexpected lines of investigation, and yet if Ischomachus approves of their way of life, then he will tolerate them. Socrates has been speaking in a mannered way throughout his conversation with Ischomachus, articulating with marked formality the moral precepts underlying his pupilage. A remark from the previous chapter shows this well. Socrates says to Ischomachus:

> Your opening remarks are admirable and not the sort to turn a listener away from his desire. And given that it is easy to learn—especially because of this—go through the matter for me. While it is not shameful for you to teach the easier matters, it is very shameful for me not to understand them, and especially if they happen to be useful. (Xen. *Oec.* 15.13)

Socrates appears to want to show that his learning is morally appropriate and, by mentioning at 16.9 those engaging in higher thought, that it has an intellectual provenance admissible to his interlocutor.

All this leaves the question whether Socrates is saying of himself that he is a philosophical man and that it is because he is one that he asks these questions, or, by contrast, that he is asking a kind of question made legitimate by the habit philosophical men have of asking it. He has made a provocative claim relevant to this point five chapters earlier in the *Oeconomicus*. Socrates has just asked Ischomachus to teach him about the activities of a gentleman. Ischomachus says that he will, with the hope of getting correction (μεταρρυθμίσῃς) from Socrates where he needs it. Socrates demurs; he has gained the reputation for being a man who prattles on, beats about in airy meditation, and is called poor (ἀδολεσχεῖν . . . καὶ ἀερομετρεῖν . . . πένης καλοῦμαι).[73] Socrates must be referring to the claims made against him in Aristophanes's *Clouds* and in Eupolis's work (Eup. fr. 386, 388 *PCG*), and that Plato reprises in his *Apology*.[74] In Aristophanes's play, Socrates is not called *philosophos*; we do not know about Eupolis's play. In Plato's dialogue, as well as in *Memorabilia* 1.2.31, he is accused of talking and investigating the sky as people think all so-called philosophizers do. In the *Oeconomicus*, Socrates is admitting to having the reputation he has elsewhere, of a silly, impractical, not-very-gentlemanly person. But he

---

[73] Xen. *Oec.* 1–3. Interestingly, ἀερομετρεῖν is found in Greek literature only here. Perhaps Xenophon misremembered ἀεροβατεῖν (Ar. *Nub.* 225; Pl. *Ap.* 19c4); more probably he recalled or coined a derivative joke made about Socrates.

[74] Cf. Pomeroy 1994, 309.

says this without reference to *philosophia*, and none of his possible meanings of "philosophical man"—about the pleasure in learning in sequence, or in preparation, or for no reason at all—overlap with the accusations reported at 11.3 that supposedly disqualify him as a judge of Ischomachus's gentlemanliness.

In light of these considerations, I think that Socrates is saying that he is a "philosophical man" to the extent (at least) that he knows the value of pursuing certain kinds of questions (for one of the five reasons listed above). Whether Socrates is to be considered a *philosophos* in the more precise ways described elsewhere does not arise.

Having now looked at all of Xenophon's Socratic writings, ought we say that Xenophon's Socrates is a *philosophos* or "philosophizes a philosophy"? Doing so would be fine, in one respect. Socrates wants to learn about justice and the other virtues through methodical conversation; he wants to be successful on the basis of that learning, which is to be prioritized over other topics of learning (perhaps excluding the *Oeconomicus*, where he claims to want to learn about farming); he applies himself vigorously to his projects; and he does something like teaching. But the fact that *we* may call Socrates a philosopher stands in a remarkable relation with the fact that Xenophon does not, in his own voice, call him *philosophos*. As we have seen, the name has a powerful rhetorical function. The Critias and Antiphon examples show it to be involved in disparagement. The *Symposium* examples show it to be concerned with the production of clever speeches. When Euthydemus situates himself within the intellectual life as someone "philosophizing," he reveals his self-blinding political aspirations. Xenophon never denies that Socrates is a *philosophos*. But whereas many others seemed quite ready to associate Socrates with *philosophia*, he appears to have been diffident, even consciously diffident, about the matter.

Xenophon discusses *philosophoi* infrequently but with a sort of realism, recognizing that a self-styled or oft-lambasted group of so-called *philosophoi* is part of Athenian society and provides an ideal of practice or pedagogy among a subset of that society. Socrates spends time within or alongside this subset. He shares many of its habits or aspirations: accumulating knowledge, talking well, toilsome self-improvement, and confidence in the importance of discipleship. But there is something marked about membership among *philosophoi*, who are subject to politically or culturally motivated criticism. Xenophon had enough work defending Socrates from criticism. It seems likely to me that Xenophon intends to avoid linking Socrates too expressly with that current of contemporary intellectual association.

Conclusion: Plato's Reasons Not to Call Socrates *Philosophos*

Historians of ancient philosophy often take Plato to have transformed the term *philosophos* from something quite general, referring to the person who cares about intellectual cultivation or wisdom broadly conceived, to something quite precise, referring to the person who contemplates the eternal verities. In doing so Plato is thought to have spearheaded the formation of philosophy as a discipline, one with self-consciously philosophical and disciplinary practitioners. As adjunct, instrument, or central component of this effort, with all but one of his dialogues featuring Socrates, Plato advanced Socrates as an ideal. An ideal of what? The answer looks obvious: "an ideal of the *philosophos*." It would be perverse to separate Plato's admiration for philosophy and his admiration for Socrates (though some readers do believe that Plato eventually admires certain non-Socratic philosophers above Socrates). All the same, close attention to the relationship between *philosophoi* and Socrates in Plato's dialogues requires we wedge apart that admiration, even if just a little. Plato takes a cautious line in attributing to Socrates the self-appellation *philosophos*.[75] Presumably he does so given its pejorative aspect in fifth-century BCE Athens.

It is clear that Plato controls his use of *philosophos*-group words, doling them out only when the situation demands them. Many of his dialogues do not mention *philosophia* or *philosophoi* or *philosophein* at all. Among the trial-and-death dialogues these include *Euthyphro* and *Crito*. Among others, these include *Meno, Laches, Ion, Menexenus, Hippias Major, Alcibiades, Clitophon*, and *Republic* Books 1–2. Many scholars think that Plato wrote most or all of these dialogues after the *Apology*, so he could have used the term *philosophos* to refer to Socrates had he wanted to. He seems uninterested in establishing Socrates as a *philosophos*. The example of Socrates as a practitioner of the way of life admired or analyzed by Plato counts for more than Socrates as a model of *philosophia*. It also seems clear that Plato does not aim to vindicate Socrates by transferring the positive evaluation of *philosophia* to the man.

We saw above, in the summary of Plato's *Apology*, that Socrates presents himself as harmed thanks to the term *philosophein*. Having gotten a bad reputation for himself by interrogating those in the city most reputed as *sophoi*, he recognizes that people think he is evil and corrupts the youth; but when they are asked by doing what and by teaching what, "they can say nothing, and are ignorant, but in order that they not seem at a loss, they say the things ready at hand against all those who philosophize, namely that they study the things

---

[75] See Peterson 2011 and 2019 for views sympathetic to my remarks in this section.

in the sky and the things below the earth, and do not believe in the gods, and make the worse argument the better" (Pl. *Ap.* 23d1–7). Socrates denies this charge and reaffirms his accusers' ignorance (23d10). He does not here say whether they are wrong to class him among *philosophoi* or wrong to assume a unity of philosophical practice. Yet some pages later he relents and admits to philosophizing, albeit in a different fashion. The god stationed him, as he "thinks and understands it, to live philosophizing and examining [him]self and others" (28e9–10). He obviously does not mean philosophizing in the way others mean it, as studying the things in the sky and so forth. Thus "examining himself and others" must be his gloss of "philosophizing." Socrates does not seem to be boasting that he philosophizes. Either he must think that "philosophizing," properly understood, does name his activity, or rather than dispute with his accusers that he philosophizes, he accepts the name with a qualification, as Thucydides's Pericles did. Socrates soon imagines that the jurors might wish to acquit him, as long as he stops, as he imagines their words, "spending time in this search (ἐν ταύτῃ τῇ ζητήσει διατρίβειν) and philosophizing" (29c9–10). He imagines them accepting, if provisionally or dubiously, his reinterpretation of "philosophizing." In his response to this imagined plea bargain, he reinforces this reinterpretation: "I shall not stop philosophizing and urging you and showing you" that they should care for virtue, etc., by means of cross-examining them (29d5–30a2). Again, Socrates ensures that "philosophizing," which apparently will be attributed to him whether he likes it or not, is to be understood as he understands it. Thus his use is primarily capitulative; and neither the original understanding nor his accommodated understanding of the term is explicitly or even approximately interpreted as "loving wisdom." From the perspective of Plato's writing this work, fictional as it may be, we can see the beginning of the redemptive project, but one that has, as yet, no putative etymological dependence.

In the *Theaetetus*, which purports to take place just before the *Euthyphro*, Socrates refers to himself as a *philosophos* only once. As Theaetetus and he dispute Protagoras's man-is-the-measure thesis, he worries that they are acting contentiously (ἀντιλογικῶς) or as competitors (ἀγωνισταί) rather than as the *philosophoi* they claim (φάσκοντες) to be (Pl. *Tht.* 164c7–10).[76] *Philosophoi* must engage in conversation with a goal of agreement and mutual understanding rather than with a goal of personal glory or victory. But even here, as

---

[76] Socrates presents this self-criticism as from the perspective of Protagoras, who says that you should not be unfair to your interlocutors—you should instead help them to see their own errors and thereby take refuge in the practice of *philosophia*. Doing so allows your interlocutors to escape their former selves. Protagoras observes that most teachers cause their students to hate *philosophia* (Pl. *Tht.* 167d–168c).

Plato continues his redemptive project, Socrates speaks of *philosophoi* in the first-person plural; he appeals to Theaetetus's esteem of *philosophia* and thus desire to be a *philosophos*. He tells him that Theaetetus's wonder shows him to be a *philosophoi*, since *philosophia* begins in wonder (155d1). His esteem for *philosophia* was probably instilled by his teacher, Theodorus. Theodorus seems to consider geometry the whole or part of *philosophia* (143d1–4),[77] and the description of the *philosophos* of the Digression, which famously seems not to describe Socrates, instead formalizes Theodorus's idea of the *philosophos*.[78]

In neither the *Sophist* nor the *Statesman*, the two dialogues dramatically most closely linked to the *Theaetetus*, does Socrates call himself a *philosophos*. In the former, he does express interest in the nature of *philosophoi*, and the visitor has views, but there is not even the suggestion that Socrates is asking about himself.[79] In the *Phaedo*, dramatically the last of this dialogue-sequence, Socrates twice says he does *philosophia*. At its beginning, he says that he had for a long time obeyed a dream that he should strive to practice music (μουσικὴν ποίει καὶ ἐργάζου) by philosophizing; but now, near death, he is trying to take it literally, by versifying (Pl. *Phd.* 61a5). Late in the dialogue, he worries, as he did in the *Theaetetus*, that in wanting to win an argument he fails to be philosophical (91a). Elsewhere in the dialogue Socrates talks about *philosophia*—as the preparation for death—without expressly identifying himself as a practitioner.[80]

In this span of dialogues, Plato gives considerable attention to *philosophia*; and in others, he gives even more. So there is no doubt that Plato is interested in *philosophia*, and values it. He is also interested in Socrates, and values him. Elsewhere he links him to *philanthrôpia* (Pl. *Euthphr.* 3d7), being *philomathês* (Pl. *Phdr.* 230d3), and even being *philologos* (Pl. *Phdr.* 236e5). But it is remarkable the degree to which Plato foregoes to call Socrates a *philosophos* or to have Socrates call himself *philosophos*. Perhaps Plato thinks that Socrates was inadequately good to deserve the name *philosophos*. But were *philosophos* a human practical ideal, it would be odd to have Socrates featured in all

[77] Socrates says that, were he polite, he would ask Theodorus whether any young men from Cyrene are studying geometry "or any other/the rest of/general *philosophia*" (ἢ τινα ἄλλην φιλοσοφίαν). On the translation, see above, p. 114n39.

[78] The digression (starting at Pl. *Tht.* 172c) appeals to Theodorus's view of *philosophia*: see 175d10–e2, with Peterson 2011, 59–89, and *Soph.* 216a1–c1, where Theodorus takes the Eleatic visitor to be quite the *philosophos*, and the whole class of *philosophoi* as θεῖος.

[79] Socrates's questions are at Pl. *Soph.* 216c; the Stranger's views are expressed most clearly at 253b–254a, 259e–260a, 268b.

[80] E.g., Pl. *Phd.* 61c5 ("if Evenus is the *philosophos* I thought he was, he would do as I say"); 63e10 (about the courage of "those who truly spend time in *philosophia*"); 82d (being a *philosophos* as a prerequisite for communing with gods); 95c1 (the proof of the *philosophos*'s serenity); 102a1 (if Cebes is a *philosophos*, he will do as Socrates suggests). See Peterson 2011, 166–95.

but one Platonic dialogue and not count as the ideal. Indeed, when describing *philosophia* (see chapter 8), Socrates comes out as its exemplary practitioner. Or perhaps Plato's use of the term *philosophos* has become so technical that it no longer applies to Socrates. But in many places in which Plato does not call Socrates a *philosophos*, we have no evidence that Plato also has a technical meaning of the term he wants to keep separate and unsullied. Indeed, as we will see two chapters hence, I am doubtful about claims of the word's technicality in Plato. The best explanation, I think, is the one adumbrated in the *Apology*: that Socrates died because he was deemed a *philosophos*.

Non-Academic *Philosophia*

Varieties of Philosophical Experience in the Fourth Century

In subsequent chapters, we will study Plato's, Aristotle's, and ultimately Heraclides's visions of *philosophoi* and *philosophia*. Though these Academic visions differ among themselves, and in Aristotle in particular we observe great internal variety, they represent only one form those visions might have taken. How *philosophia* looked to other Socratics, such as Antisthenes, Phaedo, and Aristippus, and to non-Socratics, such as Alcidamas and Isocrates, is quite different. Yet all these groups took themselves to be using the words in the *philosophos* group plausibly and comprehensibly, either directly following their linguistic forebears or spinning the idea in a reasonable though increasingly positive direction. Because *philosophia* became a discipline in the Academy, however, as I will argue in chapter 9, philosophers (so called because of their disciplinary association) share the Academic vision rather than that of, say, Antisthenes or Isocrates. This does not directly vindicate Plato's rhetorical or argumentative skill. Plato's vision did not win the battle against his rhetorical competitors because his was evidently more appealing, conducive to happiness, or historically plausible. Rather, he founded a long-lived school and research center, one that relied on concerted discussion rather than charismatic speeches, and his competitors did not.

This chapter opens the way to understanding Heraclides's picture of philosophy, and perhaps our own, by studying the alternatives. I begin with the fragmentary Socratic material, where modification of desire appears to be the leading consideration, focusing on the work of Phaedo and Antisthenes. I then turn to the *Dissoi Logoi*, a kind of technical manual for "*philosophoi*" that gives content to the practice mentioned by Gorgias. Then I turn to Alcidamas and Isocrates, for both of whom *philosophia* means a kind of teaching through speeches conducive to living well; by contrast with the Academic model of *philosophia*, with which it shares the basic idea, it mostly ignores (self-)examination and the pursuit of non-political issues.

Phaedo of Elis and Therapeutic Self-Improvement

Many readers of ancient philosophy know Phaedo of Elis as the Pythagorean-izing friend of Socrates whom Plato has narrate Socrates's final day on earth. What honor this represents or what dialectic point it makes, especially in a dialogue saturated with talk about "philosophy" and "real philosophers," we cannot know. At a minimum, however, it suggests the plausibility that the historical Phaedo would in fact talk about Socrates and the nature of philosophy. As it turns out, we know that Phaedo did write about Socrates and the nature of philosophy, in a dialogue called the *Zopyrus*; he may have done so again in another dialogue, called the *Simon*, the same cobbler we met in chapter 5.[1]

Zopyrus treats of a visiting physiognomist who judges of Socrates's visage, a topic apparently also broached by the Socratic we will study next, Antisthenes (DL 6.16). On the basis of Socrates's bull neck, Zopyrus diagnoses him as stupid and obtuse; his bulging eyes testify to his cupidity for women. Alexander of Aphrodisias (a late second-century CE Peripatetic), one of our sources for the content of this dialogue, provides the story:

> When Zopyrus the physiognomist said something outlandish regarding Socrates the philosopher, something far off from his actual way of life, and these things were ridiculed by Socrates's associates, Socrates rejoined that actually Zopyrus wasn't at all mistaken, for he would indeed have been that way, by nature, as [Zopyrus diagnosed him], had he not become better than his nature through the practice of *philosophia* (ἐκ φιλοσοφίας ἄσκησιν). (Alex. Aphrod. *De fato* 6 = Euseb. *Praep. evang.* 6.9.22)

If Alexander of Aphrodisias is quoting Phaedo at the end, then Socrates says that *philosophia* contributed to the improvement of himself beyond the allotments of nature. Either he rids himself of his cognitive weakness and passionate exacerbation, or he suppresses them. The exact contribution provided by *philosophia* itself is unclear. Some kind of *askêsis* ("exercise," "endeavor") does the rehabilitative work; *philosophia* somehow generates that

---

[1] For the dialogue names: DL 2.105. Simon in the *Simon* probably represented a life of *sophia* and *sôphrosunê* less austere and self-depriving than the ideal propounded by Antisthenes (*Soc. Ep.* 12–13). For all fragments relevant to *Zopyrus*, see Rossetti 1980; his 2015b, at 83–84, 93–96, is also helpful, suggesting that the dialogue is a protreptic to philosophy. Boys-Stones 2004, except at 10, focuses on the nature of the soul presupposed by the claim here. See Di Lanzo 2018 for an effective overview of Phaedo's life and writings.

askêsis.[2] If *philosophia* is a sort of conversation, as the context of Socrates as practitioner might suggest, then the *askêsis* might be the result of practical syllogisms. If *philosophia* is instead a sort of acceptance of new norms, for which conversation is only useful preparation, then the *askêsis* might be governed or motivated by those norms. In either case, *philosophia* underwrites a practice that transforms one's desires in radical ways. It is hardly a matter of mere self-cultivation; it is a remaking of one's self.

Another key testimony to *Zopyrus*, from Julian the Apostate (fourth-century CE Roman Emperor), provides further insight into Phaedo's picture of *philosophia*:

> Phaedo of Elis . . . judged there to be nothing incurable by *philosophia*; and by it everybody is to be purified in all their manners of life, their habits, their desires—of absolutely everything of that sort. For if it nurtured only those of good birth and excellent upbringing, there would be nothing so remarkable about *philosophia*; but if it can lead up to the light people in such a state [as Phaedo, i.e., a bad one], then it seems to me supremely remarkable. (Julian *Ep.* 82, 445a, trans. Wright)

Julian implies that Phaedo wrote explicitly about *philosophia*, treating it as a sort of panacea.[3] It cures and purifies (cf. Xen. *Symp.* 1.4), targeting a person's way of life no matter what it happens to be. The passage does not specify a relationship between *philosophia* and thoughts, beliefs, theories, or reasoning. It only praises its power; it does not articulate its structure. What we see, however, is a completely laudatory notion of a *philosophia* that is generative, through exercise, of the improvement of one's competences, dispositions, and quasi- or non-rational desires. This parts from views focused on debate and politics of Thucydides and Gorgias, or the view focused on cosmology and theory of the author of *On Ancient Medicine*. It seems to develop a distinct line of influence from our hypothesized Pythagorean tradition (a tradition in which Phaedo seems to have seen himself): regimens connected to ethical and spiritual self-improvement. We saw this in Empedocles's writings on "purification," with hints in Lysias's remarks about a "philosophizing" to get oneself out of trouble. Spiritual regimens may well require speech or discussion for

---

[2] The translation of Boys-Stones 2004, 8 ("through the practice of philosophy"), preempts asking questions about the relationship between philosophy and *askêsis*; that of Rossetti 2015b, 84 ("askesis that comes from philosophy"), does not answer the questions but at least allows them. See Smyth 1920 §1688c for ἐκ as "generated from, sourced in."

[3] The contrast might be with Isocrates, who claimed effectiveness for *philosophia* only among the already well-off (Isoc. *C. soph.* 17, 21).

their delineation and encouragement, and so we may expect that, for Phaedo, Socrates's *philosophia* does have a communicative component. The important point is that Phaedo's vision of philosophy seems to treat any mode of communication—debate skills, definition, systematization, etc.—as secondary relative to the overcoming of one's defective nature. Antisthenes and readers seem to have had a similar view.

Antisthenes of Athens and Heroic Self-Mastery

Whereas Plato gives to Phaedo the retelling of their master's final conversation, about a *philosophos*'s purification at death into an immortal rational soul, Plato famously writes nothing about Antisthenes (ca. 445–365 BCE), among Socrates's first important followers.[4] But we know about him from a range of other contemporary and later sources. In Xenophon's *Symposium*, Antisthenes argues for typically Socratic positions: against the desire for money; in favor of self-reliance as a source of pleasure; and about the benefit of generosity and congeniality over jealousy and irascibility.[5] A biographical sketch of Socrates probably by Antisthenes or an immediate follower, found in a recently published papyrus, disvalues luxury and urges the restraint of base desires (μοχθηρῶν ἐπιθυμιῶν) not through reason (τοῦ λόγου) but through training (τῶν ἐθισμῶν).[6]

These sources do not use *philosophos*-group words. Though possibly a result simply of having lost all but a fraction of his written work, this lexical silence could mean that Antisthenes spoke rather little of *philosophia* explicitly; after all, as we saw in the last chapter, many of Plato's dialogues include no reference to it, and many others have the word only on a few occasions. Still, a contemporaneous source that appears to depend on Antisthenes talks of *philosophein* and *philosophia*, and late gnomological literature attributes several sayings about *philosophia* to Antisthenes; together this probably means that Antisthenes discussed *philosophia* and that we can recover something of his use of the term.

Diogenes Laertius sums up Antisthenes's conception of the good life by observing that happiness requires only virtue combined with Socratic strength (Σωκρατικῆς ἰσχύος), and that it manifests itself in deeds, needing neither much talk nor much learning (μήτε λόγων πλείστων δεομένην μήτε μαθημάτων).

---

[4] See V A 12–21 *SSR*.

[5] Xen. *Symp.* 4.33–44.

[6] *PHib.* 2.182, frr. a (col. ii.) and f (col. x); text and attribution from McOsker 2017; see also Dorandi 2018, 788–91.

Antisthenes uses martial language to describe this view, calling virtue "an irremovable armor" (ἀναφαίρετον ὅπλον ἡ ἀρετή), reasoning (φρόνησις) "a strongest wall" (τεῖχος ἀσφαλέστατον), and calculation (λογισμός) "an indissoluble wall we must prepare" (τείχη κατασκευαστέον ἐν τοῖς αὐτῶν ἀναλώτοις).[7] A passage from a papyrus held at the university library of Erlangen-Nuremberg recently attributed to Antisthenes (in 2014) corroborates this martial language: a character uses the metaphor of a sword-blade (ξίφους ἀκμή) unable to puncture something "more solid" (στερεωτέρωι) to represent a self-inflicted "bitter" (πικρά) cure of the "hubristic and wicked."[8] Diogenes tells us that Antisthenes uses the example of Heracles, a steadfast warrior, to prove that hardship (πόνος) is a good thing, to take strong anti-hedonist line, and to exhort a "life in accordance with virtue"—and from a list of his books, we know that Antisthenes wrote one or several books about Heracles. Trudging miles daily to visit Socrates, Antisthenes learned to be steadfast and imperturbable (τὸ καρτερικὸν . . . καὶ τὸ ἀπαθές). He thought that virtue could be acquired, and, as he says in the *Heracles*, persists inalienably.[9] Other authors emphasize Antisthenes's arguments against sexual pleasure and lauding of discipline above all other virtues.[10]

This background allows us to see the plausibility of a *philosophia*-related influence on an early fourth-century BCE historian. This is Herodorus of Heraclea, a contemporary of Heraclides's father. An omnivorous reader of mythography, geography, Pythagorean literature, and sophistic pamphlets, we know him especially for having written a long and famous rationalizing treatise on Heracles, one in which he both addresses the increasingly intellectualized accounts found in fifth-century BCE authors and apportions the prolific stories of his exploits among homonymous men. One passage in particular, paraphrased or quoted by a Byzantine compiler, John Malalas (491–578 CE), includes several uses of *philosophos*-group words, and these uses seem to be Antisthenic.

---

[7] DL 6.11–13. On *logismos* in Antisthenes see Decleva Caizza 1966, 110, and Prince 2014, 394. On "walls": Alcidamas seems to have called *philosophia* the "bulwark [lit. 'walls-against'] of the laws" (ἐπιτείχισμα τῶν νόμων, Arist. *Rh.* 1406b). The precise meaning is unclear: an *epiteichisma* is a defensive fort placed at the enemy's frontier (Thuc. 8.95; Xen. *Hell.* 5.1.2); with a genitive it means "commanding [over]" (Dem. 4.5); so as LSJ s.v. A.2 admits, Alcidamas means that philosophy is either "a barrier against, or a bulwark in defense of, the laws": that is, taking laws as its enemy or the thing it protects. Aristotle's probable quotation of Alcidamas in the *Rhetoric* (see p. 115 above), where he says that Solon's laws and Theban *philosophoi* helped their respective cities flourish, suggests but does not prove that *philosophia* supports laws.

[8] *PErl.* 4.41–46 (first published 1942), attribution by Luz 2014, 187–89.

[9] DL 6.2, 3, 104, 2, 10, 105.

[10] Clem. *Strom.* 2.20.107.2–3; Theod. *Cur. graec. aff.* 3.53 (τὴν σωφροσύνη περὶ πλείστου ποιούμενος); cf. DL 6.103, ascribing to Antisthenes the view that disciplined people will forgo reading from the fear of distraction by others.

And Zeus brought about another son, Heracles by name, with Alcmene of Thebes, who was called "three-evening." This Heracles showed how to do the following: to philosophize in the evening places, or, really, the sun-setting [sc. western] ones. Those kin of his who apotheosized him after his end called a constellation "the star-clad Heracles," using his name. They depict it wearing, instead of a chiton, a lion's hide and bearing a club and seizing three apples. These three apples he grabbed, they relate, once he slew the dragon with the club, that is, triumphing over the impoverished and variegated calculation of sharp desire through the club of philosophy (νικήσαντα τὸν πονηρὸν καὶ ποικίλον τῆς πικρᾶς ἐπιθυμίας λογισμὸν διὰ τοῦ ῥοπάλου τῆς φιλοσοφίας), having as wrapping a noble mind (γενναῖον φρόνημα), like the lion's hide. And thus he grabbed the three apples, which are three virtues: not getting angry, not being avaricious, and not being indulgent (τὸ μὴ ὀργίζεσθαι, τὸ μὴ φιλαργυρεῖν, τὸ μὴ φιληδονεῖν). For, through the club of a steadfast soul (καρτερικῆς ψυχῆς) and the hide of the boldest disciplined calculation (θρασυτάτου καὶ σώφρονος λογισμοῦ), he triumphed in the earthly contest of base desire (γήϊον τῆς φαύλης ἐπιθυμίας ἀγῶνα), philosophizing until death (φιλοσοφήσας μέχρι θανάτου), as wisest Herodorus wrote down, who also reveals there to have been seven other Heracleses. (Joh. Mal. *Chronographia* 1.14)

Elsewhere I have argued that the material in the latter half of this excerpt probably represents Herodorus's original account well.[11] For Herodorus, philosophizing is characterized by a steadfast soul, which in Heracles's case is peacefulness and patience, indifference to the accumulation of money, and restraint of an otherwise prodigious sexual appetite. Success in life comes from his wholehearted and stable possession of these virtues. Philosophizing also involves, though apparently only as a failsafe measure, the ability to reflect actively on one's desires and convince oneself not to accept one's (base) desires as reasons for action. Heracles's completion of this labor, and his valorization and purported apotheosis thereafter, testifies to the heroism of philosophy.

The connection to Antisthenes is apparent. Antisthenes treats Heracles as exemplar of the good life. He uses the language of "armor" and "walls" in relation with *logismos* and *phronêsis*. He speaks of bad desires to be put down, prioritizing training in virtue over calculating ratiocination. His key virtues are discipline (*sôphrosunê*), steadfastness (*karteria*), and the concomitant freedom from a passionate attachment to anger, money, and pleasure. Furthermore, Herodorus had to get his material from somewhere, and

[11] Moore 2017.

we know no other fifth- or early fourth-century BCE source on Heracles to have treated Heracles in this fashion. I conclude that we can take Herodorus's picture of *philosophein* as that of Antisthenes. In that case, for Antisthenes, philosophy is the training of oneself toward desire-control, and the possession of such virtue explains the apotheosis—divinization—of someone like Heracles. Talk, argumentation, or even demonstrative reasoning play at best subsidiary, occasional, or defensive roles, as the example of Heracles emphasizes. Antisthenes appears to have been more impressed by Socrates's military heroism, hardiness of body and spirit, general imperturbability, and continued care for his soul than by his nattering with friends. In this way, Antisthenes's view may even seem consonant with Phaedo's: treating the modification of desires as supreme, and the route to desire-modification as of only secondary importance.

That this is Antisthenes's view of the *philosophos* gets some support by the three late attributions of *philosophos*-group terms to his name. The sixth-century CE anthologist Stobaeus tells the following story: asked by someone what he will teach his son, Antisthenes replies, "if he is to live with the gods, [to be] a *philosophos*, if with men, a *rhêtor*" (εἰ μὲν θεοῖς μέλλει συμβιοῦν, φιλόσοφον, εἰ δὲ ἀνθρώποις, ῥήτορα).[12] This remark is challengingly ambiguous. Antisthenes could be seen as praising the practical value of rhetoric, denigrating *philosophia* as suitable only for those undergoing apotheosis, who are fleeing their natural environment.[13] A Hellenistic tradition associated Antisthenes with rhetoric, both directly and through the tutelage of Gorgias, and with a distaste for theoretical pursuits.[14] Later florilegia also attribute this riposte to Demosthenes, who presumably stood more than anyone for the value of rhetoric.[15] Yet a Hellenistic tradition had Antisthenes abandoning rhetoric for an association with Socrates,[16] which would allow Antisthenes to mean quite the opposite here: whereas rhetoric has no better than mundane and instrumental value, *philosophia* elevates, allowing one to live more like the unperturbed gods.[17] Some might hear the immortalizing effects of *philoso-*

---

[12] Stob. 2.31.76. A similar response is found at Gnom. Vat. 7.

[13] Cf. Dodds 1959, 4: Athenian democracy is dangerous; you need rhetoric to defend yourself!

[14] Rhetoric: DL 6.2; Jer. *Adv. Iovinian.* 2.14; Gnom. Vat. 4; *Suda* α 2723. Gorgias: DL 6.1. See Prince 2014, 41–48.

[15] Flor. Monac. 182.

[16] DL 6.2, Gnom. Vat. 4.

[17] Goulet-Cazé 1996, 69, takes this line, glossing Antisthenes as saying that "only philosophy enables a man to surpass the human level and reach that of the divine," and linking the divine and philosophy with (normatively excellent) unity and nature. This reasoning follows Pl. *Phdr.* 274a1–2.

phia as distinctly Platonic, presented most vividly in the *Theaetetus* and eventually treated as core Platonic doctrine by later interpreters. This gives too much credit to Plato; the relationship between *philosophia* and becoming like a god—as a purified immortal soul—goes back to the self-understanding of its earliest practitioners, most notably Empedocles, and probably Pythagoras, too. Further, a central element of the Heracles hero-journey is that Heracles underwent (putative) apotheosis, and there is no reason to think Antisthenes, in discussing his acquisition of virtue, would have ignored that part. So if he attributed *philosophein* to Heracles as Herodorus did, we would expect him to say that *philosophoi* intend to live with the gods, and that orators prepare themselves rather to deal with people.

Diogenes Laertius relates another anecdote about Antisthenes and *philosophia*. When Antisthenes "was asked what he gained from *philosophia*, he said that it was the ability to converse with himself (τὸ δύνασθαι ἑαυτῷ ὁμιλεῖν)."[18] This evidently recalls Socrates's description of thought in Plato's *Theaetetus* as "talk that the soul has with itself" (λόγον ὃν αὐτὴ πρὸς αὐτὴν ἡ ψυχὴ διεξέρχεται), which includes conversing, questioning, answering, affirming, deciding, agreeing, and holding an opinion with itself.[19] Both Plato and Antisthenes could have gotten the idea from Socrates, and could have taken it in their own directions, Plato toward the idea of internal coherence (cf. 190a8–e4), Antisthenes toward the idea of self-sufficiency.[20] We might take this as consistent with the riposte in Stobaeus: rhetoric involves convincing others and being convinced by them; but only when one thinks for oneself does one qualify to live divinely. Herodorus's psychologizing internal battle, with the soul's steadfastness and its backup *logismos* defeating the "impoverished and variegated" *logismos* of sharp desire, might have been treated discursively by Antisthenes as a sort of internal debate. At any rate, Antisthenes is not said to have gained from *philosophia* any knowledge of the world, or wisdom of the cognitive sort, or a love for abstractions (any of which we might expect were *philosophia* to mean "intellectual cultivation"), but only a better orientation toward himself.

A final piece of (potential) evidence for Antisthenes's view of *philosophia* comes from an ostracon—a potsherd—found in the sands of Egyptian

---

[18] DL 6.6. Answers to this question, "what is gained from philosophy," are also attributed to Plato (Gnom. Vat. 430), Diogenes of Sinope (DL 6.63: "to be prepared for anything"), Aristotle (DL 5.20: "to live without the force of law"), and Aristippus (see below, p. 203n25).

[19] Pl. *Tht.* 189e6–7, 189e8–190a6.

[20] For this anecdote as concerned with self-sufficiency, see Prince 2014, 334–35. For a contemporary reflection, see Moran 2018, ch. 10.

Oxyrhynchus, and now in Cologne.[21] Stobaeus had already attributed to Antisthenes the following slogan: "those intending to become good men must exercise their body with gymnastics and their soul with education (παιδεύσει)."[22] The ostracon, probably the work of a student exercise, prints: "While the farmer tames (ἐξημεροῖ) his land, the *philosophos* tames his nature (φύσιν). Those intending to become good men must exercise their body with gymnastics and their soul with talk (λόγοις)." The first sentence had already been known anonymously in a Florentine florilegium; its juxtaposition with the line that Stobaeus attributes to Antisthenes and its language suggests that it could also be of Antisthenes.[23] Of particular note is the first verb, ἐξημερόω. In its only other Athenian usage, in Euripides's *Heracles*, it twice refers to Heracles's labors (πόνους) as a whole, the removal of savage beasts from the world.[24] For Herodorus's "philosophizing" Heracles, the task is precisely the taming of one's wild beasts in the improvement of one's nature. Thus the many pieces of evidence about Antisthenes's view of *philosophia* fit together, and even resonate with Phaedo's, as a laborious and serious process of desire-modification in the interest of self-control and orientation toward what is actually valuable. While treating it as a kind of discipline, with a goal of self-mastery or self-sufficiency, it does not assume a foundation in theoretical contemplation, dialectical testing, the increase in knowledge of the world, or more rigorous analytical methods.

It is plausible that Phaedo's and Antisthenes's usage has Pythagorean provenance tempered through several generations of reapplication. The Pythagorean regimen appears to have emphasized emotion control. This emotion control may have been completely distinct from argumentative skill, love for wisdom, concern for the abstract, or other modes of mental development. That for the Pythagoreans emotion control might be only one ingredient in a complete life of *philosophia* does not mean that for Phaedo and Antisthenes *philosophia* must be so expansive. After all, the passage about Heracles mentions neither knowledge nor truth, learning nor wisdom, debating nor studying. It treats philosophizing instead as attainment of the virtues of restraint, an attainment that involves training primarily in steadfastness and secondarily in the self-directed calculation appropriate for withstanding the siren call of one's desires. A more complicated view, but one basically consistent with these ones,

---

[21] Cologne inv. no. 04.

[22] Stob. 2.31.68.

[23] Henrichs 1967; Decleva Caizzi 1966, 110; Prince 2014, 547–49.

[24] Eur. *Heracl.* 20: ἐξημερῶσαι γαῖαν; 851–52: ἄβατον δὲ χώραν καὶ θάλασσαν ἀγρίαν | ἐξημερώσας. At Hdt. 1.26.1, it refers to the clearing of a "thorny" (ἀκανθώδης) tract of land; in Theophr. *Hist. pl.* 2.2.12, in the passive, it means to be domesticated.

is found in another first-generation Socratic, Aristippus (ca. 425 BCE–ca. 350 BCE), to whom Diogenes Laertius attributes six distinct answers to the question about the nature of *philosophia*. The answers are too heterogenous and insecure in their ascription to risk reconstructing a unitary view; but they do show what sorts of views of *philosophia* are conceivable for a Socratic, and the frequency with which such views are attributed to Aristippus may reflect the frequency with which he discussed *philosophia* explicitly.[25]

The *Dissoi Logoi* and Debate about Fundamental Norms

The fragments of Phaedo and Antisthenes do not treat *philosophoi* as members of a distinctive group, but we know that Gorgias and Xenophon did (chapters 5 and 6). Gorgias, in particular, spoke of debates of philosophical speeches, implying that participants in these debates were identifiable as such in the way *meteôrologoi* or political or forensic speakers were. These participants make their appearance in an anonymous text conventionally called *Dissoi Logoi*, from its opening words, often dated to around 400 BCE, in the generation of Gorgias's students.[26] The *Dissoi Logoi* gives us much more detail about the nature of these groups than Gorgias's incidental remark did.

[25] Asked what is "gained from" (περιγέγονεν ἐκ) *philosophia*, Aristippus answers, "the ability to speak confidently with everyone" (τὸ δύνασθαι πᾶσι θαρρούντως ὁμιλεῖν) (DL 2.68). What advantage do *philosophoi* have? "Should all the laws ever be repealed, we would keep living as we do" (2.68). Why do *philosophoi* go to the doors of the rich, but the rich no longer go to their doors? "The [*philosophoi*] know what they need; the others do not" (2.69). Why are *philosophoi* always seen at the doors of the rich? "And doctors at those of the sick; but nobody would wish to be sick rather than a doctor" (2.70). Once, sailing to Corinth, they hit a storm and he lost his composure; asked why *philosophoi* are scared when common people (οἱ ἰδιῶται) are not, he said: "the souls of each are not comparable" (2.71). Finally, he said that those who got a general education but not philosophy were like the suitors of Penelope; they get her maids but are not able to marry the lady herself (2.79; this answer is also attributed to Gorgias, Gnom. Vat. 743 n. 166 (= B29/P22)). Plutarch presents Aristippus's relation with Socrates in a passage that scholars attribute to yet another first-generation Socratic, Aeschines (*De curios.* 516c; attributed potentially to his *Telauges* at VI A 90–91 *SSR*; see also Hershbell 1988, 367, for the *Miltiades*): learning of Socrates's powerful effect on others, Aristippus went to Athens to study the man, his words, and his *philosophia*, "the latter of which involved coming to recognize one's vices and to expunge them" (ἧς ἦν τέλος ἐπιγνῶναι τὰ ἑαυτοῦ κακὰ καὶ ἀπαλλαγῆναι); this view stands closest to those found in Phaedo and Antisthenes.

[26] See Wolfsdorf forthcoming a for the dating. Robinson 1979, 34–41, conjectures ca. 403–395 BCE (earlier scholarship discussed at 41–50); similarly, Levi 1940; Ramage 1961. Schiappa 2005, 146, 148, dates the work earlier, given the absence of the terms *rhetorikê* and *dialektikê*. Silvermintz 2008, 147, puts it as late as mid-fourth century BCE, thinking it "directly responds to some Platonic dialogues," but the opposing direction of influence seems just as plausible. Conley 1985 and Burnyeat 1998 consider it could be much later; in this they follow scholarship from Stephanus to Gruppe.

The text opens with this striking statement: "Opposed arguments are given in Greece by those philosophizing about the good and bad" (*Diss. Log.* 1.1).[27] Only its first nine chapters exist; the final chapter, quite fragmentary, begins with this statement: "The greatest and most excellent discovery for life is found in memory, useful for everything, both for philosophy and for wisdom, . . . for when you go with it [sc. your memory], your mind gets a better and more unified picture of what it has learned" (9.1–2).[28] These two uses of *philosophos*-group words certify the text's overall concern with "philosophizing." As we read between them, the text presents "philosophizing" as the activity of debating, in the abstract, the nature of value, judgment, morality, truth, learning, democratic procedure, and the sophistic ideal. The text repeatedly juxtaposes the objective and the relativist perspectives on some of these issues, and collates examples meant to support or refute either side. No meteorological or public policy topics arise.[29] These look exactly like the *philosophoi logoi* spoken of by Gorgias and the *philosophoi* referred to by Xenophon.

The content of the text is at once disappointing and intriguing. It wallows in the eristic paradoxes familiar from Plato's *Euthydemus*. For example, it tells us that some argue that the "the wise" (τοὶ σοφοί) and the "ignorant" (τοὶ ἀμαθεῖς) are the same because, among other things, they use the same words for common objects: "earth," "human," "horse," "fire." It then presents the other side, which claims that those who argue this are wrong, and would end up admitting as much, "if someone were to ask whether wisdom differs from ignorance; [for] they would say: 'yes'" (*Diss. Log.* 5.1–8). The concern is not with common-sense plausibility but the sort of debaters' arguments that require cleverness and quickness of judgment to rebut. But this yoke of arguments is intriguing because it shows both the range of cross-domain analogizing that those who are "philosophizing" use and the abstractness of the questions that are taken as familiar: first, in addressing the difference between the wise and the ignorant, the text appeals to phonological differences in words, arithmetic, and the nature of relativizing or qualifying phrases (5.10–15); and second, the first chapter of the text claims that some who philosophize "say that the good is one thing, the bad

---

[27] *Diss. Log.* 1.1: δισσοὶ λόγοι λέγονται ἐν τῇ Ἑλλάδι ὑπὸ τῶν φιλοσοφούντων περὶ τῶ ἀγαθῶ καὶ τῶ κακῶ. Silvermintz 2008, 147, translates φιλοσοφούντων as "profess philosophy," despite the lack of evidence that the author refers to teachers.

[28] *Diss. Log.* 9.1–2: μέγιστον δὲ καὶ κάλλιστον ἐξεύρημα εὕρηται ἐς τὸν βίον μνάμα καὶ ἐς πάντα χρήσιμον, ἐς φιλοσοφίαν τε καὶ σοφίαν . . . διὰ τούτω παρελθοῦσα <ἀ> γνώμα μᾶλλον αἰσθησεῖται σύνολον ὃ ἔμαθες. Wilamowitz emended the text to read ἐς τὰν σοφίαν τε καὶ ἐς τὸν βίον, having wrongly taken *philosophia* to be the same as *sophia*.

[29] Contra Wolfsdorf forthcoming a, which offers that *philosophia* in 9.1 has a cosmological implication.

another," and others say that "they are the same thing, the things that are good and the things that are bad" (1.1).[30]

The text's fragmentary end links *sophia* to *philosophia*. Both rely on memory, which presumably means on mnemonic or autodidactic techniques (*Diss. Log.* 9.1–5). *Sophia* requires comprehensive learning and recalling; earlier passages corroborate this—the *sophoi* say the right thing at the right moment (5.9–10). Speech that is better at some moments than others is probably advice-speech. In the next chapter, the author says that *sophia* and virtue are taught by *sophoi sophistai* ("wise sophists"), just as competent writing and music teachers teach writing and music, and the Anaxagoreans and Pythagoreans are broadly acknowledged to have been successful at teaching *sophia* (6.8). The content of their *sophia* he does not identify, except to align it with virtue; we might suppose that it has political, social, and personal relevance.

It is against this background that we can infer, for the *Dissoi Logoi*, who *philosophoi* are. Thomas Robinson's views, in the fullest commentary on the text, have been influential—but they are not decisive. Robinson thought that because professional "philosophers" could have no special need for memory, *philosophia* (*Diss. Log.* 9.1) must refer instead to "general education," with *sophia* as "the practical wisdom of the sophist-rhetor."[31] He takes a related view about the opening sentence of the text: *philosophoi* must refer to "thinking people" in general, since related arguments about the good and the bad are also made by Herodotus and Euripides, and it would be worthless for the author to discuss problems that concern only "professional" *philosophoi*.[32] I disagree. Dedicated *philosophoi* certainly would need memory, as we saw from Gorgias and in more detail from *Dissoi Logoi* itself, to store and recall the pieces of evidence and counter-evidence for their broad-ranging debates. As we have already mentioned, the *Dissoi Logoi* says that *philosophoi* give endless examples about the objectivity or relativity of goodness, the admirable, the just, and the true, and unspool long sequences of arguments about virtue, teaching, political constitution, and epistemology. Memory, especially hierarchical, organized, and rationalized memory, will be essential for the *philosophos*, in his quick-minded debates with others.[33] Also, Robinson assumes too strict a contrast between *philosophia* as a professional pursuit and as general education. Not all self-organizing groups of people, such as *philosophoi*, need be considered "professionals," which implies formal or informal credentials, a

---

[30] On the nature of these arguments, see Gera 2000; Scholz 2003 (and similarly in 2004); Bailey 2008.

[31] Robinson 1979, 238.

[32] Robinson 1979, 147–48.

[33] Cf. Aristotle's comments about Gorgias's educational system at *Soph. el.* 183b37–184a1.

source of income and livelihood, and quasi-legal or at least powerful social status in a polity.

The category of *philosophoi*, for the *Dissoi Logoi*, comprises people who practice and carry out debates about the abstract nature of fundamental norms of life, both privately and publicly. They recognize themselves as *philosophoi*, as *Diss. Log.* 1.1 and 9.1 recognize. They may or may not teach *philosophia* to others—though if they do they count as *sophistai*—and the benefit of their *philosophein* seems to be in their victory in contests; at any rate, no other benefit is cited or implied. But obviously they are not debating simply for the sake of debating, for this would not explain their topic. To explain the topic we might appeal to Plato's *Protagoras*, where Socrates contends that everybody in a democratic society is simply assumed to be ready for discussions about virtue and life, given that goodness and justice and so forth are not technical topics suitable for analysis only by professionals (*Prt.* 319b5–d6). Thus facility in philosophical debate begins not in a deep well of esoteric knowledge, even if it goes in that direction, but in something shared; excellence in the sport thus represents insight and commitment, not a lucky background. We might also appeal, to explain the specific topic of philosophical debates, to a feeling of significance in these debates, that even if the explicit purpose of the debate is victory, a nice subsidiary outcome is improved understanding of basic life-guiding principles.

But we must also ask about the source of the name *philosophoi* for the people in these debates. The author of *Dissoi Logoi* never treats *philosophein* as the pursuit of *sophia*, even if some practitioners treat it as an offshoot of the activity. Even less does he treat it as the lack of *sophia*, or a fascination with the nature of the *kosmos*, or an inquiry into *ta meteôra* and the things beneath the earth. The best explanation, as I see it, is the historically contingent one traced in chapter 5, from the rhetorical-political notoriety of the Pythagoreans through Empedocles to Gorgias and to here, where for each practitioner his canniness in speech was paired with a brightly manifested curiosity about fundamental questions concerning the direction and practice of one's life.

Alcidamas and the Educational Foundation for Extemporaneous Political Practice

Whereas for the *Dissoi Logoi*, which appears to manifest a Gorgianic image of *philosophoi*, I said that *philosophia* is not mere education, for Alcidamas of

Elaia, an actual student of Gorgias, it may be.[34] (We ought not be surprised by this difference, especially since Alcidamas, who seems to have lived in Athens, might never have met the author of the *Dissoi Logoi*, which is written in an mixed Doric dialectic.) Alcidamas serves our history of *philosophia* in several ways. He provides one of the earliest extant doxographies of fifth-century BCE *philosophoi*, as we have already seen in the discussion of Empedocles in chapter 5 and will see again in chapter 9. He also followed Gorgias in writing paradoxical encomia, which may have represented a certain early route for philosophy.[35] He may have described *philosophia* as the "bulwark [lit. 'walls-against'] of the laws," but, as we have seen (p. 198n7), it is unclear whether this means "a barrier against, or a bulwark in defense of, the laws." His most important contribution comes from his use of *philosophos*-words in his one intact work, written around 390 BCE, at the time of Isocrates's *Against the Sophists* (discussed below), known as *On the Sophists* or *On Those Who Write Written Speeches*.[36] In this several-page-long speech, he promotes extemporaneous address over reading from memorized scripts.

The speech begins with an important background claim: "Some (τινες) of those being called (τῶν καλουμένων) sophists neglect research (ἱστορίας) and study (παιδείας) and have as little experience speaking as private people do. All the same, they think highly of themselves and mistake a part of the skill [i.e., writing] for the whole of it" (*Soph.* 1). Alcidamas treats "sophist" as a laudatory name given to people by those who esteem them, as he does again at the end of the next paragraph (*Soph.* 2). He says that a sophist should care about investigation and enculturation. But some sophists care only about clever textual assemblages, creating which requires the following: spending a long time, correcting at leisure, bringing together the ideas and works of the earlier sophists (τῶν προγεγονότων σοφιστῶν), cribbing clever expressions, and revising in the light of the attention of others and one's own

---

[34] Student of Gorgias: *Suda* α 1283, γ 388, δ 454. N. O'Sullivan 2005, 15, suggests that Alcidamas might have met Gorgias in 427 BCE during the latter's embassy, as Alcidamas sought out teachers (or students) for himself.

[35] The works of Alcidamas: *Encomium on Death* (Cic. *Tusc.* 1.48.116), *On Proteus the Dog* and *On Poverty* (Men. Rhet. *Division of Epideictic Speeches* 3.346.9–18; possibly the same work), and *On Nais* (Ath. 13.592c). See Barney 2016 for Gorgianic paradoxology and early philosophy.

[36] For this dating, see Milne 1924, 21–53 (who seems [9–20] to judge rightly that Plato read Alcidamas before writing the *Phaedrus*); Muir 2001, xv (who believes [xiv, 61] the reading went the other way); Mariss 2002, 55; Edwards 2007, 47. N. O'Sullivan 2005, 15–16, expresses skepticism about any specific dating. Van Hook 1919, 89–91, addresses the conflict with Isocrates; Liebersohn 1999 and McCoy 2009, 46–53, interpret the work but with no attention to *philosophia*.

attentions (*Soph.* 4). This is not enough to deserve such a grand name, and those who forego *historia* and *paideia* should be called "makers" or "producers" (προσαγορεύεσθαι ποιηταί) rather than "sophists." More specifically, they "have left out much of *rhetorikê* and *philosophia*" (*Soph.* 2). Learning those two things allows a sophist to speak well spontaneously, appropriately at any moment, with a resourceful swiftness (ταχεία . . . εὐπορίᾳ) of argument and vocabulary (*Soph.* 3). The Gorgianic language from *Helen* 13 is evident: *philosophia* is knowing how to respond, without hesitation or the leisure of a composer, to any argumentative proposition and rejoinder. Rhetoric appears to be the verbal or articulating counterpart to *philosophia*. Research and study must be the way, put abstractly, that one acquires rhetoric and *philosophia*.[37]

Midway through the speech, Alcidamas repeats his critique in similar words, bemoaning the "one laying claim to (τὸν ἀντιποιούμενον) *philosophia* and promising to educate others, who can demonstrate his *sophia* only if he has his writing tablet or book but cannot if he lacks them" (*Soph.* 15). Philosophy provides the (teachable) education necessary for excellent speaking, in particular the flexibility, creativity, and insight required for many of the most important speech contexts, as we saw in Herodotus and Thucydides. Impressively written documents may appear to reflect the rumination of a philosophical speaker or teacher, but they may rather reflect a laborious and workaday construction. In Alcidamas's verb "lay claim to," he reveals that people by his time referred to themselves as possessors or practitioners of *philosophia*, and in doing so celebrated themselves for their speechmaking and talking ability.

Near the end of the speech, Alcidamas responds to a hypothetical objection, explaining why someone who gives himself over to (διατρίβοντα) *philosophia* would vaunt spontaneous speeches (αὐτοσχεδιαστικοὺς λόγους) over those composed with forethought and care (*Soph.* 29)—which must be the presumed virtues of philosophy. His answer is simple: he of course recommends preparing ideas and arrangement in advance of a speech, but extemporaneous verbal expression has the virtue of timeliness, a virtue that outweighs the lesser virtue of technical polish (*Soph.* 33).

---

[37] Mirhady 2004, 332, wonders, plausibly, whether we are to associate *historia* (which appears contrasted with writing [*graphein*], and perhaps to be equated with thought) with *rhêtorikê* (which is concerned with invention), and *paideia* with *philosophia* (concerned with education and culture generally, and perhaps with language), where "enquiry and education" seem to constitute the art as a whole. I do not understand the putative modesty of Muir 2001, 42, when he writes: "Alcidamas probably meant no more than good background knowledge allied to the capacity to use it for practical purposes—not so far from Isocrates's usage" (which Muir has as: "both the methodical treatment of a subject . . . , and the human activity involved in pursuing it").

This speech of Alcidamas points, only somewhat more hazily than the *Dissoi Logoi* does, to a nascent sense of a group of *philosophoi*. Sophists constitute an easily acknowledged group. *Philosophia* is a topic that some of them study, but it is also a study that others lay claim to as well. *Philosophoi* then would be a sort of secondary group, concerned more for self-improvement connected to understanding and demonstration than with the run-of-the-mill sophists, who focus on the technicalities of pedagogy or elocution.

There is another speech historically attributed to Alcidamas, called the *Odysseus*. It has sometimes but not always been judged inauthentic;[38] its uses of *philosophos*-group words probably supports athetizing. Odysseus says that Palamedes and he have never quarreled heretofore; but now Odysseus will have to accuse him, and unfortunately "the man [Palamedes] is clever and philosophical" (ὁ δὲ ἀνήρ ἐστι φιλόσοφός τε καὶ δεινός, *Odyss.* 4). This means argumentative cunning to the point of devious insincerity. Odysseus returns to this theme, calling Palamedes a sophist and drawing attention to his notable powers of reason and insight; "he happens to make use of his philosophizing (φιλοσοφῶν) on the things he ought least to do" (*Odyss.* 12)—that is, his cognitive and argumentative capacities for dubious purposes. Finally, Odysseus says he will recount "what he tried even to philosophize, that is, deceiving and cajoling the youth about" (ἃ καὶ φιλοσοφεῖν ἐπικεχείρηκεν ἐξαπατῶν τοὺς νέους καὶ παραπείθων, *Odyss.* 22), namely his self-proclaimed invention of military formations, letters, numbers, measures, weights, checkers, dice, the arts, currency, and fire-beacons. Once again, philosophizing represents tricky talking. This use of "philosophizing" is not current at the end of the fifth and beginning of the fourth centuries, and is found again only in the late pseudo-Lysias 8. The theme of the speech is familiar to that period (as Gorgias's *Palamedes* proves). But the use of *philosophos*-group words is not the one we see in Alcidamas's *On the Sophists*; and whereas *On the Sophists* employed only the abstract noun *philosophia*, *Odysseus* never employs it. To be sure, Alcidamas could have shifted his patterns of use over the decades between these two speeches, and *philosophia* as "valuable education" and as "devious argument" might be thought to share *some* underlying features; all the same, we can add to the other difficulties in attributing *Odysseus* to Alcidamas this one concerning *philosophos*-group words.

---

[38] Muir 2001, xvii–xviii, is disposed to accept it, followed by Edwards 2007, 49–51, and Knudsen 2012, 43–48, but N. O'Sullivan 2008 argues persuasively that two grammatical constructions tell against classical authorship.

Isocrates and a Pedagogy for Political Speech-Making

The speech with which Alcidamas's *On the Sophists* seems in conversation is Isocrates's taxonomic *Against the Sophists* (390 BCE). The two authors use the term *philosophoi* (and cognates) in a similar way: to refer to groups of people distinctively and with a concerted focus on the deep and wide-ranging study of ethical, cultural, and political matters for the sake of effective political speech-making. In *Against the Sophists*, Isocrates distinguishes two basic groups of *sophistai*, "intellectuals," that he finds frequently conflated: the *philosophoi* and the *logographoi*. The latter group, teachers of political speechwriting, he disdains; while they look fancy with their technical vocabulary and apparent public-spiritedness, they cannot really hide their cynical instruction in "meddling and grasping" (πολυπραγμοσύνης καὶ πλεονεξίας).[39] All *philosophoi*, by contrast, at least aim to teach virtue, discipline, and wisdom—that is, what is true rather than what is merely appealing. But a range of people go under the name *philosophoi*, and Isocrates has to subdivide this category, since some, unfortunately, have given the whole class of practitioners a bad reputation. Many *philosophoi*, in seeking students, claim unreasonably to teach what is unteachable, such as knowledge of the future and justice, and once they have students they put them through pointless exercises. They promise to teach students the knowledge they need for deciding how to live, and thereby to become happy, but subsequently train them only to find inconsistencies in words rather than actions, what Isocrates calls "freewheeling and hairsplitting" talk (ἀδολεσχίαν καὶ μικρολογίαν). Some even use eristic, captious and misleading quasi-logical maneuvers (λογίδια). For students to be able to care for their souls, which is their goal, Isocrates asserts that they must learn instead about the present and to appraise their own beliefs. The subdivision of *philosophoi* Isocrates himself represents fits somewhere between the small-minded speech writers and the overpromising *philosophoi*. He teaches his students to learn speech composition with precision, study the people who speak well, adjust their speech arrangement to the circumstances, deploy *enthumêmata* ("argumentation"), speak rhythmically and musically, and have a brave and imaginative soul. The focus is not on *rhêtoreia* ("oratoricality"), he says, but on *epieikeia* ("reasonableness").[40]

---

[39] Isoc. *C. soph.* 9, 19–20; cf. *Antid.* 226–28.

[40] Isoc. *C. soph.* 1, 6–7, 20 (what *philosophoi* claim to teach); 11 (issue of bad reputation); 1–2 (pointless exercises); 3 (promises about happiness); 7–8 (freewheeling, etc., talk); 8 (learn about the present), 16–18 (brave soul, etc.), 21 (the focus). For further discussion, see McCoy 2009, 54–58.

External evidence that Isocrates takes this self-constructed middle way comes from Plato's *Euthydemus*. Late in the dialogue, Socrates quotes Prodicus as describing a class of men "who straddle the fence (μεθόρια) between *philosophos* and *politikos*" (Pl. *Euthyd.* 305c7). Context suggests that Socrates takes Prodicus's straddling class to include Isocrates and that Prodicus's characteristic distinction between words—his three-way division of "politicians," *philosophoi* (as presented in Socrates's protreptic speeches in the *Euthydemus*), and an unnamed middle class—maps onto Isocrates's three-way division of intellectual practitioners. Isocrates acknowledges a large group of people called *philosophoi* who share an interest in teaching virtue and knowledge, with the goal of happiness, by means of certain types of talking, where the internal variation concerns the type of talking this goal calls for. At this point Isocrates does not say that *philosophoi* comprise a professional class; many, he says, have remained private citizens. But some have become skilled speakers, and others focus primarily on the improvement of their students' abilities (Isoc. *C. soph.* 14, 21). Thus, for Isocrates, *philosophoi* constitute at least a distinctive social group and a subset of *sophistai*.

The subdivisions within *philosophia* get rehearsed again in Isocrates's *Helen*, which perhaps takes inspiration from Gorgias's speech of the same name (studied in chapter 5). Some people, Isocrates says, practice *philosophia* in the fashion of the earlier *sophistai*, among whose number he mentions Protagoras, Gorgias, Zeno, and Melissus. Such thinkers defended crazy paradoxes, including the impossibility of false or contradictory speech, or the unity, teachabiliy, and epistemization of virtue (Isoc. *Hel.* 1–3, 6). This disputatious hairsplitting and apparent refutation is easy for its practitioners, insofar as it takes on unfamiliar topics, where there is less risk of common sense rebuttal; and it is fun, since the fantasy-oriented youth, prone to excess, like it; but it is also useless, conducive neither to public nor private good (*Hel.* 4, 7–8). Isocrates's mode of philosophizing, by contrast, actually pursues truth, educates students about civic affairs, develops their political experience, deploys reasonable conjecture about what is important rather than seeking exact knowledge about what is trivial, and strives for small but valuable improvements rather than expansive but superficial improvements (*Hel.* 4). As he did in *Against the Sophists*, Isocrates portrays *philosophia* as a large tent, in which some practitioners succeed and some do not, and warns listeners not to judge philosophy harshly on the errors of the latter (*Hel.* 66–67). But the tent does not cover the historical past: he treats these *philosophoi* as contemporary with himself, calling Protagoras and the other fifth-century BCE thinkers "sophists," aiming to avoid linguistic anachronism but desirous to track intellectual trends nonetheless.[41]

The defense of *philosophia* against resentment and attack recurs in the *Busiris* (quoted in chapter 4 as a testimony for Pythagoras). Isocrates treats this speech as a critique of Polycrates, who, like Isocrates, is trying to make a living teaching and practicing *philosophia*, but unlike Isocrates risks making a worse name for it (Isoc. *Bus.* 1, 42, 49). Isocrates claims that *philosophoi* who discuss political matters discuss Egypt (*Bus.* 17), and so he goes on to laud Egyptian philosophy as the precursor to Greek philosophy, given its concern for people's souls, orientation toward legislation, and investigation of reality. That investigation, which includes astronomy, arithmetic, and geometry, aids in the tasks of civilization and the development of virtue (*Bus.* 22, 30).

Isocrates's other speeches reiterate these themes. In *To Demonicus*, Demonicus's eagerness for education overlaps with his preparedness for *philosophia*, which Isocrates will teach him (Isoc. *Ad Dem.* 3). This education in *philosophia* comprises both encouraging students into speechmaking and showing them how to become renowned as serious about the virtuous constitution of their character, knowing what to strive for, what to avoid, with whom to spend time, how to manage their lives, and, in the pedagogical arena, how to love learning, guard what one knows, listen to discussions, accumulate lessons, and travel to study with others (*Ad Dem.* 4–5, 7–8, 18–19). *Philosophia* teaches one to foresee what is advantageous (*Ad Dem.* 40). In *To Nicocles*, *philosophia* shows one the path to the precise knowledge for rulership and the cultivation of one's soul, even if its practitioners disagree about the path itself (Isoc. *Ad Nic.* 35, 50–52). Similarly, in the later *Nicocles*, Isocrates notes that while people often reinterpret the claim made by *philosophoi*, that they pursue virtue and skill in speaking, as a marketing ploy to yield for themselves tuition payments and social status, in fact *philosophoi* in general do help one pursue piety, justice, and virtue; it is just that, like any other possession, *philosophia* can be misused, and the practitioner himself, not the practice, is to be blamed. Indeed, *philosophia*, which involves persuasion and clarification, refutation and praise, debate and investigation, in public and in private, is education at its core (*Ad Nic.* 1–9). Isocrates says virtually the same thing in the *Evagoras*, emphasizing the importance of emulating models of living well (Isoc. *Evag.* 8–10, 76–81). And in the *Areopagiticus*, Isocrates puts *philosophia* on a parallel with horse-training, gymnastics, and hunting as parts of an education at which

---

[41] Isoc. *Bus.* 2–3. *Philosophoi* are again later than ancient *sophistai* (who use logical tricks) at *Antid.* 283–85.

some become preeminent but thanks to which the rest at least avoid dissipation (Isoc. *Areopag.* 45).

Isocrates's grandest statement on *philosophia* comes in the *Antidosis* of the late 350s BCE, in which he imagines his defense against the charges made against Socrates: making weaker arguments stronger and corrupting the youth.[42] For the most part, in that speech Isocrates elaborates on claims about *philosophia* he made in earlier speeches; and because it coincides with Plato's late and Aristotle's early work, it describes a period that we document later in this book. But in his protreptic to *philosophia* he makes three points worth noting. First, he acknowledges four distinct outcomes of a philosophical education: remaining a private citizen, though with an improved soul; becoming a competitor, apparently in the debates described by Gorgias and featured in the *Dissoi Logoi*; becoming a teacher, recapitulating one's own teacher; and becoming a judge and advisor, by which Isocrates apparently means being politically engaged (Isoc. *Antid.* 201). Second, he describes his own pedagogy in more detail. He teaches philosophy by giving his students knowledge and experience in *schemata* ("moves"), just as a wrestling teacher teaches holds and drops, and requiring laborious practice in them, which yields their synthesis and the ability to deploy them when the time is right. While he cannot convey perfectly precise knowledge, he can at least encourage close attention to and a sensitive understanding of the consequences of action (*Antid.* 183).[43] Third, Isocrates tempers his views about the other practitioners of *philosophia* he adumbrated in *Against the Sophists* and *Helen* while engaging in somewhat more jealous guarding of the term itself. He claims that some of "those serious about eristic" (τῶν περὶ τὰς ἔριδας σπουδαζόντων, *Antid.* 258) impugn him, but that he does not want to respond in kind. He admits that when they teach eristic, and when others teach astrology, geometry, and other *mathêmata*, though this looks to many like "freewheeling and hairsplitting" talk (ἀδολεσχίαν καὶ μικρολογίαν, *Antid.* 262), useless and readily forgotten, they do benefit students, even if less than they promise (*Antid.* 261). True, once students have mastered these subject matters, they do them little good unless they are in turn to become teachers of them, but while learning them they develop in cognitive ability, especially precision, persistence, and comprehension (*Antid.* 265).

---

[42] Isoc. *Antid.* 15, 30. Like Socrates (Pl. *Ap.* 17b–d), he denies the general suitability of his "wide-ranging discussions and expositions about *philosophia* and its power" for law-court disputes (9, cf. 2).

[43] Wersdörfer 1940 and Wilcox 1943 study the normative terminology associated with Isocrates's practice. Jebb 1893, 2.34–50, and Merlan 1954, 62–75, remain good sources on Isocratean *philosophia*; see also, more recently, Nightingale 1995, 26–41; Wareh 2012, 30–54; and Collins 2015, 171–81.

Thus doing the mental gymnastics of studying the "older sophists" like Empedocles, Ion, Alcmaeon, Melissus, Gorgias, and Anaxagoras, who debated the number of fundamental elements of the world, suits young people, and prepares them for *philosophia*, but this should not really be called *philosophia* at all (*Antid.* 266–70).

This third remark deserves the most commentary. In the *Antidosis*, Isocrates expands his prosopography of sophistry-philosophy from his four-entry list in *Helen* to this list of six thinkers. He displaces the charge of "freewheeling and hairsplitting" talk from himself, in his nearly four-decade-old *Against the Sophists*, onto unnamed critics and admits to seeing some benefit in their teaching, not just the right goal incorrectly pursued. But he seems now also to clarify to himself the proper referent of *philosophia*. It had never explicitly included the practice of the fussily paradoxical "older sophists," despite the copying of their theses and research programs by some *philosophoi*. Yet in *Against the Sophists*, philosophy amounted to (i) teaching (ii) the truth to (iii) improve lives, especially by conducing to (iv) virtue and wisdom. Isocrates thought he practiced *philosophia* better than many others, who overpromised and underperformed, waylaid by fictions of omniscience, the corrosive charm of eristic, and the crutch of externally imposed notions. Yet he took his competitors, even if they were giving philosophy a bad name, and thus too the practice he shared with them, genuinely to be sharing the practice. Now in the *Antidosis*, however, he retracts that broader notion, a retraction the preparation for which we saw in his *Helen*. In the 350s BCE, he thinks that a benefit to one's life is not criterion enough for some practice to count as *philosophia*; geometry improves one's mind, and thus one's access to truth, but counts only as a propaedeutic. *Philosophia* has become, in his late years, to stand for his own brand of teaching toward a resolutely public life, one of speechmaking and audience cultivation, in which one aims to become *sophos* ("totally competent") with the best *doxai* ("views," "beliefs") by means of a maximally efficient course of study (*Antid.* 271). This efficiency condition erases the "philosophy" label from his competitors, as does the full-bore commitment to a democratically active vocation.

We come to see strong opposition to Isocrates's view of *philosophia*—that is, of the best means of education—in Plato and Aristotle. Plato's Socratic dialogues depict the benefit of nit-picking, argument-following, and refutation-currying conversations; they are necessary for jolting people out of their false conceits of knowledge and complacency. Aristotle argues for the intrinsic value, pleasure, and self-realization of so-called paradox-mongering. Of course they are all talking about *philosophia*. But there are differences besides these three judgments about the benefit any sort of *philosophia* must and can have. They differ in what sort of enterprise they take *philosophia* to be. For Isocrates, it is a kind of teaching. For Plato, as I argue in the next chapter, it is a kind of conversation. For Aristotle, and thus too for Heraclides, it is a discipline. All three views have roots, it would seem, in the early period of *philosophoi*, where powerful teaching, earnest and prolonged conversation, and emulation and study of one's predecessors probably stuck out as characteristic of Pythagorean or quasi-Pythagorean activity.

Still, even if it comes from a shared background, we might wonder about the source of Isocrates's apparently distinct view of *philosophia*. Gorgias's view of *philosophia*, as we studied it in chapter 5, looks too far from that of Isocrates, even if they do both present *philosophoi* as members of a broadly dispersed club or pastime.[44] A borrowing from Alcidamas, his contemporary, seems unlikely. Socrates, as Plato and Xenophon present him, emphasizes the self-examining and other-examining aspects of *philosophia*, which Isocrates notoriously elides.[45] Apparently, then, the conception in the political circles known to Thucydides and his readers as late as the 390s BCE, in which philosophizing prepares one for civic exigencies and explains Athens's military and imperial successes, is responsible. The *Panegyricus*'s similarity with the Periclean Funeral Oration strengthens this connection, especially the claim that *philosophia* was taught by the Athenians to the Greeks.[46] Isocrates thus draws from (elite, policy-making, Athenian) popular usage. That is, not the pseudo-Lysianic "contrivance" meaning found in colloquial dispute, or even the Aristophantic "cleverness" meaning found in similar situations, but a (newly seen as) good orientation toward democratic decision-making, especially in light of frequent emergencies. We need not say, then, that Isocrates tried to "define" *philosophia*, as though he wanted to posit a homonymous neologism.[47] Instead, he would have drawn from past or common usage, and pulled out the

---

[44] Gorgias, with Prodicus and Tisias, is said to have been one of Isocrates's teachers (Dion. Hal. *Isoc.* 1).

[45] Halliwell 1997b; Morgan 2004, 146–50, emphasizes Isocrates's inconsistent application of his own principles. See Murphy 2013, 314, 316, 320, 330, for Isocrates's distinction of himself from the eristics, to whom he assimilates the Socratics (cf. Isoc. *Bus.* 6).

[46] Isoc. *Paneg.* 47–50; see further Livingstone 2007, 28–30.

[47] This is the view of, among others, Timmerman 1998, 145, 149, 155–56. Cahn 1989, 128, 134, says that Isocrates used the name *philosophia* to deny the possibility of a technical rhetoric, but does not explain how it gained that power. Poulakos 2001 summarizes Isocratean *philosophia* as training in successful use of *doxai*; Sullivan 2001 argues that *idea*, another key term in Isocratean *philosophia*, pertains to technical rhetoric; and Livingstone 2007, 20–34, argues reluctantly for three (or four: 33) Isocratean "uses" of the term *philosophia*—(i) commonsense intellectual exertion and self-cultivation; (ii) formal education; and (iii) Isocrates's own teaching—but does not explain how the word could tolerate all three uses. See further Morgan 2004, 125–36, and for bibliography, López Cruces and Fuentes Gonzalez 2000, 905–6.

features he took as salient or core by the late 390s BCE. This need not involve boundary-policing, which treats certain contemporary uses as simply too distant from the archetypes to deserve sharing its name, though late in his career Isocrates did adopt this stance on occasion. Rather, it reconstructs the normative elements—that *philosophia* conduces to usefulness, that it depends on *logoi*, that it involves teaching and learning, that it has a *polis*-context, and that it is not exclusively about meteorology or a forensic contest, and that it differs in key ways from sophistry and the political art—that undergird the main public uses of the term.

Conclusion: A Battle over the Word *Philosophia*?

This analysis clarifies the familiar notion that Isocrates battled with Plato and Aristotle over the term *philosophia*. No doubt they battled over students, or more generally, the hearts and minds of a populace in which those students might grow up. This battle concerned the term *philosophia* insofar as these leaders of schools debated the properties of *philosophia* that make it useful. Or rather, they debated what, if one wanted to do *philosophia*, one ought to do, and why. These debates deployed a range of types of argument, including etymology, which Isocrates does not use, and explanations for popular beliefs about *philosophia*, which Isocrates does use. But the conflicts between Isocrates and Plato in particular need not manifest a jealousy about the word *philosophia*, as though either wishes to make a public term a private brand name. The purported fact that Isocrates "lost" the battle with Plato is a result, as I have said, not of Plato's persuasiveness but of the fact that the discipline *philosophia* formed around Plato's Academics and their argumentative precursors and successors; thus *their* conception of *philosophia* followed Plato more than Isocrates. While Isocrates's school may have had the best attendance in Athens, his style of *philosophia* seemed relatively accessible, his mode of higher education practically defined the liberal arts to come, yet while the core of his training as speechmaking would have given his *philosophia* a practical edge, Isocrates still failed to create a discipline. Perhaps his students went into public rather than teaching careers,[48] and the end of Athens's civic autonomy in 323 BCE may have devalued the leadership potential of philosophical-political speech (as Isocrates's *Letter to Alexander* and *Panegyricus* suggest).

[48] Isocrates provides his own list of eight students (*Antid.* 93–94); Zosimos's *Life of Isocrates* picks out, from among his "many students," Theopompus and Ephorus (historians); Hypereides, Isaeus, and Lycurgus (orators); and Philiskos, Isocrates, Androtion, and Python of Byzantium (not known to be philosophical researchers).

Isocrates saw himself not as a member of a self-sustaining, socio-cultural mode of life, with shared or archived concepts and fluid participation, but as a unique teacher with identifiable paying students, whose thought-world would quiesce with his own death. His "competitors" presented themselves as part of a discipline, a continuous conversation with the refinement of methods and language, one shaped largely as a shared Socratic tradition, a tradition (Socratic, Academic, Peripatetic, and Hellenistic) from which Isocrates explicitly and continually separated himself.

Anyway, Plato's victory was a limited one, scorching only the disciplinary terrain. Other uses of *philosophos*-group terms, as in Sage maxims or anthropology, lived unscathed in the neutral territory of quotidian language (see chapter 10). So while for *philosophoi* then and now, *philosophia* pertains (approximately, for the most part, usually) to argument, (self-)examination, and criticism, and not toward the immediate production of political savvy but toward the long-term expansion of knowledge of the world and our capacity to know it, for Greek speakers as much as for English speakers, what we now translate "philosophy" hearkens to a moment before or to the side of that Isocratean-Platonic sally of precisifications.

ACADEMY

8

Plato's Saving of the Appearances

Radical Revision or Explanatory Reconstruction?

A standard view about the history of *philosophia*, propounded by Walter Burkert, Andrea Nightingale, John Cooper, and many others, is that Plato radically overhauled the term *philosophos* and its cognates.[1] The term once meant intellectual cultivation and could apply to anyone so moved to such self-improvement. Then Plato reinvented it as a technical pursuit of actual knowledge, distinguishing it from other putatively self-improving modes by its reliance on dialectic, norms of explanatory rigor, and assumptions about reality. He propounded this view in the Academy, and, indeed, its institutional structure, encouraging research in mathematics and methodology, assumed it. But this novel view of *philosophia* neither spoke for itself nor settled all questions. Those who did not yet follow it needed to see it as valuable, and those who already did needed to negotiate its relative focus on theoretical reflection and practical application. Heraclides's Pythagoras story assumes the Platonic picture of *philosophia* as the pursuit of a comprehensive and deep understanding of the world; the rest of *On Diseases*, as we can reconstruct it, suggests that *philosophia* has both intrinsic value and eminently useful application.

Much of this account is impossible to deny. We see nothing like Plato's reflections on *philosophia* in the extant writings of his contemporaries, and Isocrates even confirms the distance between Plato's and his own. Plato had unique cause to found an institution of research and teaching that would not only outlive him but also, even while he lived, produce materials independent of his hand. He reflected on Socrates's intellectual commitments, methods, and results with a profound concentration and seriousness unseen elsewhere, even in the most notable Socratics. And the fifth-century BCE attestations of *philosophos*-group words hardly even hint at the ideas we see in Plato's literary conversations about epistemology, metaphysics, or cosmology, the ideas that accompany his vision of *philosophia*.

[1] Cooper 2007, 23n4.

A primary contention of this book is that this standard view nevertheless still misses something. The view of *philosophia* presented in Plato's dialogues shows as much continuity as rupture with earlier views. Plato, it seems, asked himself about the characteristics of the practices heretofore called *philosophia*, and to the extent that one would intentionally pursue them, about their point. His answer, as dialogues written across his career reveal, is that *philosophia* amounts to a practice of conversation that conduces to virtue, or knowledge, or flourishing. This is consistent with much fifth-century BCE usage as well as with early fourth-century BCE usage, even if his contemporaries emphasize teaching or political deliberation over conversational success. Where Plato goes beyond his contemporaries is in thinking rigorously and adventurously about the conditions for virtue or flourishing—and thus about the conditions for such conversations that might conduce to virtue or flourishing. On the one side is Socrates's vigilance about conceits of knowledge, his refutative exchanges simultaneously pursuing knowledge and avoiding error. On the other side is the hypothesis of unchanging objects of knowledge and reflection on the way they might be known, a solution to skepticism about finding stable life-directing principles. Plato's innovation comes, it appears, from thinking about the prerequisites for *philosophia*, should the practice actually benefit its practitioners. His vision of *philosophia* is then largely continuous with that of his predecessors; it is his vision about the source of the promise of *philosophia* that differs. Granted, we cannot with complete satisfaction distinguish *philosophia* from its conditions of success. But recognizing commonalities among fifth- and fourth-century BCE approaches to *philosophia* makes better sense of Plato's project: he is defending *philosophia*, not defiantly adopting a dubious name for an obscure practice. It is with a study of the early career of the term that we understand Plato's work, and the way his reconstruction contributed to a valorized discipline.

Plato's dialogues do not just continue the story; they add another element. They contain the earliest extant etymologies or quasi-etymologies of *philosophia*. Their existence supports the two leading claims of this book: that the meaning of *philosophos* would not have been transparent or obviously positive to ancient Greek speakers; and that because the term may have started out as something other than a term of approbation, fourth-century BCE apologists for the *philosophos* life sought to redeem it. Plato's writings contain four distinct instances of linguistic attention to the word: minimally in the *Phaedrus*, more robustly in the *Lysis*, with theoretical intensity in the *Symposium*, and impressively, if baroquely, in the *Republic*. Their variety speaks to the freedom of Plato's invention and also to the perceived value of the effort. Most of those who have thought that *philosophos* means "lover of wisdom" are vindicating Plato's efforts.

Accordingly, this chapter has the following structure. I begin with several dialogues in which we see Plato presenting *philosophia* as continuous with a (positive) reconstruction of its late fifth-century BCE usage, a practice of concentrated and semiformal conversations about matters conducing to virtue and flourishing. I turn to the *Phaedrus*, traditionally considered a mature work, as the clearest case for the combination of a familiar vision of *philosophia* defined as a social-cultural practice with new reflections on the epistemic and even metaphysical conditions for successful philosophizing. *Philosophoi* are contrasted with *sophoi* but with compliments to the *philosophoi*. I then show that several other dialogues thought to come from late in Plato's career continue the pattern of acceptance already discovered. Finally comes the study of Plato's etymological work on *philosophos*, culminating in Socrates's stunning argument about the *philosophoi*-kings in *Republic* Book 5. I conclude with a reflection on Plato's contribution to thinking about *philosophia*.

Charmides: *Philosophia* as a Conversation for Self-Improvement

Plato's *Charmides*, a dialogue about discipline (*sôphrosunê*) and self-knowledge, uses *philosophos*-family terms twice; both times they refer to the kinds of virtue-conducing conversation depicted in this and in other dialogues. In neither case does Socrates state explicitly what he believes *philosophia* is; this means that he should be taken as using it in a familiar and uncontroversial way. The first usage shows up in the opening scene; the second shows up during the introduction to Charmides, the first of two respondents to Socrates's elenchic questions.

The dialogue depicts Socrates, at some unspecified time, narrating his return in 429 BCE from a several-year campaign in northeastern Greece.[2] Desiring to visit his usual haunts (τὰς ξυνήθεις διατριβάς) and see his friends, he goes immediately to a palaestra. He finds there a large group of people, most of whom he knows (Pl. *Chrm.* 153a1–d2). After answering their questions about the terrible siege of Potidaea, he asks two of his own. He wonders "about *philosophia*, how it's going now" (περὶ φιλοσοφίας ὅπως ἔχοι τὰ νῦν) and about the young men, whether any has distinguished himself in wisdom (σοφίᾳ), beauty, or both (153d2–4).[3] He gets an answer perhaps to both at once, because

---

[2] For the date, see Planeaux 1999; for the dialogue, see Moore and Raymond 2019.

[3] It is Socrates as narrator who uses the word *philosophia*; he does not say what word he in fact used in 429 BCE. Probably he narrates this conversation close to the end of his life. But as we will see later, Plato does not quibble about attributing certain uses of the term *philosophia* to the late fifth century BCE.

at that moment Charmides and his admirers walk in—it is he who has so distinguished himself in beauty and who we later learn has become notable as *philosophos* as well (153d5–154a6).

Though the spectacle of youth leaves Socrates's first question hanging, its position and pairing with the other do explain its meaning. *Philosophia* must refer to the activity sustained by Socrates's group of friends, including Chaerephon and Critias, at the palaestra among Socrates's other accustomed meeting places. This activity admits new participants, especially the city's distinguished teenagers as they mature, though it must also maintain stability over the years. The ensuing conversation must typify that activity of *philosophia*, given that nobody observes that anything Socrates or any of his interlocutors says is out of the ordinary. For their conversation they take as a topic the definition of discipline (Pl. *Chrm.* 157a6–b7). Success at defining it, the procedure for which everyone seems already to know, is taken to correlate with its possession (e.g., 158e7–159a4, 160d5–e1). From this we may infer that the conversations constitutive of *philosophia* address virtue-terms with a goal of learning more about the virtue and diagnosing the interlocutors' degree of virtue, urging them to become more virtuous (if the diagnosis is only lukewarm), and modeling the behaviors that may manifest or bring about the virtue.

The term *philosophos* then arises in a subsequent scene that Socrates reports in direct speech. Critias and Chaerephon have noted Charmides's exceptional good looks. They agree that he has a beautiful face. Beneath his robes, they say, he has a wonderful body. Yet this physical beauty, Socrates responds, matters only if Charmides's soul also happens to be well developed (εὖ πεφυκώς, Pl. *Chrm.* 154d1–5, 154e1). He suggests that they assess its development by having Charmides lay bare his soul and letting them look at it. "For," Socrates says, "I suppose he is quite of the age to be willing to join a conversation (ἐθέλει διαλέγεσθαι)" (154d5–7). Critias heartily agrees, "since as a matter of fact he's also *philosophos* and, as it seems to others and to himself, quite expert in poetry" (ἐπεί τοι καὶ ἔστι φιλόσοφός τε καί, ὡς δοκεῖ ἄλλοις τε καὶ ἑαυτῷ, πάνυ ποιητικός). Socrates accepts Critias's praise by saying that this fine trait (τὸ καλόν)—"being *philosophos* and expert in poetry"—has its roots in their ancestor Solon (154e8–155a3).

This passage tells us that being *philosophos* means having the ability to join the conversations typical of Socrates, Critias, Chaerephon, and their friends, one that can reveal the nature and quality of one's soul, with the hope that it matters to one's attainment of virtue. We learn that Charmides has imbibed the customs of the group. Most strikingly, he answers definitional questions "in a word," and it really is one word.[4] When he fails to defend one definition, he comes up with an alternative. He answers questions with yes or no, never accuses Socrates of tricking him, and comes to recognize his argumentative inadequacies. He accepts that the topic of the conversation—the nature of *sôphrosunê*—demands abstractness and profound thought, neither belittling it nor falling stunned into overawed silence.

Curiously, Critias added to his description of Charmides as *philosophos* that he is "expert in poetry," *poiêtikos*. Because of its collocation, this must mean having some conversational ability related to being *philosophos*, which we just found to be the ability to give, defend, and abandon definitions—and knowing the meaning of *poiêtikos* may help to establish the boundaries of *philosophos*. Critias's use of *poiêtikos* is among the earliest extant uses of the term.[5] Its contemporary uses and those in the next quarter century have a range of meanings.[6] One meaning was "productive of poetry," emphasizing versification, pleasure-inducement, and imitation.[7] But this seems an unlikely meaning in this case, for there is neither evidence of his writing nor relevance to the dialogue.[8] Isocrates used the term to refer to speaking in any genre with creativity and panache.[9] In this case, Charmides would be said to be a fluent and appealing speaker; but our evidence presents him rather as a diffident and even laconic type. In a third possibility, known from Plato's *Ion*, poetic expertise picks out the capacity to discuss poetry and other literary genera in

---

[4] Pl. *Chrm.* 159b5, 160e4–5.

[5] It would vie with Pl. *Ion* 532c8 and Isoc. *C. soph.* 12.

[6] Late in that time frame, *poiêtikos* came to mean "productive" in general: Pl. *Soph.* 219b11, 219d1, 265a4–266d5; *Def.* 411c8, 411d4, 411d5, 413b12, 414e12, 416a29. For Aristotle, "the skill of poetry" (ἡ ποιητικὴ τέχνη) came to mean giving a systematic account of the nature of poetry; see Ford 2002, 4–5.

[7] Pl. *Phdr.* 245a6, 248e1, 257a5, 265d4; *Grg.* 502c12; *R.* 387b3, 387b4, 393d8 (specifically versifying), 600e5, 601a4, 606d4, 607a2, 607b6 (poetry's quarrel with *philosophia*), 607c5, 607d7 (contrasted with *philopoiêtai*, who love and defend poetry in meterless speeches), 608b7; *Phlb.* 62d5; *Tim.* 19d5; *Leg.* 656c3, 660a4, 682a3, 700d4, 778d6 ("the poet"), 802b6; *Minos* 320e4. Relatedly, it could mean "given to riddling" (*R.* 332b9, *Alc. II* 147b9) or describe those lacking knowledge and akin to diviners and soothsayers (*Meno* 99d1).

[8] This has not stopped translators from assuming it means this, e.g., Lamb 1927, 15, "quite a poet"; Dorion 2004, "tres doué pour poésie"; Nails 2002, 91, "a young poet"; Lampert 2010, 161, having "poetic capacity"; Tuozzo 2011, 110, "quite a poet" (although also "quite poetical" [107]). Cf. Tulli 2000, who argues that Charmides and Solon are associated with the poets who write encomia for good men and hymns for gods. Critias was himself a poet, to be sure. But contra Nails 2002, 91, who cites only Pl. *Chrm.* 155c as evidence, no other ancient reference to Charmides mentions poetry. Hippothales (in the *Lysis*), by contrast, does compose poetry for his beloved Lysis (Pl. *Lys.* 204d7–206c8).

[9] Isoc. *C. soph.* 12; *Antid.* 47. Though not citing Isocrates, this might be the idea found in Friedländer 1964, 67, and Levine 2016, 38–40.

relevant ways.[10] Plato's *Protagoras* calls this ability—"being skilled concerning verses" (περὶ ἐπῶν δεινόν)—"the greatest part of a man's education." It includes knowing what the poets have written correctly, how to pick those writings apart (διελεῖν), and how to answer questions about them (ἐρωτώμενον λόγον δοῦναι). Protagoras adds that this skill concerns virtue as much as definitional conversation does.[11] As it turns out, Plato says that Charmides followed Protagoras, and both Charmides and Critias heard Protagoras give this speech (*Prt.* 315a1, 316a7). The *Charmides* includes several judgments and analyses of poetic or gnomic language.[12] So it must be that people judge Charmides good at such poetic assessments. His competence here overlaps in part with his competence in *philosophia*. Both consist in holding one's own in analytic conversations that address and conduce to virtue. They differ in the focal point of those conversations and the strength with which they scour the interlocutors' settled beliefs.

Thus the dialogue's two uses of *philosophos*-group words match up. The adjective *philosophos* applies to the capacity to carry on the engagements picked out by the noun *philosophia*. These social-communicative engagements purport to enable moral improvement. They do so, in the weak case, because they reveal one's understanding of virtue in light of definitions proposed in the conversation (in the strictly "philosophical" case) and claims made in literature (in the strictly "poetic" case). They do so at a theoretically richer level as well when they encourage the performance of the very behaviors symptomatic of the possession of those virtues: perseverance, courage, insightfulness, listening to others and giving them their due, and appreciating the divine and rational purpose of such exchange.[13]

This description of Platonic *philosophia* leaves two important questions open. First, do the interlocutors engaged in *philosophia* pursue their conversations with the end of cooperation or of competition? In non-philosophical

[10] In the *Ion*, Socrates challenges a rhapsode's claim to be able to analyze Homer's poetry and yet nobody else's. "If this ability comes thanks to a *technê*," Socrates reasons, "then you would be able to speak about all other poets—for the poetic one (ποιητική, sc. *technê*), I suppose, is a whole" (Pl. *Ion* 532c8–9). Ion's *poiêtikos* skill at interpreting Homer turns on his understanding of Homer's composition of his poems. Compare *Ap.* 28a8–c6, where, in response to Socratic questioning, poets are said to flunk self-exegesis—Socrates and his audience must assume that the poetic power, to the extent it qualifies as a skill, would have both a productive and an explanatory aspect.

[11] Pl. *Prt.* 338e7–a6. Cf. Pl. *Hp. mi.* 365c10–d3, where Socrates asks Hippias to justify Homeric views about justice and deception.

[12] Socrates asks whether Homer "speaks well" concerning the sense of shame (Pl. *Chrm.* 161a2–3); Critias glosses Hesiod's verse concerning work (163b2–c10); and Critias glosses the sage maxim "Know yourself" (164d5–165a7).

[13] Moore 2012, 7–9.

speech contexts we can readily decide. Antilogical forensic pleading and eristic exchange aim only to win the audience to one's side or to confute the opponent; small talk and blandishments aim only to promote a shared practical
framework and comity. We cannot so readily decide in the context of philosophical conversation. Socrates repeatedly undermines the definitions that Charmides and Critias provide him. From this perspective, and from the perspective of a Critias hurt by such refutations, *philosophia* looks competitive.[14] It
shares this competitiveness with the various games of verbal disputation found
in contemporary Athens. But Socrates repeatedly affirms that in fact he talks
not for the sake of triumph or honor, but for his own and the group's advantage. Responding to Critias's accusation that Socrates is trying to refute him,
he says:

> What a person you make me out to be, when you suppose that if I really am re-
> futing you, it is for any but the same reason I interrogate myself about my own
> claims: the fear that someday I will fail to notice that I think I know something
> that I don't actually know. In fact, that's what I claim to be doing right now—
> looking into the argument mostly for my own sake, though perhaps also for the
> sake of my friends. Don't you think it is a good shared by virtually everyone
> whenever the way something is comes to light? (Pl. *Chrm.* 166c7–d6)

Conversation has a cooperative function, a coming together necessary for each
person's own advance and to help the others with their advance. It would appear, then, that *philosophia* somehow combines the ambition and spirit of vig-
orous correction typical of competition with the self-criticism and marked
goodwill typical of cooperation.

This cooperative conversationality does leave one spark of competition
aflame. Socrates competes with Critias for influence on Charmides, and this
requires that Socrates does more than reveal Critias's flaws, but less than show
his own perfection. He must get Charmides to recognize that success on his
own terms comes only by practicing a Socrates-inflected *philosophia*, not the
ersatz version of his cousin Critias. With this recognition Socrates wins no
prize of honor or pride, only the satisfaction that he might continue in productive philosophical conversation with a young man he thinks might be suited
for such conversations.

The description of *philosophia* in the *Charmides* leaves another harder question open. How do conversations about virtue-terms conduce to knowledge

---

[14] Critias's accusation of Socratic competitiveness: Pl. *Chrm.* 166c3–6; cf. 162c1–d4,
165a7–b3, 169c6–d1.

about virtue, then to virtuous practice, and then to the good life? I mentioned two ways: the revelation of deficiencies may prod improvement; and the performance of conversational actions themselves in accord with virtue or vice allows small-scale modeling for virtuous action in the other departments of life. Yet these contributions may seem inadequate for explaining the benefits of the specific kinds of talking depicted in the *Charmides*. And while talking about the nature and importance of virtue may turn interlocutors toward virtue, the real work of education and self-improvement may seem to have to come from elsewhere. A closer reading of the dialogue might begin to outline some hypotheses; but we will now leave it for another dialogue.

Protagoras: Some Questions about Philosophical Conversation

The *Protagoras* provides two perspectives on *philosophia* discussions that complement and deepen those provided by the *Charmides*: they specifically address the role of competition and cooperation. This dialogue takes place several years before the dramatic action of the other. Alcibiades has just come of age, and Socrates has only now risen to prominence. The latter has brought the zealous young Hippocrates to a donnish party at Callias's house. There they hope to test the wares of Hippocrates's inamorato, Protagoras of Abdera. The prudent Protagoras appreciates Socrates's sensitivity to the danger of private audiences, so the entire crowd attends as Protagoras propounds an etiological myth that purports to illustrate the teachability of virtue, then naturalizes that myth, then opens the floor to questions. Socrates wonders about the unity of virtues. He and Protagoras make concerted headway, even as the elder figure finds the arguments for the coincidence of justice and piety, and of wisdom and discipline, hardly compelling. But their sympathies falter when Protagoras resists Socrates's assimilation of wisdom to justice. He does so by defending the relativity of goodness at such length and with such a litany of examples as to imitate a handbook of the *Dissoi Logoi* genre. Hearing the speech out, and abiding the flattering applause it wins, Socrates rebukes Protagoras for filibustering. He pleads the impossibility of comprehending such diatribes. Protagoras balks at this charge. He accuses Socrates of beseeching him to sheathe his long-form addresses, making him ill-poised to maintain his hard-won reputation. Against this accusation, Socrates threatens to forfeit: should Protagoras not shorten his responses, Socrates will leave (Pl. *Prt.* 334a1–335a7).

Callias taps in to block Socrates's departure. The party's host forebodes a dimming of conversational light and avows his supreme pleasure (ἥδιον) in hearing Protagoras and Socrates talk (διαλεγομένων). This halts Socrates, who appreciates the admission: "I have always admired your *philosophia* (φιλοσοφίαν ἄγαμαι), and I praise and cherish it now" (335d10). *Philosophia* can refer only to Callias's commitment to and organization of conversations of the sort that Protagoras and Socrates have pursued.[15] The current example shows orderly, publicly beneficial, and—at times guardedly, at times openly— agonistic exchanges about matters that are universally significant to the human experience, including culture, education, virtue, and goodness, that the inter-locutors effect through epideictic, analytic, and refutative exchange. Thus Callias as impresario curates the sort of *philosophia* discussion groups that we saw in organic homeostasis in the *Charmides*. As with the conversations in the *Charmides*, these too blend the competitive and cooperative. From one angle, Socrates and Protagoras cooperate to deliberate over the virtues' teach-ability and to characterize their inner relations. From another angle, Socrates competes with Protagoras for Hippocrates's tutelage and for the broader audi-ence's esteem. The conversation ends with ameliorating phrases of joint effort and mutual admiration, but only Socrates's irrepressible march to argumenta-tive victory brought on that end.

Callias's guests take turns striving to integrate *philosophia*'s self- and other-directed striving. Alcibiades, Critias, Prodicus, and Hippias each plead for new conversational ground rules. On Socrates's advice they resolve to give Protagoras a chance to ask Socrates whatever he wishes, after which he will resume his role as answerer. Protagoras makes the best of a less-than-satisfactory result by dragging Socrates into his wheelhouse. As we discussed earlier in the context of being *poiêtikos*, Protagoras believes that one's powers of poetic analysis diagnose the fullness of one's education—and these diagno-ses serve as much as instruments of ambition as measures of health. So Pro-tagoras asks Socrates to rectify an apparent contradiction in a song by Simo-nides. Rectification requires reinterpretation. After an initial sally, Socrates explains the song's rhetorical situation. Because Protagoras locates the song's contradiction in Simonides's takedown of the maxim attributed to Pittacus the Sage, "Hard it is to be good," Socrates marshals deep background on the com-petitive use of gnomic phrases.

It is at this point that Socrates mentions *philosophia* for a second time with, in the end, the same contours. "*Philosophia* is most ancient and most plentiful among the Greeks in Crete and in Sparta, and the most sophists on earth are

---

[15] On Callias's enthusiasm for colloquia and lessons from sophists, see chapter 6, p. 182n64. Aeschines's *Callias* has Callias spend money on Prodicus and Anaxagoras (Ath. 5.220c). At the opening of the *Hippias Minor*, the coordinator of Hippias's speech (at the conclusion of which the dialogue starts) asks Socrates, who heard it, to praise or refute parts of it, now that those of us who "have a share in the practice (διατριβῆς) of *philosophia*" are alone (Pl. *Hp. mi.* 363a2–6).

there" (Pl. *Prt.* 342b8).[16] "Sophists" refers to teachers, of the sort Protagoras styles himself.[17] The Spartan citizens have meetings to study with their sophists.[18] Spartan preeminence in Greece is to be attributed to the "wisdom" consequent to those meetings. Socrates glosses this wisdom "education" (παιδεύσει) and reiterates that the Spartans have "an excellent education in *philosophia* and discussion (λογούς)," and that being Laconic is a matter of "philosophizing rather than of athletic training (φιλογυμναστεῖν)," as is usually assumed (342d3, 342d5–6, 342e6). Spartan *philosophia* emits, through cracks in its mute façade, perfectly debilitating zingers, clinched phrases that stun their interlocutors into silence. Even the Seven Sages of Greece armed themselves with these sweet little missiles, so perfectly do they fold up more expansive fields of thought. Those Sage maxims, like "Know yourself" and "Nothing in excess," supervene on "ancient *philosophia*" (τῶν παλαιῶν τῆς φιλοσοφίας). The competition in gnomic maxims found in Simonides poem, the analysis of which turns to the deepest questions of virtue, endurance, personal success, forbearance, and hope, exemplifies that period's *philosophia*.[19]

Socrates's account of *philosophia* begins an answer to Protagoras's challenge, but remains faithful to the way he used the terms earlier in the *Protagoras* and in the *Charmides*. *Philosophia* comprises educational conversations with teachers that conduce to a communicational and mental excellence that Socrates analogizes to gymnastics' goal of bodily excellence. He introduces only one novel element: linking private philosophical conversation to its public condensation. But the brachylogic volleys associated with Spartan confrontation and Sage posturing mean less for the nature of *philosophia* than for the color of its packaging. *Philosophia* is a case of learning ahead of time. The volleys are competitive. It is uncertain whether, as with Callias's beloved *philosophia*, the education that constitutes *philosophia* and that serves those volleys, is itself competitive. Probably it has at least a tincture of sport and parry, in the fashion of gymnastic exercise; teachers might need to inculcate the spirit for such exercise.

Thus Plato uses *philosophos*-group terms in the *Protagoras* as he uses them in the *Charmides*. Being *philosophos* refers to the capacity for conversations, and *philosophia* to the conversations themselves, ones that follow norms of pro-

---

[16] In Plato's *Hippias Major*, Socrates needles Hippias for his inability to sell a range of his lectures in Sparta by presenting Spartans as a society of choosy learners (283b5–286a2).

[17] Earlier in the dialogue, the name *sophistai* refers to those characterized by knowledge of wisdom (Pl. *Prt.* 312c8), who nourish souls on *mathêmata* (313c5–7), and who teach people to become better (316c5–317c5).

[18] In four lines Socrates uses συγγενέσθαι, συγγιγνόμενοι, and συγγίγνονται (342c4–8), leaving no question about the parallel he draws between Sparta and Callias's house.

[19] For more on this topic, see Moore 2016.

ductive engagement and that concern virtues and the possession or transmission of them. These conversations often include sequential and hard-pressing questions about definitions and the relationship between similar concepts or the testing of one another's literary and gnomic interpretations. In general, *philosophia* includes a self-consciousness about the conversations themselves, including an explicit concern for their rules, goals, and educational content.

Already we can see Plato's conception of *philosophia* as a redemptive and quasi-formal version of the conceptions we saw in Gorgias, Thucydides, *Dissoi Logoi*, and the rhetorical teachers. Socrates cards the skein of tactical retorts into the smoother plaits of step-wise argumentation. The drills of preparation assume an intrinsic value. Victory over an ignorant opponent becomes victory over one's ignorant self. The implication throughout is that Plato is emphasizing the self-cultivation and group work that must always have justified the sublimation of the fighting instinct into the fast-paced and clever exchange of words. This emphasis impressed itself on a tightly circumscribed group. We now turn to the broader sell.

Phaedrus: Two Varieties of *Philosophia*, or Practice and Justification?

The *Phaedrus* can seem to provide the clearest and best contrast between Plato's innovative construction of *philosophia* and Isocrates's construction or a mundane cultural version of it. So, anyway, much scholarship has assumed. Close scrutiny of the dozen or so uses of *philosophos*-group terms in the dialogue undermines this assumption. Rather than two varieties of *philosophia*, the dialogue presents both the practice and a hypothesis about the background psychology and metaphysics that would explain the practice's capacity to make a person better through conversation.[20]

Plato's *Phaedrus*, set some decades after the *Charmides* and *Protagoras*, depicts Socrates's conversation with his younger friend Phaedrus, an aspiring orator and devotee of the speechwriter Lysias. The ending of the dialogue reflects explicitly on the meaning and application of the term *philosophos*, with the goal of giving content to that to which Socrates hopes Phaedrus and Lysias might aspire. We should call "*philosophos*, or something like that" (Pl. *Phdr.* 278b), Socrates says, whoever can compose speeches with knowledge and not mere opinion, and who can then defend those speeches while still admitting their limited value. *Philosophos* has a laudatory sense: Socrates treats this

---

[20] For more detail on this section, see Moore 2016.

lesson as a chastening of Lysias, who according to him has not yet earned the name (ἐπωνυμία). He also means the term to inspire Phaedrus, who might yet strive to deserve to be called it. Phaedrus reveals his excitement to try his best; but he also feels the dig against his erstwhile mentor. In response to Socrates's judgment about his favorite, Phaedrus asks Socrates what kind of person they might call *his* favorite, Isocrates. Socrates responds by praising Isocrates as by nature better than Lysias in speeches, as more nobly blended in character, and as more promising than anyone now alive (279a3–7)—and then adds that there is by nature within Isocrates's mind (διανοίᾳ) some (τις) *philosophia*, and because of this, a more divine impulse could lead him to better things, should he want so to be led.

In the course of the conversation that leads up to these closing remarks, Socrates has already said much about the meaning of the name *philosophos* that is to be relayed to Lysias. His mythical palinode speech—which pictures the course of the soul in love as a charioteer with two horses—links *philosophoi* with truth-discovery, and he later outlines an argument that assumes that philosophizing involves knowing how things really are, not just how they seem to be (Pl. *Phdr.* 261a3–262c4). Socrates's discussion of reading, and his continued request for answers and revised answers, shows the importance of defending one's views (275d4–276a7). His doubt that he could ever give a proper account of the soul, or of himself, suggests that human existence calls for deep modesty and reserve (246a4–6, 266b3–c1).

We might wonder, however, about the *philosophia* mentioned in the dialogue's closing lines that resides by nature within Isocrates's mind. Does it refer to the same *philosophia* that Socrates wants Phaedrus to recommend to Lysias, which includes investigating reality, giving reasoned arguments in support of one's positions, and recognizing the meagerness of any written account? From one perspective, it seems it must. Socrates never explicitly taxonomizes or ranks versions of *philosophia*. Further, the proximity between the two remarks about *philosophia* suggests a continuity in meaning between them. From another perspective, however, it might seem that Isocrates's *philosophia*, whatever its degree, must differ from the kind that Socrates encourages Phaedrus to acquire. We might expect that Socrates and Plato find Isocrates's teachings anathema to their vision of good education. Socrates, after all, cleaves popular rhetorical training from the training he recommends for Phaedrus. Isocrates's extant speeches, as we saw in the previous chapter, use the term *philosophia* to refer to his practice by contrast with the overwrought and captious arguments of the Socratics and Aristotelians. Surely Isocrates and Plato competed for students and did so by advancing distinct visions of *philosophia.*[21] Recent scholarship simply assumes that Isocrates's *tis philosophia* differs from Socrates's or Plato's vision.[22]

There are, therefore, reasons both for accepting and for rejecting the idea that Plato uses a single idea of *philosophia* on the final page of the *Phaedrus*, and by extension, in the dialogue as a whole. As the palinode ends, Socrates tells Phaedrus to settle on one way of life and to give himself "wholly over to love accompanied by philosophical talk" (Pl. *Phdr.* 257b6). Two pages later, Socrates warns Phaedrus that the cicadas singing overhead tell the muses which humans spend time in philosophy and which in sheep-like sleep (259b3). Again two pages later, Socrates tells some *logoi* to persuade Phaedrus that lest he practice *philosophia* well, he will never be able to speak well (261a4). What then is the object of Socrates's encouragement? Once again, as in the *Charmides* and *Protagoras*, Socrates never explicitly defines *philosophia*, the *philosophos*, or the activity of *philosophein*. We can tell only by looking at his uses of them.

The first occurrence of *philosophia* in the *Phaedrus*, a crucial one, comes during Socrates's attempt to one-up Lysias's speech lauding the non-lover as the best lover: he will not subject his beloved to the oppressive strictures of jealousy. Among the reasons Socrates gives against spending time with a jealous lover is that such a lover tries to keep his beloved away from those associations that would make him strong rather than weak, wise (σοφός) rather than unlearned (ἀμαθής), courageous rather than cowardly, eloquent (ῥητορικός) rather than incapable of speech, and shrewd (ἀγχίνος) rather than slow (239a2–4).[23]

---

[21] For the *Phaedrus* as Plato's contest with Isocrates, see also Howland 1937; Coulter 1967; Burger 1980, 115–26; Nehamas 1990; Goggin and Long 1993; McAdon 2004; Cooper 2004; Nightingale 2004, 14–35; McCoy 2009.

[22] De Vries 1969 ad 279a9: "Socrates refers to Isocrates with "mordant sarcasm," and "Plato leaves it to his readers to decide whether they will take . . . φιλοσοφία in the Platonic or the Isocratic sense"; see also De Vries 1953, 40–41, and De Vries 1971, 388. Yunis 2011 ad 279a8–b2: The τις "suggests that Isocrates occupies an ambiguous position between the (conventional) *philosophia* that he promotes and the (true Platonic) *philosophia* that remains for him an as yet unrealized possibility." Werner 2012, 230n162: "it is likely that Plato is using the term φιλοσοφία here as a way of taunting Isocrates, and is deliberately leaving it ambiguous as to which sense of the term is meant"; see also 120n40 and 228–29. Similar views about two opposed senses of *philosophia* are held by Brown and Coulter 1971, 411–14, and Griswold 1986, 286n18. McAdon 2004, 32–35, supports his view that Isocrates's view of philosophy is different from Plato's in the *Phaedrus* by appeal only to Plato's uses of the term "philosophy" found outside the *Phaedrus*.

[23] We have no reason to think Socrates rejects the meaning of the words in this section, despite his rejection of the authorship of this speech (contra De Vries 1969 ad 239b4; Brown and Coulter 1971; Rowe 1986 ad 239b3–4; Yunis 2011 ad 239b4).

Keeping him away from many useful associations (συνουσιῶν . . . ὠφελίμων) that would make him most a man (μάλιστ᾿ ἀνήρ), he is cause of a great harm; and greatest of them are those from which he would become most thoughtful (φρονιμώτατος)—and this is divine *philosophia*. (Pl. *Phdr.* 239a7–b4)

So *philosophia* is a kind of social arrangement identical to that described in the *Charmides* and *Protagoras*. Whereas other associations conduce to maturity as venues for the growth of strength, skill, experience, courage, fluency in public address, and cleverness, this association helps people become more thoughtful, reasonable, and insightful. It is a distinctly beneficial association. Its satisfactions cause participants to turn their backs on other putative relationships and obligations, as the jealous lover fears (cf. 252a1–b1).

Instances of the *philosophos* word group next arise in Socrates's second speech (the "Palinode"), one that many readers take as decisive for Plato's views of philosophy. Socrates has represented the life of the gods as souls in chariots endlessly circling the world. Mortals in this representation, by contrast, stop circling the world once they lose sight of reality (τῆς τοῦ ὄντος θέας), which sooner or later they will (*Phdr.* 248b4). This means that every human soul has in fact seen the realities (τὰ ὄντα), difficult as keeping an eye on them may be, but that each eventually loses track of the truth, suffering from distraction and badness (λήθης . . . κακίας), and falls to the ground (248c7). Fortunately, not all is lost; souls are transplanted into human lives, each in one of nine ordered classes. Into the premier class go the *philosophoi*:

The [soul] that sees the most [is put] into a seed of a man who will become a *philosophos* or a *philokalos* or a dedicatee of culture and love (φιλοσόφου ἢ φιλοκάλου ἢ μουσικοῦ τινος καὶ ἐρωτικοῦ). (Pl. *Phdr.* 248d2–4)

This passage emphasizes something other than what the instances of *philosophia* found in *Charmides*, *Protagoras*, and the passage at 239a–b emphasizes, namely that philosophy is a conversational and mutually improving or benefiting group practice. It treats the *philosophos* as someone who pursues a distinct way of life, perhaps as a master of the practice of a certain kind of conversation. Along with its focus on the *philosophos*'s way of life is the palinode's linking of that way of life to two others: that of the *philokalos* and of the person of *mousikê* and *erôtikê*.[24] Socrates does not say how these types of life are related, whether as identical, or as varieties of the philosophical life, or as distinct species of a common genus of which *philosophos* is just one species—

---

[24] Scholarship on this passage often ignores these companion lives, as in Werner 2012, 119.

knowing which would help us understand *philosophia*. We can look to the eight lower classes, most of which also have related ways of life, for clues.

Just below the *philosophos* and his two or three siblings we find the law-bound king (βασιλέως ἐννόμου) and the military and ruling person (ἤ πολεμικοῦ καὶ ἀρχικοῦ). The connective structure seems to distinguish three kinds of life here. The next level down includes the *politikos* and the people involved in estate management and business; the fourth, the hardworking man of the gymnasium[25] and the person who knows healing for bodies; the fifth, the soothsayer and the person concerned with certain rituals; the sixth, the poet and the person concerned with *mimêsis*; the seventh, the city- and earth-workers; the eighth, the person engaged in sophistry or crowd-rallying; and the ninth, the tyrant (*Phdr.* 248d4–e3). Some patterns reveal themselves.[26] Members at the same level do differ; the city- and earth-workers (craftsmen and farmers) provide the clearest case. Yet the members at each level also share a general concern: management of a city; management of smaller groups of people; the well-being of the body; religious observance; creation of art; skilled mechanical production of goods and services; and persuasion of people. The entries in a level mentioned later are not defective, derivative, or secondary forms of the first entry. The second, fourth, and sixth levels prove this.

This pattern suggests that the three named lives at the first level are neither avatars of the noble *philosophos* nor his bastard relatives. There are no reasons for thinking the life of the *philosophos* is being treated as better than or logically prior to the lives of beauty (τὸ καλόν) or of culture (μουσική) and love (ἐρωτική). They are different ways of life connected by a general concern. In a passage quoted and studied in chapter 5, Thucydides links the activities of the first two types of life. "We *philokaloumen* with economy, and we *philosophoumen* without weakness." Pericles must pair the charges of *philokalein* and *philosophein* because they result from similar appearances—indulging in building and in talking, in wasting money and time—and have similar goals: self-cultivation in the preparation for what may come. The Athenians have accumulated adequate resources, both in buildings and in thought. From this perspective, the palinode's pairing of the *philosophos* and the *philokalos* is unsurprising. Both sorts of people have good practical reasons for acting in ways that seem, to outsiders, to be idle talk or the decadent expansion of one's affairs.

The linkage with those dedicated to *mousikê* and *erôtikê* is unsurprising. The *Phaedo* presents Socrates saying that he repeatedly dreamt he was

---

[25] Burnet 1901 supplies a conjectured disjunction, φιλοπόνου <ἢ> γυμναστικῶν, which would allow for three distinct people at this level, not merely two.

[26] Yunis 2011, 114–15, conjectures an interesting account of the groupings.

instructed to make *mousikê* (Pl. *Phd.* 60e3, 7). He said he took this dream to be cheering him on in his present activity, thinking that his *philosophia* constituted *mousikê*, indeed of the greatest kind (61a4). Admittedly the usual view of *mousikê* has it as the production of poems (61b1), not doing what Socrates does. Yet he still thought philosophy fit. This might seem paradoxical; on the ladder of lives in the palinode, the philosophical life is perched five levels above the poetical life. But *mousikê*, rather, involves a special attitude toward the Muses and high culture. Socrates says that he composed a hymn to Apollo, and then versified the stories of Aesop.[27] The *Phaedrus* shows that the Muses may be propitiated in still further ways, including with poetry that teaches each generation the splendid works of the ancients (Pl. *Phdr.* 245a1–8) and with "other practices" (259d3).

Throughout the dialogue, then, Socrates draws complex overlaps between *philosophia*, *philokalia*, and an interest in *mousikê* and *erôtikê*. The lover of beauty (ὁ ἐρῶν τῶν καλῶν) is called a lover (ἐραστὴς καλεῖται) when he partakes in *mania* (μετέχων τῆς μανίας, Pl. *Phdr.* 249e3–4). Socrates often attributes to himself knowledge of *ta erôtika*.[28] Somehow doing philosophy is similar to these other socially and politically salient practices. All four share a certain civic piety, a seriousness of deliberate preparation, a concern for conveying cultural norms to later generations, and an orientation toward wisdom and its best guise, beauty, and attention to living well (cf. 250a5–e1).

Granted, the crucial point may appear to be that *philosophoi* have seen the most of "what is." *Philosophia* is to be defined in connection to the really real. In the palinode, the really real is the set of universals, that which is ascertainable only by mind, for example the universals of justice, discipline, and knowledge (*Phdr.* 247c5–e2). "[We] followers of Zeus look for beloveds who are *philosophoi* and leaders (*hêgimonikos*) by nature" (252e3), in that "we" are *philosophoi*, too, and gaze at the whole, simple, unchanging, and blissful revelations in a pure light (250b7–8). Yet a unique connection between *philosophia* and the universals vanishes in the solvent of the passage's details. The *philosophos* saw in a previous life more of "what is" than others but, all the same, failed to keep seeing it. The previous incarnations of the other ways of life on the nine-level scale also saw a measure of the really real. Essentially, the *philokaloi* and dedicatees of culture and love saw the same amount of the really real as the *philosophoi*. So the *philosophos* cannot be defined solely by his (past self's) connection to the really real; everyone else shares in that connection.

[27] See Betegh 2009; Kurke 2011, 251–55 with 259–64.
[28] Cf. Belfiore 2012.

For none of the lives does the palinode stipulate the actions constitutive of those connections. It does not say how one "philosophizes." The soul observes the really real; it struggles to stay high in the shared orbit; then it falls to earth. But it gives no earthly correlate to this metaphorical observing. This interpretative gap means that we cannot simply assume that the human way to seek to know reality is different from any other purportedly non-Platonic method of accessing reality, as long as that method aims to reveal the nature of justice, discipline, and knowledge. Conversation, modeling, apprenticeship, speech-training, and mathematics seem plausible candidates. All that the palinode suggests is that the method of observation and contention practiced by *philosophoi* must share something with the practice of the *philokaloi* and the dedicatees of culture and love.

The palinode uses the verb *philosophein* in ways that treat *philosophia* as a pedagogical practice (249a1–2). Its most complex discussion of a *philosophos* comes immediately after, when describing the conditions for reincarnation as a human.

> For a [soul] that has never seen the truth will never arrive into this shape [of a human]. For a human must comprehend a thing said in accord with a form (συνιέναι κατ' εἶδος λεγόμενον), it coming from many perceptions into one, being brought together by reasoning (ἐκ πολλῶν ἰὸν αἰσθήσεων εἰς ἓν λογισμῷ συναιρούμενον): and this is recollection of those things that the soul of us once saw, having accompanied god and looked askance at what we now claim is real, and coming up to what is really real. It is for this reason that the mind (διάνοια) of the *philosophos* alone becomes winged: he is always, thanks to his memory, as near as he can be to these things, the proximity to which things makes even god divine. And indeed, a man using such reminders correctly, being continually initiated into completed mystery rites, alone becomes really completed [i.e., initiated]. And standing outside the realm of things that it is human to take seriously, and becoming next to the divine, he is censured by the many as being deranged, but in fact he is possessed, as escapes the notice of the many. (Pl. *Phdr.* 249b5–d3)

Humans collate and abstract—they reason—and thereby reach the truth more readily; *philosophoi* distinguish themselves by doing this most consistently. The passage describes the process by which individual experiences become something linguistic and do so only in their unification.

As the passage continues, the *philosophos* is described as living in the human way best. Like all other humans, the *philosophos* is engaged with the universals, the things said in accord with a form, but unlike non-*philosophoi* he is "always" engaged with them, to such an extent that he seems bizarre to many people.

Of course, as the run-up to the first use of *philosophia* in the palinode makes clear, the *philosophos* fails to maintain complete focus on the really real, even if he does not fail as soon as others do. So, too, here, the "always" is qualified as *kata dunamin*, "as far as [the soul] is able." The difference is quantitative. Since absolute attendance on the really real is divine—it makes any divine thing (such as gods) divine—all humans share in, or ought to share in, something divine. The *philosophos*, in seeking to select or bring together perceptions into unifying speeches, shares most in what is most human: paradoxically, in being divine.

We should pause to note similarities between this and earlier passages. The "divine *philosophia*" mentioned in Socrates's first speech reveals itself as a richer concept. *Philosophia* is not just of the deepest importance. It is, as least in this most recent expression, the practice that contributes most directly to being divine. Also in that earliest use, Socrates said that *philosophia* made one most thoughtful (φρονιμώτατος). Here too *philosophia* involves recollecting the most; amplifying one's understanding, reason, and deliberation; and having a mind (*dianoia*) most cognizant with the sort of unities typical of divine rationality. Thus Socrates uses the word *philosophia* in his second speech in much the same way he uses it in his first speech. Nor is it so surprising that the *philosophos*, though really manifesting what is best in humans, seems strange to most humans. As we saw in the discussion of the first use in the palinode, *philosophoi* are grouped with others who are avid about what is most significant in culture—beauty, art, love—and these people look strange.

The palinode's last two uses of *philosophos*-group words suggest that *philosophia* is a way of life devoted to proper self-integration. It first addresses the ideal case. Good lovers

> strain against [the embraces of the beloved] through shame and speech (μετ᾽ αἰδοῦς καὶ λόγου ἀντιτείνει); if, in leading to a well-ordered life (τεταγμένην τε δίαιταν) and *philosophia*, the best part of their mind should prevail, they lead (διάγουσιν) a blessed and mentally integrated (ὁμονοητικόν) life, being masters of themselves and well-ordered (ἐγκρατεῖς αὐτῶν καὶ κόσμιοι), enslaving that by which badness enters the soul, and liberating that by which virtue enters. (Pl. *Phdr.* 256a6–b3)

The palinode then proceeds to the non-ideal but still admirable case:

> If to a coarser and unphilosophical life (διαίτῃ φορτικωτέρᾳ τε καὶ ἀφιλοσόφῳ) [they turn], and are dedicated to honor (φιλοτίμῳ δὲ χρήσωνται) . . . [these people may choose what people *call* blessed (sc. sex) and] do things not approved by the whole mind (ἅτε οὐ πάσῃ δεδογμένα τῇ διανοίᾳ πράττοντες). (Pl. *Phdr.* 256b7–c7)

Philosophia is identified in the first of these two quotations with being well-ordered, directed by reason, self-controlled, integrated, and protective of the prerogatives of virtue. There is no reduction of *philosophia* to a concern for the really real or to a professional approach to theoretical inquiry, even if such a concern is, in some way, a condition of *philosophia*, as it is of any human life, and such an approach would be an appropriate vehicle for that concern. There is a repeated emphasis on the traits linked to discipline, the very virtue on which the *Phaedrus* closes (279c3). The subsequent passage coordinates *philosophia* with the absence of coarseness, contrasts it with the concerns for honor and bodily pleasure, reiterates its oddness in the public eye, and treats it as the result of wholehearted attention alone. Just as at the end of the *Phaedrus*, where Socrates prays that his outside and inside are coordinate,[29] here the palinode states that *philosophia* means acting (publicly) as the mind decides (privately).

At the close of the palinode, Socrates expresses his wish that Phaedrus turn to *philosophia*. He prays to *Erôs*, using *philosophia* group words twice in close succession:

> Blaming Lysias as father of the [first] speech, stop him from [making] such speeches, and turn him to *philosophia*, just as Polemarchus, his brother, has been turned. (Pl. *Phdr.* 257b2–4)

> [Do this] so that this lover of him no longer wavers as he does now, but wholly toward love accompanied by philosophical speeches he may make his life. (257b4–6)

We may not know exactly why Lysias's speechmaking does not count as philosophical; Socrates obfuscates his critique of Lysias's speech to the unloved (234e5–235a8). But Socrates says that Polemarchus has turned toward *philosophia*. The *Phaedrus* tells us nothing else about Polemarchus; but in the *Republic*, we see that Polemarchus engages Socrates well in conversation.[30] Polemarchus opens the *Republic* by having his slave restrain Socrates; Socrates learns that he wishes to force him into joining him and others in a discussion at his house followed by the observation of some new races (Pl. *R.* 1.327a1–328a10). He interrupts Socrates to defend his father, Cephalus, when his father fails to answer Socrates's questions about justice consistently; he observes that Simonides's verses support Cephalus's contention. For several

---

[29] On this closing prayer, see Clay 1979; Griswold 1986, 226–29; Yunis 2011, 246–49; Werner 2012, 230–35.

[30] On Polemarchus's character, see Page 1990; see Gifford 2001 and Howland 2004 on the historical events involving Polemarchus alluded to in *Republic* Book 1.

pages Polemarchus acts the poetic expert, expounding Simonides's view but graciously modifying it when Socrates shows the untenability of those interpretations. When he fails to defend even these modifications, he says that he would gladly join Socrates in battle against those who believe justice means harming one's enemies (1.331d3–336a8). Some books later, Polemarchus and Adeimantus whisper to each other. We learn that they were complaining that Socrates did not explain how the community of wives and children, the idea for which follows from the view that friends hold possessions in common, should be manifest in the city he describes (5.449a7–450a1). This evidence presents Polemarchus as an interlocutor who loves conversation with Socrates, caring about the most plausible views of justice, graciously accepting Socrates's questions and refutations, and curious about the practical details of this theoretical model.

Phaedrus sees value both in the life Lysias models and in the life Socrates describes. The latter is the life not expressly of *philosophia* but of "love accompanied by philosophical speeches." This suggests that *philosophia* names a kind of conversation with a friend or beloved. From the conversations with Polemarchus depicted in the *Republic*, we see that such conversations will be those that press a person to express what he finds most valuable and true, and then to undergo testing of those views he expresses.

Socrates's exhortation to *philosophia* continues even after the palinode. He turns from his explicit concern with speech competition and the nature of love to the nature of good speaking and writing. Perhaps because he intends to continue with less rhetorical brilliance than before, he tells Phaedrus that their continued conversations remain beloved by the divine and in particular by the Muses.

> The cicadas report to the most senior Muses, Calliope and Ourania, who among humans spends time in *philosophia* and honoring their music (μουσικήν), a music that is a talk (λόγους) both human and divine and that has the most beautiful sound. (Pl. *Phdr.* 259d3–8)

Philosophia honors the Muses' sonorous talk. This talk is both human and divine; as we have learned before, these coincide at the level of the concern for virtue. Socrates treats what he has said as reasons that they continue to talk (λεκτέον). This suggests that *philosophia* honors the gods by mirroring their speech, on the human though still aspirationally divine plane.

The philosophical conversation to which Socrates encourages Phaedrus's commitment proceeds, for the remainder of the dialogue, as a meandering inquiry into the nature of speaking well. A good speaker needs only to know what an audience finds persuasive, Phaedrus tells Socrates (*Phdr.* 260a1–4). Socrates shows in return that Phaedrus does not really believe this (260b1–d1). But in showing him this, Socrates worries that he has spoken too harshly against the partisan of rhetoric (260d3–9). So he brings forth some arguments (λόγοι) to represent a more nuanced position. He addresses those *logoi*:

> Come to us, noble creatures, and persuade our beautiful-child Phaedrus that unless he philosophizes adequately (ἱκανῶς), he will never be adequate at speaking (ἱκανός ποτε λέγειν) about anything. (Pl. *Phdr.* 261a4–5)

Philosophizing is a condition for being a good orator. The *logoi* go on to claim that perfect deception requires perfect knowledge about everything (261d10–262c3). So it would seem that *philosophia* is knowledge of the details of everything in the world, so that, as the *logoi* say, one may know how exactly everything differs. But this argument is itself deceptive, because it is invalid, and deliberately so.[31] Furthermore, nothing in the previous uses of *philosophos*-group words has suggested that philosophizing involves becoming omniscient. Indeed, the few instances relating *philosophia* to contact with the really real suggest distancing oneself from the bulk of things one could possibly know to focus on the most fundamental aspects of the world. Even more tellingly, the conversation between Socrates and Phaedrus that follows, which seems to epitomize good discussion—Socrates, after all, persuades Phaedrus—does not require Socrates to know everything. So the *logoi*, not surprisingly given their name, "[mere] arguments," do not satisfactorily link *philosophia* and omniscience.[32]

Yet the *logoi*'s invalid, unprecedented, and incongruous discussion of *philosophia* has a positive lesson. It seems likely that both Phaedrus and we are to remember that philosophizing is something quite different from knowing the details of everything in the world (a similar lesson is given by the Platonic *Rival Lovers*; see chapter 10). *Philosophia* seems perhaps a response to the fact that we do *not* know all those details. As philosophers we are instead to maintain a critical consciousness in conversation, to make sure to say what we really believe, and to ask questions when our interlocutors' remarks become unclear or too abstract.

We now return to the end of the *Phaedrus*. At the beginning of this section, I quoted part of Socrates's closing remarks. The longer remark appears to make an etymological play on the word *philosophos*:

---

[31] Moore 2013a.

[32] On the status of *logoi* as reified speeches in fourth-century BCE Athens, see Ford 2008.

> If a person composed these [sc. speeches] knowing how the truth stands, is able to support in argument what he has written, and can show, with his own avowals, that his writings are effectively worthless . . . to call this person *sophos* seems to me to be grand and appropriate for god alone; but either *philosophos* or something like that would be more fitting and apt for him. (Pl. *Phdr.* 278c4–d6)

The second and third criteria for *philosophos*-hood are simple enough. Defending a view is a central part of any productive conversation, especially those about one's possession of virtues. The Platonic dialogues show little else besides conversations containing defenses of such positions. And showing that one's composed words are of little value requires only the awareness and self-awareness described in the *Apology*, that the world is harder to know than mortals tend to think. This awareness comes especially through conversation, the reciprocal testing of views.

Controversy attends the first criterion. What truth must a philosophical speaker know? It cannot be the truth of the really real, since only gods are in this state of wisdom, and *philosophoi* differ from the gods. Nor was there ever a satisfactory argument in favor of the *philosophos* being omniscient, knowledgeable about absolutely anything a person might talk about. It is not obvious what remains. It is apparently a deliberate *aporia* in the dialogue, what the good speaker should know. This *aporia* follows Socrates everywhere; it is never obvious what he knows—besides, perhaps, his own ignorance and *ta erôtika*—such that his conversations and life go the way they do. What seems more obvious is that a philosophical speaker would know, besides the ways both to defend a speech and to abandon a speech, *about what* to make a speech. One should talk about what really matters, what would really honor the gods (*Phdr.* 277d10–278b4). For the *philosophos*, knowing the truth may amount to knowing (i.e., truly) what to talk about.

Socrates does not make much of the fact that this is the *philosophos*'s activity. Some other name would work just as well.[33] The etymological connection implied between *sophos* and *philosophos*, which recurs in Heraclides's story of Pythagoras and the subsequent tradition, is playful, but provides little information. The *philosophos* may have some relationship to the wise person (*sophon*) or to wisdom (*sophia*), but the prefix *phil-* does not establish the tenor of that relationship with any determinacy, except that it is not one of identity.

We find the final use of the dialogue's freighted term, *philosophia*, in Socrates's closing remarks about Isocrates, cited at the beginning of this

---

[33] Yunis 2011 ad loc. gives a list of alternative names culled from the dialogue.

section. Here I quote the entire passage. Socrates has just told Phaedrus to relate the above results concerning *philosophia* to Lysias:

> PHAEDRUS: And you—what? How will you proceed? For we must not at all leave aside your companion.
>
> SOCRATES: Who is this?
>
> PHAEDRUS: Isocrates the beautiful; what will you report to him, Socrates? What will we call him?
>
> SOCRATES: Isocrates is still young, Phaedrus; but what I prophesy for him, I am willing to say.
>
> PHAEDRUS: What is it?
>
> SOCRATES: Compared to Lysias, he seems naturally better at speeches. He also seems more nobly blended in character, and so as he grows older it would hardly be amazing were the difference in speechwriting between him and past or present-day speechwriters to grow wider than that between a man and boys. And wider even than that, if he were unsatisfied with doing only that, and some diviner impulse led him to greater things; for there is some *philosophia* naturally in the mind of that man. (Pl. *Phdr.* 278e5–279b1)

This is Plato's sole explicit reference to Isocrates in his dialogues. What explains Plato's silence everywhere else is hard to say. What seems clear is that up to this point, Socrates has not distinguished between multiple distinct types of *philosophia* or *philosophoi*. He has done quite the opposite, observing that many types of people not explicitly named *philosophoi* share in the essential features of *philosophia*. There are no grounds for the reader to assume, then, that Socrates here refers to a special, heretofore unmentioned *philosophia*. It is in fact easy to understand Socrates's point about Isocrates while assuming that *philosophia* means here what it has meant throughout the dialogue. Socrates may be saying that Isocrates knows what he should be talking about, the education and well-being of people; knows how to defend his positions, giving arguments of a varied nature; and knows the relative poverty of his wisdom, presuming a modesty of pedagogical power.[34] It may even be that young Isocrates seeks to know about the nature of justice and discipline and knowledge, at least to a degree of precision he finds acceptable. Perhaps Plato's disappointment with Isocrates has even more pathos given his belief that Socrates would have approved of the young Isocrates.[35] The similarity in the

---

[34] Johnson 1959 attempts a reconstruction of Isocrates's thoughtful pedagogical method.

[35] Werner 2012, by contrast, asserts on unspecified evidence that "Plato was *angered* by Isocrates's use of the term φιλοσοφία" (227–30 and n158; my italics).

names of Socrates and Isocrates is probably not lost on Plato (cf. Pl. *Plt.* 258a1), and so too the similarities, and dissimilarities, in their intellectual practices.

In summary, we have found that there are no obvious bifurcations in the term *philosophos*'s use, where some instances would have a "conventional" or "rhetorical" meaning and others would have a "technical" or "Platonic" meaning. We might posit instead two aspects of the same enterprise, what we might call the "empirical" aspect, what one does and seeks when doing *philosophia*, and the "theoretical" aspect, what explains the condition for and value of doing *philosophia*. Thus the *Phaedrus* can count both as a work of *philosophia*, namely as a practical and theoretical framework for those already committed to the practice, and as a protreptic to *philosophia*, namely, as an exhortation to the practice articulated in the practical and theoretical registers. Without doubt Plato innovates, but this is in the conditions for successful *philosophia*, not in what most fundamentally it looks like.

Parmenides and *Philebus*: Corroboration of the Conversation View

The lesson from the *Phaedrus*, that *philosophia* is a kind of conversation concerned with mutual self-improvement, finds a pair of summaries in two perhaps unlikely dialogues, which are Plato's dialectically and metaphysically most erudite. The *Parmenides*, Plato's dramatically earliest dialogue, opens when one Cephalus of Clazomenae asks for the famed story of the young Socrates's conversation with Zeno and Parmenides in 449 BCE.[36] He wants to regale his friends with it, whom he calls "highly philosophical" (μάλα φιλόσοφοι, Pl. *Prm.* 126b8). Apparently they share with the *Protagoras*'s Callias a love of hearing and perhaps reflecting on or learning from certain kinds of conversation, in particular those between outstanding thinkers. Early in that conversation between Socrates and his elders, Socrates admits his difficulties with the concept of universal forms. He cannot get over his prejudice against putative forms of mud or other execrables. Parmenides diagnoses this blockage: on account of his youth, "*philosophia* has not yet taken hold (ἀντείληπται)" and so has not yet liberated him from the grip of public opinion (130e2). In Parmenides's mouth, *philosophia* means going through arguments on their own terms, in a conversation embargoing outside judgments of honor or disgrace. The criteria of good philosophical conversation, which include the norms of

---

[36] This is not the Cephalus of Syracuse, host in the *Republic*. The dramatic date of the dialogue's frame is in the late 380s BCE. See Nails 2002, 83–84, 308–9.

logic, explanatory clarity, interpretative fairness, and a shared motivation, come from the participants to the exchange. Parmenides goes on to encourage Socrates's development of a coherent theory of the forms. Without forms, conversation would be altogether impossible, he claims.[37] And without conversation, whither *philosophia* (135c5)? The implication is: it would be vanquished, undercut, impossible. Fortunately, Socrates has a noble impulse (ὁρμή) toward talking (λόγος), Parmenides says, and so he will want to preserve conversation and, accordingly, *philosophia* (135d). Thus in the *Parmenides*, *philosophia* is good conversation (Plato's first point), and conversation may depend, for any success, on knowable universals (Plato's second point).

We get a similar picture from the *Philebus*, Plato's dialogue about the relative roles of pleasure and reason in the best life. Socrates gets his primary interlocutor, Protarchus, to agree that there are two kinds of arithmetic, calculation, and measurement: the kind practiced by the many, including builders and traders; and the kind practiced by those philosophizing or working in the manner of *philosophia*. The former kind deals with irregular units, the latter with identical ones. Protarchus is brought to infer that skills may have two forms, such that the skill "of those philosophizing" is more precise in clarity and purity than that of those not philosophizing. This means that the *technai* animated by the *philosophos*'s motivation (ὁρμήν) are more precise and true in terms of measure and counting. The most precise comprehension of being, reality, and that which is always same comes through philosophy's métier, "the power of conversation" (ἡ τοῦ διαλέγεσθαι δύναμις).[38] *Philosophia* is not itself this comprehension, but the best route to it. Protarchus makes this clear when he cites Gorgias as claiming for himself the greatest power with the skill of persuasion (ἡ τοῦ πείθειν [τεχνή]), which is simply the route to the good thing itself, making all things subject to oneself. The dialogue comes to an end with Socrates's final denigration of hedonists, who treat "the love felt by beasts" as better grounds for deciding on the good life than the love of arguments that keep coming to light (μεμαντευμένων ἑκάστοτε λόγων) thanks to the philosophic muse (ἐν μούσῃ φιλοσόφῳ).[39] Even when divinized, *philosophia* provides the norms for productive conversation. And so in the *Philebus*, as in *Parmenides* and *Phaedrus*, *philosophia* is a mode of conversation that edifies because, as we learn here, it differs from other practices in its orientation toward the stability, purity, and excellence of actual reality.

---

[37] Against this translation, see Gill 2012, 18n1, with bibliography.

[38] This is often translated "the art of dialectic," but for that we would need *technê dialektikê*.

[39] Pl. *Phlb.* 57c2–3 (two forms), 57d1 (in terms of measurement and counting), 58a2–3 (what is the most precise comprehension), 57e6–7 (power of conversation), 59d1–8 (best route to comprehension), 58a7–b1 (parallel to Gorgias), 67b5–6 (philosophical muse).

For reasons any reader may see, Plato did not intend a broad public to give the *Parmenides* serious study, and a sympathetic readership for the *Philebus* might need considerable toleration for metaphysics and moral-psychological questions and distinctions. And yet they present *philosophia* so named in the same way that Plato's more accessible dialogues do. This suggests that throughout his work, he deploys a commonplace view of *philosophia*, even if he does much more than is common to understand how, if it is to work, *philosophia* does work.

Lysis and *Symposium*: Two More Protreptic Etymologies

From the evidence of the *Apology* discussed in chapter 6, I have assumed that Plato takes up a name that Socrates and his friends have been called, reconstructs or rediscovers the positive sense of it, retrojects that positive notion onto the stories he tells of Socrates's conversations, and then at times explains the conditions for or the benefit of *philosophia*. The rediscovery is for those stuck with the name *philosophoi*, or those sensitive to its charge, or those curious about the group that its limits of application seem to circumscribe. From this perspective, Plato treats the name as opaque, defined ostensively by those to whom it applies. His characters use the term naturally, and through their use they assert the range of application: the practices, the people, the intentions. As long as we see their use as basically popular, their changes in emphasis can sink in. Their repetition helps acculturate readers to the shift.

In four dialogues, Plato's Socrates presents reflections on the composition of the word *philosophia*. We have already seen those in the *Phaedrus*, where he juxtaposes the name *sophos* with *philosophos* and treats the latter as inferior in epistemic authority or confidence. He treats the *phil-* prefix only implicitly, as contributing to that inferiority. In three other dialogues, however, Socrates gives more robust and affirmative consideration to the prefix.

This is obvious especially in the *Lysis*, Plato's dialogue about the nature of friendship, *philia*. Socrates begins the conversation there by convincing Hippothales that he should get his beloved, Lysis, to recognize that he lacks the wisdom that serves as foundation for the freedom and happiness he desires (Pl. *Lys.* 207d5–210d10). He continues the conversation with Lysis's closest friend, Menexenus. Impressed at Menexenus's friendship with Lysis, he exclaims how much he desires a friend and how little he knows about getting one, and in doing so he introduces *phil-* prefixed terms into the discussion. This occasions the first of two steps in revaluing *philosophia*: spinning another once negative *phil-* prefixed term, *philetairos* ("companion"). This lays the ground-work for another case of positive spin:

Since childhood I've been desiring (ἐπιθυμῶν) a certain possession (κτήματός του), as one person desires one thing, another person another. This man desires to possess horses, that one dogs, another gold, another honor. But whereas I feel pretty calm (πρᾴως ἔχω) toward those things, toward the possession of friends I am extremely desirous (πάνυ ἐρωτικῶς), and I would wish (βουλοίμην) for myself a good friend more than the finest quail or rooster a person might own—and yes, by God, even more than a horse and a dog, so it seems—and, by the Dog, I think I would much sooner welcome a companion (ἑταῖρον) than the gold of Darius, more even than Darius himself: it is in this way I am sort of (τις) *philetairos*. (Pl. *Lys.* 211d7–e8)

Desiring a companion (*hetairon*) is like desiring any other possession, either weakly or powerfully. Socrates is "extremely desirous."[40] He says that this makes him "sort of *philetairos*." The qualifier *tis* shows that he uses the word in an unusual way. Thucydides and Aeschines use the term as something neg-ative, to refer to a vain loyalty, a pride in a sense of belonging and the apparent willingness to sacrifice even though the benefits will really accrue entirely to one's honor.[41] Xenophon similarly glosses it as a keenness to serve others with ulterior motives: to the ultimate end of receiving benefits in return.[42] Ar-istotle collocates it with *philophiloi* as the attributes of children in their exces-sive pleasure from spending time with others, caring nothing for the profit or loss of such relationships, and indeed as a symptom of their wide-ranging disposition to excess.[43] So, in the fourth century BCE, *philetairos* has a not altogether positive sense, and it never otherwise means "desiring a friend," or even "lacking a friend." Socrates is saying, as Aristotle said about the *philau-tos* (chapter 3), that we *could* construe *philetairos* this way, even though it has never actually meant this.

Not long after, Socrates generalizes from his playful reconstruction of *philetairos*. Having argued from the hypothesis that friendship requires the partners to the friendship to return the love or friendship, he concludes that this means there are no *philippoi* if their object of love, horses, do not love them in return. Glossing *philippoi* as "friends/lovers of horses" is fictive and

---

[40] Cf. Sappho 16.1–4 *PLF*.
[41] Thuc. 3.82.4; Aeschin. 1.110 (*Against Timarchus*).
[42] Xen. *Cyr.* 8.3.49.
[43] See chapter 3, p. 77.

tendentious, since Socrates cannot believe it generally means either "lacking horses," or "wanting to be friends" with horses, or even "feeling love" for horses.[44] Socrates then lists, as those who will not actually be friends unless their objects befriend them in return, the friends-of-quail (φιλόρτυγες), friends-of-dogs (φιλόκυνες), friends-of-wine (φίλοινοι), friends-of-exercise (φιλογυμνασταί), and, finally, friends-of-*sophia* (φιλόσοφοι) (*Lys.* 212d6–7). This hectic play on *phil-* prefixed terms is suspicious. Socrates acts as though they all take the form "friend of/desire for *x*." That purported homogeneity is fictitious. His rhetorical aim is clear: it prepares for a new gloss on *philosophos*, one connected to being desirous for a *sophia* that one lacks.[45]

That Socrates gives a new gloss to the *philosophos* word group here is clear from the one time he uses the term naturally, where he uses it to refer to conversation and conversationality in just the way he does in the *Protagoras*, *Charmides*, and *Phaedrus*. The dialogue begins with Socrates talking to Lysis, getting him to admit his lack of wisdom, and then to Menexenus, taking an erudite line about the subjectivity or objectivity of the state of being "a friend." At the point of Menexenus's refutation, Lysis chimes in, observing that Menexenus's view cannot be sustained. Hearing this, Socrates acknowledges his delight in Lysis's *philosophia* (Pl. *Lys.* 213d8). This must mean Lysis's competence at this sort of self- and other-examining conversation about fundamental matters, such as *sophia* and *philia*. That is because Lysis has revealed his careful attention to the conversation (213d4–5), his willingness to critique views advanced in the conversation, even those from his friend (213d2–3), and his openness to undergoing conversation himself, staying with it even to the point of admitting ignorance. So in its unmarked use in the dialogue, *philosophia* denotes the familiar Socratic conversations of the Platonic dialogues, not the lack of, desire for, and special friendship with *sophia*.

Socrates's new gloss does not explain what *philosophia* has always meant. We cannot say that these special kinds of conversations, and the competence in their engagement, are so called *because* they were always practical or interpersonal expressions of an intense desire for *sophia*. The previous chapters of this book have shown that this could not have been the meaning.[46] What we can say is that Socrates is advancing a lighthearted yet novel interpretation of

---

[44] It generally means "equestrian," often as a national trait, e.g., the people of Aetna (Pind. *Nem.* 9.32), the people of Thrace (Eur. *Hec.* 9, 428; Soph. fr. 582), or Trojans (Eur. fr. 935; Soph. fr. 859), but also as a personal trait, e.g., Hieron of Syracuse, who won a chariot race (Bacchyl. 3.69), and Cyrus, φιλιππότατος καὶ τοῖς ἵπποις ἄριστα χρῆσθαι (Xen. *An.* 1.9.5.4). The implication is probably "horsey," inclined to spend a lot on horses or horse racing, perhaps as a sign of wealth and leisure.

[45] E.g., Pl. *Lys.* 209c4, 209e2, 210a6, 210a8–d9.

[46] Cf. Peterson 2011, 247–48, on more plausible words to express "lover of wisdom."

those conversations and the disposition to hold them. We can understand them *as* expressions of a desire for *sophia*, even if the practitioners neither felt or identified such a desire, nor had any attitude toward *sophia* as such, and even if the word came from a name meaning something like "emulating *sophoi*." This radical reinterpretation depends on a familiar linguistic sophism: generalize by assuming that morphologically similar words are morphosemantically similar, then decompose by asserting an unsubstantiated but appealing morphosemantics for *phil-* prefixed terms. Socrates uses specious etymologizing to revalue philosophy.

As the argument in the *Lysis* about *philia* progresses, Socrates returns once again to etymologizing. Rejecting the assumption that similars attract, such that good would be friend with good, or bad with bad, Socrates supposes instead that the friend of the good must be a person who is neither good nor bad (Pl. *Lys.* 216e2–3). Badness crowds the gates, however; only a desire for the good keeps it away (217e8–9). We may conclude, Socrates says, that neither the *sophoi* nor the badly ignorant philosophize, only those who, while unlearned, realize that they are unlearned and want to rid themselves of that potentially bad condition (218a5–b1). Socrates caps this by saying that they have now discovered what a friend is and to whom (or what) it is a friend (218b7–10).

Why Socrates ends up talking about *philosophia* here, he does not say: does it serve as a mere example of a *phil-* prefixed name, or as part of an interesting but inessential digression, or as the crucial case? Socrates had already linked friendship and wisdom in the early conversation with Lysis, and he had implied that *philosophia* involves engaging well in conversations with friends. If wisdom is the best good, and *philia* aims ultimately for goodness, as the discussion of the *Lysis* goes on to suggest, then *philia* in its best or most abstract formulation is love or friendship for wisdom. In that case, Socrates's appeal to philosophizing in his analysis serves both as example and as relevant ideal.

Of course, from the etymological perspective the important thing is that Socrates again decomposes a *phil-* prefixed word. He treats *philein* as a desire for something one lacks. This maps imperfectly to friendship, which occurs more than at the moment of lack. Socrates helps us forget this, proclaiming his unusual state of no friends but the desire for one. So his personal revelation further positions philosophizing as the practice of the self-knowing, epistemically modest, pedagogically optimistic, *sophia*-admiring person. It is not simply contemplation, which wise people or gods could presumably do, or rote acquisition, which people without a desire could presumably do.

Famously, we see these etymological moves in the *Symposium* as well. There *Erôs* is called a *philosophos* (Pl. *Symp.* 202d6), which represents an intermediate state between *sophia* and and *amathia* ("ignorance"). We learn that "not one of the gods philosophizes or desires to become wise (ἐπιθυμεῖ σοφὸς γενέσθαι)—for each already is—and, if anyone else is wise, he does not philosophize" (204a1–7). The badly ignorant do not philosophize either. So far, the *Lysis*. Diotima adds, however, that the love of wisdom is the love of beauty. This establishes more firmly the relationship between a loving relationship and *philosophia*.[47] More impressively, it links *philosophia* to the *Symposium*'s so called "ladder of love" (210a4–212a7), which represents coming to a wholehearted commitment to virtue. Thus Socrates's incremental etymological play in *Lysis* and *Symposium* deploys fallacious linguistic reasoning to reorient his interlocutors'—and Plato's readers'—understanding of *philosophia*. To the extent that people treat Socrates's arguments as somehow insightful or useful, Plato can claim success in having shifted thinking about *philosophia*.

Republic: The *Philosophoi*-Kings

A more elaborate version of the etymological re-semanticization of *philosophia* that we see in the *Lysis* and *Symposium* is seen on the larger stage of the *Republic*, at the end of Book 5. Plato does not redefine *philosophia* as much as he shows Socrates defending it by presenting the word as though it means something other than it really does.

This move occurs in the context of Socrates's proposition that only *philosophoi*-kings could bring about the happy city. He and Glaucon imagine the withering responses this proposition would occasion: ridicule and disrepute (Pl. *R.* 5.474a5, cf. 5.473c8), assault and battery (5.474a1–3), and legal charges (ἀμυνῇ τῷ λόγῳ; δώσεις δίκην, 5.474a4–5). This last imagined response is the relevant one; Socrates presents himself as having to provide a defense of *philosophoi* as politically authoritative. In Book 6, he will respond to a different concern, voiced by Adeimantus, that *philosophoi* tend to be useless or positively harmful, by providing a sociology of education, explaining the ways philosophically promising youth get diverted from the better path. Here, by contrast, he foregoes sociology for morphosemantics. He is going to defend the word *philosophos*. His lexical effort will have him defining or distinguishing (διορίσασθαι, 5.474b7; cf. ὁρίζεσθαι, 5.474c5) and clarifying (διαδήλων, 5.474b10) the term.

---

[47] We have seen a connection of *philosophein* and *philokalein* at Thuc. 2.40.1 and Pl. *Phdr.* 248d2–4.

Readers of the *Republic* already got a hint of this kind of maneuver in Book 2, when Socrates jokingly presents *philosophoi* as dogs: they love only those they know. His argument depends on his treating the term *philosophos* as an unproblematic synonym for *philomathês* (*R.* 2.376b8). He then treats *philomathês* as valuing knowing, as though it means *philôn to manthanein*; then implicitly as valuing what one knows, as though it means *philôn mathê-mata*; then implicitly as valuing *only* what one knows, as though it means *philôn oudên allo ê mathêmatôn*. This is the property attributed to the dog who welcomes and takes as its own only whom it knows (ὃν . . . ἂν γνώριμον, ἀσπάζεται: 2.376a6; τό . . . οἰκεῖον, 2.376b6). Obviously these are not valid inferences, so there is no reason to accept that *philosophos* really means "loving only those one knows."

Socrates's set of comparanda in Book 5 for *philosophos* includes *philomathês* but also much else: in his implied analysis of *phil-* prefixed names there, he gives attention to at least ten such names: *philopaides, philoinoi, philotimoi, philositoi, philomathêtai, philotheamones, philêkooi, philotechnoi, philomathoi,* and *philodoxoi*. Socrates begins by speaking of "loving" (φιλεῖν): he asserts that "loving something" (φιλεῖν τι) does not mean loving some but not all of it; it means, instead, "cherishing everything" (πᾶν στέργοντα). Glaucon should recall the relevant principle, Socrates says: they have already discussed how *epithumia*, a desire such as thirst or hunger, is always for the entire object of the desire, not part of or a variety of that desire (4.437d8–e8). In this passage Socrates has moved fluidly and unmarkedly between three verbs of affection, *philein, epithumein,* and *stergein*; this suggests that *philosophein* is not stuck meaning only or especially *philein + sophia*. We also see, perhaps more importantly, that Socrates knows that the meaning of *philosophos* is not transparent from its morphology or the semantics of its apparent parts; otherwise he would not have to say any of these things. He must gloss *philein* and establish the constraints it puts on its putative objects. The novelty of Socrates's argument comes out in Glaucon's confusion about the general scope of *philein*; he must see *philia* as particularistic in its attentions rather than as a putative affection for an entire class.

Socrates turns to examples. His first is of the *philopais* (*R.* 5.474d3), that is, the *erôtikos* (5.474d2, 5.475a4), for whom all boys seem worthy of his welcome (ἀσπάζεσθαι) and care, and whose otherwise unappealing qualities will be spun positively. His second is of the *philoinoi*, who welcome (ἀσπαζομένους) all wine, even plonk (5.475a6–8). His third: the *philotimoi*, who cherish being honored (τιμώμενοι ἀγαπῶσιν) even by inferior people, since they desire honor generally (ὡς ὅλως τιμῆς ἐπιθυμηταὶ ὄντες) (5.475a10–b2). From these three cases of "being desirous of something" (τινος ἐπιθυμητικόν), Socrates infers the apparently surprising or non-obvious conclusion about the *philosophos*: he is the one who is "desirous (ἐπιθυμητικήν) of *sophia*" (5.475b8–9). Socrates then gives a brief related argument. We do not call those who chafe at learning (τὸν . . . περὶ τὰ μαθήματα δυσχεραίνοντα) *philomathês* or *philosophos*, just as we do not call those who decline to eat certain things *philositos* (5.475b10–c5). The one who is gladly willing to taste all learning, and can hardly get his fill, is a *philosophos* (5.475c7–10)—a distinctive individual, and not one we have seen before, to be sure.

Glaucon notes that this cannot complete the definition. For if it did, *philosophoi* would include two further groups, both of whom "enjoy learning" (καταμανθάνειν χαίροντες), namely the *philotheamones* ("theater fans") and the *philêkooi* ("music fans") (*R.* 5.475d1–4); and this would be quite strange (ἀτοπώτατοί), because "those ones would not voluntarily be willing to go to discussions and such activities (πρὸς . . . λόγους καὶ τοιαύτην διατριβήν)," as apparently would befit *philosophoi*, "but only to choral festivals wherever they are offered" (5.475d4–9). Glaucon worries that if we understand *philosophoi* as *mathêtikoi tinôn*, "learners of anything," then the category even includes learners of the "minor crafts" (τεχνυδρίων) (5.475e1–2).[48] In brief, Glauon sees Socrates's novel construction of *philosophos* as too broad; its real meaning is more tightly linked to the idea of conversation.

Socrates accepts this concern and narrows the meaning, saying that *philosophoi* are *philotheamones* only to the extent those spectators attend (as perhaps they generally do not) exclusively to "the truth" (τῆς ἀληθείας) (*R.* 5.475e7). This puts *philosophoi* on the one side, *philotheamones* (traditionally so called), *philêkooi, philotechnoi,* and *praktikoi* on the other (5.476a10–b2). Only the *philosophoi* can see and welcome (ἀσπάσασθαι) beauty itself, that is, true beauty. Socrates then gives an argument for treating beauty itself as a proper object of *knowledge*, and instances of it only objects of mere belief (through 5.479e10; the same holds for other abstractions). So *philosophoi*, he summarizes, welcome and love (ἀσπάζεσθαί τε καὶ φιλεῖν) that which they *know* (γνῶσίς); non-*philosophoi* love and concern themselves with (φιλεῖν τε καὶ θεᾶσθαι) that of which they have only belief (δόξα). "We would not be inapt to call them [sc. the latter group] *philodoxoi* rather than *philosophoi*"—even if they would take being so called quite hard (5.480a6).

The contrast with the *Symposium* account of the word *philosophos* is evident. In that dialogue, *philosophoi* lack *sophia* but know it, and so they pursue

---

[48] This word is *hapax* in classical literature. At Ath. 10.714, this passage is confusingly conflated with Pl. *R.* 5.479b10–17 and paraphrased as "*philosophoi* of minor crafts are like those at a feast who waffle [about their food]" (τοὺς τῶν τεχνυδρίων φιλοσόφους τοῖς ἐν ταῖς ἑστιάσεσιν ἔφη ἐπαμφοτερίζουσιν ἐοικέναι), and treated as Plato's allusion to a riddle.

sophia; *sophia* is a presumed good, and ignorance of one's ignorance is a presumed bad. Here, had Socrates deployed the same reasoning, *philosophoi*-kings would excel by alone realizing they lack wisdom. (Perhaps this wisdom would help them avoid acting in error and also pursue wisdom.) This is not Socrates's approach in the *Republic*. Instead, he proceeds in two steps, the second prompted by Glaucon. First, he argues from the prefix *phil-*: it implies a desire for all that the second element stands for, not just some of it. He does not say why he argues for this; the implication might be that successful leaders require knowledge (*mathêmata*) not just of a subset of things; they must know all things. Those who are not designated with a *phil-* prefix may ignore the apparently unattractive; in the case of *mathêmata*, it may be hard-to-learn topics. *Philosophoi* eagerly learn even what seems pointless or unpleasant to learn.

Following the reformulation of the *phil-* prefix, *philosophos* came across as unacceptably broad, so Socrates then gave a reformulation of the *-sophos* second element. Remarkably, he does not say that he is giving an analysis of *sophia* or being *sophos*. Perhaps remarkably, too, he does not say that the *philosophos* pursues the truth, or is *philalethês*, and he does not say why he speaks of the *philosophos* rather than the *philomathês*. He says rather that the *philosophos* is *philotheamones* of the truth, and then argues that this requires that the *philosophos* alone pursue what is always true, namely, knowledge.

It is clear that Socrates is taking a distinctive route to defining the *philosophos*. He wants to assert that *philosophoi* pursue knowledge, first, no matter how unappealing or difficult its attainment is, and, second, of what is stable and fundamental. He wants to clarify the attitude and the object. Why not just say so? The reason, it seems, is that this is not what the term *philosophos* originally means, and Socrates cannot just make up a new meaning and then announce it. He has to shift incrementally.[49] Socrates recognizes that the name *philosophos* sounds bad, as most *phil-* prefixed names do—we see Aristotle arguing this in the *Nicomachean Ethics* (see chapter 3). Socrates's approach to renovating the term *philosophos* is to have Glaucon *hear* other *phil-* prefixed terms differently, in a novel way, such that they can sound okay, even admirable, and so too *philosophos*. Then Socrates paves the way to thinking of new referents for the second element of *phil-* prefixed names, such that treating *philosophos* as concerning truth and knowledge comes across as a legitimate discovery.

Socrates's analysis of the other *phil-* prefixed names shows this. Each such term, rare and thus likely ethically charged, seems to start out bearing a

---

[49] Socrates makes a series of similar incremental shifts in the *Phaedrus*; see Moore 2013a, 2014a, 2014c.

negative intimation and then is revised to sound positive. Each in miniature replays the history of the term *philosophos*, only here in an explicit and
tendentious way. Indeed, the elucidation of Socrates's method here provides
core evidence for one of this chapter's main claims, that Plato is not really
asserting a new meaning of *philosophia*; either he is saving the appearances
(*Charmides* and *Protagoras*), or he is attending to its conditions of success
(*Phaedrus*), or he is defending the practice through rhetorical fancy, the playful provision of a not-true etymology. I turn to seven of the *phil-* prefixed
terms in this passage.

Φιλόπαις ("boy") has, in its earliest uses, a sense of being dubiously "flir-
tatious" or "lustfully unrestrained."[50] Socrates redeems it, treating it as a
label for the unjudgmental appreciator of young men.

Φίλοινος ("wine") has, starting in the fifth century BCE, a sense of intem-
perance.[51] Socrates presents it instead as describing the aficionado of all wine.

Φιλότιμος ("honor") began, as we saw in chapter 3, with the negative connotation of overweening ambition. Socrates presents it instead as describing
one who aspires to honor in all its forms.

Φιλόσιτος ("cereal") does not predate Plato, but cannot be his invention,
since while the second element of the term would appear to refer specifically
to those concerned with "cereal," "grain," Socrates's interpretation of it as describing the man who loves all food shows that the synecdoche "cereal-food"
must predate Socrates's usage. Its earliest meaning is obscure, though notably
its only other classical usage, in Xenophon, parallels it to two other *phil-* prefixed names: being *philogeôrgos* and *philoponos* (Xen. *Oec.* 20.25–27). This
collocation, and its rarity, suggests that it hardly can be taken to have meant
something so neutral as "hungry" or "food-enjoying," for it if did we might
expect it rather more frequently.

Φιλοθεάμων ("sights") again does not appear before Plato, but Glaucon's
casual and derivisive usage of it as fanboy or spectacle-monger shows that it
cannot have been a Platonic coinage.[52] The term *philotheamôn* seems to have

[50] In Simonides, it is collocated with a drunk φιλάκρητος ("drinker of unmixed wine"),
and the φιλόκωμος ("avid reveler") (Simon. fr. 7.25 ll. 5–6). Hellenistic use has it connected
to illness: Alexander the Great is *philopais ekmanôs* (Dicaerchus in Ath. 13.603a–b); Callima-
chus speaks of someone being "struck by the *philopais* illness (ἐκκόπτει τὰν φιλόπαιδα νόσον)"
(Epigr. 46.6).

[51] In Euripides's *Antiope*, Zethus describes the bad qualities (κακῶν) introduced by music,
which include being *philoinos* in addition to being idle (ἀργόν), neglectful (χρημάτων ἀτημελῆ),
and perhaps also disadvantageous (ἀσύμφορον) and out of place (ἄτοπον) (Eur. fr. 183). People
argue whether it is worse to be *philoinos* than *philoglukus* (fond of sweet wine) (ps-Arist. *Prob.*
875b3), suggesting that neither is good.

[52] Meinwald 2017 argues that *philotheamones* are people who seek to understand the world
through the dramatic performances they watch. Additional evidence against a Platonic coinage

an almost exact synonym, *philotheôros*; this term appears in Aristotle in reference to the fan of *theama*.[53] As we saw in chapter 3 (pp. 77–79), Aspasius (a commentator on Aristotle) observes that just as *philotimos* has a positive sense—even as it also has a negative sense—for Aristotle, again, the negative one precedes the positive—so too *philêkoos* and *philotheamôn* have negative meanings, even if they appear positively in the *Ethics*.

Φιλοδόξος ("reputation," "belief"), yet another word that does not appear before Plato, must predate Plato, and generally refers to an excessive desire for reputation (*doxa*). In the *Rhetoric*, Aristotle claims that *philodoxoi* are envious (φθονεροί) regarding whatever it is they desire a reputation for, as the *doxosophoi* desire reputation for *sophia* (Arist. *Rh.* 1387b32–34). Aristotle must be relying on colloquial usage. I discuss Socrates's radical departure below.

Φιλομαθής ("learning"), in its earliest extant appearance, shows up in a maxim collected by Isocrates, "if you are *philomathês*, you will be *polumathês*" (ἐὰν ᾖς φιλομαθής, ἔσει πολυμαθής, Isoc. *Ad Dem.* 18), which seems a justification for an otherwise dubious curiosity. In the *Phaedrus*, Socrates excuses himself for his unfamiliarity with the countryside by claiming he is *philomathês*, which causes him to want to stay in the city (Pl. *Phdr.* 230d3). In both cases, the idea seems to be "peculiarly curious" in the sense of "nosy" or "busy." By later in the fourth century BCE, to be sure, it specifies the intellectually curious person.[54] Socrates here is anticipating that reformed and positive usage.

The majority if not all of the *phil*- prefixed parallels to *philosophos* seem to have started out with either a negative or at least wry inflection. The second element is often synecdochal, pointing as it were indirectly at some socially relevant behavior that one must voluntarily regulate. My suggestion is that Socrates acknowledges the similarity of the term *philosophos* to these *phil*-prefixed names. There is something wry *built into the name*, given its membership in the genre of *phil*- prefixed name-calling names. Why does he draw attention to this fact? He is redeeming the name in two ways. First, he is presenting as positive a quality of some traits referred to by *phil*- prefixed names: they're not choosy! Second, he is overhauling them, effectively a momentary

---

is its natural pairing with *philêkooi*, which appears elsewhere in Plato (Pl. *Lys.* 206c10; *Euthyd.* 274c3, 304c6; cf. *R.* 7.535d5, 8.548e5); Isocrates (1.18.5); and collections of sage maxims that date to the fourth century BCE—Stob. 3.1.172 (φιλήκοον εἶναι καὶ μὴ πολύλαλον, 1.4 [Demetrius's collection]; cf. DL 1.92); Stob. 3.1.173 (φιλήκοος ἔσο [Sosiades's collection]).

[53] Arist. *Eth. Nic.* 1099a10. It is also a word found in the Middle Comic Alexis, without context.

[54] Arist. *Eth. Nic.* 1175a14: just as the *mousikos* person especially *agapein* sounds and songs, the *philomathês* especially *agapein* thinking through abstract matters. See, generally, Xen. *Cyr.* 1.2.1, 1.4.3, 1.6.8; *An.* 1.9.5.

re-semanticization. For example, *philêkoos* surely first meant "given to passive listening," being a wallflower, not contributing to conversation. But Glaucon spins it as an active decision—*wanting* to hear everything and thereby to learn. The *philomathês*, a term probably already undergoing unconscious re-semanticization, is shifted in sense from "curious," "nosy," "given to investigation rather than action" to an active learning of as much as possible that is important. Socrates's use of *philodoxos* provides the clearest case of re-semanticization, in which the second element is almost wholly changed in sense: from "concerned with *doxa* qua reputation," to "pursuing [all] *doxa* qua belief." We are then to see Socrates performing an identical operation for Glaucon and Adeimantus on *philosophos*. The outcome is "pursuing even difficult *sophia* qua knowledge." What did it start from? Well, something wry or even negative about some unreasonable excessiveness. Did Plato('s Socrates) redefine *philosophia*? Not really; he is presenting *philosophia* in a new way, though not *as* new, for the particular apologetic argument about *philosophoi*-kings here.

Conclusion: Plato and the Origin of *Philosophia*

I have argued that Plato did not utterly innovate—"before Plato, the father of philosophy, came the word's inventor, Pythagoras," says Saint Ambrose (*De Abr.* 2.7.37). Instead, he renovated, retrojected, and reappropriated. He saved the appearances, justified the practices, and encouraged their advance. We have seen Thucydides's Pericles rebut the notion that philosophizing leads to weakness and off-footedness, and Isocrates and Alcidamas locate *philosophia* in the education needed by any highly effective person. We have seen Socrates pinned as *philosophos* but then trying to rectify the term's sense. And we have seen other Socratics, such as Phaedo and Antisthenes, vindicating *philosophia* through appeal to its unexpected intra- and interpersonal benefits. None seeks to deny the entirety of earlier usages, as though one could simply rechristen the term with a new meaning. Instead, each emphasizes as salient some heretofore less prominent feature in the constellation of behaviors, norms, and contexts associated with *philosophia*. Thucydides's Pericles accepted that in philosophizing, people talked about non-emergent issues, but then argued that those issues prepared Athenians for political and military crisis. The rhetoricians took the same angle, equating *philosophia* with a broadly appealing *paideia*. Socrates explained his concern for *logoi*, his strange religious statements, and his curiosity about the nature of things as instrumental to his life-supporting self-examination and philanthropic examination of others. His followers found martial and heroic precedent in the *sôphrosunê*-increasing effects of philosophizing.

Something similar goes for Plato. He reconstructs *philosophia* as a beneficial conversational-educational activity. He fuses the Athenian model of competitive verbal games to a universal model of leisured self-improvement. He does so by having his fifth-century BCE interlocutors refer offhandedly to their semiformal and advice-sharing discussion groups as "philosophizing." In many dialogues, *philosophia* retains a colloquial sense, referring to a certain kind of edifying talking with like-aspiring people.

But this explains only some of Plato's uses of *philosophos*-group words. Other instances appear to present a notion of *philosophia* distinct from edifying conversation. Such are the instances where philosophizing means coming into contact with the forms, orienting oneself toward virtue, coming out of the cave and looking toward the sun, driving one's chariot high into the heavens, and preparing for death. Even here, however, Plato has not rejected the colloquial sense as symptomatic of a squishy and dilettantish culture, replacing it with a hardheaded and technical sense of the term. He has not moved altogether beyond Socratic method or incremental conversational improvement. He has instead reflected on the conditions for conversation to edify, for the exchange of words to burnish one's moral and intellectual personality. The norms of philosophical conversation were assumed from the start to deserve commitment and exhortation just because it would be by following them that one might move toward knowledge and human excellence—but why is this? Plato's dialogues animate conversations that suggest possibilities.

I cannot demonstrate systematically that Plato's two sorts of description of *philosophia* match. I have wanted mainly to make plausible the idea that Plato does not create a new technical notion of *philosophia* from whole cloth and that what he does create he does not simply oppose to the everyday or rhetorical notion of *philosophia*. Plato, as far as we can tell from the tenor of his interlocutors' exchanges, takes doing *philosophia* as something more or less set by his predecessors and contemporaries: talking about fundamental issues necessary for improving oneself and others. That tenor differs from that found in other authors in terms of explanation, the tolerance for precision, and the expected benefits. But we have no evidence that he repudiates other modes of *philosophia* so called, even if he does repudiate other modes of teaching, discussing, and valuing aspects of life.[55]

[55] The ways that he takes up and repudiates non-philosophical modes or genres are the great lesson of Nightingale 1995.

I have so far spoken of Plato's two-movement legitimation and justification of *philosophia*. We might call this the dimension of appropriation. The audience of this terminological appropriation includes those already called *philosophoi* or those who associate with or model themselves on so-called *philosophoi*. Some may have even already deigned to accept the name-calling, finding ease in acquiescence or even a bit of ornery pride. But a label little helps constitute personal or group identity while its application remains acerbic or pointed. Appropriation, especially with the help of wishful etymologies, allows a person to take himself to be choosing to govern himself by certain norms, and, in the case of a group, to be among others who share in that choice and thereby can share in the burdens that such a choice sets upon them all. In institutional terms, appropriation allows for the self-conscious adoption and practice of a discipline. A discipline defines a common endeavor delimited by specific practices, expectations, and goals. A name for the discipline, paired with a promising semantic archaeology of that name, allows for coordination and critical maintenance of those specific elements. Thus appropriation fosters disciplinization. This also means that it fosters specialization, technicalization, and other forms of elaboration. The people advancing these articulations must explain and defend themselves only to their disciplinary fellows, who already value fine-tuned shifts in focus and approach. Disciplines grow up with a goal at times transparent to those outside the discipline; but the reasons for their inner divisions and digressions become increasingly opaque to all but co-practitioners.

Appropriation always has its audience: in the case above, those already called *philosophoi* or inclined to the life of those so called. *Philosophia* must be legitimated to them only because they are not yet in the discipline—necessarily so, for an inchoate discipline only now coagulates. Platonic *philanthrôpia* motivates efforts to present *philosophia* as good and desirable to those not yet practicing it, or to those hovering near competing pedagogues or research programs. A practice beneficial to some as humans is a practice actually beneficial to all as humans; only a perverse schadenfreude would try to keep such a public good private. "That all should philosophize!" This mode of thinking has its precursors in exhortations to justice; we find these in the Platonic *Alcibiades* and *Clitophon*.[56] To Platonic *philanthrôpia* we must add the unavoidable sense of *philautia*, the benefit to the discipline—practiced by Plato and his associates—in increasing its numbers. A discipline needs a critical mass of practitioners to generate network benefits,[57] to induct subse-

---

[56] See Moore 2012 and 2015b, 101–35.
[57] Collins 2000.

quent generations, to capture resources, and to resist encroachment by mass culture or antagonistic movements. On the arguments that Plato's Socrates deploys, *philosophia* need not be sold only in uncut form, as a total reorientation and rigorization of life. The audience of these efforts toward disciplinary expansion need not be only those so positioned or so prepared for the self-sufficient academic life. A moderate path still yields moderate benefits. We measure along the dimension of expansion in the protreptic moments of Plato's dialogues. These present *philosophia* as appealing to those beyond a core constituency. Some dialogues find structure in the protreptic genre: the *Phaedrus* in particular, but also the *Euthydemus* and the *Phaedo*. Others look rather to include protreptic passages, the *Gorgias* and the *Republic* most notably. It is in these places we see claims beyond the "Philosophizing amounts to this, what you're already doing, and though you already believe it's good to do it, here are the reasons"—Plato's mission seen on the dimension of appropriation— but all the way to "Whoever you are, and whatever your current goals, you should philosophize!"—Plato's mission seen on the dimension of expansion. Put briefly, by making an idiosyncratic activity normative, the activity loses its idiosyncrasy; what is normative for some is normative for all.

Aristotle's Historiography of *Philosophia*

The Idea of the Discipline Named *Philosophia*

I have argued in this book that, from its beginning, the term *philosophos* picked out those groups of people who investigated fundamental matters with persistence and in concert, despite the apparent risk of enervation or self-defeat. Their *philosophia* was, for some, an identifiable avocation, as we have seen in Gorgias's *Helen*, the *Dissoi Logoi*, and Isocrates's *Antidosis*. I then argued that it awaited the lifetime of Plato for the term *philosophia* to purport to pick out the emotional-evaluative state paraphrased as the "love of wisdom." We have seen Socrates engaged in varieties of such etymological fancy in the *Lysis*, *Symposium*, and *Republic*. In this chapter, I argue that it awaited the time of the Early Academy, in the second quarter of the fourth century BCE, for the term *philosophos* to acquire the meaning used or self-applied by much of this book's readership: a member of the discipline called *philosophia*, a discipline with a lineage of expositors and critics, writers and readers, teachers and students, that goes back, for example, to Thales. Though earlier authors spoke of earlier thinkers as doing something similar to themselves, they did not call both themselves and their predecessors *philosophoi*. Aristotle, by contrast, calls certain predecessors *philosophoi*, treats their statements as pertinent to his own philosophical pursuits, and provides a theory for understanding that pertinence. This does not mean that Aristotle invented the discipline of *philosophia*; rather, he reveals and sharpens ideas developed in the colloquia of the mid-fourth-century BCE Academy, an environment that his colleague Heraclides would have shared when writing his *On Diseases*.

The first part of this chapter discusses the way certain pre-Aristotelian writers wrote about those eventually to be called *philosophoi*; I focus on Heraclitus, Hippias, and those of Plato's generation, Plato included. Their efforts consolidated a canon of relevant thinkers, but did not yet explicitly name them *philosophoi* or treat of them as sharing in a discipline understood as historically extended backwards and forwards. The second part of the chapter discusses the way Aristotle thought about the history of his practice: he called *philosophoi* those with whom he could "share opinions" about the matters central to his own investigations and who, before him, presumably shared opinions with those before themselves. The third part of the chapter clarifies the notion of a historically extended discipline.

Pre-Disciplinary *Philosophoi* in Heraclitus, Hippias, Plato, and Their Contemporaries

Heraclitus and Competition with Sophoi

Heraclitus of Ephesus serves as our earliest source for remarks about those eventually in the philosophical canon. He writes about Homer, Hesiod, Archilochus, Bias, Thales of Miletus, Xenophanes of Colophon, Hecataeus of Miletus, and Pythagoras of Samos.[1] Except for Bias, whom he admires, and Thales, whom he classifies as an astronomer, he excoriates the rest, as we saw in chapter 2.[2] All eight have important connections to the later canons of philosophy, even if by Aristotle's time fewer than half were seen as core figures.[3] This selection has added glory given that nobody would have treated Hesiod, Xenophanes, Hecataeus, and Pythagoras as members of a single cabal or school or tradition of thought. Heraclitus picks them out for representing the height of *sophia* in his contemporaries' eyes, and for making the same epistemic mistake: vaulting with their long pole of polymathic wisdom right past *noos*. Heraclitus, who vaunts his own singular wisdom, sourced in self-knowledge rather than extensive research, takes them as his cultural competitors. So, Heraclitus distinguishes himself not from a discipline, not from a corporate body, not from a lineage of thinking, but from those with the best Panhellenic reputation for (both old and new) wisdom.

Though Heraclitus does not have a disciplinary conception of *philosophia*, he presages it. He picks on many of those who have been eventually accreted into the discipline. He himself comes to be so accreted even if as on a spur. He chooses as criteria of judgment the possession of a unitary *sophia* and the understanding of the *logos*, both terms elemental to later philosophical discourse. Most remarkably, as we saw in chapter 2, Heraclitus said that *philosophoi* men

---

[1] B38 (Thales), B39/D11 (Bias), B40/D20 (Hesiod, Pythagoras, Xenophanes, Hecataeus), B42/D21 (Homer, Archilochus), B56/D22 (Homer), B57/D25a (Hesiod), B81/D27 ([Pythagoras]), B105/D24 (Homer), B106/D25b (Hesiod), B129/D26 (Pythagoras).

[2] See Morgan 2000, 53–58, for an interesting account of Heraclitus's reasons.

[3] Hesiod appears in many *sophos* lineages (see below, pp. 265–66); he was even called a *philosophos* (DL 9.22, with Koning 2010, esp. ch. 6). Hecataeus retains his fame for *sophia* into the Roman period (Ael. *VH* 13.20). Archilochus becomes the subject of a book by Heraclides (DL 5.87) and before that has a fifth-century BCE play named after him, which refers to Homer and Hesiod as *sophistai* (DL 1.12).

really have got to be researchers into much. We saw that the term *philosophoi* likely referred to Pythagoreans or their ilk. Heraclitus condemns as polymaths Hesiod, Xenophanes, and Hecataeus just as he does the Pythagoreans. Plausibly, then, he would call them *philosophoi*, too. Had he done so, he would not thereby be constituting a discipline; he would simply be generalizing a handy label. What we do see in his use of *philosophoi* and in his excoriation of those he judges the most influential teachers of Greeks is a first step in the development of a history of philosophy.

Hippias and Sophos Lineages

An historical sensibility about *sophoi* gets its most important realization in the work of Hippias of Elis.[4] He traces lines of doxastic family resemblance among authors from as early as memory would allow until his own time, including himself. He must have done so for the public fascination such archaeology affords and to dignify the new as no worse than the old or the old as the source of the new. The perhaps unintended effect was the publication of a map of *sophoi* past and present and increased appreciation for the continuities and discontinuities in Greek thought as it developed over the centuries. Without theorizing *philosophia* or delineating its course, Hippias provided the eminently relevant prosopography from which such a theory and delineation could be built. Because of his centrality for providing the historical material and sensibility necessary for the disciplinary self-understanding of classical *philosophoi*, we should understand him and his works as best we can.

Plato presents Hippias as competent and of high repute across the fields of theoretical inquiry known to fifth-century BCE Athenians.[5] At Callias's

---

[4] For Hippias's work, see Pfeiffer 1968, 51–54; Patzer 1986; Morgan 2000, 95–96; Zhmud 2006, 50 ("first treatise on the history of ideas"); *BNJ* 6; Rossetti 2015a, 140–44. Mansfeld 1986 argues that glimmers of historiography arose in Gorgias (see also Palmer 2009, 35–36), Protagoras, and the Hippocratic writers; but they were neither obviously earlier nor more influential, and their work remains in quantities that are too small to explore the historiographical attitudes that they assumed. The fifth-century BCE historian Xanthus of Lydia wrote about his contemporary, Empedocles (DL 8.63), as well as about the age of Zoroastrianism (DL 1.2), but we do not know whether he wrote anything genealogical; see Schepens and Theys 1998; Kingsley 1995. Glaucus of Rhegium wrote a history of music, and because early practitioners of music theory later became canonical philosophical figures, he in effect wrote a partial history of *philosophia*, with information about Musaeus (Harp. s.v. Μουσαῖος), Empedocles (DL 8.52), and Democritus (DL 9.38), but our evidence about its form, motivation, and reception is too fragmentary to interpret; see Huxley 1968, 47–48, 51–52; Ford 2002, 140–42; *BNP* s.v. "Glaucus [7]"; Zhmud 2006, 28, 49–50; and Barker 2014, 33–37, 43–45.

[5] Protagoras suggests that Hippias, whom he nevertheless esteems (Pl. *Prt.* 317c9–d8), teaches what he would not: arithmetic (λογισμοί), astronomy, geometry, and musical culture (318e2); cf. Xen. *Mem.* 4.4.6.

party in the *Protagoras*, a crowd surrounds him, peppering him with questions "about nature and astronomical phenomena"; he gives careful and full
answers to each.[6] He takes his expertise as his license in *sophia*. He accepts
Socrates's calling him "Hippias the *sophos*" and, more grandiosely, speaks
about those present as "most *sophoi*" of all Greeks, here in "the headquarters
of *sophia*," we who know "the nature of things."[7] So, in Plato's reconstruction,
Hippias takes himself to have knowledge about physical and other kinds of inquiry, judges this knowledge to make him *sophos*, and identifies as his peers a
class of *sophoi*. This suggests that Hippias provides a cooperative, optimistic,
and localized formation of *sophoi*, at least as seen in contrast to Heraclitus's
unstructured class of competitive or independent putative *sophoi*. This reflects
a camaraderie more than a discipline. Another Platonic dialogue shows us
more about Hippias's lineages.

Plato appears to echo or parody Hippias's writings throughout the beginning of his *Hippias Major*. As in the *Protagoras*, Socrates calls Hippias *sophos*,
and does so repeatedly, as though Hippias had flamboyantly included himself
under the concept he spent so much time writing about.[8] Indeed, the dialogue
opens with Socrates calling Hippias ὁ καλὸς τε καὶ σοφός ("the beautiful and
wise"), no mere intellectualized variation of *kalokagathos* but likely a quotation from his work: we know that he deemed a person included in his lineage,
the Milesian Thargelia, πάνυ καλὴ καὶ σοφή ("most beautiful and wise").[9]
Socrates soon brings up that lineage. Having exclaimed at the variety of diplomatic and political tasks Hippias has undertaken, he wonders what Hippias
makes of the fact that many or all of Hippias's forebears (οἱ παλαιοὶ ἐκεῖνοι),
"whose names are called great in *sophia*"—Pittacus, Bias, those around (τῶν
ἀμφὶ) Milesian Thales, and on down to Anaxagoras—refrain from political
matters.[10] That Hippias has a prepared answer implies that Socrates's list
comes from him.[11] Hippias soon confirms the implication, saying that he publicly praises (these) forebears for their wisdom, even as he privately believes

[6] Pl. *Prt.* 315c5–7: περὶ φύσεώς τε καὶ τῶν μετεώρων ἀστρονομικά . . . διέκρινε . . . διεξῄει;
cf. *Hp. mi.* 363c4–d3, 364b8–c2; *Hp. mai.* 283b7–285b7, 286e6, 287b2–3.

[7] Pl. *Prt.* 337c8–338b2. On Hippias's confidence in *sophia*, cf. *Hp. mi.* 364a3, 364a10. That
he was an ambassador (*Hp. mai.* 281a) and involved in political activities (cf. Brunschwig 1984;
Dusanic 2008) is consistent with his being a *sophos*.

[8] Pl. *Hp. mai.* 281b6, 286d7. See Kurke 2011, 344–58, for a remarkable argument to this effect.

[9] Pl. *Hp. mai.* 281a1; Ath. 13.608f. See Patzer 1986, 100–5; Gera 1997, 179–86 (Thargelia
of Miletus), 180–81 (Hippias's reference to her).

[10] Pl. *Hp. mai.* 281c7. As we saw in chapter 3, the *sophoi* were surely not so quiescent; but
fourth-century BCE authors liked to argue contrariwise, as Heraclides did in a dialogue featuring Thales (DL 1.25).

[11] His preparation is indicated by the introduction of his response: "What do you think
but . . ." (τί δ'οἴει . . . ἄλλο).

that contemporary *sophia* renders the value of older instances nugatory.[12] Socrates reiterates that Hippias concerns himself with "the earlier ones leading up to Anaxagoras" (τῶν προτέρων περὶ Ἀναξαγόρου).[13] Plato must be playing up Hippias's lineage of *sophoi*, one that extends from at least the sixth-century BCE Seven *Sophoi* to an Athenian exiled not long ago.[14] Hippias has fortified it with Thales's associates and successors, maybe Anaximander or similar Milesians.[15] Socrates refrains from putting Hippias at the end of this list only because he wants Hippias to explain his financially evidenced superiority to the other *sophoi*.[16]

Plato leads us to believe that Hippias's *sophos*-list fits a broader category of "origin tales" (ἀρχαιολογίαι) that Hippias tends to tell. Hippias says that the Spartans want to hear his accounts of the families (γενῆ) of heroes and of men and of the foundations of cities. Plutarch tells us Hippias had an Olympic Victors list.[17] Hippias delineates personages into subjects apparently to provide an eminent field against which to show off one's excellence. He sets out his horizontal lines—contemporary, tuition-charging sophists—for the same reason. In neither case does it appear that he puts the people he writes about into constructive conversation; while he presents present-day *sophoi* in something of a congress, we do not have evidence that he showed dialectical connections among the earlier ones. Socrates upbraids his work as storytelling (μυθολογῆσαι, Pl. *Hp. mai.* 286a1).

More information about Hippias's lineages comes from Plato's *Cratylus*, which presents Socrates's etymologizing the names of gods. Making hay about *ousia* and Hestia, Socrates brings in Heraclitus for support, and then refers to Rhea and Kronos. Acknowledging that he and his interlocutors have already discussed Kronos, he pauses, then exclaims that he is being attacked by "some swarm of *sophia*." Heraclitus, he observes, has spoken with an ancient wisdom (παλαί᾿ . . . σοφὰ λέγοντα) that they can date to Homer and even earlier, to the very naming of Kronos and Rhea. Heraclitus says that

[12] Pl. *Hp. mai.* 281d5–282a10.

[13] Pl. *Hp. mai.* 283a1. This is in the context of Socrates's expressing wonder that earlier *sophoi* neglected money.

[14] Jaeger 1962, 129, thus shortchanges Hippias when he attributes to Aristotle instead "the historical insight to put the Seven Wise Men at the head of this succession of commanding intellectuals [found in *On Philosophy* 1], whose influence on the development of Greek thought seemed to him so important."

[15] On Anaximander as in Thales's sphere, see DL 1.13, 1.122. Other sources confirm that Hippias discussed Thales: Arist. *De an.* 405a19 and DL 1.24; see further Snell 1944.

[16] Socrates likens Hippias to Gorgias and Prodicus as men who also perform public service and charge for private tutelage (Pl. *Hp. mai.* 282b1–d5); Hippias accepts the comparison only to brag that he earns more than they do.

[17] Plut. *Num.* 1.6.

everything moves (ῥοῇ) like a river (ποταμόν), Socrates reports, and claims that those who named the gods thought the same when they called them by the names of streams (ῥευμάτων). Homer likewise speaks of "Oceanus origin of gods" and "Mother Tethys" (*Il.* 14.201, 302). Hesiod too, and Orpheus as well. Socrates says that these all agree (συμφωνεῖ) and tend toward Heraclitus's perspective (πρὸς τὰ τοῦ Ἡρακλείτου πάντα τείνει) (Pl. *Cra.* 401c–402c). Thus each "speaks wisely" in a similar way, namely about water as the world's key principle.

The swarm of wisdom seems to fly from Hippias's research into like-minded *sophoi*.[18] The implication from the *Cratylus* gains corroboration from Clement of Alexandria. He quotes the opening of Hippias's book:

> Of these things perhaps some have been said by Orpheus, some by Musaeus in lines here and there (κατὰ βραχὺ ἄλλῳ ἀλλαχοῦ),[19] some by Hesiod, some by Homer, some by other poets, some by prose writers, some by Greeks, and some by foreigners. What I will do, having collected the best and most categorizable (ὁμόφυλα) from all these, is to compose this new and multifaceted writing. (Clem. *Strom.* 6.15.1–2)

Others testify independently to Hippias's discussion of etymologies and Homer, to his interest in the sea god Oceanus and the Oceanid nymphs, and to other divine beings.[20] Socrates's remarks about rivers and etymology suggest excerpts from Hippias's selection of "lines here and there" from canonical authors, and his bringing of Heraclitus into the mix sounds of a piece with Hippias's bringing in Anaxagoras and the Milesians around Thales.

Doubtless Hippias drew from a growing consensus about canonical *sophoi*. His contemporaries, including Pherecydes, Hellanicus, and Damastes of Sigeion, but also Herodotus and Aristophanes, argued about the relative ordering of Orpheus, Musaeus, Homer, and Hesiod.[21] As we noted above, Cratinus in his *Archilochoi* called those around Homer and Hesiod *sophistai* (DL 1.12). In Plato's *Apology*, Socrates says that, were he to have an afterlife in Hades, he

---

[18] See Mansfeld 1983, in response to Snell 1944 and (effectively) Patzer 1986.

[19] LM 2.7, by contrast, translate this as "to put it briefly, by each one in a different place," but this seems overly obvious for the opening line, insofar as it notes only that Hippias has not relied on an earlier compilation.

[20] Etymology: B9/D26; Homer: Pl. *Hp. mi.* 363c2; Oceanus: B8/D28; other divine beings: B13/D35, B14/D29; see *BNJ* 6 ad F9–11 for commentary.

[21] For the first three, see Procl. *Chrestomathy* 1.4. Damastes wrote a Περὶ ποιητῶν καὶ σοφιστῶν ("On Poets and *Sophistai*") (*Suda* δ 41); likely this is a key source. For the next two, see Hdt. 2.53.2–3; Ar. *Ran.* 1032–36.

would anticipate philosophizing with Orpheus, Musaeus, Hesiod, and Homer (Pl. *Ap.* 41a6–7).

Where Hippias seems to have innovated in ways relevant to developing a disciplinary consciousness for philosophy was in adding *sophoi*, their wise ideas, and the relations between those ideas, perhaps motivated by goals of systematicity, completeness, and usefulness. He may have had two sources of inspiration for this. First, this retailer of Trojan stories may have noticed the naturalizing common denominators in contemporary Homeric allegoresis, notably by Theagenes of Rhegium and Metrodorus of Lampsacus, who reduced the Trojan conflict to strife between the basic elements or celestial phenomena.[22] This would allow him to identify meaningful parallels between the earlier poets and later physicists, and thereby assemble a canon of doctrinally related *sophoi* down to the fifth century BCE, a chronological and thematic list of the great advisors and teachers. People already accepted relations between certain poets, such as Homer and Hesiod, and between certain researchers, such as Parmenides and Empedocles.[23] Additionally, there was increasing sensitivity to the idea of a cogent *historia peri phuseôs* ("investigation into nature").[24] Hippias could then generalize, positing pedagogical lineage or at least a meaningful ordering between the remainder of the names. Second, the flourishing of ever-elaborated lore about the Seven Sages and the circulation of rhetorical handbooks must have included sayings attributable to wise authorities and citable at any instance; in the latter case, organized collections would have provided resources both of content and form from which Hippias could construct his historical taxonomy.

We know Hippias's book to have been a great success; for many Greeks of the fifth and fourth centuries it reconstructed a course of intellectual discovery, agreement, and contention, and it published the "greatest hits" of that history. But he did not constitute the discipline of philosophy. We do not know him to have used the word *philosophos* or *philosophia*. No later author took him up as a member of the discipline,[25] and presumably disciplines are formed

---

[22] On Theagenes, see Morgan 2000, 63; Ford 2002, 68–75; Naddaf 2009; for Metrodorus, see Richardson 1975, 68–70; Califf 2003.

[23] Most 2007.

[24] See Leszl 2006, 367–69; Laks 2018, 2–12. The texts: Eur. fr. 910; *Diss. Log.* 8; Pl. *Lys.* 214b; *Prt.* 315c; *Phd.* 96a; Xen. *Mem.* 1.1.11, 1.1.14.

[25] There are two apparent minor exceptions. *Suda* ι 543 calls Hippias *sophistês kai philosophos*, but Pausanias (5.25.4) is probably right that the Greeks called Hippias (only) *sophos*. Plato and Xenophon include Hippias in conversations that may count as *philosophia* to their authors, but they include many others, too, who were even more obviously never deemed *philosophoi*. Notably, Aristotle cites Hippias only as a source of information, never as a person with views or a way of life worth discussing.

by their practitioners. Finally, while we see him having created his *sophos* lineage, we do not know him to have engaged critically and productively with the ideas recorded in it. Olympic victors do not constitute a discipline simply by having their names written down on a list. The discipline of philosophy awaits a higher sun for its growth. Yet Hippias's work sows some seeds and fertilizes the ground.

Philosophical Historiography at the Time of Plato

By early in the fourth century BCE, the framework for disciplinary formation comes into view. As we saw two chapters earlier, in Isocrates's *Busiris*, probably from the 380s BCE, Pythagoras is said to have learned *philosophia* from the Egyptians.[26] This points to an early interest in the sources of *philosophia*, and the sense that "Greek" *philosophia* descends from Pythagoras. In his *Encomium of Helen*, from sometime in the first quarter of the fourth century BCE, Isocrates mentions the paradoxes of Protagoras, Gorgias, Zeno, and Melissus.[27] All four of Isocrates's figures remain canonical, two as *philosophoi*, each advancing incredible claims about the nature of knowledge, language, and being. In the *Antidosis*, from the late 350s BCE, Isocrates situates himself against other purported teachers of *philosophia*: their encouragement to slog through astronomical and geometrical subtleties has as much benefit as the encouragement to practice anything does: as preliminaries to the real effort. Isocrates's vision of *philosophia* foregoes the disputes found in "the arguments of past sophists" (τοὺς λόγους τοὺς τῶν παλαιῶν σοφιστῶν), who differ among themselves concerning the number of fundamental "beings": an infinite number, or Empedocles's four (with strife and love), or Ion's maximum of three, or Alcmaeon's two, or Parmenides's and Melissus's one, or Gorgias's none—all of which enumeration counts as sheer mystification (περιττολογίας . . . θαυματοποιίαις) (Isoc. *Antid.* 265–68).[28] We have already seen that Isocrates's concern for *philosophia* does not lead to a disciplinary conception of it; indeed, he seems to contrast his approach with that of adversarial research. By the 350s BCE, Isocrates can rely on five decades of reflection on *philosophia*'s past.

Three other contemporaries of Plato reflect something of an inchoate disciplinization. While Xenophon treats himself as external to *philosophia*, and (as we saw in chapter 6) even treats Socrates as marginal to the practice, he

[26] Isoc. *Bus.* 18; see Livingstone 2001 ad loc.

[27] Isoc. *Hel.* 1–8.

[28] Such taxonomizing gets an apparent defense in *PVindob.* G.26008 fr. B col. II; see Most 1992; Megino Rodriguez 2008; HJ 63.

appreciates the burgeoning "inquiries into nature" epitomized by Anaxagoras and the extensive debates about the nature of justice.[29] Simmias of Thebes, famous from Plato's *Phaedo*, is said to have written an *On Philosophy*; though we know nothing of its contents, Simmias studied with Philolaus, the most important Pythagorean of his generation, and so he would be well placed to discuss both contemporary and historical *philosophia*.[30] The most pertinent source is Alcidamas, the rhetorician whose remarks on *philosophia* we studied in chapter 7. Aristotle cites him for the claim that every town, no matter how anti-intellectual it may seem, honors its wise (*sophoi*): for example, the Chians honor Homer, the Spartans honor Chilon, the Italians honor Pythagoras, and the Lampsacans honor Anaxagoras.[31] This list looks Hippian, or at least it appears to have a common source in rhetorical collections of *topoi*. More interesting is the next quotation (which we have already seen), the sole fragment of Alcidamas's *Physics*:

> Alcidamas, in the *Physics*, says that Zeno and Empedocles studied with (ἀκοῦσαι) Parmenides at the same time, that later they separated from him, and that, whereas Zeno philosophized on his own (κατ᾿ ἰδίαν φιλοσοφῆσαι), the other continued on to work with (διακοῦσαι) Anaxagoras and Pythagoras, emulating (ζηλῶσαι) the latter in his dignity (σεμνότητα) of life and bearing, and the former in his physical investigations (φυσιολογίαν).[32]

We see here the coordination of four figures regularly appearing in the rear-view mirrors of Alcidamas's contemporaries. He connects them pedagogically

[29] At the end of the opening paragraph of the *Life of Xenophon*, Diogenes Laertius writes: ἀλλὰ καὶ ἱστορίαν φιλοσόφων πρῶτος ἔγραψε (DL 2.48). Hicks 1925's influential translation as "Moreover, he was the first to write a history of philosophers" is implausible, on various factual (Xanthus of Lydia had probably already written about Empedocles), generic (the *Memorabilia* is about Socrates alone, whom Xenophon does not explicitly treat as a philosopher), and linguistic grounds (we would expect περὶ τῶν φιλοσόφων ἱστορίαν; cf. Ath. 4.54.29); this unusual locution surely means "Besides that, he was the first among philosophers to write history" (for φιλοσόφων πρῶτος, see Gal. *De nat. facult.* 2.38.13 Kuhn)—rightly, Mensch 2018, 88.

[30] DL 2.125. The work would be short; it fits, with twenty-two others, in a single volume. Plato's Socrates says that Simmias has generated more speeches than anyone he knows (Pl. *Phdr.* 242b), and that he is energetic and ingenious in debate (Pl. *Phd.* 85c, 86d). Rankin 1983, 184, suspects that Simmias is some years older than Plato. On Simmias's discipleship with Philolaus, see Zeller 1931, 38–40.

[31] Arist. *Rh.* 1398b11–16. The reference in the manuscripts to Pythagoras is deleted by Kassel 1971, 139–40, followed by Muir 2001.

[32] DL 8.56. The work's date is unknown; Alcidamas wrote at least until 369. Milne 1924, 17–18, speculates that it was written on the model of Gorgias's *On Non-Being*, which she claims to have used the dialectical method of Zeno and Melissus, allowing Plato's "Eleatic Palamedes" to refer to Alcidamas (cf. Quint. *Inst.* 3.1.10).

(who learns from whom), doxographically (whose views differ from whose), and characterologically (who acted similarly to whom).[33] He implies that all four men *philosophein* (on the assumption that the source is quoting him) and three other things: that philosophizing by oneself, while conceivable, goes against the norm; that *phusiologia* counts as a kind of philosophizing; and that philosophizing both modifies one's comportment and pursues understanding. Each reflects a disciplinary perspective. Various people engage in the same activity; that activity is both personally enculturated and impersonally advanced in concert with others; that activity is directed toward at least one type of discovery or creation; and, again, there is something of a way of life related to the discipline. In presenting Zeno, Empedocles, and the rest in this way, Alcidamas has gone beyond Hippias in constructing a history of philosophy, braiding lines of "philosophical" influence expressly so called, and noting subdisciplinary divisions and varieties in the modes of practice. Whether he took those steps unaided we cannot say, since he was writing into the 360s BCE; he may simply have reflected popular discussions of these thinkers. And though he considered himself engaged with *philosophia* we cannot readily ascribe him to the discipline of *philosophia* himself, and thereby to an internal understanding of its leading concerns. All the same, he provides in a convenient encapsulation something of the view of *philosophoi* necessary for constructing a disciplinary conception.[34]

In the last chapter, I argued that we do not see, in most of Plato's dialogues, a fully disciplinary and historical view of philosophy. Plato depicts *philosophia* instead as present-tense conversations structured by the pursuit of excellence, virtue, or goodness, as the *Symposium* most vividly depicts. The parties to *philosophia* are the parties to a conversation, which involves the present interlocutors. The interlocutors can talk about absent thinkers, such as Protagoras or Simonides, but centripetal forces bring the conversation back to the interlocutors themselves.[35] Talk of books similarly becomes talk of the reader or listener: Socrates dramatizes his reaction to reading Anaxagoras's book (Pl. *Phd.* 97b8–99d2); Zeno's reading gets the conversation of the *Parmenides* going

---

[33] Whether Alcidamas's account defies accepted chronology depends on the meaning of *akousai* and *diakousai*, which mean either "study with" (in person) or "study" (not necessarily in person), and on the meaning of "Pythagoras," which could mean either Pythagoras himself (or his "works" themselves), or later thinkers who took up Pythagoras's brilliant white mantle. Alcidamas may himself not have known the precise connections between these men; he probably drew inferences from hearsay and from similarities in their works.

[34] Alcidamas seems also to have written one of the earliest doxographies of poets, the *Mouseion* ("house of the Muses"), which probably included the *Certamen*, the contest between Homer and Hesiod; see *Suda* α 1283; Muir 2001, xx.

[35] Pl. *Prt.* 347e with *Meno* 71d (Gorgias); *Hp. mi.* 365d (Homer). Cf. Ford 1994, 212–14.

(*Phd.* 127c3–e4). Plato's Socrates does not ignore the past, but it gets flattened and relativized to those currently discussing it.[36] *Philosophia* is principally a matter of one's being challenged in one's views by the unpredictable and compelling questions and rebuttals of one's interlocutors. This can have a virtual realization in inner dialogue, but cannot be reduced to it, in light of Socrates's definition of *philosophia* as "examination of oneself and others" (Pl. *Ap.* 29a1). This is the way "self-knowledge," which takes conversation with others, is at the heart of the Platonic philosophical enterprise.[37] Just as the search for self-knowledge comes to no proper end, a proper conversation cannot be exhausted, as we know from our lives and from Socrates's saying so at the end of many Platonic dialogues. A refutation ends a game or contest, but in conversation, and thus in philosophy, it merely spurs further talking.

Plato does, of course, mention practically all the people Aristotle eventually calls *philosophoi*, even without presenting himself as canvassing or articulating or positing the history of *philosophoi*. We saw that Plato esteems Anaxagoras for contributing to Socrates's thought about rational or teleological explanation at the cosmic level. Socrates reports Empedocles's views about effluences in order to seduce Meno in a "Gorgianic" register of persuasion, and attributes views about "strife and love" to "later Ionian and Sicilian muses" (Pl. *Men.* 76c4; *Soph.* 242d7–243a1). Xenophanes is a prominent member of "the Eleatic tribe," in holding to the thesis that "all are one" (*Soph.* 242d5). Heraclitus comes up in the *Cratylus*, as we saw, and Heracliteans zing in and out of the *Theaetetus* (*Tht.* 179e3–180b3). Pythagoras and Pythagoreans are mentioned twice, in the *Republic*. Parmenides and Zeno travel together and teach Socrates in the *Parmenides*; Parmenides is also in the *Theaetetus* (183e5–184b1), joined elsewhere in that dialogue by Protagoras, Homer, Heraclitus, and his followers). Most are mentioned simply for a slogan or way of talking. The Eleatics of the *Parmenides* give Socrates a lesson in thinking, not a synopsis of their ontological writings. We learn about Anaxagoras's views only from the perspective of Socrates's excitement and disenchantment. And the term *philosophoi* generally refers to participants in Socrates's discussion circle or to those who have adopted an estimable attitude toward learning.

All the same, we do see the lineaments of a historical disciplinary thinking in Plato. Sometimes he clumps thinkers together: Empedocles and Gorgias, Ionians, Sicilians, Heracliteans, Parmenides, and Zeno (or "Eleatics"). Usually he says little about tilling these clumps into rows, but he does say something.

---

[36] Thus DL 3.25, which says that Plato initiated rebutting (ἀντειρηκώς) his predecessors' views.

[37] Cf. Moore 2015b.

In one case, from the *Theaetetus*, we see an echo of the Hippias-reliant *Cratylus* discussed above. Socrates says that many people believe that all being is really becoming: "and regarding this, all the *sophoi* except Parmenides are to be gathered in order (ἑξῆς . . . συμφερέσθων), Protagoras and Heraclitus and Empedocles, and the leading (ἄκροι) poets in each kind of poetry, Epicharmus in comedy and Homer in tragedy, who said 'Oceanus origin of gods and mother Tethys' (*Il.* 14.201, 302), said that all things are born from flow and motion" (*Tht.* 152e1–8). This list of *sophoi* is not yet a list of *philosophoi*, but it is a list of thinkers presented for reflection. In another case, a paragraph from the *Sophist*, cited in the previous paragraph (*Soph.* 242c7–243a4), the Eleatic visitor gives us what looks like a partial source for Isocrates's *Antidosis*. He rebukes Parmenides and "everyone else" (including Eleatics, Ionians, and Sicilians) who urge critical delineation (ἐπὶ κρίσιν . . . διορίσασθαι) of the number and nature of "beings": "Now, whether or not all the things they said were true, it would be harsh and discordant to make any great censure of these famous and ancient men (κλεινοῖς καὶ παλαιοῖς ἀνδράσιν)." We can say that "they spoke without caring whether we could follow them" (οὐδεν . . . φροντίσαντες εἴτ' ἐπακολουθοῦμεν αὐτοῖς λέγουσιν). The Eleatic visitor thus provides an historical taxonomy of those who wrote about "beings" (τὰ ὄντα), drawing subtle distinctions, and judging them on their ability to hold a conversation with their successors. Most scholars of Platonic dialogues believe that Plato wrote the *Sophist* late in his career, with the Academy already established. We can say, then, that we see inchoately in Plato the historical disciplinary conception that finally comes into mature view with Aristotle.

Aristotle's History of *Philosophia* as Diachronic Conversation

Aristotle moves back from the present. He affixes the conversational web to historically distant branches. *Philosophia* for him is a long-term joint effort pursuing *sophia* defined in a distinctive way. No longer is it solely a matter of personal heroism or self-improvement; Aristotle never defines *philosophia* in terms of self-knowledge. For him, *philosophia* is understanding and explaining everything most fundamentally, either considered broadly, such that *philosophia* includes all *epistêmai*, or narrowly, such that *philosophia* takes up the undergirdings of all *epistêmai*. Like Plato, he thinks this requires a communal effort.[38] But that community includes those no longer present. Thus *philosophia*

---

[38] Contra, e.g., Jordan 1990, 5–7, who mistakenly believes that Greek philosophers "had no conception that the tasks of philosophy were shared in common."

does not occur only in local instances. It takes a cumulative effort, with the burden shared by all those we can conceive of as having contributed to that cumulative effort. We stand on giants' shoulders. But this does not simply allow us to look farther. The giants have seen and thought in their own incisive ways; while we are borne up by them, their views bear on our own. They are less like stools than friends who, giving us a lift, still have something to say.

Plato assumes that one cannot know what the ancients really meant, and so one may as well focus on oneself; this is a principle of epistemic humility. Aristotle assumes that the ancients were really wise, and so one ought to reconstruct their arguments as well as possible; this is a principle of epistemic charity. Doing this charitable reconstruction allows earlier practitioners to contribute to the cumulative effort.[39] Scholarship has long disputed Aristotle's virtues and vices in his reconstruction of his predecessors. The stakes of the battle concern the usefulness of Aristotle's works as witness to his predecessors for our independent work in ancient philosophy.[40] But Aristotle's reliability and the meaning of his testimony matter little to the present chapter. What matters is that however tendentiously or dialectically or teleologically Aristotle treats his predecessors, when he calls them *philosophoi* and treats them as worthy of respectful analysis, he reveals a disciplinary conception.[41]

In this, too, as we have already seen in this chapter, Aristotle the historiographer stands on the shoulders of historiographical giants. Already Heraclitus, Hippias, Alcidamas, and Plato had sieved and sorted the best intellectuals and thinkers of the generations within memory or record. Contemporaries might put up other past thinkers for candidacy, constructing and reconstructing the canon, such as the fifth-century BCE Hippo whom Aristotle considers and rejects as unworthy for charitable reconstruction. Thus Aristotle labored in fields long furrowed, happy to call the acreage a farm and apply himself to its cultivation. The best conversational partners, like the best soils, repay many seasons of work. Even the idea of a diachronic conversation preceded Aristotle. Socrates imagined Hades as a timeless place for conversation between

---

[39] Aristotle's *Protrepticus* encourages, in the case of the fragmentary remains of philosophical Pythagoreanism, "setting out from small glimmers (αἰθυγμάτων), building such things into a corpus (ὁρμωμένους σωματατοποιεῖν), helping make it grow" (Iambl. *DCMS* 22.68,7–24).

[40] Cherniss 1951 and McDiarmid 1953 doubt the usefulness; Guthrie 1957 recuperates Aristotle; Stevenson 1974 clarifies the stakes; Collobert 2002 and Hussey 2012 describe Aristotle's historical methods.

[41] Jaeger opens his *Aristotle* (1962, 3–4) with the claim that "Aristotle was the first thinker to set up along with his philosophy a conception of his own position in history; he thereby created a new kind of philosophical consciousness." Seeing oneself in history requires seeing there to be a history, and in Aristotle's case, a history of *philosophia*; I am describing the texture of the consciousness of that history. (Cf. Barney 2012, 104, who gives an appealing argument for Aristotle's status as "the first historian of philosophy.")

his most esteemed forebears and himself. Aristotle's discipline of *philosophia* embraces these conversations as the ones most fruitful for each member's objectives.[42] The factors contributing to his ability to make *philosophia* into a discipline structured in this way include his relatively late date, his ecumenical interests, his ravenous appetite for books, and, most importantly, his two decades in Plato's Academy. The Academy formalized the Socratic discussion circles depicted in the *Charmides* and the more general discussion circles depicted in the *Protagoras*. Participants other than Socrates could now give full-time attention to philosophical pursuit and conversation, and they could proceed more linearly and systematically than a part-time or intermittent discussion club would allow. Each researcher would bring his or her own historical understanding; together they could provide, orally or in their personal libraries, the material for Aristotle's historiography.

The next sections vindicate one part of this view, that Aristotle consolidated certain of his predecessors into *philosophoi* and thus as practitioners in the discipline of *philosophia*. We will see that he shapes up a long history of *philosophia*, periodizes and striates it, and explains the roles of its ancillary members. Aristotle contributes much else to the disciplinary formation of *philosophia*, especially in methodology, treatise-writing, use of research associates, highly fruitful cross-disciplinary investigation, and sheer analytic brilliance, bringing *aporiai* into focus, and providing the most provocative answers.[43] In our focus on the *philosophos* word group, we must let those innovations speak for themselves.

Histories of the Sophoi

Aristotle's conventions for naming intellectual practitioners look jumbled and ill-defined. He switches among *philosophoi, hoi philosophountes, phusikoi, phusiologoi, sophoi, theologoi*, and *poiêtai*. Often Aristotle prefers shorthand

---

[42] Simplicius, commenting on Aristotle's *Physics* 184b15 (*In Phys.* 36,25–37,6), presents the spirit of continuity most vigorously: "Since we will hear even of Aristotle refuting (ἐλέγχοντος) the views (δόξας) of earlier philosophers, and before Aristotle Plato appears to be doing this and before them both Parmenides and Xenophanes, one must know that these men, concerned for their more superficial audience, quite refute (διελέγχουσίν) instances of apparent oddness in their [forebears'] writings, the ancients usually revealing their thought in an enigmatic way. Nevertheless, Plato is obviously impressed (θαυμάζων) with Parmenides, whom he seems to quite refute (διελέγχειν δοκεῖ). . . . And Aristotle apparently intuits (ὑπονοῶν) the depth of his wisdom, when he says that 'But Parmenides seems to speak <with sharper sight> (μᾶλλον βλέπων, *M*. A.5 986b27).' Thus these men, though sometimes they fill out what has been omitted, sometimes clarify what has been said unclearly, sometimes distinguishing what has been said about the intelligibles [in such-and-such ways], still they merely seem to refute (ἐλέγχειν)."

[43] See, for example, Barnes 1982 and Natali 2013.

temporal deictics, like *hoi nun* ("those now") and *tôn proterôn* ("those earlier"). Sometimes he mixes and matches. At *Metaphysics* N, for example, Aristotle expresses the popularity of the idea that beauty and goodness came into existence after other things came into existence by attributing it to the *theologoi* and *hoi nun* (N 1091a29–b15). In Book Λ, he attributes this idea to Pythagoras and Speusippus (Λ 1072b31). Speusippus surely counts as "among those now." Does Pythagoras count as a figure among the *theologoi*? Aristotle seems to mention his predecessors in an ad hoc or arbitrary way.

In fact his orderings are coordinate and clear: he is drawing from preexisting categories and, at times, consolidating them under new guises. To see the structure of Aristotle's chronography we might start with the passage in *Metaphysics* N. There he pares down his history to two categories. Continuing on the subject of people who believe that the advent of goodness postdates the first principles, he calls the earliest group of such people "the early poets" (οἱ ποιηταὶ οἱ ἀρχαῖοι). They treat Night, Heaven, Chaos, and Ocean as "the first things," which are ethically neutral, and posit as somewhat later a "reigning and ruling" Zeus who serves as the origin of all ethical norms. The later group he calls "those who do not speak exclusively in myth" (οἵ μεμιγμένοι . . . τῷ μὴ μυθικῶς πάντα λέγειν). Aristotle includes three sub-categories here. There is Pherecydes and the others who speak of the *ariston* ("the best").[44] Then there are the Magi, for whom no information is given. Finally, "among the later *sophoi*" (τῶν ὑστέρων δὲ σοφῶν) he mentions Empedocles and Anaxagoras, who posit love and mind as the later normative principles. Hence we have a mixed bag of appellations and groups: cosmogonic poets; the miracle-mongering Pherecydes and those who share his concept of a superlative ideal; some Persian intellectuals; and two students of nature from the fifth century BCE. There may seem to be no shared name, only a shared view about a two-step origin of the world. But then we might wonder why Aristotle chooses these people to list, or knows to interpret them allegorically or so charitably. Perhaps they do share something else; and we can come to see that they in fact do share a name. Aristotle must call them all *sophoi*; his usage "among the later *sophoi*" admits as much. The "earlier" *sophoi* must be the "early poets," Pherecydes and his ilk (who are not much earlier than Empedocles), and the Magi (knowledge of whom may date to Xerxes's crossing of the Hellespont in the early fifth century BCE).[45]

[44] This is the only reference to Pherecydes in the *Metaphysics*, but Apollonius *Mir.* 6 may cite Aristotle (= *On the Pythagoreans* fr. 1 Ross) for the claim that Pythagoras followed Pherecydes, and like him engaged in miracle-mongering (τερατοποιίας).

[45] Chroust 1973a, 2.209, 424n16, believes that Aristotle might be summarizing his *On Philosophy*. For more on the Magi in the Academy, see Horky 2009.

But the important dichotomy in this passage is not between the "earlier" and "later" *sophoi*. It is between those who speak entirely in myth and those who do not. The first group are the poets, who speak in terms of Night, Heaven, and so forth. They write genealogical stories and animate characters, and as *sophoi* their works must have been either understood as providing models for human life or interpreted allegorically or symbolically. Elsewhere in the *Metaphysics* Aristotle refers to those who speak in terms of Night and Heaven as *theologoi*, though this category might be somewhat larger than "poets," if it includes Pythagoras (Λ 1071b27). Aristotle finds the *theologoi* difficult to deal with; he includes Hesiod and the like (Ἡσίοδον καὶ πάντες ὅσοι θεολόγοι) among them. They concern themselves with first principles, but enthralled by their own experience with language and imagery, they forget to make comprehensible their claims about those principles (a complaint similar to that of the Eleatic visitor in Plato's *Sophist*). This matters if gods are to be taken as first principles. Aristotle grows impatient, complaining that "it's not worth giving serious investigation (σπουδῆς σκοπεῖν) to their mythical expressions of wisdom (τῶν μυθικῶς σοφιζομένων); we ought rather to learn from and interrogate those who speak via demonstration (δι᾽ ἀποδείξεως λεγόντων δεῖ πυνθάνεσθαι διερωτῶντας)" (B 1000a18–22). But we see that even in his frustration at their indirection, Aristotle includes these *poiêtai* and *theologoi* among the *sophoi*, and thus as relevant to his study into fundamental explanation.

The second group, those who speak "not . . . exclusively in myth," includes those who carry on certain aspects of the poetic tradition, though to a lesser extent: at least Pherecydes and Empedocles. Thus Aristotle observes the rise of some non-imagistic or non-dramatic elements, either the positing of abstract forces or reasoning through sequential argument. The stories of the poets may lend themselves to this reformation. Aristotle elsewhere says that poetry is more philosophical than history; and cosmogonies, while superficially historical, in fact unfold necessarily or plausibly—they comprise claims readily infused with notions of forces and logical requirement.[46] Empedocles retains a Hesiodic drama in his accounts of Love and Strife; Anaxagoras incants the tale of the Mind's whirling world.

Aristotle thus provides in *Metaphysics* N a miniature history of the *sophoi*. Aristotle defines the *sophoi* at the beginning of *Metaphysics* A as those who know as much as possible though without knowing every individual item,[47] who can comprehend difficult matters and especially those not learned through sense perception, and who tend to be accurate and good at explanation (*M. A*

---

[46] Arist. *Poet.* 1451b1–7; see Powell 1987, 348, for subtleties in Aristotle's view of history.

[47] Cf. Arist. *An. post.* 79a5: we may understand the universal but by lack of observation have ignored some instances.

982a8–13).[48] In other words: they have high-level understanding without being polymaths; they are insightful about abstract and conceptual matters; and they have the intellectual virtues of error-correction in the service of knowledge and articulation in the service of understanding. In a lost work Aristotle expresses this view in an etymological key. *Sophia* is a sort of "clarity" (σάφειά) for "making all things clear" (σαφηνίζουσα); clarity is something light (φαές), so called from the terms for light (τὸ φάος καὶ φῶς); and brings hidden things to light. Matters of the intelligible and divine realm (τὰ νοητὰ καὶ θεῖα) are most clear in themselves but our bodies prevent us from seeing them; *sophia* was so called for bringing those things to light.[49]

Aristotle does not use the *philosophos* word group in any of these *sophos*-histories. Yet he calls Empedocles and Anaxagoras *philosophoi* elsewhere. We may then wonder about the relationship between *sophoi* and *philosophoi*, and even of the relevance of the former to the latter. As we will soon see, Aristotle repurposes his history of the *sophoi* for his history of the *philosophoi*. The *philosophoi* constitute a proper subset of the *sophoi*, specifically the group in *Metaphysics* N of those who speak "not . . . exclusively in myth."

History of the Philosophoi

Aristotle presents the middle of *Metaphysics* A (983a23–993a23) as giving historical proof to his claim in the *Physics* that there are exactly four kinds of causal explanation. He shows that previous thinkers concerned themselves with none other than these four. This follows his analysis of the *sophos* near the book's beginning, and thus we are to deem as *sophoi* all who follow. He confirms this when he summarizes the most important chapters, A.3 and 4; he says he has drawn his results "from the *sophoi* who already themselves talked through these matters" (τῶν συνηδρευκότων ἤδη τῷ λόγῳ σοφῶν), that is, what he just discussed (A.5 987a2–3). These *sophoi* include Thales, Anaxagoras, Empedocles, Leucippus, Democritus, Anaximenes, Diogenes of Apollonia, Hippasus of Metapontum, Parmenides, Melissus, the Pythagoreans, Alcmaeon, and Xenophanes.

Yet Aristotle also refers to all these men as *philosophoi* (*M.* A.3 983b2, A.10 993a16). Thus all *philosophoi* are *sophoi*. Nearly all the *sophoi* he mentions in this chapter are *philosophoi*. We are left to ask about the exceptions and the sources of differentiation. We will see that the *philosophoi* belong to the discipline of *philosophia*. While a discipline has lines of internal differentiation, it

---

[48] On this section see Broadie 2012, esp. 53–62, and Cambiano 2012. HJ suggest this section is from the *Protrepticus*, and thus pre-350 BCE.

[49] Arist. *On Philosophy* fr. 8 Ross (from Philoponus). For discussion, see Gerson 2005, 68–70.

is more importantly a community of discussion (συνηδρεύειν τῷ λόγῳ), such that everybody can be taken as talking with one another. It excludes those *sophoi* who cannot be taken as talking to others in the discipline, such as the poets at whom we have already seen Aristotle grumble.

This explains Aristotle's treatment of Thales as the "initiator" (ἀρχηγός) of one kind of *philosophia*, the one that accepts a material principle and that attracted "most of the early philosophizers" (*M.* A.3 983b6, 983b20). Some scholars have wanted to show that Thales really did usher in a totally new method of investigation.[50] Others, by contrast, have doubted it, ascribing the real innovation to Anaximander or judging Thales merely a clever and practical *sophos*.[51] But Aristotle does not support his assertion by appeal to Thales's qualitative novelty, theoretical purity, or intellectual profundity. Thales's status as initiator comes, according to Aristotle, from his having been first to put forth the claim that water is the material principle. Aristotle recognizes the controversy in his claim.[52] Some people say that the "earliest theologizers" (πρώτους θεολογήσαντας), from quite long ago (τοὺς παμπαλαίους καὶ πολὺ πρὸ τῆς νῦν), even before Thales, had already accepted water as the first thing, and thus as equivalent to the material principle. This can be inferred from their making Oceanus and Tethys parents of creation and from the tradition of swearing an oath on Styx, which would imply that this river is the oldest thing (A.3 983b18–32).[53] But it is "unclear" (ἄδηλον, A 984a2) whether the *theologoi* really believed that water was the first principle; even if they had views about first principles (N 1091b4–7), Aristotle seems unable to read them as having made an assertion about water of the sort he takes Thales to have made.[54] Accordingly, Thales is the first *sophos* to have a stated view

[50] E.g., Rosen 1962; West 1963, 172–76; Panchenko 1993; O'Grady 2002; Sassi 2018 [2006], 21–26 (Thales's "clarity" and dispensing of divine-agent explanations).

[51] E.g., Kahn 1960; Dicks 1959.

[52] De Cesaris 2018, 185–87, discusses some interesting translation issues here. A similar controversy arises for the introduction of a second principle, Mind. Anaxagoras of Clazomenae adopted this view, but it is said that his semi-legendary country-mate Hermotimus of Clazomenae had already done so (Arist. *M.* A 984b18–19). Aristotle does not try to settle the issue, adding only that Hesiod, Parmenides, and Empedocles could be included as adopters (984b23–985a10). The same intra-Clazomenaean confusion arises again when Aristotle observes that people do not know whether Anaxagoras or Hermotimus said "for intellect is the god in us" (*Protrepticus*, in Iambl. *Pro.* 8.48,16). Hermotimus was said to be a pre-incarnation of Pythagoras (DL 8.5); Lucian calls him a Pythagorean (*Encom. musc.* 7; cf. Pliny *HN* 7.42) and names a play after him.

[53] At *Mete.* 347a6–8, Aristotle says that the ancients spoke riddlingly of Ocean; at 353a34–b1 he says that those who spent time in *theologia* considered the origins of the seas and the rivers to be deep under the Earth.

[54] Admittedly, Aristotle has limited information about Thales's views of water, relying mostly on prior accounts (as seen, e.g., at *Cael.* 294a28–b6); he knows a bit more about

of the sort that Aristotle can take as open to critique, and thus involved, no matter how inchoately (cf. *Soph. el.* 183b29), in the sequence of debates found in the later *philosophoi*, down to his own time and himself.[55] It may be that Aristotle judged Thales "the first ... to break with the tradition of divine genealogies,"[56] and he may have been famous as an exemplary figure for nearly two centuries already,[57] but the important point is that Thales could be taken as saying things that, as sparse as they may have been, could be readily formulated, without allegoresis, as answers to the questions about nature that Aristotle has.[58] In other words, Hippias's *sophos* lineage, on which Aristotle probably draws, is unexceptionable as a list of *sophoi*, but it does not adumbrate a discipline; hermeneutic obstacles leave some members dialectically and conversationally cut off.[59] Aristotle creates the discipline of *philosophia*

Thales's view of souls and god, at *De an.* 405a19 relying on Hippias for Thales's attribution of souls to inanimate objects and at 411a8 quoting Thales's "Everything is full of gods." LM 5.772 argue that Aristotle in fact constructed Thales's views (at least of water) from the doctrines of Hippo, the fifth-century BCE Pythagoreanizing thinker whom Aristotle maligns as not worth considering in his history of *sophoi/philosophoi*, "given the thinness (εὐτέλειαν) of his thinking" (*M. A* 984a4). Someone must have included him in a history of *sophoi*, plausibly Hippias himself (recently, Barney 2012, 87–92, 104). Aristotle elsewhere includes him among the "more superficial" writers (*De an.* 405b2) who "tried to refute" those (including Critias of Athens) who say that soul is blood. Aristotle was not the first to criticize Hippo; the comic playwright Cratinus got there in the late 430s BCE (Cratin. *Panoptai* fr. 167 *PCG* = Hippo A2/ DRAM. T15 + 16a).

[55] Theophrastus appears to have taken a different view: people indeed investigated nature before Thales, but Thales put them all in the shade (Simpl. *In Phys.* 23,21–33). This suggests, incidentally, that when Theophrastus interprets Prometheus's giving fire to humans as his giving them a share in *philosophia* (Σ Ap. Rhod. *Argon.* 2.1248–50; discussion in Fortenbaugh 2014, 150–56), he is making an allegorical rather than a historical claim.

[56] *BNP* s.v. "Thales"; cf. Mansfeld 1985.

[57] Thales is discussed as significant, exemplary, or a first-discoverer by many before Aristotle: Alcaeus (Him. *Or.* 28.2 [= A11a/R5], but see Wöhrle 2014, 273n2, for difficulties), Pherecydes (Arist. *On Poets* fr. 3 Ross [= DL 2.46], *Suda* φ 214.1–9), Xenophanes (DL 1.23, 9.18.11–12), Heraclitus (DL 1.23), Choerilus of Samos (DL 1.24, but see again Wöhrle 2014, 29n1, for difficulties), Democritus (DL 1.22), Herodotus (Hdt. 1.74, 1.75, 2.20 [apparently including him among "some Greeks wishing to become distinguished by their *sophia*" (Ἑλλήνων ... τινὲς ἐπίσημοι βουλόμενοι γενέσθαι σοφίην)]), Aristophanes (*Nub.* 180; *Av.* 1009), Plato (*Tht.* 174a4–b6 [cf. *Phdr.* 249d7–8]; *Prt.* 342e4; *Hip. mai.* 281c5; *R.* 600a4–7; *Ep.* II.311a1–7), Andron (Clem. *Strom.* 1.21.129.3–4), and Eudoxus of Cnidus (DL 1.29).

[58] For related views, see Mogyoródi 2000, 339–41; Palmer 2000, 184–91, 202; Leszl 2006b; Barney 2012. For a contrasting view, see Finkelberg 2017, 10–12.

[59] Aristotle probably drew on Hippias's work for his (lost) *Sophist*, which word he and Hippias sometimes use for *sophos*. After all, it is in that work that Aristotle is said to have called Zeno and Empedocles inventors of dialectic and rhetoric. Other commentators (e.g., Jaeger 1962, 30–31; cf. Chroust 1973a, 2.24–25) have assumed that this work imitated Plato's *Sophist*, which, as we have seen, also includes a list of *sophoi* (Pl. *Soph.* 242c–244b; we have seen that this list may itself benefit from Hippias's work), but there is no evidence that Aristotle has here written about not-being or the sophist *qua* dissembler—maybe he has simply updated Hippias's work.

by seeing with whom he can fruitfully engage. He entered a preexisting debate about the origins of *phusiologia* and provided a new criterion for settling the question about *philosophia*.

One group with whom we know he could fruitfully engage were the "so-called Pythagoreans" (οἱ καλούμενοι Πυθαγόρειοι, Arist. *M.* A 985b23); he dedicates to critical interpretation of them many chapters in the *Metaphysics* (including, in Book A, 989b29–990a35). Aristotle refers specifically to their view as a *philosophia* and locates it with those of Xenophanes, Melissus, Parmenides, and Alcmaeon in the "Italian *philosophia*" (A 987a31).[60] They stand apart from the materialist *phusiologoi*, having made their principles and elements "more subtle" (ἐκτοπωτέροις)—that is, immaterial (A 989b30).[61] Aristotle gives them a mixed review, applauding their endeavor to define the "what is" (τί ἐστιν), but critiquing the result as too simple (λίαν δ᾽ ἁπλῶς) and superficial (ἐπιπολαίως). Like everyone at their time, they lacked dialectic, which may have begun with Zeno and Socrates but came into its own with Plato's "investigations into the types of arguments" (A 987b32). Elsewhere Aristotle attributes to Pythagoras all kinds of miracle-mongering.[62] Still, he never treats the Pythagoreans as anything less than as *philosophoi*.

Throughout *Metaphysics* A, Aristotle emphasizes the capacity and distinctiveness of the practice designated by *philosophia*. Functionally speaking, Aristotle notes at the volume's beginning, *philosophia* involves investigating reality; but phenomenologically speaking, it means experiencing wonder and seeking explanation (*M.* A 982b11–22).[63] Some instances of wonder are experienced only by specialists; these *aporiai* motivate Aristotle's more abstruse discussions. But close-to-hand wonders (τὰ πρόχειρα τῶν ἀπόρων, A 982b13–14) count, too: "the *philosophos* is somehow a myth-lover too" (καὶ φιλόμυθος ὁ φιλόσοφός πως ἐστιν, A 982b18–19).[64] At the volume's end, Aristotle evaluates the practitioners of *philosophia* whose work he has summarized. "All

---

[60] Aristotle reports that Parmenides may have been the student of Xenophanes (*M.* A 986b21); Xenophanes and Melissus were a bit unrefined (μικρὸν ἀγροικότεροι) in their views, and Parmenides seems to speak having somehow seen better (μᾶλλον βλέπων ἔοικέ που λέγειν, 986b18–28). On the fourth-century BCE reception of Xenophanes, see Mansfeld 1987; Palmer 1998 and 2000, 182–87.

[61] They were the first to take up mathematics, whence they decided to set numbers as first principles (Arist. *M.* A 985b23–986a2).

[62] See his *On the Pythagoreans* frr. 1–3 Ross; Philip 1963.

[63] In a lost work, Aristotle imagined subterranean men seeing the earth, sea, and sky for the first time, and, presumably awed by them, inferred their divine origins (already being primed to believe in a divine agent): Cic. *Nat. D.* 2.37.95–96. On wonder in Aristotle, see Gadamer 1982, 143–45; Nightingale 2004, 228–29, 253–68.

[64] For discussion, including of the uncertain text of this passage, see Broadie 2012, 62–67. Aristotle's examples of such wonders are puppets, incommensurable diagonals, and solstices.

seem to search out (ζητεῖν) causes, the ones spoken of in the *Physics*," and while in one way they have talked about those causes, in another way they have not, speaking "too vaguely" (ἀμυδρῶς). "The earliest *philosophia* seems to have spoken falteringly (ψελλιζομένη) regarding everything" (A 993a11–16).[65] While vagueness and inarticulacy hinders conversational fluency, it does not foreclose discussion.

Aristotle's Historiographical Theory

We just pieced together Aristotle's disciplinary vision from offhand comments, and found that he includes in *philosophia* all those whose views about fundamental explanation he can interrogate, reconstruct, and critique. We can also see that he believes that *philosophoi* improved in articulacy and self-consciousness over time. We turn now to Aristotle's explicit remarks about the history of *philosophia*.

He provides them in a short volume written independently of *Metaphysics* A and now collated as *Metaphysics* α.[66] There he states quite directly that philosophy is the study of truth (ἡ περὶ τῆς ἀληθείας θεωρία, *M.* α 993a35). Nobody can be self-sufficient in the work of studying the truth, but neither can anybody altogether fail. Each person says *something* about nature (λέγειν τι περὶ τῆς φύσεως, α 993b1), and while each contribution on its own counts for little or nothing, together they can be martialed into something great (συναθροιζομένων . . . τι μέγεθος, α 993b3).[67] Therefore, *philosophia* is necessarily a group endeavor, and the numbers that are needed exceed those who are alive in a single generation.

Aristotle has not yet explained the nature of this group endeavor, and thus has not yet shown how *philosophia* is a discipline. Nor has he described how to think about the members of the group he judges vague or confused. To social attitudes he now turns. We should be grateful (χάριν ἔχειν) to those with whom we share opinions (τις κοινώσαιτο ταῖς δόξαις) but also to those with superficial opinions (τοῖς ἐπιπολαιότερον). The latter have just as much contributed to the group endeavor, having prepared our habits of thinking (ἕξιν προήσκησαν) (*M.* α 993b12–14). In the art world, Phrynis allowed Timotheus

---

[65] Aristotle uses the same verb to describe Empedocles's inarticulate idea of the efficient cause (*M.* A 985a6).

[66] See Menn unpublished, §1a5, 38–45, for this work's authenticity and source.

[67] The verb συναθροίζω often refers to the assembling of (otherwise scattered) soldiers (Xen. *An.* 7.2.8; similarly horsemen at 6.5.30), where only when they work together do they have effect, or of naval vessels of (otherwise far-flung) allies (Lys. 2.34), or the military forces of (otherwise geographically dispersed) Greeks and barbarians (Pl. *Menex.* 243b); but it may also have been used in the festival analogy of Iambl. *VP* 12; see chapter 4, p. 118.

to make the music we enjoy.[68] Just so, among those concerned with truth, some give us opinions (παρειλήφαμέν τινας δόξας, α 993b18) that we can use, and others have enabled them to do so. As Aristotle explains it, *philosophia* is a discipline when we "share opinions." Sharing opinions does not mean that everybody accepts the same views; it means having a common set of opinions which we can explore and about which we can debate. This is how we investigate nature: by creating, articulating, testing, and revising our ideas in concert with others.[69] This we see at a length of hundreds of pages in the *Metaphysics*. Obviously we can share opinions with people living or dead; Aristotle shares maximally with Empedocles, the Pythagoreans, and Plato. There are some people with whom we hardly share opinions. Aristotle may be thinking of Xenophanes and Hippo, both of whom he cites as having superficial thoughts, but perhaps also of Thales, whose views scarcely remain. Yet it would be obtuse to exclude them from the discipline. So Aristotle relativizes the sharing of opinions. Xenophanes shared opinions with Parmenides; Hippo may have shared opinions with Empedocles or some other Pythagoreans. Opinion-sharing lacks transitivity; but disciplinarity does not. The discipline is the ongoing joint effort of retrospective and contemporary conversation with those others who are taken to participate in the same project. It advances like a rope, twined from short filaments, few of which go the entire length, its strength varying with the density of connections between those strands. A consequence of this view is that there need be no absolute starting point for philosophy.[70] But the starting point, such as it is, will certainly be frayed. The further back in time one goes, those thinking about nature will not know with whom they share (relevant) opinions. The term *philosophia* provides a sightline along which to braid its constituting strands.

Aristotle helped articulate not only *philosophia* as a discipline but also dialectic and rhetoric, among other fields.[71] He did so in the same way. He observes that the originators of dialectic advanced only a little, and now progress has been made bit by bit, and the art has been enlarged; it now has a magnitude

---

[68] Aristotle speaks about the importance of Timotheus again in *PVindob.* G26008, fr. A 27, on which fragment see Janko 1987, 62, 191; Most 1992; Megino Rodriguéz 2008.

[69] Barney 2012, 185–88, calls this "clarification dialectic."

[70] There need be no conclusion to it either, but disciplines can come to an end, as wagon-construction did with the advent of the motorcar. Possibly Aristotle mistakenly predicted the imminent end of his discipline: "And so Aristotle in upbraiding the philosophers of old for thinking, according to him, that thanks to their genius philosophy had reached perfection, says that they have been guilty of extreme folly or boastfulness; all the same he adds that he saw that, as a consequence of the great advance made in few years, philosophy would be absolutely complete" (Cic. *Tusc.* 3.28.69, trans. King). I note that Aristotle here retrojects his disciplinary attitude onto his forebears.

[71] For Aristotle's disciplinary articulation of physics, for example, see Hussey 2012, esp. 18.

(Arist. *Soph. el.* 184b27). Cicero observes that Aristotle collected all the ancient writers on the *rhetorikê technê*, from its inventor Tisias down to his time, and summarized each practitioner's precepts or maxims, which took much interpretative effort and acumen, with the goal of understanding each person's method (Cic. *Inv. rhet.* 2.2.6–7). Naturally, we might subsume all this to Aristotle's dialectical method, his saving of the appearances, appealing to the views of the *sophoi* on any particular question.[72] This is not, however, an argument against his disciplinary approach. Disciplines comprise the *sophoi* whose appearances one saves.

Conclusion: The Academy and Retrospective Self-Constitution of Disciplines

Plato and his contemporaries ended up preserving the word *philosophia* for posterity. Isocrates's tuition-payers learned *philosophia*, Plato's research fellows studied *philosophia*, the first-generation fringe Socratics and friends spent their time talking *philosophia*. Thus *philosophia* grew up on a matrix of quasi-formal pedagogical, reflective, and social institutions. It could be sought out by name, association, or habitual location. But it needed a history before it could qualify as a discipline.

Disciplines have both practitioners and names, as the Hippocratic author of *On Ancient Medicine* boasts for medicine.[73] The names *philosophoi* and *philosophia* do not at first refer to certain people defined by their participation in a discipline or to a discipline as such. But gradually they do so increasingly refer, as people so named, or using that name, grow conscious of others as similarly so named, and come to see themselves as defined, or defining others, by the norms productive of that shared naming. A name shifts from being a label—a semantically vacuous slander or praise—to a description of a potentially idiosyncratic way of life and then to a description of a membership in an enterprise coordinated by continuous reference to the name itself.

That philosophy needs a history of its discipline to become a discipline may not drive us into paradox. Still, it may sound implausible, judging from parallel disciplines. Take the disciplines of mythography, poetics, historiography,

---

[72] Descriptions of dialectical method: Arist. *Top.* 100b21–23, 101a36–b4, 104a8–15, 105a34–b18; arbitrating among conflicting opinions, *M.* B 995a24–b4; *Cael.* 279b7–12; *Phys.* 206a12–14.

[73] Hippoc. *VM* 5.1–2. Cf. Schiappa 1999, 23–28, who argues the point for rhetoric.

rhetoric, or philology.[74] All arose in the fifth and fourth centuries BCE, and all arose thanks to overlapping forces: centralization of cultural activity, inflation of the value of speechmaking in democratic and diplomatic debate, and anxieties about Panhellenic anomie in the face of Persian meddling. They became disciplines in the same way: by using a word in a new way, they isolated chunks of embedded speech, turning them into discrete objects demanding autonomous analysis. Thus the practices and structures constituting *poiêtikê technê* formed around the word *poiêmata* and the flat linguistic data it extracted from festival performances or sympotic revelries, as most vividly depicted by Andrew Ford (2002). Mythography required consciousness of *muthoi*, of there being such a thing as "myth" to describe, collate, rectify, allegorize, or whatever. Likewise historiography, with *historiai*, "histories"; rhetoric, with oratory; and philology, with texts and editions. In each case, the word jostles what had been unconscious acceptance of the variety and just-so-ness of experience into a closer scrutiny, and that scrutiny gives rise to the discipline. In previous chapters I have shown how the name *philosophos* functioned in the rise of the discipline, and the rise of other disciplines lends plausibility to that demonstration. We can add that these other disciplines require acknowledged practitioners and a vocabulary or a set of practices.[75] Rhetoric speaks of "proem" and "counter-refutation." Philology uses "commentary" and "obelizing." It might not seem, however, that any discipline requires for its disciplinarity that it have a conception of its own history or details of the intentions and habits of its practitioners at its various stages of development. Yet each discipline does need predecessors, to build up the library of texts, the list of diacritical marks, the corpus of local chronicles, and to have started dicing the world into the linguistic units that absorb its attention. It may seem that once the discipline has its material to work on, such as poems, myths, speeches, historical records, or editions of Homer, and the skills to work on that material, it can cut loose from its past. But this is not so. The materials and the skills never achieve final or objective form; their identity and nature require continued reestablishment, and that reestablishment requires attention to their original establishment and all subsequent efforts. Deciding what counts as Homer's poems requires thinking through the decisions of one's predecessors in poetry analysis. So, while these disciplines attend to linguistic objects apparently external to the discipline, that externality is an illusion; those objects are continually objectified by the discipline itself.

---

[74] Mythography: Fowler 2011; Martin 2012; poetics: Ford 2002; historiography: Lloyd 2009, 58–70; rhetoric: Cole 1991; Schiappa 1999; Timmerman and Schiappa 2010; Enos 2012; Bod 2013, 58–62; philology: Pfeiffer 1968; Turner 2014, 5–14.

[75] See Bromberg 2012 with bibliography.

The historical obligation seen in the non-philosophical disciplines binds philosophy even tighter to its unique shape. This is because philosophy, as it matured into a discipline, found that it does not really work on objects even apparently external to its disciplinary practice, like the Homeridae's bardic performances or Ionian stories about Zeus.[76] It is registered in something rather more internal: the practices of philosophers themselves.[77] The linguistic objects sliced from the world and laid on the *philosophos*'s specimen slide are the arguments, claims, performances, attitudes, or ideals of other *philosophoi*. These words, actions, and norms may of course be taken to refer to something in the world, or even to the whole world itself; they may be taken to manifest patterns of reasoning or ideational constructs; and they may be practical or theoretical. But as the observable or inferable material, only the *philosophos*'s work undergoes philosophical analysis.

As it turns out, the philosopher does sometimes study the world itself, as the philologist of Homer sometimes studies Aegean trade routes or the poetry analyst sometimes studies the dances of Asia Minor. But when a student of the world, the philosopher is doing astronomy or physics, not philosophy per se; the student of Aegean trade routes is doing maritime geography, not Homeric analysis per se; and the student of Persian dances is doing comparative choreography, not poetry per se. When philosophers take what other philosophers say as their point of focus, those words constitute their exclusive concern, as we see from parallels with other fields. The poetry analyst cares for more than her predecessors' categories and analyses of poetry; she also cares for the poems she studies: what they are about, what their composition means, what their qualities and effects are. So too the philosopher cares about the truth of philosophical statements, the assumptions they rely on, and their power in relieving philosophical confusions. But these concerns operate through an unmitigated attention to philosophical speech and work. Hence the necessity of philosophy's *history* to its being a discipline, for that history records what has counted as philosophy and provides the material on which to train its ongoing attention, even as such attention is conditioned by contemporary observations and novel considerations. Without history, only a tiny contemporary slice of philosophy would command a philosopher's involvement, and she could

---

[76] Aristotle says that philosophy differs from all other *technai* in needing for its work "neither tools nor places" (in Iambl. *DCMS* 26.82,27–28); though this makes a distinct point, it is on the right pathway.

[77] This work can remain accessible to and directed toward non-philosophers if those philosophical practices to which philosophers respond diverge relatively little from quotidian practices; but in time that work may become wholly esoteric and unfamiliar; on this shift in ancient Greek philosophy, see Most 1999, 336. For the historical nature of philosophy considered from a more recent perspective, see Godlovich 2000, esp. 14–18.

as much be called someone who is interested in philosophy as would be an analyst of poetry who cared only about those poems published in the most recent journals. And perhaps neither the poet nor the philosopher can see what counts as poetic or philosophical writing without a deep corpus of material against which to judge cases. The analyst of poetry, without a historical sensibility, would instead be a pundit about contemporary literary events. So too philosophy, seen as a discipline, needs a sweeping view of the temporally expansive realm of philosophical activity.

Above, I offered an analogy between philosophy and poetics in support of the claim that philosophy needs its history to be a discipline. We might now assess a potential disanalogy. Poetics and mythography are taken to analyze the productions of others; they feed those objects through their examining machines. Philosophy, by contrast, seems not simply to analyze or receive; it also creates and sends out. Perhaps it may seem to do this principally. This is a view common enough to those contemporary philosophers who take themselves to be spending their philosophical time applying brute mental force to puzzles and problems. This view depends on two mistakes. First, those other disciplines may also seem, to some of their practitioners, primarily creative: the writing of histories, the creation of generic taxonomies, and the memorizing and performance of speeches. That creative side does not subordinate the analytic reception of "poems" and "histories" and "oratory" to pre-disciplinary raw material. Those disciplines are still constituted by those activities, even if not wholly. Second, the philosophers who take themselves to have a purely present-tense or prospective orientation forget that the puzzles they address have been articulated, prompted, or revealed in prior philosophical work that they take to be philosophical, and that they write for an ongoing discussion that makes sense only as an historical phenomenon. Their history may not go deep, but a wade or a swim makes for as much a historical orientation as a dive. The prominence of philosophical successions shows this. Philosophy is unavoidably critical; material to critique requires recognizing others besides oneself to be philosophers; and this is what the historical consciousness raised by a history of philosophy allows.

So, a discipline requires an historical consciousness and what I called "conversationality" in chapter 8: an engagement among members of the discipline. This suggests a sort of institutional theory of the disciplines (on the model of the institutional theory of art), in which membership depends on the judgment of its members, perhaps after the fact, and open to revision. Such a theory allows the possibility of "outside philosophers," those never or not for a long time recognized as philosophers; irrespective of the ingenuity or rigor of their thought, they do not become "philosophers" until those in the discipline acknowledge them as such. (Refusal to acknowledge those who ought to be acknowledged will be a disciplinary failure, of inconsistency or of irrationality.) But only time and goodwill can force that acknowledgment; there are no objective, ahistorical internal criteria of membership. What contingent, historical criteria there are, and to what use one might put earlier or other members of the discipline, remain the most heated matters of dispute through the history of philosophy.[78]

It is worth admitting that "discipline" does not translate a Greek word, but I do not claim that Aristotle had a conception of a "discipline," only that we find in Aristotle a conception of philosophy contiguous with our own disciplinary conception. The closest term might be *epistêmê*, which by Aristotle's time could mean "science" in the way we mean it, as a constellation of interrelated research questions along with lines and methods of investigation. Aristotle does think of *philosophia* as an *epistêmê*. But he does so from considerations of the knowability of its principles, and thus from the epistemological status of its argumentative outputs, for which he argues. Our notion of "discipline" may not entail any such epistemological commitments; it exists somewhere between an *epistêmê* ("knowledge"), *epitêdeuma* ("pursuit"), *technê* ("technical skill"), *askêsis* ("effortful exercise"), *paideia* or *paideusis* ("educational program"), *diatribê* ("pastime"), *praxis* ("practice"), and *sunousia* ("association").

One thing that our term "discipline" does importantly entail, however, is the existence of disciples. Disciplines allow no untutored geniuses, only tutored genius. Fine art is not a discipline, but art theory and academic art are. Disciples acquire the accoutrements of a discipline: in the case of the learned disciplines, they get introduced through time into the canon, questions, methods, and other historically assembled norms, taking what their teachers and teachers' teachers do as normative for themselves. This rigorous "discipline" involves learning things that at the moment may not seem practical or personally salient (e.g., extensive footnoting) but end up coloring perception, valuation, and activity. Schools or departments institutionalize the discipline, assigning mentors for the efficient induction of students into its deep and recent past. Competition among schools within a discipline is not necessary for a discipline,[79] but results from the institutionalization of the discipline and the situation that certain disciplinary topics thus far fail to receive consensus. Thus in mathematics nowadays (I suppose) there is less inter-school conflict, but even so, there is conflict about what to focus on.

---

[78] See Catana 2016 for bibliography concerning analytical philosophy's puzzlement about the history of philosophy.

[79] On the historical fact and productivity of such competition, see Collins 2000.

This chapter has argued that the discipline of philosophy depends on its own history; its evidence is the history of its historiography. I have tracked the changing characterizations by several intellectuals of the relationship among those who were eventually canonized as philosophers constituting the discipline of philosophy. The earliest figures present fellow thinkers in competition, lineages of similarity, and synchronic conversation. But none of these presentations is historical in the requisite way. Only with Aristotle do we come to see philosophy treated as a web of diachronic conversations; treating it this way requires a historical sensibility, and is what finally constitutes philosophy as a discipline.

Ambivalence about *Philosophia* beyond the Discipline

The Evidence of Heraclides's Protreptic Story

This book has followed the discipline called *philosophia* from its obscure head-waters at the end of the sixth century BCE, through its backwaters and eddies in the fifth century BCE, until the construction of the waterworks of the fourth-century BCE schools. As this concluding chapter will show, however, Plato and his intellectual peers channeled only some of the current; much remained to water broader fields. The disciplinary sense of *philosophia* established itself, and provided our modern word "philosophy," by concentrating one use of *philosophia*. But the common use, too, lived on, in both the way familiar from the earliest history of the term and in a relatively more laudable inflection familiar from at least the time of Lysias at the start of the fourth century BCE. This book's previous chapters have charted the relations between the proto-disciplinary and the proto-common uses of the term *philosophia*. In the fourth century BCE, as the disciplinary form grows increasingly robust and responsive to intradisciplinary discussion, those relations attenuate. They do not, however, disappear altogether. Aspects of the discipline of *philosophia*, its practice, and its self-understanding continue to depend on popular beliefs about *philosophia*.

We may see those dependence relations in a variety of contexts—a complete study of *philosophia* in the fourth century BCE, which this book cannot provide, would make them especially clear. Heraclides's *On Diseases* (mid-350s BCE), as a protreptic to *philosophia* told through the history of its term and practice, allows one vantage point. At both disciplinary and general cultural levels, the idea of being *philosophos* has finally had its day: many people finally approve of being *philosophos* or seek to become *philosophos*. Hence the reasonableness of Heraclides's writing the dialogue—not only would he seem to believe the core of what he wrote to be true; he would seem to believe that people outside the discipline could contemplate themselves joining the discipline of *philosophia*. But that the dialogue is a protreptic at all, not simply an engagement in theoretical contemplation (or whatever) *in medias res*, shows that not all people are turned toward the discipline. There must still have been considerable resistance to *philosophia*. Hence the motivation for Heraclides's writing the dialogue—he seems to believe that people were not yet totally sympathetic to the idea of *philosophia*. The remainder of this chapter will describe some of the ongoing cultural ambivalence about *philosophia* that is necessary for Heraclides's protreptic, an ambivalence best understood, even if only incompletely, by the kind of account of the term *philosophia*'s origin that the previous nine chapters have provided.

Those chapters have helped us to see something about Heraclides's protreptic besides the cultural ambivalence necessary for its construction and promulgation. His version of the Pythagoras story, which we see well in Cicero, excerpted in Iamblichus, and compressed and reconfigured in Sosicrates, depends on two fourth-century BCE innovations in thinking about *philosophia*. The first is best seen in Plato, even if the tradition precedes it: the reconstructive etymology of the word *philosophos*. The second is best seen in Aristotle, even if again the tradition precedes it: a historical consciousness of a discipline. By contrast, the non-Heraclidean version, on view in Diodorus and in Diogenes Laertius's preface, relies on related but distinct and probably earlier innovations. The first, well-known from Hippias, is the historical consciousness not of a discipline of *philosophia* but of lineages of *sophoi*. The second, well-known from Pindar, is the conception of a *sophos* such that the word *philosophos* would be coined in relation to it.

Both Pythagoras stories are protreptic, albeit in different ways. Heraclides points to Pythagoras and Empedocles, along with their respective interests, observation of and reflection on the *kosmos*, and their respective accomplishments, foreseeing and healing human disease. The other authors of the Pythagoras stories point to the legendary *sophoi*, and their respective functions, solving major human problems, and their respective characters, as akin to the gods as is possible. These differences speak, without doubt, to important variety in the proclivities and assumptions in Greek intellectual and para-intellectual culture. Yet here their similarities matter more than the differences. The stories speak equally to Pythagoras's position in accommodating the term *philosophos* and the redemption of the identity, practice, or (eventually) discipline from an image of idleness, uselessness, quietism, or vulgarity. They do not themselves establish the practical or institutional norms for the pursuit of *philosophia*, but they make pursuing a familiarity with *philosophia* seem reasonable enough, even admirable.

What protreptics do is turn people toward activities they are not currently engaged in but about which they already have, to some extent, some positive feeling. They respond to the cultural ambivalence that is instantiated in a person.

Audience members of protreptics—neither committed acolytes nor self-satisfied philistines—need to be made to feel better about making an aspirational commitment to philosophy.[1] Any discipline-governed person, who foregoes familiar desire-satisfactions for long-term self-modification and investigation, looks silly to onlookers, who cannot run the cost-benefit analysis that would vindicate what otherwise appears to be mindless repetition, wishful thinking, or the refusal of publically acceptable norms. Protreptics attempt to vindicate an obtuse-seeming practice. They appeal to aims that a person already has, trying to show that adopting the norms of some discipline, no matter how bizarre, annoying, or counterproductive they may seem, will in fact help that person to achieve those standing goals. They are not mere instances of persuasion, which urge a one-off decision. They urge a continuous flow of decisions, to act in ways that will eventually create new and as-yet-unseen norms for action. Protreptics to *philosophia* work if a person already has reasons to accept some value of *philosophia*, but are otiose if that person already accepts all the value.

Philosophia is the consummate protreptic-demanding discipline. It has very little obvious value, given its similarity to daydreaming or captiousness; yet it has as its goal the most widely admired state, personal and/or civic flourishing, during or after death. It already proceeds in the register of persuasive speech, so that its prosecution will be contiguous with its promotion; and the wholehearted orientation toward a new constellation of values that protreptic aims to effect is much the same as the very goal of *philosophia* itself, so that its promotion will be coextensive with its prosecution.[2]

This chapter sketches a few points in the topology of fourth-century BCE talk of *philosophia*. I begin with the highest, the ascendency of *philosophos* to the commonplace Greek ethic as articulated across the Hellenic world. Then I focus on the shallow, the relentless merrymaking about *philosophoi* in Athenian comedy of the later fourth century BCE. A particular cut through this shallow is explicit apotreptic to *philosophia*, speeches persuading people to turn away from it despite their inclinations to give it a try; such apotreptics get preserved or recreated in a range of fourth-century BCE philosophical texts, and I give close attention to one from a recently published Oxyrhynchus papyrus. Against the bivalent background of universal esteem for being *philosophos* and the persistent bemusement at the same, we can see two alternatives to Heraclides's protreptic. The first, from Aristotle's *Protrepticus*, is a totalizing protreptic to *philosophia* in the "self-contradiction" genre; it works only if the term *philosophia* has a positive mundane sense and an unpleasant intensive sense. The second,

---

[1] On the conditions for aspiration, see Callard 2018, especially 1–36.
[2] See Moore 2012 for an argument to this effect.

from the Platonic *Rival Lovers*, is an aporetic protreptic in the Socratic genre; here, enthusiasm about *philosophia* proves sometimes to be deeply misunderstood, but worth trying to get right. The epilogue to the book wonders at the relevance of the history of *philosophia* to the present-day practice of philosophy.

The Universal Success of the Term *Philosophos*: From Delphi to Bactria

The success of the word *philosophos* in the fourth century BCE has its clearest evidence in a stunning archaeological discovery in the 1960s, one that indicated, unbeknownst at the time, the existence of the maxim *philosophos ginou* ("be philosophical!") at Delphi by the late fourth century BCE. This proves that *philosophos* could have a completely positive and universal sense—indeed, a practically anodyne and commonsensical one—not so long after almost the opposite was true, and it can mean this at exactly the same time that, for Aristotle, being *philosophos* could mean doing the abstrusest metaphysics. It provides the clearest evidence for a complex and pluralistic history of the term, since in its anodyne sense it has nothing of the fourth-century BCE (Platonic) disciplinary notion and can hardly be thought to mean "be a lover of wisdom"; it probably means, novelly, "think before you act."

On October 22, 1966, a French archaeological team had been digging for two years at Ai Khanoum, at the confluence of the Oxus and Kokcha rivers in northeastern Afghanistan. Twenty-three hundred years earlier, this point in Bactria marked the extreme eastern edge of the Seleucid empire, one of the four kingdoms established after the death of Alexander the Great. Its king, Antiochus I, established here a garrison and a trading outpost in lapis lazuli.[3] The archaeologists were unearthing the entrance to the town's *heroön*, a structure that celebrates the city's founder. They found, turned against a wall and repurposed as a post-stand, a two-foot-long limestone block. On the upper third of its face were two inscriptions. On the left they read a four-line epigram:

These wise sayings of legendary men
    are set up in most holy Pytho–
Clearchus, having transcribed them there with care,
    places them here, conspicuous, in Cineas's *temenos*.[4]

[3] For its history, see Mairs 2014b, 57–101; it came to be rediscovered in the nineteenth and twentieth centuries: Morgan 2015.

[4] ἀνδρῶν τοι σοφὰ ταῦτα παλαιοτέρων ἀνάκει[τα]ι | ῥήματα ἀριγνώτων Πυθοὶ ἐν ἠγαθέαι· | ἔνθεν ταῦτ[α] Κλέαρχος ἐπιφραδέως ἀναγράψας | εἴσατο τηλαυγῆ Κινέου ἐν τεμένει.

The inscription refers to the Sage maxims found at the entrance to the Temple of Delphi in Apollo, "Pytho," the Panhellenic navel of the Greek world. A man named Clearchus claims to have copied them at their source, three thousand miles to the west, and to have brought them to adorn the burial chamber of Cineas. He does so to mark Cineas's establishment of this place, eventually called Ai Khanoum. On the right the archaeologists read five more lines:

As a child, be orderly
A youth, self-controlled
An adult, just
Older yet, a good counselor
And dying, without pain.[5]

These five lines have an evident connection with the four to their left. They epitomize Sage wisdom, universal commonsense imperatives concerned for the good, successful, and fitting life. The epigrapher Louis Robert (1904–85) recognized this linked set of Sage maxims from Greek literature.[6] In the florilegium of Stobaeus, in the section called *On Virtue*, there is a work by Demetrius of Phalerum, the late fourth-century BCE Athenian politician, Peripatetic, and inspiration for the Alexandrian library. That work apportioned one hundred twenty-five pieces of Sage wisdom among the Seven Sages.[7] After Demetrius's work, Stobaeus inserts a work by the otherwise unknown Sosiades. This "Advice of the Seven" collates its one hundred forty-seven pieces of wisdom into a single list.[8] The five maxims from Ai Khanoum are found in almost identical form as the five final maxims of Sosiades's list.[9] The physical evidence suggested to Robert that the block with the two inscriptions served as a base for a stele and that this stele contained all the Sage maxims found in Sosiades's list. This stele would reproduce those maxims in three columns, each forty-seven and forty-eight maxims long, with the last five, which are the only linked set, overflowing or pushed down onto the base.

Clearchus's display at Cineas's *heroön* of these maxims and his authorizing remarks about that display would advance Ai Khanoum's civic self-constitution in a range of ways. Clearchus's trek would connect the far-flung Bactrian pe-

---

[5] παῖς ὤν κόσμιος γίνου | ἡβῶν ἐγκρατής | μέσος δίκαιος | πρεσβύτης εὔβουλος | τελευτῶν ἄλυπος.

[6] Robert 1968.

[7] Stob. 3.1.172 (apportioned into groups of 21, 20, 19, 20, 12, 17, 16). DL 5.80–81 does not include this among Demetrius's list of works.

[8] Stob. 3.1.173.

[9] There are two differences: in Sosiades, the first line ends with ἴσθι, an alternative form of "be," and the fourth line ends with εὔλογος, an alternative form of "(a) reasonable (person)."

riphery with its Aegean center by a palpable image. That attenuated geographical link between desert highland and pelagic homeland would be strengthened by a normative and intellectual thread: "what the Greeks do there we do here." The inscriptions would help ensuing generations of settlers in this marginal entrepôt preserve or reclaim a Greek national identity, a shared conception of the good.[10] A more complete and contemporaneous stele, though baseless, was found in 1906 in Mysian Cyzicus, east of the Hellespont.[11] Both panels of maxims express a near-universal expansion of Greek sensibility coordinate with the near-universal expansion of Greek political rule.

But Robert's hypothesis of a list of 147 maxims in Ai Khanoum would be insecure were it to depend solely on evidence from the base. Fortunately, the French archaeologists found, a meter away from the rear-turned block, what must be the lower-left corner of its supported stele.[12] The start of two lines could be discerned:

E]
ΦΙΛΟΣΟΦ]

Remarkably, items forty-seven and forty-eight on Sosiades's list are:

ΕΥΛΟΓΕΙ ΠΑΝΤΑΣ   speak well of all
ΦΙΛΟΣΟΦΟΣ ΓΙΝΟΥ   *be philosophical*

No other recorded Sage maxim matches φιλόσοφ], and, if Sosiades's list were divided into thirds, the first (left-hand) column would end just at φιλόσοφος γίνου.[13] Thus this corner-piece confirms Robert's theory.[14]

---

[10] On the inscriptions implying a Delphic or non-Seleucid foundation for Ai Khanoum, see Kosmin 2014, 237–38; Mairs 2014a. On their preserving or instilling Greek identity and morality, see Bernard 1967, 89; Institut Fernand-Courby 1971, 183–85 (n. 37); Posch 1995, 29–31; Martinez-Sève 2014.

[11] Hasluck 1907, 62–63; Hense 1907, 765; Mendel 1909, 402–4; Dittenberger 1915, 3 §1268.

[12] This is Kabul Museum object 05.42.190; photograph in Cambon 2006.

[13] The only other *phil-* prefixed maxim on Sosiades's list is φιλοφρόνει πᾶσιν, "be courteous to all."

[14] Canali de Rossi 2004, 225 (n. 383), mistakenly saw a circular letter above the E, which he took to mean that the previous line could not be Sosiades's ΔΟΛΟΝ ΦΟΒΟΥ, thus undermining Robert's theory. But the mark he thought he saw was too far to the left to be part of a letter; it must have been a blemish in the stone badly represented in and then misinterpreted from Robert's published photograph (and perhaps the paper cast at the Fonds Louis Robert at the Institute of France); see Rougemont 2012, 201. The stele corner did not return to public display until 2006, for Europeans in the exhibit *Afghanistan, Les Trésors retrouvés*, organized by the Musée Guimet. These two pieces from Ai Khanoum, owned by the National Museum of Afghanistan,

For Robert, the maxim *philosophos ginou* ("be philosophical") identified the Ai Khanoum sayings with those of Sosiades and furnished him with an argument about Hellenistic culture. For us, it furnishes the sole instance of this maxim on stone, visible to all those who might turn their eyes toward it. Already the citation in Stobaeus was essentially the lone extant instance of the maxim from the entirety of the pre-modern Greek world, a citation, I might note, that has received almost no scholarly attention over its millennium and a half of availability.[15] But an inscription, in contrast to a compilation in a multivolume anthology, gives us a date of promulgation, a place and context of its use, and a hint that it had more than catalogical interest. The inscription charges anybody and everybody in this sun-parched hinterland, at the extreme eastern reaches of an eastern kingdom, to "be philosophical." So, not only does the panel in Ai Khanoum tell its reader, in absolutely the most general terms, what to do in the five stages of life, and to "follow god" (ἕπου θεῷ), "obey the law" (νόμῳ πείθου), and "respect your parents" (γονεῖς αἰδοῦ)—maxims 1, 2, and 4 on Sosiades's list—but also to "be philosophical."[16] "Be[ing] philosophical" is treated as on a par with one's basic religious, political, and domestic duties.

Settlers in faraway Bactria received such instruction. So did others. The monument to Cineas discharges its function only in replicating other distant monuments. The base found at the *heroön* claims for itself the status of verified facsimile, pointing west to its original, a panel at famous Delphi.[17] This means that a stele with identical contents stood there.[18] This in turn means that the great many Greeks who traveled to Delphi by the end of the fourth century BCE could themselves be charged to "be philosophical." And if Clearchus provided a facsimile of the Delphic maxims to Ai Khanoum, hardly a uniquely situated city, likely so too did others to their own cities.

---

in Kabul, were hidden or lost during the previous decades of war; see Cambon 2006, which supersedes Tissot 2006.

[15] The maxim has been also been found (and reconstructed) in the codex Vratislavensis Rehdigeranus gr. 12, #18 (φιλόσοφος <γίνου>) and the Second Recensio Parisina (φιλό<σοφο>ς γίνου), both published in Tziatzi-Papagianni 1994.

[16] Of all published work on these finds, only Rougement 2012, 201, discusses the meaning of *philosophos ginou*, though only to justify his translation of *pratique la sagesse*. Guarducci 1974 3.78–80 and 1987, 270–71, and Wieshöfer 1996, 112–14, ignore the corner piece on which it was inscribed.

[17] The long maxim list at Miletopolis cited above is missing large portions; and the lists in the gymnasium at Thera (IG XII 3, 1020) and on the now-missing and quite mutilated P. Univ. Athens 2782 are too short even to hint at their complete contents. For the relations between these and later maxim lists, see Oikonomides 1980, 1987; Tziatzi-Papagianni 1994; Tziatzi-Papagianni 1997; Führer 1997; YC 2.42–67; Verhasselt forthcoming, §5.

[18] This fact is already appreciated by Kurke 2011, 109–10.

I conjecture that this would have occurred by the second half of the fourth century BCE, and thus at a time relevant to our story of protreptics to *philosophia* in classical Athens. According to the best dating of the Cineas *heroön*'s construction, the stele in Ai Khanoum would have gone up in 281–61 BCE.[19] A panel in Delphi must then predate this. Louis Robert surmised that this Clearchus was the Peripatetic from Soli, in Cyprus, who lived from the 340s BCE at least till the 270s.[20] That Clearchus cultivated a serious interest in maxims, writing works called *On Proverbs* and *On Riddles*, perhaps specifically those attributed to the Sages, as his *Lives* might suggest. These works probably gave taxonomies of maxims, organized their sources, and assessed their respective purposes.[21] Clearchus also wrote about Indian, Persian, and Jewish philosophical traditions.[22] His dates and passions would therefore support the conjecture that it was he who replicated the Delphic stele in Bactria. External evidence cannot disprove a journey to Bactria; other philosophically minded men traveled broadly in the wake of Alexander's conquests and the diplomacy of the Successors.[23]

The evidence for the chronology of the maxim-inscription at Delphi is inconclusive; the best we can say is that the *gnôthi sauton* was probably first, probably by the early fifth century BCE, and two more, *mêden agan* and *egguê, para d'atê*, by the dramatic date of Plato's *Charmides*, 429 BCE. We know even less about the accretion of Sage maxims from one, to three, to one hundred forty-seven. I suspect that people dedicated individual maxims or lists of maxims at Delphi, which somebody transcribed and consolidated and then perhaps added to from other circulating lists of maxims. This consolidation would explain both the haphazard organization of Sosiades's list and the small patterns

[19] This is the reign of Antiochus I Sotor. The best studies are Lyonnet 2012, 157–58, and Martinez-Sève 2014, which tell against Narain 1974; Narain 1987; and Lerner 2003. The otherwise useful Rougement 2012 gives an earlier date, relying on epigraphy rather than the newest archaeological (especially pottery) evidence.

[20] Ath. 6.235a says that Clearchus studied with Aristotle (though Clearchus may have been too young for this to be possible); Josephus says that he wrote a dialogue *On Sleep* that featured Aristotle as a main character (*Ap.* 1.22). Among those sympathetic to Robert in identifying the Ai Khanoum Clearchus with Clearchus of Soli, see Institut Fernand-Courby 1971, 183–85; Guarducci 1974, 3.78–80, and 1987, 270–71; Burstein 1985, 67; Wieshöfer 1996, 112–14; Holt 1999, 37–47; Merkelbach and Stauber 2004, 6–7; Hiebert and Cambon 2008, 94–96; Taifacos 2008; Bar-Kochva 2010, 41–78; Rougement 2012, 201; Tsitsiridis 2013, 5–8; Verhasselt forthcoming, §5. Fortenbaugh 2014, 206–7, expresses uncertainty.

[21] On such works see Fortenbaugh 2014, 125–26.

[22] On the Jews in particular, see Joseph. *Ap.* 1.176–83 with Bar-Kochva 2010, 40–89; his contemporaries also wrote about Jews, as we see from Theophrastus (Porph. *Abst.* 2.26) and from Megasthenes (Clem. *Strom.* 1.15.72.5).

[23] For example, Dicaearchus (a Peripatetic), Hecataeus of Abdera (a Pyrrhonian?), and Megasthenes (unaligned?).

to be found within it.[24] For example, "follow god" (ἕπου θεῷ) and "revere the gods" (θεοὺς σέβου) are in position 1 and 3. Another version of the *egguê, para d'atê* is "flee pledges" (ἐγγύην φεῦγε, 69).[25] This spate of dedications could reflect pieces of advice that petitioners to Delphi found most helpful and thus valuable, and perhaps paralleling the dedication of body part sculptures at Epidauros celebrating cases of successful healing.[26]

The consolidation of inscriptions of maxims already at Delphi or akin to those dedicated at Delphi would provide an explanation for the position of *philosophos ginou* (48), which is found next to "speak well of all" (47) and "choose holiness" (ὅσια κρῖνε, 49). Because *philosophos ginou* has a relatively early spot on the list, perhaps it was inscribed at Delphi initially in unconsolidated form. Getting to forty-eight dedications might have taken a while. I would think that the dedication of maxims beyond the "big three" postdate 370 BCE and that *philosophos ginou* would not be in the initial spate of secondary maxims. Speaking very approximately, then, I would target the years following 350 as those during which *philosophos ginou* found its way onto Sage lists, and thence onto the Delphic panel. The temple fell to an earthquake in 373, the sanctuary was sacked in the Third Sacred War in 356, and the temple was rebuilt finally in 330. Rebuilding could occasion the reorganization of the maxims and their literary preservation.

What the Delphic *philosophos ginou* shows us is that there was at least a trio of fourth-century BCE senses for the term *philosophos*. There is no reason to think that *philosophos* began with this bland meaning; it does not fit the earliest testimony, lexical parallels, or phenomena of re-semanticizing etymologies in the fourth century BCE. We can see the Delphic sense rather as the result of semantic evolution, much of which we have already traced. It has not been completely traced, to be sure, given the inadequacy of the evidence, given the fact that most early fourth-century BCE uses are (pre-)disciplinary, and given the possibility that the Delphic sense does not have (immediate)

---

[24] Only one maxim in the first eighty-eight is negative, whereas fourteen of the next fifty-four are. Only five of the first ninety-one are in three or more words (excluding three-word maxims with μή), whereas sixteen of the remaining are. The last five maxims form a coherent unit. Susan Prince wonders to me about the consistency of its views on fortune: "acknowledge fortune" (τύχην νόμιζε, 68); "do not trust in fortune" (τύχη μὴ πίστευε, 143); "love fortune" (τύχην στέργε, 77)—and about its cowardly or mercantile ethics: "fear power" (τὸ κρατοῦν φοβοῦ, 109) and "seek profit" (τὸ συμφέρον θηρῶ, 110).

[25] Cousins or glosses of *gnôthi sauton* show up scattered through the first column: "know what you've learned" (γνῶθι μαθών, 6); "understand yourself" (or "be yourself," ἴσθι σαυτόν, 8); "consider your mortality" (φρόνει θνητά, 11); "govern yourself" (ἄρχε σεαυτοῦ, 14); "do what you know" (γνοὺς πρᾶττε, 50); "examine your character" (ἦθος δοκίμαζε, 52). A similarly sporadic set of maxims concerns friendship (15, 20, 28).

[26] On such medical dedications, see Dillon 1997, 169–77.

Attic roots—clearly, *philosophos*-group terms had a life of their own across the Aegean. Still, we have seen the coevolution of a disciplinary and pejorative uses, none of which cancelled other uses out, even if they influenced one another in important ways.

The Derision Continues: Alexis and His Laughable *Philosophoi*

Our best non-philosophical evidence for the pejorative use of *philosophos*-group terms from after 350 BCE comes from Alexis (ca. 375–275 BCE), a playwright of Middle and New Comedy in Athens. In perhaps his earliest such extant use,[27] in a fragment from his *Galateia*, a servant says:

> My master, a teenager, used to pass the time
> with speeches and attempted to
> philosophize. There was a Cyrenaic there,
> so they say, Aristippus, a ready-witted sophist,
> who back then rather excelled all the rest,
> and in licentiousness stands out among men now.
> My master gave him big bucks to become
> his student. And while he did not altogether master
> the curriculum . . . [28] (fr. 37 *PCG*)

The servant presents philosophizing as a cogent course of study (τέχνη) for those soon to be of age (μειρακίσκος); and given that it is a study in speech-making for the wealthy (cf. τάλαντον), it is presumably for those seeking a life in politics. Alexis's critical purchase against *philosophein* has three points: philosophizing is time-consuming and expensive; it attracts dreamers, those with unachievably big ambitions (οὐ πάνυ | ἐξέμαθε); and its exemplary practitioners end up exemplary for "licentiousness" (ἀκολασία). Philosophizing thus looks to fourth-century BCE Athenian audiences as a putatively promising

---

[27] The dating (late 360s–340s BCE) depends mainly on the reference to Aristippus (Arnott 1996, 141n1). Though I restrict my survey to uses of *philosophos*-group terms, Middle Comedy also includes humor about Plato (Alexis *Meropis* fr. 151; Amphis *Amphikrates* fr. 6; Aristophon *Platon* fr. 8), his Academy (Epippus *Nauagos* fr. 14; Epicrates fr. 10), and Pythagoreans (Alexis [and Cratinus?] *Pythagorizousa*; Aristophon *Pythagoristes*; Alexis and Cratinus *Tarantinoi*). For bibliography, see Arnott 1996, 305–8.

[28] Ὁ δεσπότης οὑμὸς περὶ λόγους γάρ ποτε | διέτριψε μειρακίσκος ὢν καὶ φιλοσοφεῖν | ἐπέθετο· Κυρηναῖος ἦν ἐνταῦθά τις, | ὥς φασ', Ἀρίστιππος, σοφιστὴς εὐφυής, | μᾶλλον δὲ πρωτεύων ἁπάντων τῶν τότε, | ἀκολασίᾳ τε τῶν γεγονότων διαφέρων. | τούτῳ τάλαντον δοὺς μαθητὴς γίγνεται | ὁ δεσπότης. καὶ τὴν τέχνην μὲν οὐ πάνυ | ἐξέμαθε.

route to civic success, which its novices fail to follow while its experts fail as models of that success.

Our fragment from the *Galateia* presents the external view of *philosophein*, one that I surmise differs little from the earliest impressions observers had of those they deemed *philosophoi*. Another fragment, from perhaps around the same time, presents an apparently internal view:[29]

> While walking from the Piraeus, through evils
> and puzzlement, it comes to me to philosophize.
> It seems to me, to put it as briefly as possible,
> that the painters are ignorant of Love,
> at least those who make images of this divinity.
> For it is neither female nor male, and again,
> neither god nor man, and yet again, neither stupid nor insightful,
> but, combining material from everywhere,[30]
> it brings many forms into one outline.
> For it is the daring of man, the cowardice of woman,
> the ignorance of mania, the reasoning of thought,
> the intensity of a beast, the toil of steel, the ambition of divinity.
> And these things, by the Athenians and the gods,
> I do not know what they are, but—all the same—there's something
> of this sort, and I've nearly got the name.[31] (fr. 247 *PCG*)

Likely a parody of Plato's *Symposium*,[32] this passage is presented as a plausible if risible response to amatory difficulties. Embracing complexity, it runs to paradox; seeking general principles, it runs to abstraction; working toward completeness, it runs to excess. The speaker's heterodox bombast, which might seem to give fresh insight into a topic, stalls in a farrago of high ideas: the climax

---

[29] Arnott 1996, 692, gives a date of 345–320 BCE very tentatively.

[30] The verb συννενησμένος has long been disputed by editors; the idea is presumably the one at Pl. *R.* 6.488a5–7.

[31] Πορευομένῳ δ' ἐκ Πειραιῶς ὑπὸ τῶν κακῶν | καὶ τῆς ἀπορίας φιλοσοφεῖν ἐπῆλθέ μοι. | καί μοι δοκοῦσιν ἀγνοεῖν οἱ ζωγράφοι | τὸν Ἔρωτα, συντομώτατον δ' εἰπεῖν, ὅσοι | τοῦ δαίμονος τούτου ποιοῦσιν εἰκόνας. | ἔστιν γὰρ οὔτε θῆλυς οὔτ' ἄρρην, πάλιν | οὔτε θεὸς οὔτ' ἄνθρωπος, οὔτ' ἀβέλτερος | οὔτ' αὖθις ἔμφρων, ἀλλὰ συννενησμένος | πανταχόθεν, ἑνὶ τύπῳ τε πόλλ' εἴδη φέρων. | ἡ τόλμα μὲν γὰρ ἀνδρός, ἡ δὲ δειλία | γυναικός, ἡ δ' ἄνοια μανίας, ὁ δὲ λόγος | φρονοῦντος, ἡ σφοδρότης δὲ θηρός, ὁ δὲ πόνος | ἀδάμαντος, ἡ φιλοτιμία δὲ δαίμονος. | καὶ ταῦτ' ἐγώ, μὰ τὴν Ἀθηνᾶν καὶ θεούς, | οὐκ οἶδ' ὅ τι ἐστίν, ἀλλ' ὅμως ἔχει γέ τι | τοιοῦτον, ἐγγύς τ' εἰμὶ τοὐνόματος.

[32] Details and qualifications at Arnott 1996, 692–94.

is a self-caused confusion and a loss for words. From the inside, according to an outsider, then, philosophizing is taking the long way around fundamental human problems, seeking untold conceptual distinctions and taxonomies that look impressive but, in the end, do not get to the basic issues.

Finally, in Alexis's undatable play *Linus*, Linus is showing off his library to Heracles:

LINUS: Go up

and take whatever book you want there,

and then you can read it—at any rate, look through

the titles, and take your time; nobody will bother you.

Orpheus is there, Hesiod, tragedy,

Choerilos, Homer, Epicharmus, prose works

of every kind. It'll make clear what your nature is,

the one toward which you most incline.

HERACLES: I'm taking this one.

L: Show me what it is first.

H.: A cook book, so the title shows.

L.: You're some *philosophos*, that's quite clear:

having passed over so many books,

you grab the *Art* of Simus.

H. Who's this Simus?

L. A supremely ready-witted man. He now inclines more

toward tragedy, and among actors

is far and away the superior chef, as his associates

deem him—and among chefs, the superior actor.

—A cattle-sized hunger is this man!

H.: Say what you wish:

for I am hungry, know this well.[33] (fr. 140 *PCG*)

---

[33] ΛΙΝ. Βιβλίον | ἐντεῦθεν ὅ τι βούλει προσελθὼν γὰρ λαβέ, | ἔπειτ' ἀναγνώσει, πάνυ γε διασκοπῶν | ἀπὸ τῶν ἐπιγραμμάτων ἀτρέμα τε καὶ σχολῇ. | Ὀρφεὺς ἔνεστιν, Ἡσίοδος, τραγῳδία, | Χοιρίλος, Ὅμηρος, Ἐπίχαρμος, συγγράμματα | παντοδαπά. δηλώσεις γὰρ οὕτω τὴν φύσιν, | ἐπὶ τί μάλισθ' ὥρμησε. ΗΡ. τουτὶ λαμβάνω. | ΛΙΝ. δεῖξον τί ἐστι πρῶτον. ΗΡ. ὀψαρτυσία, | ὥς φησι τοὐπίγραμμα. ΛΙΝ. φιλόσοφός τις εἶ, | εὔδηλον, ὃς παρεὶς τοσαῦτα γράμματα | Σίμου τέχνην ἔλαβες. ΗΡ. ὁ Σῖμος δ' ἐστὶ τίς; | ΛΙΝ. μάλ' εὐφυὴς ἄνθρωπος. ἐπὶ τραγῳδίαν | ὥρμηκε νῦν, καὶ τῶν μὲν ὑποκριτῶν πολὺ | κράτιστός ἐστιν ὀψοποιός, ὡς δοκεῖ | τοῖς χρωμένοις, τῶν δ' ὀψοποιῶν ὑποκριτής. | βούλιμός ἐσθ' ἄνθρωπος. ΗΡ. ὅ τι βούλει λέγε. πεινῶ γάρ, εὖ τοῦτ' ἴσθι. There is some uncertainty about the apportioning of the final few lines.

Linus presents the familiar (Hippian) canon of *sophoi*, a canon that we saw in the last chapter,[34] and uses it to diagnose Heracles's tastes.[35] When Heracles chooses a cookbook, Linus calls him a *philosophos*. The joke can be read in two ways. It could cut against Heracles: Arnott calls Linus's remark "pedantic sarcasm," reasoning that a *philosophos* would choose just about any book but a cookbook.[36] This view is uncertain. In its favor is lore connecting Pythagoreans with austerity, both in comedy and in Plato's *Phaedo*: nice food preparation is not a leading concern. Against it is the passage from Xenophon's *Oeconomicus* studied in chapter 6, where Socrates's self-ascription of *philosophos* comes up only when talking about growing food, and in the same chapter, the passage from Philemon's *Philosophoi*, where food austerity leads to clever dietary economies. So, another way to read the joke is as cutting against *philosophoi* in general: no doubt exaggerating, it treats them as mightily concerned with matters of diet. Their putative obsession with high-flown concepts simply obscures what they actually care about: eating in the right way. The Pythagorean dietary regimen, Aristippus's (and later Epicurus's) concern for pleasure, even Socrates's self-sufficient "hunger is the best sauce" (Cic. *Fin.* 2.28) all put gustatory matters high on the philosopher's agenda. On either reading, the *philosophoi* do not come out looking good: either Heracles could number among them, or they could find their exemplar in Heracles. In either case, they have a strained, countercultural, and obtuse attitude toward the most mundane elements of human life.

None of these fragments of Alexis specifically argues against the value of being *philosophos*. But none admires *philosophoi*, none treats *philosophia* as the love of wisdom or a general concern with intellectual cultivation, and none promotes *philosophein* as an effective route to maturation or problem-solving. Each presents *philosophia* as an established practice, appealing to a certain set of (often young) people, responsive to understandable goals of problem-solving or self-improvement, but basically silly in its procedure. Granted, this is comedy; but comedy exaggerates parts of life already subject to suspicion.

---

[34] Choerilus of Samos wrote a poem about Persia, which came to be read with the Homeric poems at the Panathenaea (see *BNP* s.v. "Choerilus"); he appears also to have spoken about Thales (DL 1.24, though on the reliability of this claim, see Wöhrle 2014, 29n1).

[35] For δηλώσεις γὰρ οὕτω τὴν φύσιν, compare Socrates's attempt to diagnose Strepsiades at Ar. *Nub.* 478–80 (with Moore 2016).

[36] Arnott 1996, 412, without argument.

The Perseverance of Apotreptics to *Philosophia*

Comedy provides implicit charges against *philosophia*: its practitioners take enervatingly roundabout and teeteringly ambitious approaches to self-improvement and problem-solving. From the same period we also know explicit charges against it, generally from philosophical or para-philosophical literature. Those accounts present *philosophia*'s foibles more forcefully, as unreliable, ineffectual, or dangerous—that is, as nearly useless, actually useless, or worse than useless. We studied the earliest such apotreptic in chapter 5, in our study of the Hippocratic *On Ancient Medicine*, likely from the last quarter of the fifth century BCE. Its author asserts that those tending toward *philosophia* take a foolish approach to medical practice: to explain instances of disease they appeal to cosmic-scale and hidden hypotheses, such as the four elements or speculative anthropogenesis, rather than to meso-scale and readily visible abnormalities of diet and environment. The philosophical approach suits "*graphikê*" better than actual curing; whatever the author means by this word, connected to "painting," "writing," or "depicting," it implies excellence in appearance rather than in practical application. *Philosophia*, howsoever interesting, provocative, and even insightful as it may be, does not take the direct route to proper medical practice.

We studied the opposite sort of criticism in chapter 6, in our discussion of Plato's *Apology of Socrates*, from after 399 BCE. Socrates asserts that some of his interlocutors and observers, unable to understand his ability to refute them or their neighbors, accuse him of "whatever is handy against the *philosophoi*." In this he includes three items: studying the things above the sky and below the earth; making the worse argument better; and not believing in the gods that the city believes in. These are accusations not of incompetence or irrelevance but of positive harmfulness: impiety, injustice, and immorality. As Socrates portrays it, these are not accusations inferred from his own practice, but rather tagged to *philosophoi* in general.

One of the best-known classical Greek apotreptics to *philosophia*, Callicles's speech in Plato's *Gorgias* (first third of the fourth century BCE), combines all three forms. Callicles, apparently a deep beneficiary of philosophical education (Pl. *Grg.* 487c2–d1) who comes to reject conventional values as contrary to hedonistic self-assertion, allows that *philosophia* has a certain charm when practiced by young people, in the way that speaking with a lisp does: something of a debilitation that has its upside (485a4–d1). But at a certain age, *philosophia* is just a lot of talking with young men in a corner: something quite useless (485d7). And indeed, it is not just useless; it hinders the pursuit of the higher political and personal goods, and is therefore positively harmful (486c4–d1). In the *Republic* Adeimantus shares a similar worry, though voicing it as someone else's possible charge against *philosophia*: while those who study *philosophia* during their youth are fine, those who keep doing it become "quite odd (πάνυ ἀλλοκότους), if not utterly depraved (παμβονήρους); while even the most reasonable (ἐπιεικεστάτους) seeming people . . . become useless (ἀχρήστους) to their cities" (Pl. *R.* 6.487c–d). In the decades around Socrates's death, then, we see a range of doubts that people have about *philosophoi*.

In 1984, the Egypt Exploration Society published a papyrus fragment, unearthed at Oxyrhynchus in the 1890s but long unread. That fragment contains a previously unknown apotreptic to philosophy, one which, for reasons discussed below, may date to the time of Heraclides's *On Diseases*. It is among the most vivid of such arguments, and seems to owe its sentiments, here in prose, to the versified Middle Comedy that we have just studied. Torn papyrus puts us somewhere along a vociferous complaint about *philosophoi*:

> (dis)agreement . . . nor do they agree *there*—not even about silver, though what could be whiter than silver? Still, Thrasyalkes claims it to be black. Thus when even the whiteness of silver counts as uncertain, why marvel when deliberators disagree about war and peace, alliances and revenues and payments and the like? Oh, and what about the *philosophoi* themselves? If you confined them to a single house and put an equal number of madmen in a neighboring house, you would get far, far greater howls from the *philosophoi* than from the madmen! In fact, this one, this Antisthenes here, says he would rather feel madness than pleasure; and Aristippus, what . . . is mad . . . and what Plato . . . [37] (*POxy.* 3659)

Our narrator presents *philosophoi* as contentious, obtuse, excitable, inarticulate, and life-denying. From the formal perspective, they constitute a delineated

---

[37] [. . .]φωνεῖν, συμφωνοῦσιν δὲ οὐ δ' οὕτως, ἀλλὰ καὶ τὸν ἄργυρον—καίτοι τί γένοιτ᾽ ἂν ἀργύρου λευκότερον;—ἀλλ᾽ ὅμως τοῦτον ὁ Θρασυάλης φησὶν εἶναι μέλανα. ὅτε τοίνυν καὶ τὸ λευκὸν τοῦ ἀργύρου πρὸς τὸ ἄδηλον, τί θαυμαστὸν τοὺς ἀνθρώπους ὑπὲρ εἰρήνης καὶ πολέμου, ὑπὲρ συμμαχίας καὶ προσόδων καὶ ἀναλωμάτων καὶ τῶν <τοιούτων> βουλευομένους διαφέρεσθαι; τί δὲ αὐτοὺς τοὺς φιλοσόφους; οὓς εἴ τις ἐν τῷ αὐτῷ οἴκῳ καθαίρξε[ι]ε καὶ ἐν ἑτέρῳ παρακειμέ[ν]ῳ μαινομένους ἰσαρίθ[μ]ους, πολὺ . . .] πολὺ μείζους κραυγὰς ἐκ τῶν φιλοσόφων ἢ τῶν μα]ινομένων προσδοκα . . .] οὗτος γοῦν οὗτος ὁ Ἀντισθέ]νης ἀσμεναίτερον ἂν μα]νῆναί φησιν ἢ ἡσθῆναι· ὁ δὲ Ἀ]ρίστιππος τί . . . [10 letters] . . . μαίνεσθαι . . . [11 letters] . . . η· τί δὲ Πλάτων, *POxy.* 3659.1–31; text from Cockle 1984, 59–62 (edited with commentary by Parsons and Hughes); see also Adorno 1989, 240 (18T3). Prince 2014, 369–70, reads αὐτὸς γοῦν οὗτος ὁ Ἀντισθέ]νης; the difference concerns the role Antisthenes played in the earlier, lost part of the narration. Both Parsons and Hughes and Prince conjecture that Aristippus is being said to be "mad for pleasure."

group of men from a range of generations, represented by important names, each of whom has tagline views on set topics. The connection between their thinking and matters of public decision-making is at once tenuous and noteworthy. As for the narrator's occasion for talking about *philosophoi*, he seems to be responding to a visitor's amazement about the polarization of political debate in a democratic city (presumably Athens, given the relevance of the Socratics). The civic constitution and its constituent norms, probably the norms of *parrhêsia* and *isonomia*, give citizens freedom to disagree about matters affecting their lives and livelihoods. Though he does not say so, the redemption of such disagreement is that it can and does come to an end, through formal methods of decision-making, such as majority voting. Not so the disagreement among *philosophoi*, which makes political difference trivial: *philosophoi* have no avenues for resolution, and seem even to revel in discord, in disagreements concerning at once the most vapid and the most profound issues. *Philosophoi* are both embarrassing and useless.

This fragment may well come from the mid-fourth century BCE. The papyrus's original editors, who left it undated, offered parallels for this text from the Second Sophistic; but Susan Prince, in her recent edition of Antisthenes, has suggested an early Peripatetic source.[38] In their study of Aristotle's *Protrepticus*, Hutchinson and Johnson have moved its likely date slightly earlier, suggesting that it served as proem to Aristotle's dialogue of 353 BCE.[39] They point to several internal details: the reference to Thrasyalkes, the precision of the thought experiment, and the "Socratic" locution of "counts as uncertain" (πρὸς τὸ ἄδηλον).[40] The even stronger evidence of Hutchinson and Johnson comes from several external details. Lucian cites the "howling philosopher" in his satire of earlier protreptics to *philosophia* (*Hermotimus* 11). Other parts of Aristotle's *Protrepticus* return to the themes of disagreement, madness, stupidity, and pleasure. Finally, the *Protrepticus*'s self-contradiction argument, which presents those who provide carefully reasoned arguments against *philosophia* as a way of life as already committed to doing *philosophia* (which involves giving carefully reasoned arguments as a way of life), would seem to work perfectly against this exasperated but technically meticulous speaker.[41]

---

[38] Cockle 1984, 60; Prince 2014, 370 (allowing Hellenistic authorship).

[39] Their view (in HJ) is followed by Collins 2015, 253. The dating comes from the relationship to Isocrates's *Antidosis*, which is datable.

[40] Found at Xen. *Mem.* 4.2.13–18, concerning two columns, "what counts as just" and "what counts as unjust"; I note that Aristotle attributes a two-column diagram to the Pythagoreans, especially Alcmaeon, at *M.* A 986a22–b3.

[41] Hutchinson and Johnson 2018, 113n6. I note that the narrator is so exercised by the physical theorists' disagreements that he appears to have a stake in them; he sounds like Plato's characters Clitophon and Callicles, who are drawn powerfully to philosophy but are chary to follow

Further circumstantial evidence for Aristotelian authorship could be added to the evidence that is adduced by Hutchinson and Johnson. The fourth century BCE is the last century during which we would imagine the differentiation of philosophical views to be represented by first-generation Socratics rather than by the founders of the Hellenistic schools. We know that Aristotle wrote about Aristippus and about Thrasyalkes and that few later authors wrote about the latter.[42] Anaxagoras had argued that snow is black and Democritus had theorized about the colors of metals.[43] Aristotle reflects frequently on the color of silver in arguments about the definability and describability of things, including reference to Antisthenean views on the subject, and on black and white as opposites.[44] Plato would have recently observed that disagreements about "justice and goodness" were more to be expected than those about "iron and silver."[45] Just as the speaker believes that the *philosophoi* are "crazy" because they believe that opposites are the same, for example that silver (ἄργυρος) is black—Greeks judged it white or of light color[46]—and that the admirable life appears to them unlike what it actually is, for example as free of pleasure, so also Aristotle argues that *mania* is believing that, for example, fire and ice are the same thing, and failing to perceive what is actually admirable.[47] Aristotle elsewhere uses the apparently Pythagorean technical vocabulary of "an equal number."[48] If Antisthenes and Aristippus were among the earliest authors to have written protreptics to philosophy, we might well expect Aristotle's *Protrepticus* to

---

its arguments when they hamper their quest for power. For commentary on self-contradiction arguments in Aristotle, see Castagnoli 2010, 68–94, 187–96.

[42] Aristippus: Arist. *M.* B.2 996a31–36; *Rh.* 2.23 1398b30–32. Thrasyalkes has only two entries in DK: Strabo 1.29 and 17.790; in one, Posidonius says that Aristotle developed Thrasyalkes's views of winds. Thrasyalkes comes from Thasos, but like his country-mates Stesimbrotus (470–420 BCE) and Leodamas (mathematician friend of Plato's, DL 3.24; Procl. *In Eucl.* 66.16) he may have emigrated to Athens, perhaps after Athens's siege of his hometown ca. 463 BCE.

[43] Anaxagoras: Cic. *Acad.* 2.100; Sen. *QNat.* 4b.3.6; Sext. Emp. *Pyr.* 2.244, with Hine 1980 and Williams 2012, 155–57. Democritus: Theophr. *Sens.* 73–74, 76, 80.

[44] Arist. *M.* H 1043b23–27 (Antistheneans say things can be described but not defined, for example silver as white, etc.); *M.* I 1054b12–13 (silver is like tin in being white; gold is yellow and red; but there are textual difficulties here); I 1053b31, 1055b33–34, etc. (relationship of white to black).

[45] Pl. *Phdr.* 263a6–11.

[46] See Eur. fr. 542.1; ἀργός simply means "white" or "bright" (Arist. *Top.* 149a7).

[47] Arist. *Gen. Corr.* 1.8 325a20–23.

[48] *Isarithmos*: Arist. *Eth. Nic.* 1156a7 (three kinds of friendship and three loveable properties); *M.* N 1093a30 (Pythagorean obsessions with finding equivalences between numbers and groups). See also Pl. *Tim.* 41d8 (heightened language about the Demiurge making as many souls as stars); *Leg.* 845a3 (a proportional theory of punishment).

deal immediately with them.[49] Finally, other Aristotelian works, notably bits of the *Protrepticus*, have already been found at Oxyrhynchus.[50]

Should this fragment be Aristotelian, then we get a vibrant impression of the popular views of *philosophoi* at the time of Heraclides and the early Academy, even if filtered through Aristotle's internal understanding of *philosophia* and constructed for his dialectical purposes. We see two things in particular. There is a disciplinary conception of *philosophia*, as constituted by a history of (absurd) thinkers who tussle (ineffectually) over fundamental questions, for example the reliability of sight and the value of madness—that is, appealing to history and canonical practitioners. And there is the acute worry that such tussles lead to social irrelevance, providing even less practical political or private advice than madmen could give.

Against this background, several features of Heraclides's *On Diseases* stand out. First, Heraclides's defense of *philosophia* appeals to historical practitioners of the discipline rather than solely to contemporary efforts, which might be a more intuitive route. Pythagoras is explicitly one such historical practitioner; he has an early role in the discipline, at the time when it first became possible to call oneself *philosophos*. Empedocles, whom Heraclides must also treat as explicitly a *philosophos*, since otherwise the emphasis on the Pythagoras story would not make sense, is also being treated as a historical practitioner, since it is his death, at least two generations earlier, that constitutes a key event of the work. Second, Heraclides presents *philosophia* as entirely relevant to the life of a citizen and free person, and thus as eminently useful. The Pythagoras story speaks to the *philosophos*'s superiority over athletes and merchants—or in the language of the Oxyrhynchus fragment, those concerned with the honor of political deliberation and the financial success of trade deals. Then the Empedocles story speaks to the *philosophos*'s superiority over doctors—or in the concerns of the Oxyrhynchus fragment, physicists concerned with the physiological phenomena (of sight and sanity). It is the old-fashioned Sicilian doctors, presumably, who disagreed ineffectually with one another, struggling to resuscitate the unbreathing woman; the *philosophos* Empedocles alone, a scholar of the nature of soul after the fashion of Pythagoras, could solve the medical problem.

Even a third aspect of the *On Diseases* protreptic argument, its interest in the word *philosophos* itself, may respond to the distaste of philosophy expressed in the Oxyrhynchus apotreptic. The fragment speaks of *philosophoi*

---

[49] DL 6.2, 6.16 (Antisthenes, with Prince 2014, 137–39), 2.85 (Aristippus); see Alieva 2013, 128–31.

[50] *POxy.* 666 (from *Protrepticus*), 2402 (from *Nicomachean Ethics*), 2403 (from *Categories*); and about a dozen more fragments in Egypt.

as a group of people with no obvious work; it does not glorify their actions as *philosophein* or their putative subject matter as *philosophia*. It compares them directly to madmen, a comparison that befits those with *phil-* prefixed names, as we saw in our examination of Aristophanes's *Wasps* (chapter 3, pp. 90–93). The term *philosophos* is possibly being used as a name-calling one, for people who gabble crazily about matters that seem existentially important—the reliability of our senses, the value of pleasure and the value of being out of one's mind—but for whom repetition is more typical than conclusion. Heraclides's Pythagoras story admits that the term is not transparent and that it applies to a distinctive kind of person, not merely a particular taste. Pythagoras's long analogy and explanation suggest further that Heraclides does not want to present *philosophia* as merely a commitment to mental cultivation or a desire to be competent in giving advice. Heraclides's Pythagoras is presented as decisive for the term's meaning—its eventual or normative meaning—as referring to a surprising way of life, one that looks lazy but does so only because the best way to understand the world, which is an assumed great good, is to refrain from the urgent business of the lesser types.

Aristotle's Perfect Protreptic Argument: Multiple Meanings of *Philosophia*

Hutchinson and Johnson conjecture that the fragment in *POxy.* 3659 comes from the introduction to Aristotle's *Protrepticus* (late 350s BCE). They believe that it would make sense for the narrator to be the recipient of philosophy's most famous protreptic argument, what I call the "perfect protreptic argument." That argument, I propose, deploys the non-disciplinary use of the term *philosophia* to lever its audience into adopting the norms of the discipline, ones that the remainder of the *Protrepticus* takes considerable pains to elucidate, negotiate, and praise. My view is that philosophical protreptic is called for only when something about a commitment to *philosophia*, in the disciplinary sense of the word, seems wrong; yet there is a non-disciplinary and non-pejorative meaning of *philosophia*; and these two meanings have enough continuities, even if very few, to allow equivocation in an argument about them.

Aristotle's argument has a simple basic form. If the members of one's audience accept that they should philosophize, then they should philosophize; even if they reject the claim that they should philosophize, still they should philosophize; so no matter what, they should philosophize. At any rate, this is the lowest common denominator of the witnesses to Aristotle's argument. In this form, however, the second premise does not make sense; we have as yet no reason to appreciate the connection between rejecting the norm "you should philosophize" and being governed by it. In particular, were we to take philosophizing in its disciplinary sense, the premise would simply be false. Just as I can reject some other skilled pursuit, for example, number theory or ship-piloting, without thereby committing myself to that very pursuit, it would seem that I can reject philosophizing without thereby committing myself to it. So, too, were we to taking philosophizing in a technical "Platonic" sense (by contemplating the really real), or as "loving wisdom" (by contrast to other leading apparent goods), or as "intellectual cultivation" (by contrast to other leading cultivations), the premise would also be obviously false. Because Aristotle must have intended the argument to seem at least somewhat plausible to many readers of the dialogue—and the later commentators from whom we infer the argument do not express incredulity at it—"philosophizing" must have meant something else.

All witnesses say Aristotle's premises and conclusion took a protreptic form: "you should [not] philosophize" (χρὴ [μὴ] φιλοσοφεῖν or φιλοσοφητέον).[51] Some leave it at that.[52] But others get at the nub of the issue. Those who reject the claim that they should philosophize admit, despite themselves, that they should philosophize; after all, they think they should respond to the claim effectively and do so by philosophizing. Clement says that when you reject the claim "you should philosophize," you reveal that you disdain (καταγνοίη) philosophizing, but disdaining requires knowing or recognizing or realizing (ἐγνωκάς), and knowing or recognizing or realizing just is philosophizing (Clem. *Strom.* 6.18.5). Lactantius says that rejecting the claim means saying what to do in life, and yet *philosophia* just is such discussion about what to do in life (*quid in vita faciendum vel non faciendum sit disputare*, Lactant. *Div. inst.* 3.16.396b). Alexander of Aphrodisias says that philosophizing involves "investigating (ζητεῖν) this very thing, whether one ought to philosophize or not" (Alex. Aphrod. *In Top.* 149,15).[53] Though he seems not to suppose that philosophizing is as narrowly defined as investigating whether one ought to philosophize, he does not state whether he takes it to be any investigation at all, or investigation into the sorts of thing a person ought to do, or something else. But he also says, a bit circularly, that philosophizing involves participating

[51] The term φιλοσοφητέον ("one should philosophize") is already found in Pl. *Euthyd.* 288d; Isoc. *Antid.* 285.

[52] Olymp. *In Alc.* 144.15–17 = *Protrepticus* fr. 2 Ross; *Schol. in An. Pr.*, cod. Paris. 2064 f. 263a = *Protrepticus* fr. 2 Ross; Anon. *On the General Forms of the Syllogism* (pp. ix–xii of CIAG 5.6, ed. Wallies), xi.19–21 (not in Ross).

[53] This argument is picked up at *Suda* φ 414 (s.v. φιλοσοφεῖν). For the form of argument, see Kneale 1957, 62; Rohatyn 1977, 196; Castagnoli 2010, 187–96.

in philosophical study (τὸ τὴν φιλόσοφον θεωρίαν μετιέναι), and that this activity is "proper to humans" (οἰκεῖον τῷ ἀνθρώπῳ). Thus while "searching" *simpliciter* could be proper to humans, Alexander might have in mind something more reflexive, namely searching into that which is proper to humans. So, according to Lactantius and Alexander, the audience of Aristotle's perfect protreptic argument assumes that philosophizing is figuring out what life requires of us—a notion of philosophizing that, notably, reflects the practices we have hypothesized underwrote the term's coinage. According to Clement, not so dissimilarly, philosophizing involves knowing or recognizing or realizing, especially as the result of an investigation.

Two further witnesses contribute something distinct to this general agreement. Elias (late sixth century CE) accepts that philosophizing is investigating (ζητεῖν), but then he glosses the question about action with one about existence. We should philosophize concerning whether we should or should not philosophize, he says, "for if there is philosophizing (εἰ μὲν γὰρ ἔστι), we definitely have to philosophize, given that it exists; but if there isn't philosophizing (εἰ δὲ μὴ ἔστι), even then we have to investigate why there isn't *philosophia*, and in investigating we philosophize, for searching is the cause of *philosophia*."[54] The implication is that if philosophizing does exist, then for that very reason we should philosophize. It is possible, because we can investigate into its nonexistence, and investigation is philosophizing. So we should do it.

Elias must assume that there is a goal of human life. Say that goal is *eudaimonia*. Then one must seek it. The way to seek it is by philosophizing. So one must philosophize. In this way philosophizing is necessary for humans; otherwise, we could not pursue the happiness that is our goal and realization. But suppose some pessimist says that philosophizing never works, there being no investigative route to happiness. Yet it would be the human lot to assess this claim, to investigate whether such investigation were in fact impossible. For only with such investigation could we know whether to abandon the search for the route to happiness. Of course we can investigate the possibility of *philosophia*, and we do so in the pursuit of happiness. Thus we must philosophize even then.

The perfect protreptic argument sounds imperfect if we think of *philosophia* disciplinarily, if Aristotle is saying that deniers have to deal rigorously with Heraclitus and Plato simply to deny the necessity of *philosophia*. This could hardly convince the denier. But if we think of *philosophia* non-disciplinarily, then the argument sounds much better. To deny something's importance, es-

---

[54] Elias *Proleg. phil.* 3.17–23; cf. Olymp. *In Alc.* 144.15–17 and David *Proleg. phil.* 9.2–12, the latter who actually goes through the arguments against Skepticism about the possibility of *philosophia* as knowledge of great things.

pecially something that has *prima facie* plausibility, takes propounding the greater importance of something else, or diagnosing the mistake in one's interlocutor's argument. Either task takes dialectical argument concerning human value or logical relations: that is, reasoning connected to what one should do or to someone else's reasoning. We long ago saw in Thucydides, Lysias, and Aristophanes—and in slightly more formalized guise in Gorgias and in the Socratic dialogues—this non-disciplinary notion of philosophy, a notion of non-naïve argumentation. We see it in its starkest form in the Delphic *philosophos ginou*. It is this notion that Aristotle appeals to in his perfect protreptic argument.

Aristotle does so, as it were, illicitly. For the *Protrepticus* does not deploy its dozens of pages of fine-grained argument to encourage the barest reflection on one's goals. To make the argument valuable, it would have to end up at something more involved than the Delphic injunction to "be philosophical." It coaxes one into accepting *philosophia* of the most disciplinary sort: the reasoning about first principles as we see depicted in the fourteen books of the *Metaphysics*. In effect, Aristotle's *Protrepticus* has two stages of argument: (1) you should philosophize$_{easy}$; and (2) if you should philosophize$_{easy}$, you should philosophize$_{hard}$. He deploys the "perfect" argument for the first stage; but as we have seen, he almost does not need to. Either by that time, or within a few decades, someone has inscribed *philosophos ginou* at Delphi, acknowledging its universality as a norm. A few decades later than that, Epicurus can start his *Letter to Menoeceus* with an argument so logically simple as practically to be otiose:

> Let nobody young delay philosophizing, nor being old weary of philosophizing. For nobody is it too early or too late to concern himself with his soul's health. The one saying either that it is not yet the age to philosophize or that the age has past is like the one saying that the age for happiness has not come or is no longer. Thus one should philosophize, both young and old, the latter so as, when growing old, to keep young on account of the grace of the things having been, and the former so as, while young, to be old at the same time in being fearless about the things to come. Thus one ought to care to do the things connected to happiness: if they are present, we have everything; if they are absent, we do everything toward having it. (Epicurus *Ep. Men.* 1)

If *philosophia* conduces to a soul's health, and to happiness, then one should philosophize. Further, for those who think philosophizing is valuable but only for the youth, Epicurus has an argument that it is also valuable for the elderly, and vice versa. As with Aristotle's *Protrepticus*, of course, Epicurus's actual process of philosophizing is much more involved and complicated than is implied here. Indeed, his *On Nature* was in thirty-seven papyrus rolls! So, like Aristotle, Epicurus uses the lever of the non-disciplinary (positive) form of *philosophia* to turn people toward the disciplinary (positive) form of *philosophia*—or with another metaphor, an exoteric bait and a switch to the esoteric—the more so, I would argue, because the discipline is not just difficult, as all disciplines are, but because it coexists with, and may even be the internal realization of, the imputation of a sophomoric way of life.

A Fourth-Century Dialogue about *Philosophia* and Its Ambivalence

My final piece of evidence about *philosophia*'s ambivalence in the fourth century BCE comes from a dialogue plausibly attributed to Plato, though some ascribe it instead to an anonymous early Academic.[55] This short dialogue, the *Rival Lovers*, has usually been studied, whenever it has been studied, in the way that Heraclitus's Pythagoras story has been studied—as a contribution to later fourth-century BCE school debates about the right sort of intellectual life, in this case on the side against the polymathic life of science. It more powerfully articulates, however, the mixed attitudes toward *philosophia* in the time of Heraclides and Aristotle that we have just studied, as estimable or not, as disciplinary or not, as valuable or not.

The dialogue opens with a nod to the disciplinary conception of *philosophia*. Socrates sits down next to an acquaintance in a schoolyard and notices some attractive and well-born young men. They are drawing circles, bending their hands in imitation of various celestial inclinations, and debating (ἐρίζοντε) something, all this with real intensity (μάλ᾽ ἐσπουδακότε). They appear to Socrates to be working through astronomical theories, apparently those of Anaxagoras or Oenopides.[56] Socrates asks his acquaintance about their intensity: "is it something great and admirable, whatever they're so intense about?" The acquaintance laughs at the suggestion; really what they are

---

[55] Platonic authorship: Yxem 1846, 6–7; Grote 1865, 447–53; Evans 1976; Davis 1984; Bruell 1987, 92, 106; Monserrat Molas 1999, 19–25; Pageau St-Hilaire 2014, 3–7. Possibly Platonic authorship: Annas 1985, 112; Hutchinson 1997, 618; Peterson 2011, 201–2, and 2018. Non-Platonic authorship: Schleiermacher 1836, 325–26; Stallbaum 1836, 265–68; Heidel 1896, 14, 59–63; Werner 1912; Souilhé 1930, 13.2.107–12; Isnardi 1954, 137–38; Carlini 1962 and 1964; Merlan 1963; Ledger 1989, 144; Centrone 2005, 37; Männlein-Robert 2005; Thesleff 2009, 13, 129; Dillon 2012, 50; Brisson 2014, 15–17, 306.

[56] On Anaxagoras, see chapter 6, pp. 158–64; on Oenopides, see Bodnár 2007.

doing is "harping on about the things in the sky, blathering—philosophizing" (ἀδολεσχοῦσι . . . περὶ τῶν μετεώρων καὶ φλυαροῦσι φιλοσοφοῦντες).[57] He seems here to be recapitulating an observation made a century earlier, the very observation that this book conjectures to have occasioned the coinage of the word *philosophos*.

This brief scene captures brilliantly the external and internal faces of *philosophia*, how philosophy looks to observers and its practitioners. The boys have a characteristic appearance: they are given to vociferous disputation, distinctive gesture, and, presumably, earnest or good-spirited visage. Their talk, maybe technical, sounds aimless and indistinct. Socrates's acquaintance has been watching them a while and, though he has heard words concerning *ta meteôra* bandied about, he observes mostly that they talk incessantly, in disagreement, and not about the normal subjects concerning which people usually pass the time. The internal content, by contrast, includes competing assessments of some astronomical theory. The boys' intensity of focus and shared project of explanation show that they see great significance in articulating and accepting the truth about such cosmic matters. What from the outside looks like "harping on" is surely from the inside the methodical, stepwise clarification or correction of a conversation; and "blathering" may label the extensive preliminary or adjunct discussions in preparation for addressing the key issue.

Despite being unable to hear the content of the conversation, much less contribute to it, Socrates can infer it. This ability depends on philosophy's historically extended disciplinarity. Talking philosophy can involve talking about certain other people, those considered the canonical or most provocative philosophers. Those people's theories or observations come under certain kinds of scrutiny or elaboration. Thus Socrates can see that the boys' diagrams and gesticulations most likely refer to the leading theoretical astronomers of the mid-fifth century BCE. As we saw when we looked at Plato's *Charmides* and especially his *Protagoras* (chapter 8), cooperative clarification and even self-understanding comes through agonistic questioning and examination. The boys' intensity and competition must be in the interest of joint understanding, persuading, correcting, and explaining in turn. Socrates can see the displayed vigor as expressions of enthusiasm and a seriousness of purpose rather than as sparks of angry frustration or ambitions for glory. Socrates must have considerable familiarity with philosophy to see in the boys' gabbling and babbling a conversation with one's predecessors concerning questions about the fundamental nature of the world.

---

[57] Cf. Pl. *Phdr.* 270a1 (see above, chapter 6, p. 168) and the participial use of the verb *philosophein* to gloss the rest of the sentence in Hdt. 1.30 (see above, chapter 5, p. 131).

Socrates's companion in the dialogue does not have an internal, disciplinary attitude toward philosophy; he cannot understand the boys' activity from their (and their fellow practitioners') point of view. But why, after all, should he be able to? He has spent his life in a different discipline, training in wrestling and sport (*RL* 132c9, 132d3). From that sort of life, in which bodily strength and girth matter, and identifiable victories in matches matter even more, the anemic chattering of these boys is beyond silly; it is a waste of time. So much the worse for them, he thinks, given their attractiveness and family credentials. Socrates ends up with a certain esteem for this wrestler's unprepossessing attitude (132d1–6). Indeed, he has already been drawn to him, perhaps for his sincerity and directness. Something else absorbs the wrestler's judgments of value, in an authentic way; his disparagement of philosophizing simply reflects the wholeheartedness with which he pursues his own ambitions.[58] Philosophy amounts to its own integrated set of norms, and he simply does not share them.

This was the opening of the dialogue; the disputation heats up with the introduction of a second interlocutor. This one has an affinity for cultural affairs, an intellectual bent (περὶ μουσικὴν διατετριφώς, *RL* 132d1–2). He contradicts the wrestler: accepting that the boys are philosophizing, he disagrees that their doing so is "shameful," as he paraphrases his opponent. He then goes even further: not only does he admire philosophy; he judges such admiration an essential and universal part of being human: "If ever I should think philosophizing is shameful, neither would I take myself to be human, nor anybody else who thought that way" (133a8–b1). In effect, one must philosophize. The imperative, like the (near-)contemporaneous one at Delphi, is categorical. As is claimed by Aristotle's perfect protreptic argument, or by Epicurus's ages-of-life argument, it cannot be avoided. So, the dialogue presents someone who has internalized the value of philosophy. For what reason, one might wonder— and Socrates does wonder. The story of the dialogue is that the intellectual does not know. He does not appeal to the disciplinary explanation suggested by the boys' example (and articulated in Aristotle's *Protrepticus*), that hashing out problems in theoretical astronomy or other canonical issues has intrinsic and instrumental value. Nor does he appeal to human nature, to explain its constitutive role in human existence. The suspicion is that he has come to esteem a practice from the outside, in effect for its countercultural value, as something people commonly disparage but serious people esteem, without

[58] DL 3.4: Plato studied at the school depicted in this dialogue and was an able wrestler. Sandra Peterson wonders whether the wrestler is Plato. Thrasylus thought the intellectual was Democritus (DL 9.37).

throwing himself into the practice itself, insofar as he is interested only in presenting himself as serious.[59]

Anyway, the intellectual at least tries to explain his admiration for philosophy. In response to Socrates's question, "What is it?," he quotes Solon's "Ever aging, learning plenty" (γηράσκω δ᾽ αἰεὶ πολλὰ διδασκόμενος). He interprets Solon's verse as making the sensible claim, one we have seen Epicurus to promulgate, that learning is age-independent. Then, in a fallacious inference reminiscent of Socrates's joking about philosophical dogs in *Republic* Book 2 (chapter 8, p. XXX), the intellectual says that Solon is encouraging one's "learning as much as possible in life" (ὡς πλεῖστα ἐν τῷ βίῳ μάθῃ, *RL* 133c7). From the proposition that one ought always to keep on learning, he equivocates in the "keep on," from "as one grows older" to "as one is learning." Hardly a disciplinary or methodical view, this amounts simply to equating *philosophia* with a basic epistemic orientation, the idea that we are always benefitted by knowing more. Plato's Socrates once said that the unexamined life is not a human life (Pl. *Ap.* 38a5–6); so maybe *philosophia* can really be understood as the desire for knowledge.

So we might think; but Socrates shows here the naïveté of this position. The intellectual agrees that he has made *philosophia* distillable to *polumathia*. Yet this makes the idea less appealing, once he realizes that he shares Heraclitus's suspicions of *polumathia* (*RL* 133c10–133d1). The bodily parallel, *philogumnastia*, with its coordinate *polu*- definition, *poluponia* ("much effort"), sets a bad precedent (133d6–e2). The wrestler tells him that a lot of effort (τῶν πολλῶν πόνων) is worse for the health of the body than only a measured amount (μετρίων, 134a8–b2); the same holds for food and everything else (134c10–d2). Thus too for the soul, it would seem: one should not learn "everything or many things" (135a9–10).[60] So, if one wishes to praise *philosophia*, one should not equate it with *polumathia*. The result is that philosophy is not simply learning; it is not simply a humble but optimistic epistemic attitude; it is not simply unquenchable curiosity. It must be something more specific.

Socrates asks the intellectual to help him list the topics (τῶν μαθημάτων) to be learned in philosophy (*RL* 134a8–9). In his answer the intellectual abandons the Solonic epistemic model and adopts a reputational model; and yet he still avoids answering Socrates well. He identifies the philosopher as a layman who participates in expert discussions better than any other layman: that is, without the laborious effort of becoming expert himself, but with the appearance of knowledge surpassing all but the expert's knowledge (135b1–d8,

[59] Compare Clitophon's external valuation of justice in the *Clitophon* (see Moore 2012).

[60] An identical argument against broad learning is elsewhere attributed to Aristippus (DL 2.71).

136a8–b2). In so doing the intellectual caps the quantity or quality of learning at a level just above that of the next-best amateur and definitely below that of the expert. He relativizes the topics to be learned by specifying them as those in which his comparative advantage most yields him esteem. The intellectual has hereby replaced a psychical model (self-improvement) with a social one (improvement in popularity), replacing the intrinsic value of knowledge with its (balanced) instrumental value. He appears to have in mind just the esteem due to the *Sophoi*, those all-around advisors known as experts in nothing but admired by all. He seems in fact to recapitulate the earliest coiners of the term *philosophos*, using it to denote those prone to avid discussions abstracted from the day's issues, who might all the same become politically or socially influential; but unlike those who seem to find such activity off-putting or at least remarkable, he finds it enviable.

This new explanation of *philosophia*'s value brings the intellectual no dialectical advantage. The previous model committed him to a detrimental overwork, the opposite of benefit. His current attempt, meant to avoid the harm of overwork, commits him now to uselessness, benefit's other opposite. As Socrates points out, the intellectual has imagined a philosopher as a pentathlete, effective on average but a loser in any particular contest— nobody will ever ask *his* advice (*RL* 135e1–137b3). And he has ignored the content of philosophizing, insofar as he is satisfied with external appearance. He does not mention the theoretical astronomy practiced by the boys of whom he is so fond or the questions of valuation and conversational method on display in his conversation with Socrates himself. Perhaps he does so from disdain for disciplinary specialization and a concomitant valuation of the leisured ideal. Perhaps, like the wrestler, he does not see the benefit in debating Anaxagoras's theories or in clarifying the use of moral or definitional inquiry.

Socrates continues the conversation by showing how philosophy would have to be were it to be good, as the intellectual assumes it to be. By a stepwise argument, he gets the intellectual to equate benefit with a person's improvement, which involves punishing what is bad about him, which in turn involves distinguishing (γιγνώσκειν, διαγιγνώσκειν) what is bad from what is good. One can rightly claim this skill, called "justice," if one can make these distinctions in any individual case; and one's own good and bad qualities count as one of those individual cases. This means that the ability to benefit, which is to exercise justice, involves the ability to benefit oneself—which Socrates says is to exercise discipline (*sôphronein*). And as in the general case justice means knowing people, in the personal case discipline *means* "knowing oneself" (ἑαυτὸν γιγνώσκειν). "This then," Socrates says, "is what the Delphic inscription urges" (*RL* 138a8). Obeying the Delphic inscription is essential to being good and beneficial. The intellectual claimed that *philosophia* is good and beneficial. So in accepting the argument the intellectual must believe that practicing *philosophia* is a matter of obeying the Delphic inscription.[61]

So on the intellectual's understanding of *philosophia* as clarified by Socrates, the name *philosophos* refers not to a disciplinary practitioner but to one who obeys a Delphic inscription.[62] What that means is that "being philosophical" amounts to fulfilling the expectations of the commonplace Greek ethos. We have no reason to find the intellectual utterly idiosyncratic in his view of philosophy, and the existence of a dialogue depicting his comeuppance in fact suggests its popularity. That Socrates's examination of the intellectual's views does not direct his attention to disciplinarity means, too, that Socrates finds something about his views respectable. Philosophy, if not taken as encyclopedic learning or leisured amateurism, can be something good that everybody should do: knowing oneself.[63]

The *Rival Lovers*, as I take it, speaks to an ambiguity in Greek conceptions of *philosophia* during its great century of revaluation and self-assertion, as both a meaningful, historically anchored discipline and a gnomic obligation for all human beings. As with all triumphs, there are the triumphalists, those for whom the win takes the place of the practice itself. It is as easy to

---

[61] The *Charmides* suggests a similar view; for detail, see Moore and Raymond 2019.

[62] We must emphasize, with Peterson 2011, 201, that Socrates (or the author) does not present his own final positive account of *philosophia*, but only part of a *reductio* argument for his interlocutor; contrast, e.g., Hutchinson 1997, 618. Brisson 2014, 15–17, 305, as part of his argument against Platonic authorship, seems to identify—quite bizarrely, to my mind—the intellectual with Socrates and/or Plato; he argues that the dialogue "does not hesitate to reduce philosophy to an accumulation of knowledge, and rejects it in favor of bodily exercise," and yet he also asserts that Plato always vaunts the soul over the body. Yet Brisson is right that Socrates's sympathy for the wrestler is remarkable (cf. Yates 2005, 37, and the provocative observation in Davis 1984, 80, that the boys who debate Anaxagoras and Oenopides move their arms like wrestlers).

[63] On the connection here of *philosophia* and the goodness of self-knowledge, see Moore 2015b, 236–39. Also emphasizing the dialogue's concern for self-knowledge is Souilhé 1930, 105–7, 125; Theslef 2009, 362, 365; Pageau St-Hilaire 2014, 2. There is a textual problem concerning whether Socrates ever calls himself *philosophos* in the dialogue. At *RL* 137a2, the MSS have ὡπολογήσαμεν καλὸν εἶναι τὴν φιλοσοφίαν καὶ αὐτοὶ φιλόσοφοι εἶναι ("we agreed that philosophy is excellent and that we ourselves are philosophers"). Yet Socrates and the intellectual never did agree to this. If it went without saying, then Socrates is a *philosophos*, merging apparently disciplinary and non-disciplinary personae. But the focus of the conversation tells against its going without saying. (I note that the intellectual is never called and never calls himself *philosophos*, despite the claims of Bruell 1987.) Burnet 1901 retains the Greek but notes in apparatus the seclusion of the whole line by Forster (1765) and Schanz (1882); Lamb 1927 brackets; Souilhé 1930, Mitscherling in Cooper 1997, and Brisson 2014 exclude it from their translations. Carlini 1964 (following C. Schmidt) conjectures καὶ αὖ τὸ φιλοσοφεῖν ("and philosophizing too [we agreed to be excellent]") in place of καὶ αὐτοὶ φιλόσοφοι εἶναι—I find this persuasive.

mistake the value of philosophy as it is to mistake its disvalue. Philosophy proper includes thinking through—and thus appraising the reasons in favor of doing—philosophy: thus it includes the appearance, and reality, that philosophy always involves protreptics to itself. Indeed, if philosophy really is a kind of talking that conduces to self-improvement, there is always a pair of risks: that we do not see how it could possibly work and that we assume it to be so easy that we do not go through the exercises and lessons necessary for it. (Trying to know oneself runs the same risks of seeming impossibility and conceits of ease, as I argue in my 2015 book, *Socrates and Self-Knowledge*.) Presumably we can eradicate neither risk entirely. Indeed, it is presumably the recognition of those twin risks—of hopelessness about the acquisition of wisdom and of wishful thinking that one has already acquired enough—that both impelled the formation of the discipline and maintains its current energy. Just as *Rival Lovers* offers up the problem of these two risks, the Pythagoras story that we see in Heraclides's *On Diseases* and elsewhere offers up reassurances in the face of these risks, claiming that humans may attain an efficacious wisdom, even as doing so befits extraordinary distinction in investigation and self-composure. Convincing people to pursue philosophy may require convincing them that in doing so they would in fact be *loving wisdom*: all can feel love, but doing so well—upholding a commitment to someone and a sunny disposition toward another through thick and thin—is hard; and wisdom has its many exemplars, but exemplifying it in oneself—disciplining oneself against distraction and avoiding self-deception—is even harder. But both are possible; and so one ought to try.

Epilogue
Contemporary Philosophy and the History of the Discipline

This book has aimed to historicize our interpretation of the concept *philosophia* and thus of philosophy. It has investigated the meaning of the term in its earliest situations of use. Wonder and awe may have given rise to the investigations typical of Western philosophy; or perhaps something else did: the Greek democratic *polis*, currency minting, Ionian multiculturalism, whatever. In any event, those investigations got consolidated and refined only in some socio-linguistic setting. Cicero spoke imprecisely when he said that though the name is new, philosophy is old; the name and the practice grew up together, and only retrospectively can we spot rudiments of the practice before the unifying name.

This study may have indirect relevance to contemporary discussions about the meaning of philosophy. Diverse candidates get floated: thinking about thinking, knowing at the deepest and most systematic level, conceptual analysis, concept creation, social critique. This diversity should surprise nobody. If each candidate meaning is offered as the best interpretation of the efforts of practitioners over the discipline's two-and-a-half millennia, or even of practitioners in one's immediate conversational circle, or even of oneself, we can hardly avoid uncertainty, disagreement, and shifts in emphasis. Each of us sees something else, takes something else as central, and interprets the unmet ideals differently. Some will take a minimalist line, trying to account as capaciously as possible for all activities called philosophy; others will take a maximalist line, trying to articulate the precise processes and substances of philosophy. Consensus will fail even if philosophy is to be defined along the *via negativa*, as what differentiates it from other disciplines. Indeed, we probably do not see all the disagreement, given the dominance of the institutional definition—"whatever people do in university philosophy departments" or "whatever people publish in university presses' philosophy list"—with recapitulation in "Introduction to Philosophy" classes and the interhireability of students from major graduate programs.

I suspect that there is nothing that "philosophy" (or *philosophia*) naturally or essentially or necessarily takes as its object, whether it be *kosmos* or being or self or thinking. I am less inclined to doubt Aristotle's view that the activity of philosophy amounts to explanation, especially fundamental explanation— but that is because I take explanation to be constitutive of any discipline whatsoever, and the role of explanation in philosophy is even more salient insofar as this discipline lacks other important anchors, like rocks for geologists or poems for theorists of poetry. At the same time, I think that philosophy is basically the practice of talking, with the goal of becoming a better person. This method and this aim raise a central question: How is this self-improvement through discussion and study supposed to work? There is nothing to turn to for answers except what other *philosophoi* have done and talked about. Thus I take philosophy to be, crucially and not propaedeutically, the interpretation of prior experiments in philosophy—its methods, concepts, arguments, and ideals—from those you take to be your ilk, philosophers, such that by understanding them one might come to live better. Now, probably every discipline has as a goal the flourishing of people. But the discipline of philosophy differs in believing that understanding (or disposition) comes from the interpretation of claims and views, not from understanding productive activities or natural or artificial objects in the world. I thus take philosophy to be inseparable from the history of philosophy.

The relevance to contemporary discussion of philosophy of an account of the name's coinage and early centuries of use is, if narrow, still important. It disabuses us of the notion that the term has always meant "lover of wisdom," or that this is even a meaningful or stably meaningful claim, or that this is the "natural" sense of philosophy (even if it is *a* meaning, as posited or interpreted later on). It cultivates an appreciation that the dubiety people feel about philosophy has always been felt, a sense that the value of philosophy was in dispute and contention from the start. It shakes up Hellenocentrism in a certain way, in that we can accept the Greekness of the name and certain canonical personages, but also in that we can accept that the ideas, practices, and goals may well have been foreign, and continually modified by foreign influence, and could just as well have parallels in other civilizations with no prejudice to those parallels (compare Justin E. H. Smith's 2016 book, *The Philosopher: A History in Six Types*). Most importantly for me, it gives a humble nobility to an origin story for (our) discipline connected with the *sophoi*, with political action, with curiosity, with a contrarian spirit of self-cultivation, with conversation and fellow feeling, with concentrated and enduring attention to detail, validity, and truth, with personal responsibility, and with the hope for a better life. No mere story of a word can vindicate a way of life, of course, but when that story has been about ways of life themselves, and so has drawn attention to them as proper objects of our deliberate concern, we might make some progress.

APPENDIX: VERSIONS OF THE PYTHAGORAS STORY

Sosicrates *Successions* (in Diogenes Laertius *Lives of Eminent Philosophers* 8.8) (second century BCE)

Σωσικράτης δε ἐν Διαδοχαῖς φησιν αὐτὸν ἐρωτηθέντα ὑπὸ Λέοντος τοῦ Φλιασίων τυράννου τίς εἴη, φιλόσοφον εἰπεῖν. καὶ τὸν βίον ἐοικέναι πανηγύρει· ὡς οὖν εἰς ταύτην οἱ μὲν ἀγωνιούμενοι, οἱ δὲ κατ᾽ ἐμπορίαν, οἱ δέ γε βέλτιστοι ἔρχονται θεαταί, οὕτως ἐν τῷ βίῳ οἱ μὲν ἀνδραποδώδεις, ἔφη, φύονται δόξης καὶ πλεονεξίας θηραταί, οἱ δὲ φιλόσοφοι τῆς ἀληθείας.

For translation, see p. 4.

Diodorus Siculus *Library of History* 10 fr. 24 (fl. 60–30 BCE)

ὅτι Πυθαγόρας φιλοσοφίαν, ἀλλ᾽ οὐ σοφίαν ἐκάλει τὴν ἰδίαν αἵρεσιν. καταμεμφόμενος γὰρ τοὺς πρὸ αὐτοῦ κεκλημένους ἑπτὰ σοφοὺς ἔλεγεν ὡς σοφὸς μὲν οὐδείς ἐστιν ἄνθρωπος ὢν καὶ πολλάκις διὰ τὴν ἀσθένειαν τῆς φύσεως οὐκ ἰσχύων πάντα κατορθοῦν, ὁ δὲ ζηλῶν τὸν τοῦ σοφοῦ τρόπον τε καὶ βίον προσηκόντως ἂν φιλόσοφος ὀνομάζοιτο.

For translation, see p. 69.

Cicero *Tusculan Disputations* 5.3.8–9 (work: 45 BCE)

A quibus ducti deinceps omnes qui in rerum contemplatione studia ponebant, sapientes et habebantur et nominabantur, idque eorum nomen usque ad Pythagorae manauit aetatem, quem, ut scribi auditor Platonis Ponticus Heraclides, uir doctus in primis, Phliuntem ferunt uenisse eumque cum Leonte, principe Phliasiorum, docte et copiose disseruisse quaedam; cuius ingenium et eloquentiam cum admiratus esset Leon, quaesiuisse ex eo qua maxime arte confideret; at illum artem quidem se scire nullam, sed esse philosophum. Admiratum Leontem nouitatem nominis quaesiuisse quinam essent philosophi, et quid inter eos et reliquos interesset; Pythagoram autem respondisse similem sibi uideri uitam hominum et mercatum eum qui haberetur maxumo ludorum apparatu totius Graeciae celebritate; nam ut illic alii corporibus exercitatis gloriam et nobilitatem coronae peterent, alii emendi aut uendendi quaestu et lucro ducerentur, esset autem quoddam genus eorum idque uel maxime ingenuum, qui nec plausum nec lucrum quaererent, sed uisendi causa uenirent studioseque perspicerent quid ageretur et quo modo, item nos quasi in mercatus quandam celebritatem ex urbe aliqua sic in hanc uitam ex alia uita et natura profectos alios gloriae seruire, alios pecuniae; raros esse quosdam qui ceteris omnibus pro nihilo habitis rerum naturam studiose intuerentur; hos se appellare sapientiae studiosos (id est enim philosophos); et ut illic liberalissimum esset spectare nihil sibi adquirentem, sic in uita longe omnibus studiis contemplationem rerum, cognitionemque praestare.

For translation, see pp. 13–14.

Valerius Maximus *Memorable Deeds and Sayings* 8.7 ext 2 (fl. 14–37 CE)

Atque ut ad vetustiorem Industriae actum transgrediar, Pythagoras perfectissimae opus sapientiae a iuventa <scientiae> pariter et omnis honestatis percipiendae cupiditate ingressus—nihil enim quod ad ultimum sui perventurum est finem non et mature et celeriter incipit—, Aegyptum petiit, ubi litteris gentis eius adsuefactus, praeteriti aevi sacerdotum commentarios scrutatus, innumerabilium saeculorum observationes cognovit. inde ad Persas profectus, magorum exactissimae prudentiae se formandum tradidit, a quibus siderum motus cursusque stellarum et uniuscuiusque vim proprietatem effectum benignissime demonstratum docili animo sorpsit. Cretam deinde et Lacedaemona navigavit, quarum legibus ac moribus inspectis ad Olympicum certamen descendit, cumque multiplicis scientiae maximam inter totius Graeciae admirationem specimen exhibuisset, quo cognomine censeretur interrogatus, non se sapientem—iam enim illud septem excellentes viri occupaverant—sed amatorem sapientiae, id est Graece philosophon edidit. in Italiae etiam partem, quae tunc maior Graecia appellabatur, perrexit, in qua plurimis et opulentissimis urbibus effectus studiorum suorum adprobavit. cuius ardentem rogum plenis venerationis oculis Metapontus aspexit oppidum, Pythagorae quam suorum cinerum nobilius clariusque monumentum.

For translation, see p. 72.

Quintilian *Institutes of Rhetoric* 12.1.19 (work: 95 CE)

Nam et Pythagoras non sapientem se, ut qui ante eum fuerunt, sed studiosum sapientiae uocari uoluit.

Pythagoras desired to be called not wise, like those who preceded him, but a lover of wisdom.

Nicomachus of Gerasa *Introduction to Arithmetic* 1.1 (60–120 CE)

Οἱ παλαιοὶ καὶ πρῶτοι μεθοδεύσαντες ἐπιστήμην κατάρξαντος Πυθαγόρου ὡρίζοντο φιλοσοφίαν εἶναι φιλίαν σοφίας, ὡς καὶ αὐτὸ τὸ ὄνομα ἐμφαίνει, τῶν πρὸ Πυθαγόρου πάντων σοφῶν καλουμένων συγκεχυμένῳ ὀνόματι, ὥσπερ καὶ τέκτων καὶ σκυτοτόμος καὶ κυβερνήτης καὶ ἁπλῶς ὁ τέχνης τινὸς ἢ δημιουργίας ἔμπειρος· ἀλλ᾽ ὅ γε Πυθαγόρας συστείλας πάντων τὸ ὄνομα ἐπὶ τὴν τοῦ ὄντος ἐπιστήμην καὶ κατάληψιν καὶ μόνην τὴν ἐν τούτῳ γνῶσιν τῆς ἀληθείας σοφίαν ἰδίως καλέσας εἰκότως καὶ τὴν ταύτης ὄρεξιν καὶ μεταδίωξιν φιλοσοφίαν προσηγόρευσεν, οἷον σοφίας ὄρεξιν. ἀξιοχρεώτερος δέ ἐστι τῶν ἄλλως ὁριζομένων, παρ᾽ ὅσον ἰδίου ὀνόματος καὶ πράγματος ἔννοιαν δηλοῖ· καὶ ταύτην δὲ τὴν σοφίαν ὡρίζετο ἐπιστήμην τῆς ἐν τοῖς οὖσιν ἀληθείας. . . .

The ancients, the ones who first dealt methodically with knowledge, following the leadership of Pythagoras defined *philosophia* as the love of wisdom (*philia sophias*), as the very name even expresses. All those before Pythagoras who were called *sophos* were so titled in an unprincipled way, as with the builder, the shoemaker, the pilot, and in effect any person experienced in some art or craft: but Pythagoras, at any rate, circumscribed the name for all these to the knowledge and understanding of what is, and calling the recognition of the truth in this the only wisdom properly so called, reasonably enough, and its desire and pursuit of this *philosophia*, that is, desire for wisdom (*sophias orexis*). He is more credible than those giving other definitions inasmuch as he makes clear the sense of the proper term and the thing itself—and this *sophia* he defined as knowledge of the truth in what there is. . . .

Aëtius 1.3.7 (first or early second century CE) = Ps-Plutarch *Placita Philosophorum* 1.3 876e, Stobaeus 1.10.12

πάλιν δ᾽ ἀπ᾽ ἄλλης ἀρχῆς Πυθαγόρας Μνησάρχου Σάμιος, ὁ πρῶτος φιλοσοφίαν τούτῳ τῷ ῥήματι προσαγορεύσας.

And again, from another origin [sc. he deduces the principles of all things], Pythagoras son of Mnesarchus, a Samian, the first one to have called *philosophia* by that name.

Apuleius *Florida* 15.22 (ca. 125–after 170 CE)

Tot ille doctoribus eruditus, tot tamque multiiugis calicibus disciplinarum toto orbe haustis, vir praesertim ingenio ingenti ac profecto super captum hominis animi augustior, primus philosophiae nuncupator et conditor. . . .

Educated by so many masters, and after draining so many cups of knowledge of such different kinds throughout the world, that master of truly great genius [sc. Pythagoras], more venerable than the human mind can encompass, the first to give a name and foundation to philosophy. . . . (trans. Jones)

————*Apologia* 4.7

Pythagoram, qui primum sese philosophum nuncuparit. . . .

Pythagoras himself, the first to name himself *philosophos*. . . .

Diogenes Laertius *Lives of Eminent Philosophers* 1.12 (second–third century CE)

φιλοσοφίαν δὲ πρῶτος ὠνόμασε Πυθαγόρας καὶ ἑαυτὸν φιλόσοφον, ἐν Σικυῶνι διαλεγόμενος Λέοντι τῷ Σικυωνίων τυράννῳ (ἢ Φλιασίων, καθά φησιν Ἡρακλείδης ὁ Ποντικὸς ἐν τῇ Περὶ τῆς ἄπνου)· μηδένα γὰρ εἶναι σοφὸν {ἄνθρωπον} ἀλλ᾽ ἢ θεόν. θᾶττον δὲ ἐκαλεῖτο σοφία, καὶ σοφὸς ὁ ταύτην ἐπαγγελλόμενος, ὅς εἴη ἂν κατ᾽ ἀκρότητα ψυχῆς ἀπηκριβωμένος, φιλόσοφος δὲ ὁ σοφίαν ἀσπαζόμενος.
     For translation, see pp. 17–18.

Clement *Stromata* 1.14.59.1; 1.14.61.4 (150–215 CE)

Φασὶ δὲ Ἕλληνες μετά γε Ὀρφέα καὶ Λίνον καὶ τοὺς παλαιοτάτους παρὰ σφίσι ποιητὰς ἐπὶ σοφίᾳ πρώτους θαυμασθῆναι τοὺς ἑπτὰ τοὺς ἐπικληθέντας σοφούς, . . . ὀψὲ δὲ Πυθαγόρας ὁ Φερεκύδου γνώριμος φιλόσοφον ἑαυτὸν πρῶτος ἀνηγόρευσεν.

The Greeks say that, after Orpheus and Linus and the most ancient of the poets of their period, the first to be admired for *sophia* were the so-called Seven *Sophoi*. . . . And at a late date, Pythagoras, the pupil of Pherecydes, was the first to refer to himself as *philosophos*.

————*Stromata* 4.9.1

ᾗ μοι δοκεῖ καὶ Πυθαγόρας σοφὸν μὲν εἶναι τὸν θεὸν λέγειν μόνον . . . ἑαυτὸν δὲ διὰ φιλίαν τὴν πρὸς τὸν θεὸν φιλόσοφον. διελέγετο γοῦν Μωυσεῖ, φησίν, ὁ θεὸς ὡς φίλος φίλῳ.

For which reason it seems to me that Pythagoras says that god alone is *sophos* . . . and that, because of his friendship (*philia*) with god, he is himself *philosophos*.

Iamblichus *Protrepticus* (*"Exhortation to Philosophy"*) 9
(245–325 CE)

[4,9–13] Ἀπὸ τοῦ βουλήματος τῆς φύσεως ἔφοδος εἰς προτροπὴν κατὰ τὴν Πυθαγόρου ἀπόκρισιν, ἣν εἶπε τοῖς ἐν Φλιοῦντι πυνθανομένοις τίς ἐστι καὶ τίνος ἕνεκα γέγονε· ταύτῃ γὰρ ἑπομένως συλλογιζόμεθα τὴν προτροπὴν ὅλην.

[51,6–8] καὶ τοῦτό ἐστι τῶν ὄντων οὗ χάριν ἡ φύσις ἡμᾶς ἐγέννησε καὶ ὁ θεός. τί δὴ τοῦτό ἐστι Πυθαγόρας ἐρωτώμενος, "τὸ θεάσασθαι" εἶπε "τὸν οὐρανόν," καὶ ἑαυτὸν δὲ θεωρὸν ἔφασκεν εἶναι τῆς φύσεως καὶ τούτου ἕνεκα παρεληλυθέναι εἰς τὸν βίον.

[53,19–54,5] ὥσπερ γὰρ εἰς Ὀλυμπίαν αὐτῆς ἕνεκα τῆς θέας ἀποδημοῦμεν, καὶ εἰ μηδὲν μέλλοι πλεῖον ἀπ' αὐτῆς ἔσεσθαι (αὐτὴ γὰρ ἡ θεωρία κρείττων πολλῶν ἐστι χρημάτων), καὶ τὰ Διονύσια δὲ θεωροῦμεν οὐχ ὡς ληψόμενοί τι παρὰ τῶν ὑποκριτῶν ἀλλὰ καὶ προσθέντες, πολλάς τε ἄλλας θέας ἑλοίμεθα <ἂν> ἀντὶ πολλῶν χρημάτων· οὕτω καὶ τὴν θεωρίαν τοῦ παντὸς προτιμητέον πάντων τῶν δοκούντων εἶναι χρησίμων. οὐ γὰρ δήπου ἐπὶ μὲν ἀνθρώπους μιμουμένους γύναιακαὶ δούλους, τοὺς δὲ μαχομένους καὶ θέοντας, δεῖπορεύεσθαι μετὰ πολλῆς σπουδῆς ἕνεκα τοῦ θεάσασθαι αὐτούς, τὴν δὲ τῶν ὄντων φύσιν καὶ τὴν ἀλήθειαν οὐκ οἴεσθαι δεῖν θεωρεῖν ἀμισθί.

For translation, see p. 120.

────*On the Pythagorean Way of Life* 12 (§58–59)

Λέγεται δὲ Πυθαγόρας πρῶτος φιλόσοφον ἑαυτὸν προσαγορεῦσαι, οὐ καινοῦ μόνον ὀνόματος ὑπάρξας, ἀλλὰ καὶ πρᾶγμα οἰκεῖον προεκδιδάσκων χρησίμως. ἐοικέναι γὰρ ἔφη τὴν εἰς τὸν βίον τῶν ἀνθρώπων πάροδον τῷ ἐπὶ τὰς πανηγύρεις ἀπαντῶντι ὁμίλῳ. ὡς γὰρ ἐκεῖσε παντοδαποὶ φοιτῶντες ἄνθρωποι ἄλλος κατ' ἄλλου χρείαν ἀφικνεῖται (ὃ μὲν χρηματισμοῦ τε καὶ κέρδους χάριν ἀπεμπολῆσαι τὸν φόρτον ἐπειγόμενος, ὃ δὲ δόξης ἕνεκα ἐπιδειξόμενος ἥκει τὴν ῥώμην τοῦ σώματος· ἔστι δὲ καὶ τρίτον εἶδος καὶ τό γε ἐλευθεριώτατον, συναλιζόμενον τόπων θέας ἕνεκα καὶ δημιουργημάτων καλῶν καὶ ἀρετῆς ἔργων καὶ λόγων, ὧν αἱ ἐπιδείξεις εἰώθεσαν ἐν ταῖς πανηγύρεσι γίνεσθαι), οὕτως δὴ κἂν τῷ βίῳ παντοδαποὺς ἀνθρώπους ταῖς σπουδαῖς εἰς ταὐτὸ συναθροίζεσθαι· τοὺς μὲν γὰρ χρημάτων καὶ τρυφῆς αἱρεῖ πόθος, τοὺς δὲ ἀρχῆς καὶ ἡγεμονίας ἵμερος φιλονεικίαι τε δοξομανεῖς κατέχουσιν. εἰλικρινέστατον δὲ εἶναι τοῦτον ἀνθρώπου τρόπον, τὸν ἀποδεξάμενον τὴν τῶν καλλίστων θεωρίαν, ὃν καὶ προσονομάζειν φιλόσοφον. καλὴν μὲν οὖν εἶναι τὴν τοῦ σύμπαντος οὐρανοῦ θέαν καὶ τῶν ἐν αὐτῷ φορουμένων ἀστέρων εἴ τις καθορῴη τὴν τάξιν· κατὰ μετουσίαν μέντοι τοῦ πρώτου καὶ τοῦ νοητοῦ εἶναι αὐτὸ τοιοῦτον. τὸ δὲ πρῶτον ἦν ἐκεῖνο, ἡ τῶν ἀριθμῶν τε καὶ λόγων φύσις διὰ πάντων διαθέουσα, καθ᾽ οὓς τὰ πάντα ταῦτα συντέτακταί τε ἐμμελῶς καὶ κεκόσμηται πρεπόντως, καὶ σοφία μὲν ἡ τῷ ὄντι ἐπιστήμη τις ἡ περὶ τὰ καλὰ τὰ πρῶτα καὶ θεῖα καὶ ἀκήρατα καὶ ἀεὶ κατὰ τὰ αὐτὰ καὶ ὡσαύτως ἔχοντα ἀσχολουμένη, ὧν μετοχῇ καὶ τὰ ἄλλα ἂν εἴποι τις καλά· φιλοσοφία δὲ ἡ ζήλωσις τῆς τοιαύτης θεωρίας. καλὴ μὲν οὖν καὶ αὕτη παιδείας ἦν ἐπιμέλεια ἡ συντείνουσα αὐτῷ πρὸς τὴν τῶν ἀνθρώπων ἐπανόρθωσιν.

For translation, see pp. 118–19.

———On the Pythagorean Way of Life 8 (§44)

Σχεδὸν γὰρ ταῖς ἀγωγαῖς διαφέρειν τοὺς μὲν ἀνθρώπους τῶν θηρίων, τοὺς δὲ Ἕλληνας τῶν βαρβάρων, τοὺς δὲ ἐλευθέρους τῶν οἰκετῶν, τοὺς δὲ φιλοσόφους τῶν τυχόντων, ὅλως δὲ τηλικαύτην ἔχοντας ὑπεροχήν, ὥστε τοὺς μὲν θᾶττον τρέχοντας τῶν ἄλλων ἐκ μιᾶς πόλεως τῆς ἐκείνων ἑπτὰ κατὰ τὴν Ὀλυμπίαν εὑρεθῆναι, τοὺς δὲ τῇ σοφίᾳ προέχοντας ἐξ ἁπάσης τῆς οἰκουμένης ἑπτὰ συναριθμηθῆναι. ἐν δὲ τοῖς ἑξῆς χρόνοις, ἐν οἷς ἦν αὐτός, ἕνα φιλοσοφίᾳ προέχειν τῶν πάντων· καὶ γὰρ τοῦτο τὸ ὄνομα ἀντὶ τοῦ σοφοῦ ἑαυτὸν ἐπωνόμασε.

For translation, see pp. 121–22

Eusebius *Praeparatio evangelica* 10.4.12–13 (work: 314–324 CE)

ἐνταῦθά που νέοι τῷ χρόνῳ οἱ ἑπτὰ γενόμενοι σοφοὶ ἐπὶ κατορθώσει μνημονεύονται ἀγωγῆς τῆς ἠθικωτέρας, ὧν πλέον οὐδὲν τῶν βοωμένων ἀποφθεγμάτων μνημονεύεται. ὀψὲ δε τι καὶ μᾶλλον τοῖς χρόνοις ὑποβεβηκότες οἱ παρ᾽ Ἕλλησι φιλόσοφοι διαπρέψαι μνημονεύονται. ὧν Πυθαγόρας πρῶτος, Φερεκύδου γνώριμος, τὸ φιλοσοφίαν ἀνευρὼν ὄνομα . . .

The Seven *Sophoi*, who belong to that time, are remembered for succeeding at improving ethical conduct; nothing more is remembered than their celebrated maxims. Later, after much time had passed, the *philosophoi* of the Greeks are remembered to have come to eminence. First among them was Pythagoras, the pupil of Pherecydes, who invented the name *philosophia* . . .

———Preface to St. Jerome's *Chronicle* 14,2–4 (work: ca. 311 CE)

Porro Liber et reliqui quos mox inferemus, post CC annum Cecropis fuerunt; Linus scilicet, et Zetus, et Amphion, Musaeus, Orpheus, Minos, Perseus, Aesculapius, gemini Castores, Hercules, cum quo Apollo servivit Admeto, post quos facta est Troianae urbis eversio: quam Homerus longo sequitur intervallo;

Homerus autem Solone et Thalete Milesio, caeterisque, qui cum iis septem Sapientes appellati sunt, multo prior reperitur. Deinde Pythagoras exstitit, qui se non sapientem, ut priores, sed philosophum, id est, amatorem sapientiae, dici voluit; quem secutus Socrates, Platonem erudivit: a quo famosa in partes philosophia divisa est. Horum singulos juxta ordinem sequentis historiae suis locis inseremus.

Again, Liber and the rest whom we will bring in next, lived 200 years after the year of Cecrops; Linus certainly, and Zetus, and Amphion, Musaeus, Orpheus, Minos, Perseus, Asclepias, the twin Castors, Hercules, with whom Apollo served Admetus, after which the fall of the Trojan city happened: which Homer follows after a long interval; but Homer is found to have lived long before Solon or Thales of Miletus and the others who together with them have been called the Seven Sages. Then Pythagoras appeared, who wished it to be said that he was not a Sage, as those earlier, but a philosopher, that is, a lover of wisdom; Socrates followed him, who taught Plato; by whom philosophy was divided into its well-known parts. We shall put each of these in its place according to the order of the following history. (trans. Pearse)

Ambrose of Milan *On Abraham the Patriarch* 2.7.37 (work ca. 380 CE)

Quanto prior quam ipse pater philosophiae Plato, vel eius inventor nominis Pythagoras!

Much earlier than the very father of philosophy, Plato, was the inventor of the word, Pythagoras!

Augustine *On the Trinity* 14.1.2 (work: 400–428 CE)

Nonne terrebimur exemplo Pythagorae qui cum ausus non fuisset sapientem profiteri, philosophum potius, id est amatorem sapientiae, se esse respondit, a quo id nomen exortum ita deinceps posteris placuit ut quantalibet de rebus ad sapientiam pertinentibus doctrina quisque uel sibi uel aliis uideretur excellere non nisi philosophus uocaretur.

Pythagoras, since he did not venture to profess wisdom, answered that he was rather a philosopher, that is, a lover of wisdom. Thus arose this name which so pleased succeeding generations that from then on, no matter how greatly anyone might seem either to himself or to others, to excel in subjects pertaining to wisdom, yet he should only be called a philosopher. (trans. McKenna)

———*City of God* 8.2 (work: 413–426 CE)

Italicum genus auctorem habuit Pythagoram Samium, a quo etiam ferunt ipsum philosophiae nomen exortum. Nam cum antea sapientes appellarentur, qui modo quodam laudabilis vitae aliis; praestare videbantur, iste interrogatus, quid profiteretur, philosophum se esse respondit, id est studiosum uel amatorem sapientiae; quoniam sapientem profiteri arrogantissimum videbatur.

Pythagoras of Samos is said to be the founder of the Italian school and also the originator of the word "philosophy." Before his time, any person of outstanding achievement was called a wise man. But when Pythagoras, who considered it arrogance to call one's self wise, was asked his profession, he replied that he was a philosopher, that is to say, a student or lover of wisdom. (trans. Walsh, Zema, Monahan, and Honan)

Hermias *Commentary on Plato's "Phaedrus"* 278b (ca. 410–450 CE)

Πάντων δὲ τῶν πρὸ Πυθαγόρου καὶ περί τι ἐπιστημόνων σοφῶν καλουμένων, ὁ Πυθαγόρας ἐλθὼν τὸ θεῖον μόνον σοφὸν ἐκάλεσεν, ὡς ἐξαίρετον τὸ ὄνομα τῷ θεῷ ἀπονείμας, τοὺς δὲ ὀρεγομένους σοφίας φιλοσόφους ἐκάλεσεν. Οὕτως καὶ ἐν τῷ Συμποσίῳ σοφὸν ἐκάλεσε τὸν Ἔρωτα ὁ Σωκράτης, φιλόσοφον δὲ οὔ· "θεῶν γὰρ, φησὶν, οὐδεὶς φιλόσοφος." τίνες οὖν οἱ φιλόσοφοι; οἱ ὀρεγόμενοι τῆς σοφίας.

Before Pythagoras, anyone expert in something was called *sophos*, but when Pythagoras came he called the divine alone *sophos*, . . . and he called those desiring *sophia philosophoi*. Thus even in the *Symposium* Socrates calls Eros *sophos*, but not a *philosophos*—"For none of the gods," he said, "is *philosophos*." Thus who are the *philosophoi*?—the ones desiring *sophia*.

Ammonius *Commentary on Porphyry's "Isagoge"* Proem 9,7–9, 16–18 (435/445–517/526 CE)

Ὁ μέντοι Πυθαγόρας φησι "φιλοσοφία ἐστὶ φιλία σοφίας" πρῶτος τῷ παρὰ τοῖς παλαιοτέροις ἐπιστὰς ἁμαρτήματι. ἐπειδὴ γὰρ ἐκεῖνοι σοφὸν ὠνόμαζον τὸν ἡντιναοῦν μετιόντα τέχνην . . . μεθίστησι τὴν προσηγορίαν ταύτην ἐπὶ τὸν θεὸν ὡς μόνον ἐκεῖνον καλεῖσθαι σοφόν, τὸν θεόν φημι, σοφίαν τε καὶ τὴν τῶν ὄντων ἀιδίων γνῶσιν.

Pythagoras, however, says "*Philosophia* is the love of wisdom (*philia sophias*)," being the first to charge an error against those in the past—for they called *sophos* a person who practiced any *technê* whatsoever . . . he [by contrast] transfers this appellation to God, as he calls him alone *sophos*—God, I mean—having *sophia* and recognition of eternal things.

Isidore of Seville *The Etymologies* 8.6.1.2 (560–636 CE)

Nomen Philosophorum primum a Pythagora fertur exortum. Nam dum antea Graeci veteres sophistas, id est sapientes, aut doctores sapientiae semetipsos iactantius nominarent, iste interrogatus quid profiteretur, verecundo nomine philosophum, id est amatorem sapientiae se esse respondit, quoniam sapientem profiteri arrogantissimum videbatur.

The term "philosopher" is reported to have originated with Pythagoras. Indeed, before that, the older Greek sophists called themselves, ostentatiously, the wise men, or teachers of wisdom; he [sc. Pythagoras], asked what he professed to be, replied with a modest term, "philosopher," that is, a lover of wisdom; and that professing to be wise seemed quite arrogant.

———*The Etymologies* 14.6.31

Pythagoras Samius, a quo philosophiae nomen inventum est.

Pythagoras the Samian, who invented the word *philosophia*.

CLASSICAL USES OF *PHILOSOPH-*
DISCUSSED IN THIS BOOK

Name and source	Date	Pages
Heraclitus		
B35/D40	>475	22, 26, 37–66, 261–62
Zeno		
Against the Philosophoi [title]	>430	151–53
[Hippocrates]		
On Ancient Medicine 20.1	ca. 420s	135–42
Herodotus		
History 1.30	425–415	128–32
Gorgias		
Helen 13	441–380	143–47
Thucydides		
History 2.40.1	>396 or 431	132–35, 168, 170
Anonymous		
Dissoi Logoi 1.1, 9.1	ca. 400	204–6
Simon the Shoemaker		
On Philosophy [title]	>399	153–55
Democritus		
"*Philosophia*" [nickname]	>370?	155–56
Aristophanes		
Ecclesiazusae 571	391	147–48
Prodicus		
B6/D7 = Pl. *Euthyd.* 305c7	>395	211
Lysias		
24.10	403–380	149
[8.11]	<300	149n73, 209
Alcidamas		
On Nature	>369?	141, 268–69
On the Sophists	390	207–9
in Aristotle [two sayings]	>350?	115–16, 198, 207
[*Odysseus*]	<300	209

Antisthenes		
in Diogenes Laertius, etc.	>365	31, 197, 203
[several sayings]		
Aristippus		
in Diogenes Laertius,	>356	203
etc. [six sayings]		
Aeschines the Socratic		
Telauges[?]	>350	203n25
Simmias		
On Philosophy [title]	>370	268
Phaedo		
Zopyrus	>360	195–97
Isocrates		
Against the Sophists	390	210
Busiris	390–385	212
Panegyrius	380	215
To Demonicus	374–372	212
Evagoras	374–372	212
To Nicocles	374–372	212
Nicocles	374–372	212
Helen	ca. 370	211
Areopagiticus	355	212–13
Antidosis	354–353	149n73, 213–14
Plato		
Apology	≥ 399	165–66, 301
Charmides	>347	223–28, 315n61
Gorgias	>347	301–2
Lysis	>347	246–49
Parmenides	>347	244
Phaedo	>347	192
Phaedrus	>347	231–44
Philebus	>347	245–46
Protagoras	>347	228–31
Republic	>347	250–56, 302
Rival Lovers	4th c.	310–16
Sophist	>347	192
Symposium	>347	249–50
Theaetetus	>347	191–92

Xenophon

Anabasis	>350	177–78
Cyropedia	>350	177
Memorabilia	>350	166, 172–82
Oeconomicus	>350	186–89, 300
Poroi	>350	180
Symposium	>350	132n21, 182–86

Herodorus

Fr. 14 *BNJ*	400–350	198–200

Aristotle

Metaphysics	>323	276–80
Poetics	>323	275
Protrepticus [with *POxy.* 3659?]	353	80n36, 302–9

Heraclides

On Diseases	360–353	288–90, 305–6

Demosthenes

[*Erotikos*] 50.5	350–330	132n21
[*Against Olympiodorus*] 49	341/0	150n73

Aeschines

Against Ctesiphon 108, 257	ca. 330	43n20, 132n21
Against Timarchus 41	ca. 345	43n20, 132n21

Alexis

Galateia fr. 37	ca. 350?	297–98
Linus fr. 140	>275	299–300
unnamed play fr. 247	345–320?	298–99

Philemon

Philosophoi fr. 88	>262	174

Temple of Apollo at Delphi

Ai Khanoum inscription	350–261	291–97

PHIL- PREFIXED WORDS
APPEARING IN THIS BOOK

Adjectival form	Second element and LSJ entry	Page
aphilosophos	σοφός: "skilled in any craft or art, clever"	238
aphilotimos	τιμή: "worship, esteem, honor"	77, 79
philagathos	ἀγαθός: "good, well-born, gentle"	82
philaglaos	ἀγλαός: "splendid, shining, bright"	87
philaimatos	αἷμα: "blood"	87
philaitios	αἰτία: "responsibility, accusation, cause"	6, 88
philakrêtos	ἄκρατος: "unmixed"	254
philalethês	ἀληθής: "unconcealed, true"	253
philanthrôpos	ἄνθρωπος: "human"	78
philaretos	ἀρετή: "goodness, excellence"	74
philarguros	ἄργυρος: "white metal, silver"	88
philautos	αὐτός: "self"	80–82
philêdonês	ἡδονή: "enjoyment, pleasure"	81
philêkoos	ἀκοή: "hearing, sound heard"	255–56
philêliastês	ἡλιαία: "supreme court"	91–92
philêretmos	ἐρετμόν: "oar"	84–85
phileris	ἔρις: "strife, quarrel"	80
philetairos	ἑταῖρος: "comrade, companion"	77, 247
philichthus	ἰχθῦς: "fish"	76
philippos	ἵππος: "horse"	74, 76, 248
philochrêmatos	χρήματα: "goods, property, money"	81–82
philodeipnos	δεῖπνον: "meal"	76
philodespotos	δεσπότης: "master, lord"	87
philodik(ai)os	δίκη: "custom, right, justice"	74, 78
philodoxos	δόξα: "expectation, notion, opinion"	255–56
philogeôrgos	γεωργός: "farming, farmer"	254
philoglukus	γλυκύς: "sweet"	254
philogumnastês	γυμνασία: "exercise"	230, 248, 313
philogunaios	γυνή: "wife, woman"	92
philoinos	οἶνος: "wine"	254
philokalos	καλός: "beautiful"	74, 79, 133–34, 234–37, 250
philokerdês	κέρδος: "gain, profit"	87
philokertomos	κέρτομος: "mocking, delusive"	86

Adjectival form	Second element and LSJ entry	Page
philokteanos	κτέανα: "possessions, property"	86
philokubos	κύβος: "cubical die"	91–92
philokuôn	κύων: "dog"	248
philologos	λόγος: "talk"	84
philoloidoros	λοίδορος: "railing, abusive"	78, 92
philomachos	μάχη: "battle, combat"	87
philomathês	μάθημα: "lesson, learning"	255–56
philo(m)mêdês	μῆδος: "plans, prudence" or "genital"	85
philommeidês	μείδημα: "smile"	85
philomolpos	μολπή: "dance, song"	90
philomômos	μῶμος: "blame"	87
philomuthos	μῦθος: "word, speech"	279
philon(e)ikios	νίκη: "victory"	78, 87
philopaigmôn	παῖγμα: "play, sport"	86–87
philopais	παῖς: "child"	254
philophilos	φίλος: "beloved, dear, friend"	77, 247
philophrôn	φρήν: "mind" (non-standard case)	87
philoploutos	πλοῦτος: "wealth"	88
philopoiêtês	ποίημα: "poetry"	225
philoponos	πόνος: "toil"	74, 235, 254
philopotês	ποτής: "drink"	87, 91–92
philopragmôn	πρᾶγμα: "deed, act"	78
philopseudês	ψευδής: "lying, false"	85–86
philopsogos	ψόγος: "fault, blame"	88
philopsuchos	ψυχή: "soul"	82
philoptolemos	πόλεμος: "war, battle"	86
philortux	ὄρτυξ: "quail"	248
philositos	σῖτος: "grain, bread"	254
philoskômmôn	σκῶμμα: "jest"	92
philosophos	σοφός: "wise (person)"	passim
philostephanos	στέφανος: "crown"	85
philostorgos	στοργή: "affection"	80
philotechnos	τέχνη: "art, skill"	251–52
philotheamôn/-ros	θέαμα: "sight, spectacle"	74, 77–78, 254–55
philothutês	θυσία: "sacrifice"	91–92
philotimos	τιμή: "worship, esteem, honor"	75, 81, 87, 254–55
philotoioutos	τοιοῦτος: "a such"	73–82
philoxenos	ξένος: "guest-friend"	86, 91–92
philozôos	ζωός: "living"	81–82
philupnos	ὕπνος: "sleep"	92

(For proper names and conjectured Mycenaean equivalents, see pp. 89–90.)

BIBLIOGRAPHY

Adler, Ada, ed. 1928. *Suda Lexicon*. Leipzig: Teubner.

Adorno, Francesco, ed. 1989. *Corpus dei papiri filosofici greci e latini: Testi e lessico nei papiri di cultura greca e latina: Pt. 1 Autori noti. Vol. 1.1 [A–C]*. Firenze: L. S. Olschki.

Alieva, Olga. 2013. "Protreptic in the Socratics: In Search of a Genre." In *Socratica III: Studies on Socrates, the Socratics, and the Ancient Socratic Literature*, edited by Alessandro Stavru and Fulvia de Luisa, 41–55. Berlin: Akademie Verlag.

Andrewes, Antony. 1956. *The Greek Tyrants*. London: Hutchinson.

Annas, Julia. 1985. "Self-Knowledge in Early Plato." In *Platonic Investigations*, edited by Dominic J. O'Meara, 121–38. Washington, DC: Catholic University of America Press.

Anonymous, ed. 1833. *Diogenis Laertii De Vitis Philosophorum. Libri X Cum Indice Rerum. Ad Optimorum Librorum Fidem Accurate Editi*. Leipzig: C. Tauchnitz.

Anonymous, trans. 1758. *Diogène Laërce: Les vies des plus illustres philosophes de l'antiquité: Avec leurs dogmes, leurs systemes, leur morale, et leurs sentences les plus remarquables*. Amsterdam: J. H. Schneider.

Arnott, W. Geoffrey. 1996. *Alexis: The Fragments: A Commentary*. Cambridge: Cambridge University Press.

Asheri, David, Alan B. Lloyd, and Aldo Corcella. 2007. *A Commentary on Herodotus Books I–IV*, edited by Oswyn Murray and Alfonso Moreno. Oxford: Oxford University Press.

Audring, Gert, ed. 1992. *Xenophon: Ökonomische Schriften*. Berlin: Akademie Verlag.

Aura Jorro, Francisco, ed. 1993. *Diccionario micénico*. 2 vols. Madrid: Consejo Superior de Investigaciones Científicas.

Bailey, Dominic. 2008. "Excavating *Dissoi Logoi* 4." *Oxford Studies in Ancient Philosophy* 35: 249–64.

Barker, Andrew. 2014. *Ancient Greek Writers on Their Musical Past: Studies in Greek Musical Historiography*. Pisa: F. Serra.

Bar-Kochva, Bezalel. 2010. *The Image of the Jews in Greek Literature: The Hellenistic Period*. Berkeley: University of California Press.

Barnes, Jonathan. 1982. *The Presocratic Philosophers*. Rev. ed. London: Routledge.

Barney, Rachel. 2012. "History and Dialectic." In *Aristotle's Metaphysics Alpha: Symposium Aristotelicum*, edited by Carlos G. Steel, 69–104. Oxford: Oxford University Press.

———. 2016. "Gorgias's *Encomium of Helen*." In *Ten Neglected Classics of Philosophy*, edited by Eric Schliesser, 1–25. Oxford: Oxford University Press.

Baron, Christopher. 2013. *Timaeus of Tauromenium and Hellenistic Historiography*. Cambridge: Cambridge University Press.

Bartlett, Robert, ed. 1996. *Xenophon: The Shorter Socratic Writings: "Apology of Socrates to the Jury," "Oeconomicus," and "Symposium."* Ithaca, NY: Cornell University Press.

Bartonek, Antonin. 1999. "Mycenaean Common Nouns in the Disguise of Proper Names." In *Floreant Studia Mycenaea: Akten des X. Internationalen Mykenologischen Colloquiums vom 1.–5. Mai 1995 in Salzburg*, edited by Sigrid Deger-Jalkotzy, Stefan Hiller, and Oswald Panagl, 121–29. Vienna: Verlag der Österreichischen Akademie der Wissenschaften.

Beekes, Robert. 2010. *Etymological Dictionary of Greek*. 2 vols. Leiden: Brill.

Belfiore, Elizabeth. 2012. *Socrates' Daimonic Art: Love for Wisdom in Four Platonic Dialogues*. Cambridge: Cambridge University Press.

Belloni, Luigi, ed. 2000. *Erodoto: Il regno di Creso*. Venice: Marsilio.

Benardete, Seth. 1965. "XPH and ΔEI in Plato and Others." *Glotta* 43: 285–98.

———. 1969. *Herodotean Inquiries*. The Hague: Martinus Nijhoff.

Bergk, Theodor, ed. 1872. *Aristophanis Comoediae*. 2nd ed. 2 vols. Leipzig: Teubner.

Bernard, Paul. 1967. "Aï Khanum on the Oxus: A Hellenistic City in Central Asia." *Proceedings of the British Academy* 53: 71–95.

Betegh, Gábor. 2009. "Tale, Theology and Teleology in the *Phaedo*." In *Plato's Myths*, edited by Catalin Partenie, 77–100. Cambridge: Cambridge University Press.

———. 2013. "Socrate et Archélaos dans les *Nuées*: Philosophie naturelle et éthique." In *Comédie et philosophie: Socrate et les «Présocratiques» dans les Nuées d'Aristophane*, edited by André Laks and Rossella Saetta-Cottone, 87–106. Paris: Éditions Rue d'Ulm.

———. 2014. "Pythagoreans, Orphism and Greek Religion." In *A History of Pythagoreanism*, edited by Carl Huffman, 149–66. Cambridge: Cambridge University Press.

———. 2016. "Archelaus on Cosmogony and the Origins of Social Institutions." *Oxford Studies in Ancient Philosophy* 51: 1–40.

Billings, Joshua and Christopher Moore, eds. Forthcoming. *The Cambridge Companion to the Sophists*. Cambridge: Cambridge University Press.

Bischoff, Heinrich. 1932. "Der Warner bei Herodot." Diss., Marburg.

Blaydes, F.H.M., ed. 1881. *Aristophanis Comoediae*, Vol. 3, *Ecclesiazusae*. Halle: Orphanotropheum.

Bloomer, W. Martin. 1992. *Valerius Maximus and the Rhetoric of the New Nobility*. Chapel Hill: University of North Carolina Press.

Bod, Rens. 2013. *A New History of the Humanities: The Search for Principles and Patterns from Antiquity to the Present*. Oxford: Oxford University Press.

Bodnár, István. 2007. *Oenopides of Chius: A Survey of the Modern Literature with a Collection of the Ancient Testimonia*. Berlin: Max-Planck-Institut für Wissenschaftsgeschichte.

Boedeker, Deborah. 1974. *Aphrodite's Entry into Greek Epic*. Leiden: Brill.

Boisacq, Émile. 1938. *Dictionnaire étymologique de la langue grecque*. 3rd ed. Heidelberg: Winter.

Bollack, Jean, and Heinz Wismann, eds. 1972. *Héraclite ou la séparation*. Paris: Les Éditions de Minuit.

Bollansée, Jan. 1998a. "Writers on the Seven Sages (1005–1007)." In *Die Fragmente der griechischen Historiker Continued. Part IV. Biography and Antiquarian Literature. IV A. Biography. Fascicle 1. The Pre-Hellenistic Period*, edited by Guido Schepens. Leiden: Brill.

———. 1998b. "Andron of Ephesos (1005)." In *Die Fragmente der griechischen Historiker Continued. Part IV. Biography and Antiquarian Literature. IV A. Biography. Fascicle 1. The Pre-Hellenistic Period*, edited by Guido Schepens. Leiden: Brill.

———. 1999. "Fact and Fiction, Falsehood and Truth: D. Fehling and Ancient Legendry about the Seven Sages." *Museum Helveticum* 56: 65–75.

Bouchard, Elsa. 2015. "Aphrodite *Philommêdês* in the *Theogony*." *Journal of Hellenic Studies* 135: 8–18.

Bowen, Anthony, ed. 1998. *Xenophon: Symposium*. Warminster: Aris & Phillips.

Bowra, Cecil. 1961. *Greek Lyric Poetry: From Alcman to Simonides*. 2nd ed. Oxford: Clarendon Press.

Boys-Stones, George. 2004. "Phaedo of Elis and Plato on the Soul." *Phronesis* 49: 1–23.

Bréal, Michael. 1897. *Essai de sémantique (Science des significations)*. Paris: Hachette.

Bresson, Alain. 1979. *Mythe et contradiction: Analyse de la VIIe Olympique de Pindare*. Paris: Les Belles Lettres.

Brisson, Luc, ed. 2014. *Écrits attribués à Platon*. Paris: Flammarion.

Broadie, Sarah. 2012. "A Science of First Principles." In *Aristotle's Metaphysics Alpha: Symposium Aristotelicum*, edited by Carlos G. Steel, 43–67. Oxford: Oxford University Press.

———, and Christopher Rowe, eds. 2002. *Aristotle: Nicomachean Ethics*. Oxford: Oxford University Press.

Bromberg, Jacques. 2012. "Academic Disciplines in Aristophanes' *Clouds* (200–3)." *Classical Quarterly* 62: 81–91.

Brown, Eric. Forthcoming. "Plato's Socrates and his Conception of Philosophy." In *The Cambridge Companion to Plato*, edited by Richard Kraut. 2nd ed. Cambridge: Cambridge University Press.

Brown, Malcolm, and James Coulter. 1971. "The Middle Speech of Plato's *Phaedrus*." *Journal of the History of Philosophy* 9: 405–23.

Bruell, Christopher. 1987. "On the Original Meaning of Political Philosophy: An Interpretation of Plato's *Lovers*." In *The Roots of Political Philosophy: Ten Forgotten Socratic Dialogues*, edited by Thomas L. Pangle, 91–110. Ithaca, NY: Cornell University Press.

Brumbaugh, Robert. 1991. "Simon and Socrates." *Ancient Philosophy* 11: 151–52.

Buck, Carl. 1949. *A Dictionary of Selected Synonyms in the Principal Indo-European Languages: A Contribution to the History of Ideas*. Chicago: University of Chicago Press.

Burger, Ronna. 1980. *Plato's "Phaedrus": A Defense of a Philosophic Art of Writing.* Tuscaloosa, AL: University of Alabama Press.

Burkert, Walter. 1960. "Platon oder Pythagoras? Zum Ursprung des Wortes «Philosophie»." *Hermes* 88: 159–77.

——. 1972. *Lore and Science in Ancient Pythagoreanism.* Translated by Edwin L. Minar. Cambridge, MA: Harvard University Press.

——. 1992. *The Orientalizing Revolution: Near Eastern Influence on Greek Culture in the Early Archaic Age.* Translated by Margaret E. Pinder. Cambridge, MA: Harvard University Press.

Burnet, John, ed. 1901. *Platonis Opera*, Vol. 2, Oxford: Clarendon Press.

——. 1930. *Early Greek Philosophy.* 4th ed. London: Macmillan.

Burnyeat, Myles. 1998. "*Dissoi Logoi.*" In *Routledge Encyclopedia of Philosophy*, edited by Edward Craig, 3.106–7. 10 vols. London and New York: Routledge.

——. 2007. "Other Lives." *London Review of Books*, February 22, 2007, 3–6.

Burstein, Stanley. 1976. *Outpost of Hellenism: The Emergence of Heraclea on the Black Sea.* Berkeley: University of California Press.

——. 1985. *The Hellenistic Age from the Battle of Ipsos to the Death of Kleopatra VII.* Cambridge: Cambridge University Press.

Bywater, Ingram. 1876. "Aristotle's Dialogue 'On Philosophy.' " *Journal of Philology* 7: 64–88.

——, ed. 1877. *Heracliti Ephesii Reliquiae.* Oxford: Clarendon Press.

Cahn, Michael. 1989. "Reading Rhetoric Rhetorically: Isocrates and the Marketing of Insight." *Rhetorica* 7: 121–44.

Califf, D. J. 2003. "Metrodorus of Lampsacus and the Problem of Allegory: An Extreme Case?" *Arethusa* 36: 21–36.

Calogero, Guido. 1938. "L'autenticità dell'*Ipparco* Platonico." *Annali della Scuola Normale Superiore di Pisa* 7: 13–27.

Cambiano, Giuseppe. 2012. "The Desire to Know." In *Aristotle's Metaphysics Alpha: Symposium Aristotelicum*, edited by Carlos G. Steel. Oxford: Oxford University Press, 1–42.

Cambon, Pierre, ed. 2006. *Afghanistan, les trésors retrouvés: Collections du Musée National de Kaboul. Musée National des Arts Asiatiques-Guimet. 6 Décembre 2006–30 Avril 2007.* Paris: Editions de la Réunion des Musées Nationaux.

Cameron, Alister. 1938. *The Pythagorean Background of the Theory of Recollection.* Menasha, WI: George Banta Publishing Company.

Canali De Rossi, Filippo, ed. 2004. *Iscrizioni dello estremo oriente greco: Un repertorio.* Bonn: Rudolf Habelt.

Caponigri, A. Robert, trans. 1969. *Diogenes Laertius: Lives of the Philosophers.* Chicago: Regnery.

Carlini, Antonio. 1962. "Alcuni dialoghi Pseudoplatonici e l'accademia di Arcesilao." *Annali della Scuola Normale Superiore di Pisa* 31: 33–63.

——, ed. 1964. *Platone: Alcibiade, Alcibiade secondo, Ipparco, Rivali.* Turin: Boringhieri.

Cast, David. 2008. "Simon the Shoemaker and the Cobbler of Apelles." *Source: Notes in the History of Art* 28: 1–4.

Castagnoli, Luca. 2010. *Ancient Self-Refutation: The Logic and History of the Self-Refutation Argument from Democritus to Augustine.* Cambridge: Cambridge University Press.

Catana, Leo. 2016. "Doxographical or Philosophical History of Philosophy: On Michael Frede's Precepts for Writing the History of Philosophy." *History of European Ideas* 42: 170–77.

Cavaignac, Eugène. 1919. "A propos d'un document nouveau sur les Orthagorides." *Revue des études grecques* 32: 62–66.

Centrone, B. 2005. "Die *Anterastai* und Platons erotische Dialoge." In *Pseudoplatonica: Akten des Kongresses zu den Pseudoplatonica vom 6.–9. Juli 2003 in Bamberg,* edited by Klaus Döring, Michael Erler, and Stefan Schorn, 37–50. Stuttgart: F. Steiner.

Chantraine, Pierre, ed. 1949. *Xénophon: Économique.* Paris: Les Belles Lettres.

———. 1968. *Dictionnaire étymologique de la langue Grecque: Histoire des mots.* Paris: Klincksieck.

Cherniss, Harold. 1951. "Characteristics and Effects of Presocratic Philosophy." *Journal of the History of Ideas* 12: 319–45.

Chiesara, Maria Lorenza, ed. 2001. *Aristocles of Messene: Testimonia and Fragments.* Oxford: Oxford University Press.

Christ, Matthew. 1998. *The Litigious Athenian.* Baltimore: Johns Hopkins University Press.

Chroust, Anton-Hermann. 1947."Philosophy: Its Essence and Meaning in the Ancient World." *Philosophical Review* 56: 19–58.

———. 1964. "Some Reflections on the Origin of the Term 'Philosopher.' " *New Scholasticism* 28: 423–34.

———. 1973. *Observations on Some of Aristotle's Lost Works.* Notre Dame: University of Notre Dame Press.

Cipriano, Palmira. 1990. *I composti Greci con ΦΙΛΟΣ.* Viterbo: Universita della Tuscia Instituto di Studia Romanzi.

Clay, Diskin. 1979. "Socrates' Prayer to Pan." In *Arktouros: Hellenic Studies Presented to B. M. W. Knox,* edited by Glen Bowersock, Walter Burkert, and Michael Putnam, 345–53. Berlin: De Gruyter.

Clements, Ashley. 2014. "The Senses in Philosophy and Science: Five Conceptions from Heraclitus to Plato." In *A Cultural History of the Senses,* Vol. 1, *Antiquity,* edited by Jerry Toner, 115–38. London: Bloomsbury.

Cobet, Carel Gabriel, ed. 1878a. *Diogenis Laertii De Clarorum Philosophorum: Vitis, Dogmatibus et Apophthegmatibus Libri Decem.* Paris: Didot.

———. 1878b. *Collectanea Critica Quibus Continentur Observationes Criticae in Scriptores Graecos.* Leiden: Brill.

Cockle, Helen, ed. 1984. *The Oxyrhynchus Papyri,* Vol. 52, London: Egypt Exploration Fund.

Cole, Thomas. 1991. *The Origins of Rhetoric in Ancient Greece*. Baltimore: Johns Hopkins University Press.

Collins, James. 2015. *Exhortations to Philosophy: The Protreptics of Plato, Isocrates, and Aristotle*. Oxford: Oxford University Press.

Collins, Randall. 2000. *The Sociology of Philosophies: A Global Theory of Intellectual Change*. Cambridge, MA: Harvard University Press.

Collobert, Catherine. 2002. "Aristotle's Review of the Presocratics: Is Aristotle Finally a Historian of Philosophy?" *Journal of the History of Philosophy* 40: 281–95.

Conche, Marcel, ed. 1987. *Héraclite: Fragments*. 2nd ed. Paris: Presses Universitaires de France.

Conley, Thomas. 1985. "Dating the So-Called *Dissoi Logoi*: A Cautionary Note." *Ancient Philosophy* 5: 59–65.

Connor, W. Robert. 1993. "The *Histor* in History." In *Nomodeiktes: Greek Studies in Honour of Martin Ostwald*, edited by Ralph M. Rosen and Joseph Farrell, 3–15. Ann Arbor, MI: University of Michigan Press.

Consigny, Scott Porter. 2001. *Gorgias, Sophist and Artist*. Columbia, SC: University of South Carolina Press.

Constantinidou, Soteroula. 2008. *Logos into Mythos: The Case of Gorgias' "Encomium of Helen."* Athens: Kardamitsa.

Cook, Albert. 1975. "Heraclitus and the Conditions of Utterance." *Arion* 2: 431–81.

Cooper, John. 1997. *Plato: Complete Works*. With the assistance of D. S. Hutchinson. Indianapolis, IN: Hackett.

———. 2004. "Plato, Isocrates, and Cicero on the Independence of Oratory from Philosophy." In *Knowledge, Nature, and the Good*, 65–80. Princeton: Princeton University Press.

———. 2007. "Socrates and Philosophy as a Way of Life." In *Maieusis: Essays in Ancient Philosophy in Honour of Myles Burnyeat*, edited by Dominic Scott, 20–43. Oxford: Oxford University Press.

Cornford, Francis. 1912. *From Religion to Philosophy: A Study in the Origins of Western Speculation*. London: Arnold.

Coulter, James. 1967. "*Phaedrus* 179a: The Praise of Isocrates." *Greek, Roman and Byzantine Studies* 8: 225–36.

Couprie, Dirk. 2011. *Heaven and Earth in Ancient Greek Cosmology: From Thales to Heraclides Ponticus*. New York: Springer.

Crisp, Roger, trans. 2014. *Aristotle: Nicomachean Ethics*. Cambridge: Cambridge University Press.

Cunliffe, Richard. 1963. *A Lexicon of the Homeric Dialect*. Norman, OK: University of Oklahoma Press.

Curd, Patricia. 1991. "Knowledge and Unity in Heraclitus." *The Monist* 74: 531–49.

———. 2007. *Anaxagoras: Fragments and Testimonia*. Toronto: University of Toronto Press.

———. 2015. "Anaxagoras." *Stanford Encyclopedia of Philosophy* (Fall 2015 edition), edited by Edward N. Zalta. https://plato.stanford.edu/archives/fall2015/entries/anaxagoras.

Darbo-Peschanski, Catherine. 2007a. *L'historia: commencements grecs.* Paris: Gallimard.

———. 2007b. "The Origin of Greek Historiography." In *A Companion to Greek and Roman Historiography*, edited by John Marincola, 27–38. Malden, MA: Blackwell.

Davies, Malcolm. 1989. "Sisyphus and the Invention of Religion ('Critias' TrGF 1 (43) F 19 = B 25 DK)." *British Institute of Classical Studies* 36: 16–32.

Davis, Michael. 1984. "Philosophy and the Perfect Tense: On the Beginning of Plato's *Lovers.*" *Graduate Faculty Philosophy Journal* 10: 75–97.

De Cesaris, Giulia. 2018. "Iamblichus' Investiture of Pythagoras." *Méthexis* 30: 175–96.

Decleva Caizzi, Fernanda, ed. 1966. *Antisthenis Fragmenta.* Milan: Varese.

Deichgräber, Karl. 1935. "Original und Nachahmung: Zu Ps. Aristoteles *Magna Moralia* und Ps. Hippokrates *ΠΑΡΑΓΓΕΛΙΑΙ.*" *Hermes* 70.1: 106–10.

Delatte, Armand, ed. 1922. *La vie de Pythagore de Diogène Laërce.* Bruxelles: M. Lamertin.

De Sélincourt, Aubrey, trans. 1954. *Herodotus: The Histories.* London: Penguin Books.

Desideri, Paolo. 1991. "Cultura Eracleota: Da Erodoro a Eraclide Pontico, I." In *Pontica I: Recherches sur l'histoire du Pont dans l'antiquité*, edited by Bernard Rémy, 7–27. Saint-Étienne: Université Jean Monnet.

De Vogel, Cornelia. 1966. *Pythagoras and Early Pythagoreanism: An Interpretation of Neglected Evidence on the Philosopher Pythagoras.* Assen: Van Gorcum.

De Vries, G. J. 1953. "Isocrates' Reaction to the *Phaedrus.*" *Mnemosyne* 6: 39–45.

———. 1969. *A Commentary on the "Phaedrus" of Plato.* Amsterdam: Hakkert.

———. 1971. "Isocrates in the *Phaedrus*: A Reply." *Mnemosyne* 24: 387–90.

Diels, Hermann. 1901. *Herakleitos von Ephesos.* Berlin: Weidmann.

Di Lanzo, Danilo. 2018. "Phaedo of Elis: The Biography, *Zopyrus*, and His Intellectual Profile." In *Socrates and the Socratic Dialogue*, edited by Alessandro Stavru and Christopher Moore, 221–34. Leiden: Brill.

Dilcher, Roman. 2013. "How Not to Conceive Heraclitean Harmony." In *Doctrine and Doxography: Studies on Heraclitus and Pythagoras*, edited by David Sider and Dirk Obbink, 263–80. Berlin: De Gruyter.

Dillon, John. 2003. *The Heirs of Plato: A Study of the Old Academy, 347–274 B.C.* Oxford: Oxford University Press.

———. 2012. "Dubia and Spuria." In *The Continuum Companion to Plato*, edited by Gerald A. Press, 49–52. London: Continuum.

———. 2014. "Pythagoreanism in the Academic Tradition." In *A History of Pythagoreanism*, edited by Carl Huffman, 250–73. Cambridge: Cambridge University Press.

Dillon, Matthew. 1997. *Pilgrims and Pilgrimage in Ancient Greece.* London: Routledge.

Dinan, Andrew C. 2005. "Fragments in Context: Clement of Alexandria's Use of Quotations from Heraclitus." PhD Diss. Catholic University of America.

Dindorf, Wilhelm, ed. 1826. *Aristophanis Comoediae*. Oxford: Oxford University Press.

Dittenberger, Wilhelm, ed. 1915. *Sylloge Inscriptionum Graecarum*. 4 vols. Leipzig: S. Hirzel.

Dodds, E. R., ed. 1959. *Plato: Gorgias*. Oxford: Oxford University Press.

Dorandi, Tiziano, ed. 2013. *Diogenes Laertius: Lives of Eminent Philosophers*. Cambridge: Cambridge University Press.

———. 2018. "Socrates in the Ancient Biographical Tradition: From the Anonymous *PHib.* 182 to Diogenes Laertius." In *Socrates and the Socratic Dialogue*, edited by Alessandro Stavru and Christopher Moore, 787–98. Leiden: Brill.

Dorion, Louis-André, ed. 2003. *Xénophon: Mémorables. Introduction générale. Livre I*. Paris: Les Belles Lettres.

———. 2004. *Platon: Charmide, Lysis*. Paris: Flammarion.

———. 2011. *Xénophon: Mémorables. Livre IV*. Paris: Les Belles Lettres.

Dougan, Thomas, and Robert Henry, eds. 1934. *M. Tulli Ciceronis Tusculanarum Disputationum Libri Quinque: A Revised Text with Introduction and Commentary and a Collation of Numerous MSS*. 2 vols. Cambridge: Cambridge University Press.

Douglas, Alan, ed. 1990. *Tusculan Disputations II & V: With a Summary of III & IV*. Warminster: Aris & Phillips.

———. 1995. "Form and Content in the *Tusculan Disputations*." In *Cicero the Philosopher: Twelve Papers*, edited by J. G. F. Powell, 197–218. Oxford: Clarendon Press.

Dover, Kenneth, ed. 1968. *Aristophanes: Clouds*. Oxford: Clarendon Press.

———. 1974. *Greek Popular Morality in the Time of Plato and Aristotle*. Berkeley: University of California Press.

———. 1976. "The Freedom of the Intellectual in Greek Society." *Talanta* 7: 24–54.

———. 1986. "Ion of Chios: His Place in the History of Greek Literature." In *Chios: A Conference at the Homereion in Chios, 1984*, edited by John Boardman and C. E. Vaphopoulou-Richardson, 27–37. Oxford: Clarendon Press.

Drozdek, Adam. 2005. "Anaxagoras' Cosmic Mind." *Estudios clásicos* 127: 23–35.

———. 2011. *Athanasia: Afterlife in Greek Philosophy*. Zurich: Olms.

Dumont, Jean-Paul, ed. 1988. *Les Présocratiques*. Paris: Gallimard.

Dunbabin, Thomas. 1948. *The Western Greeks: The History of Sicily and South Italy from the Foundation of the Greek Colonies to 480 B.C.* Oxford: Oxford University Press.

Dunn, Francis. 2005. "On Ancient Medicine and Its Intellectual Context." In *Hippocrates in Context*, edited by P. J. Van der Eijk, 49–67. Leiden: Brill.

Dušanić, Slobodan. 1999. "Isocrates, the Chian Intellectuals, and the Political Context of the *Euthydemus*." *Journal of Hellenic Studies* 119: 1–16.

Ebert, Theodor. 2001. "Why Is Evenus Called a Philosopher at *Phaedo* 61c?" *Classical Quarterly* 51: 423–34.

Edmonds, John. 1931. *Elegy and Iambus*. Cambridge, MA: Harvard University Press.

Edmunds, Lowell. 2006. "What Was Socrates Called?" *Classical Quarterly* 56: 414–25.

Edwards, Michael. 2007. "Alcidamas." In *A Companion to Greek Rhetoric*, edited by Ian Worthington, 47–57. Malden, MA: Blackwell.

Emlyn-Jones, C. J. 1980. *The Ionians and Hellenism: A Study of the Cultural Achievement of Early Greek Inhabitants of Asia Minor.* London: Routledge.

Engels, Johannes. 2010. *Die Sieben Weisen: Leben, Lehren und Legenden.* Munich: Verlag C. H. Beck.

Enos, Richard. 2012. *Greek Rhetoric before Aristotle.* Rev. ed. Anderson, SC: Parlor Press.

Evans, Dale Wilt. 1976. "Plato's *Minos, Hipparchus, Theages* and *Lovers*: A Philosophical Interpretation." PhD Diss., Pennsylvania State University.

Farnell, Lewis. 1932. *The Works of Pindar*, Vol. 2, *Critical Commentary.* London: Macmillan.

Faulkner, Andrew, ed. 2008. *The Homeric Hymn to Aphrodite.* Oxford: Oxford University Press.

Fehling, Detlev. 1985. *Die Sieben Weisen und die frühgriechische Chronologie: Eine traditionsgeschichtliche Studie.* Bern: P. Lang.

Fennell, Charles, ed. 1893. *Pindar: The Olympian and Pythian Odes.* New ed. Cambridge: Cambridge University Press.

Fernandez-Galiano, Manuel, ed. 1956. *Pindaro: Olimpicas.* 2nd ed. Madrid: C. Bermejo.

Filonik, Jakub. 2013. "Athenian Impiety Trials: A Reappraisal." *Dike* 16: 11–96.

Finkelberg, Aryeh. 2017. *Heraclitus and Thales' Conceptual Scheme: A Historical Study.* Leiden: Brill.

Floyd, Edwin. 1990. "The Sources of Greek Ἵστωρ 'Judge, Witness.'" *Glotta* 68: 157–66.

———. 2012. "The Etymology and Early Use of Greek Sophos 'Wise.'" Presented at the International Linguistic Association, New York City, NY, November 2012.

Ford, Andrew. 1993. "Platonic Insults: Sophistic." *Common Knowledge* 2: 33–48.

———. 1994. "Protagoras' Head: Interpreting Philosophic Fragments in *Theaetetus.*" *American Journal of Philology* 115: 199–218.

———. 2002. *The Origins of Criticism: Literary Culture and Poetic Theory in Classical Greece.* Princeton: Princeton University Press.

———. 2008. "The Beginnings of Dialogue: Socratic Discourses and Fourth-Century Prose." In *The End of Dialogue in Antiquity*, edited by Simon Goldhill, 29–44. Cambridge: Cambridge University Press.

Fornara, Charles. 1971. "Evidence for the Date of Herodotus' Publication." *Journal of Hellenic Studies* 91: 25–34.

Fortenbaugh, William. 2014. *Theophrastus of Eresus. Commentary*, Vol. 9.2, *Sources on Discoveries and Beginnings, Proverbs et al. (Texts 727–741).* Leiden: Brill.

Fowler, Robert. 1997. "Polos of Akragas: Testimonia." *Mnemosyne* 50: 27–34.

———. 2011. "*Mythos* and *Logos.*" *Journal of Hellenic Studies* 131: 45–66.

Fränkel, Hermann. 1938. "A Thought Pattern in Heraclitus." *American Journal of Philology* 59: 309–37.

Frede, Michael. 2000. "The Philosopher." In *Greek Thought: A Guide to Classical Knowledge*, edited by Jacques Brunschwig and G.E.R. Lloyd, 3–19. Translated by Catherine Porter. Cambridge, MA: Harvard University Press.

―――. 2004. "Aristotle's Account of the Origins of Philosophy." *Rhizai* 1: 9–44.

Freeman, Kathleen. 1938. "Portrait of a Millionaire—Callias Son of Hipponicus." *Greece and Rome* 8: 20–35.

Freese, John, trans. 1926. *Aristotle: Rhetoric.* Loeb Classical Library. Cambridge, MA: Harvard University Press.

Friedländer, Paul. 1964. *Plato, 2: The Dialogues, First Period.* Translated by Hans Meyerhoff. New York: Pantheon Books.

Friedrich, Paul. 1982. *The Meaning of Aphrodite.* Chicago: University of Chicago Press.

Frisk, Hjalmar. 1954. *Griechisches etymologisches Wörterbuch.* Heidelberg: Winter.

Fronterotta, Francesco. 2013. *Eraclito: Frammenti.* Milan: BUR Classici greci e latini.

Fuentes González, Pedro Pablo, and Javier Campos Daroca. 2000. "Hérodore d'Héraclée." In *Dictionnaire des philosophes antiques*, edited by Richard Goulet, 3.671–75. Paris: Centre National de la Recherche Scientifique.

Führer, Rudolf. 1997. "Zur handschriftlichen Anordnung der inschriftlichen 7-Weisen-Sprüche." *Zeitschrift für Papyrologie und Epigraphik* 118: 153–61.

Gadamer, Hans-Georg. 1982. "On the Natural Inclination of Human Beings toward Philosophy." In *Reason in the Age of Science*, translated by Frederick G. Lawrence, 139–50. Cambridge, MA: MIT Press.

Gagarin, Michael. 1986. *Early Greek Law.* Berkeley, CA: University of California Press.

Gauthier, René Antoine, and Jean Yves Jolif, eds. 1959. *Aristote: L'Éthique à Nicomaque: Introduction, traduction et commentaire.* Louvain: Publications Universitaires de Louvain.

Gemin, Marco. 2017. "L'influenza di Anassagora sull'oratoria di Pericle." *Rhetorica* 35: 123–36.

Gentili, Bruno, ed. 2013. *Pindaro: Le olimpiche.* Rome: Fondazione Lorenzo Valla.

Gera, Deborah Levine. 1997. *Warrior Women: The Anonymous "Tractatus de Mulieribus."* Leiden: Brill.

―――. 2000. "Two Thought Experiments in the *Dissoi Logoi*." *American Journal of Philology* 121: 21–45.

Gernet, Louis, and André Boulanger. 1970. *Le génie grec dans la religion.* 2nd ed. Paris: La Renaissance du Livre.

Gerson, Lloyd. 2005. *Aristotle and Other Platonists.* Ithaca, NY: Cornell University Press.

―――. 2009. *Ancient Epistemology.* Cambridge: Cambridge University Press.

Giannattasio Andria, Rosa. 1989. *I frammenti delle "Successioni dei filosofi."* Naples: Arte Tipografica.

Gifford, Mark. 2001. "Dramatic Dialectic in *Republic* Book 1." *Oxford Studies in Ancient Philosophy* 20: 35–106.

Gigon, Olof. 1935. "Untersuchungen zu Heraklit." Diss., Basel.

Gildenhard, Ingo. 2007. *Paideia Romana: Cicero's "Tusculan Disputations."* Proceedings of the Cambridge Philological Society Supplementary 30. Cambridge: Cambridge Philological Society.

Gildersleeve, Basil L., ed. 1885. *Pindar: Olympian and Pythian Odes*. Cambridge: Cambridge University Press.

Gill, Mary Louise. 2012. *Philosophos: Plato's Missing Dialogue*. Oxford: Oxford University Press.

Gilula, Dwora. 1983. "Four Deadly Sins? (Arist. *Wasps* 74–84)." *Classical Quarterly* 33: 358–62.

Godlovitch, Stan. 2000. "What Philosophy Might Be About: Some Socio-Philosophical Speculations." *Inquiry* 43: 3–19.

Goggin, Maureen, and Elenore Long. 1993. "A Tincture of Philosophy, a Tincture of Hope: The Portrayal of Isocrates in Plato's *Phaedrus*." *Rhetoric Review* 11: 301–24.

Gomme, Arnold. 1945. *A Historical Commentary on Thucydides,* Vol. 1, *Introduction and Commentary on Book 1*. Oxford: Clarendon Press.

Goodell, Thomas. 1914. "XPH and ΔEI." *Classical Quarterly* 8: 91–102.

Gostoli, Antonietta, ed. 2007. *Omero: Margite*. Pisa: F. Serra.

Gottschalk, H. B. 1980. *Heraclides of Pontus*. Oxford: Clarendon Press.

Goulet-Cazé, Marie-Odile. 1996. "Religion and the Early Cynics." In *The Cynics: The Cynic Movement in Antiquity and Its Legacy*, edited by Robert Bracht Branham and Marie-Odile Goulet-Cazé, 47–80. Berkeley: University of California Press.

———. 1997. "Les titres des oeuvres d'Eschine chez Diogène Laërce." In *Titres et articulations du texte dans les oeuvres antiques: Actes du Colloque International de Chantilly, 13–15 décembre 1994*. Collection des études Augustiniennes série antiquité, edited by J.-C. Fredouille, M.-O. Goulet-Cazé, P. Hoffmann, P. Petitmengin, and S. Deléani, 167–90. Paris: Institut d'Études Augustiniennes.

Graham, Daniel. 1997. "Heraclitus' Criticism of Ionian Philosophy." *Oxford Studies in Ancient Philosophy* 15: 1–50.

———. 2006. *Explaining the Cosmos: The Ionian Tradition of Scientific Philosophy*. Princeton: Princeton University Press.

———. 2008. "Socrates on Samos." *Classical Quarterly* 58: 308–13.

———. 2010. *The Texts of Early Greek Philosophy: The Complete Fragments and Selected Testimonies of the Major Presocratics*. 2 vols. Cambridge: Cambridge University Press.

Granger, Herbert. 2004. "Heraclitus' Quarrel with Polymathy and *Historiê*." *Transactions of the American Philological Association* 134: 235–61.

———. 2007. "The Theologian Pherecydes of Syros and the Early Days of Natural Philosophy." *Harvard Studies in Classical Philology* 103: 135–63.

Gray, Vivienne. 1992. "Xenophon's *Symposion*: The Display of Wisdom." *Hermes* 120: 58–75.

Griffin, Audrey. 1982. *Sikyon*. Oxford: Clarendon Press.

Griswold, Charles. 1986. *Self-Knowledge in Plato's "Phaedrus."* New Haven, CT: Yale University Press.

Grote, George. 1867. *Plato, and the Other Companions of Sokrates*. 3 vols. London: John Murray.

Guarducci, Margherita. 1974. *Epigrafia greca*. Vol. 3. Rome: Istituto Poligrafico dello Stato.

———. 1987. *L'epigrafia greca dalle origini al tardo impero*. Rome: Istituto Poligrafico dello Stato.

Guthrie, W. K. C. 1952. *Orpheus and Greek Religion: A Study of the Orphic Movement*. London: Methuen.

———. 1957. "Aristotle as a Historian of Philosophy: Some Preliminaries." *Journal of Hellenic Studies* 77: 35–41.

———. 1962. *A History of Greek Philosophy*, Vol. 1, *The Presocratic Tradition from Parmenides to Democritus*. Cambridge: Cambridge University Press.

———. 1971. *A History of Greek Philosophy*, Vol. 3, *The Sophists*. Cambridge: Cambridge University Press.

———. 1978. *A History of Greek Philosophy*, Vol. 5, *The Later Plato and the Academy*. Cambridge: Cambridge University Press.

Hackforth, Reginald, ed. 1945. *Plato's Examination of Pleasure: A Translation of the "Philebus."* Cambridge: Cambridge University Press.

Hadot, Pierre. 2002. *What Is Ancient Philosophy?* Translated by Michael Chase. Cambridge, MA: Harvard University Press.

Halliwell, Stephen, trans. 1997a. *Aristophanes: Birds, Lysistrata, Assembly-Women, Wealth*. Oxford: Clarendon Press.

———. 1997b. "Philosophical Rhetoric or Rhetorical Philosophy? The Strange Case of Isocrates." In *The Rhetoric Canon*, edited by Brenda Deen Schildgen, 107–25. Detroit, MI: Wayne State University Press.

Hammond, N. G. L. 1956. "The Family of Orthagoras." *Classical Quarterly* 6: 45–43.

Hasluck, Frederick. 1907. "Inscriptions from the Cyzicus District, 1906." *Journal of Hellenic Studies* 27: 61–67.

Havelock, Eric. 1963. *Preface to Plato*. Cambridge, MA: Harvard University Press.

———. 1983. "The Linguistic Turn of the Presocratics." In *Language and Thought in Early Greek Philosophy*, edited by Kevin Robb, 7–82. La Salle, IL: Hegeler Institute.

Hawes, Greta. 2014. *Rationalizing Myth in Antiquity*. Oxford: Oxford University Press.

Heberlein, Friedrich. 1980. *Pluthygieia: Zur Gegenwelt bei Aristophanes*. Frankfurt: Haag und Herchen.

Heidel, W. H. 1896. "Pseudo-Platonica." PhD Diss., University of Chicago.

———. 1940. "The Pythagoreans and Greek Mathematics." *American Journal of Philology* 61: 1–33.

Henrichs, Albert. 1967. "Zwie Fragmente über die Erziehung (Antisthenes)." *Zeitschrift für Papyrologie und Epigraphik* 1: 45–53.

Hense, Otto. 1907. "Die Kyzikener Spruchsammlung." *Berliner Philologische Wochenschrift* 24: 765–68.

Hershbell, Jackson P. 1988. "Plutarch's Portrait of Socrates." *Illinois Classical Studies* 13: 365–81.

Hicks, R. D., trans. 1925. *Diogenes Laertius: Lives of Eminent Philosophers*. Loeb Classical Library. Cambridge, MA: Harvard University Press.

Hiebert, Fredrik, and Pierre Cambon, eds. 2008. *Afghanistan: Hidden Treasures from the National Museum, Kabul.* Washington, DC: National Geographic.

Higgins, William. 1977. *Xenophon the Athenian: The Problem of the Individual and the Society of the Polis.* Albany, NY: SUNY Press.

Hine, Harry. 1980. "Seneca and Anaxagoras on Snow." *Hermes* 108: 503.

Hock, Ronald. 1976. "Simon the Shoemaker as an Ideal Cynic." *Greek, Roman, and Byzantine Studies* 17: 41–53.

Hoffman, David. 2006. "Structural Logos in Heraclitus and the Sophists." *Advances in the History of Rhetoric* 9: 1–32.

Hölscher, Uvo. 1993. "Paradox, Simile, and Gnomic Utterance in Heraclitus." In *The Pre-Socratics: A Collection of Critical Essays*, edited by A. P. D. Mourelatos, 229–38. Garden City, NY: Anchor Press.

Holt, Frank. 1999. *Thundering Zeus: The Making of Hellenistic Bactria.* Berkeley, CA: University of California Press.

Hooker, James. 1987. "Homeric φίλος." *Glotta* 65: 44–65.

Horky, Phillip Sidney. 2009. "Persian Cosmos and Greek Philosophy: Plato's Associates and the Zoroastrian *Magoi*." *Oxford Studies in Ancient Philosophy* 37: 47–103.

———. 2013. *Plato and Pythagoreanism.* Oxford: Oxford University Press

———. 2016. "*Empedocles Democraticus*: Hellenistic Biography at the Intersection of Philosophy and Politics." In *Bios Philosophos: Philosophy in Ancient Greek Biography*, edited by Mauro Bonazzi and Stefan Schorn, 37–71. Leuven: Brepols.

How, W. W., and J. Wells. 1912. *A Commentary on Herodotus.* Oxford: Clarendon Press.

Howland, Jacob. 2004. "Plato's Reply to Lysias: *Republic* 1 and 2 and *Against Eratosthenes*." *American Journal of Philology* 125: 179–208.

Howland, R. L. 1937. "The Attack on Isocrates in the *Phaedrus*." *Classical Quarterly* 31: 151–59.

Huber, Joachim. 1974. *Zur Erklärung und Deutung vom Aristophanes' "Ekklesiazusen."* Heidelberg: Huber.

Hudson, John, ed. 1720. *Flavii Josephi Quae Reperiri Potuerunt Opera Omnia Graece et Latine.* 2 vols. Oxford: E Theatro Sheldoniano.

Huffman, Carl. 2008. "Heraclitus' Critique of Pythagoras' Enquiry in Fragment 129." *Oxford Studies in Ancient Philosophy* 35: 19–47.

———. 2014. "The Peripatetics on the Pythagoreans." In *A History of Pythagoreanism*, edited by Carl Huffman. Cambridge: Cambridge University Press, 274–95.

Hülsz Piccone, Enrique. 2013. "Heraclitus on Logos: Language, Rationality, and the Real." In *Doctrine and Doxography: Studies on Heraclitus and Pythagoras*, edited by David Sider and Dirk Obbink. Berlin: De Gruyter, 281–301.

———. 2014. Review of *Eraclito: Frammenti* by Francesco Fronterotta. *Bryn Mawr Classical Review* 2014.07.35. https://www.bmcreview.org/2014/07/20140735.html.

Hunt, A. S. 1911. *Catalogue of the Greek and Latin Papyri in the John Rylands Library, Manchester*, Vol. 1, *Literary Texts.* Manchester: University of Manchester Press.

Huß, Bernhard. 1999. *Xenophons "Symposion": Ein Kommentar.* Stuttgart: Teubner.

Hussey, Edward. 1982. "Epistemology and Meaning in Heraclitus." In *Language and Logos: Studies in Ancient Philosophy Presented to G. E. L. Owen*, edited by Malcolm Schofield and Martha Nussbaum, 33–59. Cambridge: Cambridge University Press.

———. 2012. "Aristotle on Earlier Natural Science." In *The Oxford Handbook of Aristotle*, edited by Christopher Shields, 17–45. Oxford: Oxford University Press.

Hutchinson, D. S. Introduction to *Rival Lovers*. In *Plato: Complete Works*, edited by John Cooper, 618–19. Indianapolis: Hackett.

Hutchinson, D. S., and Monte Ransome Johnson. 2018. "Protreptic and Apotreptic: Aristotle's Dialogue *Protrepticus*." In *When Wisdom Calls: Philosophical Protreptic in Antiquity*, edited by Olga Alieva, Annemaré Kotzé, and Sophie Van der Meeren, 111–54. Turnhout: Brepols.

———, eds. Forthcoming. *Aristotle: Protrepticus*. Cambridge: Cambridge University Press.

Huxley, George. 1965. "Ion of Chios." *Greek, Roman, and Byzantine Studies* 6: 29–46.

———. 1968. "Glaukos of Rhegion." *Greek, Roman, and Byzantine Studies* 9: 47–54.

Ilievski, Petar H. 1983. "Some Structural Peculiarities of Mycenaean-Greek Personal Names." In *Res Mycenaeae: Akten des VII. Internationalen Mykenologischen Colloquiums vom 6.–10. April 1981 in Nürnberg*, edited by Alfred Heubeck and Günter Neumann, 202–15. Göttingen: Vandenhoeck & Ruprecht.

Institut Fernand-Courby, ed. 1971. *Nouveau Choix D'inscriptions Grecques*. Paris: Les Belles Lettres.

Intrieri, Maria. 2013. "Intessere relazioni. Osservazioni sull'itinerario di philia (I. Dalle origini al V sec. a.C.)." *Historiká* 3: 213–72.

Inwood, Brad, ed. 2001. *The Poem of Empedocles: A Text and Translation with an Introduction*. Rev. ed. Toronto: University of Toronto Press.

Isnardi, Margherita. 1954. "Note al dialogo pseudoplatonico *Anterastai*." *Parola del passato* 9: 137–43.

Jackson, Kassandra. 2010. "Father-Daughter Dynamics in the *Iliad*: The Role of Aphrodite in Defining Zeus' Regime." In *Brill's Companion to Aphrodite*, edited by Amy Smith and Sadie Pickup, 151–63. Leiden: Brill.

Jacoby, Felix. 1947. "Some Remarks on Ion of Chios." *Classical Quarterly* 41: 1–17.

Jaeger, Werner. 1947. *The Theology of the Early Greek Philosophers*. Translated by Edward S. Robinson. Oxford: Clarendon Press.

———. 1962. *Aristotle: Fundamentals of the History of His Development*. 2nd ed. Translated by Richard Robinson. Oxford: Clarendon Press.

Janko, Richard, ed. 1987. *Aristotle: Poetics*. Indianapolis, IN: Hackett.

Jebb, Richard Claverhouse. 1893. *The Attic Orators from Antiphon to Isaeus*. 2nd ed. London: Macmillan.

Jennings, Victoria, and Andrea Katsaros. 2007. *The World of Ion of Chios*. Leiden: Brill.

Johnson, R. 1959. "Isocrates' Methods of Teaching." *American Journal of Philology* 80: 25–36.

Johnstone, Mark. 2014. "On *Logos* in Heraclitus." *Oxford Studies in Ancient Philosophy* 47: 1–29.

Joly, Robert. 1956. *Le thème philosophique des genres de vie dans l'antiquité classique.* Brussels: Palais des Académies.

Jordan, William. 1990. *Ancient Concepts of Philosophy.* London: Routledge.

Kahn, Charles. 1960. *Anaximander and the Origins of Greek Cosmology.* New York: Columbia University Press.

———. 1979. *The Art and Thought of Heraclitus.* Cambridge: Cambridge University Press.

———. 2001. *Pythagoras and the Pythagoreans.* Indianapolis, IN: Hackett.

Kassel, Rudolf. 1971. *Der Text der aristotelischen Rhetorik.* Berlin: De Gruyter.

———, ed. 1976. *Aristotelis Ars Rhetorica.* Berlin: De Gruyter.

Ker, James. 2000. "Solon's *Theôria* and the End of the City." *Classical Antiquity* 19: 304–29.

Kerferd, G. B. 1950. "The First Greek Sophists." *Classical Review* 64: 8–10.

———. 1976. "The Image of the Wise Man in Greece in the Period before Plato." In *Images of Man in Ancient and Medieval Thought*, edited by Gérard Verbeke and Fernand Bossier, 17–28. Leuven: Leuven University Press.

———. 1981. *The Sophistic Movement.* Cambridge: Cambridge University Press.

Kingsley, Peter. 1990. "The Greek Origin of the Sixth-Century Dating of Zoroaster." *Bulletin of the School of Oriental and African Studies, University of London* 53: 245–65.

———. 1995. "Meetings with Magi: Iranian Themes among the Greeks, from Xanthus of Lydia to Plato's Academy." *Journal of the Royal Asiatic Society* 5: 173–209.

Kirk, Geoffrey. 1961. "Sense and Common-Sense in the Development of Greek Philosophy." *Journal of Hellenic Studies* 81: 105–17.

———. 1962. *Heraclitus: The Cosmic Fragments.* Cambridge: Cambridge University Press.

Kirk, Geoffrey, John Raven, and Malcolm Schofield. 1977. *The Presocratic Philosophers: A Critical History with a Selection of Texts.* Cambridge: Cambridge University Press.

Kneale, William. 1957. "Aristotle and the *Consequentia Mirabilis*." *Journal of Hellenic Studies* 77: 62–66.

Knudsen, Rachel Ahern. 2012. "Poetic Speakers, Sophistic Words." *American Journal of Philology* 133: 31–60.

Konstan, David. 1985. "The Politics of Aristophanes' *Wasps*." *Transactions and Proceedings of the American Philological Association* 115: 27–46.

———, trans. 2006. *Aspasius: On Aristotle's "Nicomachean Ethics" 1–4, 7–8.* Ithaca, NY: Cornell University Press.

Konstantakos, Ioannis M. 2005. "Amasis, Bias and the Seven Sages as Riddlers." *Würzburger Jahrbücher für die Altertumswissenschaft* 29: 11–46.

Kosmin, Paul J. 2014. *The Land of the Elephant Kings: Space, Territory, and Ideology in the Seleucid Empire.* Cambridge, MA: Harvard University Press.

———. 2018. *Time and Its Adversaries in the Seleucid Empire.* Cambridge, MA: Harvard University Press.

Kranz, Walther. 1934. "Vorsokratisches I and II." *Hermes* 69: 114–19 and 226–28.

Kucharski, Paul. 1964. "Anaxagore et les idées biologiques de son siècle." *Revue philosophique de la France et de l'Étranger* 89: 137–66.

Kurke, Leslie. 2011. *Aesopic Conversations: Popular Tradition, Cultural Dialogue, and the Invention of Greek Prose.* Princeton: Princeton University Press.

Laks, André. 2002. "Philosophes présocratiques: Remarques sur la construction d'une catégorie de l'historirgraphie philosophique." In *Qu'est-ce que la philosophie présocratique?*, edited by André Laks and Claire Louguet, 17–38. Villeneuve-D'Ascq: Presses Universitaires du Septentrion.

———. 2018. "Diogenes Laertius and the Pre-Socratics." In *Diogenes Laertius: Lives of the Eminent Philosophers*, edited by James Miller, 588–92. New York: Oxford University Press.

Lallot, Jean. 1971. "Une invective philosophique (Héraclit, fr. 129 et 35 D.-K.)." *Revue des études anciennes* 73: 15–23.

Lamb, W. R. M., trans. 1927. *Plato: Charmides. Alcibiades. Hipparchus. Lovers. Theages. Minos. Epinomis.* Loeb Classical Library. Cambridge, MA: Harvard University Press.

Lambert, W. G. 1957. "Ancestors, Authors, and Canonicity." *Journal of Cuneiform Studies* 11: 1–14.

———. 1962. "A Catalogue of Texts and Authors." *Journal of Cuneiform Studies* 16: 59–77.

Lampert, Laurence. 2010. *How Philosophy Became Socratic: A Study of Plato's "Protagoras," "Charmides," and "Republic."* Chicago: University of Chicago Press.

Landau, Oscar. 1958. *Mykenisch-griechische Personennamen.* Göteborg: Almqvist & Wiksell.

Landfester, Manfred. 1966. *Das griechische Nomen "Philos" und seine Ableitungen.* Hildesheim: Georg Olms Verlag.

Lang, Mabel. 1978. *Socrates in the Agora.* Princeton: American School of Classical Studies at Athens.

Lassalle, Ferdinand. 1858. *Die Philosophie Herakleitos des Dunklen von Ephesos.* Leipzig: E. Schirmer.

Lattimore, Richmond. 1939. "The Wise Advisor in Herodotus." *Classical Philology* 34: 24–35.

Leahy, Desmond. 1968. "The Dating of the Orthagorid Dynasty." *Historia* 17: 1–23.

Leão, Delfim F. 2010a. "Investidura de tales como sophos em Atenas?" *Humanitas* 62: 23–32.

———. 2010b. "The Seven Sages and Plato." In *Il quinto secolo. Studi di filosofia antica in onore di Livio Rossetti*, edited by Stefania Giombini and Flavia Marcacci, 403–14. Passignano sul Trasimeno: Aguaplano.

Ledger, Gerard R. 1989. *Re-Counting Plato: A Computer Analysis of Plato's Style.* Oxford: Clarendon Press.

Lee, H. D. P. 1936. *Zeno of Elea.* Cambridge: Cambridge University Press.

Lefebvre, David. 2011. "Avoir un *èthos* et être *philotoioutos*. Sur le sens de la notion d'*èthos* dans les *Éthiques* d'Aristote." In *Aristote: Rationalités.* Cahiers de l'ERIAC. Série "Rencontres philosophiques," edited by Annie Hourcade and René Lefebvre, 155–72. Mont-Saint-Aignan: Publications des Universités de Rouen et du Havre.

Legrand, Philippe-Ernest, ed. 1932. *Hérodote: Histoires. Tome I. Livre I.* Paris: Les Belles Lettres.

Lehnus, Luigi. 1972. "Note stesicoree (*Pap. Oxy.* 2506 e 2619)." *Studi Classici e Orientali* 21: 52–55.

Lenzi, Alan. 2008. "The Uruk List of Kings and Sages and Late Mesopotamian Scholarship." *Journal of Ancient Near Eastern Religions* 8: 137–69.

Lerner, J. D. 2003. "Correcting the Early History of Ay Kanom." *Archaeologische Mitteilungen aus Iran (und Turan)* 35/36: 373–410.

Lesher, James. 1983. "Heraclitus' Epistemological Vocabulary." *Hermes* 111: 155–70.

———. 1994. "The Emergence of Philosophical Interest in Cognition." *Oxford Studies in Ancient Philosophy* 12: 1–34.

———. 2001. *Xenophanes of Colophon: Fragments.* Toronto: University of Toronto Press.

———. 2016. "Verbs for Knowing in Heraclitus' Rebuke of Hesiod (DK 22B57)." *Ancient Philosophy* 36: 1–12.

Levi, Adolfo. 1940. "On 'Twofold Statements.'" *American Journal of Philology* 61: 292–306.

Levine, David. 2016. *Profound Ignorance, Plato's "Charmides," and the Saving of Wisdom.* Lanham, MD: Lexington Books.

Lévy, Isidore. 1926. *Recherches sur les sources de la légende de Pythagore.* Paris: E. Leroux.

Linforth, Ivan. 1936. "Diodorus, Herodorus, Orpheus." In *Classical Studies Presented to Edward Capps on His Seventieth Birthday*, 217–22. Princeton: Princeton University Press.

Livingstone, Niall. 2001. *A Commentary on Isocrates' "Busiris."* Leiden: Brill.

———. 2007. "Writing Politics: Isocrates' Rhetoric of Philosophy." *Rhetorica* 25: 15–34.

Lloyd, G.E.R. 1970. *Early Greek Science: Thales to Aristotle.* London: Chatto & Windus.

———. 2002. *The Ambitions of Curiosity: Understanding the World in Ancient Greece and China.* Cambridge: Cambridge University Press.

———. 2006. Review of *Hippocrates: On Ancient Medicine* by Mark J. Schiefsky. *Bulletin of the History of Medicine* 80: 365–66.

———. 2009. *Disciplines in the Making: Cross-Cultural Perspectives on Elites, Learning, and Innovation.* Oxford: Oxford University Press.

Lobel, Edgar, ed. 1957. *The Oxyrhynchus Papyri.* Vol. 24. London: Egypt Exploration Fund.

Lolos, Yannis A. 2011. *Land of Sikyon: Archaeology and History of a Greek City-State.* Princeton: American School of Classical Studies at Athens.

Long, Herbert, ed. 1964. *Diogenis Laertii Vitae Philosophorum.* Oxford: Clarendon Press.

Longrigg, James. 1963. "Philosophy and Medicine: Some Early Interactions." *Harvard Studies in Classical Philology* 67: 147–75.

López Cruces, Juan Luis, and Pedro Pablo Fuentes González. 2000. "Isocrate d'Athènes." In *Dictionnaire des philosophes antiques,* edited by Richard Goulet, 3.891–938. Paris: Centre National de la Recherche Scientifique.

Louden, Bruce. 2011. "Phaeacians." *The Homer Encyclopedia,* edited by Margalit Finkelberg, 2.649–51. Malden, MA: Wiley-Blackwell.

Luz, Menahem. 2014. "The Erlangen Papyrus 4 and Its Socratic Origins." *International Journal of the Platonic Tradition* 8: 161–91.

Lyonnet, Bertille. 2012. "Questions on the Date of the Hellenistic Pottery from Central Asia (Ai Khanoum, Marakanda and Koktepe)." *Ancient Civilizations from Scythia to Siberia* 18: 143–73.

Macan, Reginald, ed. 1895. *Herodotus: The Fourth, Fifth, and Sixth Books.* London: Macmillan.

MacDowell, Douglas, ed. 1971. *Aristophanes: Wasps.* Oxford: Clarendon Press.

———. 1982. *Gorgias: Encomium of Helen.* Bristol: Bristol Classical Press.

———. 1986. *The Law in Classical Athens.* Ithaca, NY: Cornell University Press.

Mackenzie, M. M. 1988. "Heraclitus and the Art of Paradox." *Oxford Studies in Ancient Philosophy* 6: 1–37.

Mairs, Rachel. 2014a. "The Founder's Shrine and the Foundation of Ai Khanoum." In *Foundation Myths in Ancient Societies: Dialogues and Discourses,* edited by Naoíse Mac Sweeney, 103–28. Philadelphia: University of Pennsylvania Press.

———. 2014b. *The Hellenistic Far East: Archaeology, Language, and Identity in Greek Central Asia.* Berkeley: University of California Press.

Malingrey, Anne-Marie. 1961. *"Philosophia": Étude d'un groupe de mots dans la littérature grecque, des Présocratiques au IVe siècle après J.-C.* Paris: Klincksieck.

Mallan, Claude. 2005. "Il était une fois la philosophie." *Archives de philosophie* 68: 107–26.

Männlein-Robert, Irmgard. 2005. "Zur literarischen Inszenierung eines Philosophiekonzeptes in den pseudoplatonischen *Anterastai.*" In *Pseudoplatonica: Akten Des Kongresses Zu Den Pseudoplatonica Vom 6.–9. Juli 2003 in Bamberg,* edited by Klaus Döring, Michael Erler, and Stefan Schron, 119–34. Stuttgart: F. Steiner.

Mansfeld, Jaap. 1979. "The Chronology of Anaxagoras' Athenian Period and the Date of His Trial: Part I: The Length and Dating of the Athenian Period." *Mnemosyne* 32: 39–69.

———. 1980. "The Chronology of Anaxagoras' Athenian Period and the Date of His Trial: Part II: The Plot against Pericles and His Associates." *Mnemosyne* 33: 17–95.

———. 1983. *"Cratylus* 402a–c: Plato or Hippias?" In *Atti del Symposium Heracliteum 1981*, edited by Livio Rossetti, 43–55. Rome: Edizioni dell'Ateneo.

———. 1985. "Myth Science Philosophy: A Question of Origins." In *Hypatia: Essays in Classics, Comparative Literature, and Philosophy Presented to Hazel E. Barnes on Her Seventieth Birthday*, edited by William M. Calder, Ulrich K. Goldsmith, and Phyllis B. Kenevan, 45–65. Boulder, CO: Colorado Associated University Press.

———. 1986. "Aristotle, Plato, and the Preplatonic Doxography and Chronography." In *Storiografia e dossografia nella filosofia antica*, edited by Giuseppe Cambiano, 1–59. Turin: Tirrenia Stampatori.

———. 1987. "Theophrastus and the Xenophanes Doxography." *Mnemosyne* 40: 286–312.

———. 1989. "Fiddling the Books: Heraclitus on Pythagoras (DK 22 B 129)." In *Ionian Philosophy*, edited by K. J. Boudouris, 229–34. Athens: International Association for Greek Philosophy.

Marcovich, Miroslav, ed. 1967. *Heraclitus: Greek Text with a Short Commentary.* Merida: Los Andes University Press.

———, ed. 1999. *Diogenis Laertii Vitae Philosophorum.* Leipzig: Teubner.

Mariss, Ruth. 2002. *Alkidamas: Über diejenigen, die schriftliche Reden schreiben, oder über die Sophisten. Eine Sophistenrede aus dem 4. Jahrhundert v. Chr., eingeleitet und kommentiert.* Münster: Aschendorff Verlag.

Martin, Richard. 1993. "The Seven Sages as Performers of Wisdom." In *The Cultures within Ancient Greek Culture: Contact, Conflict, Collaboration*, edited by Carol Dougherty and Leslie Kurke, 108–28. Cambridge: Cambridge University Press.

———. 2012. "The Myth before the Myth Began." In *Writing down the Myths*, edited by Joseph F. Nagy, 45–66. Turnhout: Brepols.

Martinez-Seve, Laurianne. 2014. "The Spatial Organization of Ai Khanoum, a Greek City in Afghanistan." *American Journal of Archaeology* 118: 267–83.

Mazzara, Giuseppe. 1999. *Gorgia: La retorica del verosimile.* Sankt Augustin: Academia Verlag.

McAdon, Brad. 2004. "Plato's Denunciation of Rhetoric in the *Phaedrus.*" *Rhetoric Review* 23: 21–39.

McCoy, Marina Berzins. 2009. "Alcidamas, Isocrates, and Plato on Speech, Writing, and Philosophical Rhetoric." *Ancient Philosophy* 29: 45–66.

McDiarmid, J. B. 1953. "Theophrastus on the Presocratic Causes." *Harvard Studies in Classical Philology* 61: 85–156.

McKirahan, Richard D., ed. 2010. *Philosophy before Socrates: An Introduction with Texts and Commentary.* Indianapolis, IN: Hackett.

McNeal, Richard, ed. 1986. *Herodotus: Book 1.* Lanham, MD: University Press of America.

McOsker, Michael. 2017. "Anonymous, On Sokrates (*P. Hibeh* II 182) (1133)." In *Die Fragmente der griechischen Historiker Continued. Part IV. Biography and Antiquarian Literature. IV A. Biography. Fascicle 8. Anonymous Biographical Papyri*, edited by James H. Brusuelas, Dirk Obbink, and Stefan Schorn. Leiden: Brill.

Megino Rodríguez, Carlos. 2008. "Propuesta de atribución de dos fragmentos del papiro de Viena *PVindob*. G 26008." *Emerita* 76: 87–104.

Meineke, Augustus, ed. 1860. *Aristophanis Comoediae*. Leipzig: B. Tauchnitz.

Meissner, Torsten, and Olga Tribulato. 2002. "Nominal Composition in Mycenaean Greek." *Transactions of the Philological Society* 100: 289–330.

———. 2006. *S-Stem Nouns and Adjectives in Greek and Proto-Indo-European: A Diachronic Study in Word Formation*. Oxford: Oxford University Press.

Mejer, Jørgen. 1978. *Diogenes Laertius and His Hellenistic Background*. Wiesbaden: Steiner.

———. 2009. "Heraclides' Intellectual Context." In *Heraclides of Pontus: Discussion*, edited by William W. Fortenbaugh and Elizabeth Pender, 27–40. New Brunswick, NJ: Transaction Publishers.

Mendel, Gustave. 1909. "Catalogue des monuments grecs, romains et byzantins du Musée Impérial Ottoman de Brousse." *Bulletin de correspondance hellénique* 33: 245–435.

Menn, Stephen. 2002. "Plato and the Method of Analysis." *Phronesis* 47: 193–223.

———. n.d. "The Aim and the Argument of Aristotle's *Metaphysics*." Accessed May 10, 2019. https://www.philosophie.hu-berlin.de/de/lehrbereiche/antike/mitarbeiter/menn/contents.

Merkelbach, Reinhold, and Josef Stauber, eds. 1998. *Steinepigramme aus dem griechischen Osten*. Vol. 3. Leipzig: Teubner.

Merlan, Philip. 1954. "Isocrates, Aristotle and Alexander the Great." *Historia* 3: 60–81.

———. 1963. "Das Problem der *Erasten*." In *Horizons of a Philosopher: Essays in Honor of David Baumgardt*, edited by Joseph Frank, 297–313. Leiden: Brill.

Milne, Marjorie Josephine. 1924. "A Study in Alcidamas and His Relation to Contemporary Sophistic." PhD Diss., Bryn Mawr College.

Minar, Edwin. 1942. *Early Pythagorean Politics in Practice and Theory*. Baltimore: Waverly Press.

Mirhady, David C. 2004. "Alcidamas on the Sophists," review of *Alkidamas* by Ruth Mariss. *Classical Review* 54: 331–33.

———, and Yun Lee Too, trans. 2000. *Isocrates I*. Austin: University of Texas Press.

Monserrat Molas, Josep. 1999. "Rivals i amants: rivals d'amor. Comentari al platònic *Anterastai*." *Anuari de la Societat Catalana de Filosofia* 11: 19–55.

Montiglio, Silvia. 2000. "Wandering Philosophers in Classical Greece." *Journal of Hellenic Studies* 120: 86–105.

Moore, Christopher. 2008. "Socratic Persuasion." PhD Diss., University of Minnesota.

———. 2012. "Socrates and Clitophon in the Platonic *Clitophon*." *Ancient Philosophy* 32: 257–78.

———. 2013a. "Deception and Knowledge in Plato's *Phaedrus.*" *Ancient Philosophy* 33: 97–110.

———. 2013b. "Socrates among the Mythographers," review of *Myth and Philosophy in Plato's "Phaedrus"* by Daniel Warner. *Polis* 30: 106–17.

———. 2014a. "Arguing for the Immortality of the Soul in the Palinode of Plato's *Phaedrus.*" *Philosophy and Rhetoric* 47: 179–208.

———. 2014b. "How to 'Know Thyself' in Plato's *Phaedrus.*" *Apeiron* 47: 390–418.

———. 2014c. "Socrates Psychagogos (*Birds* 1555, *Phaedrus* 261a7)." In *Socratica III*, edited by Livio Rossetti, Alessandro Stavru, and Fulvia de Luisa, 41–55. Sankt Augustin: Akademie Verlag.

———. 2015a. "*Promêtheia* (Forethought) until Plato." *American Journal of Philology* 136: 381–420.

———. 2015b. *Socrates and Self-Knowledge*. Cambridge: Cambridge University Press.

———. 2016. "Spartan Philosophy and Sage Wisdom in Plato's *Protagoras.*" *Epochê* 30: 281–305.

———. 2017. "Heracles the Philosopher (Herodorus Fr. 14)." *Classical Quarterly* 67: 1–22.

———. 2018a. "Heraclitus and 'Knowing Yourself.'" *Ancient Philosophy* 38: 1–21.

———. 2018b. "Xenophon on 'Philosophy' and Socrates." In *Xenophon and Plato: Comparative Studies*, edited by Gabriel Danzig, David M. Johnson, and Donald Morrison, 128–64. Leiden: Brill.

———. 2018c. "Xenophon's Socratic Education in *Memorabilia* Book 4." In *Socrates and the Socratic Dialogue*, eds. Alessandro Stavru and Christopher Moore, 500–520. Leiden: Brill.

———, and Christopher C. Raymond, eds. 2019. *Plato: Charmides. Translated with Introduction, Notes, and Analysis.* Indianapolis, IN: Hackett.

Moran, Richard. 2018. *The Exchange of Words: Speech, Testimony, and Intersubjectivity.* Oxford: Oxford University Press.

Morgan, Kathryn A. 2000. *Myth and Philosophy from the Presocratics to Plato.* Cambridge: Cambridge University Press.

———. 2004. "The Education of Athens: Politics and Rhetoric in Isocrates and Plato." In *Isocrates and Civic Education*, edited by Takis Poulakos and David Depew, 125–54. Austin: University of Texas Press.

———. 2015. *Pindar and the Construction of Syracusan Monarchy in the Fifth Century B.C.* Oxford: Oxford University Press.

Morgan, Llewelyn. 2015. "An Archaeological Whodunnit." *Lugubelinus* (blog). September 21, 2015. https://llewelynmorgan.wordpress.com/2015/09/21/an-archaeological-whodunnit.

Morpurgo Davies, Anna. 2000. "Greek Personal Names and Linguistic Continuity." *Proceedings of the British Academy* 104: 15–39.

Morrison, J. S. 1956. "Pythagoras of Samos." *Classical Quarterly* 6: 135–56.

———. 1958. "The Origins of Plato's Philosopher-Statesman." *Classical Quarterly* 8: 198–218.

Mosshammer, Alden. 1976. "The Epoch of the Seven Sages." *California Studies in Classical Antiquity* 9: 165–80.

Most, Glenn W. 1992. "Some New Fragments of Aristotle's *Protrepticus*?" In *Studi su codici e papiri filosofici. Platone, Aristotele, Ierocle. Studi e testi per il corpus dei papiri filosofici greci e latini 6*, 189–216. Florence: Leo S. Olschki Editore.

———. 1999. "The Poetics of Early Greek Philosophy." In *The Cambridge Companion to Early Greek Philosophy*, edited by Anthony A. Long, 332–62. Cambridge: Cambridge University Press.

———. 2007. "Ἄλλος δ᾽ ἐξ ἄλλου δέξεται: Presocratic Philosophy and Traditional Greek Epic." In *Literatur und Religion: Wege zu einer mythisch-rituellen Poetik bei den Griechen*, edited by Anton Bierl, Rebecca Lämmle, and Katharina Wesselmann, 271–302. Berlin: De Gruyter.

———. 2018. "Diogenes Laertius and Nietzsche." In *Diogenes Laertius: Lives of the Eminent Philosophers*, edited by James Miller, 619–22. New York: Oxford University Press.

Mourelatos, Alexander. 1965. "The Real, Appearances and Human Error in Early Greek Philosophy." *Review of Metaphysics* 19: 346–65.

———. 2008. *The Route of Parmenides*. Rev. ed. Las Vegas, NV: Parmenides.

Muir, John, ed. 2001. *Alcidamas: The Works and Fragments*. London: Bristol Classical Press.

Müller, Carl Werner. 1965. *Gleiches zu Gleichem: Ein Prinzip frühgriechischen Denkens*. Wiesbaden: Harrassowitz.

Munn, Mark. 2000. *The School of History: Athens in the Age of Socrates*. Berkeley, CA: University of California Press.

Murphy, David. 2013. "Isocrates and the Dialogue." *Classical World* 106: 311–53.

Murray, Penelope. 1981. "Poetic Inspiration in Early Greece." *Journal of Hellenic Studies* 101: 87–100.

Naddaf, Gerard. 2009. "Allegory and the Origins of Philosophy." In *Logos and Muthos: Philosophical Essays in Greek Literature*, edited by William Wians, 99–131. Albany, NY: SUNY Press.

Nails, Debra. 2002. *The People of Plato: A Prosopography of Plato and Other Socratics*. Indianapolis, IN: Hackett.

Narain, A. K. 1974. "On the Greek Epigraphs from Ai Khanoum." *Studies in Indian Epigraphy* 1: 97–103.

———. 1987. "On Some Greek Inscription from Afghanistan." *Annali dell'istituto universitario orientale di Napoli* 47: 269–92.

Natali, Carlo. 2013. *Aristotle: His Life and School*. Edited by D. S. Hutchinson. Princeton: Princeton University Press.

Nauck, August, ed. 1884. *Iamblichi De Vita Pythagorica Liber*. St. Petersburg: Eggers & S. et I. Glasunof.

Nehamas, Alexander. 1990. "Eristic, Antilogic, Sophistic, Dialectic: Plato's Demarcation of Philosophy from Sophistry." *History of Philosophy Quarterly* 7: 3–16.

Nestle, Wilhelm. 1942. *Von* Mythos *zum* Logos. *Die Selbstentfaltung des griechischen Denkens von Homer bis auf die Sophistik und Sokrates.* 2nd ed. Stuttgart: Kröner.

Nightingale, Andrea. 1995. *Genres in Dialogue: Plato and the Construct of Philosophy.* Cambridge: Cambridge University Press.

———. 2004. *Spectacles of Truth in Classical Greek Philosophy:* Theoria *in Its Cultural Context.* Cambridge: Cambridge University Press.

———. 2007. "The Philosophers in Archaic Greek Culture." In *The Cambridge Companion to Archaic Greece*, edited by H. A. Shapiro, 169–98. Cambridge: Cambridge University Press.

Norlin, George, trans. 1928. *Isocrates.* Loeb Classical Library. Cambridge, MA: Harvard University Press.

Noussia-Fantuzzi, Maria. 2010. *Solon the Athenian: The Poetic Fragments.* Leiden: Brill.

Nussbaum, Martha. 1972. "ΨΥΧΗ in Heraclitus, I & II." *Phronesis* 17: 1–16, 153–70.

Nutting, H. C., trans. 1909. *Cicero: Tusculan Disputations I, II, V.* Boston: Allyn and Bacon Press.

O'Brien, Denis. 1968. "The Relation of Anaxagoras and Empedocles." *Journal of Hellenic Studies* 88: 93–113.

Oikonomides, A. N. 1980. "The Lost Delphic Inscription with the Commandments of the Seven and *P. Univ. Athen.* 2782." *Zeitschrift für Papyrologie und Epigraphik* 37: 179–83.

———. 1987. "Records of *The Commandments of the Seven Wise Men* in the 3rd century B.C." *Classical Bulletin* 63: 67–76.

Ollier, François, ed. 1961. *Xénophon: Banquet. Apologie de Socrate.* Paris: Les Belles Lettres.

Osborne, Catherine. 2004. *Presocratic Philosophy: A Very Short Introduction.* Oxford: Oxford University Press.

Osthoff, Hermann. 1878. *Das Verbum in der Nominalcomposition im deutschen, griechischen, slavischen und romanischen.* Jena: H. Costenoble.

O'Sullivan, Lara. 2008. "Athens, Intellectuals, and Demetrius of Phalerum's Socrates." *Transactions of the American Philological Association* 138: 393–410.

O'Sullivan, Neil. 1995. "Pericles and Protagoras." *Greece and Rome* 42: 15–23.

———. 2005. "Alcidamas." In *Classical Rhetorics and Rhetoricians: Critical Studies and Sources*, edited by Michelle Ballif and Michael G. Moran, 14–18. Westport, CT: Praeger.

———. 2008. "The Authenticity of [Alcidamas] *Odysseus*: Two New Linguistic Considerations." *Classical Quarterly* 58: 638–47.

Page, Carl. 1990. "The Unjust Treatment of Polemarchus." *History of Philosophy Quarterly* 7: 243–67.

Pageau St-Hilaire, Antoine. 2014. "La double signification de la philosophie politique socratique dans les *Amoureux Rivaux*." *Ithaque* 14: 1–24.

Paley, F. A., trans. 1868. *The Odes of Pindar.* Cambridge: Deighton, Bell, and Co.

Palmer, John. 1998. "Xenophanes' Ouranian God in the Fourth Century." *Oxford Studies in Ancient Philosophy* 16: 1–32.

———. 2000. "Aristotle on the Ancient Theologians." *Apeiron* 33: 181–205.

———. 2012. *Parmenides and Presocratic Philosophy*. Oxford: Oxford University Press.

Pape, Wilhelm, and Gustav Benseler. 1863–70. *Wörterbuch der griechischen Eigennamen*. Braunschweig: Friedrich Vieweg.

Parker, Victor. 1992. "The Dates of the Orthagorids of Sicyon." *Tyche* 7: 165–75.

———. 1994. "Some Aspects of the Foreign and Domestic Policy of Cleisthenes of Sicyon." *Hermes* 122: 404–24.

Patzer, Andreas. 1986. *Der Sophist Hippias als Philosophiehistoriker*. Freiburg: K. Alber.

Pearson, Lionel. 1952. "*Prophasis* and *Aitia*." *Transactions and Proceedings of the American Philological Association*: 205–23.

Pendrick, Gerard, ed. 2002. *Antiphon: The Fragments*. Cambridge: Cambridge University Press.

Peterson, Sandra. 2011. *Socrates and Philosophy in the Dialogues of Plato*. Cambridge: Cambridge University Press.

———. 2018. "Notes on *Lovers*." In *Socrates and the Socratic Dialogue*, edited by Alessandro Stavru and Christopher Moore, 412–31. Leiden: Brill.

———. 2019. "Plato's Reception of Socrates: One Aspect." In *Brill Companion to the Reception of Socrates*, edited by Christopher Moore, 98–123. Leiden: Brill.

———. Forthcoming. "Philosophia e Socrate negli scritti di Senofonte." *Magazzino di filosofia* n. 34.

Pfeiffer, Rudolph. 1968. *History of Classical Scholarship: From the Beginnings to the End of the Hellenistic Age*. Oxford: Clarendon Press.

Philip, James. 1966. *Pythagoras and Early Pythagoreanism*. Toronto: University of Toronto Press.

Planeaux, Christopher. 1999. "Socrates, Alcibiades, and Plato's τὰ Ποτειδεατικά. Does the *Charmides* Have an Historical Setting?" *Mnemosyne* 52: 72–77.

Pomeroy, Sarah B., ed. 1994. *Xenophon: Oeconomicus: A Social and Historical Commentary*. Oxford: Clarendon Press.

Posch, Walter. 1995. *Baktrien zwischen Griechen und Kuschan: Untersuchungen zu kulturellen und historischen Problemen einer Übergangsphase*. Wiesbaden: Harrassowitz.

Pouilloux, Jean, and François Salviat. 1983. "Lichas, Lacédémonien, archonte à Thasos, et le livre VIII de Thucydide." *Comptes rendus des séances de l'Académie des Inscriptions et Belles-Lettres* 127: 376–403.

———. 1985. "Thucydide après l'exil et la composition de son histoire." *Revue de philologie, de littérature et d'histoire anciennes* 59: 13–20.

Poulakos, Takos. 2001. "Isocrates' Use of *Doxa*." *Philosophy and Rhetoric* 34: 61–78.

Powell, C. Thomas. 1987. "Why Aristotle Has No Philosophy of History." *History of Philosophy Quarterly* 4: 343–57.

Powell, John. 1938. *A Lexicon to Herodotus*. Cambridge: Cambridge University Press.

Pradeau, Jean-François, ed. 2002. *Héraclite: Fragments*. Paris: Flammarion.

Prince, Susan, ed. 2014. *Antisthenes of Athens: Texts, Translations, and Commentary*. Ann Arbor: University of Michigan Press.

Pritzl, Kurt. 1985. "On the Way to Wisdom in Heraclitus." *Phoenix* 39: 303–16.

Proust, Marcel. 1927. *Le temps retrouvé*. Paris: Gallimard.

Rabe, Hugo, ed. 1896. *Anonymi et Stephani in Artem Rhetoricam Commentaria*. Commentaria in Aristotelem Graeca. Vol. 21. Part 2. Berlin: G. Reimer.

Ramage, Edwin. 1961. "An Early Trace of Socratic Dialogue." *American Journal of Philology* 82: 418–24.

Ramnoux, Clémence. 1959. *Héraclite, ou l'homme entre les choses et les mots*. Paris: Les Belles Lettres.

Rankin, H. D. 1983. *Sophists, Socratics, and Cynics*. Totowa, NJ: Barnes & Noble Books.

Rawlinson, George, trans. 1862. *The History of Herodotus*. London: J. Murray.

Reale, Giovanni. 1987. *A History of Ancient Philosophy: From the Origins to Socrates*. Albany, NY: SUNY Press.

Redard, Georges. 1953. *Recherches sur* chrê, chrêsthai. Paris: H. Champion.

Redfield, James. 1985. "Herodotus the Tourist." *Classical Philology* 80: 97–118.

Reich, Klaus and Otto Apelt, eds. 1967. *Diogenes Laertius: Leben und Meinungen berühmter Philosophen: Buch 1–10*. Hamburg: F. Meiner.

Reiner, Erica. 1961. "The Etiological Myth of the 'Seven Sages.'" *Orientalia* 30: 1–11.

Reinhardt, Karl. 1942. "Heraklits Lehre vom Feuer." *Hermes* 77: 1–27.

Rendich, Franco. 2010. *Dizionario etimologico comparato delle lingue classiche indoeuropee*. Rome: Palombi.

Rettig, G. F. 1879. "Xenophons *Symposion* als Kunstwerk griechischen Geistes." *Philologus* 38: 269–321.

Richardson, Nicholas J. 1975. "Homeric Professors in the Age of the Sophists." *Proceedings of the Cambridge Philological Society* 201: 65–81.

Riedweg, Christoph. 2004. "Zum Ursprung des Wortes 'Philosophie' oder Pythagoras von Samos als Wortschöpfer." In *Antike Literatur in neuer Deutung*, edited by Anton Bierl, Arbogast Schmitt, Andreas Willi, and Joachim Latacz, 147–82. Munich: Saur.

———. 2005. *Pythagoras: His Life, Teaching, and Influence*. Translated by Steven Rendall. Ithaca, NY: Cornell University Press.

Robb, Kevin. 1991. "The Witness in Heraclitus and in Early Greek Law." *The Monist* 74: 638–76.

Robert, Louis. 1968. "De Delphes a l'Oxus: Inscriptions grecques nouvelles de la Bactriane." *Comptes rendus de l'Academie des Inscriptions et Belles Lettres* 112: 416–57.

Robinson, T. M., ed. 1979. *Contrasting Arguments: An Edition of the "Dissoi Logoi."* Salem, NH: Ayer.

———, ed. 1987. *Heraclitus: Fragments*. Toronto: University of Toronto Press.

Rogers, Benjamin, trans. 1906. *The Birds of Aristophanes*. London: George Bell & Sons.

Rohatyn, Dennis. 1977. "The Protreptic Argument." *International Logic Review* 8: 192–204.

Roscher, Wilhelm Heinrich. 1904. *Die Sieben- und Neunzahl im Kultus und Mythus der Griechen.* Leipzig: Teubner.

Rosenthal, Franz. 1937. "Arabische Nachrichten über Zenon den Eleaten." *Orientalia* 6: 21–67.

Roskam, Geert. 2011. "Plutarch against Epicurus on Affection for Offspring." In *Virtues for the People: Aspects of Plutarchan Ethics*, edited by Geert Roskam and Luc Van der Stockt, 175–204. Leuven: Leuven University Press.

Rossetti, Livio. 1980. "Ricerche sui 'dialoghi socratici' di Fedone e di Euclide." *Hermes* 108: 183–200.

———. 2004. "The *Sokratikoi Logoi* as a Literary Barrier: Toward the Identification of a Standard Socrates through Them." In *Socrates: 2400 Years since His Death (399 B.C.–2001 A.D.)*, edited by Vassilis Karasmanis, 81–94. Athens: European Cultural Centre of Delphi.

———. 2011. "L'*Euthydème* de Xénophon." In *Le dialogue socratique*, 55–99. Paris: Encre Marine/Les Belles Lettres.

———. 2013. "When Pythagoras Was Still Living in Samos (Heraclitus, Frg. 129)." In *On Pythagoreanism*, edited by Gabriele Cornelli, Richard D. McKirahan, and Constantinos Macris, 63–76. Berlin: De Gruyter.

———. 2015a. *La filosofia non nasce con talete e nemmeno con Socrate.* Bologna: Diogene Multimedia.

———. 2015b. "Phaedo's *Zopyrus* (and Socrates' Confidences)." In *From the Socratics to the Socratic Schools: Classical Ethics, Metaphysics, and Epistemology*, edited by Ugo Zilioli, 82–98. New York: Taylor & Francis.

———. 2018. "Philosopher Socrates? Philosophy at the Time of Socrates and the Reformed *Philosophia* of Plato." In *Socrates and the Socratic Dialogue*, edited by Alessandro Stavru and Christopher Moore, 268–98. Leiden: Brill.

Rothwell, Kenneth. 1990. *Politics and Persuasion in Aristophanes' "Ecclesiazusae."* Leiden: Brill.

Rougemont, Georges, ed. 2012. *Inscriptions grecques d'Iran et d'Asie Central.* Corpus Inscriptionum Iranicarum. London: School of Oriental and African Studies.

———, and Denis Rousset, eds. 1971. *Nouveau choix d'inscriptions grecques.* Paris: Les Belles Lettres.

Rowe, Christopher, ed. 1986. *Plato: Phaedrus.* Warminster: Aris & Phillips.

Rowett, Catherine. 2014. "The Pythagorean Society and Politics." In *A History of Pythagoreanism*, edited by Carl Huffman, 112–30. Cambridge: Cambridge University Press.

Rubincam, Catherine. 1998. "Did Diodorus Siculus Take Over Cross-References from His Sources?" *American Journal of Philology* 119: 67–87.

Rusten, J. S. 1985. "Two Lives or Three: Pericles on the Athenian Character (Thucydides 2.40.1–2)." *Classical Quarterly* 35: 14–19.

Ryan, Paul. 2012. *Plato's "Phaedrus": A Commentary for Greek Readers.* Norman: University of Oklahoma Press.

Sacks, Kenneth. 1990. *Diodorus Siculus and the First Century*. Princeton: Princeton University Press.

Sage, Paula Winsor. 1985. "Solon, Croesus and the Theme of the Ideal Life." PhD Diss., Johns Hopkins University.

Sandbach, F. H. 1958. "Ion of Chios on Pythagoras." *Proceedings of the Cambridge Philological Society* 5: 36.

Santoni, Anna. 1989. *Senofonte: Memorabili*. Milan: Rizzoli.

Sassi, Maria Michela. 2018. *The Beginnings of Philosophy in Greece*. Translated by Michele Asuni. Princeton: Princeton University Press.

Sauge, André. 2014. "Le poète contre le philosophe: primauté de la vie sur l'être. Sophocle: *Antigone*, Choeur, 332 suivants; Heidegger: *Einführung in die Metaphysik*. . . ." *Syntaktika* 47: 1–32.

Schepens, Guido. 2014. "History and *Historia*: Inquiry in the Greek Historians." In *A Companion to Greek and Roman Historiography*, edited by John Marincola, 39–55. Malden, MA: Blackwell.

Schepens, Guido, and Els Theys. 1998. "Xanthos of Lydia (1001)." In *Die Fragmente Der Griechischen Historiker Continued Part IV. Biography and Antiquarian Literature. IV A Biography. Fascicle 1. The Pre-Hellenistic Period*, edited by Guido Schepens. Leiden: Brill.

Schiappa, Edward. 1999. *The Beginnings of Rhetorical Theory in Classical Greece*. New Haven, CT: Yale University Press.

———. 2005. "*Dissoi Logoi*." In *Classical Rhetorics and Rhetoricians: Critical Studies and Sources*, edited by Michelle Ballif and Michael G. Moran, 146–48. Westport, CT: Praeger.

Schibli, Hermann. 1990. *Pherekydes of Syros*. Oxford: Clarendon Press.

Schiefsky, Mark. 2006. *Hippocrates: On Ancient Medicine*. Leiden: Brill.

Schleiermacher, Friedrich. 1836. *Introductions to the Dialogues of Plato*. Translated by William Dobson. Cambridge: J. & J. J. Deighton.

Schofield, Malcolm. 1975. "*Doxographica Anaxagorea*." *Hermes* 103: 1–24.

———. 1980. *An Essay on Anaxagoras*. Cambridge: Cambridge University Press.

———. 1991. "Heraclitus' Theory of Soul and Its Antecedents." In *Psychology*, edited by Stephen Everson, 13–34. Cambridge: Cambridge University Press.

Scholz, Peter. 2003. "Philosophizing before Plato: On the Social and Political Conditions of the Composition of the *Dissoi Logoi*." In *Ideal and Culture of Knowledge in Plato: Akten der 4. Tagung der Karl-und-Gertrud-Abel-Stiftung vom 1.–3. September 2000 in Frankfurt*, edited by Wolfgang Detel, Alexander Becker, and Peter Scholz, 201–30. Stuttgart: Franz Steiner Verlag.

———, and Alexander Becker, eds. 2004. *"Dissoi Logoi": Zweierlei Ansichten: Ein sophistischer Traktat*. Sankt Augustin: Akademie Verlag.

Schorn, Stefan. 2014. "Pythagoras in the Historical Tradition: From Herodotus to Diodorus Siculus." In *A History of Pythagoreanism*, edited by Carl Huffman, 296–314. Cambridge: Cambridge University Press.

Schuster, Paul. 1872. *Heraklit von Ephesus: Ein Versuch dessen Fragments in ihrer ursprunglichen Ordnung wiederherzustellen*. Leipzig: Teubner.

Schütrumpf, Eckart, ed. 2008. *Heraclides of Pontus: Texts and Translations*. New Brunswick, NJ: Transaction Publishers.

Sellars, John. 2001. "*Socraticorum Maximus*: Simon the Shoemaker and the Problem of Socrates." *Pli: The Warwick Journal of Philosophy* 11: 253–69.

———. 2003. "Simon the Shoemaker and the Problem of Socrates." *Classical Philology* 98: 207–16.

Seymour, Thomas D., ed. 1889. *Selected Odes of Pindar*. Boston: Ginn & Company.

Shapiro, Susan. 1996. "Herodotus and Solon." *Classical Antiquity* 15: 348–64.

Sharp, Kendall. 2004. "From Solon to Socrates: Proto-Socratic Dialogues in Herodotus." In *La costruzione del discorso filosofico nell'età dei Presocratici*, edited by Maria Michela Sassi, 82–102. Pisa: Edizioni della Normale.

Sider, David. 1980. "Did Plato Write Dialogues before the Death of Socrates?" *Apeiron* 14: 15–18.

———. 2005. *The Fragments of Anaxagoras*. 2nd ed. Sankt Augustin: Akademie Verlag.

Sigurdarson, Eiríkur. 2003. "Studies in *Historia*." PhD Diss., University of Cambridge.

Silvermintz, Daniel. 2008. "The *Double Arguments*." In *The Sophists: An Introduction*, edited by Patricia O'Grady, 147–53. London: Duckworth.

Skalet, Charles. 1928. *Ancient Sicyon*. Baltimore: Johns Hopkins University Press.

Slater, William. 1969. *Lexicon to Pindar*. Berlin: De Gruyter.

Slings, S. R. 2000. "Literature in Athens, 566–510 BC." In *Peisistratos and the Tyranny: A Reappraisal of the Evidence*, edited by Heleen Sancisi-Weerdenburg, 55–75. Amsterdam: J. C. Gieben.

Smith, J. R., trans. 1903. *Xenophon: Memorabilia*. Boston: Ginn & Company.

Smith, Justin E. H. 2016. *The Philosopher: A History in Six Types*. Princeton: Princeton University Press.

Smyth, Herbert Weir. 1956. *Greek Grammar*. Revised by Gordon M. Messing. Cambridge, MA: Harvard University Press

Snell, Bruno. 1943. *Leben und Meinungen der Sieben Weisen*. Munich: Heimeran.

———. 1944. "Die Nachrichten über die Lehren des Thales und die Anfänge der griechischen Philosophie- und Literaturgeschichte." *Philologus* 96: 170–82.

Solin, Heikki. 2003. *Die griechischen Personennamen in Rom: Ein Namenbuch*. 2 vols. Berlin: De Gruyter.

Sommerstein, Alan, trans. 1998. *Aristophanes: Ecclesiazusae*. Warminster: Aris & Phillips.

Souilhé, Joseph, ed. 1930. *Platon: Oeuvres complètes*. 14 vols. Paris: Les Belles Lettres.

Spatharas, Dimos. 2001. "Gorgias: An Edition of the Extant Texts and Fragments with Commentary and Introduction." PhD Diss., University of Glasgow.

Stadter, Philip. 1991. "Pericles among the Intellectuals." *Illinois Classical Studies* 16: 111–24.

Stallbaum, Gottfried, ed. 1836. *Plato: Opera Omnia: Meno, Euthyphro, Erastai, Hipparchus*. Gotha: Hennings.

Stamatopoulou, Zoe. 2016. "Constructing Periander in Plutarch's *Symposium of the Seven Sages*." *CHS Research Bulletin* 5. http://nrs.harvard.edu/urn-3:hlnc .essay:StamatopoulouZ.Constructing_Periander.2016.

Starkie, W.J.M., ed. 1897. *The Wasps of Aristophanes*. London: Macmillan.

Stavru, Alessandro. 2018. "Aristoxenus on Socrates." In *Socrates and the Socratic Dialogue*, edited by Alessandro Stavru and Christopher Moore, 623–64. Leiden: Brill.

Stein, Heinrich, ed. 1871. *Herodoti Historiae*. 2 vols. Berlin: Weidmann.

Stevenson, J. G. 1974. "Aristotle as Historian of Philosophy." *Journal of Hellenic Studies* 94: 138–43.

Steward, John. 1892. *Notes on the "Nicomachean Ethics" of Aristotle*. Oxford: Clarendon Press.

Stokes, Michael. 1971. *One and Many in Presocratic Philosophy*. Washington, DC: Center for Hellenic Studies.

Strassler, Robert B., ed. 2007. *The Landmark Herodotus: The Histories*. Translation by Andrea Purvis. New York: Pantheon.

Strauss, Leo. 1970. *Xenophon's Socratic Discourse: An Interpretation of the "Oeconomicus."* Ithaca, NY: Cornell University Press.

Sulimani, Iris. 2011. *Diodorus' Mythistory and the Pagan Mission: Historiography and Culture-Heroes in the First Pentad of the "Bibliotheke."* Leiden: Brill.

Sullivan, Robert. 2001. *"Eidos/idea* in Isocrates." *Philosophy and Rhetoric* 34: 79–92.

Szegedy-Maszak, Andrew. 1978. "Legends of the Greek Lawgivers." *Greek, Roman, and Byzantine Studies* 19: 199–209.

Taifacos, Ioannis. 2008. "Klearkhos of Soloi." In *The Encyclopedia of Ancient Natural Scientists: The Greek Tradition and Its Many Heirs*, edited by Paul T. Keyser and Georgia L. Irby-Massie, 477. New York: Routledge.

Taylor, C. C. W., trans. 2006. *Aristotle: Nicomachean Ethics: Books II–IV*. Oxford: Clarendon Press.

Tell, Håkan. 2007. "Sages at the Games: Intellectual Displays and Dissemination of Wisdom in Ancient Greece." *Classical Antiquity* 26: 249–75.

———. 2011. *Plato's Counterfeit Sophists*. Washington, DC: Center for Hellenic Studies.

———. 2015. "Solon and the Greek Wisdom Tradition." *Trends in Classics* 7: 8–23.

Thesleff, Holger. 1961. *An Introduction to the Pythagorean Writings of the Hellenistic Period*. Åbo: Åbo Akademi.

———. 2009. *Platonic Patterns: A Collection of Studies*. Las Vegas, NV: Parmenides.

Thomas, Rosalind. 1989. *Oral Tradition and Written Record in Classical Athens*. Cambridge: Cambridge University Press.

Thompson, Dorothy. 1960. "The House of Simon the Shoemaker." *Archaeology* 13: 234–40.

Thorburn, John. 2005. "Philocleon's Addiction." *Classics Ireland* 12: 50–61.

Timmerman, David. 1998. "Isocrates' Competing Conceptualization of Philosophy." *Philosophy and Rhetoric* 31: 145–59.

Timmerman, David, and Edward Schiappa. 2010. *Classical Greek Rhetorical Theory and the Disciplining of Discourse.* Cambridge: Cambridge University Press.

Tissot, Francine. 2006. *Catalogue of the National Museum of Afghanistan 1931–1985.* Paris: UNESCO.

Todd, Stephen, trans. 2000. *Lysias.* Austin: University of Texas Press.

Tomin, Julius. 1997. "Plato's First Dialogue." *Ancient Philosophy* 17: 31–45.

Tribulato, Olga. 2015. *Ancient Greek Verb-Initial Compounds: Their Diachronic Development within the Greek Compound System.* Berlin: De Gruyter.

Tsitsiridis, Stavros. 2013. *Beiträge zu den Fragmenten des Klearchos von Soloi.* Berlin: De Gruyter.

Tulli, Mauro. 2000. "*Carmide* fra poesia e ricerca." In *Plato: Euthydemus, Lysis, Charmides. Proceedings of the V Symposium Platonicum,* edited by T. M. Robinson and Luc Brisson, 259–64. Sankt Augustin: Academia Verlag.

Tuozzo, Thomas M. 2011. *Plato's "Charmides": Positive Elenchus in a "Socratic" Dialogue.* Cambridge: Cambridge University Press.

Turner, James. 2014. *Philology: The Forgotten Origins of the Modern Humanities.* Princeton: Princeton University Press.

Tziatzi-Papagianni, Maria. 1994. *Die Sprüche der sieben Weisen: Zwei byzantinische Sammlungen.* Leipzig: Teubner.

———. 1997. "Eine gekürzte Fassung der delphischen Sprüche der sieben Weisen." *Hermes* 125: 309–29.

Untersteiner, Mario. 1963. *Zenone, testimonianze e frammenti. Introduzione, traduzione e commento.* Florence: La Nuova Italia.

Ussher, R. G., ed. 1986. *Aristophanes: Ecclesiazusae.* Bristol: Bristol Classical Press.

Vahlen, Johannes, ed. 1903. *De Scholiis in Aristotelis Rhetoricam.* Berlin: Schade.

Van der Eijk, Philip. 2009. "The Woman Not Breathing." In *Heraclides of Pontus: Discussion,* edited by William W. Fortenbaugh, Elizabeth E. Pender, and Eckart Schütrumpf, 237–50. New Brunswick, NJ: Transaction Publishers.

Van Dijk, Jan. 1962. "Die Inschriftenfunde." In *Vorläufiger Bericht über die von dem deutschen archäologischen Institut und der deutschen Orient-Gesellschaft aus Mitteln der deutschen Forschungsgemeinschaft Unternommenen Ausgrabungen in Uruk-Warka: Winter 1959–60,* edited by Heinrich Jakob Lenzen, 44–52. Berlin: Gebr. Mann.

———, and Werner Mayer. 1980. *Texte Aus Dem Rēš-Heiligtum in Uruk-Warka.* Berlin: Gebr. Mann.

Van Hook, LaRue. 1919. "Alcidamas versus Isocrates." *Classical Weekly* 12: 89–94.

Van Leeuwen, Jans, ed. 1905. *Aristophanis Ecclesiazusae.* Leiden: Sijthoff.

Verdenius, W. J. 1947. "Notes on the Presocratics." *Mnemosyne* 13: 271–89.

———. 1955. "Notes on Plato's *Phaedrus*." *Mnemosyne* 8: 265–89.

———. 1972. *Pindar's "Seventh Olympian Ode": A Commentary.* Amsterdam: Noord-Hollandsche U.M.

———. 1983. "The Principles of Greek Literary Criticism." *Mnemosyne* 36: 14–59.

Verhasselt, Gertjan. Forthcoming. "The Seven Sages and the Inscription of Aï Khanoum." In *Clearchus of Soli: Text, Translation, and Discussion*, edited by David C. Mirhady.

Vernant, Jean Pierre. 1982. *The Origins of Greek Thought*. Ithaca, NY: Cornell University Press.

Vernhes, Jean-Victor. 2014a. "Une étymologie pour σοφός?" *Connaissance hellénique* 137 (March 2014), https://ch.hypotheses.org/834.

———. 2014b. "Retour sur l'étymologie de σοφός ou Le marteau et le sabot." *Connaissance hellénique* 139 (November 2014), https://ch.hypotheses.org/1070.

Vitali, Renzo. 1971. *Gorgia: Retorica e filosofia*. Urbino: STEU.

Vlastos, Gregory. 1950. "The Physical Theory of Anaxagoras." *Philosophical Review* 59: 31–57.

Von Fritz, Kurt. 1940. *Pythagorean Politics in Southern Italy: An Analysis of the Sources*. New York: Columbia University Press.

———. 1945. "ΝΟΥΣ, ΝΟΕΙΝ, and Their Derivatives in Pre-Socratic Philosophy (Excluding Anaxagoras): Part I. From the Beginnings to Parmenides." *Classical Philology* 40: 223–43.

Von Velsen, Friedrich, ed. 1883. *Aristophanis Ecclesiazusae*. Leipzig: Teubner.

Voss, Otto. 1896. "De Heraclidis Pontici Vita et Scriptis." Diss., University of Rostock.

Walzer, Richard. 1939. *Eraclito: Raccolta dei frammenti e traduzione italiana*. Firenze: G.C. Sansoni.

Wardy, Robert. 1996. *The Birth of Rhetoric: Gorgias, Plato, and Their Successors*. London: Routledge.

Wareh, Tarik. 2012. *The Theory and Practice of Life: Isocrates and the Philosophers*. Washington, DC: Center for Hellenic Studies.

Watkins, Calvert. 2000. *The American Heritage Dictionary of Indo-European Roots*. 2nd ed. Boston: Houghton Mifflin.

Watson, J. S., trans. 1857. *Xenophon's Minor Works*. London: Henry G. Bohn.

Węcowski, Marek. 2004. "The Hedgehog and the Fox: Form and Meaning in the Prologue of Herodotus." *Journal of Hellenic Studies* 124: 143–64.

Wehrli, Fritz. 1969. *Die Schule des Aristoteles:* Vol 7: *Herakleides Pontikos*. 2nd ed. Basel: Schwabe & Co.

Werner, Daniel. 2012. *Myth and Philosophy in Plato's "Phaedrus."* Cambridge: Cambridge University Press.

Werner, Wilhelm. 1912. "De *Anterastis* Dialogo Pseudoplatonico." PhD Diss., Darmstadt.

Wersdörfer, H. 1940. *Die Φιλοσοφία des Isokrates im Spiegel ihrer Terminologie*. Leipzig: Harrassowitz.

West, Martin. 1963. "Three Presocratic Cosmologies." *Classical Quarterly* 13: 154–76.

———. 1971. *Early Greek Philosophy and the Orient*. Oxford: Clarendon Press.

———. 1985. "Ion of Chios." *British Institute of Classical Studies* 32: 71–77.

West, Stephanie. 1991. "Herodotus' Portrait of Hecataeus." *Journal of Hellenic Studies* 111: 144–60.

Wheelwright, Philip E. 1959. *Heraclitus*. Princeton: Princeton University Press.

White, Mary. 1958. "The Dates of the Orthagorids." *Phoenix* 12: 1–14.

Whitehead, David. 1983. "Competitive Outlay and Community Profit: Φιλοτιμία in Democratic Athens." *Classica et Mediaevalia* 34: 55–74.

Wickkiser, Bronwen Lara. 2008. *Asklepios, Medicine, and the Politics of Healing in Fifth-Century Greece: Between Craft and Cult*. Baltimore: Johns Hopkins University Press.

Wiersma, W. 1933. "The Seven Sages and the Prize of Wisdom." *Mnemosyne* 1: 150–54.

Wiese, Hermann. 1963. "Heraklit bei Klemens von Alexandrien." Diss., Christian-Albrechts-Universität zu Kiel.

Wilamowitz-Moellendorff, Ulrich von. 1880. *Philologische Untersuchungen: Aus Kydathen*. Berlin: Weidmann.

———. 1922. *Pindaros*. Berlin: Weidmann.

Wilcox, Joel. 1991. "Barbarian *Psyche* in Heraclitus." *The Monist* 74: 624–37.

Wilcox, Stanley. 1943. "Criticisms of Isocrates and His Φιλοσοφία." *Transactions and Proceedings of the American Philological Association* 74: 113–33.

Williams, Gareth D. 2012. *The Cosmic Viewpoint: A Study of Seneca's Natural Questions*. Oxford: Oxford University Press.

Wiltshire, David. 2007. "The Semantics of Χρή in Aeschylus." MA Thesis, University of North Carolina.

Winans, Samuel, ed. 1881. *Xenophon: Symposium*. Boston: J. Allyn.

Wöhrle, Georg. 2014. *The Milesians: Thales*. Translated by Richard D. McKirahan. Berlin: De Gruyter.

Woldinga, G. J. 1938. *Xenophons "Symposium": Prolegomena en Commentaar*. Hilversum: J. Schipper.

Wolfsdorf, David Conan. 1998. "The Historical Reader of Plato's *Protagoras*." *Classical Quarterly* 48: 126–33.

———. Forthcoming a. "Remarks on the Unity of the *Dissoi Logoi*." In *Early Greek Ethics*, edited by David C. Wolfsdorf. Oxford: Oxford University Press.

———. Forthcoming b. "'*Sophia*' and '*Epistêmê*' in the Archaic and Classical Periods." In *Philosophy of Knowledge: A History*. Vol. 1. Edited by N. D. Smith, 11–29. New York: Bloomsbury.

Woodbury, Leonard. 1981. "Anaxagoras and Athens." *Phoenix* 35: 295–315.

———. 1985. "Ibycus and Polycrates." *Phoenix* 39: 193–220.

Yates, Velvet. 2005. "*Anterastai*: Competition in Eros and Politics in Classical Athens." *Arethusa* 38: 33–47.

Yonge, C. D., trans. 1901. *Diogenes Laërtius: The Lives and Opinions of Eminent Philosophers*. London: George Bell & Sons.

Yunis, Harvey, ed. 2011. *Plato: Phaedrus*. Cambridge: Cambridge University Press.

Yxem, Ernst Ferdinand. 1846. *Über Platons "Kleitophon."* In *Jahresbericht Friedrich-Wilhelms-Gymnasium*, 1–35. Berlin: A. W. Hahn.

Zeller, Eduard. 1931. *Outlines of the History of Greek Philosophy*. Revised by Wilhelm Nestle, translated by L. R. Palmer. 13th ed. London: Routledge.

Zevort, Charles, trans. 1847. *Diogène de Laerte: Vies et doctrines des philosophes de l'antiquité*. Paris: Charpentier.

Zhmud, Leonid. 2013. "Pythagorean Communities: From Individuals to a Collective Portrait." In *Doctrine and Doxography: Studies on Heraclitus and Pythagoras,* edited by David Silver and Dirk Obbink, 33–52. Berlin: De Gruyter.

———. 2017. "Heraclitus on Pythagoras." In *Heraklit im Kontext*, edited by Enrica Fantino, Ulrike Muss, Charlotte Schubert, and Kurt Sier, 171–86. Berlin: De Gruyter.

INDEX

Abderites, 156. *See also* Democritus of
Abdera; Hecataeus of Abdera; Protagoras
of Abdera

abstraction, 7, 101–2, 105, 135, 138, 225,
237–38, 252, 298; and emotional
control, 202; "philosophizing" and,
168, 171–72, 176–77, 204–5; research
and, 51, 207–8; *sophia* and, 54, 94, 101–2,
275–76

The Academy, 28–30, 271; and defense
of *philosophia*, 29–30; as expression
of a vision of philosophy, 28–29, 194,
221, 273; Heraclides as member of, 9,
28; and historical consciousness, 3; and
historiography of philosophy, 30, 32–33;
and *philosophia* as discipline, 29–30,
194, 216, 273, 282–87; and Pythagoras
as subject of discussion, 22; and use of
philosophia as term, 260

Adeimantus, 240, 250, 256, 302

Adler, Ada, 152

advice: as competitive arena, 123–24; and
mantic forecasting, 129n9, 139, 142,
169–70; as meddling, 165–66; political
advisory roles (*see under* politics); practical or personal, 104, 127–28, 149; sage
advice about good life, 127–28; *sophoi* as
advisors, 100–104, 123–24, 150, 266, 314;
"wise advisor" trope, 24, 105

Aeschines (orator), 149, 247

Aeschines of Sphettus (Socratic), 20n53,
114n36, 154n92, 203n25, 247

Aëtius, 3–4; *Placita Philosophorum*,
untranslated text, 323

Against the Philosophoi (Zeno), 151–53

Against the Sophists (Isocrates), 207,
210–11, 213–14

Agariste of Sicyon, 20n53

"Ages of Man" (Solon), 97–98

agriculture, 39, 105, 144, 183–84, 186–87,
189, 202, 272

Ai Khanoum, inscription at, 291–97

Aischines of Sicyon, 20n53

Alcibiades (Plato), 258

Alcidamas: and history of philosophy as
a discipline, 206–9, 268–69, 272; and
the probably spurious *Odysseus*, 209;
Pythagoras in, 115–16, 140; and "sophist" as laudatory term, 207, 209; uses of
philosophos in, 5, 28–29, 150, 157, 194,
198n7, 209

Alcmaeon, 109, 161, 267, 276, 279

Alexander of Aphrodisias, 195

Alexis, 30, 297–301

Al-Mubassir, 152

Alyattes, 103, 129

Amasis, 92n81, 129–30

ambiguity: and ambivalence toward
philosophia, 77–78; in Heraclitus, 50,
58–61, 63–64; and Platonic *vs.* Isocratean
notions of *philosophia*, 233n22; poetry
or gnomic language and, 229; in *Rival
Lovers*, 315–16

ambition, 109n13, 118; and philosophizing,
172–73; *philosophoi* and excessive, 1, 6,
61, 72–73, 77–79, 78–79, 123–24, 146–47,
150; *phil-* prefixed terms related to excessive, 254–55

ambivalence toward *philosophia*: ambiguity
and, 77–78; and polymathy in Heraclitus,
38–41; and protreptics, 288–90

Ambrose of Milan, 3–4, 256; *On Abraham
the Patriarch*, 327

Ammonius, *Commentary on Porphyry's*
Introduction, 328–29

Anabasis (Xenophon), 177

Anacharsis of Scythia, 131

anachronism, 1, 210–11; and *sophia*, 80n36

Republic (Plato), 116–17; and etymologies of *philosophia,* 222; *philosophos* in, 222; re-semanticizing of *philosophos* in, 250–56

reputation, 109n13; of Anaxagoras, 162–64; modesty and *sophos,* 95–96; peril caused by envy, 159; *philosophoi* as disreputable, 166–67, 178–80, 206–7, 210; and *philosophos* as charge, 159–64; *phil-* prefixed terms related to, 254–55; of Pythagoras, 21, 40, 72, 116–17; Socrates on his own, 188–89, 190–91

research, 26; and abstraction, 51, 207–8; as beginning point, 50; Clement on research as essential practice, 26, 48n35; connotations of, 64–65; and direct experience, 46; as hearsay, 60; Heraclitus on, 38–39, 48n35, 62–63, 261–62; *historia* as, 58–60; as hubris, 105; learning as pleasurable, 186–87; limitations of relying on, 51–57, 60, 172–75; and "love of wisdom," 48–49, 62; and oratory, 143; over-dependence on books, 173–75; *philosophein* and, 135; *philosophos* and inquiry, 128; polymathy and, 40–41, 47–49, 261–62; practical problem solving and, 136, 142, 149; as purported path to wisdom, 110–11; Pythagoras as "inquirer," 39n29; and self-improvement, 318; Socrates and, 162, 172–73; and *sophia,* 205–6

resemanticizing of *philosophos,* 250–56

retrojection, errors of, 1, 21, 24–25, 62, 93, 108, 246, 256

rhetoric: Alcidamas as rhetorician, 115, 140–41, 150, 206–9, 268; and Anaxagorean pedagogy, 168–70; Antisthenes and, 199–201; and competition among *philosophoi,* 194; as defensive instrument, 149, 200; Empedocles and, 141, 206, 278n59; extemporaneous, 194, 206–9; Gorgias and, 143–47, 200–201, 206; and memory, 205–6; in non-Academic philosophy, 194; Pericles as perfect in, 168–69; persuasion and, 201; and *philosophia,* 145–46, 150, 166, 172, 200, 208, 232, 256; in Plato's *Phaedrus,* 223, 231–32; as political instrument, 168–69, 186, 200; Pythagoras or Pythagoreans and, 108, 141, 206;

research and preparedness for, 143, 208; rhetorical contexts of *philosophia,* 28; Socrates and, 232, 240–41, 254; technical rhetoric as *philosophia,* 215n47

Rhetoric (Aristotle), 75, 77, 255

Riedweg, Christoph, 19n51, 25n67, 68n3, 131n15, 158n4

Rival Lovers (Plato), 30, 290–91, 310–16

Robert, Louis, 292–95

Robinson, Thomas, 42, 47–48, 205–6

sages. *See* Seven Sages; *sophoi* (sages or wise people)

"sage-wannabes," 1, 7, 105

Samos, 103; as home of Pythagoras, 19–20n53, 103, 108n6, 112, 113

Sandanis of Lydia, 129

sapientes, 13, 67; *philosophoi* as replacement for, 67

sarcasm, 58, 64, 300

Satyrus, 141

"Sayings of the Seven *Sophoi*" (Demetrius), 95–96

"self-contradiction" genre, 290–91

self-discipline: and self-knowledge, 314–415; as virtue, 102. *See also* discipline of the self

self-improvement, 72, 108–9, 174, 221, 256, 257, 271, 314, 316, 318; conversation and, 223–28, 244–46; learning as pleasurable, 186–87; and modification of desire, 20, 194, 196, 200; Phaedo of Elis and, 195–97; as Pythagorean preoccupation, 195–97, 209; value of moderate effort and, 259

selfishness, 80, 81n41

self-knowledge, 52, 56–57, 97, 261, 270; "know yourself" as maxim, 226n12, 230, 295, 296n25

self-reliance, 46–47, 108, 197, 201

self-sufficiency, 201

Seven Sages (Seven *Sophoi*): Babylonian precursors for, 8, 94, 98–99, 104; Cicero and association of Pythagoras with, 68; competition and status of, 95; dating of, 94–95; Diodorus on, 68–69; as distinct group, 67, 103–4, 129; and expertise, 104;

and the "art of words," 167–68, 170–72, 203–4; and *philosophoi* as group identity, 171–72, 177; and philosophy as a discipline, 267–69; and *phil-* prefixed words, 247, 254; and "purified souls," 182–83; Socrates in, 157–58

youth: immaturity and excess of, 76–77, 179, 211; *philosophein* as activity of, 134, 302, 309–10; and *philosophoi,* 178, 250; *phil-* prefixed terms related to boys, 254; influence of Pythagoras on, 109, 115, 121; Socrates's trial for corruption of, 160, 165–66, 183n66, 190, 213; study of astronomy and geometry by, 114

Zaleucus, 109
Zalmoxis, 15n42, 108–9, 113
Zeller, Eduard, 21, 23
Zeno of Elea, 22, 51, 141, 143, 150–53, 160n10, 211, 244, 267–70, 278n59, 279
Zeno of Rhodes, 99–100
Zopyrus, 9n18
Zopyrus (Phaedo of Elis), 195–97

INDEX LOCORUM

396 INDEX LOCORUM